Reading Law

Reading Law

The Interpretation
of Legal Texts

Antonin Scalia & Bryan A. Garner

The views expressed in this book are those of the authors as legal commentators. Nothing in this book prejudges any case that might come before the United States Supreme Court.

© 2012 Antonin Scalia & Bryan A. Garner

Published by Thomson/West
610 Opperman Drive
P.O. Box 64526
St. Paul, MN 55164-0527
1-800-328-9352

ISBN: 978-0-314-27555-4

Printed in the United States of America

Library of Congress Cataloguing-in-Publication Data
Antonin Scalia & Bryan A. Garner
Reading Law: the interpretation of legal texts — 1st ed.
        p.   cm.
Includes bibliographical references and index.
1. Law—interpretation and construction.
2. Judicial Process—United States.
3. Law—philosophy.
4. Statutes—United States.
5. Jurisprudence.
6. Law—methodology.
I. Scalia, Antonin, 1936–
I. Garner, Bryan A., 1958–
II. Title

First printing

"*Verbis legis tenaciter inhaerendum.*"
—Medieval legal maxim meaning
"Hold tight to the words of the law."

"[L]aw, without equity, though hard and disagreeable, is much more desirable for the public good, than equity without law: which would make every judge a legislator, and introduce most infinite confusion."
—William Blackstone
1 *Commentaries on the Laws of England* 62
(4th ed. 1770).

"Various and discordant readings, glosses, and commentaries will inevitably arise in the progress of time, and, perhaps, as often from the want of skill and talent in those who comment, as in those who make the law."
—James Kent
1 *Commentaries on American Law* 437 (1826).

"[J]udges must be aware today that there are currents of ferment in the legal world that seek to revise or even overthrow traditional notions of judicial interpretation."
—William H. Rehnquist
"The Nature of Judicial Interpretation,"
in *Politics and the Constitution:*
The Nature and Extent of Interpretation 3, 3 (1990).

"What is of paramount importance is that Congress be able to legislate against a background of clear interpretive rules, so that it may know the effect of the language it adopts."
—*Finley v. United States,*
490 U.S. 545, 556 (1989) (per Scalia, J.).

To Maureen McCarthy Scalia

and

Karolyne H.C. Garner

Short Table of Contents

Full-Length Table of Contents

Acknowledgments

We are grateful to our many learned friends who contributed in myriad ways, from suggesting interesting problems, to advising on particular points, to reading and commenting on the manuscript. We are especially indebted to the following friends who commented critically and copiously on the manuscript:

Paul H. Anderson	Paul J. Kiernan
Lackland H. Bloom Jr.	Steve Leben
Edward H. Cooper	John F. Manning
David M. Dorsen	Caleb Nelson
Mark Evans	William D. Popkin
Ward Farnsworth	Sir Christopher Ricks
Karolyne H.C. Garner	Eugene Scalia
Scott Gessler	Ann Taylor Schwing
Harris L. Hartz	Michael F. Sturley
Tony Honoré	Jeffrey S. Sutton
Melissa Lin Jones	Edward Whelan

Along the way, we have benefited from the logistical help and the perceptive suggestions of these scholars, lawyers, and judges: Edwin Anderson, Hans W. Baade, Rachel E. Barkow, Michael Boudin, Brian D. Boyle, Daniel A. Bress, Richard P. Bress, Steven G. Calabresi, Andrew Christensen, Gail Daly, Susan E. Engel, Louis Feldman, Noel J. Francisco, W. Royal Furgeson Jr., Curtis E. Gannon, Neil C. Gosch, Nathan L. Hecht, C. Scott Hemphill, Gregory Ivy, Kumar Percy Jayasuriya, Christine Jolls, Daniel R. Karon, Brett Kavanaugh, Gary S. Lawson, Lawrence Lessig, Victoria A. Lowery, Scott Martin, Stephen A. Miller, Gary Muldoon, David Nahmias, Regina L. Nassen, Andrew J. Nussbaum, John C. O'Quinn, Lee Liberman Otis, G.P. Pagone, Vince Parrett, John Phillips, William H. Pryor Jr., Michael D. Ramsey, Jane Richards Roth, D. John Sauer, Patrick J. Schiltz, Gil Seinfeld, Kannon K. Shanmugam, Donna F. Solen, John R. Trimble, and Henry Weissman.

At LawProse, Inc. in Dallas, we had the benefit not only of a fine law library but also of several accomplished legal researchers: Tiger Jackson, Jeff Newman, Becky R. McDaniel, Heather C. Haines, Timothy D. Martin, and Eliot Turner. Other LawProse staffers who contributed were Ryden McComas Anderson, Scott Keffer, and Melissa Foster Sanz.

The Garner Law Scholars at the Southern Methodist University Dedman School of Law briefed dozens of cases for our consideration. They were Salman Bhojani, Gregory A. Brassfield, Levi M. Dillon, Andrew J.M. Johnson, Carrie Xuan Nie, Abel Ramirez Jr., Derric Smith, Ben A. West, and Kimberly Winnubst. Bryan Garner in particular thanks Dean John Attanasio for creating the Garner Law Scholar program. Dean Attanasio also provided the resources to amass over 1,500 scholarly articles on statutory interpretation. Gregory Ivy at the SMU Underwood Law Library oversaw the compiling of the articles by Brandon Michael Duck, David Thomas Khirallah, Lauren Elizabeth Maluso, Daniel Osterland, and Ryan Christopher Storey. We thank Daniel P. Rosati and William S. Hein & Co. for permitting use of the HeinOnline database, which was necessary for this ambitious endeavor.

Both Karen Magnuson of Portland and Shmuel Gerber of New York copyedited the manuscript with great skill and insight. We are grateful.

Among our predecessors in this vineyard, we especially express gratitude to Henry Campbell Black, Max Radin, and Frederick J. de Sloovère for their incomparably helpful work.

A.S.

B.A.G.

Foreword

Frank H. Easterbrook[1]

"[S]trict construction . . . is not a doctrine to be taken seriously" (p. 356). Many people will be surprised to read this line, which is elaborated in an entire chapter (§ 62) of a book by two textualists who think that statutory language is both the start and the finish of the interpretive process. But no one who has paid close attention to how textualists decide cases (on the bench) or explain their methods (on or off the bench) *should* be surprised. Some texts proclaim that they should be read "strictly" (i.e., narrowly); others demand a broad or general application. The text's author, not the interpreter, gets to choose how the language will be understood and applied. The court's job is to carry out the legislative project, not to change it in conformity with the judge's view of sound policy.

Those who favor a more open-ended judicial role often quote a passage from Chief Justice John Marshall, who is usually accounted the greatest of our Justices—and whose status as a member of the founding generation (he participated in Virginia's ratifying convention) gives him a claim to represent the original understanding about interpretive method. Chief Justice Marshall once wrote: "Where the mind labours to discover the design of the legislature, it seizes every thing from which aid can be derived."[2] This passage has been used to argue for resort to legislative history, the (imputed) intent of the legislators, and a dominant role for the judge's sense of whether a given reading produces good consequences (if a judge can determine what the consequences will be, often a hard task even for social scientists who can draw on data unavailable to a court making a prediction).

That's not remotely what Chief Justice Marshall meant, however. Here is the full sentence: "Where the mind labours to dis-

---

1   Chief Judge, United States Court of Appeals for the Seventh Circuit.
2   *United States v. Fisher*, 6 U.S. (2 Cranch) 358, 386 (1805) (per Marshall, C.J.).

cover the design of the legislature, it seizes every thing from which aid can be derived; and in such case the title claims a degree of notice, and will have its due share of consideration." He was advocating, not a departure from statutory text, or a role for extra-statutory materials, but consideration of *all* the enacted text rather than a subset of it. This book takes the same position (§ 24). It is brimming with quotations from Chief Justice Marshall, all of which support a textualist approach to interpretation.

What Chief Justice Marshall knew—what this book develops—is that the more the interpretive process strays outside a law's text, the greater the interpreter's discretion. Extra materials are bound to look in multiple directions. Legislators' talk (whether on the floor or in a committee report) is not as precise as statutory language, and it is not adopted by the process for creating laws (bi-cameral approval plus signature by the chief executive). Legislative intent is a fiction, a back-formation from other and often undisclosed sources. Every legisla*tor* has an intent, which usually cannot be discovered, since most say nothing before voting on most bills; and the legisla*ture* is a collective body that does not have a mind; it "intends" only that the text be adopted, and statutory texts usually are compromises that match no one's first preference.

If some legislators say one thing and others something else, if some interest groups favor one outcome and others something different, how does the interpreter choose which path to follow? Direction often comes from the interpreter's sense of wise policy. That sense may be mistaken—the Law of Unintended Consequences applies to judicially created rules as much as it does to those with origins in the legislature or an agency—but the real problem lies in a transfer of authority from elected officials to those with life tenure. The legislature acts first, the executive branch (or private parties) second, and the judiciary third. If the final decision-maker exercises significant discretion, then it rather than the legislature (or the executive) is the real author of policy. Yet in a democracy, policy-makers are supposed to be on short leashes: for the federal government two years (the House), four years (the President and his appointees), or six years (the Senate). Judges serve for 20 years or more and never face the voters. Democratic choice under the constitutional plan depends on interpretive methods that curtail judicial discretion.

Curtail does not mean "eliminate." Interpretation is a human enterprise, which cannot be carried out algorithmically by an expert system on a computer. But discretion can be hedged in by rules, such as those that this book covers in detail, and misuse of these rules by a crafty or willful judge then can be exposed as an abuse of power. A more latitudinarian approach to interpretation, by contrast, makes it hard to see when the judge has succumbed to the Dark Side of Tenure—which, like the Dark Side of The Force in *Star Wars*, is marked by self-indulgence. Tenure is designed to insulate the judge from popular will, so that the judge will be more faithful to a text that may have been adopted by a political coalition that is now out of favor. But tenure can also liberate the judge from those texts. A system of interpretation is good to the extent that it makes this kind of misuse more visible—both to the interpreter (who often thinks that his ideas of wise policy really just *must* be the same as the legislature's) and to the public.

Political scientists, editorial page writers, and cynics often depict judges as doing nothing other than writing their preferences into law. Careful observers of the judiciary do not make that mistake. The Supreme Court of the United States decides about 80 cases a year, a tiny fraction of the nation's litigation. The Justices choose most of those 80 because they pose questions that have divided other judges. In other words, the 80 cases present the questions that the legal system finds hardest to address, and in which decent arguments can be made for different resolutions. Yet the Justices resolve almost half of their cases unanimously, and many of the others by lopsided votes.[3] The amount of real disagreement has not increased in the last 70 years.[4] Judges of the courts of appeals, whose cases are (on average) less contentious,

---

3 *See* Paul H. Edelman, David E. Klein & Stefanie A. Lindquist, *Consensus, Disorder, and Ideology on the Supreme Court*, 9 J. Empirical Legal Studs. 129 (2012).

4 *See* Frank H. Easterbrook, *Agreement Among the Justices: An Empirical Note*, 1984 Supreme Court Rev. 389. Edelman, Klein & Lindquist show that the numbers have been stable since that analysis was conducted.

agree even more often.[5] Recently the Supreme Court issued a unanimous decision in a reapportionment dispute that had different political parties (and different ethnic groups) at each others' throats.[6] Professional norms—including norms about interpretive method—produce much more consensus than would be expected if judges' decisions mirrored the disagreement in legislative bodies or political debates.[7]

It is tempting to say that the approach reflected in this book is the source of this substantial agreement, though that cannot be verified empirically. What is certain is that the rate of agreement would be higher if the authors' methods were more widely followed. This would not push the body of American law to either the left or the right on the political spectrum. Just as well-defined property rights permit people to pursue their own goals through contracts or trade, so well-defined interpretive principles permit legislators to pursue their goals with confidence that the political bargains will be enforced. Some sessions of the legislature are liberal, some conservative, and some reach compromises that include benefits for all sides. The more straightforward the rules of interpretation, the better this process can work—and the easier the people will find it to change public policy by electing persons who support their views.

The textualist method of interpretation cannot produce judicial unanimity across the board, however. One reason is the selective nature of litigation. People will pay lawyers to press their cases in courts of appeals, or the Supreme Court, only if they see a chance of prevailing. Litigation is expensive, and no one but a zealot or madman throws good money after bad by taking a pointless appeal or filing a doomed petition for certiorari. So the cases available for decision by an appellate tribunal depend on the prevailing interpretive method. Imagine a Supreme Court comprising Justice Scalia and eight near clones. That Court would find lots of cases

---

5   Frank B. Cross, *Decision Making in the U.S. Courts of Appeals* (2007) (finding a disagreement rate of about 6%).

6   *Perry v. Perez*, 132 S.Ct. 934 (2012) (per curiam).

7   Karl Llewellyn, one of the original legal realists, developed a similar proposition in *The Common Law Tradition: Deciding Appeals* (1960).

to be hard; this book shows the sorts of interpretive issues that might cause the Justice Scalia of 2011 to disagree with the Justice Scalia of 2012. It would grant review of those hard cases and decide many of them five to four (Scalia I to V versus Scalia VI to IX). Cases that the Warren Court found hard and decided 5–4, this hypothetical Court would find easy and decide 9–0; lawyers would stop presenting those disputes. But they would bring more and more of the disputes that divide textualists—and there are lines of division among textualists, as footnote 4 on page 247 of this book demonstrates.

Another reason why textualists are bound to disagree among themselves is built into the rule that meaning depends on the enacted text rather than what the text's authors meant, intended, planned, or expected the text to accomplish. Words don't have intrinsic meanings; the significance of an expression depends on how the interpretive community alive at the time of the text's adoption understood those words. The older the text, the more distant that interpretive community from our own. At some point the difference becomes *so* great that the meaning is no longer recoverable reliably. Perhaps that point has been reached for the Cruel and Unusual Punishments Clause of the Constitution's Eighth Amendment and some of the Constitution's other grand generalities.

When it becomes hard to understand how the original interpretive community heard a text, a court must choose from among three options: (1) it can give that text a new meaning; (2) it can attempt a historical reconstruction; or (3) it can declare that meaning has been lost, so that the living political community must choose. The second of these methods is bound to produce disagreement, as happened a few years ago when the Supreme Court tackled the Second Amendment and all nine Justices tried to understand the original meaning of a text that concerned a form of organization (the 18th-century militia) alien to the modern interpretive community.[8]

---

8   *District of Columbia v. Heller*, 554 U.S 570 (2008) (per Scalia, J.).

The first of these methods—the way of the "Living Constitution"—is often praised as preferable to rule by the dead. But the "Dead Hand" is not the opposite of the "Living Constitution." When the judiciary is suitably modest about its ability to understand an interpretive community of long ago, the alternative is *neither* rule by the dead nor rule by living (but tenured) judges; it is democracy, rule by the people through their representatives.[9] The Constitution prevails over a statute to the extent that the Constitution contains a legal rule. When the original meaning is lost to the passage of time—or when it was never really there but must be invented—the justification for judges' having the last word evaporates. The alternative is choice through the Constitution's principal means of decision: a vote among elected representatives who can be thrown out if their choices prove to be unpopular. That outcome should be welcomed rather than feared.

This book is a great event in American legal culture. One of your coauthors is the preeminent legal lexicographer of our time. As for your other coauthor, not since Joseph Story has a sitting Justice of the Supreme Court written about interpretation as comprehensively as in the book you are holding. And Justice Story's magisterial *Commentaries on the Constitution of the United States* (1833) dealt principally with substance rather than interpretive method. Every lawyer—and every citizen concerned about how the judiciary can rise above politics and produce a government of laws, and not of men[10]—should find this book invaluable.

---

9 *See* Frank H. Easterbrook, *Textualism and the Dead Hand*, 66 Geo. Wash. L. Rev. 1119 (1998).

10 Although the origin of this phrase is lost to time, it states a goal common to this nation's founding generation and those alive today.

Preface

Our legal system must regain a mooring that it has lost: a generally agreed-on approach to the interpretation of legal texts. In this treatise we seek to show that (1) the established methods of judicial interpretation, involving scrupulous concern with the language of legal instruments and its meaning, are widely neglected; (2) this neglect has impaired the predictability of legal dispositions, has led to unequal treatment of similarly situated litigants, has weakened our democratic processes, and has distorted our system of governmental checks and balances; and (3) it is not too late to restore a strong sense of judicial fidelity to texts.

Both your authors are textualists: We look for meaning in the governing text, ascribe to that text the meaning that it has borne from its inception, and reject judicial speculation about both the drafters' extratextually derived purposes and the desirability of the fair reading's anticipated consequences. We hope to persuade our readers that this interpretive method is the soundest, most principled one that exists. But even those who are unpersuaded will remain, to a large degree, textualists themselves—whether or not they accept the title. While they may use legislative history, purposivism, or consequentialism at the margins, they will always begin with the text. Most will often end there.

Hence the importance, to all of us, of textual meaning. How is that meaning to be determined? By convention. Neither written words nor the sounds that the written words represent have any inherent meaning. Nothing but conventions and contexts cause a symbol or sound to convey a particular idea. In legal systems, there are linguistic usages and conventions distinctive to private legal documents in various fields and to governmental legislation. And there are jurisprudential conventions that make legal interpretation more than just a linguistic exercise (see especially §§ 48–51 [private-right canons], 54 [prior-construction canon]).

Anglo-American law has always been rich in interpretive conventions. Yet since the mid-20th century, there has been a breakdown in the transmission of this heritage to successive generations of lawyers and lawmakers—indeed, a positive disparagement of the conventions by teachers responsible for their transmission. The result has been uncertainty and confusion in our systems of private ordering and public lawmaking—and, to the extent that judicial invention replaces what used to be an all-but-universal means of understanding enacted texts, the distortion of our system of democratic government.

The descent into social rancor over judicial decisions is largely traceable to nontextual means of interpretation, which erode society's confidence in a rule of law that evidently has no agreed-on meaning. Nontextual interpretation, which makes "statesmen" of judges, promotes the shifting of political blame from the political organs of government (the executive and the legislature) to the judiciary. The consequence is the politicizing of judges (and hence of the process of selecting them) and a decline of faith in democratic institutions. It was with characteristic foresight that George Washington declared: "I have always been persuaded, that the stability and success of the National Government and consequently the happiness of the people of the United States, would depend, in a considerable degree, on the *interpretation and execution of its laws.*"[1]

We seek to restore sound interpretive conventions. The "fair reading" approach that we endorse will not make judging easy. (Easier, perhaps, but never easy.) Nor will it produce an absolute sameness of results. But it will narrow the range of acceptable judicial decision-making and acceptable argumentation. It will curb—even reverse—the tendency of judges to imbue authoritative texts with their own policy preferences. It will also discourage legislative free-riding, whereby legal drafters idly assume that judges will save them from their blunders.[2] Many of these interpretive goals

---

1   George Washington (1790), in *Maxims of Washington* 128 (1909) (emphasis added).

2   *See* Daniel A. Farber, *Statutory Interpretation and Legislative Supremacy*, 78 Geo. L.J. 281, 298 (1989) ("Judges must not allow legislators to use statutes to strike poses, knowing that courts will bail them out later."); Felix Frankfurter, *A Symposium on Statutory Construction: Foreword*, 3 Vand. L. Rev. 365, 368 (1950) ("Judicial expansion of meaning beyond the limits indicated is reprehensible because it encourages slipshodness in draftsmanship and irresponsibility in legislation.").

can be achieved—especially in fields other than constitutional law—even by a diluted strain of textualism. As for what we have called pure textualism, we hope to convince the reader of that as well.

Our approach is consistent with what the best legal thinkers have said for centuries. Textualism will not relieve judges of all doubts and misgivings about their interpretations. Judging is inherently difficult, and language notoriously slippery.[3] But textualism will provide greater certainty in the law, and hence greater predictability and greater respect for the rule of law. A system of democratically adopted laws cannot endure—it makes no sense—without the belief that words convey discernible meanings and without the commitment of legal arbiters to abide by those meanings. As one commentator aptly puts the point: "[I]t is not too much to say that the preference for the rule of law over the rule of men depends upon the intellectual integrity of interpretation."[4] And as Chief Justice John Marshall put it:

> Judicial power, as contradistinguished from the power of the laws, has no existence. Courts are the mere instruments of the law, and can will nothing. When they are said to exercise a discretion, it is a mere legal discretion, a discretion to be exercised in discerning the course prescribed by law; and, when that is discerned, it is the duty of the Court to follow it. Judicial power is never exercised for the purpose of giving effect to the will of the Judge; always for the purpose of giving effect to the will of the Legislature; or, in other words, to the will of the law.[5]

---

3   *See McCulloch v. Maryland*, 17 U.S. (4 Wheat.) 316, 414 (1819) (per Marshall, C.J.) ("Such is the character of human language, that no word conveys to the mind, in all situations, one single definite idea . . ."). *See also* Richard A. Epstein, *Design for Liberty* 15 (2011) ("Hard cases are endemic to all legal regimes, no matter what their substantive commitments.").

4   Gary L. McDowell, Introduction to *Politics and the Constitution: The Nature and Extent of Interpretation* vii, vii (1990).

5   *Osborn v. Bank of the U.S.*, 22 U.S. 738, 866 (1824) (per Marshall, C.J.). *See* Lackland H. Bloom Jr., *Methods of Interpretation: How the Supreme Court Reads the Constitution* 3 (2009) (showing that "for Marshall the underlying rationale for judicial review itself was dependent on an understandable and legally applicable text").

Our basic presumption: legislators enact;[6] judges interpret.[7] And *interpret* is a transitive verb: judges interpret texts. We propose to explain how they should perform this task.

One final personal note: Your judicial author knows that there are some, and fears that there may be many, opinions that he has joined or written over the past 30 years that contradict what is written here—whether because of the demands of stare decisis or because wisdom has come late. Worse still, your judicial author does not swear that the opinions that he joins or writes in the future will comply with what is written here—whether because of stare decisis, because wisdom continues to come late, or because a judge must remain open to persuasion by counsel. Yet the prospect of "gotchas" for past and future inconsistencies holds no fear.

A.S.
B.A.G.

---

6   *See* U.S. Const. art. I, § 1 ("All legislative Powers herein granted shall be vested in a Congress of the United States").

7   *See id.* art. III, § 1 ("The judicial Power of the United States, shall be vested in one supreme Court, and in such inferior Courts as the Congress may from time to time ordain and establish."); Alexander Hamilton, *The Federalist*, No. 78 ("The interpretation of the laws is the proper and peculiar province of the courts.").

Introduction

A. The Why of This Book

The Flood-Control Case

You be the judge—the appellate judge—for a moment. Here is the case: There has been a tragic incident at a reservoir near New Orleans. Two honeymooning waterskiers have died. A federal employee was sitting atop a tower that looked down on the reservoir. With full knowledge that there were skiers nearby, he opened the huge floodgates to let out water. There was no particular need to drain any water. Yet he did it. The force of the current he created sucked two married couples through the gates, and one member of each couple—one husband and one wife—died. The surviving spouses have sued the federal government. After a trial, the district judge found that the government employee's actions went "beyond gross negligence" and "constituted a classic example of death and injuries resulting from conscious governmental indifference to public safety."

The 1952 Federal Tort Claims Act broadly authorized most tort actions against the federal government, but it expressly excluded actions prohibited by the 1928 Flood Control Act, which said that "no liability of any kind shall attach to or rest upon the United States for any damage from or by floods or flood waters at any place." The issue—whether this statutory immunity embraces the loss of human life—is a question of interpretation.

The lawyers in the case, as well as your two colleagues on the bench, have urged you to consider all kinds of factors:

- The contents of the reservoir are "flood waters" under the statute, because a prior Supreme Court opinion has so held.

- The immunizing statute is dated 1928, and the recent trend is against tort immunities.

- The purpose of the statute was to prevent a rash of lawsuits against the federal government for massive flood-control measures taken after the devastating Mississippi flood of 1927.

- The statute has not been the subject of reported litigation since 1942. One of your colleagues insists that the 1928 statute is defunct.

- It is well established that waivers of sovereign immunity are to be narrowly construed. This means, one of your colleagues asserts, that the 1928 exemption from the Federal Tort Claims Act should be broadly construed.

- The record suggests that the surviving spouses are of extremely modest means, and it does not show whether the decedents had any life insurance.

- The legislative history suggests that the overriding concern was with the federal government's destruction of farmland by flooding it to create reservoirs. Nowhere does it contain any reference to a loss of life.

- The original drafters of the immunity, as far as appears, never foresaw a day in which flood-control reservoirs would be used recreationally (as they have been since the 1950s). One of your colleagues has invited you to "imaginatively reconstruct" what those members of Congress would want if they were here today; they would never, he thinks, have intended immunity. He has also suggested that today's Congress would never endorse such an immunity.

- The Flood Control Act's immunity-conferring language is sweeping: no liability of *any* kind for *any* damage at *any* place.

Your two appellate colleagues are split, and you have the deciding vote. How should you decide? And (more important) why? What should you consider?

Those are the types of questions that we propose to answer in this book. And at the end of this introduction, we will give our own answers to those very questions in this hypothetical flood-control case—based on a case that was actually decided by the Supreme Court of the United States. Look now if you must (p. 44). But we invite you to ruminate about the case as we first discuss some fundamental points of interpretation.

The Need for a Sound Approach

Ours is a common-law tradition in which judicial improvisation has abounded. Statutes were a comparatively infrequent source of English law through the mid-19th century. Where statutes did not exist, the law was the product of judicial invention, at least in those many areas where there was no accepted common law for courts to "discover." It is unsurprising that the judges who used to be the lawgivers took some liberties with the statutes that began to supplant their handiwork—adopting, for example, a rule that statutes in derogation of the common law (judge-made law) were to be narrowly construed and rules for filling judicially perceived "gaps" in statutes that had less to do with perceived meaning than with the judges' notions of public policy.[1] Such distortion of texts that have been adopted by the people's elected representatives is undemocratic. In an age when democratically prescribed texts (such as statutes, ordinances, and regulations) are the rule, the judge's principal function is to give those texts their fair meaning.[2]

---

1   *See, e.g.*, John F. Manning, *Textualism and the Equity of the Statute*, 101 Colum. L. Rev. 1, 36–52 (2001) (arguing that the blurring of judicial and legislative functions in premodern England explains the embrace of judicial policymaking); Max Radin, *The Doctrine of the Separation of Powers in Seventeenth Century Controversies*, 86 U. Pa. L. Rev. 842, 844 (1938) ("Separation of powers had no place in the common law.").

2   Timothy Walker, *Introduction to American Law* 61 (Clement Bates ed., 10th ed. 1895) (codification in statutes makes our laws "more conformable to the theory of our government, which vests legislative power in the legislature alone, and not in the judiciary"). *See also* Cass R. Sunstein, *Interpreting Statutes in the Regulatory State*, 103 Harv. L. Rev. 405, 415 (1989) ("According to the most prominent conception of the role of courts in statutory construction, judges are agents or servants of the legislature."); Nicholas S. Zeppos, *Legislative History and the Interpretation of Statutes: Toward a Fact-Finding Model of Statutory Interpretation*, 76 Va. L. Rev. 1295, 1313 (1990) ("Traditional democratic theory suggests that the court interpreting a statute must act as the faithful agent of the legislature's intent.").

Some judges, however, refuse to yield the ancient judicial prerogative of making the law, improvising on the text to produce what they deem socially desirable results—usually at the behest of an advocate for one party to a dispute. The judges are also prodded by interpretive theorists who avow that courts are "better able to discern and articulate basic national ideals than are the people's politically responsible representatives."[3] On this view, judges are to improvise "basic national ideals of individual liberty and fair treatment, even when the content of these ideals is not expressed as a matter of positive law in the written Constitution."[4]

To the extent that people give this view any credence, the notion that judges may (even should) improvise on constitutional and statutory text enfeebles the democratic polity. As Justice John Marshall Harlan warned in the 1960s, an invitation to judicial lawmaking results inevitably in "a lessening, on the one hand, of judicial independence and, on the other, of legislative responsibility, thus polluting the bloodstream of our system of government."[5] Why these alarming outcomes? First, when judges fashion law rather than fairly derive it from governing texts, they subject themselves to intensified political pressures—in the appointment process, in their retention, and in the arguments made to them. Second, every time a court constitutionalizes a new sliver of law— as by finding a "new constitutional right" to do this, that, or the other—that sliver becomes thenceforth untouchable by the political branches. In the American system, a legislature has no power to abridge a right that has been authoritatively held to be part of

---

3   Thomas C. Grey, "Do We Have an Unwritten Constitution?" in *Stanford Legal Essays* 179, 182 (1975).

4   *Id.*

5   John M. Harlan, *The Evolution of a Judicial Philosophy: Selected Opinions and Papers of Justice John M. Harlan* 291 (1969). *Cf.* William Van Alstyne, "Clashing Visions of a 'Living' Constitution: Of Opportunists and Obligationists," in *Cato Supreme Court Review 2010–2011* 13, 20 (2011) ("The more courts transform constitutional clauses without needing actual amendments to do so—*that is*, the more they do not require new text—the less necessary new text seems to be. But then exactly to the extent that courts do not require new text, neither may it be safe to provide it, for to the extent such text is provided to record a *definite* change, one may rightly be wary—merely reacting in tutored fear of the administration of that new text, given what the Court has previously presumed *already* to do.").

the Constitution—even if that newfound right does not appear in the text. Over the past 50 years especially, we have seen the judiciary incrementally take control of larger and larger swaths of territory that ought to be settled legislatively.

It used to be said that judges do not "make" law—they simply apply it. In the 20th century, the legal realists convinced everyone that judges do indeed make law. To the extent that this was true, it was knowledge that the wise already possessed and the foolish could not be trusted with. It was true, that is, that judges did not really "find" the common law but invented it over time. Yet this notion has been stretched into a belief that judges "make" law through judicial interpretation of democratically enacted statutes. Consider the following statement by John P. Dawson, intended to apply to statutory law:

> It seems to us inescapable that judges should have a part in creating law—creating it as they apply it. In deciding the multifarious disputes that are brought before them, we believe that judges in any legal system invariably adapt legal doctrines to new situations and thus give them new content.[6]

Now it is true that in a system such as ours, in which judicial decisions have a stare decisis effect, a court's application of a statute to a "new situation" can be said to establish *the law applicable to that situation*—that is, to pronounce definitively whether and how the statute applies to that situation. But establishing this retail application of the statute is probably not what Dawson meant by "creating law," "adapt[ing] legal doctrines," and "giv[ing] them new content." Yet beyond that retail application, good judges dealing with statutes do *not* make law.[7] They do not "give new content" to the statute, but merely apply the content that has been there all along, awaiting application to myriad factual scenarios. To say that they "make law" without this necessary qualification is to

---

6   John P. Dawson, "The Functions of the Judge," in *Talks on American Law* 19, 19 (Harold J. Berman ed., 2d ed. 1971).

7   *See* William Geldart, *Introduction to English Law* 9 (9th ed. 1984) ("[T]o say that a judge in deciding is ever doing anything analogous to legislation is really doing violence to the facts.").

invite the taffy-like stretching of words—or the ignoring of words altogether.

There is no doubt that some courts—many courts—have accepted the invitation. All too true is the observation of Edward H. Levi: "[T]he fact is that in our society the law court is a powerful instrument for effecting changes that the legislature will not enact or for preventing, for some time at least, the changes that the legislatures do enact."[8] There is no constitutional justification for such a judicial hegemony.

Lawyers emboldened by the courts' adventurism in social reform actively encourage more of it, as with the lawyers who in 2011 filed suit against SeaWorld, trying to establish that the Thirteenth Amendment's prohibitions of slavery make the aquarium's keeping of killer whales unconstitutional.[9] Such "give-it-a-try litigation"[10] will be spawned by a corps of judges, or even a significant minority of them, who are willing to veer from text and tradition.

One object of this treatise is to remove a facile excuse for judicial overreaching—the notion that words can have no definite meaning. As we hope to demonstrate, most interpretive questions have a right answer.[11] Variability in interpretation is a distemper.[12] It is not true, as some commentators have claimed since the mid-20th century, that "[a]ll legislative language is ambiguous and usually susceptible of several reasonable readings."[13] Even further from

---

8   Edward H. Levi, "The Nature of Judicial Reasoning," in *Law and Philosophy: A Symposium* 263, 279 (Sidney Hook ed., 1964).

9   Greg Moran, "Orcas Make a Splashy Legal Debut with Suit," *San Diego Union-Trib.*, 27 Oct. 2011, at A1.

10   *See Lehnert v. Ferris Faculty Ass'n*, 500 U.S. 507, 550–51 (1991) (Scalia, J., concurring in the judgment in part and dissenting in part) (criticizing the creation of three-prong tests that involve "substantial judgment call[s]" because they are "calculated to perpetuate give-it-a-try litigation").

11   *See* Cass R. Sunstein, *Interpreting Statutes in the Regulatory State*, 103 Harv. L. Rev. 405, 442 (1989) ("When taken in their setting—in their context and culture—statutes are usually susceptible to only one plausible meaning.").

12   *See* Cesare Beccaria, *An Essay on Crimes and Punishments* 25 (1793) ("The disorders that may arise from a rigorous observance of the letter of penal laws, are not to be compared with those produced by the [variable] interpretation of them.").

13   Joseph P. Witherspoon, *Administrative Discretion to Determine Statutory Meaning: "The High Road,"* 35 Tex. L. Rev. 63, 76 (1956).

the truth is the contention that "in fact, statutes and precedents can yield up any number of plausible or permissible readings."[14] That dogma, if accepted, would annihilate critical thought about interpretive decision-making.

This treatise has another purpose as well. More serious, perhaps, than the fact that some judges knowingly persist in acting as lawgivers is the fact that many judges who believe in fidelity to text lack the interpretive tools necessary to that end. American legal education has long been devoted to the training of common-law lawyers, and hence common-law judges. What aspiring lawyers learn in the first, formative year of law school is how to discern the best (most socially useful) answer to a legal problem, and how to distinguish the prior cases that stand in the way of that solution. Besides giving students the wrong impression about what makes an excellent judge in a modern, democratic, text-based legal system, this training fails to inculcate the skills of textual interpretation. What students learn about the canons of interpretation and other principles of textual construction they learn haphazardly, when reading cases in such text-based courses as tax law, securities law, employment law, environmental law, and administrative law. Yet perhaps there exists a promising trend. In recent years, a few schools have adopted a mandatory first-year "Legislation and Regulation" course—after a long period of neglect.[15] Even so, a noted Harvard law professor, Mary Ann Glendon, has said: "Most of our fellow citizens, no doubt, would be astonished if they knew how little training the average law student receives in dealing with enacted law."[16] When your authors, as an experiment,

---

14 T. Alexander Aleinikoff & Theodore M. Shaw, *The Costs of Incoherence*, 45 Vand. L. Rev. 687, 689 n.4 (1992). *Cf.* Sanford Levinson, *Law as Literature*, 60 Tex. L. Rev. 373, 391 (1982) ("There are as many plausible readings of the United States Constitution as there are versions of *Hamlet* . . .").

15 Robert J. Martineau, *Craft and Technique, Not Canons and Grand Theories: A Neo-Realist View of Statutory Construction*, 62 Geo. Wash. L. Rev. 1, 3 n.8 (1993) ("The consensus of those who have written on the subject . . . is that law schools during the 1960–1980 period largely ignored legislation as a separate course in the curriculum.").

16 Mary Ann Glendon, "Comment," in Antonin Scalia, *A Matter of Interpretation: Federal Courts and the Law* 95, 96 (1997). *Cf.* Roscoe Pound, *The Future of the Common Law* 18 (1937) ("the common-law lawyer is at his worst when confront-

asked a group of about 600 lawyers how many knew the meaning of *ejusdem generis* (one of the oldest and most frequently applied canons [see § 32]), only about 10 had sufficient confidence in the answer to raise their hands.[17]

Although our legal system "calls and must call for increasingly skilled interpretation,"[18] the lack of training in lawyers produces a lack of competence in judges. In 1933, a leading legal philosopher, Morris R. Cohen, summed up the situation this way: "There are few branches of the law of which the theory is so confused or disorganized as in the case of the interpretation and construction of written instruments."[19] A quarter-century later, when the predicament was somewhat less disheveled than it is today, two leading commentators wrote: "American courts have no intelligible, generally accepted and consistently applied theory of statutory interpretation."[20] Hence it is hardly surprising that one can find judicial opinions, even from the highest courts, that sanction almost any approach to the interpretation of legally operative language—up to and including the remarkable principle that words need not be construed to mean what they say. A descriptive treatise on modern legal interpretation would have to read like the familiar lawbook annotations that "inform" us that Rule X is thus-and-so, but that some courts say Rule X is *not* thus-and-so. Such undiscriminating compendiums of judicial holdings might be useful to the litigator seeking some authority that will sanction the

---

ed with a legislative text"); Karl Llewellyn, *The Common Law Tradition: Deciding Appeals* 380 (1960) ("It is indeed both sobering and saddening to match our boisterous ways with a statutory text against the watchmaker's delicacy and care of a . . . Continental legal craftsman.").

17 The authors conducted this experiment at an American Bar Association function on 31 March 2011.

18 H. Wynn-Parry, Foreword to G. Granville Sharp & Brian Galpin, *Maxwell on the Interpretation of Statutes* vi (10th ed. 1953).

19 Morris R. Cohen, *Law and the Social Order: Essays in Legal Philosophy* 128 (1933).

20 Henry M. Hart & Albert M. Sacks, *The Legal Process: Basic Problems in the Making and Application of Law* 1201 (tent. ed. 1958). *Cf.* P.S. Atiyah, *An Introduction to the Law of Contract* 207 (4th ed. 1989) ("Perhaps nowhere does the law of the twentieth century seem more inadequate to its purposes than in the rules for the interpretation of written documents.").

interpretation being urged. But they exist elsewhere, and it is not our aim to expand their number. Our approach is unapologetically normative, prescribing what, in our view, courts ought to do with operative language.

The reader may well wonder: Where are all these interpretive canons to be found? Are they tidily collected somewhere in a code? Generally, no. Mostly, the canons exist within the thousands of law reports scattered through a law library, expounded at length but with questionable lucidity. One marvels at the naiveté of a 1946 statement: "The rules of interpretation of an English statute are well settled and familiar to all students."[21] That was not true in England at the time, and it was not true in America. The very next year, Justice Felix Frankfurter complained: "I do not get much nourishment from books on statutory construction, and I say this after freshly reexamining them all, scores of them."[22] We believe that our effort is the first modern attempt, certainly in a century,[23] to collect and arrange only the valid canons (perhaps a third of the possible candidates) and to show how and why they apply to proper legal interpretation.

The Prevailing Confusion

Is it an exaggeration to say that the field of interpretation is rife with confusion? No. Although the problem of tendentiously variable readings is age-old, the cause is not: the desire for freedom from the text, which enables judges to do what they want.

Distortion of text to suit the reader's fancy is by no means limited to the law. In the field of literature, T.S. Eliot warned about literary critics who forget that they are dealing with a text and instead find in a work such as *Hamlet* "a vicarious existence for their own artistic realization."[24] They substitute "their own Hamlet for

---

21 F.A. Mann, *The Interpretation of Uniform Statutes*, 62 L.Q. Rev. 278, 278 (1946).

22 Felix Frankfurter, *Some Reflections on the Reading of Statutes*, 47 Colum. L. Rev. 527, 530 (1947).

23 *See* Henry Campbell Black, *Handbook on the Construction and Interpretation of the Laws* (2d ed. 1911).

24 T.S. Eliot, "Hamlet" (1919), in *Selected Essays* 141, 141 (2d ed. 1934).

Shakespeare's."[25] The practice of injecting one's own thoughts into texts has long been given free rein in some schools of scriptural exegesis—so long, in fact, that scholars have given the practice its own disreputable name: *eisegesis*. The antonym of *exegesis*, the term *eisegesis* denotes the insertion of the reader's own ideas into the text, making the reader a full collaborator with the original author and enabling the introduction of all sorts of new material. For eisegetes, the possibilities are endless.

Liberation from text is attractive to judges as well. It increases their ability to do what they think is good. Unlike Shakespeare producers and theologians, judges are pressured by the environment in which they operate. In our adversarial system, one side—the side with a bad argument—has an incentive to urge departure from (or distortion of) text. It was about early nontextual expositors that John Locke wrote when he asked: "[Does] it not often happen that a man of an ordinary capacity very well understands a text or a law that he reads, till he consults an expositor, or goes to counsel; who, by the time he [has] explain[ed] them, makes the words signify either nothing at all, or what he pleases?"[26]

The quest for nontextual decision-making sometimes becomes a kind of mystical divination. Consider, for example, the view of Richard C. Cabot, an early proponent of nontextualist views. Preferring the spirit to the letter, he thought that we should endlessly create new meanings for the U.S. Constitution:

> The spirit of any agreement is thus disconcertingly wider and deeper than its letter, because both are parts of the human spirit, a network of interweaving purposes aware of but a fragment of its own implications. Its purposes are not sharply or permanently outlined. They grow as it grows. [What grows? the agreement? the human spirit? the fragment?] They find meaning after meaning hidden like a nest of Chinese boxes inside the one that they start with. . . . The spirit of the . . . written Constitution of the United

---

25 *Id.*

26 John Locke, *An Essay Concerning Human Understanding* 210 (1689; Kenneth P. Winkler ed., 1996).

States is something to be learned, but also something to be cultivated and to be created.[27]

What exactly this means is anyone's guess. Why Cabot used the word *disconcertingly* in the first sentence is puzzling, since he appears exuberant about the nebulous spirit to which he refers. Cabot was an unabashed enthusiast for letting the intangible, protean spirit overtake the tangible, fixed words of authoritative texts: "The labor of interpreting rigid words in light of growing purposes is a perennial human task . . . . The spirit must remake the letter again and again, not only because we forget but because we grow."[28]

But even in 1933, Cabot's theory of interpretation was not exactly new. That theory had found its apotheosis in *Holy Trinity Church v. United States.*[29] This notorious Supreme Court case involved a statute that expressly prohibited "the importation . . . of . . . foreigners . . . under contract . . . to perform labor or service of any kind in the United States."[30] The statute made exceptions for, among other occupations, professional actors, artists, lecturers, and singers, but none for clergymen. The United States sued Trinity Church, in New York City, for the penalty provided by the statute, because the church had contracted with an English minister to become its pastor. While admitting that the church's act was "within the letter" of the statute, the Supreme Court of the United States nonetheless felt that the church should not be held liable— "felt," we say, because the situation involved what is technically known as a *casus male inclusus* (that is, a situation unquestionably covered by the explicit words of the statute, but thought to be ill-advisedly covered). A result-oriented Court applied a "viperine interpretation" that killed the statute for present purposes to achieve a desired result. Its rationale: "[A] thing may be within the letter of the statute and yet not within the statute, because not within

---

27 Richard C. Cabot, *The Meaning of Right and Wrong* 209–10 (1933).

28 *Id.* at 208–09.

29 143 U.S. 457 (1892) (per Brewer, J.).

30 *Id.* at 458.

its spirit nor within the intention of its makers."[31] Nontextualists often quote this statement to justify readings that defy the text, as when Justice William Brennan used it in *United Steelworkers v. Weber*[32] to permit a racially based affirmative-action program in the face of a statute that made it unlawful to "discriminate . . . because of . . . race."[33]

Holy Trinity is a decision that the Supreme Court stopped relying on more than two decades ago.[34] Its ascendancy among theorists began in the early 20th century, when (for example) one commentator urged judges to substitute their own idealized version of what the governing text might say (but does not), touting the "imaginative comprehension of the element of ideal policy on the part of the judicial mind"[35] and decrying the "inordinate respect for procedure [that] comes to dominate legal interpretation."[36] A later theorist, still active, argues that judges should base decisions on their sense of what "community morality" provides.[37] In his view, "[s]tatutory interpretation aims to make the governance of the pertinent community fairer, wiser, and more just."[38] We do not mean to suggest that what has assertedly become the theorists' "preferred style of interpretation" has achieved predominance

---

31 *Id.* at 459. *Cf. People ex rel. Attorney-General v. Utica Ins. Co.*, 15 Johns. 358, 381 (N.Y. 1818) (stating the mantra of two-fanged viperine interpretations: "A thing which is within the intention of the makers of a statute is as much within the statute as if it were within the letter; and a thing which is within the letter of the statute, is not within the statute, unless it be within the intention of the makers."). For more on viperine interpretations, see p. 431.

32 443 U.S. 193 (1979) (per Brennan, J.).

33 *Id.* at 199 n.2; § 703(a) and (d) of Title VII of the 1964 Civil Rights Act.

34 *See* John F. Manning, *Second-Generation Textualism*, 98 Cal. L. Rev. 1287, 1313 (2010) (opining that some Justices of the United States Supreme Court have "succeeded in dispatching *Holy Trinity* from the mainstream of the Court's jurisprudence").

35 Elijah Jordan, *Theory of Legislation: An Essay on the Dynamics of Public Mind* 442 (1930; repr. 1952).

36 *Id.* at 445.

37 Ronald Dworkin, *Taking Rights Seriously* 126 (1977).

38 Ronald Dworkin, *Justice for Hedgehogs* 133 (2011). *Cf.* Ronald Dworkin, *Law as Interpretation*, 60 Tex. L. Rev. 527, 541–43 (1982) (suggesting that judges are full-fledged coauthors of chain novels, the legislature being solely responsible for only the first chapter).

within the judiciary. While a spirit-of-the-law approach occasionally rears its head (see § 58), the Supreme Court of the United States has not cited *Holy Trinity* favorably since 1989,[39] and Justice John Paul Stevens's invocation and defense of the case in a 2007 concurrence was joined by no other Justice.[40]

Modern nontextualism is based in part on an equivocal use of the word *construction*, which is the noun corresponding to *construe*. When construing a statute, one engages in *statutory construction*, which has long been used interchangeably with the phrase *statutory interpretation*. When one is construing a constitutional text, one is engaged in *constitutional construction* or, again, *constitutional interpretation*. When construing a contract, one is likewise engaged in *contractual construction*—though the more usual phrase is *contractual interpretation*. So far, so good.

Oddly enough, though, the noun *construction* answers both to *construe* (meaning "to interpret") and to *construct* (meaning "to build"). Lawyers have been known to make the embarrassing linguistic gaffe of talking about *constructing* a statute when they refer to deriving meaning from it. A book about constitutional adjudication (by a nonlawyer, we are happy to add) referred to "the Supreme Court's role in *constructing* the United States Constitution," a solecism that one of us called out in a book on legal usage.[41]

As it happens, nontextualists have latched onto the duality of *construction*. From the germ of an idea in the theoretical works of the 19th-century writer Francis Lieber,[42] scholars have elaborated a

---

39 *Public Citizen v. United States Dep't of Justice*, 491 U.S. 440, 454 (1989) (per Brennan, J.).

40 *Zuni Pub. Sch. Dist. No. 89 v. Department of Educ.*, 550 U.S. 81, 107 n.3 (2007) (Stevens, J., concurring).

41 *Garner's Dictionary of Legal Usage* 210 (3d ed. 2011) (adding that "[a] nonlawyer might think that *construction of statutes* is the business of legislatures, since they *construct* (i.e., build) statutes; but *construction* in that phrase means 'the process of construing,' which is the business of the courts").

42 *See id.* at 474. Francis Lieber, *Legal and Political Hermeneutics, or Principles of Interpretation and Construction in Law and Politics* 56 (1839) (defining *construction*, with absolutely no citation of authority, as "the drawing of conclusions respecting subjects that lie beyond the direct expression of the text, from elements known from and given in the text—conclusions which are in the spirit, though not within the letter of the text").

supposed distinction between *interpretation* and *construction*: "The academic discourse . . . increasingly distinguishes between *constitutional interpretation*, which is a hermeneutic exercise common to literature and law alike, and *constitutional construction*, which is a political and adjudicative exercise designed to fill the interstices of constitutional text."[43] Thus is born, out of false linguistic association, a whole new field of legal inquiry.

But the equivocal nature of *construction* has positively done harm in the work of constitutional theorists who wish to liberate judges from the texts they construe. One, for example, has recently written a 474-page book largely premised on the distinction: *Constitutional interpretation*, he says, is "the ascertainment of meaning,"[44] while *constitutional construction* involves "build[ing] out the American state over time,"[45] especially through all the supposed "modalities of interpretation: arguments from history, structure, ethos, consequences, and precedent."[46] These are said to be "state-building constructions."[47] He argues that when political and social movements over time "are successful, they change the mind of the general public, politicians, and courts," and that "[t]his influence eventually gets reflected in new laws, in new constitutional doctrines, and in new constitutional constructions."[48] Even some textualists have embraced the distinction so as to contrast

---

43 Jamal Greene, *On the Origins of Originalism*, 88 Tex. L. Rev. 1, 10 (2009) (emphasis added). *Cf.* Randy E. Barnett, *Restoring the Lost Constitution: The Presumption of Liberty* 99 (2004) (distinguishing interpretation, which determines the meaning of words, from construction, which "fills the inevitable gaps created by the vagueness of these words when applied to particular circumstances"); Keith E. Whittington, *Constitutional Interpretation: Textual Meaning, Original Intent, and Judicial Review* 7–11 (1999) (characterizing constitutional interpretation as "essentially legalistic" and constitutional construction as "essentially political"). *Cf.* Stanley Fish, *Is There a Text in This Class?* 327 (1980) (stating, in relation to literary criticism, that "[i]nterpretation is not the art of construing but the art of constructing," adding: "Interpreters do not decode poems; they make them.").

44 Jack M. Balkin, *Living Originalism* 4 (2011).

45 *Id.* at 5 (using, in chapter 1 alone, *constitutional construction* 17 times; *construction* 22 times; *construe* none at all; and *construct* 2 times).

46 *Id.* at 4.

47 *Id.* at 5.

48 *Id.* at 18.

the legitimacy of constitutional interpretation with the relative illegitimacy of so-called constitutional construction.[49]

But this supposed distinction between *interpretation* and *construction* has never reflected the courts' actual usage. As a scholar accurately wrote in 1914: "Some authors have attempted to introduce a distinction between *interpretation* and *construction* . . . but it has not been accepted by the profession. For practical purposes any such distinction may be ignored, in view of the real object of both interpretation and construction, which is merely to ascertain the meaning and will of the lawmaking body, in order that it may be enforced."[50] Or another in 1993: "The terms 'construction' and 'interpretation' have been used as synonyms when applied to statutes for as long as scholars have written on the subject."[51]

Textualism and Its Challengers

Theories of legal interpretation have been discussed interminably, and often so obscurely as to leave even the most intelligent readers—or perhaps especially the most intelligent readers—befuddled.[52] So why would we add to the number? In fact, we do not. Far from proposing yet another novel approach, we seek a return to the oldest and most commonsensical interpretive principle:

---

49 *See, e.g.*, Lawrence B. Solum, "We Are All Originalists Now," in Lawrence B. Solum & Robert W. Bennett, *Constitutional Originalism: A Debate* 22–24 (2011).

50 William M. Lile et al., *Brief Making and the Use of Law Books* 337 (3d ed. 1914). *See* John O. McGinnis & Michael B. Rappaport, *Original Methods Originalism: A New Theory of Interpretation and the Case Against Construction*, 103 Nw. U. L. Rev. 751, 772–80 (2009) (noting that the distinction between interpretation and construction is conceptually and historically unfounded); H.T. Tiffany, "Interpretation and Construction," in 17 *American and English Encyclopaedia of Law* 1, 2 (David S. Garland & Lucius P. McGehee eds., 2d ed. 1900) (calling the purported distinction "of little practical benefit" and noting that "the terms are used interchangeably by the courts and by the majority of text-book writers").

51 Robert J. Martineau, *Craft and Technique, Not Canons and Grand Theories: A Neo-Realist View of Statutory Construction*, 62 Geo. Wash. L. Rev. 1, 1 n.1 (1993).

52 *See* Learned Hand, "Proceedings in Commemoration of Fifty Years of Federal Judicial Service," 264 F.2d [introductory page] 28 (1959) ("[M]any sages . . . have spoken on [statutory construction], and I do not know that it has gotten us very much further.").

> In their full context, words mean what they conveyed to
> reasonable people at the time they were written—with the
> understanding that general terms may embrace later tech-
> nological innovations.

Hence a 2012 statute referring to *aircraft*, if still in effect in 2112, would embrace whatever inventions the label fairly embraces, even inventions that could not have been dreamed of in 2012. The exclusive reliance on text when interpreting text is known as *textualism*. We believe that this approach elicits both better drafting and better decision-making.

In the broad sense, everyone is a textualist. Even judges without textualist convictions habitually open their opinions by stating: "We begin with the words of the statute."[53] This statement belabors the obvious. One naturally must begin with the words of the statute when the very subject of the litigation is what the statute requires. But to say that one *begins* with the words of the statute is to suggest that one does not *end* there. Like the starting line of a boat race, the text is (on this view) thought to be a point of departure for a much longer journey. So when you read qualified introductory bows to the text, brace yourself for a nontextual solution—maybe a far-fetched one.

Textualism, in its purest form, begins and ends with what the text says and fairly implies. Its principal tenets have guided the interpretation of legal texts for centuries. To enable the reader to evaluate pure textualism with an open mind, we must lay to rest at the outset the slander that it is a device calculated to produce socially or politically conservative outcomes. Textualism is not well designed to achieve ideological ends, relying as it does on the most objective criterion available: the accepted contextual meaning that the words had when the law was enacted. A textualist reading will sometimes produce "conservative" outcomes, sometimes "liberal" ones. If any interpretive method deserves to be labeled an ideological "device," it is not textualism but competing methodologies such as purposivism and consequentialism, by which the words

---

53   *But see Chisom v. Roemer*, 501 U.S. 380, 383 (1991) (per Stevens, J.) (which begins
     not with the words of the statute but with its "central purpose"—a practice that
     one of us in dissent called "just backwards"—*id.* at 405).

and implications of text are replaced with abstractly conceived "purposes" or interpreter-desired "consequences." Willful judges might use textualism to achieve the ends they desire, and when the various indications of textual meaning point in different directions, even dutiful judges may unconsciously give undue weight to the factors that lead to what they consider the best result. But in a textualist culture, the distortion of the willful judge is much more transparent, and the dutiful judge is never *invited* to pursue the purposes and consequences that he prefers.

If pure textualism were actually a technique for achieving ideological ends, your authors would be counted extraordinarily inept at it. One of them, a confessed law-and-order social conservative, wrote the first Supreme Court opinion protesting the "enhancement" (i.e., increase) of criminal sentences on the basis of factual determinations made by judge rather than jury[54] and dissented from such "conservative" majority opinions as those setting a constitutional limit on the amount of punitive damages,[55] preventing tort suits against nonmilitary personnel by persons injured in active military service,[56] and imposing criminal punishment for "using a firearm" on a defendant whose "use" of the gun was to trade it for drugs.[57] He has cast the deciding vote or written for the Court in such "liberal" majority opinions as the one holding unconstitutional laws prohibiting the burning of the American flag[58] and the one overruling the case allowing un-cross-examined hearsay to be introduced in criminal prosecutions.[59] Your other author holds many opinions commonly seen as "liberal." He is

---

54 *Almendarez-Torres v. United States*, 523 U.S. 224, 260 (1998) (Scalia, J., dissenting). *See also Apprendi v. New Jersey*, 530 U.S. 466, 499 (2000) (Scalia, J., concurring).

55 *BMW of N. Am., Inc. v. Gore*, 517 U.S. 559, 598–99 (1996) (Scalia, J., dissenting).

56 *United States v. Johnson*, 481 U.S. 681, 692–93 (1987) (Scalia, J., dissenting) (protesting expansion of the judicially created *Feres* immunity to nonmilitary defendants—*see Feres v. United States*, 340 U.S. 135 (1950) (per Jackson, J.)).

57 *Smith v. United States*, 508 U.S. 223, 241–42 (1993) (Scalia, J., dissenting) (arguing that the ordinary meaning of *using* a gun or other instrumentality is using it for its intended purpose).

58 *Texas v. Johnson*, 491 U.S. 397 (1989) (per Brennan, J.).

59 *Crawford v. Washington*, 541 U.S. 36 (2004) (per Scalia, J.).

pro-choice, for example, and supports same-sex marriage; but he finds nothing in the text of the Constitution that mandates these policies. He also favors gun control and deplores the Second Amendment, but he believes that the majority opinion in *Heller*[60] correctly interpreted that amendment as establishing a personal right to bear firearms.

Sir Thomas More (1478–1535) well knew the discomfort that the good judge sometimes feels. Speaking of his judicial duties, he declared: "[I]f the parties will at my hands call for justice, then, all were it my father stood on the one side, and the Devil on the other, his cause being good, the Devil should have right."[61] The judge's responsibility is a hard one.

Nontextualism, which frees the judge from interpretive scruple, comes in various forms. Perhaps the nontextualists' favorite substitute for text is purpose.[62] So-called purposivism, which has been called "the basic judicial approach these days,"[63] facilitates departure from text in several ways. Where purpose is king, text is not—so the purposivist goes around or behind the words of the controlling text to achieve what he believes to be the provision's purpose. Moreover, *purpose* is taken to mean the purpose of the author (the legislature or private drafter)—which means that all sorts of nontextual material such as legislative history (see § 66) becomes relevant to revise the fairest objective meaning of the text.

The most destructive (and most alluring) feature of purposivism is its manipulability. Any provision of law or of private ordering can be said to have a number of purposes, which can be placed on a ladder of abstraction. A law against pickpocketing, for example, has as its narrowest purpose the prevention of theft from the person; and then, in ascending order of generality, the protection of private property; the preservation of a system of private ownership;

---

60 *District of Columbia v. Heller*, 554 U.S. 570 (2008) (per Scalia, J.).

61 R.W. Chambers, *Thomas More* 268 (1962).

62 *See Harris v. Commissioner*, 178 F.2d 861, 864 (2d Cir. 1949) (per L. Hand, C.J.) ("It is always a dangerous business to fill in the text of a statute from its purposes.").

63 John Bell, "Policy Arguments in Statutory Interpretation," in *Legal Reasoning and Statutory Interpretation* 55, 59 (Jan van Dunné ed., 1989).

the encouragement of productive activity by enabling producers to enjoy the fruits of their labor; and, finally, the furtherance of the common good. The purposivist, who derives the meaning of text from purpose and not purpose from the meaning of text, is free to climb up this ladder of purposes and to "fill in" or change the text according to the level of generality he has chosen.[64] Climbing the levels of abstraction is a rhetorical ploy that allows the judge to disregard text, as Judge Frank Easterbrook explains: "Shifting the level of generality—emphasizing the anticipated effects of a rule while slighting the rule itself—is a method of liberating judges from rules. . . . A corps of judges allowed to play with the level of generality will move every which way, defeating the objective of justice (equal treatment) under law."[65] The unpredictability of purposivism is inevitable, as Lord Devlin recognized: "Five judges are no more likely to agree than five philosophers upon the philosophy behind an Act of Parliament, and five different judges are likely to have five different ideas about the right escape route from the prison of the text."[66]

Early in his career as a judge, Justice Harry Blackmun understood how best to further the interests that legislation seeks to protect. He wrote: "[T]he recognized purpose and aim of the statute are more consistently and protectively to be served if the statute is construed literally and objectively rather than non-literally and subjectively on a case-by-case application."[67] That view is precisely correct—though Justice Blackmun famously came to depart from it in his later years on the Supreme Court, perhaps because of the

---

64 *See* Max Radin, *Statutory Interpretation*, 43 Harv. L. Rev. 863, 876 (1930) (explaining that "nearly every end is a means to another end" and that, if one abstracts from a statute's "immediate" purposes to its "ultimate" purposes, it becomes necessary to acknowledge that "the avowed and ultimate purposes of all statutes, because of all law, are justice and security").

65 Frank H. Easterbrook, *What Does Legislative History Tell Us?* 66 Chi.-Kent L. Rev. 441, 449 (1990). *Cf.* Larry A. Alexander, *Painting Without the Numbers: Noninterpretive Judicial Review*, 8 U. Dayton L. Rev. 447, 452 (1983) ("At some point as we ascend the ladder of generality of description and then descend again to apply the general norm to a specific, modern practice, we cross over the line from what they [the Framers] banned to what we would ban.").

66 Patrick Devlin, *The Judge* 16 (1979).

67 *Petteys v. Butler*, 367 F.2d 528, 538 (8th Cir. 1966) (Blackmun, J., dissenting).

impatience that all of us feel in seeing the slow progress of the machinery of democratic government.

The term *purposivism* suggests, wrongly, that its supposed antonym—namely *textualism*—precludes consideration of a text's purpose. That is not so. It is untrue that a texualist judge must "put on blinders that shield the legislative purpose from view."[68] As we will demonstrate, the textualist routinely takes purpose into account, but in its concrete manifestations as deduced from close reading of the text. It is when an abstract purpose is allowed to supersede text that the result is what Justice Felix Frankfurter cautioned against: "interpretations by judicial libertines"[69] who "draw prodigally upon unformulated purposes or directions."[70]

The evident purpose of what a text seeks to achieve is an essential element of context that gives meaning to words.[71] *Nail* in a regulation governing beauty salons has a different meaning from *nail* in a municipal building code. The purposivist, however, goes beyond the immediate purpose evident from the text (climbs the ladder of generality) to find another purpose[72]—often a highly abstract one—enabling him to give crabbed interpretations to limiting provisions and unrealistically expansive interpretations to narrow provisions.

Consider a simplified illustration of purposivist interpretation: A city ordinance reads, "It is a class A misdemeanor for the driver of a vehicle not to come to a complete stop at a stop sign." Someone gets stopped, arrested, and charged. The proof is incon-

---

68 William D. Popkin, *An "Internal" Critique of Justice Scalia's Theory of Statutory Interpretation*, 76 Minn. L. Rev. 1133, 1142 (1992).

69 Felix Frankfurter, *Some Reflections on the Reading of Statutes*, 47 Colum. L. Rev. 527, 529 (1947).

70 Felix Frankfurter, *A Symposium on Statutory Construction: Foreword*, 3 Vand. L. Rev. 365, 367 (1950).

71 *See* Reed Dickerson, *Statutory Interpretation: Core Meaning and Marginal Uncertainty*, 29 Mo. L. Rev. 1, 11 (1964) ("[W]here the immediate legislative purpose is clearly revealed by the pertinent statutory language read in proper context, its meaning is clear.").

72 *See, e.g., FCC v. NextWave Personal Communications Inc.*, 537 U.S. 293, 311, 313–15 (2003) (Breyer, J., dissenting) (stating that it is "dangerous . . . to rely exclusively upon the literal meaning of a statute's words" and then proceeding to derive the statute's purpose without reference to the dispositive text).

trovertible. A judge who wants to get around the language might divine the purpose as being to promote public safety and note that there are no significant public-safety issues if it is 3:00 A.M. and no pedestrians or other drivers are anywhere in the vicinity. This judge might therefore find an equitable exception to the statute as "promoting its genuine purposes" and as "being true to its spirit."

What purposivism disregards is that some statutes pursue their broadest purpose (public safety, in the previous example) in a prophylactic fashion (*always* stop at a stop sign because we don't trust *your* judgment about whether public safety requires it). And other statutes depart from their broadest purpose in the other direction. A ban on vehicles in a public park might be aimed at protecting park visitors from dangerous or fast-moving objects, for example, but ambulances might be excepted. Otherwise it would pursue that broadest goal only at the expense of harming other values that the legislature deems important. After all, no statute, and no private instrument for that matter, pursues its "broad purpose" at all costs.[73] The statute might not have won majority approval without the provisions that limit its application or that simply stop short of what it might have done. Those limiting provisions (or the absence of more expansive provisions) are no less a reflection of the genuine "purpose" of the statute than the operative provisions, and it is not the court's function to alter the legislative compromise.[74]

One thinks of A.P. Herbert's fictional Lord Mildew, who was probably exasperated with purposivist arguments when he proclaimed: "If Parliament does not mean what it says it must say so."[75]

---

73 *See Pension Benefit Guar. Corp. v. LTV Corp.*, 496 U.S. 633, 646–47 (1990) (per Blackmun, J.) ("No legislation pursues its purposes at all costs. . . . [I]t frustrates rather than effectuates legislative intent simplistically to assume that *whatever* furthers the statute's primary objective must be the law.'") (quoting *Rodriguez v. United States*, 480 U.S. 522, 525–26 (1987) (per curiam)).

74 *Federal Reserve Sys. v. Dimension Fin. Corp.*, 474 U.S. 361, 374 (1986) (per Burger, C.J.) ("Invocation of the 'plain purpose' of legislation at the expense of the terms of the statute itself takes no account of the processes of compromise."). *See* John F. Manning, *What Divides Textualists from Purposivists?* 106 Colum. L. Rev. 70, 103–09 (2006) (explaining role of semantic meaning in legislative processes).

75 *Bluff v. Father Gray* (as quoted, fictitiously of course, in A.P. Herbert, *Uncommon Law* 313 (1935)).

Another common replacement for text is consequentialism, often referred to as *pragmatism* or *workability*. The proponents of this view (we will call them *consequentialists*) urge that statutes should be construed to produce sensible, desirable results, since that is surely what the legislature must have intended. But it is precisely because people differ over what is sensible and what is desirable that we elect those who will write our laws—and expect courts to observe what has been written. There is an uncanny correspondence between the consequentialist's own policy views and his judicial decisions.[76]

Some commentators are remarkably frank about it: "[P]olicy issues, even of a controversial character, are inherent in the judicial and interpretative function, and judges must (where necessary) import their own political morality to resolve interpretative questions when the legislative intent is doubtful or (sometimes, and within limits) even when the legislative intent is just substantively bad."[77] In short, these theorists would give judges free rein to override the legislature's "bad ideas"—even the bad ideas that are not unconstitutional.

The common response of purposivists and consequentialists to criticisms of their theories is that textualism, with its cross-cutting canons and competing principles, does not always provide a clear answer and hence can also be subjectively manipulated.[78] Yet there is a world of difference between an objective test (the text)—which sometimes provides no clear answer, thus leaving the door open to judicial self-gratification—and tests that invite judges to say that the law is what they think it ought to be.

Purposivists and consequentialists often purport to give effect to what the legislature desired—the broader purpose that it had in mind, or the sensible, workable outcomes that it surely intended.

---

76 *See* Antonin Scalia, *Originalism: The Lesser Evil*, 57 U. Cin. L. Rev. 849, 863 (1989) ("[T]he main danger in judicial interpretation . . . of any law . . . is that the judges will mistake their own predilections for the law.").

77 P.S. Atiyah & Robert S. Summers, *Form and Substance in Anglo-American Law* 109 (1987).

78 *See* William N. Eskridge Jr., *Textualism: The Unknown Ideal?* 96 Mich. L. Rev. 1509, 1533–36 (1998).

On this theory, the judges are "faithful agents" of the legislative branch, giving effect to what elected representatives of the people really desired.

But this mask of judicial lawmaking has recently been cast aside as interpretive theorists have begun arguing that judges are not just "faithful agents" but "cooperative partners" with the legislature in the making of our laws.[79] Curiously enough, these theorists, none of whom is otherwise known as an advocate of originalist interpretation of the Constitution, rest this assertion (for the federal courts, at least) on the original meaning of "The judicial Power" in Article III, § 1 of the Constitution. According to their account, judicial power was understood to include (and presumably state courts were also understood to possess) the power to "depart from or compromise the words or letter of a statute."[80] In other words, "[t]o prevent injustices by the most dangerous branch, the least dangerous one—no less an agent of 'We the People' [sic]— was expected to . . . trim back unjust and partial statutes, and make legislation more coherent with fundamental law."[81]

In medieval England, when the legislative and judicial powers were commingled, judges did exercise both.[82] But the Supreme Court of the United States was firmly committed to judicial textualism as early as the chief justiceship of John Marshall. While riding circuit in 1813, Marshall wrote:

> To [the legislative] department is confided, without revision, the power of deciding on the justice as well as wisdom of measures relative to subjects on which they have the constitutional power to act. Wherever, then, their language

---

79 *See, e.g.*, William N. Eskridge Jr., *Texualism: The Unknown Ideal?* 96 Mich. L. Rev. 1509, 1522–23 (1998); William D. Popkin, *The Collaborative Model of Statutory Interpretation*, 61 S. Cal. L. Rev. 541, 585 (1988); Jonathan R. Siegel, *Textualism and Contextualism in Administrative Law*, 78 B.U. L. Rev. 1023, 1094–96 (1998).

80 William N. Eskridge Jr., *All About Words: Early Understandings of the "Judicial Power" in Statutory Interpretation, 1776–1806*, 101 Colum. L. Rev. 990, 996 (2001).

81 *Id.* at 995.

82 *See* John F. Manning, *Textualism and the Equity of the Statute*, 101 Colum. L. Rev. 1 (2001).

admits of no doubt, their plain and obvious intent must prevail."[83]

To whatever extent inherent judicial authority to revise statutes was asserted after the 18th century, it was a rare and anomalous throwback to the earlier heyday of judicial power—like the canon of interpretation that statutes in derogation of the judge-made common law were to be strictly construed (we reject this view: see § 52). How else to explain the total absence in modern judicial opinions of the concept of judge as legislating partner? This concept survives not in the real world but only in theoretical disputation over whether it was ever one of the assumed powers of judges in the United States. Any nominee to a federal judgeship, or any candidate for state judicial election, who dared assert a power to change statutory law would be soundly rejected. How is it that this magnificent judicial prerogative to legislate, supposedly present at the founding of our republic, utterly disappeared? Have our judges become less assertive, less bold, less jealous of their powers? No. Despite an occasional judicial opinion recalling bygone glories, our system of separated powers never gave courts a part in either the drafting or the revision of legislation.[84] Bills of rights, which existed at both state and federal levels, set forth with some specificity the only "fundamental law" that courts were authorized to prefer over text enacted by the people's representatives.

Some of the other rarefied theoretical attacks on textualism so defy common sense and human experience that we perhaps waste the reader's time in discussing them. Some commentators try to obliterate all distinctions between textualists and nontextualists by positing that a text has no meaning, no independent existence, apart from authorial intention—so that all interpreters are "intentionalists." This is what one commentator fallaciously urges:

> [T]here can be no "textualist" method, because there is no object—no text without writerly intention—to which would-be textualists could be faithful. And if there is no

---

83 *Evans v. Jordan*, 8 F. Cas. 872, 873 (C.C.D. Va. 1813) (No. 4,564), *aff'd*, 13 U.S. (9 Cranch) 199 (1815) (per Washington, J.).

84 *See* John F. Manning, *Textualism and the Equity of the Statute*, 101 Colum. L. Rev. 1 (2001).

object—no plain and lucid text to which interpreters could be faithful—neither is there an object to which interpreters could be unfaithful. Consequently, "judicial activism," usually defined as substituting one's preferred meaning in place of the meaning the text clearly encodes, becomes the name of a crime no one could possibly commit. After all, you can't override a meaning that isn't there.[85]

To say that words have no meaning, indeed no existence, apart from the intention of their author is a ludicrous extension of the thesis that a tree falling in a deserted forest makes no noise. *King Lear* would still be *King Lear* if it were produced by the random typing of a thousand monkeys over a thousand years. And a Bob Hope joke would still be funny if it were sculpted in sand by the action of the desert wind. To be sure, authors may use figures of speech that cause straightforward statements to mean the opposite of what they say. It is possible to write "That is a brilliant notion!" meaning to convey that the notion is quite absurd. But that the statement represents sarcasm or irony or satire is apparent from its context (the device would be ineffective otherwise)—and in any event legal texts are supposed to be straightforward expressions of denotation and not the place for literary devices that make words mean what they do not say. (For a more extended treatment of intention, see § 67.)

Another philosophical approach (if it can be called that) denies any distinction between what the text says and what the reader does with it. On this view, all interpretation is self-fulfilling:

> [M]ost [lawyers and judges] tell a story about legal interpretation that is simply a scam . . . . The truth is, there is no such thing as "just following the law." Every judge, every lawyer, every interpreter always makes the law, never finds

---

85 Stanley Fish, *Intentional Neglect*, N.Y. Times, 19 July 2005, at A21. *See* Ronald Dworkin, *Justice for Hedgehogs* 145 (2011) ("It doesn't help to say, as [Stanley] Fish does, that a poem is created by a reading and that there is therefore no text independent of a particular reading and no reading independent of a particular reader."); Christopher Ricks, "Stanley Fish: *Is There a Text in This Class?*" in *Reviewery* 192, 192 (2002) (noting that Fish's self-described "stunning proposal for a new way of thinking about the way we read' . . . would, if acted upon, lobotomise [critical thought]").

it, when reading a legal text. And their personal views inescapably play a central role in the making.[86]

One could hardly imagine a more sweeping negation of the possibility of laws that accurately represent the judgment of the people, laws whose content is predictable, and judges who subjugate their personal views to the rule of law. "A government of men, not of laws" summarizes this cynical view, which invites judges to do whatever they like, since they cannot do otherwise—the doctrine of predestination applied to judicial decisions.

Justice Felix Frankfurter recognized quite the opposite possibility when he praised Justice Oliver Wendell Holmes for his legal self-abnegation: "Probably no man who ever sat on the Court was by temperament and discipline freer from emotional commitments compelling him to translate his own economic or social views into constitutional commands."[87] This view of Holmes is neither naive nor disingenuous: It depicts an admirable quality to which more judges should aspire.

At perhaps the zenith of nontextualism, some ultramodern theorists urge judicial creation of a "text beyond the text." One noted commentator asserts: "Recently legal scholars have paid attention to what can be called 'The Constitution Outside the Constitution.'"[88] This invisible, unratified nondocument that restricts future democratic choice consists of whatever is "deeply embedded in our political order,"[89] such as "the general social safety

---

86   Robert Benson, *The Interpretation Game: How Judges and Lawyers Make the Law* xiii (2008). *See* Jeffrey M. Shaman, *Constitutional Interpretation* 7 (2001) ("The meaning that the Supreme Court creates for the Constitution finds its predominant source in the personal beliefs and values of the individual justices who comprise the Court at any given time. . . . The justices often turn inward to find values that will provide meaning for the Constitution."). *See also* (and much for the worse) Martin M. Shapiro, *Judges as Liars*, 17 Harv. J.L. & Pub. Pol'y 155, 156 (1994) ("Courts and judges always lie. Lying is in the nature of the judicial activity.").

87   Felix Frankfurter, *Mr. Justice Holmes and the Supreme Court* 21 (2d ed. 1961).

88   Mark Tushnet, *Why the Constitution Matters* 6–7 (2010). *See* Ernest A. Young, *The Constitution Outside the Constitution*, 117 Yale L.J. 408 (2007) (asking what the Constitution would include besides the canonical document if "defined . . . by function, rather than by form").

89   Tushnet, *Why the Constitution Matters* at 7.

net of the modern social welfare state [in particular the Social Security Act], the basic structure of modern environmental law, and the core provisions of our civil rights statutes."[90] This is not to say that the real Constitution (the text ratified by the people and kept in the National Archives) does not matter. It is said to matter "because it provides the structure through which we act politically to get our representatives to enact statutes that will become part of the constitution outside the Constitution."[91] This view, the commentator states, is "the conventional wisdom among scholars."[92] If so, it is yet another means by which theorists seek to avoid the constraints of a controlling text.

One judicial critic of originalism (and of purposivism, consequentialism, and all other approaches) says that there is no need for a criterion: "I have been tempted from time to time to develop a theory of my own, partly because it's just more fun to have a brightly colored banner to fly, and partly because the leading theories do have their virtues."[93] He has not succumbed but instead has developed the no-theory theory:

> What's needed is not yet another theory but an escape from theorizing. . . . [W]isdom lies simply in knowing the limits of one's knowledge, that good sense is more often displayed in collective and diverse settings than in a rarefied appellate atmosphere, and that the language, structure, and history of law serve best as mediums [sic[94]] of restraint rather than excuses for intrusion.
>
> .   .   .
>
> Restrained judges may lack the cachet of inhabiting the handsome mansion of a theory, but their modesty might some day return some greater measure of governance to those to whom it rightly belongs.[95]

---

90 *Id.* at 8.

91 *Id.*

92 *Id.* at 17.

93 J. Harvie Wilkinson III, *Cosmic Constitutional Theory* 115 (2012).

94 Unless the passage refers to clairvoyants, *media* is the proper term. *See Garner's Modern American Usage* 531 (3d ed. 2009).

95 Wilkinson, *Cosmic Constitutional Theory* at 115.

That looks much like a brightly colored banner. We have little concern that the judge who follows such advice will lack cachet, but great fear that he will lack an objective basis for judging. Do the injunctions "be modest" and "be restrained" mean always deferring to the wishes of the legislature? And if not always, then how are the appropriate occasions to be identified? By the statute's departure from what the people ratified in the United States Constitution? From long-standing, traditional practices in most states? From what the current national majority seems to desire? From what would be good for the society? From the views of the "wisest" people who are (ex officio) our judges? Judges' repudiation of what this author calls a theory and what we would call principled interpretation creates an aristocratic regime in which wise, modest judges (trust them) allow or forbid whatever they like or dislike.

For more on nontextualist stratagems—which are anything but fully developed theories of interpretation—see §§ 58–61 and 66–70.

B. The How of This Book

Some Fundamental Issues

To prescribe the principles of sound interpretation, we must resolve some fundamental issues about which there is a surfeit of disparate views. We set them forth here to declare what we believe the approach to interpretation should be.

First, and most fundamentally: Is it the goal of judicial interpretation to give effect to the drafter's subjective intent? This is traditionally said to be the case, but judges are and should be doing something else entirely. In the interpretation of legislation, we aspire to be "a nation of laws, not of men." This means (1) giving effect to the text that lawmakers have adopted and that the people are entitled to rely on, and (2) giving *no* effect to lawmakers' unenacted desires. As Justice Oliver Wendell Holmes put it: "We do not inquire what the legislature meant; we ask only what the statute means."[96] That is why the cases approving the use of legislative history (as we do not) *disapprove* of it when the enacted text is unambiguous. The same exclusionary rule applies to the interpretation of private documents. Their very object is to

---

96 Oliver Wendell Holmes, *The Theory of Legal Interpretation*, 12 Harv. L. Rev. 417, 419 (1899). *See* Felix Frankfurter, *Some Reflections on the Reading of Statutes*, 47 Colum. L. Rev. 527, 538 (1947) (quoting Holmes as saying, "Only a day or two ago, when counsel talked of the intention of the legislature, I was indiscreet enough to say I don't care what their intention was. I only want to know what the words mean."); *Holmes–Pollock Letters* 90 (Mark deWolfe Howe ed., 1961) (letter from Oliver Wendell Holmes to Frederick Pollock dated 9 Dec. 1898) ("We don't care a damn for the meaning of the writer and . . . the only question is the meaning of the words . . ."); Oliver Wendell Holmes, *The Common Law* 309 (1881) ("The law has nothing to do with the actual state of the parties' minds. In contract, as elsewhere, it must go by externals, and judge parties by their conduct."); *Rickman v. Carstairs*, [1833] 5 B. & Ad. 651, 663, 110 E.R. 931, 936 (per Lord Denman) ("The question in this and other cases of construction of written instruments is, not what was the intention of the parties, but what is the meaning of the words they have used."). *See also* R.W.M. Dias, *Jurisprudence* 237 (4th ed. 1976) ("[T]he amorphous composition of the legislative body compels a tribunal to address itself to what the *enactment* means, not what particular persons may have meant."); Frederick A. Philbrick, *Language and the Law: The Semantics of Forensic English* 29 (1949) (stating that "the meaning of the writer is quite immaterial. The question is not what the writer meant, but what he conveyed to those who heard or read.").

express the parties' intent in a binding form. Private ordering is a misnomer if judges can countermand its directives by finding unexpressed "genuine" intent—which ends up being what the judges think would be fair. So unless the text itself is ambiguous, the parol-evidence rule excludes precontractual indications of what the parties thought they were achieving.

Traditional authorities on interpretation, while repeating the mantra that the objective of interpretation is to discern the lawgiver's or the private drafter's intent, would add that this intent is to be derived solely from the words of the text.[97] We would have no substantive quarrel with the search for "intent" if that were all that was meant. But describing the interpretive exercise as a search for "intent" inevitably causes readers to think of *subjective* intent, as opposed to the objective words that the drafters agreed to in their expression of rights and duties. Subjective intent is beside the point. Speculation about it—even in the oddly anthropomorphic phrase *intent of the document*—invites fuzzy-mindedness. Objective *meaning* is what we are after, and it enhances clarity to speak that way. For a more detailed explanation of why we renounce references to *intent*, see § 67.

Second, is the objective meaning of the words the sole legitimate criterion of interpretation? In the broadest sense, yes: What we seek is textual meaning. But in a narrower sense, perhaps not: Many established principles of interpretation are less plausibly based on a reasonable assessment of meaning than on grounds of policy adopted by the courts. (These principles do not, we hasten to add, go so far as to give words a meaning they cannot bear, but merely favor one among the permissible meanings.) In statu-

---

97 *See, e.g.*, Charles Fried, *Sonnet LXV and the "Black Ink" of the Framers' Intention*, 100 Harv. L. Rev. 751, 759 (1987) ("[W]ords and text are chosen to embody intentions and thus replace inquiries into subjective mental states. . . . [T]he text *is* the intention of the authors or of the framers."); G.W. Paton, *A Textbook of Jurisprudence* § 51, at 250 (G.W. Paton & David P. Derham eds., 4th ed. 1972) ("[T]he subjective intention of Parliament cannot be considered . . . ; the intent must be gathered from the statute itself."); Alexander Hamilton, "Final Version of an Opinion on the Constitutionality of an Act to Establish a Bank" (1791), in 8 *The Papers of Alexander Hamilton* 97, 111 (Harold C. Syrett ed., 1965) ("[W]hatever may have been the intention of the framers of a constitution, or of a law, that intention is to be sought for in the instrument itself.").

tory interpretation there is, for example, the rule of lenity, whereby ambiguity in a criminal law is resolved in favor of the defendant; and in interpretation of private contracts there is the rule that ambiguity will be construed *contra proferentem*, against the party that drafted the instrument. It might be said that rules like these, so deeply ingrained, must be known to both drafter and reader alike so that they can be considered inseparable from the meaning of the text. A traditional and hence anticipated rule of interpretation, no less than a traditional and hence anticipated meaning of a word, imparts meaning. Other rules, such as the constitutional-doubt canon (see § 38), are based on judicial-policy considerations alone. We accept these oft-recited rules of interpretation unless they seem to us incoherent, not genuinely followed, or in plain violation of our constitutional structure.

Permissible Meanings

A fundamental rule of textual interpretation is that neither a word nor a sentence may be given a meaning that it cannot bear. Without the concept of permissible meanings, there is no such thing as faithful interpretation of legal texts. Through accurate knowledge of language and proper education in legal method, lawyers ought to have a shared sense of what meanings words can bear and what linguistic arguments can credibly be made about them.

Some words have two or more quite different meanings. For example, *post* can refer to a piece of timber set upright, a position of employment, or mail. More commonly, however, the interpretive issue involves not which of two totally different meanings is intended but what level of generality is to be accorded to a single meaning. In writings on the interpretation of texts, the loose norm is to refer to all uncertainties of meaning as *ambiguities*. But there is a useful and real distinction between textual uncertainties that are the consequence of verbal ambiguity (conveying two very different senses, as when *table* could refer either to a piece of furniture or to a numerical chart) and those that are the consequence of verbal vagueness (as when *equal protection of the laws* can be given a scope so narrow as to include only protection from injury, or so broad as to include equal access to government benefits). A word or phrase is ambiguous when the question is which of two or more meanings applies; it is vague when its unquestionable meaning has uncertain application to various factual situations.[98] Take, for example, the Supreme Court case applying a statute that imposed an enhanced penalty for "using a firearm" in connection with a drug crime.[99] The phrase was ambiguous: The majority thought that it referred to *any* use of a firearm, including trading one for drugs; the dissenters thought it referred to use of a firearm for the purposes for which firearms are normally employed. Even on the latter assumption, the phrase *using a firearm* was (arguably, at least) vague. Do the purposes for which firearms are normally employed include only the discharge of firearms? Or do they also include threatening with firearms? Brandishing them? Carrying them openly?

True ambiguity is almost always the result of carelessness or inattention.[100] It is rarely intentional—though there are certainly instances of statutory or contractual ambiguity in which each side, fully aware of the ambiguity, embraces it in the hope or belief that its version of meaning will ultimately prevail. This is one reason why the search for the shared "intent" of the drafters of a multi-party product is a search for something that never existed.

Vagueness, on the other hand, is often intentional, as general terms (*reasonable time*, *best efforts*, *equal protection*) are adopted to

---

98   *See* E. Allan Farnsworth, "Some Considerations in the Drafting of Agreements," in *Drafting Contracts and Commercial Instruments* 145, 146–47 (1971) ("Ambiguity, properly defined, is distinct from vagueness. A word that may or may not be applicable to marginal objects is vague. But a word [that has] . . . two entirely different connotations [is ambiguous]."). *See also* Linda D. Jellum, *Mastering Statutory Interpretation* 70 (2008) (noting that although "ambiguity is not the same as generalness, . . . judges routinely say that language is ambiguous when it is merely vague, broad, or general"); Reed Dickerson, *The Interpretation and Application of Statutes* 48–49 (1975) ("Whereas *ambiguity* in its classical sense refers to equivocation, *vagueness* refers to the degree to which, independently of equivocation, language is uncertain in its respective applications to a number of particulars.").

99   *Smith v. United States*, 508 U.S. 223 (1993) (per O'Connor, J.).

100   *See* W. David Slawson, *Legislative History and the Need to Bring Statutory Interpretation Under the Rule of Law*, 44 Stan. L. Rev. 383, 423 (1992) ("[A]mbiguities are almost always mistakes . . . . [V]agueness in statutory language is never, in itself, evidence of a mistake.").

cover a multitude of situations that cannot practicably be spelled out in detail or even foreseen. Like ambiguity, vagueness can often be clarified by context. When, for example, the general term *defendant* is used in a statute dealing with criminal procedure, it obviously refers only to criminal defendants. Most interpretive canons apply to both ambiguity (as narrowly defined) and vagueness. There are some meanings (some applications) that even the vaguest of terms cannot bear. But some canons have practical application only to ambiguous terms (e.g., the nearest-reasonable-referent canon [§ 20]) or only to vague ones (e.g., *ejusdem generis* canon [§ 32]).

The principle that the semantic content of words is limited to permissible meanings may seem too obvious to be worth insisting on. But some do not accept it: They seek to arrive at legal meanings through some method other than discerning the contextual meaning of words and sentences and paragraphs.

The "Fair Reading" Method

The interpretive approach we endorse is that of the "fair reading": determining the application of a governing text to given facts on the basis of how a reasonable reader, fully competent in the language, would have understood the text at the time it was issued. The endeavor requires aptitude in language, sound judgment, the suppression of personal preferences regarding the outcome, and, with older texts, historical linguistic research. It also requires an ability to comprehend the *purpose* of the text, which is a vital part of its context. But the purpose is to be gathered only from the text itself, consistently with the other aspects of its context. This critical word *context* embraces not just textual purpose but also (1) a word's historical associations acquired from recurrent patterns of past usage, and (2) a word's immediate syntactic setting—that is, the words that surround it in a specific utterance.[101]

Among the best historical statements of the fair-reading approach is that of Chief Justice John Marshall:

---

101 *See* I.A. Richards, *Interpretation in Teaching* viii (1938).

> To say that the intention of the instrument must prevail;
> that this intention must be collected from its words; that
> its words are to be understood in that sense in which they
> are generally used by those for whom the instrument was
> intended; that its provisions are neither to be restricted into
> insignificance, nor extended to objects not comprehended
> in them, nor contemplated by its framers;—is to repeat
> what has been already said more at large, and is all that can
> be necessary.[102]

A modern version of the fair-reading method was set forth in 1934 by Frederick J. de Sloovère, who wrote:

> [T]he demand for certainty and predictability requires an
> objective basis for interpretation which can be attained
> only (1) by a faithful reliance upon the natural or reason-
> able meanings of language; (2) by choosing always a mean-
> ing that the text will sensibly bear by the fair use of lan-
> guage; and (3) by employing a thoroughly worked out but
> rational method for choosing among the several possible
> meanings.[103]

De Sloovère's version improves on Marshall's statement by eliminating the possibly misleading references to *intention* (see § 67). He was right to insist on certainty, predictability, objectivity, reasonableness, rationality, and regularity, which are the objects of the skilled interpreter's quest.

As we have said, in a fair reading, purpose—as a constituent of meaning—is to be derived exclusively from a text. Normally, finding a purpose in text is a straightforward matter requiring no feats of subtle deduction. Generally the purpose is unmistakable. A statute imposes a tax: The purpose is to contribute to the fisc. A statute provides that anyone with three or more convictions for DUI must have his driver's license permanently revoked: The purpose is to keep those so convicted permanently off the road. (The purposivist, leaping to the more general purpose, might find it to be keeping habitual drunks off the road, that status being

---

102 *Ogden v. Saunders*, 25 U.S. (12 Wheat.) 213, 332 (1827) (opinion of Marshall, C.J.).

103 Frederick J. de Sloovère, *Textual Interpretation of Statutes*, 11 N.Y.U. L.Q. Rev. 538, 541 (1934).

evidenced by three DUI convictions—and since, to achieve that purpose, the convictions must have been valid, collateral attack is permissible.) A statute limits the time for appeal to 60 days after judgment has been entered: The purpose is to close off appeal, and terminate the litigation, after 60 days. (The purposivist might find it to be closing off appeal after a reasonable time, which is specified as 60 days in normal circumstances—but special circumstances may provide an exception.) A statute creates a private claim for harassing phone calls: Its purpose is to deter, and provide compensation for, telephone harassment. (The purposivist might find it to be deterring, and providing compensation for, *viva voce* harassment by electronic means—so that the statute might be held to apply to videos posted on the Internet.)

But there is something just as powerful as those types of elementary deductions—and indeed something that can replace them when the narrow purpose is indeed ambiguous: the prefatory material of most legal instruments—the title, preamble, purpose clause, and recital (see § 34 [prefatory-materials canon]). As Max Radin wrote in 1942:

> In modern statutes it has become increasingly common to set forth the purpose in elaborate detail in the preamble. This, it may be well to add, is far from being an innovation. At all times in English history it was an extremely common practice, notable examples of which are the Statute Quia Emptores and the Statute of Uses. But old or new, the practice gives us a fairly definite notion of what the statute means to accomplish.[104]

There is, however, an important caveat: While such provisions as a preamble or purpose clause can clarify an ambiguous text, they cannot expand it beyond its permissible meaning. If they could, they would be the purposivists' playground, since it is common for a preamble or purpose clause to invoke the most acceptable or stirring objective that the drafters had in mind—which is almost always the most general objective. ("In Order to form a more perfect Union, establish Justice, insure domestic Tranquility, provide for the common defense, promote the general Welfare, and secure

---

104 Max Radin, *A Short Way with Statutes*, 56 Harv. L. Rev. 388, 398 (1942).

the Blessings of Liberty to ourselves and our Posterity . . . ." Who could object? But should all ambiguities in the Constitution be resolved on the basis of what judges think will "form a more perfect Union"?)

A well-known example of judicial interpretation, seemingly invented by the Oxonian H.L.A. Hart and sometimes called a "chestnut" in books about statutory construction, may serve as a useful illustration of the fair-reading method. An ordinance states: "No person may bring a vehicle into the park." The example, according to Hart, illustrates that there are "debatable cases in which words are neither obviously applicable nor obviously ruled out."[105] He asks whether the no-vehicle rule applies to these items:

> airplanes
> automobiles
> bicycles
> roller skates
> toy automobiles

We might add:

ambulances	rollerblades
baby strollers	scooters
gliders	Segways
golf carts	skateboards
Heelys roller shoes	tricycles
mopeds	unicycles
motorcycles	unmotorized wheelchairs
motorized wheelchairs	

Is the application of this ordinance truly going to induce lots of hand-wringing? It should induce some critical thinking, yes. But judges who use the fair-reading method will arrive at fairly consistent answers. We do not mean to say the decisions will be easy. *Nothing* is easy. But the relevant line of inquiry is pretty straightforward.

With a terminological issue like this one, we should consult (without apology) what the lexicographers say. After all, they have studied dozens if not hundreds of instances of actual English

---

105 H.L.A. Hart, *Positivism and the Separation of Law and Morals*, 71 Harv. L. Rev. 593, 607 (1958).

usage to arrive at the core meaning of *vehicle*—the word at issue here. One meaning of the word—the very first given in some
dictionaries—is "a substance, esp. a liquid, serving as a means for
the readier application or use of another substance mixed with or
dissolved in it."[106] The context of the sign here at issue, which includes its *purpose* of excluding certain things from the park—presumably things that would otherwise commonly be introduced—
makes clear that this is not the sense that the sign bears. There is
no more reason to address intrusion into the park of mixing media
than to address intrusion of elephants. Another meaning of *vehicle*
is apt—a meaning defined in its most general sense by one current
desktop dictionary as follows: "a means of carrying or transporting
something."[107] Another dictionary says: (1) "[a] means of conveyance, usu. with wheels, for transporting people, goods, etc.; a car,
cart, truck, carriage, sledge, etc."; or (2) "[a]ny means of carriage
or transport; a receptacle in which something is placed in order to
be moved."[108]

Anything that is ever called a *vehicle* (in the relevant sense)
would fall within these definitions. But it is common usage that we
are looking for, and not *every* "means of conveyance with wheels"
and *every* "receptacle in which something is placed in order to be
moved" is commonly called a *vehicle*—not airline carry-on luggage
with wheels, for example; nor supermarket grocery carts; nor baby
carriages. A more colloquial meaning is given by another dictionary as the second meaning for the relevant sense of *vehicle*: "A self-
propelled conveyance that runs on tires; a motor vehicle."[109] But if
taken literally, this definition would embrace a remote-controlled,
miniature model car—which does not seem right. The proper colloquial meaning in our view (not all of them are to be found in
dictionaries) is simply a *sizable* wheeled conveyance (as opposed to
one of any size that is motorized). Designation of a certain roadway
for use by *vehicular traffic* might well include horse-drawn carts
and even rickshaws, but it would not include remote-controlled

---

106 *The Oxford Universal Dictionary* 2339 (1955).

107 *Merriam-Webster's Collegiate Dictionary* 1386 (11th ed. 2003).

108 *The New Shorter Oxford English Dictionary* 3554 (4th ed. 1993).

109 *American Heritage Dictionary of the English Language* 1919 (5th ed. 2011).

model cars, baby carriages, tricycles, or perhaps even bicycles. Understanding the term in such a limited, colloquial fashion is similar to the manner in which Justice Holmes found the National Motor Vehicle Theft Act inapplicable to airplane theft. "[I]t is possible," he wrote, "to use the word [*vehicle*] to signify a conveyance working on land, water or air," but "in everyday speech 'vehicle' calls up the picture of a thing moving on land."[110]

Taking the word to mean a sizable wheeled conveyance would exclude from the park only one of the five examples given by Hart: automobiles. It would permit airplanes, bicycles, roller skates, and toy automobiles. And among our additional examples it would admit to the park all except ambulances, golf carts, mopeds, motorcycles, and (perhaps) Segways.

How might the purposivist solve the same puzzle? He would not limit his determination of purpose to the one purpose unquestionably demonstrated from reading the text in context: the exclusion from the park of things that would otherwise commonly be introduced and that common usage would include within the prohibition. He would ask *why* things are excluded, and would probably conclude for one or both of two reasons: to preserve the quiet, restful atmosphere of the park, and to eliminate the danger of fast-moving mechanical objects. The former purpose alone would not lead to the exclusion of *all* motor vehicles; electrically powered automobiles, mopeds, golf carts, and Segways would be admitted. The latter purpose (eliminating the danger of speeding objects) would exclude all of these, but would also exclude scooters, bicycles, unicycles, and perhaps tricycles. Whether some of the other items would be excluded (e.g., Heelys roller shoes, rollerblades, and skateboards) would depend on how far the purposivist is willing to allow the purpose of eliminating the danger of speeding to stretch the broadest meaning of *vehicle*.

One might ask, why assume one, or the other, or both of these purposes? And if it is a hilly park, why not assume a third: preventing the danger of runaway speeding objects—which would ban baby carriages and perhaps wheelchairs? There is no basis for

---

110 *McBoyle v. United States*, 283 U.S. 25, 26 (1931) (per Holmes, J.).

the choice except the interpreter's assessment of what the purpose *ought* to be. The purposivist would probably make an exception to the noisy-vehicle ban for ambulances: What lawmaker could possibly place the objective of peace and quiet above the objective of saving a human life? What the purposivist comes up with is not (as our solution is) a selection from among the permissible meanings of *vehicle*. None of those permissible meanings includes only noisy vehicles (except ambulances) and vehicles that travel at a great speed. What the purposivist has done is to create a *new* ordinance—one that excludes vehicles *except* ambulances and vehicles that are quiet and do not go fast. This may (perhaps) make a lot of sense, but it is not the ordinance that the city council adopted.

The purposivist approach assumes that legal instruments make complete sense. Of course they should be so interpreted where the language permits—but not where it does not. Not only is legal drafting sometimes imperfect, but often the imperfection is the consequence of a compromise that it is not the function of the courts to upset—or to make impossible for the future by disregarding the words adopted. Some of the imperfections can be cured or mitigated by doctrines and devices other than the mauling of text, such as enforcement discretion, the rule of lenity (see § 49), deference to executive interpretation, or special doctrines applicable to special situations. For example, it may well be that the undeniable exclusion of ambulances by the text of the ordinance is countermanded by an ordinance or court-made rule exempting emergency vehicles from traffic rules.[111]

A final point about fair-reading textualism. Although some judges diverge from it through purposivism or consequentialism, others (less commonly, to be sure) can diverge from it by "strict constructionism"—a hyperliteral brand of textualism that we equally reject. Consider a statute that defines *white-collar crime* as "an act or series of illegal acts committed by non-physical means and by concealment or guile, to obtain money or property, to avoid the payment or loss of money or property, or to obtain business or

---

111 *Cf. Brogan v. United States*, 522 U.S. 398, 406 (1998) (per Scalia, J.) ("Criminal prohibitions do not generally apply to reasonable enforcement actions by officers of the law.").

personal advantage."[112] A hypothetical defendant accused of embezzlement establishes that to effect the embezzlement, he had to press buttons, open doors, carry cashier's checks on his person, etc. His lawyer argues that these are inarguably "physical means," taking his client's conduct out of the statute. A hypothetical strict-constructionist judge might agree that Congress got the wording wrong if it was in fact targeting anyone but spiritualists. On this view, the defendant cannot be properly charged, and Congress should be urged to redo its statutory handiwork.

But such a result would attribute to *non-physical* a permissible meaning ("not involving the use of physical means") that is inconsistent with the textually manifest purpose of the act. One accepted meaning of *physical* is "inclined to be bodily aggressive or violent,"[113] or "characterized by esp. rugged and forceful physical activity."[114] Various canons reinforce this fair reading: the weighing of context (§ 2), the presumption against ineffectiveness (§ 4), the ordinary-meaning canon (§ 6), and the historical meaning of the term being defined (*white-collar crime*) (§ 36). A good textualist uses interpretive devices to derive sound meaning from the words used.

In sum, a "viperine" construction that kills the text can result from reading it either nonliterally or hyperliterally. The soundest legal view seeks to discern literal meaning in context. *Literal* here bears a clinical sense, not a pejorative one: "A sensible literal meaning of a statute must always be followed if there is no other meaning that the words can reasonably bear."[115] Correspondingly: "If there is but a single sensible meaning, it is nearly always the literal meaning."[116] It is a slander on literalism to say, as Archibald Cox did, that "there is no surer way to misread any document than

---

112 Justice System Improvement Act § 901(a)(18), 42 U.S.C. § 3791(a)(18).

113 2 *The New Shorter Oxford English Dictionary* 2197 (4th ed. 1993).

114 *Merriam-Webster's Collegiate Dictionary* 935 (11th ed. 2003).

115 Frederick J. de Sloovère, *Textual Interpretation of Statutes*, 11 N.Y.U. L.Q. Rev. 538, 543 (1934).

116 *Id*. at 547.

to read it literally."[117] By *literally* perhaps he meant "hyperliterally." Or perhaps he was thinking of allegories or myths or satires—but the statement is incorrect with regard to legal instruments.

Scope and Organization of What Follows

Our advice in this treatise is subject to two significant limitations. First, it pertains only to what a court ought to do when it is free to interpret a text on its own. When an identical question of interpretation has previously been resolved by the same court or a superior court, the doctrine of stare decisis renders our advice irrelevant, except to the extent that it may induce a court to overrule its own precedent or to narrow the case's application. In federal courts[118] and some state courts,[119] the interpretation of a statute by the agency charged with implementing it controls so long as it is within the range of reasonable interpretation—even though it may not be what the court would have arrived at on its own. When courts subject to that limitation are reviewing agency action, our advice will be useful only in identifying the range of reasonable interpretation, not in determining the best interpretation. Second, since our subject is the *interpretation* of texts, we do not address their *validity*. So in discussing statutory texts we explain the rule that ambiguity in criminal laws will be construed in favor of the defendant (the rule of lenity), and in discussing privately created texts we mention the rule that ambiguity in a written contract will be construed against the party that drafted the instrument (*contra proferentem*). But we do not discuss the doctrine that criminal laws failing to provide adequate notice are invalid or the rule that unconscionable contracts will not be enforced. These doctrines may

---

117 Archibald Cox, *Judge Learned Hand and the Interpretation of Statutes*, 60 Harv. L. Rev. 370, 375–76 (1947).

118 *See Chevron, U.S.A., Inc. v. Natural Res. Def. Council, Inc.*, 467 U.S. 837, 842–45 (1984) (per Stevens, J.) (setting forth a two-step process for courts to follow when determining the validity of an agency's interpretation of a statute).

119 *E.g., Colbert v. District of Columbia Dep't of Emp't Servs.*, 933 A.2d 817, 822 (D.C. 2007) (deferring to the Department's "reasonable" interpretation of a workers'-compensation statute); *Mississippi Gaming Comm'n v. Imperial Palace of Miss., Inc.*, 751 So.2d 1025, 1029 (Miss. 1999) (deferring to the Commission's interpretation of the Gaming Control Act).

incidentally trigger the interpretive principle that a text should be interpreted to have a meaning that makes it valid rather than invalid (see § 5), but they do not in themselves pertain to interpretation. In other words, we are not writing a treatise on legislation or on the law of contracts or, for that matter, on the Constitution. Our subject is solely interpretation: how a legal message is to be received by those who must apply its directives.

The raw material of our study consists of legally operative texts other than judicial opinions. (The words of the latter, as opposed to their dispositions, have, strictly speaking, no legally binding effect.) Authoritative legal texts setting forth binding governmental directives (e.g., constitutions, statutes, ordinances, regulations) are, of course, not the only category of legally operative language. A second category consists of texts adopted by private persons, acting either alone (as with wills) or by agreement (as with real-estate leases). Most of the interpretive principles applicable to one category apply to the other as well—but not all of them. For example, the venerable principle that an ambiguity should be resolved against the party responsible for drafting the document (*contra proferentem*) does not apply to governmental directives. And the principle that language should be construed so as to avoid serious constitutional doubt does not usually apply to privately drafted documents.

Given these categories, the body of this treatise is divided into (1) principles that apply to all legally operative language, including both public and private texts; and (2) principles that apply specifically to governmental prescriptions such as statutes, ordinances, and regulations. We disclaim any full treatment of rules specifically applicable to language in the various types of private documents because those intricate rules would expand the text threefold with limited benefit, and they have been well covered elsewhere.[120]

---

120 *See, e.g.*, *Restatement (Second) of Contracts* §§ 200–230, at 82–191 (1981 & apps.); Joseph M. Perillo, *Calamari and Perillo on Contracts* 105–47 (6th ed. 2009); E. Allan Farnsworth, *Farnsworth on Contracts* 255–388 (2d ed. 1998); Margaret N. Kniffin, "Interpretation of Contracts," in 5 *Corbin on Contracts* §§ 24.1–24.31, at 2–341 (1998); John Edward Murray, *Murray on Contracts* 221–70 (2d rev. ed. 1974). *See also* Kenneth S. Wollner, *How to Draft and Interpret Insurance Policies* 5–58 (1999); Thomas E. Atkinson, *Handbook of the Law of Wills* 807–17 (2d ed. 1953).

The principles of interpretation here set forth are appropriate for courts in the absence of legislative prescription. (We do not regard a statute's definition of terms [see § 36] as a legislatively prescribed rule of interpretation; it is simply part of the text being interpreted.) Legislative prescription of interpretive rules can raise two constitutional problems.

First, if the prescription purports to dictate the meaning of future legislation, it raises the question of the degree to which a legislature may prescribe the speech of future legislatures. Most general definitional sections contained in codified laws finesse this difficulty by defining words to have their ordinary meanings (which is what would be assumed anyway) and including a general exception that permits future legislatures to make their intent clear however they want (such as "unless the context indicates otherwise").[121] But what if a general definitional section in the code gives a word an unusual meaning, and does not specify "unless otherwise indicated"? (See p. 275.)

Second, when the prescription directs courts how to interpret texts (even the very statute in which the prescription is contained), it raises the problem of separation of powers: To what extent *can* the legislature tell the judiciary how to do its job? The answer may depend in part on what the job at issue is. A statutory prescription concerning the interpretation of private documents is not much different from a statutory prescription that the documents must say this-or-that to be valid—clearly within the legislature's power. Statutes directing how the courts are to interpret the legislature's own handiwork are another matter. Although a legislature can abolish the doctrine of sovereign immunity, can it take the lesser step of instructing the courts no longer to require a clear statement for a waiver? Some states have enacted a repealer of the rule of lenity,[122] and the courts of some of those states have ignored such

---

121 1 U.S.C. § 1 (2006).

122 *See* Ariz. Rev. Stat. Ann. § 13-104 (repealing rule, 1978); Cal. Penal Code § 4 (same, 1872); 11 Del. Code § 203 (same, 1953); Idaho Gen. Laws ch. 5, § 2 (same, 1899); Ky. Rev. Stat. ch. 208, § 1 (same, 1942); Mich. Pub. Acts No. 328, § 2 (same, 1931); Mont. Rev. Code 94-1-102 (same, 1947); N.H. Rev. Stat. § 518:1 (same, 1973); N.Y. Penal Code § 11 (same, 1881); Or. Laws ch. 743, § 2

repealers.[123] Some states have specifically permitted[124] or even required[125] courts to consider legislative history (see § 66). The validity of such enactments is subject to reasonable debate. (See pp. 244–45.)

The Flood-Control Case Resolved

Let us now decide the case posed on page 1. If you are a textualist, you focus closely on the words. The crucial word is not *any*, but *damage*. It is inconceivable to us that a native speaker of English would refer to human deaths as "damage at a place." *Damages* might be awarded for the deaths; but the deaths cannot idiomatically be referred to as *damage*. The word *damage* (harm to property) is quite distinct in meaning from *damages* (money awarded to a victorious litigant).[126] No one who witnessed the deaths would have said, "What horrific damage there was!" Based on the text alone, the survivors should be allowed to recover because the immunity is inapplicable.

Most of the suggested rationales put forward by counsel and by your hypothetical colleagues are irrelevant:

- That the immunizing statute is dated 1928, and the trend is against tort immunities.

- That the purpose of the statute was to prevent governmental liabilities arising from flood-control projects.

- That the statute has allegedly become defunct because of nonuse (see § 57 [desuetude canon]).

- That flood-control reservoirs have been made into recreational facilities.

(same, 1971); S.D. Codified Laws § 13.0101 (same, 1939); Texas Acts, 63rd Leg., p. 883, ch. 399, § 1 (same, 1973); Utah Laws, ch. 196, § 76-1-106 (same, 1973).

123 *See, e.g., State v. Dansereau*, 956 A.2d 310, 315 (N.H. 2008); *Harrott v. County of Kings*, 25 P.3d 649, 659 (Cal. 2001); *State v. Ovind*, 924 P.2d 479, 482 (Ariz. Ct. App. 1996).

124 *See* Ohio Rev. Code § 1.49 sub. (c) (2011); Or. Rev. Stat. § 174.020(1)(b) (2011).

125 *See* N.J. Stat. § 2A:58C-1(a) (2011) (applicable only to products-liability statute).

126 *See Garner's Dictionary of Legal Usage* 242 (3d ed. 2011).

- That the plaintiffs are of limited means and may not have life insurance on the decedents.

- That the legislative history contains no mention of loss of life (see § 66).

- That the enacting Congress would have wanted liability here or that the current Congress would want it (see § 67).

- That the immunity is sweeping (*any . . . any . . . any*); it still encompasses only *damage*.

It is relevant, of course, that a Supreme Court precedent establishes that the reservoir constitutes "flood waters" under the statute. And the canon that waivers of sovereign immunity are disfavored (§ 46) is arguably relevant, but that can be used only to resolve ambiguities, not to overcome the words of the text. Here the wording of the immunity is dispositive.

In the actual case on which our hypothetical problem was based, *United States v. James,* the en banc Fifth Circuit allowed recovery,[127] but the Supreme Court of the United States reversed.[128] The Court's opinion glossed over the distinction between *damage* (harm to property) and *damages* (money awarded in a court judgment) and used them interchangeably:

> Although the Court of Appeals found, for example, that the word "damage" was ambiguous because it might refer only to damage to property and exclude damage to persons, the ordinary meaning of the word carries no such limitation. Damages "have historically been awarded both for injury to property and injury to the person—a fact too well-known to have been overlooked by the Congress."[129]

That passage verges on verbal legerdemain, similar to equating *desert* (a dry place) with *deserts* (what one deserves) or *premise* (logical foundation) with *premises* (property) or *specie* (coinage) with *species* (category under genus).

---

127 *James v. United States,* 760 F.2d 590 (5th Cir. 1985) (en banc) (per Reavley, J.).

128 478 U.S. 597 (1986) (per Powell, J.).

129 *Id.* at 605 (quoting *American Stevedores, Inc. v. Porello,* 330 U.S. 446, 450 (1947) (per Reed, J.)).

Justice John Paul Stevens filed an admirable textualist and originalist dissent,[130] noting that in a proviso to the immunity, the statute twice referred to lands "subjected to overflow and damage."[131] He distinguished *damage* from both *injury* (personal injury) and *damages* (compensation), citing legal dictionaries and encyclopedias from the appropriate era. His reasoning was linguistically astute:

> Because the preferred definition of "damage" in 1928 excluded harm to the person, one would think that the Court—in accordance with the "plain meaning" of § 3—would construe the immunity provision to bar liability only for property damage. Surprisingly, the Court reaches precisely the opposite conclusion. Its analysis, however, relies entirely on authorities which define "*damages*"— or the monetary remedy imposed on one found liable for a legal wrong—rather than "*damage*"—which is the term Congress employed to identify the liability from which the Federal Government was thereafter excused. It is therefore quite beside the point that "damages" have "historically been awarded both for injury to property and injury to the person'" for the statute bars liability for "damage," not "damages." . . . The Court thus provides no basis for thinking that Congress used "damage" other than in its common, preferred usage to mean property damage. If "plain meaning" is our polestar, the immunity provision does not bar respondents' personal injury suits.[132]

This passage exemplifies the attention to text, and specifically to its original meaning, that we seek here to promote. Alas, Justice Stevens's reasoning did not carry the day, and the surviving spouses recovered nothing.

---

130 Apart, that is, from the mention of legislative history. See § 66 of this treatise.

131 33 U.S.C. § 702c.

132 478 U.S. at 615–16 (internal citations omitted) (Stevens, J., dissenting, joined by Marshall and O'Connor, JJ.).

Sound Principles
of Interpretation

Principles Applicable
to All Texts

Prefatory Remarks

The legal instruments that are the subject of interpretation have not typically been slapped together thoughtlessly but are the considered expression of intelligent human beings. In whatever age or culture, human intelligence follows certain principles of expression that are as universal as principles of logic. For example, intelligent expression does not contradict itself or set forth two propositions that are entirely redundant. Lapses sometimes occur, but they are departures from what would normally be expected.

Most of the canons of interpretation set forth here are so venerable that many of them continue to bear their Latin names. Properly regarded, they are not "rules" of interpretation in any strict sense but presumptions about what an intelligently produced text conveys.

The canons fulfill another purpose—a self-fulfilling purpose, so to speak: They promote clearer drafting. When it is widely understood in the legal community that, for example, a word used repeatedly in a document will be taken to have the same meaning throughout, and that a change in terminology suggests a change in meaning, you can expect those who prepare legal documents competently to draft accordingly.

Sections 1–37 of this treatise deal with principles for interpreting all types of legal instruments, from constitutions to statutes to ordinances to regulations to contracts to wills. Sections 38–57 are specific to statutory interpretation.

Fundamental Principles

1. Interpretation Principle

Every application of a text to particular circumstances entails interpretation.

> "Those who apply the rule to particular cases must of necessity expound and interpret that rule."
>
> Chief Justice John Marshall
> *Marbury v. Madison,*
> 5 U.S. (1 Cranch) 137, 177 (1803).

It is sometimes said that a plain text with a plain meaning is simply applied and not "interpreted" or "construed."[1] Whether that is true is perhaps a matter of definition. As we see things, "if you seem to meet an utterance which doesn't have to be interpreted, that is because you have interpreted it already."[2] Any meaning derived from signs involves interpretation,[3] even if the interpreter finds the task straightforward. Interpretation or construction is "the ascertainment of the thought or meaning of the author of, or of the parties to, a legal document, as expressed therein, according to the rules of language and subject to the rules of law."[4]

---

1   *E.g., Caminetti v. United States*, 242 U.S. 470, 485 (1917) (per Day, J.) ("Where the language is plain and admits of no more than one meaning the duty of interpretation does not arise."); *Mautner v. Peralta*, 263 Cal. Rptr. 535, 541 (Ct. App. 1989) ("[A]mbiguity ordinarily is a condition precedent to statutory interpretation."); *Sears, Roebuck & Co. v. Poling*, 81 N.W.2d 462, 466 (Iowa 1957) ("[R]esort may be had to rules of construction only where the language of an instrument is of doubtful meaning."); *Gans v. Aetna Life Ins. Co.*, 108 N.E. 443, 444 (N.Y. 1915) ("Where the parties by their words have left no fair reason for doubt, there is no just or defensible excuse for construction.").

2   Christopher Ricks, "Stanley Fish: *Is There a Text in This Class?*" in *Reviewery* 192, 196 (2002). *See* Frank E. Horack Jr., *In the Name of Legislative Intention*, 38 W. Va. L.Q. 119, 121 (1932) ("[I]f a specific statute is applied to a specific case there must in every instance be interpretation.").

3   *See* Cass R. Sunstein, *The Partial Constitution* 104 (1993) ("[I]nterpretive principles are always at work. That is no embarrassment to constitutional law, or indeed to law itself, but instead an inevitable part of the exercise of reason in human affairs.").

4   H.T. Tiffany, "Interpretation and Construction," in 17 *American and English Encyclopaedia of Law* 1, 2 (David S. Garland & Lucius P. McGehee eds., 2d ed. 1900).

You might be tempted to say, "If the language were plain and unambiguous, we wouldn't be arguing about it, would we?" Banish the thought: Lawyers argue about plain and unambiguous language all the time. That is their job: to inject doubt when it is in their clients' interest. But more often the language is not plain and unambiguous, so that to figure out its meaning, the implicit process of interpretation that we apply to plain and unambiguous language must be made express. That process consists of this:

> Given a rule of law that [those] conditions generically described as A produce a certain legal liability or other consequence X, does the specific fact or group of facts *n* fall within the genus A?[5]

You read an authoritative legal text to discover A (a major premise). You find facts to discover *n* (the minor premise). Then you draw your conclusion. The formulator of this simple but profound paradigm, Sir Frederick Pollock, acknowledged the difficulties that inevitably arise: "[A]lthough it may at first seem easy to untrained common sense to pronounce that some acts are within the prohibition of the law and others are not, there will and must be cases near the borderline which are not obviously on either one side or the other."[6]

Let us apply Pollock's formula to a real case: In Worcester County, Massachusetts, a Panera Bread restaurant leased space in a shopping center under a written agreement that forbade the shopping center to lease space to any restaurant whose "annual sales of sandwiches" might be expected to exceed 10% of the restaurant's income. The shopping center later negotiated for lease of space to a Qdoba restaurant, which sold exclusively tacos, burritos, and quesadillas. Panera filed a declaratory-judgment action in the Massachusetts Superior Court seeking to enjoin the lease.[7]

---

5   Frederick Pollock, *A First Book of Jurisprudence for Students of the Common Law* 226 (1896). *Cf.* 3 Roscoe Pound, *Jurisprudence* 469 (1959) (stating that "the facts having been found, judicial decision according to law involves (1) finding the legal precept to be applied, (2) interpreting the precept, (3) applying the precept to the cause").

6   Pollock, *A First Book of Jurisprudence* at 224–25.

7   *White City Shopping Ctr. v. PR Restaurants*, 2006 WL 3292641 (Mass. Super. Ct. 31 Oct. 2006).

The condition that produced a legal consequence here (genus A in Pollock's formulation) was a restaurant with more than the speci-fied sales of *sandwiches*. *Sandwiches* not being a defined term in the lease, the court sensibly relied on a reputable dictionary, which defined a sandwich as "two thin pieces of bread, usually buttered, with a thin layer (as of meat, cheese, or savory mixture) spread between them."[8] The facts whose inclusion within genus A would produce the legal consequence of prohibition consisted of a res-taurant that sold *tacos, burritos, and quesadillas* (*n* in Pollock's for-mulation). The court found that these foods typically consist of a single tortilla stuffed with a choice filling of meat, rice, and beans (inexplicably neglecting to mention cheese). The injunction was properly denied on grounds that no reasonable speaker of English would call a taco, a burrito, or a quesadilla a "sandwich."[9]

8   *Id.* at *3 (quoting *Webster's Third New International Dictionary* 2002 (1961)).
9   *Id.* at *4.

2. Supremacy-of-Text Principle

The words of a governing text are of paramount concern, and what they convey, in their context, is what the text means.

"We have not traveled, in our search for the meaning of
the lawmakers, beyond the borders of the statute."
United States v. Great Northern Ry.,
287 U.S. 144, 154 (1932) (per Cardozo, J.).

When deciding an issue governed by the text of a legal in-strument, the careful lawyer or judge trusts neither memory nor paraphrase but examines the very words of the instrument. As Justinian's *Digest* put it: *A verbis legis non est recedendum*[1] ("Do not depart from the words of the law").

Of course, words are given meaning by their context, and con-text includes the purpose of the text. The difference between tex-tualist interpretation and so-called purposive interpretation is not that the former never considers purpose. It almost always does. The subject matter of the document (its purpose, broadly speak-ing) is the context that helps to give words meaning—that might cause *draft* to mean a bank note rather than a breeze. And even beyond that, it can be said more generally that the resolution of an ambiguity or vagueness that achieves a statute's purpose should be favored over the resolution that frustrates its purpose. But the textualist insists on four limitations:

First, the purpose must be derived from the text, not from extrinsic sources such as legislative history or an assumption about the legal drafter's desires.

Second, the purpose must be defined precisely, and not in a fashion that smuggles in the answer to the question before the decision-maker. Assume a text that requires the losing litigant to pay the winner's attorney's fees; and assume further that the in-terpretive question is whether expert-witness fees are included. It

---

1   *Cf. Digest* 32.69 pr. (Marcellus). *Cf.* also Unif. Statute & Rule Construction Act
     § 19 (1995) ("*Primacy of Text.* The text of a statute or rule is the primary, essential
     source of its meaning.").

is clear enough that in normal usage, expert-witness fees are not included. But if the express "purpose" of the provision is said to be making the winner whole for its costs of suit, that normal usage could be overridden. To find such a purpose in the absence of a clear indication in the text is to provide the judge's answer rather than the text's answer to the question. Positing a make-the-winner-whole purpose effectively begs the question—assuming what is to be proved: that reimbursing attorney's fees means reimbursing other expenses as well.

Third, the purpose is to be described as concretely as possible, not abstractly. For example, statutes of limitations have the purpose of ensuring that claims be brought within a specified period—they are not to be considered as having the generalized purpose of "promoting justice." Every end is a means to a further end. Letting judges interpret the words of a text so as to achieve the abstract purpose of doing justice is effectively to let them decide what the statute should mean—to decide what is justice or equity—rather than to decide what the text itself says. There are many equally tempting way stations on the path to that ultimate purpose of doing justice and producing equity. For example, a statute providing a specific protection and a discrete remedy for purchasers of goods can be said to have as its purpose "protecting the consumer." That would not justify expansive consumer-friendly interpretations of provisions that are narrowly drawn. Such a highly generalized purpose is not relevant to genuine textual interpretation.

Fourth, except in the rare case of an obvious scrivener's error, purpose—even purpose as most narrowly defined—cannot be used to contradict text or to supplement it. Purpose sheds light only on deciding which of various *textually permissible meanings* should be adopted. No text pursues its purpose at all costs. Drafters make exceptions, or leave some matters uncovered, because of competing social values (in the case of legislation) or competing desires (in the case of privately drafted documents). Or to put the point differently, the limitations of a text—what a text chooses *not* to do—are as much a part of its "purpose" as its affirmative dispositions. These exceptions or limitations must be respected, and the only way to accord them their due is to reject the replacement or supplementation of text with purpose.

3. Principle of Interrelating Canons

No canon of interpretation is absolute. Each may be overcome by the strength of differing principles that point in other directions.

> "[C]anons are not mandatory rules. They are guides that 'need not be conclusive.'"
>
> *Chickasaw Nation v. United States*,
> 534 U.S. 84, 93 (2001) (citation omitted) (per Breyer, J.).

Principles of interpretation are guides to solving the puzzle of textual meaning, and as in any good mystery, different clues often point in different directions. It is a rare case in which each side does *not* appeal to a different canon to suggest its desired outcome. The skill of sound construction lies in assessing the clarity and weight of each clue and deciding where the balance lies.

An oft-cited law-review article by Karl Llewellyn, a highly regarded 20th-century legal scholar, derides time-honored canons of construction by asserting that "there are two opposing canons on almost every point."[1] Llewellyn's supposed demonstration, however, treats as canons some silly (and deservedly contradicted) judicial statements that are so far from having acquired canonical status that most lawyers have never heard of them.[2] And some are not canons of interpretation because they reject textual interpretation as the basis of decision.[3] (To the extent that these might have become frequently expressed, they are not canons but anticanons.) The rest are not contradictions at all, but merely indications that different (noncontradictory) canons may sometimes provide

---

1   Karl Llewellyn, *Remarks on the Theory of Appellate Decision and the Rules or Canons About How Statutes Are to Be Construed*, 3 Vand. L. Rev. 395, 401 (1950). *Cf.* Carleton Kemp Allen, *Law in the Making* 578 (7th ed. 1964) (echoing Llewellyn by saying that "[t]here is scarcely a rule of statutory interpretation, however orthodox, which is not qualified by large exceptions, some of which so nearly approach flat contradictions that the rule itself seems to totter on its base").

2   *E.g.*, Llewellyn, 3 Vand. L. Rev. at 402 ("Where various states have already adopted the statute, the parent state is followed.").

3   *E.g.*, *id.* at 401 ("To effect its purpose a statute may be implemented beyond its text . . ."); *id.* at 402 ("Courts have the power to inquire into real—as distinct from ostensible—purpose."); *id.* at 404 ("The letter is only the 'bark.' Whatever is within the reason of the law is within the law itself.").

differing indications of meaning.[4] This unsurprising fact hardly renders the canons useless or obsolete: "[T]he fact that the maxims may work against each other . . . does not establish the hopeless confusion posited by Llewellyn's model. It is simply a matter of competing inferences drawn from the evidence."[5]

Some modern critics have gone Llewellyn one better in glibly disparaging the canons. One actually says, "I . . . think that most of the canons are just plain wrong,"[6] calling them "[v]acuous and inconsistent."[7] Elsewhere, the same commentator suggests—attributing an odious cynicism to all those who use the canons—"that they are fig leaves for decisions reached on other grounds."[8] Still another commentator asserts that "[r]ules and canons of statutory construction must be abolished and eliminated from the legal vocabulary."[9] Alas, these types of derogatory remarks have influenced American legal education.

Still, most current academic commentary displays an increased, if sometimes begrudging, acceptance of the usefulness of the canons.[10] This acceptance accords with the centuries-old

---

4   *E.g., id.* at 404 (citing the canon that "The same language used repeatedly in the same connection is presumed to bear the same meaning throughout the statute" [presumption of consistent usage (§ 25)], which is said to be contradicted by the proposition that "This presumption will be disregarded where it is necessary to assign different meanings to make the statute consistent" (an expression of the canon that provisions of documents are to be interpreted to be consistent rather than contradictory [harmonious-reading canon (§ 27)])).

5   Geoffrey P. Miller, *Pragmatics and the Maxim of Interpretation*, 1990 Wis. L. Rev. 1179, 1202.

6   Richard A. Posner, *Statutory Interpretation—in the Classroom and in the Courtroom*, 50 U. Chi. L. Rev. 800, 806 (1983).

7   *Id.* at 816.

8   *Continental Cas. Co. v. Pittsburgh Corning Corp.*, 917 F.2d 297, 300 (7th Cir. 1990) (per Posner, J.). *Cf.* Joel R. Cornwell, *Smoking Canons: A Guide to Some Favorite Rules of Construction*, CBA Record, May 1996, at 43, 43 (stating that some jurisprudes [we use the term advisedly here] consider the canons "little more than smoke screens covering the subtle maneuvers of the result-oriented").

9   James C. Thomas, *Statutory Construction When Legislation Is Viewed as a Legal Institution*, 3 Harv. J. on Legis. 191, 210 (1966).

10   *See, e.g.,* William N. Eskridge Jr. & Philip P. Frickey, *Foreword: Law as Equilibrium*, 108 Harv. L. Rev. 26, 66 (1994) (explaining how the canons—as part of an "interpretive regime"—provide "some degree of insulation against judicial arbitrariness . . . [and render] statutory interpretation more predictable, regular, and

wisdom that they are indeed helpful, neutral guides. Roscoe Pound endorsed them:

> [C]ommon-law canons of interpretation are grounded in experience developed by reason and tend to a better administration of justice than leaving interpretation in each case to feelings of policy on the part of the tribunal, which may or may not be those of the legislators. If the canons were sometimes applied too rigidly in the [19th] century, it was rather because of a tendency to mechanical handling of all law at that time than because of any intrinsic unsuitableness of the canons themselves.[11]

Justice Felix Frankfurter also endorsed them: "Insofar as canons of construction are generalizations of experience, they all have worth."[12] The canons influence not just how courts approach texts but also the techniques that legal drafters follow in preparing those texts. Yes, they can be abused, as every useful tool can be abused. But we should hardly abandon them.

The sound view is that "statutory interpretation is governed as absolutely by rules as anything else in the law . . . . [O]n the whole, the rules of statutory interpretation are specially stable."[13] This is not to say that it is always clear what results the principles *produce*. But the principles to be applied in reaching these results

---

coherent . . ."); Jonathan R. Macey & Geoffrey P. Miller, *The Canons of Statutory Construction and Judicial Preferences*, 45 Vand. L. Rev. 647, 672 (1992) (noting that "complete abandonment of the canons would have judges deciding complex issues of law over which they have no expertise or experience and might reduce judicial respect for the norm of legislative supremacy in lawmaking"); John F. Manning, *Legal Realism and the Canons' Revival*, 5 Green Bag 2d 283, 294 (2002) (noting that "modern scholars across a wide range of philosophical approaches . . . believe that canons of construction are worth arguing about and arguing for"); David L. Shapiro, *Continuity and Change in Statutory Interpretation*, 67 N.Y.U. L. Rev. 921, 925 (1992) (stating that the canons have "an important and valuable role to play" by helping to resolve close questions of construction "in favor of continuity and against change"); Cass R. Sunstein, *Interpreting Statutes in the Regulatory State*, 103 Harv. L. Rev. 405, 412 (1989) (rejecting the idea that the canons are "an outmoded and unhelpful guide to the courts").

11 3 Roscoe Pound, *Jurisprudence* 506 (1959).

12 Felix Frankfurter, *Some Reflections on the Reading of Statutes*, 47 Colum. L. Rev. 527, 544 (1947).

13 Joel Prentiss Bishop, *Commentaries on the Written Laws and Their Interpretation* § 2, at 3 (1882).

are "specially stable." They *should* be stable, that is, despite the efforts of many moderns to destabilize them.

4. Presumption Against Ineffectiveness

A textually permissible interpretation that furthers rather than obstructs the document's purpose should be favored.

There is a legendary story about zoning legislation stating that "no drinking saloon may exist within a mile of any schoolhouse." Misinterpreting and misapplying this provision, the court decided that a certain schoolhouse had to be moved.[1] That decision was precisely backward: The clear purpose of the statute, as gathered from the words alone ("no drinking saloon" is the prohibition), was to protect schoolhouses—not saloons.

The presumption against ineffectiveness ensures that a text's manifest purpose is furthered, not hindered. Embodying this presumption, a provision of the California Civil Code affirms that a contract "must receive such an interpretation as will make it lawful, *operative*, definite, reasonable, and *capable of being carried into effect*."[2] The italicized qualifiers essentially direct that the contract should be construed, if possible, to work rather than fail. Similarly for statutes: As expressed by the Texas Supreme Court, if the "language is susceptible of two constructions, one of which will carry out and the other defeat [its] manifest object, [the statute] should receive the former construction."[3]

This canon follows inevitably from the facts that (1) interpretation always depends on context, (2) context always includes evident purpose, and (3) evident purpose always includes effectiveness.

An oft-cited case is *The Emily & the Caroline*,[4] dealing with two ships that were being outfitted for the slave trade. The Slave Trade Act of 1794[5] forbade anyone to "build, fit, equip, load, or otherwise prepare, any ship or vessel, within any port or place of the said United States . . . for the purpose of carrying on any trade

---

1   *See* Dudley Cammett Lunt, *The Road to the Law* 187 (1932).

2   Cal. Civ. Code § 1643 (emphasis added).

3   *Citizens Bank of Bryan v. First State Bank*, 580 S.W.2d 344, 348 (Tex. 1979).

4   22 U.S. (9 Wheat.) 381 (1824) (per Thompson, J.).

5   1 Stat. 347, § 1.

or traffic in slaves"[6]—or else the ship or vessel would be forfeited. The crucial word was *prepare*: Did it mean to begin preparations, or to complete them? The evidence indisputably showed that the ships would be used to transport slaves, but the shipowners argued that the ships could not be "prepared" if they were not yet ready for use toward that purpose. The Supreme Court of the United States held that this interpretation would render "evasion of the law . . . almost certain"[7]:

> As soon . . . as the preparations have progressed, so far as clearly and satisfactorily to show the purpose for which they are made, the right of seizure attaches. To apply the construction contended for on the part of the claimant, that the fitting or preparation must be complete, and the vessel ready for sea, before she can be seized, would be rendering the law in a great measure nugatory, and enable offenders to elude its provisions in the most easy manner.[8]

In other words, the vessel would never be fully "prepared" until it set sail, and would therefore be much harder to seize.

An 1883 case provides another example.[9] A Pennsylvania statute provided that the Ridge Avenue Passenger Railway Company would pay annually to the City of Philadelphia a tax of 6% on the amounts of declared dividends that exceeded 6% of the company's "capital stock."[10] The term was susceptible of two meanings. The company contended that it referred to authorized capital stock; the city contended that it referred only to capital stock actually issued (paid-in capital). The Pennsylvania Supreme Court held for the city: "[T]he object and purpose of the statute was to create and secure a revenue to the city of Philadelphia, whose streets the corporation [was] occupying for the purposes of [its] charter."[11] The court explained that if the company's interpretation were correct, the company could manipulate the amount of authorized capital

---

6   *Id.*

7   22 U.S. at 390.

8   *Id.* at 389.

9   *See City of Philadelphia v. Ridge Ave. Passenger Ry. Co.*, 102 Pa. 190 (1883).

10   Act of March 8th 1872, § 3, P. L. 264.

11   102 Pa. at 196.

in such manner that it would never have to pay the city anything: "[T]his purpose and object of the statute, would be defeated; the absurdity of such a construction is therefore apparent."[12]

---

12 *Id.*

5. Presumption of Validity

An interpretation that validates outweighs one that invalidates (*ut res magis valeat quam pereat*).

> "[W]hen a statute is reasonably susceptible of two interpretations, by one of which it is unconstitutional and by the other valid, the court prefers the meaning that preserves to the meaning that destroys."
> *Panama Refining Co. v. Ryan*,
> 293 U.S. 388, 439 (1935) (Cardozo, J., dissenting).

The presumption of validity disfavors interpretations that would nullify the provision or the entire instrument—for example, an interpretation that would cause a future interest created by a will to violate the rule against perpetuities, that would cause an arbitration clause to be unenforceable, or that would cause a statute to be unconstitutional. The presumption might be viewed as a species of the presumption against ineffectiveness (see § 4), since an interpretation that renders a provision invalid (unlawful) "obstructs" its application to the maximum. In fact, some courts have applied the canon (wrongly) to interpretations that do not render a provision void but merely make it ineffective.[1] And some courts have even applied the presumption to interpretations that render a provision superfluous or nugatory (see § 26).[2] But these are imprecise applications.

An opinion by the formidable Justice Joseph Story on circuit exemplifies the proper application of the presumption of validity. When the recently formed United States sought to acquire land in Rhode Island for national-defense purposes, the state legislature enacted a statute authorizing any town or person in the state, with the consent of the governor, to sell lands to the United States for that purpose. The act contained a proviso "that all civil and criminal processes issued under the authority of the state . . . may be executed on the lands so ceded, and within the fortifications

---

1   *See, e.g.*, *United States v. Revis*, 22 F.Supp.2d 1242, 1255 (N.D. Okla. 1998); *May v. Saginaw County*, 32 F. 629, 632 (C.C.E.D. Mich. 1887).

2   *See, e.g.*, *Grimme v. Grimme*, 101 Ill. App. 389, 395 (Ill. Ct. App. 1902); *Steiner v. Peterman*, 63 A. 1102, 1104 (N.J. Ch. 1906); *City of Goldsboro v. Moffett*, 49 F. 213, 215 (C.C.E.D.N.C. 1892).

which may be erected thereon, in the same way and manner as if such lands had not been ceded as aforesaid."[3]

The defendant in *United States v. Cornell*[4] was a soldier at Fort Adams in Newport Harbor, a federal facility that had been acquired under this state statute. Cornell had killed another soldier on the post and was tried for murder under a 1790 federal statute that provided the death penalty for anyone who commits murder "within any fort, arsenal, dock-yard, magazine, or in any other place or district of country, under the sole and exclusive jurisdiction of the United States."[5] Cornell's counsel argued that the federal statute was inapplicable because it applied only where the United States had exclusive jurisdiction, whereas the proviso in the Rhode Island legislation authorizing the purchase retained the state's civil and criminal jurisdiction. The issue, in short, was whether the provision stating that "all civil and criminal processes issued under the authority of the state . . . may be executed on the land so ceded" reserved concurrent legislative jurisdiction in Rhode Island, or rather merely permitted service of process in cases in which Rhode Island had jurisdiction. In reasoning that the latter must be the case, Justice Story adverted to the constitutional provision authorizing Congress to "exercise [the] Authority [of exclusive legislation] over all Places purchased by the Consent of the Legislature of the State in which the Same shall be, for the Erection of Forts, Magazines, Arsenals, dock-Yards and other needful Buildings."[6] When Congress purchased land in that manner and for those purposes, he said, exclusive federal jurisdiction automatically followed. But what if Rhode Island's consent, by reason of the proviso, did not convey exclusive sovereignty? The consent, he wrote, should not be interpreted that way:

> [I]t may well be doubted whether congress [is] by the terms of the constitution, at liberty to purchase lands for forts, dockyards, &c. with the consent of a state legislature,

---

3   Laws of Rhode Island at 551 (as quoted in *United States v. Cornell*, 25 F. Cas. 646 (C.C.D.R.I. 1819) (No. 14,867)).

4   25 F. Cas. at 646.

5   Act of April 30, 1790, 1 Stat. 113, § 3.

6   Art. I, § 8, cl. 17.

where such consent is so qualified that it will not justify the "exclusive legislation" of congress there. It may well be doubted if such consent be not utterly void. "Ut res magis valeat quam pereat," we are bound to give the present act a different construction, if it may reasonably be done; and we have not the least hesitation in declaring that the true interpretation of the present proviso leaves the sole and exclusive jurisdiction of Fort Adams in the United States.[7]

This was a surgically precise use of the presumption of validity. The Rhode Island proviso had to be interpreted that way because otherwise the Rhode Island statute would be void, authorizing a conveyance that was unconstitutional. Story's use is even linguistically precise: The Latin *ut* means "in order that," which appropriately introduces the sentence in which he applies the canon.

7　25 F. Cas. at 649.

Semantic Canons

6. Ordinary-Meaning Canon

Words are to be understood in their ordinary, everyday meanings—unless the context indicates that they bear a technical sense.

> "The enlightened patriots who framed our constitution, and the people who adopted it, must be understood to have employed words in their natural sense, and to have intended what they have said."
> Chief Justice John Marshall,
> *Gibbons v. Ogden*, 22 U.S. (9 Wheat.) 1, 71 (1824).

The ordinary-meaning rule is the most fundamental semantic rule of interpretation.[1] It governs constitutions, statutes, rules, and private instruments. Interpreters should not be required to divine arcane nuances or to discover hidden meanings. Justice Joseph Story's words are as true today as they were when written in the middle of the 19th century, and they are true not just of constitutions but of all other legal instruments:

> [E]very word employed in the constitution is to be expounded in its plain, obvious, and common sense, unless the context furnishes some ground to control, qualify, or enlarge it. Constitutions are not designed for metaphysical or logical subtleties, for niceties of expression, for critical propriety, for elaborate shades of meaning, or for the exercise of philosophical acuteness or judicial research. They are instruments of a practical nature, founded on the common business of human life, adapted to common wants, designed for common use, and fitted for common understandings.[2]

---

1   *See, e.g.*, James Kent, *Commentaries on American Law* 432 (1826) ("The words of a statute are to be taken in their natural and ordinary signification and import; and if technical words are used, they are to be taken in a technical sense."); Cal. Code Civ. Proc. § 1861 ("The terms of a writing are presumed to have been used in their primary and general acceptation . . .").

2   Joseph Story, *Commentaries on the Constitution of the United States* 157–58 (1833).

This is not to say that interpretation will always be straightforward and easy—just that we should not make it gratuitously roundabout and complex.

Most common English words have a number of dictionary definitions, some of them quite abstruse and rarely intended. One should assume the contextually appropriate ordinary meaning unless there is reason to think otherwise. Sometimes there *is* reason to think otherwise, which ordinarily comes from context. And it should not be forgotten that not all colloquial meanings appropriate to particular contexts are to be found in the dictionary—as the "using a firearm" example we gave earlier (see p. 32) illustrated.

Many words have more than one ordinary meaning. The fact is that the more common the term (e.g., *run*), the more meanings it will bear—the more "polysemous" it is, as linguists put it. Hence *run* was once calculated as having more than 800 meanings.[3] Yet context disambiguates: We can tell the meanings of *he is running down the hill, she is running late, she has been running the company for four years, the car is running low on gas, his enemies kept running him down, the driver was intent on running him down*, and so on.

One scholar has suggested that the ordinary-meaning rule "presumes, wrongly, that all native listeners and readers of language always understand words to mean the same thing the speakers intended."[4] But those absolutes (*all* and *always*) mischaracterize the presumption. What the rule presumes is that a thoroughly fluent reader can reliably tell in the vast majority of instances from contextual and idiomatic clues which of several possible senses a word or phrase bears. Consider: A *check* might be an inspection, an impeding of someone else's progress, a restaurant bill, a commercial instrument, a patterned square on a fabric, or a distinctive mark-off. A *kite* might be an object flown in the sky on a string, a hawklike bird, or a predatory person—or, as a verb, *to kite* might mean "to fly," "to hurry," or "to pass (commercial paper) fraudulently." To say something nondescript such as "There was a check"

---

3   *See* John J. DeBoer, Walter V. Kaulfers & Helen Rand Miller, *Teaching Secondary English* 133 (1951) ("the little word *run*, with its compounds, has 800 meanings, from *home run* to *run on a bank* or *run in a stocking*").

4   Linda D. Jellum, *Mastering Statutory Interpretation* 64 (2008).

or "The kite was present" means nothing certain. But once you combine words in ordinary, idiomatic ways—as by referring to *check-kiting* or by saying *He checked the kite carefully before flying it*—no ordinary speaker of the language could even pretend to misunderstand.

Some theorists deny that plain meaning or ordinary meaning ever exists.[5] But common experience proves the contrary: In everyday life, the people to whom rules are addressed continually understand and apply them. Let us consider how the ordinary-meaning canon affects legal analysis. That occurs in a great variety of contexts.

Sometimes the canon governs the interpretation of so simple a word as a preposition. The Pennsylvania Supreme Court had to interpret the meaning of *into* in a statute that read: "A person commits an offense if he knowingly, intentionally, or recklessly discharges a firearm from any location into an occupied structure."[6] One James McCoy was inside the Old Country Buffet when he fired his gun. The question was whether, in ordinary English, *into* denotes the movement from outside to inside—or whether the movement of the bullet from the gun chamber into the area in which it first struck something would be sufficient for discharging "into an occupied structure." One might have analogized to other idioms: *Run into an occupied structure* suggests starting outside and going inside; while *peer into an occupied structure* suggests a continuing presence outside. On appeal, McCoy was properly held not to have fired his gun "into" the restaurant (since he was already inside), so his conviction was overturned.[7]

On a question like that one, a judicial interpreter might be tempted simply to rely on his or her own sense of the language— or *Sprachgefühl*, as the Germans call it (and, believe it or not,

---

5 *See, e.g.*, Stanley Fish, *There Is No Textualist Position*, 42 San Diego L. Rev. 629, 633 (2005) (arguing that there is no such thing as plain meaning). *See also* Steven L. Winter, *Indeterminacy and Incommensurability in Constitutional Law*, 78 Cal. L. Rev. 1441, 1468 (1990) (criticizing California Supreme Court's preference for plain-meaning arguments because "there is no such thing as 'plain meaning'").

6 18 Pa. Stat. § 2707.1(a).

7 *Commonwealth v. McCoy*, 962 A.2d 1160 (Pa. 2009).

sprachgefühl has been a word in our shamelessly pilfering English language since about 1894).[8] But lexicographers and usage commentators have explicitly dealt with questions such as the meaning of *into*, and it would be a mistake not to consult them. As the Pennsylvania court's opinion demonstrated,[9] these authorities can illuminate a question such as the precise contours of *into*. For our readers' convenience, we include as Appendix A a list of the principal dictionaries that can be consulted to determine the near-contemporaneous common meaning of words from 1750 to the present.

Courts have sometimes ignored plain meaning in astonishing ways. The Kansas Supreme Court, for example, perversely held that roosters are not "animals," so that cockfighting was not outlawed by a statute making it illegal to "subject[] any animal to cruel mistreatment."[10] Far more satisfactory is the holding of a Massachusetts appellate court that a goldfish *is* an animal for purposes of a statute prohibiting the award of "any live animal as a prize or an award in a game . . . involving skill or chance."[11] The court relied in part on dictionary definitions:

> "The word 'animal,' in its common acceptation, includes all irrational beings." This broad definition, which accords with most dictionary meanings, leaves us little to contrib-

---

8   *Merriam-Webster's Collegiate Dictionary* 1208 (11th ed. 2003).

9   962 A.2d at 1166–67 (citing *Webster's Third New International Dictionary* 1184 (1961; repr. 1984) (noting that *into* typically follows "a verb that carries the idea of motion . . . to indicate a place or thing . . . enterable or penetrable by or as if by a movement from the outside to the interior part"); *Webster's New World Dictionary* 738 (2d ed. 1984) (noting that *into* describes action "from the outside to the inside of; toward and within")). *See also Garner's Modern American Usage* 450 (3d ed. 2009) (stating that "*into* denotes movement. Thus, a person who swims . . . *into* the ocean is moving from, say, the mouth of a river."); 8 *Oxford English Dictionary* 9 (2d ed. 1989) (giving the "general sense" of *into* as "expressing motion from without to a point within limits of space, time, condition, circumstance, etc.").

10 *State ex rel. Miller v. Claiborne*, 505 P.2d 732, 733 (Kan. 1973) (noting that the cruelty-to-animals-statute had traditionally applied only to four-legged animals).

11 Mass. Gen. Laws ch. 272, § 80F (1977). *See Knox v. Massachusetts Soc'y for Prevention of Cruelty to Animals*, 425 N.E.2d 393 (Mass. App. Ct. 1981).

ute by deliberating on where the line should be drawn on any taxonomic scale.[12]

Sometimes context indicates that a technical meaning applies. Every field of serious endeavor develops its own nomenclature—sometimes referred to as *terms of art*. Where the text is addressing a scientific or technical subject, a specialized meaning is to be expected: "In terms of art which are above the comprehension of the general bulk of mankind, recourse, for explanation, must be had to those, who are most experienced in that art."[13] And when the law is the subject, ordinary legal meaning is to be expected, which often differs from common meaning. As Justice Frankfurter eloquently expressed it: "[I]f a word is obviously transplanted from another legal source, whether the common law or other legislation, it brings the old soil with it."[14]

Perhaps the most famous example of the technical-meaning exception—one that pervades legal drafting—is the presumption that *person* in legal instruments denotes a corporation and other entity, not just a human being (see § 44 [artificial-person canon]). This presumption has been known to rankle nonlawyers when they encounter it.

A case exemplifying ordinary legal meaning that diverges from everyday usage is *State v. Gonzales*,[15] which involved a Louisiana statute defining the crime of *contributing to the delinquency of a juvenile* as "the intentional enticing, aiding, soliciting, or permitting, by anyone over the age of seventeen, of any child under the age of seventeen . . . to . . . [p]erform any sexually immoral act."[16] Ernest Gonzales, an adult, was convicted of this crime after enticing a 16-year-old girl to have sex with him. Yet she had already been emancipated and twice married. Was she a "child under the age of

---

12 *Knox*, 425 N.E.2d at 396 (quoting *Commonwealth v. Turner*, 14 N.E. 130, 132 (Mass. 1887)).

13 Hugo Grotius, *The Rights of War and Peace* 177 (1625; A.C. Campbell trans., 1901).

14 Felix Frankfurter, *Some Reflections on the Reading of Statutes*, 47 Colum. L. Rev. 527, 537 (1947).

15 129 So.2d 796 (La. 1961).

16 La. Rev. Stat. Ann. § 14:92.

seventeen"? No, according to the Louisiana Supreme Court: The word *child* does not include an emancipated minor in the "ordinary accepted meaning under civil law."[17]

Another technical-meaning case involved the word *consideration*, which in general English means "something to be taken account of" or "polite thoughtfulness," but in law means "value given in exchange for a benefit." Now consider a statute that makes a felon of "[w]hoever for a consideration knowingly gives false information to any officer of any court with intent to influence the officer in the performance of official functions."[18] A criminal defendant seeking reduced bail lies to a trial court, saying that he has never before been convicted of a crime—as a result of which he gets his bail reduced. Has he lied "for a consideration"? A nonlawyer unschooled in the ways of legal terminology might well say so. But from the legal point of view, did he lie in exchange for something of value? The prosecution said that he did: The reduction in bail that he received as a consequence of his false statement was valuable to him. The defense lawyers argued that the phrase *for a consideration* means "for an *agreed* exchange" and in the context of this statute envisions "some benefit received from a third party" in exchange for false testimony. They urged that there was no agreed exchange—no legal "consideration"—when leniency is merely the consequence of false testimony. And they were right, as the Wisconsin Court of Appeals held.[19] If the court had not applied the specialized legal sense of *consideration*, it would have misconstrued the statute.

Courts as well as advocates have been known to overlook technical senses of ordinary words—senses that might bear directly on their decisions. Consider *Estep v. State*, decided in 1995 by the Texas Court of Criminal Appeals.[20] At issue was the meaning of a procedural rule that provided:

---

17 129 So.2d at 798.

18 Wis. Stat. § 946.65.

19 *State v. Howell*, 414 N.W.2d 54 (Wis. Ct. App. 1987).

20 901 S.W.2d 491 (Tex. Crim. App. 1995).

An appeal shall be dismissed on the State's motion, supported by affidavit, showing that appellant has escaped from custody pending the appeal and that to the affiant's knowledge, has not voluntarily returned to lawful custody within the State within ten days after escaping.[21]

Having been convicted of telephone harassment, Jeffrey Estep appealed. Twelve days later the state filed a motion to dismiss Estep's appeal, together with an affidavit from a prosecutor stating that Estep was taken into custody and then "mistakenly" released by the Dallas County Sheriff's Department on the same day he filed a notice of appeal. According to the affidavit, he had "not voluntarily returned to lawful custody within Texas within ten days" of leaving the Dallas County Sheriff's Department. Had he escaped? Finding that he had, the trial court granted the motion.[22]

On appeal, the crucial question was the meaning of the word *escape*. The prosecutors argued that if a convicted criminal is accidentally released—even by the intentional action of a person with authority to release him—he is considered to have escaped. The court of appeals disagreed. For its understanding of the term *escape*, the court relied on an abridged, outdated, nonscholarly dictionary—the 1980 edition of the *Oxford American Dictionary*—which defined *escape* as "to get oneself free from confinement or control."[23] The court decided not to "expand[] the concept of 'escape' to include releases authorized by persons in authority but not authorized by law."[24]

What the court overlooked, perhaps because it failed to consult a law dictionary, is that *escape* as a term of art has traditionally borne precisely the meaning that the court disclaimed—to include a release authorized by a jailer but without legal sanction. Consider one sense in which law dictionaries have consistently defined *escape* since the mid-19th century:

21　Tex. R. App. P. 60(b).

22　*See* 901 S.W.2d at 492.

23　*Oxford American Dictionary* 217 (1st ed. 1980).

24　901 S.W.2d at 495.

- **1839:** "An escape is the deliverance of a person out of prison, who is lawfully imprisoned, before such person is entitled to such deliverance by law."[25]

- **1847:** "The escaping or getting out of lawful restraint; as when a man has been arrested or imprisoned and gets away before he is discharged by due course of law. An *escape* is either negligent or voluntary; negligent, where the party escapes without the consent of the sheriff or his officer; voluntary where the sheriff or his officer permits him to go at large."[26]

- **1969:** "A criminal offense at common law, and by statute in most jurisdictions, consisting in the unlawful departure of a legally confined prisoner from custody or the act of a prisoner in regaining his liberty before being released in due course of law. The criminal offense committed by a jailer, warden, or other custodian of a prisoner in permitting him to depart from custody unlawfully."[27]

- **2009:** "At common law, a criminal offense committed by a peace officer who allows a prisoner to depart unlawfully from legal custody."[28]

This term-of-art sense, admittedly on the wane in legal usage, should have been considered in determining which sense the word bore in the rule (see § 53 [canon of imputed common-law meaning]). The court's decision may well have been correct, but not because *escape* could not possibly mean a release in which the prisoner was a passive participant.

Not always is it easy to determine whether ordinary meaning or a specialized meaning applies. For example, in *Nix v. Hedden*, the Supreme Court of the United States was presented with the question whether tomatoes were subject to the import tariff ap-

---

25 John Bouvier, *A Law Dictionary* 369 (1839).

26 Henry James Holthouse, *A New Law Dictionary* 184–85 (1847).

27 James A. Ballentine, *Ballentine's Law Dictionary* 415 (William S. Anderson ed., 3d ed. 1969).

28 *Black's Law Dictionary* 623 (9th ed. 2009).

plicable to fruit, or to the higher tariff applicable to vegetables.[29] Although botanists classify the tomato as a fruit, the American people consider it a vegetable. In a brief, straightforward opinion, the Court sided with ordinary meaning (not exactly a victory for the ordinary person, who as a result had to pay more for tomatoes). The decision was not clearly correct, since the Court had long applied a rule that ambiguities in tariff and tax statutes are to be construed in favor of the taxpayer.[30]

---

29 149 U.S. 304 (1893) (per Gray, J.).

30 *See, e.g., American Net & Twine Co. v. Worthington*, 141 U.S. 468, 474 (1891) (per Brown, J.). See § 49.

7. Fixed-Meaning Canon

Words must be given the meaning they had when the text was adopted.

"Words must be read with the gloss of the
experience of those who framed them."
United States v. Rabinowitz,
339 U.S. 56, 70 (1950) (Frankfurter, J., dissenting).

Words change meaning over time, and often in unpredictable ways.[1] Queen Anne is said (probably apocryphally) to have commented about Sir Christopher Wren's architecture at St. Paul's Cathedral that it was "awful, artificial, and amusing"—by which she meant that it was awe-inspiring, highly artistic, and thought-provoking. All three words have since undergone what linguists call *pejoration*: Their meanings have degenerated so that they now bear mostly negative connotations. It would be quite wrong for someone to ascribe to Queen Anne's 18th-century words their 21st-century meanings. To do so would be to misunderstand—or misrepresent—her meaning entirely.

Although courts routinely apply legal instruments to novel situations over time, their meaning remains fixed. Properly understood, originalism is an age-old idea in our jurisprudence for private and public documents alike.[2] But it applies mostly to older documents that continue in effect: Those are the ones whose operative terms are most likely to have undergone semantic shift. The

---

1   *See* James Bradstreet Greenough & George Lyman Kittredge, *Words and Their Ways in English Speech* 234–61 (1901). *See also* Charles Barber, *Linguistic Change in Present-Day English* 109 (1964); E.H. Sturtevant, *Linguistic Change: An Introduction to the Historical Study of Language* 85 (1917).

2   *E.g.*, Anton Friedrich Justus Thibaut, *An Introduction to the Study of Jurisprudence* 45 (Nathaniel Lindley trans., 1855) ("If the meaning of a word has changed in different times, that meaning is to be preferred which was common when the law, in which the word is found, was promulgated."); Thomas M. Cooley, *A Treatise on the Constitutional Limitations Which Rest upon the Legislative Power of the States of the American Union* 59 (1868) ("We cannot understand [constitutional] provisions unless we understand their history."); Reed Dickerson, *Statutes and Constitutions in an Age of Common Law*, 48 U. Pitt. L. Rev. 773, 779–80 (1987) (noting that "[t]he textual integrity of a constitutionally authorized statute can only be preserved by adhering to the connotations it generated at the time of its enactment."); Frank H. Easterbrook, *The Role of Original Intent in Statutory Construction*, 11 Harv. J.L. & Pub. Pol'y 59, 61 (1988).

modern repudiators of originalism deal mainly with its application to public documents—statutes and constitutions. Their newfangled theory is that 18th- and 19th-century drafters expected the meaning of their words to evolve over time—as opposed to having a consistent meaning that will be applied to new and different situations. This view is belied by legal history.

In the English-speaking nations, the earliest statute directed to statutory interpretation made it a punishable offense for counsel to argue anything other than original understanding. Enacted by the Scottish Parliament in 1427, the act was entitled "That nane interpreit the Kingis statutes wrangeouslie."[3] It read: "Item, The King of deliverance of councel, the manner of statute forbiddis, that na man interpreit his statutes utherwaies, then the statute beares, and to the intent and effect, that they were maid for, and as the maker of them understoode: and quha sa dois the contrarie, shall be punished at the Kingis will."[4] Even with its Law French ("whosoever speaks the contrary"), the original meaning of this statute is quite plain.

Similarly but less punitively, a 16th-century treatise entitled *A Discourse upon the Exposicion and Understandinge of Statutes* insisted that a statute must be read in its historical context, "for without knowledge of the ancient lawe they shall neither knowe the statute nor expounde it well, but shall, as it were, followe theire noses and groape at yt in the darke."[5] Sir Edward Coke (1552–1634) espoused this view,[6] and so did John Locke (1632–1704).[7]

Blackstone (1723–1780), the great 18th-century exponent of English law, was a thoroughgoing originalist. Consider his illus-

---

3   James I, 7th Parl., cap. 107 (1427) (Glendook ed.) (repealed by the Statute Law Revision (Scotland) Act of 1906, § 1 & schedule).

4   *Id.*

5   *A Discourse upon the Exposicion and Understandinge of Statute with Sir Thomas Egerton's Additions* 141 (ca. 1565; repr. 1942).

6   Edward Coke, *The Fourth Part of the Institutes of the Laws of England* *324–25 (1644; 15th ed. 1797) (stating that acts of Parliament "consist of the letter, and of the meaning of the makers of the Act").

7   John Locke, *An Essay Concerning Human Understanding* 133 (1801) ("Words are the marks of . . . the speaker: nor can anyone apply them, as marks, . . . to anything else but the ideas that [the speaker] hath.").

tration. A law enacted in the 11th century forbade all ecclesiastical persons to "purchase provisions at Rome."[8] To an 18th-century reader (or, for that matter, to a 21st-century reader), this—in Blackstone's words—"might seem to prohibit the buying of grain or other victual"[9] while in Rome. But the historical evidence showed that in the 11th century, "the nominations to benefices [ecclesiastical-office appointments] were called *provisions*," so that the statute was actually meant to prohibit bribes amounting to "usurpations of the papal fee."[10] To give *provision* the 18th-century meaning, or the 21st-century meaning, would be utterly wrong.

The idea that meaning itself—as opposed to the application of a stable meaning to new phenomena—might change over time was preposterous to the few 19th-century writers who even considered the idea. In 1821, James Madison, one of the architects of the Constitution and author of the Bill of Rights, correctly stated the gist of the fixed-meaning canon: "Can it be of less consequence that the meaning of a constitution should be *fixed* and *known*, than that the meaning of a law should be so? Can, indeed, a law be fixed in its meaning and operation, unless the constitution be so?"[11] Daniel Webster, the greatest American lawyer of the 19th century, said this:

> Will [our successors] think that what was thought by our fathers and grandfathers, who formed the Constitution and established the government, was wholly wrong? I suspect not. We must take the meaning of the Constitution as it has been solemnly fixed.[12]

The upshot is that new rights cannot be suddenly "discovered" years later in a document, unless everyone affected by the docu-

---

8   1 William Blackstone, *Commentaries on the Laws of England* 60 (4th ed. 1770).

9   *Id.*

10   *Id.* For the views of a Continental contemporary of Blackstone, see Cesare Beccaria, *An Essay on Crimes and Punishments* 25 (1793) ("When the code of laws is once *fixed*, it should be observed in the literal sense, and nothing more is left to the judge than to determine, whether an action be, or be not, conformable to the written law.") (emphasis added).

11   Letter from James Madison to C.E. Haynes, 25 Feb. 1821 (repr. 9 *The Writings of James Madison* 443 (Gaillard Hunt ed., 1910)).

12   2 Daniel Webster, *The Works of Daniel Webster* 164 (1851).

ment had somehow overlooked an applicable provision that was there all along. This is true of contracts and statutes as much as it is of constitutions.

The traditional view long remained unchallenged. In 1868, Thomas M. Cooley wrote: "A constitution is not to be made to mean one thing at one time, and another at some subsequent time when the circumstances may have so changed as perhaps to make a different rule in the case seem desirable."[13] In 1905, the Supreme Court of the United States applied the rule to the country's founding document: "The Constitution is a written instrument. As such its meaning does not alter. That which it meant when adopted it means now."[14]

Yet despite the sway of this principled approach, which has lasted through the centuries in Anglo-American law, modern legal literature preaches the dogma of shifting meanings. The new religion began in the mid-20th century. Here is an example from 1956:

> [T]he words used by a legislature . . . will undergo in common usage a constant process of change in meaning—or better, in ambiguity. . . . With substantial passage of time it becomes difficult for a court to grasp the earlier meanings and to avoid reading the statutory words with the later meanings they have assumed in use. . . . Since the meaning of words shifts and the standards of the statute are expressed by their means, there results a shifting in the meaning of the standards, however firm they may have been in the beginning.[15]

---

13 Thomas M. Cooley, *A Treatise on the Constitutional Limitations Which Rest upon the Legislative Power of the States of the American Union* 54 (1868).

14 *South Carolina v. United States*, 199 U.S. 437, 448 (1905) (per Brewer, J.). *Cf.* Frank H. Easterbrook, "Approaches to Judicial Review," in *Politics and the Constitution: The Nature and Extent of Interpretation* 17, 22 (1990) ("Writing means the perpetuation of the ideas of the drafters. Law means rules."); Randal N.M. Graham, *A Unified Theory of Statutory Interpretation*, 23 Statute L. Rev. 91, 95 (2002) ("[O]riginalism has become so deeply ingrained in Anglo-Canadian law that one would be hard pressed to find a decision in which the courts did not at least purport to employ originalist construction as the principal means of resolving interpretative problems.").

15 Joseph P. Witherspoon, *Administrative Discretion to Determine Statutory Meaning: "The High Road,"* 35 Tex. L. Rev. 63, 76–77 (1956). *See also* Kenmore M.

And another example from 1989: "A law does not exist in order to be understood historically," but instead "if it is to be understood properly—i.e., according to the claim it makes—must be understood at every moment, in every concrete situation, in a new and different way."[16] Over time, American law has been subjected to a drumbeat of such dogmatic assertions, especially in law schools.[17] One of the leading consequentialist texts today, entitled *Dynamic Statutory Interpretation*, encourages thoroughly modern modes of "adapting statutes to new circumstances and responding to new political preferences . . . even when the interpretation goes against as well as beyond original legislative expectations."[18]

Yet originalism remains the normal, natural approach to understanding anything that has been said or written in the past. If you want to understand now what Queen Anne was saying about St. Paul's Cathedral, you do not ask what the phrase *awful, artificial, and amusing* means today. That alone is reason enough for using originalism to interpret private documents. But where public documents—constitutions, statutes, ordinances, regulations—are at issue, there is a still more important reason: Originalism is the *only* approach to text that is compatible with democracy. When government-adopted texts are given a new meaning, the law is changed; and changing written law, like adopting written law in the first place, is the function of the first two branches of government—elected legislators and (in the case of authorized

---

McManes, *Effect of Legislative History on Judicial Decision*, 5 Geo. Wash. L. Rev. 235, 242 (1937) ("The courts should not and cannot hold themselves apart from the ever-growing changes taking place today. Legislation must be construed in the light of the times.").

16 Hans-Georg Gadamer, *Truth and Method* 308 (2d ed. 1989).

17 *See* Randal N.M. Graham, *What Judges Want: Judicial Self-Interest and Statutory Interpretation*, 30 Statute L. Rev. 38, 38 (2009) ("In the eyes of postmodern theorists, words have no 'essential' meanings; instead, words are constantly shifting variables . . ."). *See also* Erwin Chemerinsky, *Constitutional Law: Principles and Policies* 25 (2011) (stating the nonoriginalist position as being that "the framers probably did not intend that their intent would govern later interpretations of the Constitution."); T. Alexander Aleinikoff, *Updating Statutory Interpretation*, 87 Mich. L. Rev. 20, 49, 58 (1988) (suggesting that judges should interpret old legal texts as if they were adopted yesterday, rather than trying to ascertain meaning as of the date of adoption).

18 William N. Eskridge Jr., *Dynamic Statutory Interpretation* 108 (1994).

prescriptions by the executive branch) elected executive officials and their delegates. Allowing laws to be rewritten by judges is a radical departure from our democratic system. As Chief Justice William H. Rehnquist described the consequence, disregard of original meaning

> is a formula for an end run around popular government. To the extent that it makes possible an individual's persuading one or more appointed federal judges to impose on other individuals a rule of conduct that the popularly elected branches of government would not have enacted and the voters have not and would not have embodied in the Constitution, [this] version of the living Constitution is genuinely corrosive of the fundamental values of our democratic society.[19]

This is no accidental consequence of abandoning original meaning; it is the very reason for it—a surrender, as Lord Devlin put it, to the "great temptation to cast the judiciary as an elite which will bypass the traffic-laden ways of the democratic process."[20]

This corrosion of democracy occurs even when law-revising judges are elected, as they are in many states. The five or seven or nine members of a state supreme court, lawyers all, can hardly be considered a representative assembly. Moreover, when the task of judges becomes the updating of written law, not only is the function of the popular branches diminished, but also the very nature of the judicial branch and the qualifications for those who serve in it are radically altered. The process necessarily becomes politicized: "If the dominant political force for the time being may, or thinks it may, amend the constitution offhand by procuring

---

19 William H. Rehnquist, *The Notion of a Living Constitution*, 54 Tex. L. Rev. 693, 706 (1976).

20 Patrick Devlin, *The Judge* 17 (1979). *See* Edward H. Levi, *An Introduction to Legal Reasoning* 33 (1949) ("It often appears that the only hope lies with the courts. Yet the democratic process seems to require that controversial changes should be made by the legislative body."). *See also* Antonin Scalia, *A Matter of Interpretation: Federal Courts and the Law* 135–36 (1997) ("To guarantee that the freedom of speech will be no less than it is today is to guarantee something permanent; to guarantee that it will be no less than the aspirations of the future is to guarantee nothing at all."); Gary L. McDowell, Introduction to *Politics and the Constitution: The Nature and Extent of Interpretation* vii, xi (1990) ("[T]o change the Constitution's meaning through interpretation is to change our politics.").

judicial spurious interpretation, it is evident that pressure will be brought to bear on the courts to adjust constitutional provisions to the exigencies of current political policy."[21] Candidates for an office whose function is to change the law *will* be selected, as legislators are, on the basis of what changes they promise to or are likely to bring about. Hence federal candidates for nomination or confirmation are now evaluated not exclusively, or perhaps even primarily, on the basis of such traditional judicial standards as legal ability, impartiality, and judicial demeanor, but on the basis of whether (to take the most prominent qualifications) they will or will not discern an innovated constitutional right to abortion or to homosexual conduct. The selection of judges—even appointed judges—thus becomes an eminently political, results-oriented process. People want judges who will change (or not change) the law *their* way.

Sometimes the change from original meaning adopted by nonoriginalists consists in ascribing different meaning to a term that is ambiguous (in the narrow sense we have described above)—that is, to a word or phrase that can denote two different concepts. For example, the Supreme Court of the United States held in *Hudson v. McMillian*[22] that the Eighth Amendment's prohibition of *cruel and unusual punishments* covered such things as beatings by sadistic prison guards, even though until then *punishments* had been taken to refer to what the defendant was *sentenced* to undergo rather than to everything that took place during confinement. (A beating that was not part of the sentence would form the basis for a tort suit rather than a constitutional claim.) And it held in *Gregg v. Georgia*[23] that a punishment could be "cruel" within the meaning of the Constitution if it is excessive for the offense involved, even though until then the word had been thought to refer to punishments that were in their nature physically cruel (thumbscrews, for example).

Usually, however, the change produced by nonoriginalists gives a different meaning to provisions that are not ambiguous

---

21   3 Roscoe Pound, *Jurisprudence* 489 (1959).

22   503 U.S. 1 (1992) (per O'Connor, J.).

23   428 U.S. 153 (1976) (Stewart, J., plurality opinion).

but vague. Statutes often—and constitutions always—employ general terms such as *due process, equal protection, cruel and unusual punishments*. What these generalities meant as applied to many phenomena that existed at the time of their adoption was well understood and accepted. For example, the prohibition of cruel and unusual punishments in the federal Constitution was not thought to prevent categorical imposition of the death penalty for conviction of certain crimes.[24] Well into the 20th century, conviction of certain crimes (for example, murder of a police officer) resulted in an automatic death penalty.[25] Yet in *Lockett v. Ohio*,[26] the Supreme Court held that the death penalty could never be mandatory upon conviction but must always be subject to suspension by the sentencing authority after a constitutionally required consideration of all "mitigating factors."[27] What the Constitution's general term was understood to require had simply changed in light of what the Court called society's "evolving standards of decency."[28]

Originalism prevents this sort of nine-person (or indeed five-person) constitutional revision. Yet the reader should not be deluded by the caricature of originalism as a doctrine that would make it impossible to apply a legal text to technologies that did not exist when the text was created.[29] The First Amendment, it is sometimes said, would not apply to the Internet; legislation regu-

---

24 *See Woodson v. North Carolina*, 428 U.S. 280, 289 (1976) (Stewart, J., plurality opinion) ("At the time the Eighth Amendment was adopted in 1791, the States uniformly followed the common-law practice of making death the exclusive and mandatory sentence for certain specified offenses.").

25 *See* Rory K. Little, *The Federal Death Penalty: History and Some Thoughts About the Department of Justice's Role*, 26 Fordham Urb. L.J. 347, 373–74 (1999) (detailing the enactment of mandatory-death-penalty acts after *Furman v. Georgia*, 408 U.S. 238 (1972) (per curiam)).

26 438 U.S. 586 (1978) (Burger, C.J., plurality opinion).

27 *Id.* at 606–08.

28 *Trop v. Dulles*, 356 U.S. 86, 101 (1958) (per Warren, C.J.).

29 *See, e.g.*, Jack L. Landau, *Some Thoughts About Constitutional Interpretation*, 115 Penn St. L. Rev. 837, 865–66 (2011) (asserting that originalism cannot be used to determine whether an 1857 Oregon search-and-seizure statute prohibits police from planting a GPS tracker on a car without a warrant); Christopher Birch, *The Connotation/Denotation Distinction in Constitutional Interpretation*, 5 J. App. Prac. & Process 445, 467–68 (2003) (asserting that originalism prevents the Constitution from encompassing new technologies).

lating contracts would not apply to agreements to manufacture microchips; and so on. The objection is empty: Drafters of every era know that technological advances will proceed apace and that the rules they create will one day apply to all sorts of circumstances that they could not possibly envision: "A 19th-century statute criminalizing the theft of goods is not ambiguous in its application to the theft of microwave ovens."[30]

The meaning of rules is constant. Only their application to new situations presents a novelty. Professor Lon Fuller recognized this point in 1934: "Suppose a legislator enacts that it shall be a crime for anyone 'to carry concealed on his person any dangerous weapon.' After the statute is passed someone invents a machine, no larger than a fountain pen, capable of throwing a 'death ray.' Is such a machine included? Obviously, yes."[31] The category denoted by *any dangerous weapon* may include untold numbers of yet-to-be-invented harmful devices.

In *Zucarro v. State*,[32] the statute at issue prohibited Sunday operation of "theaters, variety theaters, and such other amusements." Did the statute apply to motion pictures, which did not exist when the statute took effect? Although the legislators could not possibly have had movies in mind, the court correctly held that a fair reading of the phrase *such other amusements* did indeed embrace them.[33] Broad language can encompass the onward march of science and technology: "Old laws apply to changed situations. . . . While a statute speaks from its enactment, even a criminal statute embraces everything which subsequently falls within its scope."[34]

The Fourth Amendment, with its reference to "unreasonable searches and seizures," is yet another example of encompassingly

---

30   *K Mart Corp. v. Cartier, Inc.*, 486 U.S. 281, 323 (1988) (Scalia, J., concurring in part & dissenting in part).

31   Lon L. Fuller, *American Legal Realism*, 82 U. Pa. L. Rev. 429, 445–46 (1934).

32   197 S.W. 982 (Tex. Crim. App. 1917).

33   *Id.* at 985–86.

34   *Browder v. United States*, 312 U.S. 335, 339–40 (1941) (per Reed, J.). *Cf. Crispin v. Christian Audigier, Inc.*, 717 F.Supp.2d 965 (C.D. Cal. 2010) (holding that Facebook is an Electronic Communication Service under the Stored Communication Act—a statute that predated Facebook and even the advent of the Internet).

broad language that comes to be applied to technology unknown when the operative words took effect. In 2001, the Supreme Court held that the Fourth Amendment applied to a technology well beyond the conception of any Framer (or ratifier), disapproving the warrantless use of a thermal imager to determine whether high-intensity lamps (typically needed for growing marijuana indoors) were being used in a private home.[35] The use of that device "to explore details of the home that would previously have been unknowable without physical intrusion" is a *search* that is presumptively unreasonable without a warrant.[36] And the surreptitious and trespassory attachment of a tracking device to the underbody of an automobile constituted a *search*[37] even though neither tracking devices nor automobiles existed in 1791.

A frequent line of attack against originalism consists in appeal to popular Supreme Court decisions that are assertedly based on a rejection of original meaning. We do not propose overruling all those decisions. Our prescriptions are for the future. For the past, we believe in the doctrine of stare decisis, which will preserve most of the nonoriginalist holdings on the books. Which ones will fall depends on several factors.[38] Stare decisis is beyond the scope of our discussion here, but it is germane to the present point that the relevant factors include the degree of public acceptance.

Some assert that only nonoriginalism could have produced those generally acclaimed results. The validity of that assertion is often questionable. *Brown v. Board of Education*,[39] for example—the example most often cited—purported to rely on public

---

35 *Kyllo v. United States*, 533 U.S. 27 (2001) (per Scalia, J.).

36 *Id.* at 40. *Cf. Minnesota v. Dickerson*, 508 U.S. 366, 379, 382 (1993) (Scalia, J., concurring) ("[E]ven if a 'frisk' prior to arrest would have been considered impermissible in 1791, perhaps . . . it is only since that time that concealed weapons capable of harming the interrogator quickly and from beyond arm's reach have become common—which might alter the judgment of what is 'reasonable' under the original standard.").

37 *See United States v. Jones*, 132 S.Ct. 945, 949 (2012) (per Scalia, J.) (attachment of GPS tracking device to an individual's vehicle constituted a search within the meaning of the Fourth Amendment).

38 *See infra* pp. 411–14.

39 347 U.S 483 (1954) (per Warren, C.J.).

education's new importance, its changed place in American life throughout the nation. But it is far from clear—indeed, it is probably not true—that the Court's reliance on the changed times was necessary. The text of the Thirteenth and Fourteenth Amendments, and in particular the Equal Protection Clause of the Fourteenth, can reasonably be thought to prohibit all laws designed to assert the separateness and superiority of the white race, even those that purport to treat the races equally. Justice John Marshall Harlan took this position in his powerful (and thoroughly originalist) dissent in *Plessy v. Ferguson*.[40] Recent research persuasively establishes that this was the original understanding of the post–Civil War Amendments.[41]

But this is not the most important response to those who point to the accomplishments of nonoriginalism. Nor is the most important response that for every popularly acclaimed nonoriginalist decision there is another that is popularly condemned. The most important response is, "So what?" It is in no way remarkable, and in no way a vindication of textual evolutionism, that taking power from the people and placing it instead with a judicial aristocracy can produce some creditable results that democracy might not achieve. The same can be said of monarchy and totalitarianism. But once a nation has decided that democracy, with all its warts, is the best system of government, the crucial question becomes which theory of textual interpretation is compatible with democracy. Originalism unquestionably is. Nonoriginalism, by contrast, imposes on society statutory prescriptions that were never democratically adopted. When applied to the Constitution, nonoriginalism limits the democratic process itself, prohibiting (through imaginative interpretation of the Bill of Rights) acts of self-governance that "We the people" never, ever, voted to outlaw. With nonoriginalism, those limitations will be determined, term by term, by Justices of the Supreme Court. The power to prohibit abortion, for example, was never democratically removed from the

---

40   163 U.S. 537, 552 (1896) (Harlan, J., dissenting).

41   *See generally* Michael W. McConnell, *Originalism and the Desegregation Decisions*, 81 Va. L. Rev. 947 (1995).

people's choice, but by judicial decree it is no longer a subject on which the people can seek to persuade one another and vote.

The conclusive argument in favor of originalism is a simple one: It is the only objective standard of interpretation even competing for acceptance. Nonoriginalism is not an interpretive theory—it is nothing more than a repudiation of originalism, leaving open the question: How does a judge determine when and how the meaning of a text has changed? To this question the non-originalists have no answer—or rather no answer that comes even close to being an objective test. For example, one apologist for semantic morphing states that "dynamism occurs when certain values are important enough to the statutory interpreter that they trump legislative primacy."[42] But what is important enough to one statutory interpreter may not be important enough to another. We know of no other nonoriginalist "test" that is not similarly mercurial. The choice is this: Give text the meaning it bore when it was adopted, or else let every judge decide for himself what it should mean today.

A caveat: Proper application of the fixed-meaning canon requires recognition of the fact that some statutory terms refer to defined legal qualifications whose definitions are, and are understood to be, subject to change. Giving a bad name to originalism was the 1925 Illinois case of *People ex rel. Fyfe v. Barnett*,[43] which dealt with an 1887 statute that read as follows: "The . . . commissioners . . . shall prepare a list of all *electors* between the ages of twenty-one and sixty years, possessing the necessary legal qualifications for jury duty, to be known as the jury list."[44] Because women were not *electors* in 1887 (they did not get the vote in Illinois until 1913), the Illinois Supreme Court held that only men could be on the jury list.[45] That decision was incorrect. The statutory definition of

---

42 Lawrence M. Solan, *The Language of Statutes: Laws and Their Interpretation* 131 (2010).

43 150 N.E. 290 (Ill. 1925).

44 Illinois Jury Commissioners' Act, 1887 (amended 1899) (as quoted in *id.* at 291).

45 150 N.E. at 291–92 (emphasis added). *See Commonwealth v. Welosky*, 177 N.E. 656 (Mass. 1931) (likewise holding that women remained ineligible). *But see Commonwealth v. Maxwell*, 114 A. 825 (Pa. 1921) (correctly holding that women became eligible).

elector in Illinois had been changed, and the semantic content of the jury-list law followed that change. It would be equivalently preposterous to hold that a pre-1913 statute outlawing the bribery of jurors applied only to men on juries—and that female jurors were free to accept bribes with impunity. A legal text referring to a statutorily defined term is understood to have a silent gloss, "as the definition may be amended from time to time."

Statutorily amended, that is. It is not for the courts to change definitions from time to time, as the New York Court of Appeals did in *Braschi v. Stahl Associates Co.*[46] In that case, the court had to decide the meaning of *family* in a rent-control statute that prohibited a landlord from dispossessing "either the surviving spouse of the deceased tenant or some other member of the deceased tenant's family who has been living with the tenant."[47] Did this include a cohabiting nonrelative who had had an emotional commitment to the deceased tenant? Yes, said the court, relying on secondary dictionary definitions in which *family* is defined figuratively, not literally.[48] The dissent correctly criticized this expansive interpretation, confining *family* to its traditional sense of "objectively verifiable relationships based on blood, marriage and adoption, as the State has historically done in estate succession laws, family court acts and similar legislation."[49]

ا&.   ا&.   ا&.

In legal literature, the word *originalism* has undergone pejoration to such a degree that it has become a kind of snarl-word for scholars of the left. They consider the doctrine it represents to have been thoroughly discredited. Professor Randy E. Barnett has admirably summed up this slice of academic history:

> The received wisdom among law professors is that originalism in any form is dead, having been defeated in intellectual combat sometime in the 1980s. According to this

---

46   543 N.E.2d 49 (N.Y. 1989).

47   New York City Rent & Eviction Regs., 9 N.Y.C.R.R. § 2204.6(d).

48   543 N.E.2d at 54.

49   *Id.* at 58 (Simons, J., dissenting).

story, Edwin Meese and Robert Bork proposed that the Constitution be interpreted according to the original intentions of its framers. Their view was trounced by many academic critics, perhaps most notably by Paul Brest in his widely cited article, "The Misconceived Quest for the Original Understanding" and by H. Jefferson Powell in his article, "The Original Understanding of Original Intent." Taken together, these (and other) articles represent a two-pronged attack on originalism that was perceived at the time as devastating: as a method of constitutional interpretation, originalism was both unworkable and itself contrary to the original intentions of the founders.[50]

.   .   .

If ever a theory had a stake driven through its heart, it seem[ed] to be originalism. But despite the onslaught of criticism, the effort to discern the original meaning of constitutional terms continues unabated. Indeed, by some accounts it may be the dominant method actually used by constitutional scholars—even by those who disclaim originalism. As Jack Rakove observed after listing those constitutional scholars who have offered originalist arguments, "[b]ut in truth, the turn to originalism seems so general that citation is almost beside the point." And this movement toward originalism has cut across ideological lines. "In recent years, the originalist premise has also been manifested in the emerging strain of broad originalism in liberal and progressive constitutional theory."[51]

Barnett pinpoints just why some theorists oppose adhering to original meanings: "[N]ot because it cannot be done, but because the original meaning of the text *can* be ascertained, and they find this meaning to be inadequate or objectionable. They reject the meaning of the Constitution as enacted and wish to substitute another meaning that they contend is superior."[52] The doctrine of originalism has succeeded in large measure because it is preferable to the alternatives: "It takes a theory to beat a theory and, after a decade of trying, the opponents of originalism have never con-

---

50 Randy E. Barnett, *Restoring the Lost Constitution: The Presumption of Liberty* 89–90 (2004) (internal citations omitted).

51 *Id.* at 91 (internal citation omitted).

52 *Id.* at 96.

verged on an appealing and practical alternative."[53] Further: "The inability of the most brilliant and creative legal minds to present a plausible method of interpretation that engenders enough confidence to warrant overriding the text has helped make some version of originalism much more attractive."[54]

And what is that version? It is the one that we espouse: *original meaning*, as opposed to *original intention* (which devolves into trying to read the minds of enactors or ratifiers). This brand of originalism—as opposed to the search for historical *intent*, which we renounce[55]—holds sway with many respected scholars today.[56] We hardly endorse all that these scholars have said, but we believe it to be imperative that the term *originalism* be reclaimed so that rational discourse about what it broadly represents may take place.

---

53 *Id.* at 92.

54 *Id.*

55 *See* § 67.

56 *See, e.g.*, Akhil Reed Amar, *On Text and Precedent*, 31 Harv. J.L. & Pub. Pol'y 961, 963 (2008) (stating that doctrine is subordinate to the document and siding with the "documentarians—people who believe in the primacy of the text, history, and structure" when applying precedent); R.W.M. Dias, *Jurisprudence* 228 (4th ed. 1976) (stating that plain meaning requires that words be "accorded their ordinary meaning at the time of enactment").

8. Omitted-Case Canon

Nothing is to be added to what the text states or reasonably implies (*casus omissus pro omisso habendus est*). That is, a matter not covered is to be treated as not covered.

> "Whatever temptations the statesmanship of policymaking might wisely suggest, construction must eschew interpolation and evisceration. [The judge] must not read in by way of creation."
> Felix Frankfurter,
> *Some Reflections on the Reading of Statutes,*
> 47 Colum. L. Rev. 527, 533 (1947).

The principle that a matter not covered is not covered is so obvious that it seems absurd to recite it. The judge should not presume that every statute answers every question, the answers to be discovered through interpretation.[1] As the noted lawyer and statesman Elihu Root said of the judge: "It is not his function or within his power to enlarge or improve or change the law."[2] Nor should the judge elaborate unprovided-for exceptions to a text, as Justice Blackmun noted while a circuit judge: "[I]f the Congress [had] intended to provide additional exceptions, it would have done so in clear language."[3]

Yet some authorities assert the judicial power, even the judicial responsibility, to supply words or even whole provisions that have been omitted. Some of them would have the court "reconstruct

---

1   *See* Cal. Code Civ. Proc. § 1858 ("In the construction of a statute or instrument, the office of the Judge is simply to ascertain and declare what is in terms or in substance contained therein, not to insert what has been omitted . . ."); Cal. Civ. Code § 3530 ("That which does not appear to exist is to be regarded as if it did not exist."). *See also Simmons v. Arnim*, 220 S.W. 66, 70 (Tex. 1920) ("Courts must take statutes as they find them. . . . They are not the law-making body. They are not responsible for omissions in legislation."); R.W.M. Dias, *Jurisprudence* 232 (4th ed. 1976) ("A judge may not add words that are not in the statute, save only by way of necessary implication.").

2   Elihu Root, *The Importance of an Independent Judiciary*, 72 Independent 704, 704 (1912). *See* Edward H. Levi, "The Nature of Judicial Reasoning," in *Law and Philosophy: A Symposium* 263, 274 (Sidney Hook ed., 1964) ("Granted the right and duty of the court to interpret the document, it has not been given the duty or the opportunity to rewrite the words.").

3   *Petteys v. Butler*, 367 F.2d 528, 538 (8th Cir. 1966) (Blackmun, J., dissenting).

what the enacting legislature would have wanted" if it had addressed the overlooked case.[4] (See § 60.) Others assert a judicial power entirely unconnected with a posited legislative intent:

> Statutory reform has been severely affected by [the] fiction . . . that when courts interpret and apply statutes theirs is not a creative role but only the role of finding and applying the legislature's mandate. In what is perhaps its most extreme vision, this fiction takes the form of a conclusive presumption that when a legislature undertakes to prescribe at all for a problem it prescribes in full. . . . It is too plain for argument that neither a court in laying down a decisional doctrine nor a legislature in enacting a statute can possibly foresee and provide answers for all the questions that will arise. Thus, it is a matter not of choice but of necessity that courts must act creatively when interpreting and applying statutes.[5]

The traditional view, and the one we support, is to the contrary. The absent provision cannot be supplied by the courts.[6] What the legislature "would have wanted" it did not provide, and that is an end of the matter. As Justice Louis Brandeis put the point: "A *casus omissus* does not justify judicial legislation."[7] And Brandeis again: "To supply omissions transcends the judicial function."[8]

A Maryland case—*Montgomery County Volunteer Fire-Rescue Association v. Montgomery County Board of Elections*[9]—illustrates

---

4   Kent Greenawalt, *Statutory Interpretation: 20 Questions* 221 (1999).

5   Robert E. Keeton, *Venturing to Do Justice: Reforming Private Law* 78–79 (1969).

6   *See Jones v. Smart*, [1785] 1 Term Rep. 44, 52 (per Buller, J.) ("[W]e are bound to take the act of parliament, as they have made it: a *casus omissus* can in no case be supplied by a Court of Law, for that would be to make laws.") (emphasis added); *MacMillan v. Director, Div. of Taxation*, 434 A.2d 620, 621 (N.J. Super. Ct. App. Div. 1981) ("We certainly may not supply a provision no matter how confident we are of what the Legislature would do if it were to reconsider today."). *See also* Frank H. Easterbrook, *Statutes' Domains*, 50 U. Chi. L. Rev. 533, 548 (1983) ("Judicial interpolation of legislative gaps would be questionable even if judges could ascertain with certainty how the legislature would have acted. Every legislative body's power is limited by a number of checks . . . . The foremost of these checks is time. . . . The unaddressed problem is handled by a new legislature with new instructions from the voters.").

7   *Ebert v. Poston*, 266 U.S. 548, 554 (1925) (per Brandeis, J.).

8   *Iselin v. United States*, 270 U.S. 245, 251 (1926) (per Brandeis, J.).

9   15 A.3d 798 (Md. 2011).

the point. Maryland's Election Law required that a referendum petition contain the signer's address, his printed name, and the date of signing, and that the signer sign his name "as it appears on the statewide voter registration list."[10] The statute provided that a signature must be validated and counted if these requirements and other, specified confirming requirements were met. In reviewing a petition to place a referendum on the ballot, the Montgomery County Board of Elections refused to validate many signatures because they were not legible, causing the petition to fail. In the ensuing lawsuit, the Board contended that it could not determine whether the signature represented the name "as it appears on the statewide voter-registration list" unless the signature was legible. The court decided that illegibility in itself could not be a basis for invalidity. The court noted that the legislature could have added legibility as a prerequisite for validation, as several other states have done. But in the absence of such a penmanship prerequisite, the Board could not create one.[11]

The search for what the legislature "would have wanted" is invariably either a deception or a delusion. What is a *gap* anyway? It is not a void of some kind that makes a court's decision logically impossible. Instead, it is the space between what the statute provides and what the gap-finding judge thinks it should have provided.[12] It is "nothing else than the difference between the positive law and some other order considered to be better, truer, and juster."[13] What has been omitted in the *gap* invariably turns out to be what the judge believes desirable—so gap-filling ultimately comes down to the assertion of an inherent judicial power to write the law.[14] Our rejection of such a power does not rest on a belief that "when a legislature undertakes to prescribe at all for

---

10 Md. Code Ann., Elec. Law § 6-203(a)(1).

11 15 A.3d at 808.

12 Hans Kelsen, *The Pure Theory of Law* 248 (Max Knight trans., 1967).

13 Huntington Cairns, *Legal Philosophy from Plato to Hegel* 240 (1949).

14 *See, e.g.*, Joseph Raz, *The Authority of Law* 48–50, 197 (1979) (stating that the court should fill gaps by using moral skills and that "within the admitted boundaries of their lawmaking powers courts act and should act just as legislators do, namely, they should adopt those rules which they judge best").

a problem it prescribes in full." That is a false statement of the issue. The issue is whether, *when* a legislature prescribes in a fashion that courts regard as providing only "in part" and not "in full," what remains is to be governed by preexisting law, unamended, or rather by a new law, enacted by the courts. Judicial amendment flatly contradicts democratic self-governance.

Two caveats: First, interstitial lawmaking by courts is to be distinguished from the courts' continuing exercise of their common-law powers in jurisdictions where those are retained. The fact, for example, that a state legislature changes one rule of judge-made tort law does not suggest that the courts' power over the remainder of tort law has been eliminated—and the continued exercise of that power is not filling a gap in the statute. (When, however, the statute purports to provide a comprehensive treatment of the issue it addresses, judicial lawmaking is implicitly excluded.) Second, it is possible, though rare, for a statute to leave a matter to future common-law development by the courts—either expressly or (where the statute deals with a traditional field of common-law jurisprudence) by implication. An example of the latter is the Sherman Act, whose reference to "restraint of trade" has always been taken to refer to activity (so denominated) that the common law made unlawful—and to authorize continuing development of that common law by federal courts.[15] Express commitment to common-law development (though that of the states rather than of the federal courts) is to be found in the Federal Tort Claims Act, which provides that the United States is liable to tort claims "in the same manner and to the same extent as a private individual under like circumstances."[16]

The omitted-case canon—the principle that what a text does not provide is unprovided—must sometimes be reconciled with the principle that a text does include not only what is express but also what is implicit. For example, when a text authorizes a certain act, it implicitly authorizes whatever is a necessary predicate of that act. Authorization to harvest wheat genuinely implies autho-

---

15 *Leegin Creative Leather Prods., Inc. v. PSKS, Inc.*, 551 U.S. 877 (2007) (per Kennedy, J.).

16 28 U.S.C. § 2674.

rization to enter the land for that purpose.[17] In our earlier *Montgomery County Board of Elections* illustration, legibility might well have been an implicit requirement of the statute if the statute had not required (as it did) a printed name that could be compared with the voter registration list. To hold, on the other hand, that a statute rendering certain action unlawful and imposing governmental sanctions "implies" a private right of action for violation of the statute[18] is gap-filling disguised as implication. The same can be said of implications from "penumbras," "emanations," and other legal fictions. It is part of the skill, and honesty, of the good judge to distinguish between filling gaps in the text and determining what the text implies.

Let us consider some cases of real and imagined gaps. In one case,[19] a New York statute had provided criminal penalties for a person who committed a "fraudulent insurance act," a term defined in the statute.[20] The legislature later amended the statute to add a new defined term, "fraudulent health care insurance act,"[21] but did not change the substantive part of the law to make that newly defined act unlawful. The chief operating officer of a managed-healthcare provider was charged with committing a "fraudulent healthcare insurance act"—which the prosecution argued was a subspecies of a fraudulent insurance act. The New York Court of Appeals rightly ordered the case dismissed.[22] The legislature had failed to criminalize the defined conduct; if that omission was inadvertent, the remedy lay with the legislature.

In a 1987 per curiam opinion,[23] the Supreme Court of the United States interpreted a tax statute that read: "If any part of any underpayment [of income tax] . . . is due to negligence . . . , there shall be added to the tax an amount equal to 5% of the

---

17 See § 30 (predicate-act canon).

18 *Superintendent of Ins. of N.Y. v. Bankers Life & Cas. Co.*, 404 U.S. 6, 13 n.9 (1971) (per Douglas, J.).

19 *People v. Boothe*, 944 N.E.2d 1137 (N.Y. 2011).

20 N.Y. Penal Law §§ 176.10–176.30.

21 *Id.* § 176.05(1) & (2).

22 944 N.E. 2d at 1139.

23 *Commissioner v. Asphalt Prods. Co.*, 482 U.S. 117 (1987) (per curiam).

underpayment."[24] The taxpayer underpaid taxes by $7,000, but the vast majority of the underpayment (perhaps 90%) was found by the Tax Court to have been neither fraudulent nor even negligent. The taxpayer argued that the 5% penalty should be calculated not on $7,000, but only on the $700 underpayment that was negligent. The Supreme Court refused to add to the language of the statute ("an amount equal to 5% of the underpayment") the language necessary to produce the taxpayer's perhaps-more-reasonable result ("an amount equal to 5% of the *amount of the* underpayment *attributable to negligence*"). The statute as written, unsupplemented, was properly held to control.

Although legal texts are sometimes incomplete because they fail to address matters that ought to have been addressed, few openly espouse the view that courts may remedy the incompleteness with rules of their own creation. Those who do so often use the excuse exemplified in the interpretive creed of William Robert Bishin: "[I]f we have let the legislature foist its problems upon the courts, so be it. The courts must decide the case whether or not it should have been decided by the legislature."[25] The question-begging here is apparent. Courts must "decide the case," to be sure. But does deciding the case mean determining (as Bishin assumes) which disposition would be most desirable? Or does it mean determining to what extent the statute (or the private document) alters the state of the law that would obtain if the statute did not exist? Ever since judge-made common law has been replaced by statutory law, the answer has been the latter.

ða   ða   ða

Are there *any* established exceptions to the omitted-case canon? Yes, there are. In the field of private ordering, the most

---

24 26 U.S.C. § 6653(a)(1).

25 William Robert Bishin, *The Law Finders: An Essay in Statutory Interpretation*, 38 So. Cal. L. Rev. 1, 27–28 (1965). *Cf.* Judith S. Kaye, *State Courts at the Dawn of a New Century: Common Law Courts Reading Statutes and Constitutions*, 70 N.Y.U.L. Rev. 1, 34 (1995) ("[T]o refuse to make the necessary policy choices when called upon to do so would result in a rigidity and paralysis that the common-law process was meant to prevent.").

common is the doctrine of *cy pres*, under which, when the precise object of a charitable gift can no longer be achieved—for example, because of termination of the charity that was its beneficiary—the court will supply another object that comes close to the same thing (for example, another charity with the same goals).[26] In the field of governmental prescriptions, noncompliance with nonjurisdictional time limitations on court filings is excused when it is not the fault of the filer. The most common example is the tolling of statutes of limitations because of unforeseen events that make compliance impossible—as when a natural disaster disrupted the courthouse.[27]

Other asserted exceptions are infirm. An example is the maxim that no one can benefit from his own wrong (*nullus commodum capere potest de injuria sua propria*).[28] The principle was invoked most starkly in a series of cases decided before the mid-20th century, when the question arose whether a murderer could inherit from his victims. At the time, the relevant statutes dealing with wills and intestacy did not explicitly address whether the wrongdoer could inherit. So there was no authoritative text to prevent the inheritance.

As a general matter of right and wrong, all of us recoil from the thought that a murderer could advance his heirship. In one case, a grandson murdered his grandfather to prevent changes in

---

26 *See* Edith L. Fisch, *The Cy Pres Doctrine in the United States* 1–2 (1950).

27 *See, e.g., Wagner v. New York, Ontario & Western Ry.* 146 F.Supp. 926, 929 (M.D. Pa. 1956) (statute of limitations tolled for filing of complaint because clerk's office was closed after an extraordinary flood). *See also Middleton v. Silverman*, 430 So.2d 981, 982 (Fla. Dist. Ct. App. 1983) (statute of limitations tolled because courthouse closed three hours early because of civil disturbance).

28 *Black's Law Dictionary* 1856 (9th ed. 2009) (translating the maxim "no one can gain advantage by his own wrong"); Herbert Broom, *A Selection of Legal Maxims* 233 (Joseph Gerald Pease & Herbert Chitty eds., 8th ed. 1911) (stating that "this maxim, which is based on elementary principles, is fully recognized in Courts of law and of equity, and, indeed, admits of illustration from every branch of legal procedure"); Thomas Branch, *Principia Legis et Aequitatis: Being an Alphabetical Collection of Maxims, Principles or Rules, Definitions, and Memorable Sayings, in Law and Equity* 140 (1824); 2 Edward Coke, *The First Part of the Institutes of the Laws of England, or a Commentary upon Littleton* § 222, at 148b (1628; 14th ed. 1791) ("it is a maxime of law, that no man shall take advantage of his owne wrong").

a will under which the grandson would inherit. The New York Court of Appeals decreed that he take nothing.[29] By contrast, an Illinois case essentially allowed a defendant who murdered his mother, father, and sister to become heir to their entire estates.[30] Most cases agreed with the Illinois murderer-can-inherit holding, which we believe is textually correct.[31]

Today, all states have statutes that explicitly deal with this problem—saying, for example, that a person who "feloniously and intentionally kills the decedent forfeits all benefits."[32] The universal enactment of such laws illustrates what happens when courts (as most did in this instance) apply an unwise law as written. If the defect is serious, the legislature will cure it. The statute books will become more complete, and improvised judge-made exceptions that cannot be found in the text of enacted laws will be less numerous.

---

29 *Riggs v. Palmer*, 22 N.E. 188, 189–90 (N.Y. 1889). *See Van Alstyne v. Tuffy*, N.Y.S. 173, 175 (Sup. Ct. 1918) ("[W]here the natural and direct consequence a criminal act is to vest property in the criminal, whether he be a thief or a murderer, the thought of his being allowed to enjoy it is too abhorrent for the courts of this state, or of the United States, to countenance . . ."); *Perry v. Strawbridge*, 108 S.W. 641, 642 (Mo. 1908) ("Can it be said that one, by high-handed murder can not only make himself an heir in fact, when he had but a mere expectancy before, but further shall enjoy the fruits of his own crime? To us this seems abhorrent to all reason, and reason is the better element of the law.").

30 *Wall v. Pfanschmidt*, 106 N.E. 785, 789–90 (Ill. 1914).

31 *Owens v. Owens*, 6 S.E. 794, 794–95 (N.C. 1888) (wife convicted as accessory in husband's murder retains her right to dower); *Deem v. Millikin*, 6 Ohio C. C. 357, 358 (Ct. App. 1892) (same), *aff'd*, 44 N.E. 1134 (Ohio 1895); *Shellenberg v. Ransom*, 59 N.W. 935, 941 (Neb. 1894) (that an intestate is murdered by an heir apparent does not affect plain statutory language that automatically vests title in that heir); *In re Carpenter's Estate*, 32 A. 637, 637 (Pa. 1895) (no statute provided that slayers of parent and husband would forfeit inheriting victim's estate); *Long v. Kuhn (In re Kuhn's Estate)*, 101 N.W. 151, 152 (Iowa 1904) (murderess-widow not statutorily barred from taking share of husband's estate); *McAllister v. Fair*, 84 P. 112, 112–13 (Kan. 1906) (husband who murdered his wife could inherit from her because statute's plain language that a husband inherit his wife's estate contained no exception for criminal conduct); *Eversole v. Eversole*, 185 S.W. 487, 489 (Ky. Ct. App. 1916) (no statute deprived widow who murdered husband of right to dower).

32 Ariz. Rev. Stat. § 14-2803(a). *See also, e.g.*, Alaska Stat. § 13.12.803 (referring to a person who "feloniously kills the decedent").

9. General-Terms Canon

General terms are to be given their general meaning (*generalia verba sunt generaliter intelligenda*).

Without some indication to the contrary, general words (like all words, general or not) are to be accorded their full and fair scope. They are not to be arbitrarily limited. This is the general-terms canon, which is based on the reality that it is possible and useful to formulate categories (e.g., "dangerous weapons") without knowing all the items that may fit—or may later, once invented, come to fit—within those categories.

Some think that when courts confront generally worded pro-
ons, they should infer exceptions for situations that the drafters
er contemplated and did not intend their general language to
ve. These people want courts to approach general words dif-
itly from how they approach words that are narrow and spe-
Traditional principles of interpretation reject this distinction
se the presumed point of using general words is to produce
ral coverage—not to leave room for courts to recognize ad
exceptions. It is true that literal meaning is more readily dis-
nible when the provisions are concrete and specific than when
y are abstract and general, and one is right to hesitate and pon-
r before deciding that a specific factual situation falls within the
verage of a general provision. But in the end, general words are
neral words, and they must be given general effect.

Examples of general words with general meanings can be
id in the post-Civil War amendments to the United States
onstitution. The Fourteenth Amendment, for example, guaran-
ees equal protection of the laws to "all persons." Some commentators have argued that because it was enacted for the benefit of
blacks, it should not apply to anybody else.[1] But in the first case

---

1   *See* Ward Farnsworth, *Women Under Reconstruction: The Congressional Under-standing*, 94 Nw. U. L. Rev. 1229, 1234 (2000) (quoting several Congressmen who said, in 1874–75, that the Fourteenth Amendment "barred legal discrimination against blacks and nothing more."). *Cf. Sugarman v. Dougall*, 413 U.S. 634, 649–50 (1973) (Rehnquist, J., dissenting) (arguing that the Fourteenth Amendment protects no minorities except racial ones).

to expound the meaning of the Thirteenth, Fourteenth, and Fifteenth Amendments—the *Slaughter-House Cases*[2]—the Supreme Court acknowledged the breadth of the language used, as contrasted with the immediate purpose for their passage:

> We do not say that no one else but the negro can share in this protection [of the 13th, 14th, and 15th Amendments]. Both the language and spirit of these articles are to have their fair and just weight in any question of construction. Undoubtedly while negro slavery alone was in the mind of the Congress which proposed the thirteenth article, it forbids any other kind of slavery, now or hereafter. If Mexican peonage or the Chinese coolie labor system shall develop slavery of the Mexican or Chinese race within our territory, this amendment may safely be trusted to make it void. And so if other rights are assailed by the States which properly and necessarily fall within the protection of these articles, that protection will apply, though the party interested may not be of African descent.[3]

Both text and tradition support this much of the opinion. The language of the Fourteenth Amendment—that no state may deny to any person the equal protection of the law—is very general. Scholarly commentary has long agreed. In 1922 a respected commentator accurately stated: "Although the primary purpose of the Fourteenth Amendment was undoubtedly . . . to safeguard the negro in his new status of a freeman, its actual scope is vastly wider than that, and its effect has been very far reaching."[4]

Nor could the general wording of the Fourteenth Amendment be confined to men. And it never has been. One of the arguments sometimes trotted out to show that textualists are not really evenhanded is the argument that despite the Fourteenth Amendment's guarantee of equal protection to *all* persons, women were not given the vote until adoption of the Nineteenth Amend-

---

2　83 U.S. (16 Wall.) 36 (1872) (per Miller, J.).

3　*Id.* at 72. *But see id.* at 81 ("We doubt very much whether any action of a State not directed by way of discrimination against the negroes as a class, or on account of their race, will ever be held to come within the purview of [the Equal Protection Clause]. It is so clearly a provision for that race and that emergency, that a strong case would be necessary for its application to any other.").

4　Charles Kellogg Burdick, *The Law of the American Constitution* 502 (1922).

ment. That has nothing to do with the meaning of *person* in the Fourteenth Amendment; it has to do with the meaning of *equal protection*. Not all instances of treating people differently violate that guarantee—which is why, on adoption of the Fourteenth Amendment, unisex toilets did not appear in all public buildings. And as horrible as it may seem, there is no doubt that the society that adopted the Fourteenth Amendment did not believe that the equal-protection guarantee gave women the vote, as the laws of the era demonstrate.

The general-terms canon applies to interpretive issues with great frequency. In an Eighth Circuit case,[5] the court construed a federal statute allowing the government to seize "any property, including money,"[6] that had been used for an illegal gambling business. The question arose whether "any property, including money" included real as well as personal property. The Government had begun forfeiture actions against 13 parcels of real estate that had allegedly been used in an illegal gambling business. The trial court interpreted the term *property* not to include real property and therefore dismissed the forfeiture actions. But the appellate court quite rightly held that *any property* means "any property," real and personal. It is not limited by the phrase *including money* (see § 15 [presumption of nonexclusive "include"]). An ill-considered dissent would have held that the clear language meant something other than what it said, based in part on legislative history (see § 66) and on the "spirit of the law" (see § 58).[7]

The argument most frequently made against giving general terms their general meaning is the one made (and rejected) in the *Slaughter-House* cases—that those who adopted the provision had in mind a particular narrow objective (equal protection for blacks) though they expressed a more general one (equal protection for "any person"). The conclusive response to this argument is that "statutory prohibitions often go beyond the principal evil to cover reasonably comparable evils, and it is ultimately the provisions of

---

5   *United States v. South Half of Lot 7 & Lot 8, Block 14, Kountze's 3rd Addition to the City of Omaha*, 910 F.2d 488 (8th Cir. 1990) (en banc).

6   18 U.S.C. § 1955(d).

7   *See* 910 F.2d at 491 (Heaney, J., dissenting).

our laws rather than the principal concerns of our legislators by which we are governed."[8]

In the case from which that statement derives, *Oncale v. Sundowner Offshore Services*, the statute at issue made it "an unlawful employment practice for an employer . . . to discriminate against any individual . . . because of such individual's . . . sex."[9] Joseph Oncale worked as a roustabout on an oil platform as part of an eight-man crew. He sued his employer under Title VII, alleging that his male coworkers had sexually harassed him. The lower courts rejected his claim, holding that Title VII did not cover claims by males alleging sex discrimination by other males. In the Supreme Court, however, Oncale prevailed. As the Court had held before, the statute protects men as well as women. And just as there is no textual basis for limiting its protections to women, the Court found "no justification in the statutory language or [its] precedents for a categorical rule excluding same-sex harassment claims from the coverage of Title VII."[10] The Court acknowledged that "male-on-male sexual harassment in the workplace was assuredly not the principal evil Congress was concerned with when it enacted Title VII."[11] But the statutory prohibition was broadly worded.

The other common argument against application of the canon is slightly less ambitious. It acknowledges that the general term cannot be limited to the precise evil that most concerned the lawgiver but asserts that when the situation at issue could not have been within the lawgiver's contemplation, an ambiguity exists. That was the argument made in *Pennsylvania Department of Corrections v. Yeskey*.[12] The plaintiff was a prisoner who, because he suffered from hypertension, had been excluded from participation in the prison's motivational-boot-camp program, successful completion of which would have shortened his sentence. He con-

---

8   *Oncale v. Sundowner Offshore Servs., Inc.*, 523 U.S. 75, 79 (1998) (per Scalia, J.).

9   42 U.S.C. § 2000e-2(a)(1).

10 523 U.S. at 79.

11 *Id.*

12 524 U.S. 206 (1998) (per Scalia, J.).

tended that this exclusion violated Title II of the Americans with Disabilities Act, which provided that "no qualified individual with a disability shall, by reason of such disability, be excluded from participation in or be denied the benefits of the services, programs, or activities of a public entity . . . ."[13] The Act defined *public entity* as "any department, agency, special purpose district, or other instrumentality of a State or States or local government."[14] The Department of Corrections argued that Congress could not possibly have had state prison programs in mind, that the question whether the law applied to such programs had no clear answer, and that the ambiguity should be resolved against federal interference with the running of state prisons. The Supreme Court of the United States disagreed: "[A]ssuming . . . that Congress did not envision that the [Americans with Disabilities Act] would be applied to state prisoners, in the context of an unambiguous statutory text that is irrelevant. As we have said before, the fact that a statute can be 'applied in situations not expressly anticipated by Congress does not demonstrate ambiguity. It demonstrates breadth.'"[15]

Sometimes the scope of the general term is unclear. In *People v. Williamson*,[16] decided by the Colorado Supreme Court in 2011, the defendant, charged with sexual assault, claimed that the victim consented to having sex with him in exchange for money, and sought to introduce evidence that the victim had been arrested on five separate occasions for soliciting prostitution. The prosecution sought to exclude that evidence by reason of Colorado's Rape Shield Statute,[17] which created a presumption that evidence of a victim's prior or subsequent "sexual conduct" is irrelevant and thus inadmissible. Williamson contended that solicitation of prostitution was not "sexual conduct" but merely talk. The court held to the contrary. It is a close question whether the general term *conduct* includes the proposal of conduct, but the court's task was

---

13 42 U.S.C. § 12132.

14 *Id.* § 12131(1)(B).

15 524 U.S. at 212 (quoting *Sedima, S.P.R.L v. Imrex Co.*, 473 U.S. 479, 499 (1985) (per White, J.)).

16 249 P.3d 801 (Colo. 2011).

17 Colo. Rev. Stat. Ann. § 18-3-407(1)(a) (West 2011).

made easier by application of another canon—that a change in terminology suggests a change in meaning (see § 25 [presumption of consistent usage]). While the legislature had used the term *sexual conduct* to describe the type of behavior that falls under the Rape Shield Statute's general rule of irrelevance and inadmissibility, it had used more narrow and specific terms—such as *sexual activity* and *sexual intercourse*—when it carved out exceptions to that general rule, and related statutes in the criminal code relied on and defined more specific terms, such as *sexual intrusion* and *sexual penetration*.[18]

In the field of criminal law, the general-term principle is subject to several well-established exceptions deriving from the common-law requirement of evil intent for criminal liability. Seemingly absolute criminal prohibitions ("no person may") will not be applied to government agents in the lawful execution of their duties, to defendants who have been entrapped by the government, and to those acting in self-defense or out of necessity. See § 50 (*mens rea* canon).

---

18   *See* 249 P.3d at 803.

10. Negative-Implication Canon

The expression of one thing implies the exclusion of others (*expressio unius est exclusio alterius*).

Expressio unius, also known as *inclusio unius*, is a Latin name for the communicative device known as negative implication. In English, it is known as the negative-implication canon. We encounter the device—and recognize it—frequently in our daily lives. When a car dealer promises a low financing rate to "purchasers with good credit," it is entirely clear that the rate is *not* available to purchasers with spotty credit.

Virtually all the authorities who discuss the negative-implication canon emphasize that it must be applied with great caution, since its application depends so much on context.[1] Indeed, one commentator suggests that it is not a proper canon at all but merely a description of the result gleaned from context.[2] That goes too far. Context establishes the conditions for applying the canon, but where those conditions exist, the principle that specification of the one implies exclusion of the other validly describes how people express themselves and understand verbal expression.

The doctrine properly applies only when the *unius* (or technically, *unum*, the thing specified) can reasonably be thought to be an expression of *all* that shares in the grant or prohibition involved. Common sense often suggests when this is or is not so. The sign outside a restaurant "No dogs allowed" cannot be thought to mean that no other creatures are excluded—as if pet monkeys, potbellied pigs, and baby elephants might be quite welcome. Dogs are specifically addressed because they are the animals that customers are most likely to bring in; nothing is implied about other animals. On the other hand, the sign outside a veterinary clinic saying "Open for treatment of dogs, cats, horses, and all other farm and domestic animals" does suggest (by its detail) that the circus lion

---

1   *See, e.g.*, Roland Burrows, *Interpretation of Documents* 67 (1943); Henry Campbell Black, *Handbook on the Construction and Interpretation of the Laws* 219 (2d ed. 1911).

2   Reed Dickerson, *The Interpretation and Application of Statutes* 234 (1975).

with a health problem is out of luck. (Notice how *ejusdem generis* [§ 32] also comes into play with this example.) The more specific the enumeration, the greater the force of the canon:

> [I]f Parliament in legislating speaks only of specific things and specific situations, it is a legitimate inference that the particulars exhaust the legislative will. The particular which is omitted from the particulars mentioned is the *casus omissus*, which the judge cannot supply because that would amount to legislation.[3]

Even when an all-inclusive sense seems apparent, one must still identify the scope of the inclusiveness (thereby limiting implied exclusion). Consider the sign at the entrance to a beachfront restaurant: "No shoes, no shirt, no service." By listing some things that will cause a denial of service, the sign implies that other things will not. One can be confident about not being excluded on grounds of not wearing socks, for example, or of not wearing a jacket and tie. But what about coming in without pants? That is not included in the negative implication because the specified deficiencies in attire noted by the sign are obviously those that are common at the beach. Others common at the beach (no socks, no jacket, no tie) will implicitly not result in denial of service; but there is no reasonable implication regarding wardrobe absences *not* common at the beach. They go beyond the category to which the negative implication pertains.

This interpretive canon should not be confused with other principles of law that may produce identical results. One commentator ascribes to the canon the Supreme Court's doctrine that private rights of action are not to be "implied" in federal statutes that do not expressly create them—and goes on to condemn both the canon and the doctrine.[4] But while some cases applying the presumption against implied right of action (§ 51) mention the fact that the statute in question contains an express private right

---

3   J.A. Corry, *Administrative Law and the Interpretation of Statutes*, 1 U. Toronto L.J. 286, 298 (1936).

4   Richard A. Posner, *Statutory Interpretation—in the Classroom and in the Courtroom*, 50 U. Chi. L. Rev. 800, 812 (1983).

of action separate from the implied one asserted,[5] the provision of an express right is not considered the basis for or a condition of the doctrine. Indeed, the presumption against implied right of action has been invoked in several cases in which there was no basis for applying the negative-implication canon.[6] And perhaps the most consequential "implying" of a private right of action—one for violating § 10(b) of the Securities Exchange Act—occurred with respect to a statute that did create express private rights of action for other violations, so that the negative-implication canon would have precluded the implied right of action.[7] But the United States Supreme Court's rejection of implied rights of action is based not on a negative implication from an express private right of action, but instead on the principle that federal courts do not possess the lawmaking power of common-law courts. If Congress does not create a private right of action for violating one of its laws, the courts have no power to create one.[8]

Now for some examples.

In one case, the state constitution declared that the judges of superior courts must be elected by both branches of the legislature. Then, later, a legislative act authorized the governor to appoint a temporary superior-court judge. The court applied the negative-implication canon to the constitutional language: "If one having authority prescribe[s] the mode in which a particular act [the naming of judges] is to be done, can the agent [the legislature] who executes it substitute any other? Does not the act of prescrib-

---

5   *See, e.g., Hartford Underwriters Ins. Co. v. Union Planters Bank*, 530 U.S. 1 (2000) (per Scalia, J.) (holding that a statute expressly granting a bankruptcy trustee a right to recover does not also impliedly give an administrative claimant a right to recover).

6   *See, e.g., Gonzaga Univ. v. Doe*, 536 U.S. 273, 287 (2002) (per Rehnquist, C.J.) (holding that nondisclosure provisions of Family Educational Rights and Privacy Act did not create any enforceable rights); *Lopez v. Jet Blue Airways*, 662 F.3d 593, 596–97 (2d Cir. 2011) (finding no implied private right of action for violation of Air Carrier Access Act of 1986).

7   *See Blue Chip Stamps v. Manor Drug Stores*, 421 U.S. 723, 730 (1975) (per Rehnquist, J.).

8   *See, e.g., Alexander v. Sandoval*, 532 U.S. 275, 281 (2001) (per Scalia, J.); *Touche Ross & Co. v. Redington*, 442 U.S. 560, 578 (1979) (per Rehnquist, J.).

ing the mode, necessarily imply a prohibition to all other modes?"[9] Hence the statute was held unconstitutional.[10]

A second case illustrates what can happen when a court seems not even to recognize that the doctrine applies. A Mississippi statute provided that assistant district attorneys "may be removed at the discretion of the duly elected and acting district attorney."[11] Although district attorney was an elected position, some district attorneys were appointed by the governor between elections. And so the question arose whether a gubernatorial appointee had the power to remove assistant district attorneys.[12] Did he have that power even though he had not been "duly elected"? The negative-implication canon would suggest not. Yet the Mississippi Supreme Court, without even mentioning much less considering the canon, held that "appointed" district attorneys who had not been "duly elected" were empowered to fire assistant district attorneys. It likewise did not mention or consider another canon that had obvious application: the surplusage canon (§ 26). Its interpretation deprived the words *duly elected and* of all effect.

A third case exemplifies a correct result, even though the court did not specifically cite the doctrine. A New Hampshire statute immunized municipalities from "damages arising from insufficiencies or hazards on public highways, bridges, or sidewalks . . . when such hazards are caused solely by snow, ice, or other inclement weather."[13] A person who suffered damages from a fall on ice in a public parking lot sued the city of Laconia. The city claimed a statutory immunity, arguing that (1) the parking lots are essential components of the highway system, (2) the purpose of the statute was to protect cities from lawsuits resulting from weather conditions on public property, and (3) the legislature could not be expected to enumerate in the statute every single type of public property. The plaintiff argued that a parking lot is not a highway,

---

9   *State ex rel. M'Cready v. Hunt*, 2 Hill 1, 171 (S.C. Ct. App. 1834) (per Johnson, J.).

10 *Id.* at 168, 178–79.

11 Miss. Code Ann. § 25-31-6 (1972).

12 *Allred v. Webb*, 641 So.2d 1218 (Miss. 1994).

13 N.H. Rev. Stat. § 231-92-a (1991).

not a bridge, and not a sidewalk—and that the immunity therefore did not apply. The legislature could easily have written "any public property, including highways, bridges, and sidewalks," but it did not. The New Hampshire Supreme Court correctly held that because the law specified three types of public property but omitted all others, the immunity did not bar the lawsuit.[14]

As that New Hampshire case illustrates, the negative-implication canon is so intuitive that courts often apply it correctly without calling it by name. Consider *United States v. Giordano*,[15] decided by the Supreme Court of the United States in 1974. A statute[16] established procedures for obtaining court orders authorizing the interception of wire and oral communications. It said that the "Attorney General . . . or any Assistant Attorney General . . . specially designated by the Attorney General" could authorize application for such orders.[17] In Giordano's case, it was the Attorney General's executive assistant who applied for the court-authorized wiretap. Hence Giordano argued that the conversations to be used as evidence had been "unlawfully intercepted" and should be suppressed. A unanimous Court agreed with him: The statute named two types of high-ranking officials—and all others were excluded.[18]

---

14 *Johnson v. City of Laconia*, 684 A.2d 500, 501–02 (N.H. 1996).

15 416 U.S. 505 (1974) (per White, J.).

16 Title III of the Omnibus Crime Control and Safe Streets Act of 1968, 18 U.S.C. §§ 2510–2520.

17 *Id.*, § 2516(1).

18 416 U.S. at 514.

11. Mandatory/Permissive Canon

**Mandatory words impose a duty;
permissive words grant discretion.**

The text of this canon is entirely clear, and its content so obvious as to be hardly worth the saying. The trouble comes in identifying which words are mandatory and which permissive. The traditional, commonly repeated rule is that *shall* is mandatory and *may* is permissive:

> The tenant *shall* provide written notice of an intent to vacate no fewer than 30 days before moving. (This states an obligation.)

> The tenant *may* vacate the premises on 30 days' written notice. (This grants permission, with a condition.)

When drafters use *shall* and *may* correctly, the traditional rule holds—beautifully.

But alas, drafters have been notoriously sloppy with their *shall*s, resulting in a morass of confusing decisions on the meanings of this modal verb. Volume 39 of *Words and Phrases* contains more than 55 pages of digested judicial holdings on the word—and the cases are anything but uniform. Have the courts been wayward in their holdings? Not really. The problem is that drafters have used the word improperly—even promiscuously. Consider the different types of sentences in which *shall* can appear. As you read the sentences, remember that *shall* ought to be replaceable by either *has a duty to* or *is required to*:

- Each party *shall* bear its own expenses. (The grammatical subject is charged with the duty imparted by the verb phrase *shall bear* [= has the duty to bear]. The usage is correct.)

- Each party *shall* be responsible for its own expenses. (The grammatical subject is not quite charged with a duty. [A *duty to be responsible for*? As opposed to *a duty to bear*?] *Shall* is a future-tense verb essentially equivalent to *will*, or perhaps a "false future" *shall* that should really be *is responsible for.*)

- Neither party *shall* be required to pay the other's expenses. (This could not mean "neither party is required to be required to." *Shall* essentially means *will*. An improvement would be to replace *shall be* with *is* or to delete *be required to.*)

- Neither party *shall* claim reimbursement for its expenses from the other party. (Does this really mean "neither party is required to claim reimbursement"? No. *Shall* here means *may*—as is common when a negative word such as *not* or *neither* precedes *shall.*)

- Neither party *shall* be reimbursed by the other party for its expenses. (If *shall* is mandatory here, it merely means that neither party *must* be reimbursed—leaving open the option that it *may* be. This *shall* appears to be equivalent to a future-tense *will*—or perhaps *may* or even *can* [referring to legal capability].)

Shall, in short, is a semantic mess. *Black's Law Dictionary* records five meanings for the word.[1]

Responding to this sloppy usage, courts have treated *shall* as having variegated meanings. In the Supreme Court of the United States alone, the pronouncements on its meaning have been widely diverse:

- For existing rights, *shall* means "must," but it need not be construed as mandatory when a new right is created.[2]

---

1   *Black's Law Dictionary* 1499 (9th ed. 2009). *See* Nora Rotter Tillman & Seth Barrett Tillman, *A Fragment on* Shall *and* May, 50 Am. J. Legal Hist. 453 (2010) (focusing on the historical usage of *shall* and *may* with emphasis on legal contexts); Dale E. Sutton, *Use of "Shall" in Statutes*, 4 John Marshall L.Q. 204, 204, 208 (1938–1939) (noting that *shall* "has too many meanings to make its unnecessary use safe" and that "[m]any valuable hours and needless paragraphs have been wasted on this word by courts").

2   *West Wis. Ry. v. Foley*, 94 U.S. 100, 103 (1876) (per Waite, C.J.).

- If a duty is imposed on the government, "the word 'shall,' when used in statutes, is to be construed as 'may,' unless a contrary intention is manifest."[3]

- A legislative amendment from *shall* to *may* had no substantive effect.[4]

- *Shall* may be treated as a "precatory suggestion."[5]

- The "mere use of the word 'shall'" in a statute "was not enough to remove the Secretary [of Labor]'s power to act," even though the statute stated that the Secretary *shall* act within a certain time and the Secretary did not do so.[6]

- The meaning of *shall* is not fixed: "[t]hough 'shall' generally means 'must,' legal writers sometimes use, or misuse, 'shall' to mean 'should,' 'will,' or even 'may.'"[7]

Hence there has been a movement in recent years to rewrite the federal rules—appellate, criminal, civil, evidence—to remove all the *shall*s and otherwise restyle them. (One of your authors had a leading role in this drafting reform.) Each *shall* became *must, is,* or *may.*

All this having been said, when the word *shall* can reasonably be read as mandatory, it ought to be so read. Consider a statute requiring subcontractors to provide notices of their liens (focus especially on the second sentence):

> Such claimant shall have given . . . written notices of the claim . . . to the prime contractor . . . and to the surety or sureties. Such notices *shall be accompanied by a sworn statement of account* . . . .[8]

---

3   *Railroad Co. v. Hecht,* 95 U.S. 168, 170 (1877) (per Waite, C.J.).

4   *Moore v. Illinois Cent. R.R.,* 312 U.S. 630, 635 (1941) (per Black, J.).

5   *Scott v. United States,* 436 U.S. 128, 146 (1978) (Brennan, J., dissenting).

6   *United States v. Montalvo-Murillo,* 495 U.S. 711, 718 (1990) (per Kennedy, J.).

7   *Gutierrez de Martinez v. Lamagno,* 515 U.S. 417, 432 n.9 (1995) (per Ginsburg, J.).

8   Ann. Tex. Civ. Stats. art. 5160 (Vernon 1969) (emphasis added).

A lawsuit arose when a claimant provided the surety with written notice but did not accompany it with a sworn statement of account. Incredibly, the court deciding this case held that despite the *shall*, the sworn statement was not required.[9] Yet the legislature had been admirably clear. The statute unambiguously states that a claimant *shall* provide the surety with both the written notice and a sworn statement of account.

Even if the court had properly found the sworn statement of account to be required, the case would still have presented what is a recurrent issue in the huge constellation of *shall–must* holdings: What is the effect of failing to honor a mandatory provision's terms? That is an issue for a treatise on remedies, not interpretation.

9   *United States Fid. & Guar. Co. v. Parker Bros. & Co.*, 437 S.W.2d 880, 882 (Tex. Civ. App.—Houston [1st Dist.] 1969, writ ref'd n.r.e.).

12. Conjunctive/Disjunctive Canon

And joins a conjunctive list, *or* a disjunctive list—but with negatives, plurals, and various specific wordings there are nuances.

The conjunctions *and* and *or* are two of the elemental words in the English language. Under the conjunctive/disjunctive canon, *and* combines items while *or* creates alternatives. Competent users of the language rarely hesitate over their meaning. But a close look at the authoritative language of legal instruments—as well as the litigation that has arisen over them—shows that these little words can cause subtle interpretive problems. Although these conjunctions can appear in countless constructions, we have identified six types of sentences in which they most frequently appear in legal instruments.

#1: The Basic Requirement

CONJUNCTIVE	DISJUNCTIVE
You must do A, B, and C.	You must do A, B, or C.

With the conjunctive list, all three things are required—while with the disjunctive list, at least one of the three is required, but any one (or more) of the three satisfies the requirement. Hence in the well-known constitutional phrase *cruel and unusual punishments,*[1] the *and* signals that cruelty or unusualness alone does not run afoul of the clause: The punishment must meet both standards to fall within the constitutional prohibition.[2] The same point holds true

---

1   U.S. Const. amend. VIII ("Excessive bail shall not be required, nor excessive fines imposed, nor cruel and unusual punishments inflicted.").

2   *See Harmelin v. Michigan,* 501 U.S. 957, 967 (1991) (Scalia, J., plurality opinion) ("As a textual matter . . . a disproportionate punishment can perhaps always be considered 'cruel,' but it will not always be (as the text also requires) 'unusual.'"). *See also* Meghan J. Ryan, *Does the Eighth Amendment Punishments Clause Prohibit Only Punishments That Are Both Cruel and Unusual?* 87 Wash. U. L. Rev. 567, 605 (2010) ("[F]or the 'and' to have meaning, the Clause must be interpreted as prohibiting only punishments that are both cruel and unusual.").

for the phrase *necessary and proper*[3] in Article I of the Constitution.

A common interpretive issue involves the conjunction *and*, which (if there are two elements in the construction) entails an express or implied *both* before the first element. Here it is implied: "Service shall be made upon the District of Columbia by delivering . . . or mailing . . . a copy of the summons, complaint and initial order to [both] the Mayor of the District of Columbia (or designee) and the Corporation Counsel of the District of Columbia (or designee)."[4] A plaintiff sued the District for injuries suffered when a fire truck struck her car, but her complaint was dismissed for failure to comply with the rule just quoted because she had not served the mayor.[5] She contended that the purpose of the statute was substantially satisfied by service on the corporation counsel; since that officer was a statutory agent of the mayor, service on him or her was, in legal effect, service on the mayor. The D.C. Superior Court correctly held that what the rule says, it says (see § 2 [supremacy-of-text principle]), and the *and* means that service must be effected on both corporation counsel and the mayor.[6]

Sometimes huge amounts of money can depend on these little words. In *OfficeMax, Inc. v. United States*,[7] the federal tax code imposed certain taxes on "toll telephone service," including "a telephonic quality communication for which . . . there is a toll charge which varies in amount with the distance and elapsed transmission time of each individual communication."[8] In 1965, when Congress enacted the relevant provision, AT&T was the

---

3   U.S. Const. art. I, § 8, cl. 18 ("To make all Laws which shall be necessary and proper for carrying into Execution the foregoing Powers, and all other Powers vested by this Constitution in the Government of the United States, or in any Department or Officer thereof."). *See* Gary Lawson & Patricia B. Granger, *The "Proper" Scope of Federal Power: A Jurisdictional Interpretation of the Sweeping Clause*, 43 Duke L.J. 267, 275 (1993) ("The [Necessary and Proper Clause] specifies that any laws enacted under its authority must be both necessary and proper—in the conjunctive.").

4   D.C. Super. Ct. Civ. P.R. 4(j)(1).

5   *Thompson v. District of Columbia*, 863 A.2d 814, 815–16 (D.C. 2004).

6   *See id.* at 818.

7   428 F.3d 583 (6th Cir. 2005).

8   26 U.S.C. § 4252(b)(1).

only telephone-service provider in the United States that offered long-distance calling, and it imposed a toll on long-distance calls based on variations in *both* the time and distance of the call. In the 1990s, other operators started charging long-distance rates based on time only, and AT&T adopted this approach in 1997. If the tax code required variation based on both time and distance, then no telephone-service consumers would be subject to the tax. The Government contended that the tax applied whenever toll charges varied in amount based on *either* time or distance. OfficeMax argued that the tax applied only when toll charges varied in amount based on *both* time and distance. Relying in part on dictionaries and usage guides, the Sixth Circuit correctly held that *and* is conjunctive and that the toll must therefore vary on both bases.[9]

When there is a multi-element construction with an *and* between the last two elements only, the rhetorical term for the construction is *syndeton*. Some drafters, perhaps through abundant caution, put a conjunction between all the enumerated items, as here:

> The seller shall provide:
> - (a) a survey of the property; and
> - (b) the surveyor's sworn certificate that the survey is authentic and, to the best of the surveyor's knowledge, accurate; and
> - (c) a policy of title insurance showing the boundaries of the property; and
> - (d) a plat showing the metes and bounds of the property.

This technique is called *polysyndeton*. It is a rhetorical technique merely; it does not convey a meaning different from that of the identical phrasing minus the *and*s at the end of (a) and (b). And it should be avoided by legal drafters lest, over time, it cast doubt on the meaning conveyed by the use of syndeton.

---

9   428 F.3d at 588–89.

Sometimes drafters will omit conjunctions altogether between the enumerated items, as here:

> The seller shall provide:
>> (a) a survey of the property;
>> (b) the surveyor's sworn certificate that the survey is authentic and, to the best of the surveyor's knowledge, accurate;
>> (c) a policy of title insurance showing the boundaries of the property;
>> (d) a plat showing the metes and bounds of the property.

This technique is termed *asyndeton*, and it is generally considered to convey the same meaning as the syndetic or polysyndetic formulation: It is as though *and* were inserted between the items. But because such a construction could be read as a disjunctive formulation, most drafters avoid it.

#2: *The Basic Prohibition*

CONJUNCTIVE	DISJUNCTIVE
You must not do A, B, and C.	You must not do A, B, or C.

With the conjunctive list, the listed things are individually permitted but cumulatively prohibited. With the disjunctive list, none of the listed things is allowed.

After a negative, the conjunctive *and* is still conjunctive: *Don't drink and drive.* You can do either one, but you can't do them both. But with *Don't drink or drive*, you cannot do either one: Each possibility is negated. This singular-negation effect, forbidding doing *anything* listed, occurs when the disjunctive *or* is used after a word such as *not* or *without*. (The disjunctive prohibition includes the conjunctive prohibition: Since you may not do any of the prohibited things, you necessarily must not do them all.) The principle that "not A, B, *or* C" means "not A, not B, *and* not C" is part of what is called *DeMorgan's theorem*.

#3: *The Negative Proof*

CONJUNCTIVE	DISJUNCTIVE
To be eligible, you must prove that you have not A, B, and C.	To be eligible, you must prove that you have not A, B, or C.

With the conjunctive negative proof, you must prove that you did not do all three. With the disjunctive negative proof, what must you prove? If you prove that you did not do one of the three things, are you eligible? Suppose the statute says:

> To be eligible for citizenship, you must prove that you have not (1) been convicted of murder; (2) been convicted of manslaughter; or (3) been convicted of embezzlement.

An applicant proves #3—that he has never been convicted of embezzlement—but fails to prove that he has not been convicted of both murder and manslaughter. Is he eligible? (No.) Is the requirement that he not have done one of these things, or that he have done none? (He must have done none.)

Consider a case involving two provisions of the Comprehensive Drug Abuse Prevention and Control Act[10] that gave an innocent-owner defense to forfeiture of a vehicle used in a drug crime. An owner's vehicle could not be declared forfeited "by reason of any act or omission established by that owner to have been committed or omitted without the knowledge, consent, *or* willful blindness of the owner."[11] Oscar Goodman was given a Rolls-Royce that had been used in drug activity. He had not consented to the earlier drug activity, but may have known about it at the time he took title to the car.[12] Could Goodman successfully raise the innocent-owner defense? Goodman contended that the innocent-owner defense should be read *disjunctively* to protect any owner who can prove a lack of knowledge, lack of consent, or lack of willful blindness. The Government contended that a disjunctive interpretation would lead to an absurd result that would allow

---

10   21 U.S.C. § 881(a)(4) (West Supp. 1994).

11   *Id.* § 881(a)(4)(C) (emphasis added).

12   *United States v. One 1973 Rolls Royce*, 43 F.3d 794, 803 (3d Cir. 1994).

every post-illegal-act transferee to escape the forfeiture statute by merely claiming lack of consent, regardless of his knowledge at the time of the illegal act or at the time of the transfer.[13] The Third Circuit incorrectly held that even if you knew about the illegal act, if you did not consent your car cannot be forfeited.[14] It neglected to apply DeMorgan's theorem.[15]

#4: Introduced with each or every

CONJUNCTIVE	DISJUNCTIVE
Every husband and father must report annually.	Every husband or father must report annually.
Each husband and father must report annually.	Each husband or father must report annually.

With the conjunctive *and*, proper usage would assign the adjectives *every* and *each* to both of the following nouns, so that "Every (each) husband and father" means "Every (each) husband and every (each) father." (See § 19 [series-qualifier canon].) But it is easy to mistake the meaning for "Every (each) husband-and-father"—easy enough, in fact, that the conjunctive uses here illustrated might be considered ambiguous. If the husband-and-father meaning is intended, the sentence should be recast that way, or perhaps as "Every (each) husband who is a father." In the disjunctive instances, of course, the problem of ambiguity does not arise because *husband or father* includes not only men who fall into either category but also fathers who are also husbands and husbands who are also fathers.

#5: Introduced with an Indefinite Article

CONJUNCTIVE	DISJUNCTIVE
A husband and father must report annually.	A husband or father must report annually.

13 *Id.* at 813.

14 *Id.* at 814.

15 *See id.* at 815 n.19.

With the conjunctive wording, only someone who fits both descriptions must comply. With the disjunctive wording, someone who fits either description must comply.

#6: *The Synonym-Introducing* or

> "The award of exemplary or punitive damages is the exception, not the rule."

> "An interpretation can be novel, or innovative."

In these sentences, the *or* introduces a definitional equivalent. The second item is nonrestrictive (i.e., the sentence is complete without it), so it is typically (as in the second example just quoted) set off by commas.

#7: *Variant Wordings and Variant Lead-Ins*

The wording of the lead-in may be crucial to the meaning. If the introductory phrase is *any one or more of the following*, then the satisfaction of any one element, or any combination of elements, will suffice. The introductory phrase *each of the following* is equivalent to *all the following*. But notice how the surrounding words can affect the sense:

- The member may select a remedy from among *all the following*: . . . . (Choose one, even if the listing uses *and*s.)

- Among the cumulative options available to a member are *all the following*: . . . . (Choose as many as you like [because of the word *cumulative*], even if the listing uses *or*s.)

- The sole option available to a member is the choice of *any one or more of the following*: . . . . (Choose as many as you like [because of the phrase *or more*], even if the listing uses *or*s.)

- *Each of the following* remedies is available to a member: . . . . (Choose one—probably. The phrasing is ambiguous, whether the listing uses *and* or *or*.)

- A member may select from among *the following reme-dies*: . . . . (Choose one—probably. The phrasing is ambiguous, whether the listing uses *and* or *or.*)

The blackletter rule in the main heading of this section covers the vast majority of wordings. But as with so many other interpretive issues, there is a vast array of possible permutations in phrasing. In one case, the Wyoming Supreme Court had to grapple with a statute that began with polysyndetic *or*s but then dropped the *or* between the last two enumerated items—in a provision that was ungrammatical to boot.[16] The statute allowed for a child to be adopted "without the written consent of the parent" if the nonconsenting mother or father:

(a) has been adjudged guilty by a court of competent jurisdiction of cruelty, abuse, or mistreatment of the child; or

(b) has been judicially deprived of parental rights or had parental rights terminated with respect to the child; or

(c) who [sic] has willfully abandoned such child;

(d) if it is proven to the satisfaction of the court that said father or mother, if able, has not contributed to the support of said child during a period of one (1) year immediately prior to the filing of the petition for adoption . . . .[17]

Notice the absence of the conjunction *or* between subsections (c) and (d).

The child in this case had been adopted without the written consent of his father. The trial court found that the father had not provided support for the child during the period of one year before the adoption proceeding (the requirement set forth in subsection (d)), but it did not find willful abandonment (the requirement set forth in subsection (c)). The father contended that because subsections (c) and (d) are not joined by the conjunction *or,* they must be read together as a single requirement, so that that provision ((d) without (c)) was no proper basis for allowing the adoption. The

---

16 *Voss v. Ralston* (*In re Voss's Adoption*), 550 P.2d 481 (Wyo. 1976).

17 1957 Wyo. Sess. Laws § 1-710.2.

adopting parent contended that since the first three subsections were connected by *or*, subsection (d) should be construed as if it were connected by *or* as well. Ruling for the father, the court held that subsections (c) and (d) must be read together. So adoption of a child without the father's consent required proof of both lack of support and willful abandonment.

That decision was correct. As we have said, asyndeton (absence of conjunction) is normally equivalent to syndeton (use of the conjunction *and*). Textually, there was no serious question that subsection (d) was cumulative. The only real question was whether it was cumulative with (c) alone or with (a) through (c). That did not matter for purposes of the case at hand, but the court got that right as well. Contextually, the requirement fits well with (c) but not (a) and (b). The grammar in the statute was abysmal, containing one inadvertency after another in subsections (c) and (d): The *who* in (c) is all wrong, and (d) is hopelessly unparallel. Yet the statute is intelligible, and the court's unflinching approach to interpretation was laudable. The court complied with our § 8 (omitted-case canon) by stating:

> The omission of words from a statute must be considered intentional on the part of the legislature. Words may not be supplied in a statute where the statute is intelligible without the addition of the alleged omission. Words may not be inserted in a statutory provision under the guise of interpretation.[18]

And it followed the presumption of consistent usage (§ 25):

> Where the legislature has specifically used a word or term in certain places within a statute and excluded it in another place, the court should not read that term into the section from which it was excluded. A word or words appearing in one section of a statute cannot be transferred into another section. Since the word "or" is absent we must now conclude that (c) and (d) are not separate and not alternatives. The series of alternatives was interrupted by its absence and so joinder of (c) and (d) must have been intended.[19]

---

18   550 P.2d at 485 (citations omitted).

19   *Id.* (citations omitted).

ૐ   ૐ   ૐ

What remains here is to say a word about the unfortunate hybrid *and/or*—a drafting blemish that experts often warn against[20] but legal drafters nevertheless use. The literal sense of *and/or* is "both or either," so that *A and/or B* means (1) "A," (2) "B," or (3) "both A and B."[21] So if you must do "A and/or B," you have those three choices. Although one can envision situations in which this result is desired by the drafter, that unusual consequence is obscured (and is perhaps not meant) by use of the sloppy *and/or*. When that is meant, careful drafters would say *A or B or both*—or, if several items were to be listed, they would introduce the list with *any one or more of the following.*

---

20 *See, e.g., Garner's Dictionary of Legal Usage* 57–58 (3d ed. 2011); E.L. Piesse, *The Elements of Drafting* 85 (J.K. Aitken & Peter Butt eds., 10th ed. 2004) (*"And/or* is best discarded. It does not significantly improve brevity and it sometimes makes a passage harder to follow."); Garner, *Legal Writing in Plain English* 112–13 (2001) ("Replace *and/or* wherever it appears."); Dwight G. McCarty, *That Hybrid "and/or,"* 39 Mich. B.J. 9, 17 (1960) ("[T]he only safe rule to follow is not to use the expression in any legal writing, document, or proceeding, under any circumstance."); E.A. Driedger, *The Composition of Legislation* 79 (1957) ("If *or* is used, no one would seriously urge that if one enumerated duty or power is performed or exercised, the remainder vanish; and if *and* is used, no one would say that an enumerated duty or power cannot be exercised except simultaneously with all the others."). For an amusing essay on *and/or*, see R.E. Megarry, *A New Miscellany-at-Law* 223 (2005).

21 *Local Div. 589, Amalgamated Transit Union v. Massachusetts*, 666 F.2d 618, 627 (1st Cir. 1981) (per Breyer, J.) ("the words 'and/or' commonly mean 'the one or the other or both'").

13. Subordinating/Superordinating Canon

Subordinating language (signaled by *subject to*) or superordinating language (signaled by *notwithstanding* or *despite*) merely shows which provision prevails in the event of a clash—but does not necessarily denote a clash of provisions.

Drafters often use the qualifiers *subject to* and *notwithstanding* (or *despite*). A dependent phrase that begins with *subject to* indicates that the main clause it introduces or follows does not derogate from the provision to which it refers. Suppose that § 7 of a statute says that an educational institution can operate in the state only if it qualifies as a "school," pays a fee, and displays a valid certificate issued by the state department of education. A later section of the statute provides: "Subject to § 7, a kindergarten or other preschool program may operate only from the hours of 8:00 a.m. to 5:00 p.m." This means that the permission for kindergartens and pre-school programs to operate during those hours does not eliminate the requirement that kindergartens and preschool programs comply with § 7. There is no clash between the provisions; the later one merely imposes an additional 8-to-5-only requirement, and the *subject to* phrase makes this point clear.

Subject to should never introduce a provision that completely contradicts the provision that the *subject to* phrase modifies. To say that "all minors may be admitted *subject to*" an earlier provision that "no person may be admitted" makes no sense. But *subject to* often introduces a provision that contradicts some applications of what it modifies: "all persons may be admitted *subject to*" an earlier provision that "no minors may be admitted."

Notwithstanding performs a function opposite that of *subject to*. A dependent phrase that begins with *notwithstanding* indicates that the main clause that it introduces or follows derogates from the provision to which it refers. The previous example could be reframed to say that "no minors may be admitted *notwithstanding*" an earlier provision that "all persons may be admitted." (Hence the minors included among the *persons* in the clause that the *notwithstanding* phrase modifies are inadmissible.) Like *subject to*, a *notwithstanding* often produces contradiction of some applications of a broadly framed provision—as just demonstrated.

Drafters often use *notwithstanding* in a catchall provision, where its supposed referent is unclear and perhaps even nonexistent: "Notwithstanding anything herein to the contrary, a continuing-legal-education provider approved by the state bar may conduct seminars without fulfilling any other requirement." There may be nothing to the contrary anywhere in the document—even nothing that could be *thought* to be to the contrary. But the catchall *notwithstanding* is a fail-safe way of ensuring that the clause it introduces will absolutely, positively prevail.

Whether resolving a conflict of application, signaling an addition to other requirements, or merely making assurance doubly sure, *subject to* and *notwithstanding* phrases mean what they say: The provision to which they accord priority prevails. Let us illustrate the subordinating/superordinating canon with a case for each phrase.

In *Weinstock v. Holden,*[1] a provision of the Missouri Constitution established a commission that would "fix the compensation" for all elected state officials and judges. It provided that this schedule of compensation "shall become effective" unless disapproved by concurrent resolution of the general assembly, and that "[t]he schedule shall, subject to appropriations, apply and represent the compensation for each affected person."[2] The commission's schedule for 1997 was not disapproved by the general assembly, but neither did the general assembly appropriate the necessary funds. Weinstock, a retired judge, claimed entitlement to increased compensation as the schedule provided, arguing that *subject to appropriations* meant only subject to the availability of state funds. The Missouri Supreme Court correctly held otherwise:

> [W]e must . . . allow the words "subject to appropriations" to have their full meaning. . . . Only after appropriation

---

1   995 S.W.2d 411 (Mo. 1999).

2   Mo. Const. art. XIII, § 3.8.

does the schedule become "the compensation for each affected person" in the sense that it is legally enforceable.[3]

In *Green v. Commonwealth*,[4] the defendant, a 15-year-old, was
convicted of using a firearm in the commission of a carjacking.
He had been sentenced under a Virginia statute providing that a
juvenile convicted of a violent felony will be sentenced as an adult,
but the sentence may be suspended "conditioned upon successful completion of such terms and conditions as may be imposed
in a juvenile court upon disposition of a delinquency case."[5] Yet
the Virginia statute that he had violated provided for a sentence
of three years and concluded: "Notwithstanding any other provision of law, the sentence prescribed . . . shall not be suspended in
whole or in part, nor shall anyone convicted hereunder be placed
on probation."[6] The trial court correctly ruled that the mandatory
three-year sentence applied, and the Virginia Court of Appeals
affirmed:

> The word "notwithstanding" is defined as "without preven-
> tion or obstruction from or by." *Webster's Third New Inter-
> national Dictionary* 1545 (1993). Given that understanding
> of the word, we conclude that the terms of Code § 18.2-
> 53.1 are not limited by other incongruous laws because the
> General Assembly intended Code § 18.2-53.1 to function
> "without obstruction" from them. Nothing in § 16.1-272
> contradicts this interpretation.[7]

---

3   995 S.W.2d at 418.

4   507 S.E.2d 627 (Va. Ct. App. 1998).

5   Va. Code § 16.1-272(A)(1).

6   *Id.* § 18.2-53.1.

7   507 S.E.2d at 629.

14. Gender/Number Canon

In the absence of a contrary indication, the masculine includes the feminine (and vice versa) and the singular includes the plural (and vice versa).

In the Constitution, the President is referred to many times with the pronouns *he, him,* and *his.* These references, by common grammatical understanding, refer to a President of either sex. Grammarians and lexicographers have traditionally held that the masculine includes the feminine: *He, him,* and *his* are considered third-person singular common-sex pronouns—but only when the context calls for this understanding.[1] English-language texts are rife with the generic-masculine pronoun. In recent decades, there has been a concerted effort among writers and editors, particularly in academic legal writing, to eradicate this convention.[2] But it persists.

Does the principle that the masculine includes the feminine include the reverse? Does the new politically correct "generic-feminine" pronoun (*Every judge who recuses herself is subject to this rule*) include the masculine? Yes—at least in texts adopted in the age of political correctness.[3]

---

1   *See, e.g.,* 1 Noah Webster, *An American Dictionary of the English Language* (1828) (s.v. *he* (4)) ("*He,* when a substitute for *man* in its general sense, expressing mankind, is of common gender, representing, like its antecedent, the whole human race."); Peter Bullions, *The Principles of English Grammar* (13th ed. 1845) ("[T]he masculine term has also a general meaning, expressing both male and female, and is always to be used when the office, occupation, profession, etc., and not the sex of the individual, is chiefly to be expressed.").

2   For your authors' differing views on this subject, see *Making Your Case: The Art of Persuading Judges* 116, 119 (2008).

3   *See* Alaska Stat. § 01.10.050(c) (2008) ("Words of any gender may, when the sense so indicates, refer to any other gender."); Ariz. Rev. Stat. Ann. § 1-214(D) (1973) ("Words of the feminine gender include the masculine and the neuter."); Colo. Rev. Stat. § 2-4-103 (2009) ("[E]very word importing the feminine gender only may extend to and be applied to males and things as well as females."); Conn. Gen. Stat. § 1-1(g) (1974) ("Words importing the masculine gender may be applied to females and words importing the feminine gender may be applied to males."); Nev. Rev. Stat. § 0.030(2) (2009) ("The use of a feminine noun or pronoun in conferring a benefit or imposing a duty does not exclude a male person from that benefit or duty."); S.D. Codified Laws § 2-14-5 (2004) ("Words

As for the singular–plural principle, the United States Code addresses this issue (as well as the previous one) in its rules of construction: "In determining the meaning of any Act of Congress, unless the context indicates otherwise . . . words importing the singular include and apply to several persons, parties, or things; words importing the plural include the singular; words importing the masculine gender include the feminine as well."[4] The rule is simply a matter of common sense and everyday linguistic experience: "It is a misdemeanor for any person to set off a rocket within the city limits without a written license from the fire marshal" does not exempt from penalty someone who sets off two rockets or a string of 100. If you cannot do one, you cannot do any, or many. The best drafting practice, in fact, is to use the singular number for just that reason: Each rocket unambiguously constitutes an offense.

But what if the drafter makes the reference plural? That would normally include the singular. A provision in a lease saying that "No person may set off *rockets* on the premises" would properly be interpreted to forbid the setting off of a single rocket. But the proposition that many includes only one is not as logically inevitable as the proposition that one includes multiple ones, so its application is much more subject to context and to contradiction by other canons. If the same plural *rockets* were used in a governmental proscription carrying a penalty ("It is a misdemeanor for any person to set off rockets within the city limits, etc."), there is some chance that a court would apply the rule of lenity (see § 49) to hold a single rocket harmless. An instance discussed by both Blackstone and Bentham concerned a 1278 statute establishing the penalty for "stealing horses." The English judges held that this provision did not apply to someone who stole a single horse. Bentham defended the holding as praiseworthy:

> This construction I am aware has been cited as an instance of scrupulousness carried to the extreme, but I must confess I see not with what justice. Taking the value of the

---

used in the masculine gender include the feminine and neuter. Words used in the feminine gender include the masculine and neuter.").

4   1 U.S.C. § 1.

thing stolen for the measure of the guilt of stealing, the guilt of stealing horses is at least double, to that of stealing one horse: and it follows not, that because the legislature has thought fit to annex a certain degree of punishment to a certain degree of guilt, it therefore should annex the same to half that guilt. . . . [I]n the doubt the safest decision was that which was on the mildest side: and from this no evil consequence could arise when followed by the well-imagined step that was taken next by the Judges. "They procured a new act" (says [Blackstone]) "in the following year."⁵ I honour those Judges, and, of all I know upon record, would cherish this precedent they have set us. It points to their successors the true method of giving the public the benefit of their discernment without transgressing the limits of their authority."⁶

His point is well taken—which is why books on legal drafting recommend using the singular over the plural.⁷

---

5   1 William Blackstone, *Commentaries on the Laws of England* 88 (4th ed. 1770) ("Judges . . . procured a new act for that purpose in the following year.").

6   Jeremy Bentham, *A Comment on the Commentaries: A Criticism of William Blackstone's Commentaries on the Laws of England* 141 (1776; Charles Warren Everett ed., 1928).

7   *See, e.g.*, Bryan A. Garner, *Legal Writing in Plain English* 114 (2001).

15. Presumption of Nonexclusive "Include"

The verb *to include* introduces examples, not an exhaustive list.

In normal English usage, if a group "consists of" or "comprises" 300 lawyers, it contains precisely that number. If it "includes" 300 lawyers, there may well be thousands of other members from all walks of life as well. That is, the word *include* does not ordinarily introduce an exhaustive list, while *comprise*—with an exception that we will discuss shortly—ordinarily does. That is the rule both in good English usage[1] and in textualist decision-making.[2] Some jurisdictions have even codified a rule about *include*.[3]

Often the phrase that appears is *including but not limited to*— or either of two variants, *including without limitation* and *including without limiting the generality of the foregoing*. These cautious

---

1   *See, e.g., The Random House Dictionary of the English Language* 967 (2d ed. 1987) ("To *include* is to contain as a part or member, or among the parts and members, of a whole: The list *includes* many new names. . . . To *comprise* is to consist of, as the various parts serving to make up the whole: This genus *comprises* 50 species."); H.W. Fowler, *A Dictionary of Modern English Usage* 275 (Ernest Gowers ed., 2d ed. 1965) ("With *include*, there is no presumption . . . that all or even most of the components are mentioned; with *comprise*, the whole of them are understood to be in the list."); Theodore M. Bernstein, *The Careful Writer: A Modern Guide to English Usage* 228 (1965) ("The word *include* . . . usually suggests that the component items are not being mentioned in their entirety. If all [the component items] are being mentioned, it would be better to write . . . 'were'; or, if there is an irresistible urge for a fancy word, to use *comprised*."); Bergen Evans & Cornelia Evans, *A Dictionary of Contemporary American Usage* 110–11 (1957) ("It is better to use *comprise* when all of the constituent parts are enumerated or referred to and to use *include* when only some of them are.").

2   *See, e.g., Federal Land Bank of St. Paul v. Bismarck Lumber Co.*, 314 U.S. 95, 100 (1941) (per Murphy, J.) ("the term 'including' is not one of all-embracing definition, but connotes simply an illustrative application of the general principle"); *United States v. Philip Morris USA Inc.*, 566 F.3d 1095, 1115 (D.C. Cir. 2009) (explaining that *including* indicates a nonexhaustive list but that "adding 'but not limited to' helps to emphasize the non-exhaustive nature"); *Richardson v. National City Bank of Evansville*, 141 F.3d 1228, 1232 (7th Cir. 1998) (for purposes of interpreting administrative regulations, *include* is a term of illustration, not limitation).

3   *See, e.g.*, Tex. Gov't Code Ann. § 311.005(13) (West 1989) ("'Includes' and 'including' are terms of enlargement and not of limitation or exclusive enumeration, and use of the terms does not create a presumption that components not expressed are excluded.").

phrases are intended to defeat the negative-implication canon (§ 10): "Even though the word *including* itself means that the list is merely exemplary and not exhaustive, the courts have not invariably so held. So the longer, more explicit variations are necessary in the eyes of many drafters."[4] Even so, the commonness of these belts-and-suspenders phrases does not lessen the exemplariness of *include*.

In one particular legal specialty—intellectual-property law—*comprise* is held to be synonymous with *include*. Specifically, *comprise* introduces a nonexhaustive list in the field of patent-claim drafting.[5] But this is a narrow, anomalous exception.

---

4   *Garner's Dictionary of Legal Usage* 439–40 (3d ed. 2011).

5   *See Vehicular Techs. Corp. v. Titan Wheel Int'l, Inc.*, 212 F.3d 1377, 1382–83 (Fed. Cir. 2000) ("The phrase *consisting of* is a term of art in patent law signifying restriction and exclusion, while, in contrast, the term *comprising* indicates an open-ended construction. . . . In simple terms, a drafter uses the phrase *consisting of* to mean 'I claim what follows and nothing else.' A drafter uses the term *comprising* to mean 'I claim at least what follows and potentially more.'") (emphasis added); *Genentech, Inc. v. Chiron Corp.*, 112 F.3d 495, 501 (Fed. Cir. 1997) ("*Comprising* is a term of art used in claim language which means that the named elements are essential, but other elements may be added and still form a construct within the scope of the claim.") (emphasis added); *Parmelee Pharm. Co. v. Zink*, 285 F.2d 465, 469 (8th Cir. 1961) ("The word *comprising* in the patent law is an open-ended word and one of enlargement and not of restriction. . . . In contrast, the word *consisting* is one of restriction and exclusion.") (emphasis added).

16. Unintelligibility Canon

An unintelligible text is inoperative.

> "There are sometimes statutes which no rule or canon of interpretation can make effective or applicable to the situations of fact which they purport to govern. In such cases the statute must simply fail."
>
> 3 Roscoe Pound, *Jurisprudence* 493 (1959).

A legendary Irish act provided that the material of an existing prison should be used in building a new prison and that the prisoners should continue their confinement in the old prison until the new one was completed.[1] This account is surely apocryphal, but the point it makes is revealing: To give meaning to what is meaningless is to create a text rather than to interpret one.

But we cannot press this unintelligibility principle too far. It is readily applicable when language makes no sense, or when two provisions are irreconcilable. But what about a provision that has a meaning so vague that its application to real-world events is imponderable? Or a term that is utterly ambiguous, even after all the tools of construction have been applied, but either of whose potential meanings would be workable and eminently reasonable? It would be appropriate to consider such a text unintelligible, but courts do not. They clarify the vagueness and resolve the ambiguity no matter what—subject to the principle that vague provisions restricting speech or imposing punishments are void. Indeed, in the case of statutes conferring vague or ambiguous authority on agencies, courts will permit the vagueness or ambiguity to persist, leaving it up to the agency to decide—from time to time and under different administrations—which of the various permissible interpretations it will adopt.

Consider the Mount Zion Church case.[2] One Rebecca Partlow was convicted of violating a statute prohibiting "the sale of spirituous liquors . . . within three miles of . . . Mount Zion Church in

---

1   Ex. from Ernst Freund, *Standards of American Legislation* 225–26 (1917; repr. 1965).

2   *State v. Partlow*, 91 N.C. 550 (1884).

Gaston County."[3] The problem was that Gaston County had two Mount Zion Churches—one with a black congregation and one with a white one. The North Carolina Supreme Court began its analysis by rejecting (quite properly) the testimony of a legislator who voted on the bill, who would have testified that it was the black church that had been intended.[4] (That was the one near where Partlow had allegedly sold the liquor.) "Whatever may be the views and purposes of those who procure the enactment of a statute, the legislature contemplates that its intention shall be ascertained from its words as embodied in it. And courts are not at liberty to accept the understanding of any individual as to the legislative intent."[5] That mode of resolving the ambiguity having been eliminated, the court held: "We are constrained to declare that the clause of the statute under consideration is, because of its ambiguity, inoperative and void."[6]

Interestingly, the statute would not have been ambiguous—it would have been entirely clear—if there had been only one Mount Zion Church at the time of the bill's enactment. A newly constructed church by the same name could not change the law's original meaning (see § 7 [fixed-meaning canon]). The principle is that a statute is unintelligible if its original meaning remains intractably ambiguous after all the other interpretive tools are applied. Nineteenth-century courts tended—rightly, we believe—to invoke the rule boldly when it was called for.

Another case illustrates this rigorous approach. In 1872, the Texas Supreme Court confronted an act requiring that interlocutory appeals "be regulated by the law regulating appeals from final judgment in the District Court, so far as the same may be appli-

---

3   *Id.* at 551.

4   *See Covalt v. Carey Can., Inc.*, 860 F.2d 1434, 1438–39 (7th Cir. 1988) (per Easterbrook, J.) (stating that the universal principle in federal court is to reject testimony by members of the enacting legislature but noting that California courts, unfortunately, have occasionally permitted state legislators to testify about their understanding of a bill); Lord Macmillan, *Law and Other Things* 163 (1938) ("[O]ne of the cardinal rules is that you must not ask the person who used a particular word what he meant by it.").

5   91 N.C. at 552.

6   *Id.* at 554.

cable thereto."[7] The word *thereto*, grammatically speaking, must mean "to interlocutory appeals"—as the court tacitly assumed. Yet can *any* law explicitly regulating appeals from a final judgment "be applicable" to interlocutory appeals? No. So the court concluded: "If . . . we find the Act . . . referring for its execution to other laws which can have no application, we are at a loss to know how the Act can be administered. . . . [W]hen we find ourselves totally unable to administer a law by reason of its uncertainty or ambiguity, . . . we shall not hesitate to discharge the duty which the law devolves upon us."[8] And so the court ignored the law. This approach was perhaps *too* rigorous—or at least too literal. The presumption against ineffectiveness (§ 4) suggests that "applicable" must mean not "applicable by its terms" but "susceptible of being applied."

An interesting and more recent case testing the unintelligibility canon is *AFL-CIO v. American Petroleum Institute.*[9] The federal statute at issue there required the Occupational Safety and Health Administration to promulgate standards for handling toxic material so as to ensure "*to the extent feasible*, . . . that no employee will suffer material impairment of health."[10] Interpreting that provision, a four-Justice plurality upheld the Fifth Circuit's setting aside of the agency's benzene standard on the ground that it was not supported by appropriate findings. Then-Justice Rehnquist concurred separately. After examining the legislative history, he concluded that "the feasibility requirement . . . is a legislative mirage, appearing to some Members but not to others, and assuming any form desired by the beholder."[11] It might mean "to the extent achievable without bankrupting the industry"; or "to the extent the benefits outweigh the costs"; or even "to the extent technologically possible." He therefore concluded that the provision was unconstitutional as a delegation of legislative power to OSHA. We agree that the provision was textually ambiguous, and thus left

---

7   Act of November 1st, 1871 (Pamphlet Acts, p. 17).

8   *Ward v. Ward*, 37 Tex. 389, 391–92 (1872).

9   448 U.S. 607 (1980) (Stevens, J., plurality opinion).

10   29 U.S.C. § 655(b)(5) (emphasis added).

11   448 U.S. at 681 (Rehnquist, J., concurring).

its meaning to be determined by OSHA and the courts—leaving room for a determination that it was a delegation of legislative power (if one considers the prohibition of such delegation enforceable by the courts). But if, as Justice Rehnquist's analysis assumes, a text means what the legislature intended it to mean, and if it was clear in this case that there was no meaning intended by a majority of Congress, then the product would be not an unconstitutional delegation but a meaningless and hence inoperative provision. As the textualist sees things, however, Congress enacted an intractably ambiguous phrase. It makes no difference whether a legislative majority favored a particular meaning. Justice Rehnquist was correct in believing that Congress had left the ambiguity to OSHA and the courts to resolve. One who believes in the determinativeness of "legislative intent" should hold "intentless" text to be inoperative—yet we know of no one who does so.

Sometimes, as in the *American Petroleum Institute* case, a court is presented with a text that would require more than a minor fix to make it intelligible. Although one minor emendation might be permissible (e.g., reading *pirson* as *prison*), a reconstructed text is not (see § 8 [omitted-case canon]). As the King of Hearts says in *Alice in Wonderland*: "If there is no meaning in it . . . that saves a world of trouble, you know, as we needn't try to find any."[12]

    ❧ ❧ ❧

In a curious and lengthy passage, Judge Richard A. Posner has likened a judge who follows the unintelligibility canon to a platoon commander who, on receiving a garbled message, does nothing and presumably allows his troops to be slaughtered. We quote the passage at length to impart its full flavor:

> Suppose the commander of the lead platoon in an attack finds his way blocked by an unexpected enemy pillbox. He has two choices: go straight ahead at the pillbox, or try to bypass it to the left. He radios the company commander for instructions. The commander replies, "Go—" but the rest of the message is garbled. When the platoon

---

12 Lewis Carroll, *The Complete Illustrated Works* 1, 77 (1982 ed.).

commander radios back for clarification, he is unable to get through. If the platoon commander decides that, not being able to receive an intelligible command, he should do nothing until communications can be restored, his decision will be wrong. For it is plain from the part of the message that was received that the company commander wanted him to get by the enemy pillbox, either by frontal attack or by bypassing it. And surely the company commander would have preferred the platoon commander to decide by himself which course to follow rather than to do nothing and let the attack fail. For the platoon commander to take the position that he may do nothing, just because the communication was garbled, would be an irresponsible "interpretation."

The situation with regard to legislative interpretation is analogous. In our system of government the framers of statutes and constitutions are the superiors of the judges. The framers communicate orders to the judges through legislative texts (including, of course, the Constitution). If the orders are clear, the judges must obey them. Often, however, because of passage of time and change of circumstance the orders are unclear and normally the judges cannot query the framers to find out what the order means. The judges are thus like the platoon commander in my example. It is irresponsible for them to adopt the attitude that if the order is unclear they will refuse to act.[13]

The analogy limps. Except, perhaps, for those relatively few statutes that deal with the jurisdiction and procedures of the courts themselves, legislation is an order not to the courts but to the executive or the citizenry. When its command is garbled beyond comprehension, there is no command; and in our system of separated powers, courts have no power to devise one. Second (and relatedly), unlike the subordinate officer who is the agent of his superior and is arguably authorized to do (in the absence of a clear command) what he thinks his superior would want done—or indeed even to act on his own—courts are assuredly not agents of the legislature and have no power to write laws on their own. They are agents of the people, charged with remedying the harm that a

---

13   Richard A. Posner, *Legal Formalism, Legal Realism, and the Interpretation of Statutes and the Constitution*, 37 Case Western L. Rev. 179, 189 (1986–1987).

person claims to have suffered at the hands of another person or of the government. It is no part of that charge to write laws that the legislature has not written. Third (and least important) if necessity knows no law, the necessity of taking action to win a battle or save the lives of troops committed to one's care is not comparable to the necessity of figuring out who wins a courtroom dispute.

Syntactic Canons

17. Grammar Canon

Words are to be given the meaning that proper grammar and usage would assign them.

> "This Court naturally does not review congressional enactments as a panel of grammarians; but neither do we regard ordinary principles of English prose as irrelevant to a construction of those enactments."
>
> *Flora v. United States,*
> 362 U.S. 145, 150 (1960) (per Warren, C.J.).

Although drafters, like all other writers and speakers, sometimes perpetrate linguistic blunders,[1] they are presumed to be grammatical in their compositions. They are *not* presumed to be unlettered. Judges rightly presume, for example, that legislators understand subject–verb agreement, noun–pronoun concord, the difference between the nominative and accusative cases, and the principles of correct English word-choice. No matter how often the accuracy, indeed the plausibility, of this presumption is cast in doubt by legislators' oral pronouncements, when it comes to what legislators enact, the presumption is unshakable.

Courts sometimes say that rules of grammar govern unless they contradict legislative intent or purpose.[2] This statement is entirely correct (though it should go without saying) if it refers to legislative intent or purpose manifested in the only manner in which a legislature can authoritatively do so: in the text of the enactment. The presumption of legislative literacy is a rebuttable one; like all the other canons, this one can be overcome by other textual

---

1   *See, e.g.,* Jeremy Bentham, "Nomography," in 3 *The Works of Jeremy Bentham* 231, 242–43 (John Bowring ed., 1843) ("In the examination of one statute, I have found a multitude of such gross palpable grammatical errors, as scarcely any schoolboy, who had made his way to the upper form of any school in which no language was taught besides English, would see himself convicted of without shame.").

2   *See, e.g., Costello v. INS,* 376 U.S. 120, 122–26 (1964) (per Stewart, J.); *United States v. Shirey,* 359 U.S. 255, 260–61 (1959) (per Frankfurter, J.); *United States v. Whitridge,* 197 U.S. 135, 143 (1905) (per Holmes, J.).

indications of meaning. But if the statement suggests that grammatical usage is some category of indication separate from textual meaning, it is quite wrong. Grammatical usage is one of the means (though not the exclusive means) by which the sense of a statute is conveyed: "The words [a legislator] uses are the instruments by means of which he expects or hopes to effect . . . changes [in society]. What gives him this expectation or this hope is his belief that he can anticipate how others (e.g., judges and administrators) will understand these words."[3]

Often the issue centers on syntactic relationships. In a 1989 United States Supreme Court case, a Bankruptcy Code provision stated: "[T]here shall be allowed to the holder of [an oversecured] claim, interest on such claim, and any reasonable fees, costs, or charges provided for under the agreement . . . ."[4] The question was whether "interest on such claim" was subject to the qualification "provided for under the agreement." The Court held that it was independent of the qualification, the conjunction *and* being essentially equivalent to *together with*:

> This reading is also mandated by the grammatical structure of the statute. The phrase "interest on such claim" is set aside by commas, and separated from the reference to fees, costs, and charges by the conjunctive words "and any." As a result, the phrase "interest on such claim" stands independent of the language that follows. "[I]nterest on such claim" is not part of the list made up of "fees, costs, or charges," nor is it joined to the following clause so that the final "provided for under the agreement" modifies it as well. The language and punctuation Congress used cannot be read in any other way. By the plain language of the statute, the two types of recovery are distinct.[5]

Many high-stakes cases turn on such narrow linguistic questions.

---

3   Gerald C. MacCallum Jr., *Legislative Intent*, 75 Yale L.J. 754, 758 (1966).

4   11 U.S.C. § 506(b).

5   *United States v. Ron Pair Enters., Inc.*, 489 U.S. 235, 241–42 (1989) (per Blackmun, J.) (citation and footnote omitted).

But some grammatical principles are weaker than others—
such as the preference for *that* in a restrictive relative clause and
a comma plus *which* in a nonrestrictive relative clause. A famous
example arose in the drafting of the 1984 Republican platform:

> Republicans oppose new taxes that are unnecessary. (Re-
> strictive meaning: only unnecessary new taxes are anath-
> ema.)

> Republicans oppose new taxes, which are unnecessary.
> (Nonrestrictive meaning: all new taxes are anathema.) [6]

An unfastidious wording that used *which* without a comma—one
not seriously proposed at the Convention—could have gone either
way:

> Republicans oppose new taxes which are unnecessary.
> (Ambiguous.)

This grammatical convention—preferring *that* for restrictive
clauses and comma-*which* for nonrestrictive ones—is unfortunately a weak basis for deciding statutory meaning. For while grammarians have sought heroically to establish this as a firm rule,[7]
they have been unsuccessful. Some usages of traditional English
militate against it—the fact, for example, that *that* is not just a
relative pronoun but also a stand-alone pronoun, a demonstrative
adjective, and a conjunction. Good writers avoid too many *that*s
in close proximity, and even a bad writer would never say (as the
use of *that* as the defining relative pronoun would require) "that
that I saw." What H.W. Fowler wrote in 1926 remains entirely
true today:

---

6   For more on this example, see Bryan A. Garner, *How a "That–Which" Editorial
     Decision Changed U.S. History*, 37 Student Law. 10 (May 2009).

7   Theodore M. Bernstein, *The Careful Writer* 444 (1965) ("*That* is better used to
     introduce a limiting or defining clause, *which* to introduce a nondefining or par-
     enthetical clause."); John F. Genung, *Outlines of Rhetoric* 94–95 (1894) ("There are
     many cases where, for the sake of euphony or clearness, . . . *which* has to be used
     though the meaning is restrictive. Such cases ought to be studied; and wherever
     that will go smoothly, use it. Do not be so careless in this respect as some writers
     are."); Richard Dublin, *A Selection of English Synonyms* 21 (rev. ed. 1860) ("*Which*
     is used in speaking of a class generally, and *that* when we mean to designate any
     particular *individual* of that class.").

> [I]f writers would agree to regard *that* as the defining rela-
> tive pronoun, and *which* as the non-defining, there would
> be much gain both in lucidity and in ease. Some there
> are who follow this principle now; but it would be idle to
> pretend that it is the practice either of most or of the best
> writers.[8]

Hence it is not unusual to encounter a text that disregards
the supposed *that–which* dichotomy. Consider, for example, Connecticut's good-samaritan law. Designed to immunize healthcare
providers who voluntarily render emergency aid, the law states
that such providers

> shall not be liable to [a] person assisted for civil damages for
> any personal injuries which result from acts or omissions by
> such person in rendering the emergency care, which may
> constitute ordinary negligence.[9]

Does this mean that all emergency care is immunized, or only
instances constituting ordinary negligence? If *which* is read non-
restrictively, the immunity is absolute; if it is read restrictively, only
ordinary negligence is immunized. A strict *that–which* grammarian's reading (coupled with the punctuation canon [§ 23]) creates
an absolute immunity. But only a reading that gives *which* a restrictive sense (in both its instances in the statute)—and overrides
the punctuation—gives effect to every word (see § 26 [surplusage
canon]). So a court would be textually justified in ignoring the
grammarian's reading[10]—though legal drafters would be well-ad-
vised in the future to heed Fowler's recommendation for lucidity
and ease.

---

8 H.W. Fowler, *A Dictionary of Modern English Usage* 635 (1926).

9 Conn. Gen. Stat. § 52-557b(a).

10 *See Glorioso v. Police Dep't of Burlington*, 826 A.2d 271 (Conn. Super. Ct. 2003).

18. Last-Antecedent Canon

A pronoun, relative pronoun, or demonstrative adjective generally refers to the nearest reasonable antecedent.

In 1841, President William Henry Harrison died in office—barely a month into the ninth presidency of the United States. At his inauguration, he had spoken for nearly two hours in the rain and contracted pneumonia, from which he died: a lesson to all bloviators. His vice president, John Tyler, became the new president.

Or did he?

The answer turned on the wording of Article II of the Constitution: "In Case of the Removal of the President from Office, or of his Death, Resignation or Inability to discharge the Powers and Duties of the said Office, the Same shall devolve on the Vice President." The question was what it was, precisely, that devolved. Was it the *office*, or was it *the powers and duties of said office*? From a grammatical point of view, what is the antecedent of the legalistic pronoun *same*? Did John Tyler become the tenth president, or did he remain the vice president while having the powers and duties of the presidency? Constitutional scholars long debated the point.[1]

The so-called last-antecedent canon resolves the issue favorably to Tyler: *office* is the nearest reasonable antecedent of *same*; the phrase *powers and duties* is a more remote antecedent. As a result, we can now confidently pronounce that there have been 44 presidents in the history of the United States as of 2012.

This rule is the legal expression of a commonsense principle of grammar, here rather technically expressed by a British grammarian: "It is clearly desirable that an anaphoric (backward-looking) or cataphoric (forward-looking) pronoun should be placed as near as the construction allows to the noun or noun phrase to which it refers, and in such a manner that there is no risk of ambiguity."[2]

---

1   *See* David P. Currie, *His Accidency*, 5 Green Bag 2d 151, 154 (2002). *See also Garner's Modern American Usage* 726 (3d ed. 2009).

2   Robert W. Burchfield, *Fowler's Modern English Usage* (3d ed. 1996).

In what has been called the "seminal authority"[3] on the last-antecedent canon, *Barnhart v. Thomas*,[4] the Supreme Court of the United States illustrated how the rule works. Let us say that parents warn a teenage son: "You will be punished if you throw a party or engage in any other activity that damages the house."[5] With this homey example, the Court said in a unanimous opinion: "If the son nevertheless throws a party and is caught, he should hardly be able to avoid punishment by arguing that the house was not damaged."[6] The relative pronoun *that* attaches only to *other activity*, not to *party* as well:

> The parents proscribed (1) a party, and (2) any other activity that damages the house. As far as appears from what they said, their reasons for prohibiting the home-alone party may have had nothing to do with damage to the house—for instance, the risk that underage drinking or sexual activity would occur. And even if their only concern was to prevent damage, it does not follow from the fact that the same interest underlay both the specific and the general prohibition that proof of impairment of that interest is required for both.[7]

The actual language at issue in *Barnhart* was closely analogous. A social-security disability claimant was capable of performing her old job—but her old job (that of an elevator operator) was no longer available in the national economy. The relevant statute allows benefits "only if [the claimant's] physical or mental impairment or impairments are of such severity that he is not only unable to do his previous work but cannot, considering his age, education, and work experience, engage in any other kind of substantial gainful work which exists in the national economy."[8] The claimant argued that she should be able to receive disability benefits because elevator-operator jobs were no longer available in the national economy,

---

3   Jeremy L. Ross, *A Rule of Last Resort: A History of the Doctrine of the Last Antecedent in the United States Supreme Court*, 39 Sw. L. Rev. 325, 326 (2009).

4   540 U.S. 20, 27–28 (2003) (per Scalia, J.).

5   *Id.* at 27.

6   *Id.*

7   *Id.*

8   42 U.S.C. §§ 423(d)(2)(A), 1382c(a)(3)(B).

even though she was physically capable of doing the work required by such a job. The Court rightly rejected the argument. The restrictive relative clause (*which exists in the national economy*) modified only *substantial gainful work*; it did not reach all the way back to *previous work.*[9]

The very first recital of the canon by the Supreme Court of the United States involved the demonstrative adjective *such*—in a case that arose in 1799.[10] A Virginia statute provided that "no person, his heirs or assigns, . . . shall hereafter be admitted to any warrant [entitling compensation] for . . . military service, unless he, she, or they, produce . . . a proper certificate of proof made before some court of record within the commonwealth, by the oath of the party claiming, or other satisfactory evidence that such party was bona fide an inhabitant of this commonwealth." In a footnote, Chief Justice Oliver Ellsworth stated: "The rule is, that 'such' applies to the last antecedent, unless the sense of the passage requires a different construction."[11] Here, he said, *such party* "must, in order to preserve the sense of the context," refer to the donee of the warrant, his heirs, or assigns, referred to earlier in the passage.[12]

One caveat. The last-antecedent canon may be superseded by another grammatical convention: A pronoun that is the subject of a sentence and does not have an antecedent in that sentence ordinarily refers to the subject of the preceding sentence. And it almost always does so when it is the word that begins the sentence. For example: "The commission may find that discrimination has occurred. It must be clear and explicit." The nearest potential antecedent of *it* is *discrimination*, but without some other indication of meaning its proper referent is *The commission*.

---

9   540 U.S. at 26.

10   *Sims's Lessee v. Irvine*, 3 U.S. (3 Dall.) 425 (1799) (per Ellsworth, C.J.).

11   *Id.* at 444 n.*.

12   *Id.*

19. Series-Qualifier Canon

When there is a straightforward, parallel construction that involves all nouns or verbs in a series, a prepositive or postpositive modifier normally applies to the entire series.

The Fourth Amendment begins in this way, with a prepositive (pre-positioned) modifier (*unreasonable*) in the most important phrase: "The right of the people to be secure in their persons, houses, papers, and effects, against *unreasonable searches and seizures*, shall not be violated . . . ."[1] The phrase is often repeated: *unreasonable searches and seizures*. Does the adjective *unreasonable* qualify the noun *seizures* as well as the noun *searches*? Yes, as a matter of common English. A similar question arises with the Impeachment Clause's reference to *high crimes and misdemeanors*. And the answer is the same: The misdemeanors must be "high" no less than the crimes. In the absence of some other indication, the modifier reaches the entire enumeration.[2] That is so whether the modifier is an adjective or an adverb.[3]

Consider application of the series-qualifier canon to the following phrases:

- *Charitable institutions or societies*—held, that *charitable* modifies both *institutions* and *societies*.[4]

---

1 U.S. Const. amend. IV (emphasis added).

2 *See, e.g., Lewis v. Jackson Energy Coop. Corp.*, 189 S.W.3d 87, 92 (Ky. 2005) ("[A]n adjective at the beginning of a conjunctive phrase applies equally to each object within the phrase."); *Ward Gen. Ins. Servs., Inc. v. Employers Fire Ins. Co.*, 7 Cal. Rptr. 3d 844, 849 (Ct. App. 2003) ("Most readers expect the first adjective in a series of nouns or phrases to modify each noun or phrase in the following series unless another adjective appears.").

3 *See, e.g., United States v. X-Citement Video, Inc.*, 513 U.S. 64, 68 (1994) (per Rehnquist, C.J.) (holding that the "most natural grammatical reading" of a statute is that an initial adverb modifies each verb in a list of elements of a crime).

4 *In re Schleicher's Estate*, 51 A. 329, 329–30 (Pa. 1902).

- *Internal personnel rules and practices of an agency*—held, that *internal personnel* modifies both *rules* and *practices*, and *of an agency* held to modify both nouns as well.[5]

- *Intentional unemployment or underemployment*—held, that *intentional* modifies both nouns.[6]

- *Intoxicating bitters or beverages*—held, that *intoxicating* modifies both *bitters* and *beverages*.[7]

- *Forcibly assaults, resists, opposes, impedes, intimidates, or interferes with*—held, that *forcibly* modifies each verb in the list.[8]

- *Willfully damage or tamper with*—held, that *willfully* modifies both *damage* and *tamper with*.[9]

Similar results obtain with postpositive modifiers (that is, those "positioned after" what they modify) in simple constructions:

- *Institutions or societies that are charitable in nature* (the institutions as well as the societies must be charitable).

- *A wall or fence that is solid* (the wall as well as the fence must be solid).

- *A corporation or partnership registered in Delaware* (a corporation as well as a partnership must be registered in Delaware).

The typical way in which syntax would suggest no carryover modification is that a determiner (*a, the, some,* etc.) will be repeated before the second element:

- *The charitable institutions or the societies* (the presence of the second *the* suggests that the societies need not be charitable).

---

5   *Jordan v. United States Dep't of Justice*, 591 F.2d 753, 764 (D.C. Cir. 1978).

6   *Iliff v. Iliff*, 339 S.W.3d 74, 80 (Tex. 2011).

7   *Ex parte State ex rel. Attorney Gen.*, 93 So. 382, 383 (Ala. 1922).

8   *Long v. United States*, 199 F.2d 717, 719 (4th Cir. 1952).

9   *In re John R.*, 394 A.2d 818, 819 n.1 (Md. Ct. Spec. App. 1978).

- *A solid wall or a fence* (the fence need not be solid).

- *Delaware corporations and some partnerships* (the partnerships may be registered in any state).

- *To clap and to cheer lustily* (the clapping need not be lusty).[10]

With postpositive modifiers, the insertion of a determiner before the second item tends to cut off the modifying phrase so that its backward reach is limited—but that effect is not entirely clear:

- *An institution or a society that is charitable in nature* (any institution probably qualifies, not just a charitable one).

- *A wall or a fence that is solid* (the wall may probably have gaps).

- *A corporation or a partnership registered in Delaware* (the corporation may probably be registered anywhere).

To make certain that the postpositive modifier does not apply to each item, the competent drafter will position it earlier:

- *Societies that are charitable in nature or institutions.*

- *A fence that is solid or a wall.*

- *A partnership registered in Delaware or a corporation.*

A case exemplifying the simple construction contemplated by the blackletter canon arose in Minnesota.[11] A state statute allowed medical professionals access to certain hospital records if they were "requesting or seeking through discovery data, information, or records relating to their medical staff privileges [etc.]."[12] In 1997, two doctors at Saint Cloud Hospital requested such information about themselves, and they were denied. The question was how to read the phrase *through discovery*—as modifying just *seeking* or also *requesting*. Did the statute mean "medical professionals requesting—or seeking through discovery—data, infor-

---

10 *See* Randolph Quirk & Sidney Greenbaum, *A University Grammar of English* § 9.37, at 270 (1973).

11 *Amaral v. Saint Cloud Hosp.*, 598 N.W.2d 379 (Minn. 1999).

12 Minn. Stat. § 145.64(2) (1998).

mation, or records [etc.]"? Or did it mean "medical professionals requesting or seeking—through discovery—data, information, or records [etc.]"? The Minnesota Supreme Court correctly held that the latter interpretation controlled.[13]

Sometimes the syntax gets trickier. In *United States v. Pritchett*,[14] the United States Court of Appeals for the District of Columbia Circuit had to determine the reach of the adverbial phrase *when on duty*. The District of Columbia Code prohibited carrying a concealable pistol or dangerous weapon,[15] but the prohibition did not apply to "jail wardens, or their deputies, policemen or other duly appointed law enforcement officers, or to members of the Army, Navy, or Marine Corps of the United States or of the National Guard or Organized Reserves *when on duty*."[16] A deputy jail warden was convicted of carrying a pistol when he was not on duty. The appellate court reversed the conviction because the statute did not apply to jail wardens, whether or not they were on duty: "[H]ad the drafters of the statute intended the phrase 'when on duty' to modify the earlier portion of the Act referring to deputy jail wardens, they could have . . . omitted the 'or' preceding members of the 'Army, Navy, or Marine Corps,' etc., and inserted a comma before the phrase 'when on duty' so as to separate it from the clause immediately preceding."[17] The court was right about the result and about the comma, but it was the *to* rather than the *or* that set the last phrase apart.

Perhaps more than most of the other canons, this one is highly sensitive to context. Often the sense of the matter prevails: *He went forth and wept bitterly* does not suggest that he went forth bitterly. And like all the other canons (and perhaps more than most), it is subject to defeasance by other canons. In *Phoenix Control Systems, Inc. v. Insurance Co. of North America*,[18] an insurer (INA) provided a policy that covered the insured (PCS) for the defense of all law-

---

13   598 N.W.2d at 388 (with added support from other contextual factors).

14   470 F.2d 455 (D.C. Cir. 1972).

15   D.C. Code § 22-3204 (1953).

16   *Id.* § 22-3205 (1932) (emphasis added).

17   470 F.2d at 459.

18   796 P.2d 463 (Ariz. 1990).

suits resulting from "any infringement of copyright or improper or unlawful use of slogans *in your advertising*."[19] When PCS was sued for copyright infringement in the preparation of a business proposal, INA declined to defend on grounds that the infringement had not occurred in advertising. The Arizona Supreme Court held that the modifier *in your advertising* did not reach back to *infringement of copyright*. This would seem to contradict the canon here under discussion, but the holding was justified by the rule that ambiguities in contracts will be interpreted against the party that prepared the contract (*contra proferentem*).

---

19 *Id.* at 465 (emphasis added).

20. Nearest-Reasonable-Referent Canon

When the syntax involves something other than a parallel series of nouns or verbs, a prepositive or postpositive modifier normally applies only to the nearest reasonable referent.

Although this principle is often given the misnomer *last-antecedent canon* (see § 18), it is more accurate to consider it separately and to call it the *nearest-reasonable-referent canon*. Strictly speaking, only pronouns have antecedents, and the canon here under consideration also applies to adjectives, adverbs, and adverbial or adjectival phrases—and it applies not just to words that precede the modifier, but also to words that follow it. Most commonly, the syntax at issue involves an adverbial phrase that follows the referent.

A Prohibition-era case[1] provides a striking example involving grammatically unparallel items with a postpositive modifier. Section 32 of Virginia's Prohibition Act of 1924 provided that "the provisions of this act shall not be construed to prevent any person from manufacturing for his domestic consumption *at his home* . . . wine or cider from fruit of his own raising . . . ."[2] What was modified by *at his home*? Did this mean *manufacturing at his home* or *consumption at his home*—or both? What happened is that the appellant, J.R. Harris, produced wine at his farm in Brunswick County from berries grown there. He intended to take the wine from his farm to his home in Greensville County, where he would consume it. While transporting the wine, Harris was detained and later convicted of unlawfully transporting two gallons of wine.

The Virginia Supreme Court upheld the conviction. The court stated that the "rules of grammar will not be permitted to defeat the purpose of the act,"[3] which was to "prevent the use of ardent

---

1   *Harris v. Commonwealth*, 128 S.E. 578 (Va. 1925).

2   Prohibition Act, Acts 1924, § 32, p. 593 (as quoted in *Harris*, 128 S.E. at 579) (emphasis added).

3   128 S.E. at 579.

spirits as a beverage."⁴ This was a poor, result-oriented decision. In the phrase "manufacturing for his domestic consumption" both *manufacturing* and *consumption* are nouns, but are not nouns in parallel; the second is in a prepositional phrase modifying the first. Only by a contorted reading of the statute does the prepositional phrase *at his home* modify *manufacturing* as well as *consumption* (the adjacent noun).

Another postpositive-modifier case was the Sixth Circuit's decision in *In re Sanders*,⁵ in which the court was called on to determine the reach of an adverbial *during*-clause. Under the Bankruptcy Code, a debtor could not receive a discharge of his debts under Chapter 13 if he had "received a discharge . . . in a case filed under Chapter 7 . . . *during the 4-year period preceding*" the filing of a Chapter 13 petition.⁶ Jason Sanders had filed a Chapter 7 petition on July 29, 2002, and was granted a discharge in that case on February 5, 2003. He then filed a Chapter 13 petition on January 5, 2007—which was more than four years after his Chapter 7 filing, but less than four years after his Chapter 7 discharge. Did the phrase *during the 4-year period* modify the word *discharge* or the word *filed?* Not a difficult question. *Discharge* and *case filed* are not grammatically parallel; the latter is in a prepositional phrase modifying the former. The court correctly held that the four-year period started to run on the date of the *filing* of the Chapter 7 petition. Although it invoked the last-antecedent canon (§ 18), in fact the court was indulging in the common misnomer we mentioned above: The phrasing involved a *referent*, not an *antecedent*.

---

4   *Id.*

5   551 F.3d 397 (6th Cir. 2008).

6   11 U.S.C. § 1328(f) (emphasis added).

21. Proviso Canon

A proviso conditions the principal matter that it qualifies—almost always the matter immediately preceding.

Properly speaking, a proviso is a clause that introduces a condition by the word *provided*.[1] A proviso "is introduced to indicate the effect of certain things which are within the statute but accompanied with the peculiar conditions embraced within the proviso."[2] It modifies the immediately preceding language.

Because of regular abuse of provisos, however, the rule that a proviso introduces a condition has become a feeble presumption. One now often finds *provided that* introducing not a condition to an authorization or imposition, but an exception to it, or indeed even an addition to it. And the authorization or imposition that it modifies is often found not immediately before but several clauses earlier. Because of the variable meaning and variable reach of provisos, they have come to be disfavored by knowledgeable drafters.[3]

A classic case illustrating the proviso canon is *Pennington v. United States*,[4] in which the United States Court of Claims was called on to interpret this text in an appropriations statute:

> Back pay and bounty: For payment of amounts for arrears of pay of two and three year volunteers, for bounty to volunteers, and their widows and legal heirs, for bounty under the act of July 28, 1866, and for amounts for commutation of rations to prisoners of war in rebel States, and to soldiers on furlough, that may be certified to be due by the accounting officers of the Treasury, during the fiscal year 1908, $200,000;

---

1   *Webster's Second New International Dictionary* 1995 (1934).

2   James DeWitt Andrews, "Statutory Construction," in 14 *American Law and Procedure* 1, 48 (James Parker Hall & James DeWitt Andrews eds., rev. ed. 1948).

3   *See* Bryan A. Garner, *Legal Writing in Plain English* 107 & n.1 (2001) (and authorities cited there).

4   48 Ct. Cl. 408 (1913).

> Provided, That in all cases hereafter so certified the said accounting officers shall, in stating balances, follow the decisions of the United States Supreme Court or of the Court of Claims of the United States after the time for appeal has expired, if no appeal be taken, without regard to former settlements or adjudications by their predecessors.[5]

Alexander Pennington had sought to have his military pay increased, arguing that the length of his active service should have been computed to include his years as a West Point cadet. The Comptroller of the Treasury rejected his claim, but later the Supreme Court held that cadet service should be included in term of service. The Comptroller refused to reconsider Pennington's case. Pennington contended that even though his claim did not include backpay or bounty, the proviso in this routine appropriations act functioned as an independent and permanent legislative enactment applicable to "all cases" and all "decisions of the Supreme Court." The Court of Claims rejected this sweeping contention, interpreting the proviso as qualifying only this statute's enacting clause, which involved backpay and bounty. As for Pennington's argument that the proviso required accounting officers to follow United States Supreme Court and Court of Claims decisions in *all* cases—a specification that would not have been needed if it applied only to the small number of cases affected by the enacting clause—the Court of Claims aptly said: "It would be dangerous to charge upon Congress an intention to enact independent legislation so important in its results, because of its use of a few superfluous words in a clause of a statute, named and having all of the characteristics of a proviso."[6]

---

5   *Id.* at 411.

6   *Id.* at 415.

22. Scope-of-Subparts Canon

Material within an indented subpart relates only to that subpart; material contained in unindented text relates to all the following or preceding indented subparts.

In the following passage, the material in boldface relates to all three subparts, and the *if*-clause in subpart (C) relates only to (C):

> 1.1 Xxxx xxxx xxxx xxxxxxxx xxxx xx xxxx xx xxxxxxxx xxx xxxxxxx xxx xxx xxxxxxx:
>
> (A) Xxxx xxxx xxxx xxxxxxxx xxxx xx xxxx xx xxxxxxxx xxx xxxxxxx xxx xxx xxxxxxx;
>
> (B) Xxxx xxxx xxxx xxxxxxxx xxxx xx xxxx xx xxxxxxxx xxx xxxxxxx xxx xxx xxxxxxx;
>
> (C) Xxxx xxxx xxxx xxxxxxxx xxxx xx xxxx xx xxxxxxxx xxx xxxxxxx xxx xxx xxxxxxx; if xxxx xxxx xxxx xxxxxxxx xxxx xx xxxx.
>
> **Xxxx xxxx xxxx xxxxxxxx xxxx xx xxxx xx xxxxxxxx xxx xxxxxxx xxx xxx xxxxxxx. Xxxx xxxx xxxx xxxxxxxx xxxx xx xxxx xx xxxxxxxx.**

Yet a major caveat must accompany this canon. If the circumstances in which the text was created suggest that the formatting was not something that the drafters of the text enacted, then little or no heed should be given to it. In a paper contract, the formatting has credence: the parties, after all, saw and signed the document as prepared. With a legislative assembly, the same may or may not be true. If a legislative printing office formats bills in its own way after their passage, then the formatting is simply not part of the adopted text and is irrelevant. But since the rise of computers, legislators typically vote on fully formatted provisions. So the older a legislative provision is, the less this canon can be relied on.

Let us consider some actual examples.

In *Jama v. Immigration & Customs Enforcement*,[1] the provision at issue read as follows (the crucial text being the italicized language at the end):

(E) Additional removal countries.

> If an alien is not removed to a country under the previous subparagraphs of this paragraph, the Attorney General shall remove the alien to any of the following countries:
>
> (i)   The country from which the alien was admitted to the United States.
>
> (ii) The country in which is located the foreign port from which the alien left for the United States or for a foreign country contiguous to the United States.
>
> (iii) A country in which the alien resided before the alien entered the country from which the alien entered the United States.
>
> (iv) The country in which the alien was born.
>
> (v) The country that had sovereignty over the alien's birthplace when the alien was born.
>
> (vi) The country in which the alien's birthplace is located when the alien is ordered removed.
>
> (vii) If impracticable, inadvisable, or impossible to remove the alien to each country described in a previous clause of this subparagraph, *another country whose government will accept the alien into that country.*[2]

The petitioner, who was born in Somalia, contended that he could not be removed to that country under section (E)(iv) because that country had not agreed to accept him (a condition mentioned in (E)(vii)). The Supreme Court of the United States rightly held that what happens in subpart (vii) stays in subpart (vii): "Each clause is distinct and ends with a period, strongly suggesting that each

---

1   543 U.S. 335 (2005) (per Scalia, J.).

2   8 U.S.C. § 1231(b)(2)(E) (emphasis added).

may be understood completely without reading any further."[3] So the Court concluded that the petitioner could be returned to his birth country even if its advance consent had not been obtained. The same result should have applied even if the periods had been semicolons.

Another United States Supreme Court case illuminates this canon. At issue in *United States v. Hayes*[4] was a provision of the federal Gun Control Act of 1968, which prohibited the possession of a firearm by a person convicted of domestic violence. The Act defined a misdemeanor crime of domestic violence as follows:

> [T]he term "misdemeanor crime of domestic violence" means an offense that—
>
> (i) is a misdemeanor under Federal, State, or Tribal law; and
>
> (ii) has, as an element, the use or attempted use of physical force, or the threatened use of a deadly weapon, committed by a current or former spouse, parent, or guardian of the victim . . . .[5]

The defendant had been convicted of misdemeanor battery in West Virginia. The victim of that battery was his wife, but that relationship was not an element of the crime—that is to say, it was not the misdemeanor of spousal battery. The question, therefore, was whether the phrase *committed by a current or former spouse, parent, or guardian of the victim* modified *use of force* (within the same subpart (ii)) or *offense* (much earlier in the main lead-in clause). If the former, the spousal relationship had to be an element of the crime; if the latter, no. The Court held not, essentially rewriting the statute as follows (added material italicized, deleted material struck through):

> [A] misdemeanor crime of domestic violence means an ~~offense~~ *committed by a current or former spouse, parent, or guardian of the victim* that—

---

3   *Jama*, 543 U.S. at 344.

4   555 U.S. 415 (2009) (per Ginsburg, J.).

5   18 U.S.C. § 921(a)(33)(A).

(i) is a misdemeanor under Federal, State, or Tribal law; and

(ii) has, as an element, the use or attempted use of physical force, or the threatened use of a deadly weapon, ~~committed by a current or former spouse, parent, or guardian of the victim~~.

The case is worth discussing in some detail because it provides an excellent example of how various canons of interpretation point to different outcomes, requiring sound judgment as to which have the strongest force. The Supreme Court's majority, in finding that the inclusion of the crucial phrase in subsection (ii) was merely the consequence of "less-than-meticulous drafting,"[6] relied on these points:

- It is normal usage to speak of *committing an offense*, but not *committing a use* (§ 6 [ordinary-meaning canon]).

- If included in subsection (ii), the word *committed* is superfluous (*use committed by* adds nothing to *use by*) (§ 26 [surplusage canon]).

- If the crucial phrase belonged in subsection (ii), adding another factor to that subsection, it would have been more grammatical for the earlier portion of that subsection to refer to *elements* (plural) rather than *an element* (singular) (§ 17 [grammar canon]).

- An earlier statute defining *misdemeanor crime of domestic violence*, which used the same language—though not divided into subsections—had uniformly been interpreted to apply the *committed by* provision to the earlier noun *offense* rather than the nearest noun *use* (§ 54 [prior-construction canon]).

An intelligent use of the canons. Unfortunately, the majority also relied on legislative history (the remarks of a single Senator) and the question-begging factor of "Congress' manifest purpose,"[7]

---

6   555 U.S. at 423.

7   *Id.* at 427.

which it said would be frustrated because so few statutes had as an element the use of force "by a current or former spouse, parent, or guardian of the victim."

For its part, Chief Justice Roberts's dissent relied on:

- location of the crucial phrase in the indented subsection (ii) (the canon currently under discussion);

- the nearest-reasonable-referent canon (*use of force* rather than *offense*) (§ 20); and

- the rule of lenity, which interprets ambiguous provisions to favor the criminal defendant (§ 49).

The Chief Justice wrote pointedly:

> [T]he "committed by" phrase in clause (ii) is best read to modify the preceding phrase "the use or attempted use of physical force, or the threatened use of a deadly weapon." By not following the usual grammatical rule [of the nearest reasonable referent], the majority's reading requires jumping over two line breaks, clause (i), a semicolon, and the first portion of clause (ii) to reach the more distant antecedent ("offense"). Due to the floating "that" after "offense," if "committed by" modified "offense" the text would read "offense that committed by."[8]

All in all, and on both sides, the case represents admirable use of the canons. Your judicial author joined the dissent, but the case was unquestionably close.

---

8   *Id.* at 431 (Roberts, C.J., dissenting, joined by Scalia, J.) (internal citations omitted).

23. Punctuation Canon

Punctuation is a permissible indicator of meaning.

"[T]he meaning of a statute will typically heed
the commands of its punctuation."

United States Nat'l Bank of Oregon v.
Independent Ins. Agents of America, Inc.,
508 U.S. 439, 454 (1993) (per Souter, J.).

No helpful aid to interpretation has historically received such dismissive treatment from the courts as punctuation—periods, semicolons, commas, parentheses, apostrophes. The original reason was understandable enough. Punctuation was considered of small account because it was thought to be "the work of the engrossing clerk or the printer."[1] And, again in days of yore, it was held that because many legislators voted only on the basis of bills that they heard read aloud—without seeing the printed page— they could take no notice of the punctuation marks.[2] But some modern commentators have extended that justification to posit that "[p]unctuation and other marks of emphasis are not part of the English language."[3] Perhaps not, but they are a part of our system of writing. As the title of a recent best-selling book makes amusingly clear, punctuation can even change the meaning of words. It can convert nouns into verbs, and change a description of a panda bear ("Eats shoots and leaves") into a description of Jesse James ("Eats, shoots, and leaves"). No intelligent construction of a text can ignore its punctuation.

Punctuation in a legal text will rarely change the meaning of a word, but it will often determine whether a modifying phrase or clause applies to all that preceded it or only to a part. Properly placed commas would cancel the last-antecedent canon in the example given earlier (see § 18): If the parents' note read, "You will be punished if you throw a party, or engage in any other activity, that damages the house," the added punctuation would make it

---

1   *Morrill v. State*, 38 Wis. 428, 434 (1875).

2   James DeWitt Andrews, "Statutory Construction," in 14 *American Law and Procedure* 1, 47 (James Parker Hall & James DeWitt Andrews eds., rev. ed. 1948).

3   Roland Burrows, *Interpretation of Documents* 47 (1943).

clear that the final clause modified not just *activity* but *party* as well. (Nonharmful parties are allowed.) Periods and semicolons insulate words from grammatical implications that would otherwise be created by the words that precede or follow them, and parentheses similarly isolate the material they contain.

Commentators have often said that "[p]unctuation is never permitted to control, vary, or modify the plain and clear meaning of the language of the body of the act."[4] This must be a remnant of the former denigration of punctuation that had not been adopted by the legislature; in modern times, we see no rational basis for such a rule. As is the case with other indications of meaning, the body of a legal instrument cannot be found to have a "clear meaning" without taking account of its punctuation. There is no reason to exclude punctuation from this stage of the inquiry. And we disagree with the position that the use of punctuation as an interpretive aid should be relied on only "when all other means fail."[5]

Punctuation is often integral to the sense of written language. In one famous instance, the U.S. Tariff Act of 1872[6] contained a tariff exemption in which a misplaced comma cost the United States Treasury some $1 million. A provision in that statute was supposed to exempt from tariffs the importation of semitropical and tropical fruit plants. But at some point during enactment, a comma after *fruit plants* was repositioned between those words, so that the statute referred to "fruit, plants tropical and semi-tropical."[7] Soon various fruit importers contended that all fruit could be brought into the United States duty-free. At first the Treasury Department overruled these contentions, but then it

4   Francis J. McCaffrey, *Statutory Construction* 54 (1953).

5   *United States v. Ron Pair Enters., Inc.*, 489 U.S. 235, 250 (1989) (O'Connor, J., dissenting) (quoting *Ewing's Lessee v. Burnet*, 36 U.S. (11 Pet.) 41, 54 (1837) (per Baldwin, J.)).

6   42 Cong., ch. 315, June 6, 1872, 17 Stat. §§ 230–58.

7   *Id.* ch. 315, § 5, 17 Stat. § 235.

reversed its position and decided they had merit.[8] The statute was soon amended—in 1874—to close the loophole.[9]

A comma nearly cost a Canadian company $2.13 million. Rogers Communications Inc. contracted with Aliant Inc. to string miles of Rogers's cable lines across thousands of utility poles in the Maritimes for an annual fee of $9.60 per pole. Rogers contended that this price held good for at least the first five years, but Aliant contended that the contract's termination clause could be invoked at any time. It all came down to the effect of the second comma in a provision stating that the agreement

> shall continue in force for a period of five years from the date it is made, and thereafter for successive five-year terms, unless and until terminated by one year's prior notice in writing by either party.[10]

If the second comma had not appeared, the adverbial *unless*-clause would modify only the provision about the successive five-year terms. But with the comma, the phrase *and thereafter for successive five-year terms* becomes a parenthetical element, and the *unless*-clause becomes part of the main sentence. When the issue came before the Canadian Radio-Television and Telecommunications Commission, it properly concluded that "based on the rules of punctuation," the second comma "allows for the termination of the [contract] at any time, without cause, upon one year's written notice."[11] The Commission reversed its decision after Rogers produced an equivalent French-language copy of the contract,

---

8   United States Department of the Treasury, *Synopsis of Sundry Decisions of the Treasury Department* 192 (1874).

9   Tariff Act of 1872, *amended by* 43 Cong., Sess. I, May 9, 1874, ch. 163, 18 Stat. § 43 (moving comma to its correct position). *See also* United States Department of the Treasury, *Synopsis of Sundry Decisions of the Treasury Department* 241 (1875). For a whole series of sentences in which punctuation fundamentally affects meaning, see S.H. Clark, *Interpretation of the Printed Page* 200–26 (1915).

10   Grant Robertson, "The $2 Million Comma," *Globe & Mail*, 7 Aug. 2006, at B1 (we have corrected other aspects of the punctuation by adding a hyphen and a possessive).

11   *Id.*

which had only one possible interpretation, the one favorable to Rogers.[12]

But hostility to punctuation persists. In *Hill v. Conway*,[13] the Vermont Supreme Court confronted a provision of state law dealing with the suspension of drivers' licenses. The provision said that "the suspension period for a conviction for first offense . . . of this title shall be 30 days; for a second conviction 90 days and for a third or subsequent six months, . . . but if a fatality occurs, the suspension shall be for a period of one year."[14] The Commissioner of Motor Vehicles suspended Randall Hill's driver's license for "365 days following his first offense conviction on a charge of careless and negligent operation with death resulting."[15] Hill contended that because the 30-day punishment for a first offense is set apart from the one-year fatality provision by a semicolon, 30 days should have been the limit of his suspension.

The Vermont court held that the semicolon should not prevail. The punctuation of a statute, it said, will not be more important to interpretation than the legislative intent. (See § 67.) Leaping to the most general description of legislative purpose, the court said that the statute was meant to preserve public safety and remove irresponsible drivers from the road. To bar the state from suspending for more than 30 days the license of a driver whose first offense resulted in a death would be "an absurd and irrational result, and inconsistent with the legislative objective as we construe it to be."[16] In short, the court abused the absurdity doctrine (see § 37) and disregarded the rule of lenity (see § 49). Such are the slighting indignities to which semicolons are often subjected.

Punctuation is tiny. So there must be added to the number of those who do not know the rules of punctuation the even greater number of those who are careless. Perhaps more than any other indication of meaning, punctuation is often a scrivener's error,

---

12 Catherine McLean, "Rogers Comma Victory Found in Translation," *Globe & Mail*, 21 Aug. 2007, at B2.

13 463 A.2d 232 (Vt. 1983).

14 Vt. Stat. Ann. tit. 23, § 2506.

15 463 A.2d at 233.

16 *Id.* at 234.

overcome by other textual indications of meaning. So in the case quoted at the beginning of this section, the Supreme Court, after noting that "[t]he unavoidable inference from familiar rules of punctuation" pointed in one direction, concluded that "all of the other evidence from the statute points the other way."[17]

> Against the overwhelming evidence from the structure, language, and subject matter of the 1916 Act there stands only the evidence from the Act's punctuation, too weak to trump the rest. . . . [W]e are convinced that the placement of the quotation marks in the 1916 Act was a simple scrivener's error, a mistake made by someone unfamiliar with the law's object and design. Courts, we have said, should "disregard the punctuation, or repunctuate, if need be, to render the true meaning of the statute."[18]

ᘓᕒ   ᘓᕒ   ᘓᕒ

One punctuation convention merits special mention: the serial comma—that is, the comma after the penultimate item in a series and just before the conjunction (a, b, and c). Authorities on English usage overwhelmingly recommend using the serial comma to prevent ambiguities.[19] Let us say that a testator bequeaths the residue of his enormous estate to "Bob, Sally, George and Jillian." Do the devisees take equal fourths, or do George and Jillian have to

---

17 *United States Nat'l Bank of Or. v. Independent Ins. Agents of Am., Inc.,* 508 U.S. 439, 454, 455 (1993) (per Souter, J.).

18 *Id.* at 462 (quoting *Hammock v. Loan & Trust Co.,* 105 U.S. 77, 84–85 (1881) (per Harlan, J.) (internal quotation marks and citation omitted)).

19 *See, e.g., Garner's Modern American Usage* 676 (3d ed. 2009) ("[O]mitting the final comma may cause ambiguities, whereas including it never will."); *The Chicago Manual of Style* § 6.18, at 312 (16th ed. 2010) ("Chicago strongly recommends this widely practiced usage, blessed by Fowler and other authorities, since it prevents ambiguity"); Kate L. Turabian, *A Manual for Writers of Term Papers, Theses, and Dissertations* §§ 3.68, 3.70, at 50–51 (5th ed. 1987) ("A series of three or more words, phrases, or clauses (like this) takes a comma between each of the elements, and before a conjunction separating the last two."); Patricia T. O'Conner, *Woe Is I* 137 (1996) ("[M]y advice is to stick with using the final comma."); Joseph Gibaldi, *MLA Style Manual* § 3.42b, at 67 (2d ed. 1998) ("Use a comma to separate words, phrases, and clauses in a series."); H.W. Fowler, *A Dictionary of Modern English Usage* 24 (1926) ("The only rule that will obviate . . . uncertainties is that after every item, including the last unless a heavier stop is needed for independent reasons, the comma should be used.").

split a third? If Bob and Sally become avaricious, they might argue that they take thirds, not quarters, as shown by the punctuation.

Despite the well-known semantic hazards of omitting the serial comma, some legal drafters omit it anyway. And some legislative-drafting manuals, as a matter of style, actually adopt the newspaper convention of omitting it.[20]

So although the better practice is to use the serial comma, courts should not rely much if any on its omission. The Arizona Supreme Court made this mistake in interpreting the word *enterprise*,[21] which was statutorily defined as "any corporation, partnership, association, labor union or other legal entity."[22] The court erroneously latched onto the wording *labor union or other legal entity* as a single item in the enumeration because of the lack of a comma, reasoning that "[t]he absence of a comma after the phrase 'labor union' makes a difference,"[23] so that the *other legal entity* must be one similar to a labor union and could not include the state. While the outcome seems correct for other reasons, the absence of a comma assuredly did not "make a difference." Nor did the absence affect meaning earlier in the same statute in the phrases *neglect, abuse or exploitation*[24] (*abuse or exploitation* is not a single category) or in the relative clauses *that has been employed to provide care, that has assumed a legal duty to provide care or that has been appointed by a court to provide care*[25] (a better style would be to put a comma before the *or*). The court did not seem to notice that the serial comma was consistently omitted in the statute—as required by the state's drafting manual—and wrongly attributed meaning to this fact in a particular instance.

---

20 *See, e.g., Arizona Legislative Bill Drafting Manual* 83 (2011–2012).

21 *Estate of Braden v. Arizona*, 266 P.3d 349, 352 (Ariz. 2011) (en banc).

22 Ariz. Rev. Stat. § 46–455(Q).

23 266 P.3d at 352.

24 Ariz. Rev. Stat. § 46–455(B).

25 *Id.*

Contextual Canons

24. Whole-Text Canon

The text must be construed as a whole.

> "In ascertaining the plain meaning of the statute, the court must look to the particular statutory language at issue, as well as the language and design of the statute as a whole."
>
> *K Mart Corp. v. Cartier, Inc.,*
> 486 U.S. 281, 291 (1988) (per Kennedy, J.).

Perhaps no interpretive fault is more common than the failure to follow the whole-text canon, which calls on the judicial interpreter to consider the entire text, in view of its structure and of the physical and logical relation of its many parts. Sir Edward Coke explained the canon in 1628: "[I]t is the most natural and genuine exposition of a statute to construe one part of the statute by another part of the same statute, for that best expresseth the meaning of the makers."[1] Coke added: "If any section [of a law] be intricate, obscure, or doubtful, the proper mode of discovering its true meaning is by comparing it with the other sections, and finding out the sense of one clause by the words or obvious intent of the other."[2] In more modern terms, the California Civil Code states, with regard to private documents: "The whole of a contract is to be taken together, so as to give effect to every part, if reasonably practicable, each clause helping to interpret the other."[3]

Context is a primary determinant of meaning. A legal instrument typically contains many interrelated parts that make up the whole. The entirety of the document thus provides the context for each of its parts. When construing the United States Constitution

---

1   1 Edward Coke, *The First Part of the Institutes of the Laws of England, or a Commentary upon Littleton* § 728, at 381a (1628; 14th ed. 1791). *See* Herbert Broom, *A Selection of Legal Maxims* 440 (Joseph Gerald Pease & Herbert Chitty eds., 8th ed. 1911) ("the construction must be made upon the entire instrument, and not merely upon disjointed parts of it").

2   Coke, *First Part of the Institutes of the Laws of England* at 381a.

3   Cal. Civ. Code § 1641.

in *McCulloch v. Maryland*,[4] Chief Justice John Marshall rightly called for "a fair construction of the whole instrument."[5] More than a century later, Justice Benjamin Cardozo echoed the point in the context of legislation: "[T]he meaning of a statute is to be looked for, not in any single section, but in all the parts together and in their relation to the end in view."[6]

The Supreme Court of the United States has said that statutory construction is a "holistic endeavor,"[7] and the same is true of construing any document.

Many of the other principles of interpretation are derived from the whole-text canon—for example, the rules that an interpretation that furthers the document's purpose should be favored (§ 4 [presumption against ineffectiveness]), that if possible no word should be rendered superfluous (§ 26 [surplusage canon]), that a word or phrase is presumed to bear the same meaning throughout the document (§ 25 [presumption of consistent usage]), that provisions should be interpreted in a way that renders them compatible rather than contradictory (§ 27 [harmonious-reading canon]), that irreconcilably contradictory provisions should be given no effect (§ 29 [irreconcilability canon]), and that associated words bear on one another's meaning (*noscitur a sociis*) (§ 31 [associated-words canon]).

The canon can lend itself to abuse. Properly applied, it typically establishes that only one of the possible meanings that a word or phrase can bear is compatible with use of the same word or phrase elsewhere in the statute; or that one of the possible meanings would cause the provision to clash with another portion of the statute. It is not a proper use of the canon to say that since the overall purpose of the statute is to achieve *x*, any interpretation of the text that limits the achieving of *x* must be disfavored. As we have said, limitations on a statute's reach are as much a part of the statutory purpose as specifications of what is to be done.

---

4   17 U.S. (4 Wheat.) 316 (1819) (per Marshall, C.J.).

5   *Id.* at 406.

6   *Panama Ref. Co. v. Ryan*, 293 U.S. 388, 439 (1935) (Cardozo, J., dissenting).

7   *United Sav. Ass'n of Tex. v. Timbers of Inwood Forest Assocs., Ltd.*, 484 U.S. 365, 371 (1988) (per Scalia, J.).

But the canon can also refute purposivist claims, as in *In re Stinson*,[8] a 2002 bankruptcy case decided in the Western District of Virginia. Stinson alleged that BB&T, a prospective employer, discriminated against him because of an earlier bankruptcy filing. He relied on a 1984 statute disallowing discrimination "with respect to employment,"[9] claiming that this language extended to hiring practices. Although the word *employment* is indeed broad, and might plausibly include hiring decisions, the court rightly rejected Stinson's claim. Why? Because although § 525(b) of the statute prohibited discrimination by private employers "with respect to employment," the preceding provision, § 525(a), which applied to government employment, forbade the government not only to "discriminate with respect to employment against" a person who had been a bankruptcy debtor but also to "deny employment to" or "terminate the employment of" such a person. If both sections had dealt with hiring, then the specification in subpart (a) would have been an exercise in "unwarranted superfluousness."[10] In short, the court used the whole-text canon to reject Stinson's argument that his "interpretation more fully advance[d] the apparent goals of § 525."[11]

---

8   285 B.R. 239 (Bankr. W.D. Va. 2002).

9   11 U.S.C. § 525(b).

10 285 B.R. at 248.

11 *Id.* at 247.

25. Presumption of Consistent Usage

A word or phrase is presumed to bear the same meaning throughout a text; a material variation in terms suggests a variation in meaning.

> "[T]here is a natural presumption that identical words used in different parts of the same act are intended to have the same meaning."
>
> *Atlantic Cleaners & Dyers, Inc. v. United States,*
> 286 U.S. 427, 433 (1932) (per Sutherland, J.).

The correlative points of the presumption of consistent usage make intuitive sense. The preparation of a legal instrument has traditionally been seen as a solemn and deliberative act that requires verbal exactitude. Hence it has long been considered "a sound rule of construction that where a word has a clear and definite meaning when used in one part of a . . . document, but has not when used in another, the presumption is that the word is intended to have the same meaning in the latter as in the former part."[1] And likewise, where the document has used one term in one place, and a materially different term in another, the presumption is that the different term denotes a different idea. If it says *land* in one place and *real estate* later, the second provision presumably includes improvements as well as raw land.

Yet more than most other canons, this one assumes a perfection of drafting that, as an empirical matter, is not often achieved. Though one might wish it were otherwise, drafters more than rarely use the same word to denote different concepts, and often (out of a misplaced pursuit of stylistic elegance) use different words to denote the same concept. Predictably, then, the canon has had its distinguished detractors. Justice Joseph Story called the approach "narrow and mischievous," adding: "It is by no means a correct rule of interpretation to construe the same word in the same sense, wherever it occurs in the same instrument."[2] One of

---

1   Herbert Broom, *A Selection of Legal Maxims* 443 (Joseph Gerald Pease & Herbert Chitty eds., 8th ed. 1911).

2   1 Joseph Story, *Commentaries on the Constitution of the United States* § 454, at 323 (2d ed. 1858).

Story's examples from the Constitution is *state*, which bears four meanings in the document: (1) a section of territory occupied by a political society; (2) the government established by such a society; (3) the society that is organized under such a government; and (4) the people composing such a political society.[3]

Because it is so often disregarded, this canon is particularly defeasible by context. Perhaps under his colleague Story's influence, Chief Justice John Marshall noted: "[I]t has . . . been also said, that the same words have not necessarily the same meaning attached to them when found in different parts of the same instrument: their meaning is controlled by context. This is undoubtedly true."[4] A prime example of defeasance by context was given long ago by Henry Campbell Black: A statute providing that a person who, "being married, . . . marr[ies] any other person during the life of the former husband or wife" is guilty of a felony. The first use of *marry* refers to a valid marriage, but if the statute is going to make any sense, the second use cannot mean the same thing, but must denote going through the ceremony of marriage (though ineffectually).[5] A more careful drafter might have written, in the second instance, *purports to marry* or *goes through a marriage ceremony with*.

But the presumption makes sense when applied (as it usually is) pragmatically. In a 1980 case,[6] the Supreme Court of the United States had to decide whether the word *filed* bore the same meaning in two provisions contained in the same section of the Equal Employment Opportunity Act. The respondent argued that it meant different things. The Court held: "In the end, we cannot accept respondent's position without unreasonably giving the word 'filed' two different meanings in the same section of the statute."[7] And the Court emphasized the besetting sin of short-term, expedient interpretations: "Even if the interests of justice might be

---

3   *Id.*

4   *Cherokee Nation v. Georgia*, 30 U.S. (5 Pet.) 1, 19 (1831) (per Marshall, C.J.).

5   Henry Campbell Black, *Handbook on the Construction and Interpretation of the Laws* 146–47 (2d ed. 1911).

6   *Mohasco Corp. v. Silver*, 447 U.S. 807 (1980) (per Stevens, J.).

7   *Id.* at 826.

served in this particular case by a bifurcated construction of that word, in the long run, experience teaches that strict adherence to the procedural requirements specified by the legislature is the best guarantee of evenhanded administration of the law."[8]

The presumption of consistent usage applies also when different sections of an act or code are at issue. In a 1988 case, the Iowa Supreme Court was called on to decide whether *serious mental impairment* meant the same thing in the statutory section dealing with involuntary hospitalization as it did in another section dealing with habeas corpus petitions for release from involuntary hospitalization.[9] The psychiatric hospital argued that involuntary hospitalization entailed a more stringent standard for *serious mental impairment* than did the continued commitment of a patient who challenged the prolonged hospitalization against his will. Although in one place the statute spelled out three elements for involuntary hospitalization in the first instance—(1) mental illness, (2) deficiency of judgment, and (3) dangerousness—the hospital contended that the phrase *serious mental impairment* took on a different meaning in the later provision relating to continued confinement (dropping the dangerousness requirement). The court sensibly held that the two uses of the phrase—one in § 229.13 of the Iowa Code and the other in § 229.37—bore an identical meaning that included dangerousness.[10]

Yet the presumption of consistent usage can hardly be said to apply across the whole *corpus juris*. Frequently when a court is called on to construe a statutory word or phrase, counsel for one side will argue that it must bear the well-established or unavoidable meaning that the same word or phrase has in a different statute altogether. Without more, the argument does not have much force: "[T]he mere fact that the words are used in each instance is not a sufficient reason for treating a decision on the meaning of the words of one statute as authoritative on the construction of

---

8   *Id.*

9   *B.A.A. v. Chief Med. Officer, Univ. of Iowa Hosps.*, 421 N.W.2d 118 (Iowa 1988).

10   *Id.* at 125 (citing Iowa Code § 229.1(2)).

another statute."[11] But the more connection the cited statute has with the statute under consideration, the more plausible the argument becomes. If it was enacted at the same time, and dealt with the same subject, the argument could even be persuasive.

---

11 Rupert Cross, *Precedent in English Law* 192 (1961).

26. Surplusage Canon

If possible, every word and every provision is to be given effect (*verba cum effectu sunt accipienda*[1]). None should be ignored. None should needlessly be given an interpretation that causes it to duplicate another provision or to have no consequence.

> "These words cannot be meaningless, else they would not have been used."
>
> *United States v. Butler,*
> 297 U.S. 1, 65 (1936) (per Roberts, J.).

The surplusage canon holds that it is no more the court's function to revise by subtraction than by addition. A provision that seems to the court unjust or unfortunate (creating the so-called *casus male inclusus*) must nonetheless be given effect. As Chief Justice John Marshall explained: "It would be dangerous in the extreme, to infer from extrinsic circumstances, that a case for which the words of an instrument expressly provide, shall be exempted from its operation."[2] Or in the words of Thomas M. Cooley: "[T]he courts must . . . lean in favor of a construction which will render every word operative, rather than one which may make some idle and nugatory."[3] This is true not just of legal texts but of all sensible writing: "Whenever a reading arbitrarily ignores linguistic components or inadequately accounts for them, the reading may be presumed improbable."[4]

Sometimes lawyers will seek to have a crucially important word ignored—such as *only*, *solely*, or *exclusively*—and nontextualist judges will often oblige them. In one such case, *Abright v.*

---

1   Ulpian, *Digest* 2.7.5.2 ("Words are to be taken as having an effect.").

2   *Sturges v. Crowninshield,* 17 U.S. (4 Wheat.) 122, 202 (1819) (per Marshall, C.J.). *See* Ernst Freund, *Interpretation of Statutes*, 65 U. Pa. L. Rev. 207, 218 (1917) ("[T]he legislator is presumed to, as in fact he does, choose his words deliberately intending that every word shall have a binding effect.").

3   Thomas M. Cooley, *A Treatise on the Constitutional Limitations Which Rest upon the Legislative Power of the States of the American Union* 58 (1868). *See Kungys v. United States*, 485 U.S. 759, 778 (1988) (Scalia, J., plurality opinion) (calling it a "cardinal rule of statutory interpretation that no provision should be construed to be entirely redundant.").

4   E.D. Hirsch, *Validity in Interpretation* 236 (1967).

Shapiro,[5] the New York Rent Stabilization Code excluded from rent stabilization "housing accommodations used *exclusively* for professional, commercial, or other nonresidential purposes."[6] In this particular case, which took 13 years for the courts finally to resolve, 52 physicians used their residential apartments for professional purposes, as a result of which the landlords began charging higher rent based on the fair market value of the building used as professional premises. The physicians sued on grounds that their rents had been stabilized and they were not using the premises *exclusively* for professional purposes since they also continued to live there. The Appellate Division essentially read the word *exclusively* out of the statute and allowed the landlords to have their higher rent on wholly nontextual grounds reflecting purposivism: "[R]ent stabilization was not adopted to provide a means for those with the ability to pay to avoid having to pay a market rent for premises in which to practice their profession."[7] Perhaps not. But the legislature used the adverb *exclusively*, and the court was wrong to negate its clear meaning.

Lawyers rarely argue that an entire provision should be ignored—but it does happen. For example, in *Fortec Constructors v. United States*,[8] the quality-control paragraph of a construction contract with the Army read as follows:

> All work . . . shall be subject to inspection and test by the Government at all reasonable times and at all places prior to acceptance. Any such inspection and test is for the sole benefit of the Government and shall not relieve the Contractor of the responsibility of providing quality control measures to assure that the work strictly complies with the contract requirements. *No inspection or test by the Government shall be construed as constituting or implying acceptance.*[9]

---

5   458 N.Y.S.2d 913 (App. Div. 1983), *appeal after remand*, 614 N.Y.S.2d 408 (App. Div. 1994).

6   N.Y. Rent Stabilization Code § 2520.11(n) (emphasis added).

7   614 N.Y.S.2d at 409.

8   760 F.2d 1288 (Fed. Cir. 1985).

9   *Id.* at 1292 (emphasis in original).

When the Army demanded that the contractor demolish and re-construct noncompliant work, the contractor protested that the on-site Army inspector had failed to notify Fortec of the defects and that this silence constituted an acceptance of the original work. The court correctly rejected this argument:

> To agree with Fortec's contention would render clause 10 meaningless. This court must be guided by the well accepted and basic principle that an interpretation that gives a reasonable meaning to all parts of the contract will be preferred to one that leaves portions of the contract meaningless. Therefore, Fortec's contention is rejected for being inconsistent with contract clause 10. The Corps quality assurance inspections did not constitute an acceptance of the work.[10]

More frequently, however, this canon prevents not the total disregard of a provision, but instead an interpretation that renders it pointless. Because legal drafters should not include words that have no effect, courts avoid a reading that renders some words altogether redundant.[11] If a provision is susceptible of (1) a meaning that gives it an effect already achieved by another provision, or that deprives another provision of all independent effect, and (2) another meaning that leaves both provisions with some independent operation, the latter should be preferred.

Put to a choice, however, a court may well prefer ordinary meaning to an unusual meaning that will avoid surplusage. So like all other canons, this one must be applied with judgment and discretion, and with careful regard to context. It cannot always be dispositive because (as with most canons) the underlying proposition is not *invariably* true. Sometimes drafters *do* repeat themselves and *do* include words that add nothing of substance, either

---

10 *Id.*

11 *See, e.g., Lowe v. SEC*, 472 U.S. 181, 207 n.53 (1985) (per Stevens, J.) ("[W]e must give effect to every word that Congress used in the statute."); *Reiter v. Sonotone Corp.*, 442 U.S. 330, 339 (1979) (per Burger, C.J.) ("In construing a statute we are obliged to give effect, if possible, to every word Congress used."); *Burdon Cent. Sugar Ref. Co. v. Payne*, 167 U.S. 127, 142 (1897) (per Fuller, C.J.) ("[T]he contract must be so construed as to give meaning to all its provisions, and . . . that interpretation would be incorrect which would obliterate one portion of the contract in order to enforce another part . . .").

out of a flawed sense of style or to engage in the ill-conceived but lamentably common belt-and-suspenders approach. Doublets and triplets abound in legalese: *Execute and perform*—what satisfies one but not the other? *Rest, residue, and remainder*—could a judge interpret these as referring to three distinct things? *Peace and quiet*—when is peace not quiet? A clever interpreter could create unforeseen meanings or legal effects from this stylistic mannerism. This consequence, indeed, has befallen the phrase *indemnify and hold harmless*: The two parts of the phrase are historically synonymous, but some modern courts have purported to find distinct senses.[12] The English law lords once held, quite properly, that the second part of the statutory phrase *in addition to and not in derogation of* added nothing but emphasis.[13] Before the 2007 revisions, the Federal Rules of Civil Procedure contained varying requirements *for cause, for good cause, for cause shown,* and *for good cause shown.* There was no reason to believe that, after removal of the attendant modifiers, the cause did not have to be good or did not have to be shown.

A United States Supreme Court case testing the canon's application against duplication of meaning was *Moskal v. United States.*[14] The defendant had participated in a scheme that altered the odometer readings on used vehicles, and then obtained (through the mail from another state) new titles that showed the falsified readings. The state officials who issued the new titles did not know that the readings were fraudulent. The defendant was convicted under 18 U.S.C. § 2314, which punishes anyone who, "with unlawful or fraudulent intent, transports in interstate . . . commerce any falsely made, forged, altered or counterfeited securities . . . , knowing the same to have been falsely made, forged, altered or counterfeited." The titles were obviously not "forged, altered or counterfeited"; Moskal argued that they were not "falsely made" either, since those who made them believed them to be accurate. The Court rejected this argument in part because it would make

---

12 *See Garner's Dictionary of Legal Usage* 443–45 (3d ed. 2011).

13 *Davies v. Powell Dyffryn Assoc. Collieries,* [1942] 1 All E.R. 657.

14 498 U.S. 103 (1990) (per Marshall, J.).

"falsely made" redundant with "forged" and "counterfeited," and would thus "violate[] the established principle that a court should give effect, if possible, to every clause or word of a statute."[15]

We agree with (and one of us wrote) the dissent, which explained Congress's quadrupling of near-synonyms:

> As the United States conceded at oral argument, and as any dictionary will confirm, "forged" and "counterfeited" mean the same thing. Since iteration is obviously afoot in the relevant passage, there is no justification for extruding an unnatural meaning out of "falsely made" simply in order to avoid iteration. The entire phrase "falsely made, forged, altered, or counterfeited" is self-evidently not a listing of differing and precisely calibrated terms, but a collection of near synonyms which describes the product of the general crime of forgery.[16]

Yet words with no meaning—language with no substantive effect—should be regarded as the exception rather than the rule. In one interesting case, the absurdity doctrine (§ 37) might have tempted a court to disregard a word (*male*) incorporated by reference into a statute, but that doctrine could not overcome the constitutional provision that had been incorporated. In *People ex rel. Ahrens v. English*,[17] an Illinois suffrage statute provided that any woman 21 or older could vote for school officers if she belonged to one of the three classes mentioned in Article 7 of the Illinois Constitution. Those classes consisted of (1) those who were electors in the state on April 1, 1848; (2) those who were naturalized before January 1, 1870; and (3) male citizens of the United States over the age of 21. The Illinois Supreme Court recognized that reading the word *male* as being incorporated into the statute "is wholly inconsistent with the entire scope and the manifest intent of the act,"[18] and seemed prepared, because of the absurdity, to disregard that word insofar as interpretation of the statute was concerned. It found, however, that the constitutional provision *governed* the

---

15   *Id.* at 109 (internal quotation marks omitted).

16   *Id.* at 120–21 (Scalia, J., dissenting).

17   29 N.E. 678 (Ill. 1892).

18   *Id.* at 679.

voting qualifications for the office in question, and that provision could not be disregarded.[19] The would-be voter's petition for mandamus was denied.[20]

At least one commentator has suggested that the surplusage canon is fundamentally wrong: "Statutes are not always carefully drafted. Legal drafters often include redundant language on purpose to cover any unforeseen gaps or simply for no good reason at all. And legislators are not likely to waste time or energy arguing to remove redundancy when there are more important issues to address. Thus, the presumptions [underlying this canon] simply do not match political reality."[21] We think the objection ill-founded for four reasons. First, the surplusage canon is well known: Statutes *should* be carefully drafted, and encouraging courts to ignore sloppily inserted words results in legislative free-riding and increasingly slipshod drafting. Nothing should be included in a legal instrument "for no good reason at all." Second, general language—not redundancy—is the accepted method for covering "unforeseen gaps." Third, if the legislators themselves are not mindful of ferreting out words and phrases that contribute nothing to meaning, they ought to hire eagle-eyed editors who are. (Many, in fact, do.) Finally, when a drafter *has* engaged in the retrograde practice of stringing out synonyms and near-synonyms (e.g., *transfer, assign, convey, alienate, or set over*), the bad habit is so easily detectable that the canon can be appropriately discounted: *Alienate* will not be held to mean something wholly distinct from *transfer, convey,* and *assign,* etc.[22]

---

19 *Id.* at 679–80.

20 *Id.* at 680.

21 Linda D. Jellum, *Mastering Statutory Interpretation* 104 (2008).

22 *See Garner's Dictionary of Legal Usage* 294–97 (3d ed. 2011) (s.v. "Doublets, Triplets, and Synonym-Strings").

27. Harmonious-Reading Canon

The provisions of a text should be interpreted in a way that renders them compatible, not contradictory.

> "[O]ne part is not to be allowed to defeat another, if by any reasonable construction the two can be made to stand together."
> Thomas M. Cooley,
> *A Treatise on the Constitutional Limitations*
> *Which Rest upon the Legislative Power of the*
> *States of the American Union* 58 (1868).

The imperative of harmony among provisions is more categorical than most other canons of construction because it is invariably true that intelligent drafters do not contradict themselves (in the absence of duress). Hence there can be no justification for needlessly rendering provisions in conflict if they can be interpreted harmoniously. But if context and other considerations (including the application of other canons) make it impossible to apply the harmonious-reading canon, the principles governing conflicting provisions (see §§ 28 [general/specific canon] and 29 [irreconcilability canon]) must be applied.

How does this pragmatic canon apply in practice? In *State v. Bowsher*,[1] the Arizona Supreme Court was faced with two statutory provisions that dealt with the beginning of a probated criminal sentence. One of them provided that "a period of probation commences on the day it is imposed or as designated by the court"[2]; but another provided that a probationary period must begin "without delay."[3] The trial court had sentenced Brad Bowsher to serve two consecutive four-year probationary terms. On appeal, Bowsher argued that the sentence was unlawful because the second period could not start "without delay" but must start four years after the date of sentencing. The Arizona court rightly held to the contrary. If *without delay* in the second provision prohibited even consecutive probationary periods, it would flatly contradict *or as designated by the court* in the first provision. The reconciliation was

---

1   242 P.3d 1055 (Ariz. 2010).

2   Ariz. Rev. Stat. § 13-903(A).

3   Ariz. Rev. Stat. § 13-901(A).

to interpret the first provision as allowing consecutive sentences, and to interpret the second as requiring the later sentence to commence immediately ("without delay") on expiration of the first. In short, the court read the two sections of the statute harmoniously so that one did not nullify the other.

Not every harsh result indicates a contradiction that must be "reconciled" away. Double taxation, for example. In *Commissioner v. Beck's Estate*,[4] an income-tax provision of the Internal Revenue Code treated as "income" of the grantor of a trust "any part of the income of a trust [that is] applied to the payment of premiums upon policies of insurance on the life of the grantor."[5] Meanwhile, a gift-tax provision of the Code imposed a tax on "the transfer . . . of property by gift . . . whether the transfer is in trust or otherwise, whether the gift is direct or indirect."[6] The problem in *Beck's Estate* was that a portion of the income of an irrevocable insurance trust was used to pay annual premiums for the life-insurance policies of the grantor. While the grantor agreed that he had to pay income tax on the value of those premiums, he deducted the premium amount from his gift-tax return in the year when the trust was created and funded. The IRS disallowed the gift-tax deduction. In the consequent litigation, Beck's estate argued that it would be "unbearably inconsistent . . . to tax the value of that income as a gift from him [when the trust was established] . . . and thereafter to tax those payments as his income."[7]

With Judge Jerome Frank writing for the Second Circuit, the court decided that both income taxes and gift taxes were due for the value of the premiums. The court reasoned that the gift-tax and income-tax provisions had originally been enacted as part of the same act, indicating Congress's intention that they overlap. Further, Judge Frank memorably noted that there would have been straightforward ways for legislators to arrive at Beck's estate's desired result: "For Congress knows—who would not?—how to

---

4   129 F.2d 243 (2d Cir. 1942) (per Frank, J.).

5   26 U.S.C. § 167(a)(3).

6   *Id.* § 501(a).

7   *Beck v. Commissioner*, 43 B.T.A. 147, 148 (1940).

prevent such double taxation. A short sentence would have done the trick. The familiar 'easy-to-say-so-if-that-is-what-was-meant' rule of statutory interpretation has full force here. The silence of Congress is strident."[8]

The harmonious-reading canon is just as applicable to contracts as it is to statutes. A Third Circuit case exemplifies this principle, though its application of the principle is questionable. In *J.E. Faltin Motor Transp., Inc. v. Eazor Express, Inc.,*[9] a lease for the use of a trailer contained arguably contradictory provisions. Section 1 contained broad language that "no provision in this contract shall be construed to increase the legal liability of any party hereto."[10] Section 3.5, meanwhile, stated that the lessee would indemnify the lessor "for any loss or damage [to the trailer] . . . arising out of the . . . possession of said trailer, or arising from any other cause."[11] After the trailer was destroyed by fire, the lessor, Faltin Motor, sued the lessee, Eazor, to make good on the § 3.5 indemnity. The court found no inconsistency between the two provisions: § 1 meant, it said (implausibly), that there can be no increase in liability beyond what is stated in the contract (including § 3.5). A better resolution, mentioned by the court but not dispositively,[12] would have been to hold that the specific provision (§ 3.5) governed over the general (§ 1)—which brings us to our next blackletter canon.

---

8   129 F.2d at 245.

9   273 F.2d 444 (3d Cir. 1960).

10   *Id.* at 445.

11   *Id.*

12   *Id.*

28. General/Specific Canon

If there is a conflict between a general provision and a specific provision, the specific provision prevails (*generalia specialibus non derogant*).

The general/specific canon, like the irreconcilability canon (see § 29), deals with what to do when conflicting provisions simply cannot be reconciled—when the attribution of no permissible meaning can eliminate the conflict. Which provision must yield? Or must they both be disregarded? Under this canon, the specific provision is treated as an exception to the general rule.[1] Jeremy Bentham supplied the rationale: "[T]he particular provision is established upon a nearer and more exact view of the subject than the general, of which it may be regarded as a correction."[2] Or think of it this way: the specific provision comes closer to addressing the very problem posed by the case at hand and is thus more deserving of credence.

The most common example of irreconcilable conflict—and the easiest to deal with—involves a general prohibition that is contradicted by a specific permission, or a general permission that is contradicted by a specific prohibition. Imagine, for example, a sign at the entrance to a park that reads: "No wheeled vehicles. Bicycles and baby carriages may be walked along the paths." The second sentence, which flatly contradicts the first, governs when a bicycle or baby carriage is in the park—a specific exception to the general prohibition. The same effect ordinarily occurs even when the contradictory provisions are separated by intervening text.

---

1   *See, e.g., Radzanower v. Touche Ross & Co.*, 426 U.S. 148, 153 (1976) (per Stewart, J.) ("It is a basic principle of statutory construction that a statute dealing with a narrow, precise, and specific subject is not submerged by a later enacted statute covering a more generalized spectrum."); *Morton v. Mancari*, 417 U.S. 535, 550–51 (1974) (per Blackmun, J.) ("Where there is no clear intention otherwise, a specific statute will not be controlled or nullified by a general one, regardless of the priority of enactment."). *See also* Joel Prentiss Bishop, *Commentaries on the Written Laws and Their Interpretation* § 112a, at 106–07 (1882) ("[T]he general and specific in legal doctrine may mingle without antagonism, the specific being construed simply to impose restrictions and limitations on the general.").

2   Jeremy Bentham, "A Complete Code of Laws," in 3 *The Works of Jeremy Bentham* 210 (John Bowring ed., 1843).

Note that the general/specific canon does not mean that the existence of a contradictory specific provision voids the general provision. Only its application to cases covered by the specific provision is suspended; it continues to govern all other cases. So if a lease provides in one clause that water is provided, and in another it provides that the tenant is responsible for all utilities, the tenant will still be liable to pay for all utilities other than water.

The rule applies to contradictory provisions in a single statute no less than to contradictory provisions in a contract. Consider a case from Missouri.[3] The domestic-relations statute stated: "If a party requests a decree of legal separation rather than a decree of dissolution of marriage, the court shall grant the decree in that form."[4] But a different section of the statute contained a provision dealing with the specific situation in which one of the parties claims that the marriage is irretrievably broken: "If both of the parties by petition or otherwise have stated under oath that the marriage is irretrievably broken, or one of the parties has so stated and the other has not denied it, the court, after considering the aforesaid petition or statement, and after a hearing thereon shall make a finding whether or not the marriage is irretrievably broken and shall enter an order of dissolution or dismissal accordingly."[5]

Here is what happened. Mrs. McCallister filed a petition for legal separation. In response, Mr. McCallister stated in a verified pleading (i.e., under oath) that the marriage was irretrievably broken and requested a dissolution of the marriage. Mrs. McCallister opposed dissolution and denied that the marriage was irretrievably broken, but did not do so under oath. The trial court entered a decree of legal separation. On appeal, Mr. McCallister contended that § 452.320.1 required that the denial that the marriage was irretrievably broken had to be under oath. The appellate court agreed and proceeded, quite justifiably, to treat the section dealing specifically with a claim of irretrievable breakdown as an

---

3   *McCallister v. McCallister*, 809 S.W.2d 423 (Mo. Ct. App. 1991).

4   Mo. Rev. Stat. § 452.305.2 (1986).

5   *Id.* § 452.320.1.

exception to the general rule about a party's request for a legal separation.[6]

But what about contradictory provisions in two separate statutes—an earlier general prohibition (or permission) contradicted by a later specific permission (or prohibition), or an earlier specific permission (or prohibition) contradicted by a later general prohibition (or permission)? Does the rule apply to these? And does its applicability depend on which provision is enacted later?

The reason why the canon might be thought inapplicable to seeming contradictions in successive statutes is simple: No one (or almost no one) thinks that the way contradictions are to be resolved in single instruments, including single statutes, is that the provision appearing later in the instrument prevails. But it *is* a principle of statutory construction that a later-enacted statute that contradicts an earlier one effectively repeals it (see § 55). So where there is a conflict between a general provision and a specific one, whichever was enacted later might be thought to prevail. But that analysis disregards the principle behind the general/specific canon—namely, that the two provisions are not in conflict, but can exist in harmony. The specific provision does not negate the general one entirely, but only in its application to the situation that the specific provision covers. Hence the canon does apply to successive statutes. Indeed, that is perhaps its most common application, since legislators are often—despite the presumption to the contrary—unfamiliar with enactments of their predecessors. They unwittingly contradict them.

A Nebraska case provides an example.[7] Nebraska's Age Discrimination Act, enacted in 1963, prohibited discrimination on the basis of age. In 1986, however, the legislature amended the statutes governing retirement of state employees to give retirees the choice of receiving their pensions in a lump-sum payment if they were under the age of 55, but with the forfeiture of some benefits if they were over 55. Nebraska's Equal Opportunity Com-

6   *McCallister*, 809 S.W.2d at 427.

7   *Nebraska Equal Opportunity Comm'n v. State Emps. Ret. Sys.*, 471 N.W.2d 398 (Neb. 1991).

mission sued the State Employees Retirement System on behalf of an over-55 retiree, contending that the age-based forfeiture was prohibited. The Nebraska Supreme Court correctly held that the specific provisions of the 1986 retirement legislation prevailed over the general age-discrimination prohibition of the 1963 statute. When statutes are in conflict, as when the provisions of a single text are in conflict, the specific controls over the general.[8]

The perceptive reader may have observed that this case would have come out the same way even without the benefit of the general/specific canon. For even without it, the later statute would have been an implicit repeal of the earlier statute's application to state-employee retirement. So the canon makes no difference when it is the specific provision that has been enacted later. Implicit repeal of the earlier statute's application to the specific situation would produce the same effect: The specific would prevail. But the general/specific canon makes all the difference if the general provision has been enacted later.

The Supreme Court of the United States confronted such a situation in *Morton v. Mancari*.[9] The Indian Reorganization Act of 1934[10] provided an employment preference for qualified Native Americans in the Bureau of Indian Affairs. The Equal Employment Act of 1972[11] prohibited racial discrimination in federal employment. The Supreme Court rejected the claim by non-Native American employees of the BIA that the preference had been repealed, reasoning in part as follows:

> [T]he Indian preference statute is a specific provision applying to a very specific situation. The 1972 Act, on the other hand, is of general application. Where there is no clear intention otherwise, a specific statute will not be controlled or nullified by a general one, regardless of the priority of enactment.[12]

---

8   *Id.* at 400.

9   417 U.S. 535 (1974) (per Blackmun, J.).

10   25 U.S.C. § 461 et seq.

11   42 U.S.C. § 2000e-16(a) (1970 ed., Supp. II).

12   *Morton*, 417 U.S. at 550–51.

This type of reasoning assumes two provisions of equal dignity. The Louisiana Supreme Court has misapplied it to a general constitutional provision that should have been held to nullify a statutory one. A Louisiana statute provided that all property of a specific orphans' home was "exempted from all taxation, either by the State, parish, or city in which it is situated, any law to the contrary notwithstanding."[13] Thirty-two years after that statute was passed, Louisiana adopted a new constitutional provision that "[a]ll property shall be taxed in proportion to its value."[14] When the City of New Orleans tried to tax the orphans' home, the home sued to enforce the exemption. The Louisiana Supreme Court incorrectly held that the specific provision antedating the more general provision remained operative. It limited its application of the canon by a condition with which we do not agree. It said that "[a] general statute, *without negative words*, will not repeal the particular provisions of the former."[15] In other words, while "all property shall be taxed" yielded to the canon, "no property is exempt" would not have; the specific exemption for the orphanage would have been repealed. We see no basis for this distinction. More important, though, the general/specific canon applies only to provisions that are of the same level of legal hierarchy. A specific statutory provision that contravenes a general constitutional injunction or prohibition is invalid.

Sometimes it is difficult to determine whether a provision is a general or a specific one. In *Radzanower v. Touche Ross & Co.*,[16] the Supreme Court of the United States had to decide whether a suit against a national bank for violation of the Securities Exchange Act of 1934 could be brought under the venue provision contained in that statute,[17] which allowed suit in any district where the violation occurred, or could be brought only under the exclusive-venue provision for suits against national banks established by the 1878

---

13 Act of March 12, 1836.

14 La. Const. art. 118 (1868).

15 *City of New Orleans v. Poydras Orphan Asylum*, 33 La. Ann. 850, 854 (La. 1881) (emphasis added).

16 426 U.S. 148 (1976) (per Stewart, J.).

17 15 U.S.C. § 78aa.

National Bank Act,[18] which limited venue to the district in which the bank was established. The Court held that the latter provision governed, in part because "[i]t is a basic principle of statutory construction that a statute dealing with a narrow, precise, and specific subject is not submerged by a later enacted statute covering a more generalized spectrum."[19] Yet there is great force in what Justice Stevens wrote in dissent:

> [B]oth of these statutes are special venue statutes. Neither party relies on the general venue provision in 28 U.S.C. § 1391. One relies on a special statute for one kind of litigant—national banks; the other relies on a special statute for one kind of litigation—cases arising under the Securities Exchange Act of 1934. The precise issue before us involves only a tiny fraction of the cases in either special category: Most litigation against national banks does not arise under the Securities Exchange Act; and most litigation arising under the Securities Exchange Act does not involve national banks. Thus, with equal logic we might describe either statute as creating an exception from the somewhat more general provisions of the other.[20]

---

18   12 U.S.C. § 94.

19   426 U.S. at 153.

20   *Id.* at 159 (Stevens, J., dissenting).

29. Irreconcilability Canon

If a text contains truly irreconcilable provisions at the same level of generality, and they have been simultaneously adopted, neither provision should be given effect.

When reconciliation of conflicting provisions cannot reasonably be achieved, the proper resolution is to apply the unintelligibility canon (§ 16) and to deny effect to both provisions.[1] After all, if we cannot "make a valid choice between two differing interpretations, . . . we are left with the consequence that a text means nothing in particular at all."[2]

Courts rarely reach this result. If both of the contradictory provisions have been adopted simultaneously, and if the general/specific canon cannot resolve the conflict, some authorities suggest that the later-appearing provision must prevail (on the theory that, appearing later in the text, it presumably repeals the earlier provision).[3] Others suggest, quite to the contrary, that the earlier-appearing provision must prevail (because of the "priority of its position").[4] Yet neither of those positions bears any relationship in the usual case to the text's probable meaning. Unless the text has been amended, the later provision is *not* later in time, having been adopted simultaneously with the earlier one—so it cannot realistically be thought to have repealed the earlier one.

---

1   Henry Campbell Black, *Handbook on the Construction and Interpretation of the Laws* 154–56 (2d ed. 1911). *See* Francis J. McCaffrey, *Statutory Construction* 54–55 (1953); Roland Burrows, *Interpretation of Documents* 85–86 (1943).

2   E.D. Hirsch, *Validity in Interpretation* 251 (1967).

3   *See* 1 Jabez Gridley Sutherland, *Statutory Construction* § 268, at 514 (2d ed. 1904) ("The different sections or provisions of the same statute or Code should be so construed as to harmonize and give effect to each; but, if there is an irreconcilable conflict, the later in position prevails."); Black, *Handbook on the Construction and Interpretation of the Laws* 168 (2d ed. 1911) (stating that "it is a general rule that where there is an irreconcilable conflict between different sections or parts of the same statute, the last words stand, and those in conflict with them are repealed").

4   *See* 17 Am.Jur.2d *Contracts* § 385, at 373 (2004). *See also* Cal. Civ. Code § 1070 (stating, as regards grants, that "[i]f several parts of a grant are absolutely irreconcilable, the former part prevails").

A third way of cutting this Gordian knot of irreconcilable provisions is to enforce the provision "relatively more important or principal to the [instrument]."[5] This approach, advocated by Samuel Williston, has been approved by the New York Court of Appeals.[6] It will often be unavailable, as when a loan contract contains conflicting interest rates or a construction contract contains conflicting performance dates. And where it is available, it will amount to a search for nonexistent "intent"—not much different from the approach that Joel Prentiss Bishop long ago recommended for contracts: "[T]o regard but lightly the technical rules . . . and, feeling after the intent of the parties, to discard on the one hand, and retain on the other, what in the result will best give effect to such intent."[7]

But outright invalidation is admittedly an unappealing course—especially when the matter covered by the contradictory provisions is central to the document or statute in question. One can often resort to some other rule of interpretation—in a contract with conflicting interest rates, perhaps to the rule that the document should be construed *contra proferentem* (see p. 427), imposing the lower rate of interest on the loan company that prepared the document; or in a criminal statute applying the contradictory provision that favors the defendant, under the rule of lenity (§ 49). Often there will be a background rule of law that steps in to supplant the contradictory provisions. For example, when a contract contains contradictory provisions for the time of performance, a reasonable time will be presumed; and in some jurisdictions perhaps a legal rate of interest will be presumed when interest is clearly required but its amount not specified. These devices will often save the document.

If irreconcilability occurs with penal provisions, the result should favor the accused (see § 49 [rule of lenity]). In *State v. Taylor,*[8] two sections of a statute adopted at the same time con-

---

5   *Israel v. Chabra*, 906 N.E.2d 374, 380 n.3 (N.Y. 2009) (quoting 11 Richard A. Lord, *Williston on Contracts* § 32:15, at 507–10 (4th ed. 2007)).

6   *Id.*

7   Joel Prentiss Bishop, *Commentaries on the Law of Contracts* § 386, at 151 (1887).

8   85 S.W. 564 (Mo. 1905).

flicted. One section declared it a felony to willfully and maliciously maim or wound someone else's horse,[9] and the very next section declared the same conduct a misdemeanor.[10] After maiming a horse inside a building that he broke into, Taylor was prosecuted for second-degree burglary, defined to include "breaking and entering . . . with intent to . . . commit any felony therein."[11] On appeal of his conviction, Taylor argued that because he had committed a misdemeanor under § 1988, he could not lawfully be charged with second-degree burglary. The court agreed and threw out the conviction—but on the wrong grounds: "Where there is an irreconcilable conflict between different sections or parts of the same statute, the last words stand, and those which are in conflict with them, so far as there is a conflict, are repealed; that is, the part of a statute later in position in the same act or section is deemed later in time, and prevails over repugnant parts occurring before, though enacted and to take effect at the same time."[12] By the court's reasoning, if the misdemeanor provision had come first and the felony provision second, Taylor's conviction would have been affirmed. But this result would be erroneous under the rule of lenity. Because a clash of this kind gives rise to an ambiguity, lenity should be the guiding principle.

---

9   Mo. Rev. Stat. § 1987 (1899).

10 *Id.* § 1988.

11 *Id.* § 1886.

12 85 S.W. at 567.

30. Predicate-Act Canon

Authorization of an act also authorizes a necessary predicate act.

> "[W]here a general power is conferred or duty enjoined,
> every particular power necessary for the exercise of the one,
> or the performance of the other, is also conferred."
>
> Thomas M. Cooley,
> *A Treatise on the Constitutional Limitations Which Rest upon the*
> *Legislative Power of the States of the American Union* 63 (1868).

Contrary to the praise heaped on the Shakespearean character Portia for holding that Shylock could take his pound of flesh but not spill a drop of blood ("O upright judge! . . . O learned judge!"[1]), it was a terrible opinion. She should have invoked the principle that contracts to maim are void as contrary to public policy.[2] Her supposedly brilliant rationale ignored the well-acknowledged predicate-act canon. Authorization to take the flesh surely implies the authorization to spill blood—just as permission to harvest the wheat on one's land implies permission to enter on the land for that purpose. This is just common sense—and is one of the reasons why "strict construction" is foolish (see § 62).

The predicate-act canon is ancient. In 1759, Sir Henry Finch wrote that "[w]here the king is to have mines, the law giveth him power to dig in the land."[3] Further:

> "[T]he vendee of all one's fishes in his pond, may justify the coming upon the banks to fish, but not the digging of a trench to let out the water to take the fish, for he may take them by nets, and other devices; but if there were no other means to take them, he might dig a trench."[4]

The canon applies to all manner of texts. In the context of legislation, it has long been held that "whenever a power is given by

---

1   William Shakespeare, *The Merchant of Venice* 4.1.309–10 (Stanley Wells & Gary Taylor eds., 1986).

2   *Cf.* Clarence Morris, *The Justification of the Law* 85 (1971) (noting that "[t]he case would surely have gone the same way had the clause read 'one pound, more or less, of flesh, with the necessary blood-letting appurtenant thereto'").

3   Henry Finch, *Law, or a Discourse Thereof* 63 (1759).

4   *Id.*

a statute, everything necessary to making it effectual or requisite to attaining the end is implied."[5] As for contracts, the California Civil Code (to cite but one example) mandates that "[a]ll things that in law or usage are considered as incidental to a contract, or as necessary to carry it into effect, are implied therefrom, unless some of them are expressly mentioned therein, when all other things of the same class are deemed to be excluded."[6] And as for grants: "One who grants a thing is presumed to grant also whatever is essential to its use."[7]

The Supreme Court of Illinois has properly noted two limitations on the predicate-act canon: (1) "The implication under this rule . . . must be a necessary, not a conjectural or argumentative one";[8] and (2) "where the means for the exercise of a granted power are given, no other or different means can be implied, as being more effectual or convenient."[9]

The predicate-act canon must be applied with caution, lest the tail of what is implied wag the dog of what is expressly conferred. Despite the story describing how "for the want of a nail the kingdom was lost," the authority to protect the kingdom does not reasonably imply the authority to promulgate standards for the shoeing of horses: "The incident follows the principal, and not the principal the incident."[10] Determining what is *reasonably* implied takes some judgment.

What takes *no* real judgment, though, because of its obviousness, is the point that Jeremy Bentham was at pains to make in the 19th century: "Command includes permission. To mean to command any act to be done, and not to mean to permit it to be

---

5 James Kent, *Commentaries on American Law* *464 (Charles M. Barnes ed., 13th ed. 1884).

6 Cal. Civ. Code § 1656 (and note well the negative-implication exception at the end—see § 10).

7 *Id.* § 3522.

8 *Field v. People ex rel. McClernand*, 3 Ill. 79, 83 (1839).

9 *Id.*

10 Cal. Civ. Code § 3540.

done, is impossible."[11] Hence it makes little sense to draft a legal instrument that says a person both *shall* and *may* do an act—as apparently was once common.[12] If you must do something, then you are necessarily allowed to do it.

---

11   Jeremy Bentham, "Nomography," in 3 *The Works of Jeremy Bentham* 231, 262 (John Bowring ed., 1843).

12   *Id.* at 263.

31. Associated-Words Canon

Associated words bear on one another's meaning (*noscitur a sociis*).

The Latin phrase *noscitur a sociis* means "it is known by its associates"—a classical version, applied to textual explanation, of the observed phenomenon that birds of a feather flock together. The associated-words canon could refer to the basic principle that words are given meaning by their context (see § 2)—and some authorities use this canon at that broad level of generality.[1] But we mean something more specific. When several nouns or verbs or adjectives or adverbs—any words—are associated in a context suggesting that the words have something in common, they should be assigned a permissible meaning that makes them similar. The canon especially holds that "words grouped in a list should be given related meanings."[2]

Take a line from Shakespeare's *The Tempest*, first published in 1623, in which Gonzalo says that he would not have "treason, felony, sword, pike, knife, gun, or need of any engine."[3] The mere listing provides helpful context for the meaning of *engine*, which today is considered a broad term with an entirely neutral meaning. The editors of the modern Folger edition of the play translate *engine* as "military weapon." And the *Oxford English Dictionary* details the violent associations of the term from its first use in about 1300 through the 19th century: "A machine or instrument used in warfare. Formerly sometimes applied to all offensive weapons, but chiefly and now exclusively to those of large size and having mechanism, e.g. a battering-ram, catapult, piece of ordnance, etc."[4]

If someone were to argue that *pike*, in Gonzalo's list, might refer to a freshwater fish or that *engine* might refer to the locomotive

---

1 *See* D.C. Pearce, *Statutory Interpretation in Australia* 48 (1981).

2 *Third Nat'l Bank in Nashville v. Impac Ltd.*, 432 U.S. 312, 322 (1977) (per Stevens, J.) (correctly stating the doctrine but, in our view, misapplying its import).

3 2.1.176–77.

4 5 *Oxford English Dictionary* 250 (2d ed. 1989).

car on a train, the argument could be easily dismissed by looking
to the surrounding terms. Likewise, if a statute is said to apply to
"tacks, staples, nails, brads, screws, and fasteners," it is clear from
the words with which they are associated that the word *nails* does
not denote fingernails and that *staples* does not mean reliable and
customary food items.

For the associated-words canon to apply, the terms must be
conjoined in such a way as to indicate that they have some quality
in common. The walrus's allusion to "shoes and ships and seal-
ing-wax, . . . cabbages and kings"[5] provides no occasion for *noscitur a sociis*. The common quality suggested by a listing should be
its most general quality—the least common denominator, so to
speak—relevant to the context.

There is reason to disagree with the Canadian decision holding that the statutory term *ordinances* means only laws made by
a legislative body, since it was conjoined with *Acts* in the statutory phrase *Acts and ordinances*.[6] The only quality that those words
surely have in common is a legally binding effect prescribed by a
governmental authority. There is no more reason to believe that
ordinances were meant to be similar to *Acts* in regard to the nature
of the promulgator than there is to believe that they were meant
to be different in that regard. That is to say, the phrase *Acts and
ordinances* could have meant "Acts [of the legislature] and all other
binding pronouncements [issued by *any* proper authority]."

Despite our nails-and-staples example, the most common effect of the canon is not to establish which of two totally different
meanings applies but rather to limit a general term to a subset of
all the things or actions that it covers—but only according to its
ordinary meaning. So in the case just discussed, the Canadian
court used the canon (wrongly, we submit) to restrict the term
ordinances to one of its many possible applications—namely, only
those laws made by a legislative body.

The associated-words canon has tremendous value in a broad
array of cases. Consider the Minnesota statute making it a crime

---

5   Lewis Carroll, *Through the Looking Glass* 64 (1871; repr. 1917)
6   *R. v. Markin*, (1969) 68 W.W.R. 611, ¶ 6.

to carry or possess a pistol in a motor vehicle unless the pistol is unloaded and "contained in a closed and fastened case, gunbox, or securely tied package." When police stopped Phyllis Taylor, she was found to have a pistol within her purse on the floor behind the passenger seat. On appeal, Taylor argued that her purse was a "case," which dictionaries define as "something that encloses or contains." The state argued that *noscitur a sociis* imparts a restrictive meaning to *case*: A *gunbox* is a hard, latched container; and by the terms of the statute a *package* must be a "securely tied" package; and a *case* a "closed" and "fastened" case. This listing suggests a container that does not make the gun readily retrievable. A purse, by contrast, is just where a woman would pack heat for ready access. So the Minnesota Court of Appeals rightly held that Ms. Taylor was not within the exception to the statute.[7] The outcome might have been different if the general word *case* had not been qualified by such specific adjectives.

You might well wonder why the rule of lenity (§ 49) would not save Taylor here. The answer is that the rule of lenity applies only when a reasonable doubt persists *after* the traditional canons of interpretation have been considered. There was no ambiguity here.

Although most associated-words cases involve listings—usually a parallel series of nouns and noun phrases, or verbs and verb phrases—a listing is not prerequisite. An "association" is all that is required. Consider a Texas case[8] involving a public-information act that contained an exemption from disclosure for "[a]n internal record or notation of a law enforcement agency or prosecutor that is maintained for internal use in matters relating to law enforcement or prosecution . . . if . . . release of the internal record or notation would interfere with law enforcement or prosecution . . . ."[9] An unsuccessful applicant for a position as a Fort Worth police officer submitted an open-records request for copies of the hiring-process documents relating to his application. The city refused to

---

7   *State v. Taylor*, 594 N.W.2d 533, 535–36 (Minn. Ct. App. 1999).

8   *City of Fort Worth v. Cornyn*, 86 S.W.3d 320 (Tex. App.—Austin 2002, no pet.).

9   Tex. Gov't Code Ann. § 552.108(b)(1).

provide them, contending that this information was exempt from disclosure by reason of the law-enforcement exception.

In the ensuing litigation, the city argued, reasonably enough, that the information it sought to protect *was* related to law enforcement; its officers must make well-informed hiring decisions, and if the information it obtains and records during the hiring process were readily available to the public, those third parties who provide information about the applicant would be reluctant to speak candidly. The court of appeals nonetheless denied the exemption on grounds of *noscitur a sociis*:

> In three separate instances, the statute links the words law enforcement and prosecutor. The doctrine of construction—*noscitur a sociis*—teaches that "the meaning of particular terms in a statute may be ascertained by reference to words associated with them in the statute; and that where two or more words of analogous meaning are employed together in a statute, they are understood to be used in their cognate sense, to express the same relations and give color and expression to each other."
>
> Under this rule of construction, we construe the phrases "information relating to law enforcement" and "would interfere with law enforcement" in reference to the type of information that would also "relate to prosecution" or "interfere with prosecution." So doing, we conclude that the phrase "law enforcement," in light of the immediately following words "prosecutor" or "prosecution," evidences an intent by the Legislature to include within the law enforcement exception only that type of information that relates to violations of the law.[10]

Note the slippery reference to *intent* (see § 67), as opposed to meaning. Yet on the whole, such close textual analysis is laudable.

---

10   86 S.W.3d at 327 (citations omitted).

32. *Ejusdem Generis* Canon

Where general words follow an enumeration of two or more things, they apply only to persons or things of the same general kind or class specifically mentioned (*ejusdem generis*).

The *ejusdem generis* canon applies when a drafter has tacked on a catchall phrase at the end of an enumeration of specifics, as in *dogs, cats, horses, cattle, and other animals.* Does the phrase *and other animals* refer to wild animals as well as domesticated ones? What about a horsefly? What about protozoa? Are we to read *other animals* here as meaning *other similar animals?* The principle of *ejusdem generis* essentially says just that: It implies the addition of *similar* after the word *other.*

This canon parallels common usage. If one speaks of "Mickey Mantle, Rocky Marciano, Michael Jordan, and other great competitors," the last noun does not reasonably refer to Sam Walton (a great competitor in the marketplace) or Napoleon Bonaparte (a great competitor on the battlefield). It refers to other great *athletes.* But perhaps that is too easy an example, since the general term *competitors* is so nondescript that it almost cries out to be given more precise content by the previous words. A more realistic example (and one that the books are full of) is a passage in which the enumeration is followed by *and all other persons* or *and all other property.* Take, for example, a will that gives to a particular devisee "my furniture, clothes, cooking utensils, housewares, motor vehicles, and all other property." In the absence of other indication (of which more below), almost any court will construe the last phrase to include only personalty and not real estate.

The rationale for the *ejusdem generis* canon is twofold: When the initial terms all belong to an obvious and readily identifiable genus, one presumes that the speaker or writer has that category in mind for the entire passage. The fellow who spoke of "other competitors" did so *in the context* of athletes, and that context narrows the understood meaning of the term. And second, when the tagalong general term is given its broadest application, it renders the prior enumeration superfluous. If the testator really wished the devisee to receive *all* his property, he could simply have said "all my property"; why set forth a detailed enumeration and then render it all irrelevant by the concluding phrase *all other property?* One avoids this contradiction by giving the enumeration the effect of limiting the general phrase (while still not giving the general phrase a meaning that it will not bear). As expressed by Lord Kenyon in a case holding that the statutory phrase *cities, towns corporate, boroughs, and places* applied only to places of the same sort as those enumerated: "[O]therwise the Legislature would have used only one compendious word, which would have included places of every denomination."[1]

Courts have applied the rule, which in English law dates back to 1596,[2] to all sorts of syntactic constructions that have particularized lists followed by a broad, generic phrase. Today American courts apply the rule often.[3] Some examples through the years:

- "contracts of employment of seamen, railroad employees, or any other class of workers engaged in foreign or interstate commerce"—held to include only transportation workers in foreign or interstate commerce.[4]

- "automobile, automobile truck, automobile wagon, motor cycle, or any other self-propelled vehicle not designed for running on rails"—held not to apply to an airplane.[5]

- "trays, glasses, dishes, or other tableware"—held not to include paper napkins.[6]

---

1   *Rex v. Wallis*, (1793) 5 T.R. 375, 101 Eng. Rep. 210.

2   *Archbishop of Canterbury's Case*, (1596) 2 Co. Rep. 46a, 76 E.R. 519. *See Sandiman v. Breach*, [1827] 7 B. & C. 96 (K.B.) (per Lord Tenterden—the rule of *ejusdem generis* also being known as Lord Tenterden's Rule).

3   Preston M. Torbert, *Globalizing Legal Drafting: What the Chinese Can Teach Us About Ejusdem Generis and All That*, 11 Scribes J. Legal Writing 41, 43 (2007).

4   *Circuit City Stores, Inc. v. Adams*, 532 U.S. 105, 109, 115 (2001) (per Kennedy, J.).

5   *McBoyle v. United States*, 283 U.S. 25, 26, 27 (1931) (per Holmes, J.).

6   *Treasure Island Catering Co. v. State Bd. of Equalization*, 120 P.2d 1, 5 (Cal. 1941).

- "all personal effects, household effects, automobiles and other tangible personal property"—held not to include cash.[7]

- "soldiers' and sailors' home, almshouse, home for the friendless, or other charitable institution"—held not to include a state hospital.[8]

- "gravel, sand, earth or other material" on state-owned land—held not to include commercial timber harvested on state-owned land.[9]

- Licensing requirement for "the business of a blood boiler, bone boiler, fell-monger, slaughterer of cattle, horses, or animals of any description, soap boiler, tallow melter, tripe boiler, or other noxious or offensive business, trade, or manufacture"—held not to apply to a brickmaker or a small-pox hospital, because they were dissimilar to the listed jobs or businesses.[10]

- Authorization to employ and pay "teachers, . . . janitors, and other employes of the schools"—held not to apply to employment and payment of a lawyer.[11]

- A statute authorizing removal from office for "incompetency, improper conduct, or other cause satisfactory to said board"—held to cover only a cause that related to the incumbent's fitness for office.[12]

Examples of such wordings—and of such holdings—are legion.

An especially interesting case[13] involved South Dakota's Equine Activities Act, which stated that "[n]o equine activity sponsor, equine professional, doctor of veterinary medicine, or any

---

7   *In re Pergament's Estate,* 123 N.Y.S.2d 150, 153–54 (Sur. Ct. 1953), *aff'd sub nom. In re Pergament's Will,* 129 N.Y.S.2d 918 (App. Div. 1954).

8   *In re Jones,* 19 A.2d 280, 282 (Pa. 1941).

9   *Sierra Club v. Kenney,* 429 N.E.2d 1214, 1222 (Ill. 1981).

10 *Wanstead Local Bd. of Health v. Hill,* (1863) 143 E.R. 190; *Withington Local Bd. of Health v. Manchester Corp.,* [1893] 2 Ch. 19.

11 *Denman v. Webster,* 73 P. 139, 139 (Cal. 1903) (*employes* so spelled).

12 *State ex rel. Kennedy v. McGarry,* 21 Wis. 496, 497–98 (1867).

13 *Nielson v. AT&T Corp.,* 597 N.W.2d 434 (S.D. 1999).

other person, is liable for an injury to or the death of a participant resulting from the inherent risks of equine activities"[14]—risks that were defined as "dangers or conditions which are an integral part of equine activities, including . . . [c]ertain hazards such as surface and subsurface conditions . . . ."[15]

Gregg Nielson's 19-year-old daughter was riding a horse in a pasture leased to a riding club. While running at a controlled gallop, the horse tripped and somersaulted, killing its rider. An investigation revealed that the horse had tripped because it stepped in a cable trench that had been dug by AT&T. Nielson sued the company for its negligence in failing to fill the trench properly and to warn riders of the danger the trench presented. He contended that AT&T was not involved in the sponsorship of equine activities and should therefore not be protected by the Equine Activities Act. AT&T argued that under the plain language of the statute, the phrase *any other person* provided immunity to all persons, regardless of their occupation, their status, or their foreseeable involvement in equine activities. Applying *ejusdem generis*, the court correctly held that *any other person* included only those involved in equine activities.[16] AT&T was liable.

As in all the preceding examples, *ejusdem generis* has traditionally required the broad catchall language to *follow* the list of specifics, as witness a short historical sampling of commentary:

- **1888:** "EJUSDEM GENERIS—. . . It is a rule of legal construction that general words following an enumeration of particulars are to have their generality limited by reference to the preceding particular enumeration."[17]

---

14   S.D. Codified Laws § 42-11-2.

15   *Id.* § 42-11-1(6)(c)

16   597 N.W.2d at 439–40.

17   Stewart Rapalje & Robert L. Lawrence, *A Dictionary of American and English Law* 435 (1888).

- **1900:** "[E]*jusdem generis* [requires that] general words following words of a more particular character are regarded as limited in their meaning by the former."[18]

- **1943:** "There appears to be no case where the *ejusdem generis* rule has been applied to general words which precede specific words."[19]

- **1966:** "*Ejusdem generis*. Of the same kind. If a number of things of the same kind are specified and are followed by general words, the latter may be held to be limited in their scope."[20]

- **1975:** "[E]*jusdem generis* . . . says that if a series of more than two items ends with a catch-all term that is broader than the category into which the preceding items fall but which those items do not exhaust, the catch-all term is presumably intended to be no broader than that category."[21]

- **1996:** "The ejusdem generis rule only comes into effect when dealing with general words at the end of a list."[22]

- **2007:** "The ejusdem generis canon asserts that a general phrase at the end of a list is limited to the same type of things (the generic category) that are found in the specific list."[23]

Authorities have traditionally agreed that the specific–general sequence is required, and that the rule does not apply to a general–specific sequence.[24]

---

18 H.T. Tiffany, "Interpretation and Construction," in 17 *American and English Encyclopaedia of Law* 1, 6 (David S. Garland & Lucius P. McGehee eds., 2d ed. 1900).

19 Roland Burrows, *Interpretation of Documents* 66 (1943).

20 W.A. Leach, *Legal Interpretation for Surveyors* 63 (1966).

21 Reed Dickerson, *The Interpretation and Application of Statutes* 234 (1975).

22 James A. Holland & Julian S. Webb, *Learning Legal Rules* 202 (3d ed. 1996).

23 William D. Popkin, *A Dictionary of Statutory Interpretation* 74 (2007).

24 *See, e.g.*, E.A. Driedger, *The Construction of Statutes* 86–95 (1974).

But in 1973 the editors of a leading American treatise, *Suther-land Statutes and Statutory Construction*, ill-advisedly amended its traditional explanation with this statement: "Where the opposite sequence is found, i.e., specific words following general ones, the doctrine is equally applicable, and restricts application of the general term to things that are similar to those enumerated."[25] Another commentator has erroneously suggested that applying *ejusdem generis* to general–specific sequences "appears to be the majority view."[26]

That is not so. The vast majority of cases dealing with the doctrine—and all the time-honored cases—follow the species–genus pattern. The question is whether it ought to be so limited. It might be argued that one of the rationales for *ejusdem generis* exists no less when the general term comes first than when it comes last: that when an *introductory* general term is given its broadest application, no less than when a *tagalong* term is given its broadest application, the enumeration of specifics becomes superfluous. That is perhaps not entirely true. Following the general term with specifics can serve the function of making doubly sure that the broad (and intended-to-be-broad) general term is taken to include the specifics. Some formulations suggest or even specifically provide this belt-and-suspenders function by introducing the specifics with a term such as *including* or even *including without limitation* ("all buildings, including [without limitation] assembly houses, courthouses, jails, police stations, and government offices"). But even without those prefatory words, the enumeration of the specifics can be thought to perform the belt-and-suspenders function. Enumerating the specifics before the general, on the other hand, cannot reasonably be interpreted as having such a function. This is perhaps demonstrated by the fact that there is no commonly used verbal formulation (the equivalent of *including without limitation* in the general-followed-by-specific context) that makes that function

---

25 2A *Sutherland Statutes and Statutory Construction* § 47:17 (C. Dallas Sands ed., 4th ed. 1973) (the statement having been preserved in the fifth and later editions). *See Gulf Ins. Co. v. James*, 185 S.W.2d 966 (Tex. 1945) (applying—or rather misapplying—the rule to a general–specific sequence).

26 Gregory R. Englert, *The Other Side of Ejusdem Generis*, 11 Scribes J. Legal Writing 51, 54 (2007).

clear in the specific-followed-by-general context. One never encounters a provision that reads "all assembly houses, courthouses, jails, police stations, government offices, and, *without limitation by reason of the foregoing*, all other buildings."

The other rationale for the *ejusdem generis* canon undoubtedly does not apply to a genus-followed-by-species sequence. When the genus comes first ("all buildings, assembly houses, courthouses, jails, police stations, and government offices") it is a stranger that arrives, so to speak, without an introduction saying it is limited; one is invited to take it at its broadest face value. So the *ejusdem generis* canon is properly limited to its traditional application: a series of specifics followed by a general. The Supreme Court of Canada was entirely correct in refusing to apply the canon when general words in a statutory provision preceded, rather than followed, the specifics.[27]

Courts have often gotten sloppy in stating the rule. Sometimes they confuse it with the more general rule *noscitur a sociis* (see § 31 [associated-words canon]), as when they disregard the necessary specific–general sequence in the enumeration. The Third Circuit has misleadingly said that *ejusdem generis* applies to "general words *near* a specific list,"[28] and the Supreme Court that "a general statutory term should be understood in light of the specific terms that *surround* it"[29] (an erroneous formulation duly repeated by the Fourth Circuit[30]). In all contexts other than the pattern of specific-to-general, the proper rule to invoke is the broad associated-words canon, not the narrow *ejusdem generis* canon.

---

27 *National Bank of Greece (Canada) v. Katsikonouris*, [1990] 2 S.C.R. 1029, ¶12 ("[I]n the clause under consideration, the general words precede and do not follow the specific enumeration. The clause states that coverage as to the interest of the mortgagee is valid notwithstanding 'omission or misrepresentation,' and then provides illustrative examples of such omissions and misrepresentations. The rationale for applying the *ejusdem generis* rule is accordingly absent.").

28 *Cooper Distrib. Co. v. Amana Refrigeration, Inc.*, 63 F.3d 262, 280 (3d Cir. 1995) (emphasis added).

29 *Hughey v. United States*, 495 U.S. 411, 419 (1990) (per Marshall, J.) (emphasis added).

30 *United States v. Parker*, 30 F.3d 542, 553 n.10 (4th Cir. 1994).

There are also potentially objectionable statements to the effect that *ejusdem generis* does not apply "where the intention of the legislative body is otherwise apparent"[31]—unless one takes "apparent" to mean "apparent from text and context." As we have observed, the interpreter's mission should be not to divine the *ignis fatuus* known as "drafter's intention," but instead to determine what the drafter has actually said.

Five caveats.

First, *ejusdem generis* generally requires at least two words to establish a genus—before the *other*-phrase. "Theaters and other places of public entertainment" does not invoke the canon.[32] There are decisions to the contrary. For example, the language "clerical or other error" in tax assessments was held to refer only to ministerial errors and not to errors of judgment.[33] But this is simply another instance of misusing the fairly technical *ejusdem generis* canon for the somewhat less technical associated-words canon. Why should the rule require at least two terms before *other*? A single-word lead-in certainly invokes the second of the two rationales supporting the canon: A general tag-on renders a single specific word superfluous no less than a series of words. If the word *property* is given its general connotation, the testator who devises "my car and all other property" might just as well have said "all my property." But with a single-word lead-in, the first rationale for the canon does not exist. There is no reason to conclude, from the single specification of *car*, that the testator had only personal property in mind. A sign at the entrance to a butcher shop reading "No dogs or other animals" does not suggest that only canines, or only four-legged animals, or only domestic animals are excluded; dogs may have been mentioned only because they are the most common offenders.[34]

---

31 *A.H. Jacobson Co. v. Commercial Union Assurance Co.*, 83 F.Supp. 674, 678 (D. Minn. 1949).

32 *Allen v. Emmerson*, [1944] K.B. 362, 366–67. *See also United Towns Elec. Co. v. Attorney-General for Newfoundland*, [1939] 1 All. E.R. 423, 428 (P.C.) ("The mention of a single species . . . does not constitute a genus.").

33 *Hermance v. Board of Supervisors of Ulster County*, 71 N.Y. 481, 486–87 (1877).

34 The context, entrance to a store catering to the public, shows that *animals* does not include *homo sapiens*.

A recent United States Supreme Court opinion presented the question whether the two-specifics minimum for application of the canon applied. In *Ali v. Federal Bureau of Prisons*,[35] a prison inmate sued the bureau under the Federal Tort Claims Act for the mishandling of his belongings. The government invoked a provision of the Act, stating that its waiver of sovereign immunity did not apply to the "detention of any goods, merchandise, or other property by any officer of customs or excise or any other law enforcement officer."[36] The plaintiff argued that by application of *ejusdem generis* the phrase *any other law enforcement officer* meant only other law-enforcement officers enforcing customs or excise laws.[37] The Supreme Court rightly held that the canon did not apply: "The phrase is disjunctive, with one specific and one general category, not . . . a list of specific items separated by commas and followed by a general or collective term."[38] This conclusion rests on the premise that the phrase *officer of customs or excise* refers to a single, specific type of officer—and is not equivalent to *customs officer or excise officer.* That premise was unexamined, but was probably correct. It is traditional to pair the two terms *customs* and *excise* in reference to officers who enforce exclusion restrictions and assess duties on imports. Great Britain and other countries have long had Bureaus of Customs and Excise.

Second, the doctrine often gives rise to the question how broadly or narrowly to define the class delineated by the specific items listed.[39] What sets *ejusdem generis* apart from the other canons—and makes it unpopular with many commentators—is its indeterminacy. The doctrine does not specify that the court must identify the genus that is at the lowest possible level of generality. The court has broad latitude in determining how much or how little is embraced by the general term. An ordinance that applies to owners of "lions, tigers, and other animals" might be held to

---

35 552 U.S. 214 (2008) (per Thomas, J.).

36 28 U.S.C. § 2680(c).

37 *Id.* at 218.

38 *Id.* at 225.

39 *See* John F. Manning & Matthew C. Stephenson, *Legislation and Regulation* 252–54 (2010) (examining the problem of scope).

apply only to owners of wildcats or to owners of all dangerous wild animals. Or:

- "horses, cattle, sheep, pigs, goats, and other farm animals." Must they be mammals? (Are catfish included?) Must they be quadrupeds? (Are chickens included?) Must they be hoofed? (Is a sheepdog included?)

- "LPs, CDs, DVDs, and other means of home entertainment." Must they be disks? (Not an iPod?) Must they be disks of a certain type? (A Frisbee is excluded?)

Our advice here must be a generalization: Consider the listed elements, as well as the broad term at the end, and ask what category would come into the reasonable person's mind. It seems to us that a state's reservation of "oil, gas, and other minerals" would include all fossil fuels, including coal—not just liquid and gaseous fossil fuels.[40]

But the difficulty of identifying the relevant genus should not be exaggerated. Often the evident purpose of the provision makes the choice clear. If the previously discussed ordinance required the animal owners to be instructed on the unpredictability of feline behavior—or, on the other hand, required them to adopt certain measures to prevent escape—the choice would be clear. Moreover, it will often not be necessary to identify the genus with specificity in order to decide the case at hand. If the issue is whether the above ordinance applies to the owner of a dachshund, it is inconsequential whether the genus established by the specification is dangerous wild animals or wildcats. That can await a later case involving hyenas. Because *whatever* the genus—wildcats or wild animals—it does not include Fido. So an English case dealing with a ban on importation of "arms, ammunition, gunpowder, or any other goods" held that the prohibition did not apply to pyrogallic acid.[41] It had been argued that pyrogallic acid is used in photography, which, like arms, ammunition, and gunpowder, is

---

40 *Contra State ex rel. Commissioners of the Land Office v. Butler*, 753 P.2d 1334, 1339 (Okla. 1987) (holding that the common understanding of "other minerals" is limited to those "similar in kind and class to oil and gas," which excludes coal).

41 *Attorney-General v. Brown*, [1920] 1 K.B. 773, 799–800 (per Sankey, J.).

used in war. The court did not identify what the genus was but said that it was assuredly not everything used, or used in preparing some article for use, in modern warfare—since that would include *everything*, making the specification of *arms, ammunition, and gunpowder* pointless.

Third, sometimes the specifics do not fit into any kind of definable category—"the enumeration of the specific items is so heterogeneous as to disclose no common genus."[42] With this type of wording, the canon does not apply. Thus, the general words *all manner of merchandise* were held not to be limited by a preceding enumeration of fruit, fodder, farm produce, insecticides, pumps, nails, tools, and wagons.[43] The same was held true of the phrase *for any other necessary public purposes* in a statute providing that private property could be expropriated by certain cities for "establishing, opening, widening, extending or altering any street, avenue, alley, wharf, creek, river, watercourse, market place, public park or public square, and for establishing market houses, and for any other necessary public purposes."[44]

Fourth, when the specifics exhaust the class and there is nothing left besides what has been enumerated, the follow-on general term must be read literally.[45] For example, *federal Senators, fed-*

---

42 Lord Macmillan, *Law and Other Things* 166 (1938). *See State v. Eckhardt*, 133 S.W. 321, 322 (Mo. 1910) (*ejusdem generis* not applied because "the words 'street' and 'field' . . . are not even remotely related" and "each stands as the representative of a distinct class" in a statute criminalizing the abandonment of a child in "a street, field or other place"); *McReynolds v. People*, 82 N.E. 945, 947–48 (Ill. 1907) (*ejusdem generis* not applied to enumeration of "any wharf or place of storage, or in any warehouse, mill, store or other building" because it should not be applied "where the specific words signify subjects greatly different from one another").

43 *Heatherton Coop. v. Grant*, [1930] 1 D.L.R. 975 (N.S.).

44 *See City of Caruthersville v. Faris*, 146 S.W.2d 80, 86–87 (Mo. Ct. App. 1940) (refusing to apply *ejusdem generis* because of the disparities within the enumeration) (quoting Mo. Rev. Stat. 1929, § 6852).

45 *Mason v. United States*, 260 U.S. 545, 554 (1923) (per Sutherland, J.) (*ejusdem generis* not applied to executive order withdrawing public mining land "from settlement and entry, or other form of appropriation" because the "specific words [settlement and entry] are sufficiently comprehensive to exhaust the genus and leave nothing essentially similar upon which the general words may operate"); *Danciger v. Cooley*, 248 U.S. 319, 326 (1919) (per Van Devanter, J.) (*ejusdem generis* not applied to statute regulating transport of liquor by "[a]ny railroad com-

eral Representatives, and other persons. The class represented by the specifics is obviously members of Congress—but that class consists entirely of senators and representatives; *other persons* would therefore have no effect if limited to that class, and must be given its general meaning. A case exemplifying the point is *Knoxtenn Theatres, Inc. v. McCanless*,[46] involving a state tax on liquid carbonic-acid gas "used in the preparation . . . of soft drinks or other beverages, or for any other purpose." The taxpayer, which used the gas for air conditioning in its theater, argued that *ejusdem generis* limited *any other purpose* so that it could not apply to air-conditioning use. The court quite properly held that the catchall ending language

> cannot extend the same kind or class, because the words "soft drinks or other beverages" exhaust the kind or class and the general words following "or for any other purpose," by necessity, show an intent to go beyond the whole field of soft drinks and beverages. The final general words have a sweeping, all-inclusive effect, otherwise, these final general words have no purpose whatever.[47]

In the congressional example, the outcome would be different if the text read *federal Senators, federal Representatives, and other members of Congress.* There, the concluding phrase simply cannot bear any other meaning than the one already exhausted by the preceding specifics; because it cannot be expanded beyond its permissible meaning, it must be treated as surplusage.

Fifth, since the days of Blackstone[48] and even Coke, commentators have said that the general word will not be treated as applying to persons or things of a higher quality, dignity, or worth than those specifically listed. Thus, a statute applicable to masters and fellows of colleges, deans and chapters of cathedrals, parsons,

---

pany, express company, or other common carrier, or any other person" because "[t]he words 'any railroad company, express company, or other common carrier,' comprehend all public carriers").

46 151 S.W.2d 164 (Tenn. 1941).

47 *Id.* at 165–66.

48 1 William Blackstone, *Commentaries on the Laws of England* 88 (4th ed. 1770).

vicars, and "others having spiritual promotions"[49] was held inapplicable to bishops, who were of a higher rank than those listed.[50] And a duty imposed on copper, brass, pewter, tin, and "all other metals not enumerated" was held inapplicable to gold and silver—in part because of *ejusdem generis*, but also because gold and silver are commonly referred to not as "metals" but as "precious metals."[51] Apart from protecting the interests of bishops and other illustrious persons, there seems to us little to be said for the proposition that inferiority of worth always establishes the relevant genus. Although the inferiority rule is an ancient one, it is infrequently applied and even little known in modern times.

Commentators sometimes dispute whether the *ejusdem generis* canon is beneficial. One calls for its abolition;[52] another questions its "lexicographic accuracy."[53] But others call it "a gem of common sense"[54] and say that it "expresses a valid insight about ordinary language usage."[55] The redoubtable Max Radin suggested that the canon has some "foundation in logic and in ordinary habits of speech."[56] And the high court in New Jersey has praised the rule as being "grounded in grammar, logic and reason."[57]

Whatever its intrinsic merit, the canon has sometimes been applied with a rigidity that hampered rather than helped the

---

49 13 Eliz. c. 10 § 3 ("And for that long and unfashionable leases made by colleges, deans, and chapters, parsons, vicars, and others having spiritual promotions . . .").

50 *Archbishop of Canterbury's Case*, (1596) 2 Co. Rep. 46a, 76 E.R. 519.

51 *Casher v. Holmes*, (1831) 109 E.R. 1263, 1264 (K.B.).

52 *See, e.g.*, Alex Frame, *Salmond: Southern Jurist* 93 (1995) (noting that John Salmond sought to abolish the rule in New Zealand with a legislative bill drafted in 1908).

53 Reed Dickerson, *The Interpretation and Application of Statutes* 234 (1975) ("Whether the presumption is lexicographically accurate is not entirely clear.").

54 Joel R. Cornwell, *Smoking Canons: A Guide to Some Favorite Rules of Construction*, CBA Record, May 1996, at 43, 45.

55 2A Norman J. Singer, *Statutes and Statutory Construction* § 47:18, at 291 (6th ed. 2000).

56 Max Radin, *Statutory Interpretation*, 43 Harv. L. Rev. 863 (1930). *Cf.* William D. Popkin, *Materials on Legislation* 216 (4th ed. 2005) (stating that *ejusdem generis* "is probably based on a genuine attempt to understand language").

57 *President & Dirs. of Manhattan Co. v. Armour* (*In re Armour's Estate*), 94 A.2d 286, 293 (N.J. 1953).

search for genuine textual meaning. Black regarded it as "really a rule of strict construction."[58] As stated in 1895 by Lord Justice Rigby (quoted by Beal, who obviously did not think much of the canon)[59]:

> The doctrine known as that of *ejusdem generis* has, I think, frequently led to wrong conclusions on the construction of instruments. I do not believe that the principles as generally laid down by great judges were ever in doubt, but over and over again those principles have been misunderstood, so that words in themselves plain have been construed as bearing a meaning which they have not, and which ought not to have been ascribed to them. In modern times I think greater care has been taken in the application of the doctrine . . . .[60]

This greater care springs primarily from the recognition that, like the other canons, *ejusdem generis* is not a rule of law but one of various factors to be considered in the interpretation of a text. The canon would have undoubted application to a sign at the entrance to a butcher shop that read: "No dogs, cats, and other animals allowed." It would have application, but given the context of the sign it would not carry the day. Even if the sign were expanded to read "No dogs, cats, pet rabbits, parakeets, or other animals," no one would think that only domestic pets were excluded, and that farm animals or wild animals were welcome. When the context argues so strongly against limiting the general provision, the canon will not be dispositive.

But the canon cannot be dismissed lightly. The truly knowledgeable interpreter (and drafter) knows the *ejusdem generis* canon; it has become part of the accepted terminology of legal documents. Any lawyer or legislative drafter who writes two or more specifics followed by a general residual term without the intention that the residual term be limited may be guilty of malpractice. To be sure,

---

58 Henry Campbell Black, *Handbook on the Construction and Interpretation of the Laws* 217 (2d ed. 1911).

59 Edward Beal, *Cardinal Rules of Legal Interpretation* 65–66 (A.E. Randall ed., 3d ed. 1924).

60 *Anderson v. Anderson*, [1895] 1 Q.B. 749, 755 (per Rigby, L.J.) (emphasis added).

other factors can supersede *ejusdem generis,* but the canon would carry some weight nonetheless. We see no basis (except perhaps a rejection of textualism) for Driedger's suggestion that this canon should be applied only as a last resort, after "the substantive context or the object of the Act" has failed to determine the scope of the general word.[61] *Ejusdem generis* is one of the factors to be considered, along with context and textually apparent purpose, in determining the scope. It does not always predominate, but neither is it a mere tie-breaker.

---

61 E.A. Driedger, *The Construction of Statutes* 94–95 (1974).

33. Distributive-Phrasing Canon

Distributive phrasing applies each expression to its appropriate referent (*reddendo singula singulis*).

If someone in Kansas is instructed to go to London "by rail and steamer," the listener implicitly understands to take a train to an East Coast port, then the steamer perhaps to Liverpool, and then another train to London.[1] Likewise, gifts of "$1,000 and $1,500 to Jill and Jan, respectively" are understood as meaning $1,000 to Jill and $1,500 to Jan. Because of this type of distributive phrasing, a rule stating that "Men and women are eligible to become members of fraternities and sororities" cannot reasonably be read to suggest an unconventional commingling of sexes in the club membership.[2]

Sometimes a word alone signals a distributive sense, such as *apiece, each, every, per, respective*; sometimes it is simply the sense of the passage. A leading guide to English grammar states: "Words like *each, every*, and the compounds with *every-*, can be termed distributive because they pick out the members of a set singly, rather than considering them in the mass."[3]

A simple example of the application of the distributive-phrasing canon is the 19th-century Pennsylvania case of *Commonwealth v. Cooke*.[4] Section 3 of a state statute provided that a banker or broker "who shall neglect or refuse to make the return and report required by the 1st and 2d sections of this act, shall, for every such neglect or refusal, be subject to a penalty of $1000."[5] Section 1 of the act required a return to be made of the business done, setting forth the profit and paying a 3% tax into the state treasury. Section 2 required a report of the names of people in the firm or of those engaged in the business. The defendant, having failed to make

---

1   *See Hope Natural Gas Co. v. Shriver*, 83 S.E. 1011, 1015 (W. Va. 1914) (dictum).

2   *See* Reed Dickerson, *The Interpretation and Application of Statutes* 233 (1975).

3   Randolph Quirk et al., *A Comprehensive Grammar of the English Language* 382 (1985).

4   50 Pa. 201 (1865).

5   Act of 16 May 1861, P.L. 708, 72 P.S. § 2222.

either a return or a report, was fined $2,000 and contended on appeal that he should have been fined only $1,000. The Pennsylvania Supreme Court rejected the contention, admirably analyzing the grammatical distributiveness of the word *every*:

> It is clear that the offences being different in kind, independent in act, and distinct in time, each is liable to punishment. When the legislature therefore said, every such neglect or refusal should be the subject of a penalty, it becomes very plain it did not refer to a *joint* neglect of *several* acts impossible of simultaneous performance. Had the word "every" been omitted, the language might have been dubious, but with it before us, as a part of the very letter of the act, we are admonished by the reference to resort to separate sections to ascertain the neglect or refusal referred to, and thus compelled to give the distributive word *every* a reference to each: *reddendum* [sic] *singula singulis*.[6]

A more subtle case involved a statute that was analogous to the idea that (A) men and (B) women are eligible to become members of (Y) fraternities and (Z) sororities—implying an A–Y correlation and a B–Z correlation. The statute in *Bishop v. Deakin*[7] provided that a person could not (A) be elected or (B) continue to hold office if he had been convicted of an offense (Y) within five years preceding an election or (Z) at any time since that election. The defendant in that case, a councillor, had been convicted of perjury in 1932 and been elected in 1934. The relevant statute also created a six-month limitation period for challenging an election—and the plaintiffs did not file their writ until nearly a full year after the defendant's election. If the court had allowed a pre-election offense to disallow continuation in office long after an election, it would have nullified the six-month limitation period. So the court resolved the anomaly by applying the distributive-phrasing canon and attributing a distributive relationship to the consequences of pre-election and post-election offenses. Fortunately, this sort of

---

6   50 Pa. at 207–08 (emphasis in original).

7   [1936] Ch. 409.

syntactic construction that gives rise to a distributive-phrasing in-terpretation has largely fallen into disuse.[8]

---

34. Prefatory-Materials Canon

A preamble, purpose clause, or recital is a permissible indicator of meaning.

Drafters often set forth certain facts and purposes in prefatory material—that is, a passage that precedes the text's operative terms, such as a legislative preamble. In former times, the customary format was several "Whereas" clauses, followed by "Now, therefore, be it enacted that . . . ," or (in a contract) "Now, therefore, in consideration of the mutual covenants contained herein and other good and valuable consideration, the parties agree as follows . . . ." More recently, Congress dispenses with the *whereases* and simply says, "Congress finds the following"; savvy transactional lawyers will simply put a first heading that says "Background" or "Recitals."

Of course, the function of a statute or any other legal instrument is to establish rights and duties, not to set forth facts or to announce purposes. Tuesday the 5th will remain Tuesday the 5th even if a legislated prologue announces it to have been the 4th, and a congressional expression of purpose has as much real-world effect as a congressional expression of apology. The same can be said of statements of facts and purposes in private instruments. The prologue, in other words, is in reality as well as in name *not* part of the congressionally legislated or privately created set of rights and duties. It is an aside. It is hard to imagine, for example, that any legislator who disagreed with that aside would vote against a bill containing all the dispositions that the legislator favored. As Henry Campbell Black wisely observed:

> [T]he preamble to a statute does not invariably recite the real reason for its enactment. Its statements of facts are neither infallible nor conclusive. This should operate as a restraint upon the disposition to attach too great weight to the preamble as evidencing the purpose and intention of the lawmakers.[1]

---

1   Henry Campbell Black, *Handbook on the Construction and Interpretation of the Laws* 255 (2d ed. 1911).

Again, the same could be said of the prefatory material in private instruments.

On the other hand, the prologue does set forth the assumed facts and the purposes that the majority of the enacting legislature or the parties to a private instrument had in mind, and these can shed light on the meaning of the operative provisions that follow. And this is the view that courts and judges have taken for many years. In his *Commentaries on the Constitution of the United States*, Justice Joseph Story wrote that "the preamble of a statute is a key to open the mind of the makers, as to the mischiefs, which are to be remedied, and the objects, which are to be accomplished by the provisions of the statute."[2]

Some courts and commentators have said that the prologue cannot be invoked when the text is clear.[3] This limitation is reasonable if it means that the prologue cannot give words and phrases of the dispositive text itself a meaning that they cannot bear. But the limitation is unreasonable and erroneous if it means that the prologue cannot be considered in determining which of various permissible meanings the dispositive text bears. If the prologue is indeed an appropriate guide to meaning, it ought to be considered along with all other factors in determining *whether* the instrument is clear. The factors undermining its reliability affect its weight, not its relevance.

A federal appellate case demonstrates how genuinely helpful a preamble can be. A Department of Energy regulation gave oil producers price allowances based on (among other things) the total number of "wells that produced crude oil." The oil field at issue had two types of wells: injection wells, which forced substances into the subsurface to increase pressure within the oil reservoirs;

---

2   1 Joseph Story, *Commentaries on the Constitution of the United States* § 459, at 326 (2d ed. 1858).

3   *See Jogi v. Voges*, 480 F.3d 822, 834 (7th Cir. 2007) ("It is a mistake to allow general language of a preamble to create an ambiguity in specific statutory or treaty text where none exists. Courts should look to materials like preambles and titles only if the text of the instrument is ambiguous."). *See generally* 2A Norman J. Singer & J.D. Shambie Singer, *Statutes and Statutory Construction* § 47.4, at 292 (7th ed. 2007) ("[T]he preamble cannot control the enacting part of the statute in cases where the enacting part is expressed in clear, unambiguous terms.").

and recovery wells, which brought crude oil to the surface. The question was simply whether injection wells counted as "wells that produced crude oil." The regulation's prologue (the requisite Statement of Basis and Purpose), which preceded its publication in the *Federal Register*, explicitly said no. End of case. (The court rejected the property owners' contention that the prologue should not count because it was not published in the Code of Federal Regulations.) The court correctly said:

> It is well settled . . . that the preamble to a regulation . . . should be considered in construing the regulation and determining the meaning of the regulation.
> In the construction of the Constitution of the United States, statutes and regulations, the federal rule permits and requires consideration of preambles in appropriate cases.[4]

There are, however, two serious limitations on the use of prologues. First, an expression of specific purpose in the prologue will not limit a more general disposition that the operative text contains. There is no inconsistency between the two, since legislative remedies often go beyond the specific ill that prompted the statute. Second, an expansive purpose in the preamble cannot add to the specific dispositions of the operative text. After all, no legislation or private disposition pursues its stated purposes at *all* costs. And there is no requirement that the limitations contained in the enactment must be recited in the prologue. Like other indications of purpose, the prefatory text can suggest only which *permissible* meanings of the enactment should be preferred.

Consider a statute whose prologue sets forth as its purpose "to promote quiet and safety in the park" and whose main clause is "no vehicle may be taken into the park." Somebody rides a shod horse on the park's sidewalks and is arrested. The activity is loud and unsafe, but is the horse a vehicle? Does the prologue's reference to "quiet and safety" make it so? The commentator who devised the example (after Hart—see pp. 36–39) incorrectly suggests that the horse *is* properly classifiable as a vehicle: "After all,

---

4   *Wiggins Bros., Inc. v. Department of Energy*, 667 F.2d 77, 88 (Temp. Emer. Ct. App. 1981) (citations omitted).

to so define the meaning of the vague implementing language of the statute would serve its ultimate purpose, even though it might conflict with or strain an ordinary meaning of 'vehicle.'"[5] Indeed, it would do grievous violence to the word *vehicle*—and a purpose clause cannot be used to that end.

These limitations on broad expressions of purpose do not apply only when those expressions are contained in a preface rather than the body of the text. Expressions of purpose are usually placed there, but they do not have to be. It is quite possible, for example, to eliminate the *whereas* clauses and include the same material after "It is hereby enacted as follows." That should make no difference. Just as the placement in a prologue does not eliminate the relevance of this material, placement in the text does not augment it. For example, a statute might provide that "dogs are to be muzzled for the purpose of stamping out rabies." Does the fact that this purpose has been expressed in an adverbial phrase modifying the operative language make it a necessary condition to the operative language? That is, must rabies be a continual problem in order for the muzzle law to continue in effect? No. In the words of one commentator, dogs "must continue to be muzzled so long as the statute is in force, even if rabies has been stamped out. The maxim *Cessante ratione legis cessat lex ipsa* [When the reason of the law ceases, the law itself ceases] is inapplicable to statute law."[6] Quite so. The purpose clause cannot override the operative language.

---

5   Robert S. Summers, "Statutory Interpretation in the United States," in *Interpreting Statutes: A Comparative Study* 407, 415 (D. Neil MacCormick & Robert S. Summers eds., 1991).

6   W. Nembhard Hibbert, *Jurisprudence* 95 (1932).

35. Title-and-Headings Canon

The title and headings are permissible indicators of meaning.

> "[T]he title of a statute or section can aid in resolving an ambiguity in the legislation's text."
> *INS v. National Ctr. for Immigrants' Rights, Inc.,*
> 502 U.S. 183, 189 (1991) (per Stevens, J.).

For the legal drafter, it can be quite a challenge to devise headings that adequately disclose the contents of a provision. Yet the drafter also knows that headings are useful navigational aids. Hence, given the precarious balance between the helpfulness of supplying headings and the difficulty of making them thoroughly accurate, drafters sometimes include this explicit disclaimer: "Headings are for convenience only and do not affect the interpretation of this [instrument]." Be sure to check your text or code or compilation for such a disclaimer.

Coke and many later judges refused to take into account the title of an act because it was not part of the enactment.[1] In modern practice, however, "the title is adopted by the legislature."[2] The classic statement about the use of statutory titles and headings in American law appeared in a 1947 decision of the Supreme Court:

> [The] heading is but a short-hand reference to the general subject matter involved. . . . [H]eadings and titles are not meant to take the place of the detailed provisions of the text. Nor are they necessarily designed to be a reference guide or a synopsis. . . . For interpretive purposes, they are of use only when they shed light on some ambiguous word or phrase. They are but tools available for the resolution of a doubt. But they cannot undo or limit that which the text makes plain.[3]

---

1 *Powlter's Case*, (1610) 11 Coke Rep. 29a, 33b ("[A]s to the style or title of the act, that is no parcel of the act . . ."); *Hadden v. Collector*, 72 U.S. (5 Wall.) 107, 110 (1866) (per Field, J.).

2 James DeWitt Andrews, "Statutory Construction," in 14 *American Law and Procedure* 1, 21–22 (James Parker Hall & James DeWitt Andrews eds., rev. ed. 1948).

3 *Brotherhood of R.R. Trainmen v. Baltimore & Ohio R.R.*, 331 U.S. 519, 528–29 (1947) (per Murphy, J.).

Sometimes, too, the title or heading is the longhand reference for an elliptical text. In one case, a state statute required that "vessels" have firescreens for smokestacks.[4] The question was what type of vessels the statute referred to. The Michigan Supreme Court held that because the legislative title referred to steam vessels, that permissible meaning would be adopted.[5]

In another case, the Mississippi Supreme Court was confronted with whether a certain criminal act—"concealing or harboring a prisoner or convict who has escaped"—was punishable as a felony or only as a misdemeanor. The body of the statute did not make this point clear. Yet the title of the statute began: "An Act to make it a felony for any person . . . ."[6] In holding that the statute was indeed a felony statute, the court rightly stated: "If there is any uncertainty in the body of an act, the title may be resorted to for the purpose of ascertaining legislative intent and of relieving the ambiguity."[7]

But a title or heading should never be allowed to override the plain words of a text. So we disapprove of the suggestion that the infamous *Holy Trinity* decision, which we discuss in detail at pages 11–13, can be defended on textualist grounds because of its prologue. That case, the reader will recall, held that a clergyman was not covered by a statute that prohibited "the importation . . . of . . . foreigners . . . [under contract] . . . to perform labor or service of any kind in the United States."[8] One commentator asserts that the title of the act—The Alien Contract Labor Act—created an ambiguity that enabled resort to an interpretation (a purposive interpretation) that would exclude clergymen.[9] That is not possible. The text of the statute contains no ambiguity at all: "labor and service of any kind" unambiguously includes not just labor

---

4   *Burrows v. Delta Transp. Co.*, 64 N.W. 501, 509 (Mich. 1895).

5   *Id.*

6   *Bellew v. Dedeaux*, 126 So.2d 249, 250 (Miss. 1961) (citing Miss. Laws 1952, ch. 258).

7   *Id.* (citing *Lewis v. Simpson*, 167 So. 780 (Miss. 1936)).

8   *Holy Trinity Church v. United States*, 143 U.S. 457, 458 (1892) (per Brewer, J.).

9   William N. Eskridge Jr., *Textualism: The Unknown Ideal?* 96 Mich. L. Rev. 1509, 1533, 1535 (1998).

but *service* of any kind. A shorthand title could not change that. Moreover, the act contained exemptions for services provided by people who were not laborers in the narrow sense, including actors, artists, lecturers, and singers. In any event, the commentator's analysis has the progression quite reversed: It is the unambiguous operative text ("labor and service") that clarifies the meaning of the ambiguous word *labor* in the prologue.

Sometimes courts do use titles improperly. For example, a Texas venue statute used a mandatory word, *shall*, to establish where a certain type of lawsuit could be brought: "Suits against railroad corporations . . . for damages arising from personal injuries . . . *shall* be brought either in the county in which the injury occurred or in the county in which the plaintiff resided at the time of the injury."[10] But in 1983, when the venue statutes were codified, a new heading was put on this railroad provision: "Permissive Venue." Problematically, the mandatory language was carried forward verbatim.

The provision with the new heading was soon tested. A passenger was injured when getting off a train in Amarillo (Potter County). Though he lived a few miles away in Randall County, he filed suit in Angleton (Brazoria County), more than 500 miles from Amarillo or Randall County. The railroad, Burlington Northern, filed a motion to transfer venue to the locale of the accident: Potter County. The trial court denied the transfer, and the Houston Court of Appeals bafflingly affirmed—placing great weight on the word *permissive* in the new heading.[11] The decision was linguistically naive in several respects. First, the language of the operative provision was mandatory, as prior cases had held. A new title could not give it a nonmandatory meaning, which the language could not bear. Second, it was not even clear that the new title ("Permissive Venue") *contradicted* mandatory meaning. Dictionaries define *permissive* not only as "optional" but also as "allowed, permitted" (as in the legal phrase *permissive waste*). The title of the mandatory venue statute merely listed the two places

---

10 Tex. Rev. Civ. Stat. art. 1995 (1983; repealed 1985).

11 *Burlington N. R.R. v. Harvey*, 717 S.W.2d 371, 375–77 (Tex. App.—Houston [14th Dist.] 1986, writ ref'd n.r.e.).

where venue was permissible or permitted. It did not suggest that venue was also permitted in other locales.

❧   ❧   ❧

Despite what we have said about titles of legal instruments generally, most states have a constitutional provision, called the title–body clause, that prescribes the relationship between a statute's title and its implementing language.[12] A statutory interpreter should of course consult them.

---

12 *See* Carl H. Manson, *The Drafting of Statute Titles*, 10 Ind. L.J. 155, 156 (1934).

36. Interpretive-Direction Canon

Definition sections and interpretation clauses are to be carefully followed.

> "[D]efinition by the average man or even by the ordinary dictionary with its studied enumeration of subtle shades of meaning is not a substitute for the definition set before us by the lawmakers with instructions to apply it to the exclusion of all others. There would be little use in such a glossary if we were free in despite of it to choose a meaning for ourselves."
>
> *Fox v. Standard Oil Co. of N.J.*,
> 294 U.S. 87, 96 (1935) (per Cardozo, J.).

Drafters often specify the meaning of the terms they use. Individual statutes often contain definition sections giving ordinary words a limited or artificial meaning.[1] State and federal codifications dealing with particular areas of law often contain a definition provision applicable to the entire codified field.[2] And both the federal government and some states have enacted definition sections that apply to all laws.[3] Some state definitional provisions

---

1   *See, e.g.*, W. Va. Code § 29B-1-2(1) (West 1977) ("As used in this article: 'Custodian' means the elected or appointed official charged with administering a public body."); Conn. Gen. Stat. Ann. § 23-26a (West 2002) ("'all-terrain vehicle' means a motorized vehicle, not suitable for operation on a highway that (1) is not more than fifty inches in width, (2) has a dry weight of not more than six hundred pounds, (3) travels on two or more tires specifically designed for unimproved terrain, (4) has a seat or saddle designed to be straddled by the operator, and (5) has an engine with a piston displacement of more than fifty cubic centimeters.").

2   *See, e.g.*, 11 U.S.C. § 101 (2010) (defining 55 terms applicable to the federal Bankruptcy Code, including *accountant, attorney, claim, debtor, insider,* and *transfer*); 21 U.S.C. § 802 (2009) (defining 56 terms applicable to the federal Controlled Substances Act, including *administer, felony drug offense, manufacture, narcotic drug, serious bodily injury,* and *ultimate user*); Tex. Penal Code § 1.07 (Vernon 2011) (defining 49 terms applicable to the state Penal Code, including *act, correctional facility, individual, possession,* and *reasonable belief*); N.Y. Banking Law § 2 (McKinney 2008) (defining 29 terms applicable to the state banking laws, including *bank, minor, shareholder,* and *total reserves*).

3   *See, e.g.*, 1 U.S.C. § 1 (2006) ("In determining the meaning of any Act of Congress, unless the context indicates otherwise . . . the words 'insane' and 'insane person' and 'lunatic' shall include every idiot, lunatic, insane person, and person non compos mentis; . . . 'signature' or 'subscription' includes a mark when the person making the same intended it as such . . ."); Ga. Code Ann., § 1-3-2 (2004) ("As used in this Code or in any other law of this state, defined words [enumerated in the definition section] shall have the meanings specified, unless the context in which the word or term is used clearly requires that a different meaning be used.").

apply even to private instruments,[4] so that drafters of wills, contracts, and other legal instruments must heed their lexicographic commands.

No legislature has the power to bind its successors to particular terminology (see § 45 [repealability canon]). But with respect to these general definitional provisions, it usually does not matter. They are typically limited by an expression such as "unless the context requires otherwise,"[5] and the definitions they set forth (unsurprisingly) accord with the normal, ordinary meaning of words. The result is that the words bear their ordinary meaning unless the context indicates an unusual (but permissible) meaning—which is precisely what the rule would be without the definition.

When a definitional section says that a word "includes" certain things, that is usually taken to mean that it may include other things as well[6] (see § 15 [presumption of nonexclusive "include"]). When, by contrast, a definitional section says that a word "means" something, the clear import is that this is its *only* meaning.[7] For example, the Pennsylvania Statutory Construction Act provided that "[t]he following words and phrases, when used in any law hereafter enacted, unless the context clearly dictates otherwise,

---

4 *See* Mass. Gen. Laws Ann. ch. 190B, § 2-709(b) (West 2011) ("If an applicable statute or a governing instrument calls for property to be distributed 'per capita at each generation,' the property is divided into as many equal shares . . ."). The comment to this section expressly states that it "applies to both private instruments and to provisions of applicable statutory law."

5 *See* 12 U.S.C. § 5002(20) ("Unless the context requires otherwise, the terms not defined in this section shall have the same meanings as in the Uniform Commercial Code."); Tex. Gov't Code Ann. § 311.005 (West 2011) ("The following definitions apply unless the statute or context in which the word or phrase is used requires a different definition."). *See also* Lord Macmillan, *Law and Other Things* 168 (1938) (noting that in British statutes, definitions are "all carefully guarded with the prefatory warning 'unless the contrary intention appears'").

6 *See Federal Land Bank of St. Paul v. Bismarck Lumber Co.*, 314 U.S. 95, 100 (1941) (per Murphy, J.) ("[T]he term 'including' is not one of all-embracing definition, but connotes simply an illustrative application of the general principle."); *Dunaway v. Commissioner*, 124 T.C. 80, 91 (2005) ("Generally, the word 'includes' is interpreted by the courts as a word of enlargement, not of limitation.").

7 *See Helvering v. Morgan's, Inc.*, 293 U.S. 121, 125 n.1 (1934) (per Stone, J.) ("The natural distinction would be that where 'means' is employed, the term and its definition are to be interchangeable equivalents, and that the verb 'includes' imports a general class, some of whose particular instances are those specified in the definition.").

shall have the meanings ascribed to them in this section." It then defined *domestic animal* as "any equine animal, bovine animal, sheep, goat, and pig."[8] After enacting this definition, the legislature made it a crime to kill, maim, or poison a domestic animal. A defendant, Massini, poisoned a cat and was prosecuted and convicted under the statute. On appeal, he argued that because of the statutory definition, a cat was not a domestic animal within the meaning of the statute and thus he was guilty of no crime. The prosecution argued in vain that § 33 of the Statutory Construction Act provided that "words and phrases shall be construed . . . according to their common and approved usage." That applied, the Pennsylvania Superior Court rightly said, only to words and phrases not defined in the Act; otherwise, it would "make useless all the statutory definitions formulated by the legislature."[9] The definitional listing was exhaustive, not exemplary, and felines were not included.

Ordinarily, judges apply text-specific definitions with rigor. For example, in one case the Residential Drug-Related Evictions Act of the District of Columbia provided for the eviction of public-housing tenants when "the Court has determined . . . that the rental unit is a drug haven" because, among other things, "a tenant or occupant of the rental unit has been charged with a violation of [drug laws] due to activities that occurred within the housing accommodation that contains the rental unit."[10] The Act defined *occupant* as "a person authorized by the tenant or housing provider to be on the premises of the rental unit."[11] In a properly authorized search of Raesheeda Ball's apartment (while she was not there), the police found five men (presumably acquaintances of Ball) with handguns, rifles, crack cocaine, PCP, marijuana, and drug paraphernalia. The men were arrested and charged with violating the drug laws.[12] A jury held that because Ball's apartment had been

---

8   1 Pa. Constr. Stat. § 1991.

9   *Commonwealth v. Massini*, 188 A.2d 816, 818 (Pa. Super. Ct. 1963).

10   D.C. Code § 42-3602(a)(1).

11   *Id.* § 42-3601(16).

12   *Ball v. Arthur Winn Gen. P'ship/So. Hills Apartments*, 905 A.2d 147, 149 (D.C. 2006).

used as a drug haven, she could be evicted. On appeal, Ball argued that the term *occupant* in the statute must be defined in light of landlord–tenant law as one who lives in a housing unit, and that because visitors or guests are not "occupants," the perpetrators' actions could not establish the existence of a drug haven. After all, Ball contended, application of the Act's definition would result in a rental unit's being designated a drug haven if a repairman were found in possession of drugs inside it.[13] The Government argued that the trial court had properly instructed the jury that an *occupant* was what the definition says: anyone authorized by the tenant to be on the premises of the rental unit. The court agreed and held that the established meaning of a word must yield to the statutory definition.[14]

It is very rare that a defined meaning can be replaced with another permissible meaning of the word on the basis of other textual indications; the definition is virtually conclusive. Rare, but not inconceivable. Definitions are, after all, just one indication of meaning—a very strong indication, to be sure, but nonetheless one that can be contradicted by other indications. So where the artificial or limited meaning would cause a provision to contradict another provision, whereas the normal meaning of the word would harmonize the two, the normal meaning should be applied.

Sometimes a definition itself contains a term that is not clear. When that is the case, the usual criteria of interpretation discussed in this book are brought to bear. Far and away the most important of those is the contextual factor of the word actually being defined. Since on this side of the looking-glass an entirely artificial definition is rare, the meaning of the definition is almost always closely related to the ordinary meaning of the word being defined. The definition "means nails" will bear one meaning when the defined term is *fasteners* and quite another when the defined term is *digital excrescences*. And when the federal Food, Drug, and Cosmetics Act defines *drugs* as "articles (other than food) intended to affect

---

13 *Id.* at 151.
14 *Id.* at 151–52.

the structure or any function of the body,"[15] it assuredly does not include exercise bikes.

A result-oriented case that flouts this principle is *State v. Hudson*, decided by the Maine Supreme Court.[16] Maine law authorized courts to order convicted criminals to make restitution to the victims of their crimes.[17] *Victim* was defined as a "person who suffers . . . economic loss as a result of a crime . . . ."[18] *Economic loss* included "reasonable charges incurred for reasonably needed products, services, and accommodations . . . ."[19] In this case, the defendant was convicted of animal cruelty for recklessly starving his horse. The horse was turned over to the Maine State Society for the Protection of Animals so that it could be treated and cared for. As a condition of the defendant's probation, the trial judge required him to reimburse the Society for its expenses in nursing the horse back to health. On appeal, the defendant contended that the Society was not an authorized claimant for restitution under the statute because it was not a victim.[20] The prosecution countered that the Society was a victim because it met the statutory definition of having "suffer[ed] . . . economic loss as a result of a crime"—loss from the expenses related to the care of the injured horse. The Maine Supreme Court agreed with the prosecution.[21]

That might have been a reasonable enough holding if the statute had provided for restitution to "anyone who incurred economic loss as a result of the crime." But it did not. It provided for restitution to *victims*—and it defined that term not just as anyone *incurring* economic loss, but as anyone *suffering* economic loss. In the context of defining *victim*, an organization that voluntarily takes care of an abused animal can hardly be considered to have *suffered* loss.

---

15   21 U.S.C. § 321(g)(1)(C).

16   470 A.2d 786 (Me. 1984).

17   Me. Rev. Stat. tit. 17-A, § 1324.

18   *Id.* § 1322(7).

19   *Id.* § 1322(3)(A).

20   *Hudson*, 470 A.2d at 788.

21   *Id.*

Another case, one of much greater consequence, also inter-preted a definition's vague term with no regard for the term being defined. *Babbitt v. Sweet Home Chapter of Communities for a Great Oregon*[22] put an end to logging on thousands of acres in the West and prohibited other useful human activities, such as farming, be-cause of the harm that the activity would cause to the habitat of an endangered species. The Endangered Species Act made it unlaw-ful "to . . . take any [protected] species within the United States."[23] It defined *take* as "to harass, *harm*, pursue, hunt, shoot, wound, kill, trap, capture, or collect, or to attempt to engage in any such conduct."[24] The Department of Interior's implementing regulation, in turn, defined the definitional term *harm* as follows:

> *Harm* in the definition of "take" in the Act means an act which actually kills or injures wildlife. Such act may in-clude significant habitat modification or degradation where it actually kills or injures wildlife by significantly impairing essential behavioral patterns, including breeding, feeding or sheltering.[25]

The Supreme Court of the United States erroneously held in *Bab-bitt* that this regulation was a reasonable interpretation of the Act. In fact, though, one of the reasons, perhaps the principal reason, that the Secretary's regulation was unreasonable is that it took no account of the word (*take*) that the statutory definition, including the word *harm*, was defining. We quote the dissent, which one of us wrote—and quote it at length because we like it:

> If "take" were not elsewhere defined in the Act, none could dispute what it means, for the term is as old as the law itself. To "take," when applied to wild animals, means to reduce those animals, by killing or capturing, to human control.[26] This is just the sense in which "take" is used else-

22   515 U.S. 687 (1995) (per Stevens, J.).

23   16 U.S.C. § 1538(a)(1)(B).

24   *Id.* § 1532(19) (emphasis added).

25   50 C.F.R. § 17.3 (emphasis added).

26   *See, e.g.,* 11 *Oxford English Dictionary* 37 (1933) ("*Take* . . . To catch, capture (a wild beast, bird, fish, etc.)"); *Webster's New International Dictionary of the English Language* (2d ed. 1949) (*take* defined as "to catch or capture by trapping, snaring, etc., or as prey"); *Geer v. Connecticut,* 161 U.S. 519, 523 (1896) (per White, J.)

where in federal legislation and treaty[27] . . . . It is obvious that "take" in this sense—a term of art deeply embedded in the statutory and common law concerning wildlife— describes a class of acts (not omissions) done directly and intentionally (not indirectly and by accident) to particular animals (not populations of animals).

. . .

The tempting fallacy—which the Court commits with abandon, . . . is to assume that *once defined*, "take" loses any significance, and it is only the definition that matters. . . . [I]f the terms contained in the definitional section are susceptible of two readings, one of which comports with the standard meaning of "take" as used in application to wildlife, and one of which does not, an agency regulation that adopts the latter reading is necessarily unreasonable, for it reads the defined term "take"—the only operative term— out of the statute altogether.

. . .

The verb "harm" has a *range* of meaning: "to cause injury" at its broadest, "to do hurt or damage" in a narrower and more direct sense. . . . To define "harm" as an act or omission that, however remotely, "actually kills or injures" a population of wildlife through habitat modification is to choose a meaning that makes nonsense of the word that "harm" defines—requiring us to accept that a farmer who tills his field and causes erosion that makes silt run into a nearby river which depletes oxygen and thereby "impairs [the] breeding" of protected fish has "taken" or "attempted to take" the fish. It should take the strongest evidence to make us believe that Congress has defined a term in a manner repugnant to its ordinary and traditional sense.[28]

("'[A]ll the animals which can be taken upon the earth, in the sea, or in the air,— that is to say, wild animals,—belong to those who take them.'") (quoting the *Digest* of Justinian); 2 William Blackstone, *Commentaries on the Laws of England* 411 (4th ed. 1770) ("Every man . . . has an equal right of pursuing and taking to his own use all such creatures as are *ferae naturae*").

27 *See, e.g.*, Migratory Bird Treaty Act, 16 U.S.C. § 703 (1988 ed., Supp. V) (no person may "pursue, hunt, take, capture, kill, [or] attempt to take, capture, [or] kill" any migratory bird); Agreement on the Conservation of Polar Bears, Nov. 15, 1973, Art. I, 27 U.S.T. 3918, 3921, T.I.A.S. No. 8409 (defining *taking* as "hunting, killing and capturing").

28 515 U.S. at 717–19 (Scalia, J., dissenting) (emphasis added).

Hence we disagree with the notion that the definiendum (the word being defined) has no necessary link to the definiens (the definition itself). In legal-drafting circles, it is well known that counterintuitive definitions are a bane.[29] And in legal-interpretation circles, there is a presumption against them—because the word being defined is the most significant element of the definition's context. The normal sense of that word and its associations bear significantly on the meaning of ambiguous words or phrases in the definition. So while it is true that drafters "have the power to innovate upon the general meaning of words at large free from all legal restrictions,"[30] they do not have the power to do so free from the presumption that they have not done so.

The perceptive reader will also have observed that in *Babbitt*, the Secretary's regulation, and the Court's approval of it, blatantly violated another basic canon, *noscitur a sociis* (§ 31 [associated-words canon]). All nine other verbs contained in the statutory definition of *take* ("harass, pursue, hunt, shoot, wound, kill, trap, capture, or collect") fit the ordinary meaning of *take* pretty well. What they all have in common—and share with the narrower meaning of *harm* but not with the Secretary's definition—is that they denote affirmative conduct intentionally directed against a particular animal or animals, not acts or omissions that indirectly, and perhaps unintentionally, cause harm to a population of animals.[31]

Legal drafters have the power not only to define their terms but also to limit the implications of their terms—which means that a contract or statute can exclude a canon of construction based on probable import. Legislatures do this all the time, on a

---

29 *See, e.g., Garner's Dictionary of Legal Usage* 258 (3d ed. 2011) ("[O]ne must be careful not to use counterintuitive definitions, as by saying that the word *dog* is deemed to include all horses."); Reed Dickerson, *Fundamentals of Legal Drafting* § 7.3, at 144 (2d ed. 1986) ("[I]t is important for the legal draftsman not to define a word in a sense significantly different from the way it is normally understood by the persons to whom it is addressed.").

30 *Morrison v. Wilson*, 30 Cal. 344, 348 (1866).

31 *See* Caleb Nelson, *Statutory Interpretation* 761 (2011) (noting that in this context, *harm* could be "understood to refer only to injuries associated with the assertion of control or partial control over the animal").

retail rather than wholesale basis, when they use the phrase *including without limitation*, which has the effect of excluding application of the negative-implication canon (see § 10) to what follows. And a statute or contract could provide generally that its use of the word *person* does not include corporations—altering the normal interpretive rule to the contrary (see § 44 [artificial-person canon]). Excluding interpretive rules that are not based on probable meaning is another matter. Presumably neither private parties nor legislatures can alter rules based on sheer logic—requiring, for example, that all provisions be given effect, even those that contradict each other. Logical reasoning is the duty of the courts, and not even the legislature can exclude it.

Another unremovable duty of the courts is to give private and public texts their fair meaning. It is one thing for private parties or the legislature to supply the definition of the words, and specify the implication of the words, that go into this determination of fair meaning; it is something else for them to prescribe that fair meaning will not govern. That cannot be done. So in our view a contractual provision that all ambiguities will be resolved in favor of one of the parties is ineffective—or, perhaps, effective only when, after applying all the normal tools of interpretation, an ambiguity cannot be resolved (which is never). As for the regrettably common legislative provision that a statute must be "liberally construed," does this mean anything other than "in the event of ambiguity, the plaintiff suing under this statute will win"? And can the legislature instruct judges to place a thumb on the scales in this fashion? We think not. Rather, consistently with the presumption of validity (§ 5) and the constitutional-doubt canon (§ 38), such a provision should be regarded as requiring a fair interpretation as opposed to a strict or crabbed one—which is what courts are supposed to provide anyway.

37. Absurdity Doctrine

A provision may be either disregarded or judicially corrected as an error (when the correction is textually simple) if failing to do so would result in a disposition that no reasonable person could approve.

> "[I]n construing . . . all written instruments, the grammatical and ordinary sense of the words is to be adhered to, unless that would lead to some absurdity, or some repugnance or inconsistency with the rest of the instrument, in which case the grammatical and ordinary sense of the words may be modified, so as to avoid that absurdity and inconsistency, but no farther."
>
> *Grey v. Pearson,*
> [1857] 6 H.L. Cas. 61, 106 (per Lord Wensleydale).

Some absurd outcomes can be avoided without doing real violence to the text. But sometimes there is *no* sense of a provision—*no* permissible meaning—that can eliminate an absurdity unless the court fixes a textual error. As Blackstone explained: "[W]here words bear . . . a very absurd signification, if literally understood, we must a little deviate from the received sense of them."[1] A little: If an easy correction is not possible, the absurdity stands.

No one would contend that the mistake cannot be corrected if it is of the sort sometimes described as a "scrivener's error."[2] Suppose, for example, that a passage misspells *third party* as "third partly," or inexplicably repeats the word ("third party party"). No one would suggest that the entire provision containing such an error must be disregarded because it makes no sense: The meaning is clear. Such readily identifiable "scrivener's errors" present no realistic interpretive problem. In Manitoba, publication of the banns for marriage was regulated by a statute making provision for people "in the habit of attending whorship

---

1   William Blackstone, *Commentaries on the Laws of England* § 2, at 60 (4th ed. 1770).

2   *See* Daniel A. Farber, *Statutory Interpretation and Legislative Supremacy*, 78 Geo. L.J. 281, 289 (1989) ("If the directive contains a typographical error, correcting the error can hardly be considered disobedience.").

[sic] at different churches."[3] The meaning could not have been seriously in doubt.

Is the situation different when the error (more likely a drafter's error than a scrivener's) makes entire sense grammatically but produces a disposition that makes no substantive sense (a so-called *evaluative absurdity*[4])? Consider, for example, a provision in a statute creating a new claim by saying that "the winning party must pay the other side's reasonable attorney's fees." That is entirely absurd, and it is virtually certain that *winning party* was meant to be *losing party*. May the court read it that way, in defiance of the plain text?

We agree with those authorities who say that it may. The line between reading *partly* to mean "party," and reading *winning* to mean "losing," is generally not a principled one. In both cases we are not revising the apparent meaning of the text but are giving it the meaning that it would convey to a reasonable person, who would understand that misprints had occurred.[5] What the rule of absurdity seeks to do is what all rules of interpretation seek to do: *make sense* of the text. And just as a text does not make sense if *nails* (in a context dealing with fasteners) is taken to mean "fingernails," or if *third partly* is not recognized as a scrivener's error, so also a text that assesses attorneys' fees against the winning party does not make sense unless *winning* is understood to be a drafter's error for *losing*. The difference between these three examples goes to the basis for the judgment (context versus grammar versus sanity of outcome), not to the purpose of the judgment. In all three,

---

3   *See* R.E. Megarry, *A Second Miscellany-at-Law* 183 (1973) (citing Revised Statutes of Manitoba 1970, c. M50, § 8(2)(b)).

4   *See* D. Neil MacCormick & Zenon Bankowski, "Some Principles of Statutory Interpretation," in *Legal Reasoning and Statutory Interpretation* 41, 46–47 (Jan van Dunné ed., 1989).

5   *See Amalgamated Transit Union Local 1309 v. Laidlaw Transit Serv., Inc.*, 435 F.3d 1140, 1145 (9th Cir. 2006) (holding that *less* meant *more* in 28 U.S.C. § 1453(c)(1), which required an application for appeal to be filed "not less than 7 days" after the entry of the court's remand order); *Miedema v. Maytag Corp.*, 450 F.3d 1322, 1326 (11th Cir. 2006) (same); *Pritchett v. Office Depot, Inc.* 420 F.3d 1090, 1093 n.2 (10th Cir. 2005) (same) (in 2009, the statute was amended by Pub. L. 111–16 § 6(2) to read "not more than 10 days").

what is sought is the fair meaning of the text—the meaning that causes it to make sense.

The threshold for true absurdity typically presents itself straightforwardly. Consider the case of a Texas citizen, Derrik Boone, who was convicted of driving with a suspended license. At the time of his arrest, a Texas statute provided an absolute defense to all "Chapter 601 offenses" if the accused "produce[d] in court a motor vehicle liability policy . . . that was valid at the time the offense is alleged to have occurred."[6] "Chapter 601 offenses," as they are termed in Texas, included not just driving without insurance but also driving with a suspended license. Mr. Boone urged the courts to apply this exemption as written, so that every time he was haled into court for driving with a suspended license, he could flash his insurance card and walk away with impunity. This interpretation would have encouraged scofflaws to drive long after their licenses had been suspended for any reason, simply on condition that they maintain insurance—a result that has no semblance of plausibility. "Chapter 601 offenses" was obviously an error for "driving-without-insurance offenses." Hence the court applied the absurdity rule and held that Mr. Boone had no insurance-card defense to his charge.[7] Not surprisingly, two years later, in 1999, the Texas legislature amended § 601.193 to apply only in cases involving a motorist's failure to provide proof of insurance.[8]

What is omitted from statutory text, no less than what is included, can cause it to be absurd. In 1945, the Arkansas legislature passed "An Act to Authorize and Permit Cities of First and Second Class and Incorporated Towns to Vacate Public Streets and Alleys in the Public Interest." This seems tame enough. But § 8 read as follows: "All laws and parts of laws, and particularly Act 311 of the Acts of 1941, are hereby repealed."[9] This omnibus repealer threatened to wipe out all the statutory law in the state. When that very result was in fact urged on the Arkansas Supreme

---

6   Tex. Transp. Code Ann. § 601.193(a) (West 1995).

7   *State v. Boone*, 1998 WL 344931 (Tex. App.—Dallas June 30, 1998) (mem. op., not designated for publication).

8   *See* Tex. Transp. Code Ann. § 601.193 (West 1999).

9   Act 17 of 1945 (repl. 1980; now Ark. Stat. § 14-301-301).

Court, the court held as follows: "No doubt the legislature meant to repeal all laws in conflict with that act, and, by error of the author or the typist, left out the usual words 'in conflict herewith,' which we will imply by necessary construction."[10] Some years later, Justice George Rose Smith of that court wrote a hilarious fictitious opinion purporting to hold that all pre-1945 statutes in Arkansas, including the Statute of Frauds, had been nullified.[11]

Yet error-correction for absurdity can be a slippery slope. It can lead to judicial revision of public and private texts to make them (in the judges' view) more reasonable.[12] To avoid this, the doctrine must be subject to two limiting conditions:

(1) The absurdity must consist of a disposition that no reasonable person could intend. Something that "may seem odd . . . is not absurd."[13] The oddity or anomaly of certain consequences may be a perfectly valid reason for choosing one textually permissible interpretation over another, but it is no basis for disregarding or changing the text. Justice Joseph Story made the hurdle a very high one:

> "[I]f, in any case, the plain meaning of a provision, not contradicted by any other provision of the same instrument, is to be disregarded, because we believe the framers of that instrument could not intend what they say, it must be one, where the absurdity and injustice of applying the provision to the case would be so monstrous, that all mankind would, without hesitation, unite in rejecting the application."[14]

---

10 *Cernauskas v. Fletcher*, 201 S.W.2d 999, 1000 (Ark. 1947) (per McHaney, J.).

11 *See* R.E. Megarry, *A Second Miscellany-at-Law* 185–89 (1973) (reproducing the fictitious opinion).

12 *See* John F. Manning, *The Absurdity Doctrine*, 116 Harv. L. Rev. 2387, 2476–79 (2003) (noting the Supreme Court's ill-founded use of the absurdity doctrine in the *Holy Trinity* case (1892) and correctly suggesting that modern textualists use a reasonable-user-of-language approach to assess whether a statute produces absurd results).

13 *Exxon Mobil Corp. v. Allapattah Servs., Inc.*, 545 U.S. 546, 565 (2005) (per Kennedy, J.). *See also Shady Grove Orthopedic Assocs. v. Allstate Ins. Co.*, 130 S.Ct. 1431, 1446 n.13 (2010) (per Scalia, J.) ("The possible existence of a few outlier instances does not prove [that an] interpretation is absurd. Congress may well have accepted such anomalies as the price of a uniform system of federal procedure.").

14 1 Joseph Story, *Commentaries on the Constitution of the United States* § 427, at 303

(2) The absurdity must be reparable by changing or supplying
a particular word or phrase whose inclusion or omission
was obviously a technical or ministerial error (e.g., *losing
party* instead of *winning party*).[15] The doctrine does not
include substantive errors arising from a drafter's failure to
appreciate the effect of certain provisions.

Both conditions are necessary for correct application of the absurdity doctrine. Together they absolve the doctrine of the charge
that it is an application not of textualism but of purposivism—
seeking to give the text not the meaning that it objectively conveys
but the meaning that was in the mind of the drafter.

A good example of failure of the second condition is the United States Supreme Court's decision in *Chung Fook v. White*.[16] A
provision of the Immigration Act of 1917 stated that "if the person
sending for wife or minor child is naturalized, a wife to whom
married [sic] or a minor child born subsequent to such husband
or father's naturalization shall be admitted without detention for
treatment in hospital." The appellant was not a naturalized citizen
but a native-born one who wanted to bring his alien wife into the
United States for treatment of a dangerous contagious disease. She
was denied entry.

It was admittedly absurd to exempt from detention the
wife and children of each naturalized citizen, while denying it
to spouses and children of native citizens. The Supreme Court

---

(2d ed. 1858). *See also United States v. Butler*, 297 U.S. 1, 79 (1936) (Stone, J., dissenting) ("For the removal of unwise laws from the statute books appeal lies, not
to the courts, but to the ballot and to the processes of democratic government.");
Metropolis Theater Co. v. City of Chicago, 228 U.S. 61, 69 (1913) (per McKenna, J.)
("To be able to find fault with a law is not to demonstrate its invalidity.").

15 *See* Michael S. Fried, *A Theory of Scrivener's Error*, 52 Rutgers L. Rev. 589, 607
(2000) ("Absurdity alone is insufficient to justify application of the doctrine.
Rather, there must also exist a non-absurd reading that could be achieved by
modifying the enacted text in relatively simple ways."). *See also Gilmore v. United
States*, 699 A.2d 1130, 1132–33 (D.C. 1997) (reading the word *subsection* as *section* in sentencing guidelines because of clerical error, when interpreting the statute otherwise would create a "pointlessly circular provision"); *Stanton v. Frankel
Bros. Realty Co.*, 158 N.E. 868, 870 (Ohio 1927) (reading the word *of* as *or* in
statute allowing only the "county auditor *of* any complainant" to appeal decision
of county tax board).

16 264 U.S. 443 (1924) (per Sutherland, J.).

nonetheless upheld the denial of entry, stating: "The words of the statute being clear, if it unjustly discriminates against the native-born citizen . . . the remedy lies with Congress and not with the courts. Their duty is simply to enforce the law as it is written, unless clearly unconstitutional."[17] As far as the doctrine of absurdity is concerned,[18] that result was correct. Favoring naturalized citizens over native citizens was, to be sure, absurd; but it was not an absurdity arising from the oversight of not providing similar treatment for native-born citizens *in the Immigration Act*; such a provision would have been entirely out of place there. There was, in other words, no way to regard the limitation to naturalized citizens as a mistake in the text of the Immigration Act. The doctrine of absurdity is meant to correct obviously *unintended* dispositions, not to revise purposeful dispositions that, in light of other provisions of the applicable code, make little if any sense.

---

17 *Id.* at 446.

18 Under modern equal-protection law, the disposition against native citizens might well be held unconstitutional, since it has no conceivable rational basis. *See Washington v. Confederated Bands & Tribes of the Yakima Indian Nation*, 439 U.S. 463, 501 (1979) (per Stewart, J.) ("[L]egislative classifications are valid unless they bear no rational relationship to the State's objectives.").

Principles Applicable Specifically to Governmental Prescriptions

Prefatory Remarks

The rules set forth thus far rest on normal uses of language by educated speakers and so apply to all written legal instruments. There are also rules specifically applicable to various categories of private legal instruments such as wills, deeds, and contracts. For example, the ambiguities in a contract will be construed against the party that drafted the document (*contra proferentem*). Such rules are based not on linguistic usage (otherwise, they would be universally applicable) but rather on various factors depending on the context and the field of law—factors such as preference for reflecting normal expectations, or preference for the disposition most consonant with sound public policy. Discussed below are the special rules applicable to statutes and other authoritative governmental dispositions.

As a jurisprudential matter, Anglo-American legal systems are premised on a rule of law that equates justice with conformity to law—nothing more. This notion is referred to as the positive-law theory of justice,[1] whereby the judges follow the law enacted by the legislature. There is no going around or behind the words of a statute (except, as we have seen, in the case of genuine absurdity). If a judge adheres to the social-good theory of justice[2] (holding that there is a duty to effect justice outside the positive law) or the natural-right theory of justice[3] (holding that justice is based not on positive law but on natural right, rendering each person his due as a human being regardless of the positive law), then the judge will likely seek to discount statutory provisions that do not coincide with the judge's own perception of social good or sense of natural right.

In the American system of separate and coequal powers, authoritative interpretation of the laws is the assigned role of the courts. It is an interesting question—though for the most part an academic one—how far a legislature can go in prescribing how the

---

1   *See* Otto A. Bird, *The Idea of Justice* 43–78 (1967).

2   *See id.* at 79–117.

3   *See id.* at 118–60.

243

courts interpret. It cannot, of course, direct the outcome of cases—provide that plaintiffs win, say, or that criminal defendants lose. But could it provide, either generally or with respect to a particular statute, that the courts will take account of legislative history[4]—or, for that matter, *not* take account of legislative history? Can it provide, either generally or with respect to a particular statute, that the negative-implication canon (§ 10) will not apply, or that the rule of lenity will be disregarded?

In a system of separated powers, the answers to these questions depend on whether the legislature is doing its own job or intruding upon the courts' job of applying the fair meaning of texts. Marking the constitutional line is beyond the scope of this book on interpretation, but a few things seem clear. To start with, the answer may differ when a legislature prescribes how private legal instruments are to be interpreted, as opposed to enacting rules for interpreting its own statutes. To a large extent legislatures can prohibit various private dispositions—which necessarily means that they can set forth the textual requirements for certain private agreements. For example, they can forbid charging interest above a certain amount. So why can they not, short of that, provide that any instrument providing for the charging of interest above a certain rate must be clear and unambiguous? And is it any different to provide that any provision for the charging of interest "shall be strictly construed"? Such a statutory directive is as much an instruction to lenders (how they must write) as to courts (how they must construe).

But a legislature's prescription of how courts are to interpret its own product is quite different. When the prescription applies to interpretation of only the statute in which it is contained, it can amount to nothing more than the legislature's clarification of the statute's meaning. For example, a provision excluding application of the negative-implication canon has the same effect as adding words such as *without limitation* before each passage where that canon would otherwise apply. And a directive *not* to use legislative history in the interpretation of the statute is the equivalent

---

4   *See, e.g.*, Ohio Rev. Code § 1.49.

of a provision in a private document that it represents the entire agreement between the parties. Some interpretive prescriptions contained in a statute might run afoul of the Constitution—for example, a prescription that legislative history *must* be considered[5] or (at least arguably under the Due Process Clause) that the rule of lenity does not apply.

An interpretive command applicable to *all* statutes is more problematic—more likely to be an intrusion upon the courts' function of interpreting the laws, rather than an exercise of the legislature's power to clarify the meaning of its product. That is certainly true for a previously enacted statute: The legislature has no power to "clarify" the meaning of such a statute except by amendment, which hardly seems to describe a directive to the courts. And the legislature can clarify the meaning of a later-enacted statute only to the extent that the later-enacting legislature can be assumed to accept the clarification that the earlier statute prescribes, which it is under no obligation to do. This issue is similar to that which arises when a legislature enacts a general definition of terms applicable to all future legislation. See § 36 (interpretive-direction canon).

But all this is for the most part academic. Apart from the rule-of-lenity abridgments discussed in § 49, the only common enactments directing judicial interpretation that we are aware of are those prescribing that the provisions of a statute "are to be liberally construed." This in no way clarifies what any particular provision of the statute says, but it instructs the courts, with regard to all the provisions, how to make their interpretive judgment—with a thumb on the side of the scales that produces expansive application of the statute. Such a provision should be regarded as merely rejecting "strict construction" that distorts fair meaning—which the courts should not be engaging in anyway (pp. 355–58). Since fair interpretation is what the Constitution requires, instructing

---

5   *See* Jonathan R. Siegel, *The Use of Legislative History in a System of Separated Powers*, 53 Vand. L. Rev. 1457, 1458 (2000); John F. Manning, *Putting Legislative History to a Vote: A Response to Professor Siegel*, 53 Vand. L. Rev. 1529, 1533–34 (2000).

the courts to interpret fairly may make Congress a busybody, may be ultra vires, but does not have any effect.

We proceed, then, to the special rules applicable to the interpretation of authoritative governmental dispositions—including statutes, ordinances, and regulations. Most of these rules apply as well to the interpretation of constitutions, which are assuredly authoritative governmental dispositions.[6] Some, however, such as the constitutional-doubt canon (§ 38) can logically have no application in the constitutional context. One could say (unhelpfully) that all the following rules are based on what one would normally expect the statute or constitution to say. We have grouped them, however, into four somewhat arbitrary categories based on what seem to us the principal bases generally asserted for their existence: (1) those based on what one would normally expect the statute to say (one's own policy preferences aside); (2) those pertaining to the structure of government; (3) those reflecting a regard for individual rights; and (4) those favoring the stability and continuity of the law.

---

6   *See, e.g.*, Theodore Sedgwick, *A Treatise on the Rules Which Govern the Interpretation and Application of Statutory and Constitutional Law* 24 (1857) ("[T]he general rules of interpretation are the same, whether applied to statutes or constitutions."); Thomas M. Cooley, *A Treatise on the Constitutional Limitations Which Rest upon the Legislative Power of the States of the American Union* 63 (1868) ("We are aware of no reasons, applicable to ordinary legislation, which do not apply equally well to constitutions . . ."); Joel Prentiss Bishop, *Commentaries on the Law of Statutory Crimes* § 92, at 61 (1873) ("The general doctrine is, that constitutions are to be expounded in the same way and according to the same rules as statutes.").

Expected-Meaning Canons

38. Constitutional-Doubt Canon

A statute should be interpreted in a way that avoids placing its constitutionality in doubt.

> "[W]here a statute is susceptible of two constructions, by one of which grave and doubtful constitutional questions arise and by the other of which such questions are avoided, our duty is to adopt the latter."
> *United States ex rel. Attorney General v. Delaware & Hudson Co.*, 213 U.S. 366, 408 (1909) (per White, J.).

In 1909, the Supreme Court of the United States was presented with a case[1] requiring the interpretation of the Hepburn Act of 1906. The statute's "commodities clause," if given broad effect, presented grave constitutional questions under the Commerce Clause.[2] Hence the Court read the commodities clause narrowly and sustained a statute that the lower court had held wholly void.[3] The doctrine by which the Court achieved this result—the so-called constitutional-doubt canon—would by the late 20th century be described by the Court as "beyond debate."[4]

One might think that this is simply an application of the general presumption against unconstitutionality, which is a species of the presumption of validity.[5] But this view would be mistaken because the rule goes much further than that. It militates against not only those interpretations that would render the statute

---

1   *United States ex rel. Attorney Gen. v. Delaware & Hudson Co.*, 213 U.S. 366 (1909) (per White, J.).

2   U.S. Const. art. I, § 8, cl. 3.

3   *United States v. Delaware & Hudson Co.*, 164 F. 215 (C.C.E.D. Pa. 1908).

4   *Edward J. DeBartolo Corp. v. Florida Gulf Coast Bldg. & Constr. Trades Council*, 485 U.S. 568, 575 (1988) (per White, J.). *Contra* Frank H. Easterbrook, *Do Liberals and Conservatives Differ in Judicial Activism?* 73 U. Colo. L. Rev. 1401, 1405–06, 1409 (2002) (assailing the constitutional-doubt canon as "noxious" and "wholly illegitimate," and calling it "a misuse of judicial power"). *See generally* John Copeland Nagle, Delaware & Hudson *Revisited*, 72 Notre Dame L. Rev. 1495 (1997).

5   *See supra* § 5.

unconstitutional but also those that would even raise serious questions of constitutionality.[6]

Perhaps this long-standing principle of interpretation is based, or at least was originally based, on a genuine assessment of probable meaning. In the texts that it enacts, a legislature should not be presumed to be sailing close to the wind, so to speak—entering an area of questionable constitutionality without making that entrance utterly clear. That was perhaps the original reason for the rule, and it is the reason we include it among the expected-meaning canons. But with respect to federal legislation at least—where the canon is routinely applied—that is today a dubious rationale. The modern Congress sails close to the wind all the time. Federal statutes today often all but acknowledge their questionable constitutionality with provisions for accelerated judicial review,[7] for standing on the part of members of Congress,[8] and even for

---

6   See, e.g., Crowell v. Benson, 285 U.S. 22, 62 (1932) (per Hughes, C.J.) ("When the validity of an act of the Congress is drawn in question, and even if a serious doubt of constitutionality is raised, it is a cardinal principle that this Court will first ascertain whether a construction of the statute is fairly possible by which the question may be avoided.").

7   See, e.g., the Federal Election Campaign Act (found unconstitutional in part in Buckley v. Valeo, 424 U.S. 1 (1976) (per curiam)), which provided that "the district court immediately shall certify all questions of constitutionality of this Act to the United States court of appeals for the circuit involved, which shall hear the matter sitting en banc," whose decision "shall be reviewable by appeal directly to the Supreme Court" which appeal "shall be brought no later than 20 days after the decision of the court of appeals"; and that "[i]t shall be the duty of the court of appeals and of the Supreme Court . . . to advance on the docket and to expedite to the greatest possible extent the disposition of any matter [so] certified," 2 U.S.C. § 437h (1970) (amended 1988). Other cases finding unconstitutional, in whole or in part, statutes providing for expedited judicial review include Bowsher v. Synar, 478 U.S. 714 (1986) (per Burger, C.J.) (Balanced Budget and Emergency Deficit Control Act of 1985); Reno v. American Civil Liberties Union, 521 U.S. 844 (1997) (per Stevens, J.) (Communications Decency Act of 1996); Clinton v. City of New York, 524 U.S. 417 (1998) (per Stevens, J.) (Line Item Veto Act); United States v. Playboy Entm't Group, Inc., 529 U.S. 803 (2000) (per Kennedy, J.) (Telecommunications Act of 1996); and Citizens United v. Federal Election Comm'n, 130 S.Ct. 876 (2010) (per Kennedy, J.) (Bipartisan Campaign Reform Act of 2002).

8   See, e.g., 2 U.S.C. § 692(a)(1) (Supp. II 1994) ("Any Member of Congress or any individual adversely affected by [this Act] may bring an action, in the United States District Court for the District of Columbia, for declaratory judgment and injunctive relief on the ground that any provision of this part violates the Constitution."). In Raines v. Byrd, 521 U.S. 811, 815–16, 829–30 (1997) (per Rehnquist, C.J.), the United States Supreme Court held that the portion of this provision

fall-back dispositions should the primary disposition be held unconstitutional.[9]

A more plausible basis for the rule is that it represents judicial policy—a judgment that statutes *ought not* to tread on questionable constitutional grounds unless they do so clearly, or perhaps a judgment that courts should minimize the occasions on which they confront and perhaps contradict the legislative branch. Since we favor this alternative view, we have no difficulty with the situation in which the factor that gives rise to the constitutional doubt arose *after* the statute was enacted. Such a situation arose in *Lowe v. SEC*,[10] where Justice Byron White's concurrence criticized the majority's reliance on the constitutional-doubt canon as follows: "The Court thus attributes to the 76th Congress . . . the ability to predict our constitutional holdings 45 years in advance of our declining to reach them."[11] This may well have been an accurate criticism of the majority opinion, which described the constitutional-doubt canon as implementing an actual intent of the enacting Congress to avoid constitutional difficulty. But the canon rests instead upon a judicial policy of not interpreting ambiguous statutes to flirt with constitutionality, thereby minimizing judicial conflicts with the legislature. That policy has full force whether the cases raising the constitutional doubt antedate or postdate a statute's enactment.

The constitutional-doubt canon has been amply criticized[12] and amply defended.[13] We side with its defenders. And even its

---

purporting to confer standing on individual members of Congress was unconstitutional, violating the "cases and controversies" requirement of Article III, § 2.

9   *See* Balanced Budget and Emergency Deficit Control Act of 1985, 2 U.S.C. § 922(f)(1) (Supp. III 1985) (amended 1997), providing for alternative disposition "[i]n the event that any of the reporting procedures described in [the Act] are invalidated." They were. *See Bowsher v. Synar*, 478 U.S. 714 (1986) (per Burger, J.).

10 472 U.S. 181 (1985) (per Stevens, J.).

11 *Id.* at 227 (White, J., concurring).

12 *See, e.g.*, Frederick Schauer, Ashwander *Revisited*, 1995 Sup. Ct. Rev. 71, 71–72 (1995); Richard A. Posner, *Statutory Interpretation—in the Classroom and in the Courtroom*, 50 U. Chi. L. Rev. 800, 815–16 (1983); Henry J. Friendly, *Benchmarks* 211 (1967).

13 *See, e.g.*, Matthew C. Stephenson, *The Price of Public Action: Constitutional Doctrine and the Judicial Manipulation of Legislative Enactment Costs*, 118 Yale L.J. 2,

critics acknowledge that the rule is well established. Yet it presents the difficult question: How doubtful is doubtful? This cannot be precisely answered in the abstract. At most, the mere assertion of unconstitutionality by one of the litigants is not enough. The doubt must be "substantial."[14] Unsurprisingly, the cases are many in which the majority and the dissent disagree on application of that standard.[15]

But sometimes, helpfully enough, the decision is unanimous. In 1989 the Supreme Court decided *Gomez v. United States*,[16] involving the scope of the Federal Magistrates Act. The statutory clause at issue provided that magistrates—today they are called *magistrate judges*—"may be assigned such additional duties as are not inconsistent with the Constitution and laws of the United States."[17] In *Gomez*, a magistrate was assigned to preside over jury selection in a felony trial. Defense counsel objected and demanded an Article III judge. The magistrate noted the objection, yet proceeded with the jury selection. On appeal, the Court was presented with deciding (1) whether jury selection was among the "additional duties" that a magistrate could be assigned without the defendant's consent; and (2) whether it is constitutional for a magistrate to preside over this phase of a criminal trial despite the defendant's objection. For a unanimous Court, Justice Stevens wrote: "It is our settled policy to avoid an interpretation of a federal statute that engenders constitutional issues if a reasonable alternative interpretation poses no constitutional question."[18] Hence the

---

11–16 (2008); Cass R. Sunstein, *Nondelegation Canons*, 67 U. Chi. L. Rev. 315, 331–32 (2000); Ernest A. Young, *Constitutional Avoidance, Resistance Norms, and Preservation of Judicial Review*, 78 Tex. L. Rev. 1549, 1585–93 (2000).

14   *See* William K. Kelley, *Avoiding Constitutional Questions as a Three-Branch Problem*, 86 Cornell L. Rev. 831 (2001).

15   *See, e.g., United States v. X-Citement Video, Inc.*, 513 U.S. 64, 78, 83 (1994) (per Rehnquist, C.J.) (majority and dissent disagreeing about whether the Protection of Children Against Sexual Exploitation Act raised "serious constitutional doubts"); *Rust v. Sullivan*, 500 U.S. 173, 192, 205 (1991) (per Rehnquist, C.J.) (majority and dissent disagreeing about whether statutory prohibition contained in the Public Health Service Act raised serious constitutional doubts).

16   490 U.S. 858 (1989) (per Stevens, J.).

17   28 U.S.C. § 636(b)(3).

18   490 U.S. at 864.

Court avoided the second issue by finding that jury selection was not among the "additional duties" consistent with the Magistrates Act, which gave magistrates the primary duties of (1) presiding at civil trials and criminal-misdemeanor trials, subject to the parties' consent; and (2) handling certain pretrial and posttrial rulings. The Court relied not only on the constitutional-doubt canon but also on the negative-implication canon (see § 10): "[T]he carefully defined grant of authority to conduct trials of civil matters and of minor criminal cases should be construed as an implicit withholding of the authority to preside at a felony trial."[19]

The constitutional-doubt canon is sometimes lumped together with the rule that "if a case can be decided on either of two grounds, one involving a constitutional question, the other a question of statutory construction or general law, the Court will decide only the latter."[20] The two rules together are sometimes called the "rules of constitutional avoidance."[21] But it promotes clarity to keep the two separate. The constitutional-doubt canon is a rule of interpretation; the rule that statutory grounds will be considered first is a rule of judicial procedure. Often, but not always, both rules will be invoked in the same case: In the process of considering the statute first, the court may find that one of its interpretations must be rejected as constitutionally doubtful.

---

19 *Id.* at 872.

20 *Ashwander v. Tennessee Valley Auth.*, 297 U.S. 288, 347 (1936) (Brandeis, J., concurring).

21 *See, e.g.*, Linda D. Jellum, *Mastering Statutory Interpretation* 235 (2008).

39. Related-Statutes Canon

Statutes *in pari materia* are to be interpreted together, as though they were one law.

> "We generally presume that Congress is knowledgeable about existing law pertinent to the legislation it enacts."
> *Goodyear Atomic Corp. v. Miller,*
> 486 U.S. 174, 184–85 (1988) (per Marshall, J.).

Any word or phrase that comes before a court for interpretation is part of a whole statute, and its meaning is therefore affected by other provisions of the same statute. It is also, however, part of an entire *corpus juris*. So, if possible, it should no more be interpreted to clash with the rest of that corpus than it should be interpreted to clash with other provisions of the same law. Hence laws dealing with the same subject—being *in pari materia* (translated as "in a like matter")—should if possible be interpreted harmoniously. As James Kent explained in 1826: "Several acts *in pari materia*, and relating to the same subject, are to be taken together, and compared in the construction of them, because they are considered as having one object in view, and as acting upon one system."[1]

Though it is often presented as effectuating the legislative "intent," the related-statute canon is not, to tell the truth, based upon a realistic assessment of what the legislature actually meant. That would assume an implausible legislative knowledge of related legislation in the past, and an impossible legislative knowledge of related legislation yet to be enacted. The canon is, however, based upon a realistic assessment of what the legislature ought to have meant. It rests on two sound principles: (1) that the body of the law should make sense, and (2) that it is the responsibility of the courts, within the permissible meanings of the text, to make it so.

"Statutes," Justice Frankfurter once wrote, "cannot be read intelligently if the eye is closed to considerations evidenced in affiliated statutes."[2] Part of the statute's context is the *corpus juris* of

---

1   1 James Kent, *Commentaries on American Law* 433 (1826).

2   Felix Frankfurter, *Some Reflections on the Reading of Statutes*, 47 Colum. L. Rev. 527, 539 (1947).

which it forms a part, and this corpus can be dauntingly substantial. What is required, according to a British judge, is a "conspectus of the entire relevant body of the law for the same purpose."[3]

The critical questions are these: Just how affiliated must "affiliated" be, and what purposes are the same? The cases provide—properly, in our view—a good deal of leeway. In one case, the defendant was indicted for aggravated arson, which was committed by "whosoever shall unlawfully and maliciously set fire to any dwelling-house, any person being therein." The charge against the defendant was that he himself was inside the dwelling when he started the fire. The defense objected that the statute prohibits only harm to others—not to oneself—and the court was persuaded only because another statute, the Offenses Against the Person Act (which speaks of "unlawfully and maliciously . . . wound[ing] . . . any person"), had never been understood as including self-mutilation or suicide.[4]

Consider a case[5] arising under the Minnesota Human Rights Act, which read: "It is an unfair discriminatory practice . . . for an owner . . . to refuse to sell, rent, or lease . . . any real property because of race, color, creed, religion, national origin, sex, marital status, status with regard to public assistance, disability, or familial status."[6] The Act did not define the term *marital status*. Layle French refused to let his rental house to Susan Parsons because she intended to cohabit with her fiancé before marriage, which was inconsistent with French's religious beliefs. The question was whether French violated the Act. French argued that the term *marital status* is ambiguous because it is susceptible of two meanings: one that includes cohabiting couples, and one that does not. He contended that the second meaning must be preferred because Minnesota law had always discouraged fornication in favor of protecting the institution of marriage. The Minnesota Attorney General contended that the first meaning should be preferred because

---

3   *Ealing L.B.C. v. Race Relations Bd.*, [1972] A.C. 342, 361 (H.L.) (per Lord Simon of Glaisdale).

4   *R. v. Arthur*, [1968] 1 Q.B. 810.

5   *State v. French*, 460 N.W.2d 2 (Minn. 1990).

6   Minn. Stat. § 363.03, subd. 2.

the fornication statute had fallen into complete disuse and did not accurately reflect the state's public policy. (On the impermissibility of this argument, see § 57 [desuetude canon].) Without using the phrase *in pari materia*, the Minnesota Supreme Court held that the Minnesota Human Rights Act must be read harmoniously with the anti-fornication statute. Hence it correctly held that French did not violate the Act.[7]

In Title 18 of the United States Code, two statutes have similar wordings: § 924(c)(1)(A) enhances the criminal penalty if a perpetrator carries a firearm "*during and in relation to . . .* [a] drug trafficking crime,"[8] while § 844(h)(2) enhances the penalty if the perpetrator "carries an explosive *during* the commission of any felony."[9] In *United States v. Ressam*,[10] Ahmed Ressam was carrying explosives in the trunk of his car when he arrived by ferry at Port Angeles, Washington. After he gave false information on a customs form, customs officials searched his car and discovered the explosives. The penalty imposed for Ressam's felony conviction of lying on the customs form was enhanced under § 844(h)(2). On appeal, he argued that he possessed the explosives for reasons unrelated to the underlying felony—and hence did not carry the explosives "during" the commission of that felony. The Supreme Court of the United States rightly held that *during* is a purely temporal word, especially when contrasted with the wording of the related firearm statute: *during and in relation to*.[11] In fact, Congress originally enacted § 844(h)(2) shortly after § 924(c) and used the same language—both with only the preposition *during*—and only later amended the latter to contain the additional phraseology *and in relation to*.[12] The Court correctly considered the cognate firearm provision while interpreting the explosives provision.

It is a logical consequence of this contextual principle that the meaning of an ambiguous provision may change in light of

---

7   460 N.W.2d at 11.

8   18 U.S.C. § 924(c)(1)(A) (emphasis added).

9   *Id.* § 844(h)(2) (emphasis added).

10   553 U.S. 272 (2008) (per Stevens, J.).

11   *Id.* at 274–76.

12   *Id.* at 275–76.

a subsequent enactment.[13] But can that be so even when the ambiguous provision has already been given an authoritative judicial interpretation? No, by reason of the principle of stare decisis, which has special force in statutory cases. The legislature, naturally, can change the law whose meaning the prior judicial interpretation established. But once that meaning *has* been established, the meaning cannot change "in light of" a later statute with which a different meaning would be more compatible. This would be repealer by the weakest of implications; and repeals by implication are disfavored (see § 55).

---

13 *See, e.g., United States v. Stewart*, 311 U.S. 60, 64 (1940) (per Douglas, J.) (construing Revenue Acts of 1916 and 1928 *in pari materia* to resolve "ambiguities and doubts" about meaning of language of earlier statute); *State v. Hormann*, 805 N.W.2d 883, 893 (Minn. Ct. App. 2011) (reading 2008 vehicle-title statute *in pari materia* with 1998 vehicle-tracking-device statute to clarify ambiguous term in the earlier statute).

40. Reenactment Canon

If the legislature amends or reenacts a provision other than by way of a consolidating statute or restyling project, a significant change in language is presumed to entail a change in meaning.

We oppose the use of legislative history, which consists of the hearings, committee reports, and debate leading up to the enactment in question (see § 66). But quite separate from legislative history is *statutory* history—the statutes repealed or amended by the statute under consideration. These form part of the context of the statute, and (unlike legislative history) can properly be presumed to have been before all the members of the legislature when they voted. So a change in the language of a prior statute presumably connotes a change in meaning.

For example, if a statute providing for an award to the prevailing party of "attorney's fees and expert-witness fees" has been amended to award only "attorney's fees," there would be no basis for the argument (sometimes made) that attorney's fees *include* reimbursement of the attorney's expenditures for expert witnesses.

This presumption does not apply to stylistic or nonsubstantive changes. Lawyers need not rack their brains to explain a change from *in addition* or *moreover* to *and*.

Courts have been known to misapply the rule about changed language. In one case, a statute provided standing to "a person who has had actual care, control, and possession of [a] child for not less than six months preceding the filing of the petition."[1] In a dispute over this provision, one litigant contended that the six-month period had to be immediately preceding the filing of the petition; the other litigant contended that periods of care, control, and possession could be aggregated to meet the six-month requirement. The dispositive fact should have been that the predecessor statute used the phrase *immediately preceding* and an amendment dropped the word *immediately*. The aggregating argument should have prevailed. But the court was purposivist in its approach,

---

1   Tex. Fam. Code Ann. § 102.003(a)(9) (West 1996).

reasoning that the purpose of the statute was to give standing only to people who definitely had a current relationship with the child. So the court impermissibly supplied the word *immediately*. In the process, it perverted a second canon of construction (see § 54 [prior-construction canon]), holding that the Texas Supreme Court's interpretation of the *former* statute governed the meaning of the *corrected* statute.[2]

There is a major exception to the presumption that a change in language produces a change in meaning. For ease of reference, legislatures often consolidate their statutes at large into a code divided by topic—criminal law, court jurisdiction, etc. When those codifications have been enacted into positive law, the law is the new code provision, rather than the prior statute at large.[3] Such codifications often revise the wording of the prior statute to provide for consistency of expression. But that revision does not result from legislative reconsideration of the substance of codified statutes. So recodification reverses the presumption: Instead of suggesting a new meaning, new language does not amend prior enactments unless it does so clearly. The same applies to legislative restyling exercises short of codification, such as the nonsubstantive redrafting of the Federal Rules of Appellate Procedure in 1998.[4]

The critical language in this exception is *unless it does so clearly*. The new text is the law, and where it clearly makes a change, that governs. This is so even when the legislative history consisting of the codifiers' report expresses the intent to make no change. A case in point is *United States v. Wells*,[5] which involved omission of the "materiality" requirement in the redefinition of a false-statement offense effected by the 1948 recodification of the federal criminal code. Justice David Souter wrote for a unanimous Court:

---

2   *In re Garcia*, 944 S.W.2d 725, 727 (Tex. App.—Amarillo 1997, no writ).

3   *See, e.g.*, 1 U.S.C. § 204.

4   *See* Fed. R. App. P. 1 (Advisory Committee Notes to the 1998 Amendments stating: "The language and organization of the rule are amended to make the rule more easily understood. In addition to changes made to improve the understanding, the Advisory Committee has changed language to make style and terminology consistent throughout the appellate rules. These changes are intended to be stylistic only.").

5   519 U.S. 482 (1997) (per Souter, J.).

Respondents also rely on the 1948 Reviser's Note to § 1014, which discussed the consolidation of the 13 provisions into one, and explained that, apart from two changes not relevant here, the consolidation "was without change of substance". . . . Respondents say that the revisers' failure to mention the omission of materiality from the text of § 1014 means that Congress must have "completely overlooked" the issue. . . . But surely this indication that the "staff of experts" who prepared the legislation either overlooked or chose to say nothing about changing the language of three of the former statutes does nothing to muddy the ostensibly unambiguous provision of the statute as enacted by Congress. . . . In any event, the revisers' assumption that the consolidation made no substantive change was simply wrong. . . . Those who write revisers' notes have proven fallible before.[6]

The Supreme Court's analysis did not measure up, in our view, in *Fourco Glass Co. v. Transmirra Products Corp.*[7] The case was a patent-infringement suit, in which (according to the general/specific canon [§ 28]) venue was governed by the special provision applicable to such suits rather than the general venue provision. The dispute centered on the meaning of that special provision, which had been reworded in the 1948 recodification of the judicial code, changing the permissible venue from "the district of which the defendant is an inhabitant"[8] to "the judicial district where the defendant resides."[9] The simultaneous revision of the general corporate-venue provision permitted suit "in any judicial district in which [the company] is incorporated or licensed to do business or is doing business," and continued that "such judicial district shall be regarded as the residence of such corporation for venue purposes."[10] The issue was whether *resides* in the special-venue provision should be given that meaning or should be held to mean the same thing as the previous term *inhabitant.*

---

6   *Id.* at 496–97 (citations omitted).
7   353 U.S. 222 (1957) (per Whittaker, J.).
8   28 U.S.C. § 109.
9   *Id.* § 1400(b).
10   *Id.* § 1391(c).

The Supreme Court held the latter, Justice Harlan dissenting. That holding was arguably correct, given the presumption against change by recodification (*inhabitant* and *resident* are not inherently different). But in our view the Court's opinion placed inordinate weight on the Senate and House Judiciary Committees' assertion that "every change made in the text is explained in detail in the Revisers' Notes,"[11] and on the Revisers' Notes' assertion that the "[w]ords . . . 'where the defendant resides' were substituted for 'of which the defendant is an inhabitant' because the '[w]ords "inhabitant" and "resident," as respects venue, are synonymous.'"[12]

With codification projects, it is common to enact a prologue stating that no substantive amendments are intended, so that prior caselaw will continue valid in an unbroken line. Should this be given greater weight than revisers' notes, or than the general presumption of no change that would have applied without the specification? No. When the general assertion of no change is contradicted by an unquestionable change in a specific provision, the specific will control over the general.

The Texas Supreme Court took such an approach in *Fleming Foods of Texas, Inc. v. Rylander*.[13] The state tax code specified that "[a] tax refund claim may be filed with the comptroller by the person who paid the tax."[14] The precodification statute had included the phrase *directly to the state* at the end of this language, but that adverbial qualification had been deleted in a codification project whose enacting clause stated that the new version was not to change the substantive law. In this lawsuit, an indirect taxpayer claimed the benefit of the newly reworded provision; the state argued that, as with the previous version, only direct taxpayers were entitled to the refund. The Texas Supreme Court properly held that dropping the phrase *directly to the state* was both significant and substantive, reasoning that an ordinary citizen ought to be

---

11   353 U.S. at 226.

12   *Id.*

13   6 S.W.3d 278 (Tex. 1999).

14   Tex. Tax Code Ann. § 111.104(b).

able to read the statute book and glean its meaning.[15] This is a beneficent fiction that legislative drafters should keep in the forefront of their minds.

---

15 6 S.W.3d at 284–85.

41. Presumption Against Retroactivity

A statute presumptively has no retroactive application.

> "The presumption is very strong that a statute was not
> meant to act retrospectively, and it ought never to receive
> such a construction if it is susceptible of any other."
> *United States Fid. & Guar. Co. v. United States ex rel. Struthers*
> *Wells Co.*, 209 U.S. 306, 314 (1908) (per Peckham, J.).

As a general, almost invariable rule, a legislature makes law for the future, not for the past. Judicial opinions typically pronounce what the law was at the time of a particular happening. Statutes, by contrast, typically pronounce what the law becomes when the statutes take effect. This point is basic to our rule of law. Even when they do not say so (and they rarely do), statutes will not be interpreted to apply to past events. It has long been so, as James Kent recognized in 1826: "A retroactive statute would partake in its character of the mischiefs of an ex post facto law, as to all cases of crimes and penalties;[1] and in every other case relating to contracts or property, it would be against every sound principle."[2] And Thomas M. Cooley in 1868: "Retrospective legislation, except when designed to cure formal defects, or otherwise operate remedially, is commonly objectionable in principle, and apt to result in injustice; and it is a sound rule of construction which refuses lightly to imply an intent to enact it."[3]

The presumption against retroactivity is a guide to interpretation, not a constitutional imperative, because the presumption applies even when the Constitution does not forbid retroactivity. For example, a statute reducing the penalties for a crime will be presumed to apply only to acts occurring after the statute's effective date, even though there is no constitutional difficulty in applying

---

1   Note that the federal ex post facto prohibitions (U.S. Const. art. I, § 9, cl. 3; § 10, cl. 1) have been held to apply only to criminal and penal laws. *See Collins v. Youngblood*, 497 U.S. 37, 41–42 (1990) (per Rehnquist, C.J.) (citing *Calder v. Bull*, 3 U.S. (3 Dall.) 386, 390–91 (1798) (opinion of Chase, J.)). But in general legal usage, the term *ex post facto* often applies to all retroactive laws.

2   1 James Kent, *Commentaries on American Law* 426 (1826).

3   Thomas M. Cooley, *A Treatise on the Constitutional Limitations Which Rest upon the Legislative Power of the States of the American Union* 62–63 (1868).

it to prior acts.[4] So the presumption of prospectivity is not the same as the ancient hostility to ex post facto laws.[5] The latter are a particular species of the genus of retroactive laws: those retroactive laws that, in the words of Justice Joseph Story (describing the New Hampshire Constitution's prohibition of "retrospective" laws), "take away or impair vested rights acquired under existing laws, or create a new obligation, impose a new duty, or attach a new disability, in respect to transactions or considerations already past."[6]

Since the presumption is a canon of interpretation and not a rule of constitutional law, a statute can explicitly or by clear implication be made retroactive. Its retroactive operation may, but will not necessarily, violate one of the Ex Post Facto Clauses,[7] one of the Due Process Clauses,[8] the Takings Clause,[9] or the Obligation of Contracts Clause[10] of the United States Constitution, or similar provisions in state constitutions.[11] But constitutional violations not being a matter of statutory interpretation, they are beyond the scope of our discussion.

The difficult question is: What does retroactivity consist of? All can agree that statutes imposing new civil or criminal liability

---

4   *See, e.g., Commonwealth v. Kimball,* 38 Mass. 373 (1838); *State v. Daley,* 29 Conn. 272 (1860); *Bradley v. United States,* 410 U.S. 605, 607–08 (1973) (per Marshall, J.) (dictum).

5   *See Hughes Aircraft Co. v. United States ex rel. Schumer,* 520 U.S. 939, 947 (1997) (per Thomas, J.). *See also* Gerald Garvey, *Constitutional Bricolage* 61–62 (1971).

6   *Society for the Propagation of the Gospel v. Wheeler,* 22 F. Cas. 756, 767 (C.C.D.N.H. 1814) (No. 13,156) (we have modified the tense of Story's verbs).

7   U.S. Const. art. I, § 9, cl. 3; § 10, cl. 1. *See, e.g., Stogner v. California,* 539 U.S. 607 (2003) (per Breyer, J.).

8   U.S. Const. amend. V; amend. XIV, § 1. *See, e.g., Usery v. Turner Elkhorn Mining Co.,* 428 U.S. 1, 15 (1976) (per Marshall, J.). *But see United States v. Carlton,* 512 U.S. 26, 39 (1994) (Scalia, J., concurring in the judgment).

9   U.S. Const. amend. V. *See, e.g., Eastern Enters. v. Apfel,* 524 U.S. 498 (1998) (per O'Connor, J.).

10   U.S. Const. art. I, § 10, cl. 1. *See, e.g., United States Trust Co. of N.Y. v. New Jersey,* 431 U.S. 1, 32 (1977) (per Blackmun, J.).

11   *See, e.g., A. Gallo & Co. v. McCarthy,* 2 A.3d 56, 70 (Conn. Super. Ct. 2010); *Doe v. Phillips,* 194 S.W.3d 833, 852 (Mo. 2006); *McClung v. National Carbon Co.,* 228 S.W.2d 488, 489 (Tenn. 1950); *Safford v. Metropolitan Life Ins. Co.,* 164 N.E. 351, 352 (Ohio 1928).

are presumptively inapplicable to acts engaged in before their enactment. But what about a change in the rules governing admission of evidence—for instance, elimination of the common-law disability of a wife to testify against her husband? Would it be retroactive (and thus presumably unintended) for that new rule to apply to a trial conducted *after* its enactment but dealing with an alleged crime committed *before* its enactment? No, because retroactivity ought to be judged with regard to the act or event that the statute is meant to regulate.[12] Because this law was meant to regulate the admission of evidence at trial, it would be retroactive only if applied to trials completed before its effective date.

Not all cases are so straightforward. Take, for example, a statute limiting the fees that may be awarded to lawyers who litigate prisoner lawsuits. It could theoretically be considered retroactive if it applied to any of the following events that occurred before its effective date: "(1) the alleged violation upon which the fee-imposing suit is based . . . ; (2) the lawyer's undertaking to prosecute the suit for which attorney's fees were provided . . . ; (3) the filing of the suit in which the fees are imposed . . . ; (4) the doing of the legal work for which the fees are payable . . . ; and (5) the actual award of fees in a prisoner case . . . ."[13] We would select #4 as the retroactivity event—which is what the Supreme Court held in a case presenting those facts.[14] The rationale that we have described is not what the Court relied on in that case,[15] and despite a later case seemingly embracing our rationale,[16] the Supreme Court has categorically rejected it, relying instead on Justice Story's opinion (mentioned earlier) dealing with a constitutional prohibition of retroactive legislation.[17]

---

12 *See Landgraf v. USI Film Prods.*, 511 U.S. 244, 286, 290–94 (1994) (Scalia, J., concurring in the judgment).

13 *Martin v. Hadix*, 527 U.S. 343, 362–63 (1999) (Scalia, J. concurring in part and concurring in the judgment).

14 *See generally Martin v. Hadix*, 527 U.S. 343 (1999) (per O'Connor, J.).

15 *See id.* at 362.

16 *Republic of Austria v. Altmann*, 541 U.S. 677, 697 n.17 (2004) (per Stevens, J.).

17 *See Vartelas v. Holder*, 132 S.Ct. 1479, 1486–89 (2012) (per Ginsburg, J.) (relying on *Society for the Propagation of the Gospel v. Wheeler*, 22 F. Cas. 756, 767 (C.C.D.N.H. 1814) (No. 13,156)).

The fact that retroactivity is to be judged with regard to the act or event that the statute is meant to regulate may account for what has been regarded (perhaps erroneously) as an exception to nonretroactivity. The common-law rule, as expressed by Chief Justice Marshall in 1809, was "that after the expiration or repeal of a law, no penalty can be enforced, nor punishment inflicted, for violations of the law committed while it was in force, unless some special provision be made for that purpose by statute."[18] So after the Twenty-First Amendment to the United States Constitution repealed the Eighteenth, thereby eliminating the authority for and rendering inoperative the National Prohibition Act, prosecutions for violations of the Act that had occurred while it was in effect had to be dismissed.[19] It can be argued that the act or event that the repeal of a punitive law is meant to regulate is the proceeding to impose punishment, so that the common-law rule is not really a contradiction of nonretroactivity. Some of the cases speak this way—saying, for example, that "[b]y the repeal the legislative will is expressed that no further proceedings be had under the act repealed."[20] Whether or not it constituted a genuine exception to nonretroactivity at common law, the repeal of a penal statute eliminated prosecution for past acts. The so-called abatement doctrine provided that repeal, even repeal by amendment, and even by amendment reducing the penalty, would require dismissal of the indictment under the earlier criminal statute. The United States and almost all the states have adopted saving statutes designed to eliminate the doctrine and to permit continued prosecution under the prior law.[21] The federal provision, enacted in 1871 and codified in 1947, provides: "The repeal of any statute shall not have the effect to release or extinguish any penalty, forfeiture, or liability incurred under such statute, unless the repealing Act shall so

---

18 *Yeaton v. United States*, 9 U.S. (5 Cranch) 281, 283 (1809) (per Marshall, C.J.). *See also United States v. Tynen*, 78 U.S. (11 Wall.) 88, 95 (1870) (per Field, J.).

19 *United States v. Chambers*, 291 U.S. 217, 222 (1934) (per Hughes, C.J.).

20 *Tynen*, 78 U.S. (11 Wall.) at 95.

21 *See generally* Note, *Today's Law and Yesterday's Crime: Retroactive Application of Ameliorative Criminal Legislation*, 121 U. Pa. L. Rev. 120 (1972–1973).

expressly provide."[22] Such a provision cannot deny effect to a future legislature's provision applying newly adopted lesser sentences retroactively to offenses committed before their adoption (see § 45 [repealability canon]), but it does demand that such a provision be express or clearly implied (see § 54 [presumption against implied repeal]).

---

22 Act of Feb. 25, 1871, c. 71, § 4, 16 Stat. 432 (codified as 1 U.S.C. § 109).

42. Pending-Action Canon

When statutory law is altered during the pendency of a lawsuit, the courts at every level must apply the new law unless doing so would violate the presumption against retroactivity.

Some cases hold that courts must apply the law in effect when their decisions are rendered.[1] Others hold that the law in effect when the lawsuit was filed must govern.[2] Neither view is correct. The presumption against retroactivity determines whether courts should apply the law in effect at the time of suit or the law in effect at the time of judgment—or for that matter the law in effect when the acts at issue occurred. The application of that presumption depends on what the provision in question controls: If it limits the jurisdiction of courts, the time of final judgment is the dividing line between prospective and retroactive effect.[3] If it limits the time within which suit must be brought, the filing of suit is the dividing line.[4] If it renders private action unlawful, the date of the

---

1 *See, e.g., Bradley v. School Bd. of Richmond,* 416 U.S. 696, 711 (1974) (per Blackmun, J.) ("[A] court is to apply the law in effect at the time it renders its decision, unless doing so would result in manifest injustice or there is statutory direction or legislative history to the contrary."); *Thorpe v. Housing Auth. of Durham,* 393 U.S. 268, 281 (1969) (per Warren, C.J.) (applying the "general rule . . . that an appellate court must apply the law in effect at the time it renders its decision"); *Bruner v. United States,* 343 U.S. 112, 116–17 (1952) (per Vinson, C.J.) (dismissing suit because the statute conferring jurisdiction at time of filing was repealed while case was on appeal); *Ex parte McCardle,* 74 U.S. (7 Wall.) 506, 514 (1868) (per Chase, C.J.) (holding that Court had no jurisdiction to render decision in case already argued and taken under advisement when Congress passed act regarding Court's jurisdiction); *United States v. Schooner Peggy,* 5 U.S. (1 Cranch) 103, 110 (1801) (per Marshall, C.J.) ("[I]f, subsequent to the judgment and before the decision of the appellate court, a law intervenes and positively changes the rule which governs, the law must be obeyed.").

2 *See, e.g., Doll v. Doll,* 794 N.W.2d 425, 427 n.1. (N.D. 2011) (noting that although the applicable statute had changed, the court would apply the law in effect at the time of filing).

3 *See, e.g., Sentence Review Panel v. Moseley,* 663 S.E.2d 679, 682–83 (Ga. 2008); *Dashiell v. Holland Maide Candy Shops,* 188 A. 29, 30 (Md. 1936).

4 *See, e.g., Indiana Spine Group, P.C. v. Pilot Travel Ctrs., L.L.C.,* 959 N.E.2d 789, 793 (Ind. 2011); *State v. Morales,* 236 P.3d 24, 29 (N.M. 2010).

action is the dividing line.[5] But as we said in the preceding section, if it renders lawful private action that was previously unlawful, the time of final judgment is the dividing line.[6]

Since the outcome rests ultimately on the presumption of prospectivity, it can be altered by legislative prescription that changes operation of the presumption. The California Code of Civil Procedure, for example, provides that "[j]urisdiction of the court over the parties and the subject matter of an action continues throughout subsequent proceedings in the action."[7] The background presumption that a statute eliminating jurisdiction applies to cases still pending is not strong enough to render a later jurisdictional statute an implicit repeal of this code provision (see § 55 [presumption against implied repeal]).

---

5   See, e.g., Hoare v. Allen, 2 Dall. 102, 103 (Pa. 1789); Phagan v. State, 486 S.E.2d 876, 879 (Ga. 1997).

6   See, e.g., People v. Glisson, 782 N.E.2d 251, 257–58 (Ill. 2002) (holding that repeal of statute creating offense of which defendant had been convicted did not affect the conviction).

7   Cal. Civ. Proc. Code § 410.50(b).

43. Extraterritoriality Canon

A statute presumptively has no extraterritorial application (*statuta suo clauduntur territorio, nec ultra territorium disponunt*).

> "Legislation is presumptively territorial and confined to limits over which the law-making power has jurisdiction."
> *Sandberg v. McDonald,*
> 248 U.S. 185, 195 (1918) (per Day, J.).

Since the rise of the nation-state, countries have avoided subjecting people to conflicting laws (and disrupting one another's legal systems) by international consensus that a nation's law governs action within its territorial jurisdiction—even action by other nations' citizens. This is not to say that international law forbids extraterritorial application. A country may, if it wishes, subject its own citizens to its laws wherever they are,[1] and may subject all persons in other countries to its laws with regard to action that has a substantial effect within its territory.[2] But in practice, that is the exception rather than the rule. The same principle applies to the laws of our states, though the Constitution may place some limits on extending a state's laws to the territory of sister states.[3]

It has long been assumed that legislatures enact their laws with this territorial limitation in mind. Indeed, medieval law had the maxim *Statuta suo clauduntur territorio, nec ultra territorium disponunt*—"Statutes are confined to their own territory and have no extraterritorial effect."[4] The legislature need not qualify each law by saying "within the territorial jurisdiction of this State." That is

---

1   *See, e.g.*, 18 U.S.C. § 2423(c) ("Engaging in illicit sexual conduct in foreign places.—Any United States citizen or alien admitted for permanent residence who travels in foreign commerce, and engages in any illicit sexual conduct with another person [defined to include conduct that would violate United States law] shall be fined under this title or imprisoned not more than 30 years, or both.").

2   *See* 1 *Restatement (Third) of the Foreign Relations Law of the United States* § 402(1)(c), at 237–38 (1987) ("[A] state has jurisdiction to prescribe law with respect to . . . conduct outside its territory that has or is intended to have substantial effect within its territory.").

3   *See* 1 *Restatement (Second) of Conflict of Laws* § 2 cmt. *b*, at 34 (1971).

4   *Black's Law Dictionary* 1874 (9th ed. 2009).

how statutes have always been interpreted,[5] and "[i]t is presumable that Congress legislates with knowledge of our basic rules of statutory construction."[6]

In earlier times, this extraterritoriality canon was applied with some rigor. In the 1909 *American Banana Co.* case,[7] for example, the Supreme Court unanimously held that the Sherman Act did not apply to a suit by one American corporation against another alleging predatory acts done in Central America to preserve the defendant company's domination of banana shipments to the United States. In an opinion by Justice Holmes, the Court said that "the general and almost universal rule is that the character of an act as lawful or unlawful must be determined wholly by the law of the country where the act is done."[8]

In a leading case on this issue, *Lauritzen v. Larsen,*[9] a seaman sought a maritime remedy under the Jones Act, which gave relief to "*any* seaman who . . . suffer[ed] personal injury in the course of his employment."[10] Larsen, a Dane, signed on as a crew member of a Danish ship in New York. The Danish-language contract contained a Danish choice-of-law provision, and it was subject to a Danish union's employment contracts. Injured in Cuba, Larsen sued in New York under the Jones Act, asserting that because the statute applies to "any seaman," the Act gave him an optional remedy in addition to whatever Danish law might provide. The Supreme Court unanimously rejected Larsen's claim, Justice Jackson writing that Congress simply did not, through the use of *any,* extend "our law and [open] . . . our courts to all alien seafaring

---

5 *See* B.A. Wortley, *Jurisprudence* 138 (1967) ("[L]egislation is a deliberate and formal command, an attempt to rule within a certain legal order—it purports to apply, from a definite point in time, to persons in a definite *spatial* area.").

6 *McNary v. Haitian Refugee Ctr., Inc.,* 498 U.S. 479, 496 (1991) (per Stevens, J.). *Cf. Cail v. Papayanni,* [1863] 1 Moo. P.C. (N.S.) 471, 474 (per Dr. Lushington) ("No Statute ought . . . to be held to apply to Foreigners with respect to transactions out of British jurisdiction, unless the words of the Statute are perfectly clear.").

7 *American Banana Co. v. United Fruit Co.,* 213 U.S. 347 (1909) (per Holmes, J.).

8 *Id.* at 356.

9 345 U.S. 571 (1953) (per Jackson, J.).

10 46 U.S.C. § 688 (emphasis added).

men injured anywhere in the world in service of watercraft of every foreign nation."[11] He added: "[A] hand on a Chinese junk, never outside Chinese waters, would not be beyond [the statute's] literal wording."[12] Jackson further noted that our rule is based on international law, one sovereign power being bound to respect the subjects and the rights of all other sovereigns outside its own territory: "[I]f any construction otherwise be possible, an Act will not be construed as applying to foreigners in respect to acts done by them outside the dominions of the sovereign power enacting."[13]

The idea that *any* does not mean "anywhere in the world" was reaffirmed by the Supreme Court in *Morrison v. National Australia Bank Ltd.*,[14] in which the relevant statute punished acts "in connection with the purchase or sale of *any* security registered on a national securities exchange or *any* security not so registered."[15] In that case, Australian investors—in Australia—bought stock in the National Australia Bank. They later sued the Bank and an American company, HomeSide, which National had purchased. The investors claimed that both National and HomeSide had defrauded them by overvaluing HomeSide's assets. The issue was whether § 10(b) of the Securities Exchange Act of 1934 applied to the purchase and sale abroad of stock in a foreign company not listed on an American exchange. No, it did not, and *any* did not unambiguously confer a worldwide berth. As one of us wrote for the Court: "When a statute gives no clear indication of an extraterritorial application, it has none."[16]

So what type of language suffices to create extraterritorial application? In *United States v. Weingarten*,[17] a federal statute criminalized "travel[ing] in foreign commerce . . . for the purpose of engaging in any sexual act . . . with a person under 18 years of

---

11 *Larsen*, 345 U.S. at 577.

12 *Id.*

13 *Id.* at 578.

14 130 S.Ct. 2869 (2010) (per Scalia, J.).

15 15 U.S.C. § 78j(b) (emphasis added).

16 130 S.Ct. at 2873.

17 632 F.3d 60 (2d Cir. 2011).

age."[18] Weingarten, a U.S. citizen who had lived abroad for 13 years, was convicted under the statute of molesting his 16-year-old daughter during a trip from the family's residence in Belgium to Israel, where they planned to relocate. In analyzing the issue of applicability of U.S. laws beyond the borders of the United States, the Second Circuit applied the presumption that "'Congress does not intend a statute to apply to conduct outside the territorial jurisdiction of the United States' unless it 'clearly expresses its intent to do so.'"[19] The presumption was overcome here, the court wrote, because "[s]uch a clear and affirmative indication is present."[20] The statute "manifestly expresses Congress's concern with conduct that occurs overseas, criminalizing travel in foreign commerce undertaken with the intent to commit sexual acts with minors."[21] The court went on to reverse the conviction because travel between two foreign states was not, in its view, "travel[] in foreign commerce" within the meaning of the statute.

In recent times, courts have often watered down the presumption against extraterritoriality. In some cases they have even ignored it, as federal appellate courts did for nearly 50 years with respect to extraterritorial application of the Securities Exchange Act.[22] More often, they have accepted language as having an implied prescription of extraterritorial application when it does not clearly have that import. For example, the Supreme Court held in 1993 that the Sherman Act's specification that it covers restraints of trade or commerce "among the several States, or with foreign nations"[23] (a specification that existed when *American Banana* was decided) does indeed mean that acts abroad creating such restraints (or at least some such acts) are covered: "[I]t is well established by now that the Sherman Act applies to foreign conduct that was

---

18 18 U.S.C. § 2423(b).

19 632 F.3d at 64 (quoting *United States v. Yousef,* 327 F.3d 56, 86 (2d Cir. 2003)).

20 *Id.*

21 *Id.* at 65.

22 See the discussion in *Morrison v. National Australia Bank Ltd.,* 130 S.Ct. 2869, 2877–81 (2010) (per Scalia, J.).

23 15 U.S.C. § 1.

meant to produce and did in fact produce some substantial effect in the United States."[24]

When the presumption against extraterritorial application is ignored, the courts will decide what application was "intended" on the basis of their assessment of what applications abroad will substantially further the purpose of the statute. And the same is true when something less than a clear indication of extraterritorial application is allowed to avoid the presumption. So eliminating or watering down the presumption ultimately results in purposivism (see above).

But this ignoring or watering down of the presumption is not consistent. Two years before making the statement quoted above concerning the "well established" application of the Sherman Act to acts abroad that have some substantial effect in the United States, the Supreme Court held that Title VII of the Civil Rights Act of 1964, which forbade discrimination in employment, did *not* apply to employment discrimination by a Delaware corporation against an American citizen in Saudi Arabia.[25] The Court held that the presumption against extraterritorial application was not overcome by the broad jurisdictional language (of the sort that had been invoked in the Sherman Act cases)[26] and cited many other statutes in which (it said) that did not suffice.[27] More recently, the Supreme Court has reaffirmed that the presumption against extraterritoriality applies "unless there is the affirmative intention of the Congress clearly expressed" to give a statute extraterritorial effect.[28]

Having a statutory presumption that is often applied but sometimes ignored is retrograde. Legislators must know what to expect. We favor restoring the presumption to its former banana-like state. This is not to overrule all cases previously ignoring or distorting the statute; stare decisis suffices to preserve them. But we should take the presumption seriously for the future.

---

24 *Hartford Fire Ins. Co. v. California*, 509 U.S. 764, 796 (1993) (Souter, J., plurality opinion).

25 *EEOC v. Arabian Am. Oil Co.*, 499 U.S. 244, 259 (1991) (per Rehnquist, C.J.).

26 *Id.* at 249–50.

27 *Id.* at 250–51.

28 *Morrison*, 130 S.Ct. at 2877 (quoting *Arabian Am. Oil Co.*, 499 U.S. at 248).

44. Artificial-Person Canon

The word *person* includes corporations and other entities, but not the sovereign.

Traditionally the word *person*—as well as *whoever*—denotes not only natural persons (human beings) but also artificial persons such as corporations, partnerships, associations, and both public and private organizations.[1] Though surprising to nonlawyers, this legal meaning is age-old.[2]

As always, however, much depends on context. For example, *person* was sensibly held to mean "natural person" in a statute allowing a person to defend his or her own lawsuit despite not being qualified to practice law.[3] How could it be otherwise?

And the word *person* traditionally excludes the sovereign. There exists a "longstanding interpretive presumption" to that effect.[4] The Supreme Court of the United States once explained

---

1   1 U.S.C. § 1; 5 U.S.C. § 551(2). *See Isaacson v. Dow Chem. Co.*, 517 F.3d 129, 135–36 (2d Cir. 2008) (chemical-manufacturing companies held to be *persons* under the federal-officer removal statute).

2   *See, e.g., Beaston v. Farmers' Bank of Del.*, 37 U.S. (12 Pet.) 102, 134 (1838) (per McKinley, J.) ("No authority has been adduced to show, that a corporation may not, in the construction of statutes, be regarded as a natural person: while, on the contrary, authorities have been cited which show, that corporations are to be deemed and considered as *persons*, when the circumstances in which they are placed, are identical with those of natural persons, expressly included in such statutes."); *McIntire v. Preston*, 10 Ill. 48, 63–64 (1848). *See also* 1 William Blackstone, *Commentaries on the Laws of England* 119 (4th ed. 1770) ("Persons are also divided by the law into either natural persons, or artificial . . . . [A]rtificial persons are such as created and devised by human laws for the purposes of society and government; which are called corporations or bodies politic."); F. Stroud, *The Judicial Dictionary* 582 (1890) ("Prima facie the word 'person,' in a public statute, includes a Corporation as well as a natural person.").

3   *Aberdeen Bindery, Inc. v. Eastern States Printing & Publ'g Co.*, 3 N.Y.S.2d 419, 421–22 (App. Div. 1938). *See also Rowland v. California Men's Colony*, 506 U.S. 194, 198 (1993) (per Souter, J.) (only a natural person qualifies as a *person* in a statute allowing certain persons to proceed in court *in forma pauperis*). *Cf. Law Soc'y v. United Serv. Bureau Ltd.*, [1934] 1 K.B. 343 (per Avory, J.) (*person* did not include corporations in a statute imposing a fine for a "person not having in force a practising certificate, who willfully pretends to be . . . qualified . . . to act as a solicitor").

4   *Vermont Agency of Natural Res. v. United States ex rel. Stevens*, 529 U.S. 765, 780 (2000) (per Scalia, J.). *See, e.g., Will v. Michigan Dep't of State Police*, 491 U.S. 58,

the presumption as follows: "Since, in common usage, the term 'person' does not include the sovereign, statutes employing the [term] are ordinarily construed to exclude it."[5] That explanation is not entirely adequate: In *common* usage, after all, *person* does not include artificial persons as well. So common usage is not the standard here. Legal usage is—and in this instance its treatment of the word *person* is peculiar.

In a case decided by the Supreme Court of the United States,[6] an ex-employee of the Vermont Agency of Natural Resources sued Vermont on behalf of the federal government (a *qui tam* action) for submitting false monetary claims to the Environmental Protection Agency. Vermont moved to dismiss the lawsuit, arguing that it was not a person within the meaning of the False Claims Act, which allows *qui tam* actions against any person who knowingly presents to the government a fraudulent claim for payment.[7] Applying the "longstanding interpretive presumption that *person* does not include the sovereign," the Supreme Court held for Vermont—and ordered the action dismissed.[8]

Noninclusion of the sovereign means noninclusion of agencies of the sovereign as well. The issue arose in *In re Al Fayed*,[9] in which Mohamed al-Fayed, the father of Dodi Fayed, subpoenaed the Central Intelligence Agency for documents to be used in a French proceeding investigating the automobile crash in which

---

71 (1989) (per White, J.) (a state and its officials acting in their official capacities are not *persons* under 42 U.S.C. § 1983); *South Carolina v. Katzenbach*, 383 U.S. 301, 323–24 (1966) (per Warren, C.J.) ("The word 'person' in the context of the Due Process Clause of the Fifth Amendment cannot, by any reasonable mode of interpretation, be expanded to encompass the States of the Union."); *Trinkle v. California State Lottery*, 84 Cal. Rptr. 2d 496, 498–99 (Cal. Ct. App. 1999) (a state agency is not a *person* within the meaning of the Unfair Competition Act.).

5   *United States v. Cooper Corp.*, 312 U.S. 600, 604 (1941) (per Roberts, J.).

6   *Vermont Agency of Natural Res. v. United States ex rel. Stevens*, 529 U.S. 765 (2000) (per Scalia, J.).

7   31 U.S.C. § 3729(a).

8   529 U.S. at 780. *See Director, Office of Workers' Comp. Programs, Dep't of Labor v. Newport News Shipbuilding & Dry Dock Co.*, 514 U.S. 122, 130 (1995) (per Scalia, J.) (holding that "person adversely affected or aggrieved" by a final order does not include an agency in its regulatory or policy-making capacity).

9   91 F.Supp.2d 137 (D.D.C. 2000).

Dodi was killed along with Princess Diana. The statute on which al-Fayed proceeded read as follows: "The district court of the district in which a person resides . . . may order him . . . to produce a document or other thing for use in a proceeding in a foreign or international tribunal."[10] The CIA moved to quash the subpoena because it was not a person within the meaning of the statute. The district court agreed, but the first reason it gave was mistaken: "In three of the instances in which 'person' appears, the pronouns 'him' and 'his' are used to refer to the term. The use of 'him' and 'his' mitigates[11] against interpreting the antecedent noun, 'person,' to mean 'United States' or 'agency.'"[12] Yet this point is irrelevant. The pronouns appear commonly in contexts that include so-called *artificial persons* (i.e., corporations), and they have no bearing on the human or nonhuman nature of the referent. The proper basis for the decision was simply that *person* traditionally excludes the sovereign.[13]

Hard cases arise here as elsewhere. In *United States v. Persichilli*,[14] the relevant statute provided: "Whoever . . . for the purpose of obtaining anything of value from any person . . . knowingly alters a social security card . . . or possesses a social security card or counterfeit social security card with intent to sell or alter it . . . shall be guilty of a felony . . . ."[15] The evidence at trial proved that Persichilli was attempting to alter a social-security card in order to obtain a fraudulent driver's license. Under Persichilli's view, the department of motor vehicles, from which he would have obtained the driver's license, was not a "person" and the government had therefore failed to prove that he acted with "the purpose of obtaining anything of value from any person." The Government, by contrast, argued that the term *person* embraced legal entities, including governments and governmental entities. The court held,

---

10 28 U.S.C. § 1782(a).

11 Sic: read *militates*, a common illiteracy. *See Garner's Modern American Usage* 543 (3d ed. 2009).

12 91 F.Supp.2d at 140.

13 *Id.* at 141.

14 608 F.3d 34 (1st Cir. 2010).

15 42 U.S.C. § 408(a)(7)(C).

incorrectly in our view, that as used in this statute, the term *person* included governments and governmental entities. The court noted that under the federal Dictionary Act[16] *person* usually includes nonnatural entities, such as corporations, but not necessarily governments or governmental entities. Yet the court relied on the principle that "[s]tatutes are customarily read, where the language permits, to address the mischief that is Congress' target."[17] Here, the statute targeted fraudulent social-security cards. The court believed that the most likely victim of a fraudulent social-security card was the Social Security Administration and that other governmental entities were also likely victims. Therefore, the court concluded that a reading that included governmental entities was the most plausible. On balance, we believe that the general presumption about the meaning of *person*, combined with the rule of lenity (§ 49), should have produced the opposite result. The court erroneously relied on purposivism to convict a highly unsympathetic defendant.

Despite the general rule about corporations as persons, a cognate word such as *personal* does not necessarily bear a similar sense. In 2011, the Supreme Court of the United States decided the point.[18] A trade association representing some of AT&T's competitors submitted a Freedom of Information Act request to the Federal Communications Commission requesting documents that the agency had obtained from AT&T in the course of an investigation. AT&T sought to enjoin the agency's production of the documents on the ground that they came within the exemption from FOIA production for law-enforcement records whose disclosure "could reasonably be expected to constitute an unwarranted invasion of personal privacy."[19] The FCC took the position that the personal-privacy exemption does not apply to companies, but AT&T argued that because Congress has defined *person* (in the Dictionary Act[20]) to include corporations, the derivative

---

16   1 U.S.C. § 1.

17   608 F.3d at 38.

18   *FCC v. AT&T Inc.*, 131 S.Ct. 1177 (2011) (per Roberts, C.J.).

19   5 U.S.C. § 552(b)(7)(C).

20   1 U.S.C. § 1.

adjective *personal* must also extend to corporations. The Supreme Court rejected this argument. It noted, among other things, that while *person* is a defined term, *personal* is not, and in ordinary usage that adjective describes individuals, not companies (as in *personal expenses*, *personal life*, and *personal opinion*); and that the full phrase *personal privacy* denotes "a type of privacy evocative of human concerns."[21] This holding exemplifies the crucially important maxim that words are almost invariably to be understood in their ordinary, everyday meaning (see § 6).

---

21 *FCC v. AT&T,* 131 S.Ct. at 1179.

Government-Structuring Canons

45. Repealability Canon

The legislature cannot derogate from its own authority or the authority of its successors.

The one body whose future actions a legislature has no power to affect is the legislature itself. Just as a corporate board of directors cannot adopt an immutable policy, legislators cannot make their laws irrepealable or disable themselves or their successors from taking action: "[O]ne legislature cannot bind a subsequent one . . . ."[1] This canon is traditionally known as the nonentrenchment doctrine.

Resting as it does on sheer logic, the principle dates from time immemorial. As Cicero wrote to Atticus: "When you repeal the law itself, . . . you at the same time repeal the prohibitory clause, which guards against such repeal."[2] Blackstone put the point this way: "Acts of Parliament derogatory from the power of subsequent Parliaments bind not."[3] And Chief Justice John Marshall wrote: "[O]ne legislature cannot abridge the powers of a succeeding legislature,"[4] adding: "The correctness of this principle, so far as respects general legislation, can never be controverted."[5] He also wrote that a statute is "alterable when the legislature shall please to alter it."[6] The Supreme Court of the United States has uniformly followed this principle.[7]

---

1   Joel Prentiss Bishop, *Commentaries on the Written Laws and Their Interpretation* § 147, at 134 (1882).

2   1 William Blackstone, *Commentaries on the Laws of England* § 3, at 90–91 (1765) (citing 3 Marcus Tullius Cicero, *Epistolae ad Titus Pomponium Atticum: in usum Scholar. S. J.*, 112 (Simeon Bosius ed., 1605) (Letter No. 23) ("*Cum lex abrogatur, illud ipsum abrogatur, quo non eam abrogari oporteat.*")).

3   1 William Blackstone, *Commentaries on the Laws of England* 70 (4th ed. 1770).

4   *Fletcher v. Peck*, 10 U.S. (6 Cranch) 87, 135 (1810) (per Marshall, C.J.).

5   *Id.*

6   *Marbury v. Madison*, 5 U.S. (1 Cranch) 137, 177 (1803) (per Marshall, C.J.).

7   *See, e.g., United States v. Winstar Corp.*, 518 U.S. 839, 872 (1996) (Souter, J., plurality opinion); *Reichelderfer v. Quinn*, 287 U.S. 315, 318 (1932) (per Stone, J.)

Hence there is no legal effect to a statutory provision stating that any exceptions to the statute's requirements must be express, or must specifically refer to the statute.[8] A later legislature's power—or, for that matter, the same legislature's power—to make exceptions without specific reference, and even to make exceptions by implication, cannot be eliminated. But when exception by implication is asserted, the implication must be clear enough to overcome the presumption against implied repeal (see § 55)—since the exception effectively repeals the earlier statute's application to the matter that it covers.

Nor is it permissible for a legislature to prescribe the only words that will be effective to produce an amendment. In South Australia, for example, the Real Property Act of 1886 purported to control future parliaments of South Australia in all legislation affecting land under the Real Property Act by requiring that amendments could be effective only if couched in certain words (that is, mandating that they recite the precise words *notwithstanding the provisions of the Real Property Act 1886*).[9] On this view, replacing *notwithstanding* with either *despite* or *in spite of* would result in a nugatory amendment. But as the learned commentator J.M. Finnis correctly observed: "[T]he legislature of South Australia has plenary power to couch its enactments in such literary form as it may choose. It cannot be effectively commanded by a prior legislature to express its intention in a particular way."[10]

Similarly, a legislature cannot be unalterably bound by definitions that purportedly apply to all statutes. As we have observed, a legislature has no power to dictate the language that later statutes must employ (see § 36 [interpretive-direction canon]). Statutory

---

("the will of a particular Congress . . . does not impose itself upon those to follow in succeeding years"); *Manigault v. Springs*, 199 U.S. 473, 487 (1905) (per Brown, J.) ("This law was doubtless intended as a guide to persons desiring to petition the legislature for special privileges . . . but it is not binding upon any subsequent legislature . . ."); *Newton v. Commissioners*, 100 U.S. 548, 559 (1879) (per Swayne, J.) (in cases involving public interests and public laws, "there can be . . . no irrepealable law").

8   *See, e.g.*, 5 U.S.C. § 559.

9   *See* J.M. Finnis, *1973 Annual Survey of Commonwealth Law* 11–12 (1974).

10   *Id.* at 12.

definitions usually account for this reality by (1) ascribing to words the ordinary meaning that they would bear anyway, and (2) stating that the definitions apply "unless the context indicates otherwise"[11]—the consequence of which is that the definitions accomplish nothing that ordinary principles of interpretation would not produce anyway. But when the definition set forth in an earlier statute provides a meaning that the word would not otherwise bear, it should be ineffective. It cannot be said to be part of the *corpus juris* whose provisions the court must reconcile (see § 27 [harmonious-reading canon]), since it is not itself a law but an effort to constrain future lawmakers. A definition section contained within a particular statute is quite different. That does prescribe what the statute says, and it is dispositive, barring either a clear indication that it has been ignored or the inclusion of the phrase *unless the context indicates otherwise*.[12]

Sometimes legislatures have actually tried to enact irrepealable acts. In *Boswell v. State*,[13] for example, the Oklahoma legislature tried to irrevocably pledge a portion of the gasoline excise tax to a special state fund.[14] The Oklahoma Supreme Court rightly held the statute unconstitutional.[15]

---

11 *See* 1 U.S.C. § 1 ("In determining the meaning of any Act of Congress, unless the context indicates otherwise, words importing the singular include and apply to several persons, parties, or things . . .").

12 *See supra* § 36.

13 74 P.2d 940 (Okla. 1937).

14 69 Okla. St. Ann. § 99(k)(2) (as quoted in *id.* at 943, 944).

15 74 P.2d at 943, 947.

46. Presumption Against Waiver of Sovereign Immunity

A statute does not waive sovereign immunity— and a federal statute does not eliminate state sovereign immunity—unless that disposition is unequivocally clear.

> "It is an axiom of our jurisprudence. The Government is not liable to suit unless it consents thereto, and its liability in suit cannot be extended beyond the plain language of the statute authorizing it."
> *Price v. United States,*
> 174 U.S. 373, 375–76 (1899) (per Brewer, J.).

The American states were heirs to a system in which the sovereign, the king, was not amenable to suit. Here is how Blackstone described it:

> Are then, it may be asked, the subjects of England totally destitute of remedy, in case the crown should invade their rights, whether by private injuries, or public oppressions? To this we answer, that the law has provided a remedy in both cases. And, first, as to private injuries; if any person has, in point of property, a just demand upon the king, he must petition him in his court of chancery, where his chancellor will administer right as a matter of grace, though not upon compulsion.
>
> . . . .
>
> Next, as to cases of ordinary public oppression, where the vitals of the constitution are not attacked, the law hath also assigned a remedy. For, as a king cannot misuse his power, without the advice of evil counselors, and the assistance of wicked ministers, these men may be examined and punished. . . . But it is at the same time a maxim in those laws, that the king himself can do no wrong . . . .[1]

Just as the king was amenable to "petition" only in the court of chancery that he had voluntarily created and given limited jurisdiction over him, so also the sovereign states (and the United States) were amenable to suit only when they agreed. Ordinary

---

1   1 William Blackstone, *Commentaries on the Laws of England* 236–37 (4th ed. 1770).

laws providing remedies for wrongs were not deemed applicable to the sovereign, and statutory waivers of sovereign immunity were rare.

Opinions of the Supreme Court of the United States say that a waiver of sovereign immunity "'cannot be implied but must be unequivocally expressed.'"[2] The cases in which that rule is pronounced did not contain any clear implication of waiver, and we doubt that the precise line set forth in that dictum ("unequivocally expressed") will hold—or ought to.

To be sure, the sovereign's consent to suit must be clear, but there is such a thing as utterly clear implication. Even English cases at least as early as the 1900s acknowledge that intent to include the sovereign can be implied:

> The Crown is not bound by an Act of Parliament unless specially named, or unless there is a necessary implication to be drawn from the provisions of the Act, or from the legislation on the subject, that the Crown was intended to be bound.[3]

We doubt whether an American court would be less generous. Imagine, for example, a state statute that authorizes suit for damage to real property and provides that when the losing defendant is the state, the plaintiff will be awarded attorney's fees. It is inconceivable that suit would not be allowed against the state. The implication, to be sure, must be utterly clear. Waiver cannot be found, for example, merely because one provision of an act fails to contain an express exclusion of state liability that other provisions of the act do contain.[4]

Unsurprisingly, Americans do not take kindly to the notion that the sovereign can do no wrong. Nor to the notion that suit

---

2   *Franconia Assocs. v. United States*, 536 U.S. 129, 141 (2002) (per Ginsburg, J.) (quoting *United States v. King*, 395 U.S. 1, 4 (1969) (per Black, J.)). *See United States v. Nordic Village, Inc.*, 503 U.S. 30 (1992) (per Scalia, J.) (holding that a statute lacking unequivocal expression did not waive sovereign immunity).

3   *Thomas v. Pritchard*, [1903] 1 K.B. 209, 212–13; 72 L.J.K.B. 23, 25. *See also Hornsey Urban Dist. Council v. Hennell*, [1902] 2 K.B. 73, 80; 71 L.J.K.B. 479, 482 ("[T]he intention that the Crown shall be bound . . . must clearly appear either from the language used or from the nature of the enactments.").

4   *Bombay Province v. Bombay Mun. Corp.*, [1947] A.C. 58, 65.

against the government should be forbidden entirely. At the federal level, sovereign immunity with regard to contract claims was largely eliminated by the Court of Claims Act in 1855[5] and the Tucker Act in 1887,[6] and with regard to tort claims by the Federal Tort Claims Act in 1946.[7] Suits seeking injunction or mandamus against federal executive officers acting unlawfully had long been allowed[8] (perhaps on Blackstone's theory that it was not the sovereign but the sovereign's "wicked ministers" who were being held to account), and the gaps and inconsistencies in that judicially created practice were eliminated by an amendment to the Administrative Procedure Act in 1976.[9] Some state supreme courts have judicially abolished the doctrine of sovereign immunity in the area of tort liability,[10] and the Supreme Court of the United States has spoken ill of the doctrine in general:

> The immunity enjoyed by the United States as a territorial sovereign is a legal doctrine which has not been favored by the test of time. It has increasingly been found to be in conflict with the growing subjection of governmental action to the moral judgment. A reflection of this steady shift in attitude toward the American sovereign's immunity is found in . . . observations in unanimous opinions of [the] Court . . . .[11]

---

5   10 Stat. 612 (1855).

6   24 Stat. 505 (1887).

7   60 Stat. 842 (1946).

8   *See generally* Louis L. Jaffe, *The Right to Judicial Review I*, 71 Harv. L. Rev. 401 (1958) and *The Right to Judicial Review II*, 71 Harv. L. Rev. 769 (1958); Roger C. Cramton, *Nonstatutory Review of Federal Administrative Action: The Need for Statutory Reform of Sovereign Immunity, Subject Matter Jurisdiction, and Parties Defendant*, 68 Mich. L. Rev. 387 (1970).

9   Pub. L. No. 94-574, 90 Stat. 2721 (1976).

10   *See, e.g., Stone v. Arizona Hwy. Comm'n*, 381 P.2d 107 (Ariz. 1963); *Muskopf v. Corning Hosp. Dist.*, 359 P.2d 457 (Cal. 1961).

11   *National City Bank of N.Y. v. Republic of China*, 348 U.S. 356, 359 (1955) (per Frankfurter, J.). *See also United States v. The Thelka*, 266 U.S. 328, 340–41 (1924) (per Holmes, J.) ("The reasons that have prevailed against creating a government liability in tort do not apply to a case like this, and on the other hand the reasons are strong for not obstructing the application of natural justice against the Government by technical formulas when justice can be done without endangering any public interest.").

Because of this attitude, the rigor with which courts have applied the interpretive rule disfavoring waivers of sovereign immunity has abated—rightly so. But the waiver itself must still be
express or clearly implied. That applies both to the fact of waiver
and to its precise scope. Thus, a state's consent to suit in its own
courts does not establish consent to suit on the same cause of action in federal courts.[12]

A classic old case involving the scope of an unquestioned waiver is *Price v. United States.*[13] A federal statute subjected the United
States to suit in the Court of Claims for "all claims for property
of citizens of the United States taken or destroyed by Indians."[14]
The plaintiff claimed that on June 26, 1847, while he was travel-
ing on the route from Missouri to Santa Fe, Osage Indians took
and drove away 32 head of his oxen, worth $400. He was awarded
that amount in the Court of Claims. But he contended on appeal
that the award should have been much larger because he had been
using the oxen to pull wagons, and the fair value of the wagons
and the goods they contained was $7,200, which he was forced to
sell at a loss:

> Because out in the unoccupied territory in which the taking
> of the oxen took place there was no market, and because he
> had no means of transporting the property not taken to a
> convenient market, he was subject to the whim or caprice
> of a passing traveller, and sold it to him for $1,200. The loss
> thereby entailed upon him he claims to recover under the
> provisions of the statute . . . .[15]

The Supreme Court said no:

> The property left in the possession of the petitioner was
> neither damaged nor destroyed by the action of the Indians
> in taking away the other property. . . . The damages were
> not to the property, considered as property, but simply con-
> sequential [damages] from the wrong done, and consisted
> solely in the fact that the petitioner, wronged by the taking

---

12 *Great N. Life Ins. Co. v. Read*, 322 U.S. 47, 54 (1944) (per Reed, J.).

13 174 U.S. 373 (1899) (per Brewer, J.).

14 26 Stat. c. 538, § 1.

15 *Id.* at 375.

away of certain property, was unable to realize the real value of property not taken, damaged, or destroyed.[16]

That decision was correct, and the case should be decided the
same today—the property was neither taken nor destroyed. It is
ingrained in our jurisprudence, and presumably known to legislators, that suit will not lie against the government unless there has
been a clear waiver of immunity *for the subject matter in question.* A
claim against the government for the value of property "taken or
destroyed" is simply not a claim for consequential damages caused
by the tort of taking or destroying property.[17]

It has been a corollary of the rule disfavoring waiver of sovereign immunity—or was arguably thought to be a part of the rule
itself—that "limitations and conditions upon which the Government consents to be sued must be strictly observed and exceptions thereto are not to be implied."[18] So, for example, statutes of
limitations applicable to suits against the government could not
be accorded the sorts of equitable tolling that would be allowed
in private suits.[19] This rigidity made sense when suits against the
government were disfavored, but not in modern times. It is one
thing to regard government liability as exceptional enough to require clarity of creation as a matter of presumed legislative intent.
It is quite something else to presume that a legislature that has
clearly made the determination that government liability is in the
interest of justice wants to accompany that determination with
nit-picking technicalities that would not accompany other causes
of action. The Supreme Court of the United States began to make
exceptions to this approach in the 1960s,[20] and finally signaled
complete departure in a 1990 opinion written by Chief Justice
Rehnquist:

---

16 *Id.* at 378.

17 *See also Schillinger v. United States*, 155 U.S. 163, 167 (1894) (per Brewer, J.) (suit
for government's contracting with third party for work to be done through unau-
thorized use of plaintiff's patent would not lie in Court of Claims because it was
a suit "sounding in tort" and not "upon any contract" with the government).

18 *Soriano v. United States*, 352 U.S. 270, 276 (1957) (per Clark, J.).

19 *Id.* at 275.

20 *See Honda v. Clark*, 386 U.S. 484, 501 (1967) (per Harlan, J.); *Bowen v. City of
N.Y.*, 476 U.S. 467, 479 (1986) (per Powell, J.).

> Once Congress has made . . . a waiver [of sovereign immu-
> nity], we think that making the rule of equitable tolling ap-
> plicable to suits against the Government, in the same way
> that it is applicable to private suits, amounts to little, if any,
> broadening of the congressional waiver. Such a principle is
> likely to be a realistic assessment of legislative intent as well
> as a practically useful principle of interpretation. We there-
> fore hold that the same rebuttable presumption of equitable
> tolling applicable to suits against private defendants should
> also apply to suits against the United States.[21]

The Chief Justice may have been exaggerating in saying that the Court *held* what he said—since the opinion immediately went on to say that the rules of equitable tolling applicable to private suits were of no help to this plaintiff.[22] But in fact the Court's later opinions hold to that line,[23] and we believe rightly so.

To require stricter observance of conditions attached to suits permitted against the government than of similar conditions at-tached to private suits is unjustified. But worse would be to aug-ment the proof required for the claim to which an unquestioned waiver applies. In the classic case on the subject, a New York statute permitted persons who had a lien on money owing from the state to a contractor to sue the state directly and recover the amount of the lien. When the holder of a mechanics' lien for work performed for a highway contractor proceeded under this stat-ute, the state denied that any money was owing to the contractor and asserted that the waiver of sovereign immunity should not be deemed to apply when the state contested the debt. In rejecting

---

21 *Irwin v. Department of Veterans Affairs*, 498 U.S. 89, 95–96 (1990) (per Rehnquist, C.J.).

22 *Id.* at 96.

23 *See, e.g., Franconia Assocs. v. United States*, 536 U.S. 129, 145 (2002) (per Gins-burg, J.) (rule for when a claim against the government "accrues" for statute-of-limitations purposes same as rule in private suits); *Scarborough v. Principi*, 541 U.S. 401, 420–23 (2004) (per Ginsburg, J.) (applying to 30-day deadline for fee-award application against government a relation-back rule applicable to fee-award applications in private litigation). The Court has declined to apply the *Irwin* principle to the question whether the statute-of-limitations provision of the Court of Claims Act is jurisdictional and hence must be raised by a court *sua sponte*. *See John R. Sand & Gravel Co. v. United States*, 552 U.S. 130, 138–39 (2008) (per Breyer, J.). But that holding was explicitly grounded in stare decisis.

this assertion for the New York Court of Appeals, Justice Cardozo wrote the oft-quoted line:

> The exemption of the sovereign from suit involves hardship enough, where consent has been withheld. We are not to add to its rigor by refinement of construction, where consent has been announced.[24]

In *Gomez-Perez v. Potter*,[25] a postal employee sued the Postal Service and the Postmaster General for actions taken against her in alleged retaliation for her filing an age-discrimination complaint. Section 633a(a) of Title 20 forbade "discrimination based on age" by (among other agencies) the Postal Service; and § 633a(c) authorized suit in district court for violation of that provision. The Postal Service contended that "sovereign immunity principles require that § 633a(a) be read narrowly as prohibiting substantive age discrimination but not retaliation."[26] The Court properly rejected that contention:

> Subsection (c) of § 633a unequivocally waives sovereign immunity for a claim brought by "[a]ny person aggrieved" to remedy a violation of § 633a. Unlike § 633a(c), § 633a(a) is not a waiver of sovereign immunity; it is a substantive provision outlawing "discrimination." That the waiver in § 633a(c) applies to § 633a(a) claims does not mean that § 633a(a) must surmount the same high hurdle as § 633a(c).[27]

Other legal questions raised by the doctrine of sovereign immunity do not pertain to the interpretation of texts—for example, when it is that government action such as the initiation of a law-

---

24 *Anderson v. John L. Hayes Constr. Co.*, 153 N.E. 28, 29–30 (N.Y. 1926).

25 553 U.S. 474 (2008) (per Alito, J.).

26 *Id.* at 476.

27 *Id.* at 491. *See also United States v. White Mountain Apache Tribe*, 537 U.S. 465, 472–73 (2003) (per Souter, J.); *United States v. Aetna Cas. & Sur. Co.*, 338 U.S. 366, 383 (1949) (per Vinson, C.J.).

suit[28] or participation in a federal program[29] constitutes a waiver. One last interpretive consequence of the doctrine, however, pertains to federal elimination of the states' sovereign immunity guaranteed by the Eleventh Amendment,[30] a result that Congress has power to effect under § 5 of the Fourteenth Amendment.[31] The Supreme Court has required for that purpose "an unequivocal expression of congressional intent."[32] Thus, it has held, for example, that a state is not a "person" subject to the suits authorized by 42 U.S.C. § 1983 for deprivation of constitutional rights[33] and that a provision of the federal Rehabilitation Act authorizing suit against "any recipient of Federal assistance" under the Act[34] does not authorize suit against states that receive assistance.[35] This rule requiring "unequivocal" designation of the states cannot be attributed to the mere doctrine of sovereign immunity itself (or to the presumed intent of the legislature for the sovereign whose immunity is at issue). Rather, the Supreme Court of the United States has made clear the federal structural consideration that is the proper basis for assuming that state immunity has not been eliminated unless that result is founded on clear expression:

> Our reluctance to infer that a State's immunity from suit in the federal courts has been negated stems from recognition of the vital role of the doctrine of sovereign immunity in

---

28 *See, e.g., United States v. Shaw*, 309 U.S. 495, 505 (1940) (per Reed, J.) (suit by United States in state court does not waive sovereign immunity for counter claims).

29 *See College Sav. Bank v. Florida Prepaid Postsecondary Educ. Expense Bd.*, 527 U.S. 666, 680–81 (1999) (per Scalia, J.) (mere participation in a federal program does not constitute a "constructive waiver," even when the federal program specifically provides that participation will entail state liability to suit).

30 *Seminole Tribe of Fla. v. Florida*, 517 U.S. 44, 72–73 (1996) (per Rehnquist, C.J.).

31 *Fitzpatrick v. Bitzer*, 427 U.S. 445 (1976) (per Rehnquist, J.).

32 *Pennhurst State Sch. & Hosp. v. Halderman*, 465 U.S. 89, 99 (1984) (per Powell, J.).

33 *Quern v. Jordan*, 440 U.S. 332 (1979) (per Rehnquist, J.).

34 29 U.S.C. § 794a(a)(2).

35 *Atascadero State Hosp. v. Scanlon*, 473 U.S. 234, 246 (1985) (per Powell, J.) ("A general authorization for suit in federal court is not the kind of unequivocal statutory language sufficient to abrogate the Eleventh Amendment.").

our federal system. . . . As Justice Marshall well has noted, "[b]ecause of the problems of federalism inherent in making one sovereign appear against its will in the courts of the other, a restriction upon the exercise of the federal judicial power has long been considered . . . appropriate . . . ."[36]

---

36 *Pennhurst State Sch. & Hosp.*, 465 U.S. at 99–100 (quoting *Employees of Mo. Dep't of Pub. Health & Welfare v. Missouri Dep't of Pub. Health & Welfare*, 411 U.S. 279, 294 (1973) (Marshall, J., concurring in the result)).

47. Presumption Against Federal Preemption

A federal statute is presumed to supplement rather than displace state law.

It is a reliable canon of interpretation—though sometimes dishonored in the breach—to presume that a federal statute does not preempt state law. The presumption is readily overcome if state law would require something that federal law prohibits or would prohibit something that federal law requires. That presents a clear conflict, subjecting people to contradictory commands, so by reason of the Supremacy Clause,[1] federal law prevails. Likewise, if federal law forbids what state law permits, federal law prevails. But if federal law neither prohibits nor requires what state law forbids, state law prevails.

One difficulty arises when a federal statute sets certain standards or requirements—such as for automobile passenger restraints or cigarette advertising—and a state law sets a higher standard or requirement. There is no conflict of commands, since meeting the higher state standard or requirement complies with the federal one as well. Sometimes, however, the federal statute is meant to establish a *maximum* standard or requirement on which everyone can rely, so that, for example, manufacturers serving a national market will not be compelled to comply with the law of the most restrictive state. The cases refer to this type of preemption as *field preemption*—though as the Supreme Court has pointed out, it is really "a species of conflict preemption."[2] Congress having determined that its regulation is exclusive, state laws to the contrary conflict.

Sometimes the federal statute makes its occupation of the field express. For example, in 2012 the Supreme Court held[3] that a California law regulating slaughterhouse treatment of certain animals was preempted by the Federal Meat Inspection Act,[4]

---

1   U.S. Const. art. VI, cl. 2.

2   *English v. General Elec. Co.*, 496 U.S. 72, 79 n.5 (1990) (per Blackmun, J.).

3   *National Meat Ass'n v. Harris*, 132 S.Ct. 965 (2012) (per Kagan, J.).

4   21 U.S.C. § 601 *et seq.*

which contained the following provision: "Requirements within the scope of this [Act] with respect to premises, facilities and operations of any establishment at which inspection is provided under . . . this [Act] which are in addition to, or different than those made under this [Act] may not be imposed by any State."[5]

ERISA, the Employee Retirement Income Security Act of 1974,[6] contained a similarly broad field-preemption provision, stating that it "shall supersede any and all State laws insofar as they may now or hereafter relate to any employee benefit plan" covered by the Act.[7]

Even if Congress has not enacted such an express provision, however, state law will be preempted "when Congress intends federal law to 'occupy the field.'"[8] In our view, of course, such an "intent" (see § 67) must derive from the text of the federal laws and not from such extraneous sources as legislative history. The problem here lies in ensuring certainty in the law: Too often, when such an intent will or will not be found is difficult to predict.

Field preemption is much more likely to be found when the federal statute deals with an area that the federal government has traditionally controlled, such as foreign affairs, international relations, and immigration. For example, in *Crosby v. National Foreign Trade Council*,[9] a Massachusetts statute barred from state contracts certain entities doing business with Burma. The statute was held to be preempted by a federal statute imposing certain sanctions on Burma and giving the President authority to impose or withhold further sanctions. And in *Toll v. Moreno*[10] the Supreme Court held preempted a Maryland statute declaring lawfully admitted aliens of a certain classification ineligible for instate college tuition. It relied on "the preeminent role of the Federal Government with

---

5   *Id.* § 678.

6   29 U.S.C. § 1001 *et seq.*

7   *Id.* § 1144(a).

8   *Crosby v. National Foreign Trade Council*, 530 U.S. 363, 372 (2000) (per Souter, J.).

9   *Id.*

10 458 U.S. 1 (1982) (per Brennan, J.).

respect to the regulation of aliens within our borders"[11] and the comprehensive provisions of the Immigration and Nationality Act of 1952.[12]

Field preemption is less likely when the state law in question pertains to a subject of traditional state regulation. Because most exercises of general governmental power can be said to be "traditionally" functions of a state, the principle must apply not to the *fact* of state regulation of a particular activity, but to its *purpose*. In the *Crosby* case dealing with Burma, for example, it was surely traditional for states to prescribe the qualifications of state contractors—but not traditional for states to do so in order to punish a foreign country for its inhumane activities. This focus on the purpose rather than the regulated object of the state law is suggested by some of the explicit preemption provisions that Congress has enacted. For example, the provision of the Atomic Energy Act states: "Nothing in this section shall be construed to affect the authority of any State or local agency to regulate activities for purposes other than protection against radiation hazards."[13] Similarly, a provision of the Federal Cigarette Labeling and Advertising Act declares preempted any "requirement or prohibition based on smoking and health . . . imposed under State law with respect to the advertising or promotion of any cigarettes."[14]

It is hard to know when a federal statute will be construed to effect field preemption. The Supreme Court has held[15] that a tort action against an automobile manufacturer for failing to provide an airbag was preempted by the less restrictive requirements issued by the Department of Transportation under the National Traffic and Motor Vehicle Safety Act[16]—even though a saving clause in that statute said that "[c]ompliance with" a federal safety standard "does not exempt any person from any liability under

---

11 *Id*. at 10.

12 8 U.S.C. § 110 *et seq*. (1976 & Supp. IV).

13 42 U.S.C. § 2021(k).

14 15 U.S.C. § 1334(b).

15 *See Geier v. American Honda Motor Co*., 529 U.S. 861, 865 (2000) (per Breyer, J.).

16 15 U.S.C. § 1381 *et seq*.

common law."[17] Yet the Court has held not preempted a tort action for failing to include on prescription-drug labeling a warning beyond what the Food & Drug Administration approved and required under the Food, Drug, and Cosmetic Act.[18] As for the Federal Cigarette Labeling and Advertising Act's preemption of any "requirement or prohibition based on smoking and health . . . imposed under State law with respect to the advertising or promotion of any cigarettes": The Supreme Court held that this provision resulted in preemption of state common-law failure-to-warn claims and one of two common-law fraud claims relating to cigarette advertising.[19] On the other hand, in *Altria Group, Inc. v. Good*,[20] the Court held that the same provision did not preempt a state-law statutory claim for fraudulent advertising.

While any determination about field preemption is highly fact-bound, two principles seem to us clearly required. First, the preemption canon ought not to be applied to the text of an explicit preemption provision. That is, the text ought to be given its fair meaning rather than a meaning narrowed by the presumption. The reason is obvious: The presumption is based on an assumption of what Congress, in our federal system, would or should normally desire. But when Congress has explicitly set forth its desire, there is no justification for not taking Congress at its word—i.e., giving its words their ordinary, fair meaning. So, for example, we disagree with the decision of the Supreme Court in *Cipollone* to give the preemption provision of the Federal Cigarette Labeling and Advertising Act a "narrow" meaning rather than simply the meaning that its words fairly convey.[21]

Second, it is theoretically possible for Congress to preempt state law enacted by statute or regulation but not to preempt state common law applied by juries and the courts. But such a disposition makes so little sense that it would take the clearest of statutory

---

17 *Id.* § 1397(k).

18 21 U.S.C. § 301 *et seq. See Wyeth v. Levine*, 555 U.S. 555 (2009) (per Stevens, J.).

19 *Cipollone v. Liggett Group, Inc.*, 505 U.S. 504, 530–31 (1992) (per Stevens, J.).

20 555 U.S. 70 (2008) (per Stevens, J.).

21 505 U.S. at 518. *See id.* at 544–47 (Scalia, J., concurring in the judgment in part and dissenting in part).

language to adopt it. The relevant question, after all, is whether the federal statute establishes a national standard that is meant to provide a safe harbor from liability. If it does, state departures from that standard by common-law adjudication are just as disruptive of the safe harbor as departures by statute or regulation. Indeed, they are *more* disruptive, since case-by-case jury determinations of such questions as "negligence" and "failure to warn" are not only unpredictable and inconsistent, but also usually uninformed regarding the benefits (as opposed to the costs) of the more lenient federal rule.[22] If a statute explicitly prohibiting different state requirements is not meant to establish a national standard, it is hard to imagine what it *is* meant to do. So we find questionable the Supreme Court's determination in *Cipollone* that the federal statutory provision stating that "[n]o requirement or prohibition based on smoking and health shall be imposed under State law with respect to the advertising or promotion of any cigarettes" had merely the effect of "supersed[ing] only positive enactments by legislatures or administrative agencies that mandate particular warning labels"[23]—while allowing state common-law claims that are not based on the state statute.

---

22 *See Wyeth*, 555 U.S. at 626–27 (Alito, J., dissenting).
23 *Cipollone*, 505 U.S. at 518–19.

Private-Right Canons

48. Penalty/Illegality Canon
A statute that penalizes an act makes it unlawful.

> "[W]here the statute inflicts a penalty for doing an act, although
> the act itself is not expressly prohibited, yet to do the act is
> unlawful, because it cannot be supposed that the Legislature
> intended that a penalty should be inflicted for a lawful act."
> *Powhatan Steamboat Co. v. Appomattox R.R.*,
> 65 U.S. (24 How.) 247, 252 (1860) (per Clifford, J.).

In the words of James Kent, one of the chief 19th-century expositors of American law: "If a statute inflicts a penalty for doing
an act, the penalty implies a prohibition, and the thing is unlawful, though there be no prohibitory words in the statute."[1]

Why does this canon matter? Kent's example is that of a statute imposing a penalty for the making of a usurious contract: Because the contract is held to be illegal, it is void.[2] So one cannot
enforce such a contract and just pay a fine for having made it.

Many statutory provisions penalize without expressly illegal-
izing. Consider the Massachusetts statute that read: "Whoever
sells, or offers for sale, or has in possession, a lobster less than ten
and one-half inches in length, measuring from one extreme of the
body, extended, to the other, exclusive of claws or feelers, shall
forfeit five dollars for every such lobster."[3] If the provision had read
shall be taxed instead of *shall forfeit*, the provision would be read as
a tax and not a penalty. But because *forfeit* connotes a penalty, it
would be impossible to contract legally for the delivery of nine- to
ten-inch lobsters with the understanding that each one would be
subject to a $5 governmental exaction. Any such contract, being
illegal, would be void.

---

1   James Kent, *Commentaries on American Law* 436 (1826).

2   *Id.*

3   Mass. Pub. Stat. c. 91, § 84, as amended, Mass. Stat. 1884, c. 212, § 1 (as quoted
     in *Commonwealth v. Barber*, 10 N.E. 330, 331 (Mass. 1887)).

49. Rule of Lenity

Ambiguity in a statute defining a crime or imposing a penalty should be resolved in the defendant's favor.

"Blurred signposts to criminality will not suffice to create it."
United States v. C.I.O.,
335 U.S. 106, 142 (1948) (Rutledge, J., concurring).

The rule of lenity—sometimes cast as the idea that "[p]enal statutes must be construed strictly"[1] and sometimes as the idea that if two rational readings are possible, the one with the less harsh treatment of the defendant prevails[2]—was termed by Jeremy Bentham "the subject of more constant controversy than perhaps of any in the whole circle of the Law."[3]

The rule originally rested on the interpretive reality that a just legislature will not decree punishment without making clear what conduct incurs the punishment and what the extent of the punishment will be; or at least on the judge-made public policy that a legislature *ought* not to do so. Chief Justice John Marshall explained it this way in 1820:

> The rule that penal laws are to be construed strictly . . .
> is founded on the tenderness of the law for the rights of
> individuals; and on the plain principle that the power of
> punishment is vested in the legislative, not in the judicial
> department. It is the legislature, not the Court, which is to
> define a crime, and ordain its punishment.[4]

Some authorities consider the rule to be based on constitutional requirements of fair notice and separation of powers (federal courts have no power to define crimes[5]). But application of the rule of

---

1   1 William Blackstone, *Commentaries on the Laws of England* 88 (4th ed. 1770).

2   *McNally v. United States*, 483 U.S. 350, 359–60 (1987) (per White, J.).

3   Jeremy Bentham, *A Comment on the Commentaries: A Criticism of William Blackstone's Commentaries on the Laws of England* 141 (1776; Charles Warren Everett ed., 1928).

4   *United States v. Wiltberger*, 18 U.S. (5 Wheat.) 76, 95 (1820) (per Marshall, C.J.).

5   *See United States v. Bass*, 404 U.S. 336, 348 (1971) (per Marshall, J.) ("[B]ecause of the seriousness of criminal penalties, and because criminal punishment usually

lenity, vague as it is, does not coincide with the constitutional requirement of fair notice—or even with that requirement plus the constitutional-doubt canon (§ 38). And as for the separation of powers, the rule antedates both state and federal constitutions, and it applies not only to crimes but also to civil penalties.

Consider a straightforward case. With respect to certain specified institutions, including federally insured banks, a federal statute made it a crime to "knowingly mak[e] any false statement or report" or to "willfully overvalu[e] any land, property, or security" for the purpose of influencing action "upon any application, . . . commitment, [or] loan."[6] A Louisiana bank president was convicted of writing bad checks on accounts that had insufficient funds. But were the bad checks themselves "false statements" that give rise to criminal liability under the statute? Justice Blackmun wrote for a seven-member majority of the Supreme Court of the United States in holding no: "Congress should have spoken in language that is clear and definite. . . . '[The rule of lenity] would require statutory language much more explicit than that before us here to lead to the conclusion that Congress intended to put the Federal Government in the business of policing the' deposit of bad checks."[7]

One interpretive problem sometimes arises when the same violation of law is made subject to *both* a civil or criminal penalty *and* a private claim for the injury inflicted. Is the language defining the violation to be given one meaning (a narrow one) for the penal sanction and a different meaning (a more expansive one) for the private compensatory action? That seems inconceivable. The Supreme Court of the United States says as much: "[The dissent] further suggests that lenity is inappropriate because we construe the statute today 'in a civil setting' rather than 'a criminal prosecution.' The rule of lenity, however, is a rule of statutory construction

---

represents the moral condemnation of the community, legislatures and not courts should define criminal activity.").

6   18 U.S.C. § 1014.

7   *Williams v. United States*, 458 U.S. 279, 290 (1982) (per Blackmun, J.) (quoting *United States v. Enmons*, 410 U.S. 396, 411 (1973) (per Stewart, J.), with the really strange internal end-quote as shown).

whose purpose is to help give authoritative meaning to statutory language. It is not a rule of administration calling for courts to refrain in criminal cases from applying statutory language that would have been held to apply if challenged in civil litigation."[8]

The main difficulty with the rule of lenity is the uncertainty of its application. Its operation would be relatively clear if the rule were automatically applied at the outset of textual inquiry, before any other rules of interpretation were invoked to resolve ambiguity. Treating it as a clear-statement rule would comport with the original basis for the canon and would provide considerable certainty. But that is not the approach the cases have taken. The Supreme Court of the United States expresses the consensus when it says that "[t]he rule comes into operation at the end of the process of construing what Congress has expressed, not at the beginning as an overriding consideration of being lenient to wrongdoers."[9] Fair enough. But less comprehensible is the Court's statement in a later case that the rule applies "only when the equipoise of competing reasons cannot otherwise be resolved."[10] If that were so, the rule either would never apply (when is the last time you read a decision saying that an interpretive "equipoise" could not be resolved?) or would be superfluous (if alternative meanings were in utter equipoise, the statute would be inoperative as meaningless[11]).

But not to worry: Supreme Court opinions provide an ample supply of other criteria for determining when the rule of lenity applies, ranging from when the court "can make 'no more than a guess,'"[12] to when the court is "left with an ambiguous statute,"[13]

---

8   *United States v. Thompson/Ctr. Arms Co.*, 504 U.S. 505, 518 n.10 (1992) (Souter, J., plurality opinion). *See Crandon v. United States*, 494 U.S. 152, 158 (1990) (per Stevens, J.) (applying the rule of lenity to a hybrid criminal/civil statute—in the civil context); *Leocal v. Ashcroft*, 543 U.S. 1, 11 n.8 (2004) (per Rehnquist, C.J.) (same).

9   *Callanan v. United States*, 364 U.S. 587, 596 (1961) (per Frankfurter, J.). *See United States v. R.L.C.*, 503 U.S. 291 (1992) (in which the plurality of a splintered Court unfortunately applied the rule of lenity *after* consulting legislative history—see § 66).

10 *Johnson v. United States*, 529 U.S. 694, 713 n.13 (2000) (per Souter, J.).

11 *See* § 16 (unintelligibility canon).

12 *Reno v. Koray*, 515 U.S. 50, 65 (1995) (per Rehnquist, C.J.) (citing *Ladner v. United States*, 358 U.S. 169, 178 (1958) (per Brennan, J.)).

13 *Smith v. United States*, 508 U.S. 223, 239 (1993) (per O'Connor, J.).

to when there remains "grievous ambiguity or uncertainty."[14] Given the multiplicity of expressed standards, one of your authors has said that the rule of lenity under current law "provides little more than atmospherics, since it leaves open the crucial question—almost invariably present—of how much ambiguousness constitutes an ambiguity."[15]

The criterion we favor is this: whether, after all the legitimate tools of interpretation have been applied, "a reasonable doubt persists."[16]

Vague as it is, this test seems to be more comprehensible than the others. One might believe that the provision in question is not "in equipoise" or "grievously ambiguous"—while yet acknowledging that the matter is not beyond reasonable doubt. This is, to be sure, more defendant-friendly than most of the other formulations. We prefer it because we believe that when the government means to punish, its commands must be reasonably clear. When they are not clear, the consequences should be visited on the party more able to avoid and correct the effects of shoddy legislative drafting—namely, the federal Department of Justice or its state equivalent.

Does the canon attach to tax laws? For many years, the Supreme Court of the United States subjected them to a strict construction, holding that "[i]n case of doubt [statutes levying taxes] are construed most strongly against the government, and in favor of the citizen."[17] Although many states continue to apply this rule,[18] it unfortunately can no longer be said to enjoy universal

---

14 *Muscarello v. United States*, 524 U.S. 125, 139 (1998) (per Breyer, J.).

15 *United States v. Hansen*, 772 F.2d 940, 948 (D.C. Cir. 1985).

16 *Moskal v. United States*, 498 U.S. 103, 108 (1990) (per Marshall, J.).

17 *Gould v. Gould*, 245 U.S. 151, 153 (1917) (per McReynolds, J.) (citing prior authorities going back to an 1842 opinion by Justice Story on circuit, *United States v. Wigglesworth*, 28 F. Cas. 595 (C.C.D. Mass. 1842) (No. 16,690)).

18 *See, e.g., Sane Transit v. Sound Transit*, 85 P.3d 346, 364 (Wash. 2004) (taxpayer won because statute was ambiguous); *State ex rel. Arizona Dep't of Revenue v. Capitol Castings, Inc.*, 88 P.3d 159, 161 (Ariz. 2004) (same); *Goodman Oil Co. v. Idaho State Tax Comm'n*, 28 P.3d 996, 998 (Idaho 2001) (same); *Skepton v. Borough of Wilson*, 755 A.2d 1267, 1270 (Pa. 2000) (same); *American Healthcare Mgmt., Inc. v. Director of Revenue*, 984 S.W.2d 496, 498 (Mo. 1999) (same).

approval.[19] Nor are statutes providing remedies for fraud considered penal laws subject to the canon. As Blackstone described it:

> [W]here the statute acts upon the offender, and inflicts a penalty, as the pillory or a fine, it is then to be taken strictly: but when the statute acts upon the offence, by setting aside the fraudulent transaction, here it is to be construed liberally.[20]

The rule of lenity is often overlooked when it ought to apply. Consider the Kentucky statute making it a crime to "sell, lend, or give" liquor to a minor—unless you are the minor's parent or guardian. Sixteen-year-old Davis and seventeen-year-old Rison decided to pool their money to buy and then drink whiskey. They did so, were caught, and were arrested. Davis, the younger boy, was charged with "giving" whiskey to Rison. The trial court dismissed the indictment without explanation, and the prosecution appealed to the Kentucky Supreme Court. Davis argued that he did not "sell, lend, or give" whiskey to Rison—and that *give* means "to bestow a gift." The prosecution argued that, in an expanded sense, *give* means "to furnish, provide, or supply." The court agreed with the prosecution's argument and remanded the case for trial[21]— quite erroneously. The rule of lenity militated in favor of a judgment for Davis, as did *noscitur a sociis* (see § 31 [associated-words canon]), but the court dismissed the first and missed the second.

---

19 *See, e.g., Colgate-Palmolive-Peet Co. v. United States,* 320 U.S. 422, 429–30 (1943) (per Reed, J.) (upholding government's imposition of excise tax despite ambiguity in Revenue Act of 1934); *Burnet v. Guggenheim,* 288 U.S. 280, 286 (1933) (per Cardozo, J.) (upholding imposition of tax despite ambiguity in Revenue Act of 1924); *Stryker Corp. v. Director, Div. of Taxation,* 773 A.2d 674, 684 (N.J. 2001) (recognizing well-settled rule that tax laws are construed strictly against the state, yet imposing tax because "tax laws also must be construed reasonably so that the Legislature's purpose in enacting the statute is not destroyed"); *Johnson v. State Tax Comm'n,* 411 P.2d 831, 834 (Utah 1966) (interpreting ambiguous tax statute against taxpayer to accomplish the legislative purpose and bring about "equal and non-discriminatory taxation").

20 1 William Blackstone, *Commentaries on the Laws of England* 88 (4th ed. 1770). *See also* 3 Roscoe Pound, *Jurisprudence* 498 (1959).

21 *Commonwealth v. Davis,* 75 Ky. 240, 242–43 (1876).

On the whole, it might fairly be said that the rule of lenity is underused in modern judicial decision-making[22]—perhaps the consequence of zeal to smite the wicked. The defendant has almost always done a bad thing, and the instinct to punish the wrongdoer is a strong one. But a fair system of laws requires precision in the definition of offenses and punishments. The less the courts insist on precision, the less the legislatures will take the trouble to provide it.

Naturally, the rule of lenity has no application when the statute is clear—though just as naturally counsel will try to manufacture ambiguity when there is none. In *Sullivan v. United States*,[23] the District of Columbia's Sex Offender Registration Act required registration by any person who "[c]ommitted a [sex] offense at any time and is in custody or under supervision on or after July 11, 2000" because of "[b]eing convicted of . . . an offense under the District of Columbia Official Code."[24] Two years before the Act was enacted, Sullivan was convicted of assault with intent to rape. He was jailed and later released. After the Act took effect, he was convicted of driving without a permit, was placed on supervised probation, had his probation revoked, and was jailed once again.[25] After his release, District authorities repeatedly notified Sullivan

---

22 See *James v. United States*, 550 U.S. 192, 219 (2007) (Scalia, J., dissenting) ("The rule of lenity, grounded in part on the need to give 'fair warning' of what is encompassed by a criminal statute, . . . demands that we give this text the more narrow reading of which it is susceptible."); *Almendarez-Torres v. United States*, 523 U.S. 224, 271 (1998) (Scalia, J., dissenting) ("[W]here the doctrine of constitutional doubt does not apply, the same result may be dictated by the rule of lenity, which would preserve rather than destroy the criminal defendant's right to jury findings beyond a reasonable doubt."); *United States v. O'Hagan*, 521 U.S. 642, 679 (1997) (Scalia, J., concurring in part and dissenting in part) ("While the Court's explanation of the scope of § 10(b) and Rule 10b-5 would be entirely reasonable in some other context, it does not seem to accord with the principle of lenity we apply to criminal statutes."); *Smith v. United States*, 508 U.S. 223, 246 (1993) (Scalia, J., dissenting) ("Even if the reader does not consider the issue to be as clear as I do, he must at least acknowledge, I think, that it is eminently debatable—and that is enough, under the rule of lenity, to require finding for the petitioner here.")

23 990 A.2d 477 (D.C. 2010).

24 D.C. Code § 22-4001(5)(A)(I), (9).

25 990 A.2d at 478.

that he must register under the Act, yet he repeatedly failed to do so. He was then convicted of failing to register as a sex offender.

On appeal, Sullivan (or, more properly, his lawyer) argued that he did not have to register under the Act because (1) he had been released from custody for his sex offense before the Act took effect, and (2) his post-Act conviction of driving without a license (a nonviolent traffic offense) was not the type of offense that could bring him within the reach of the Act. The District of Columbia Court of Appeals correctly held otherwise. The language "convicted of . . . an offense under the District of Columbia Official Code" was broad (see § 9 [general-terms canon]) and unambiguous, and it did not exclude any type of conviction for which a court might order a person into custody or supervision.[26] Hence, the rule of lenity had no application.

---

26 *Id*. at 482.

50. *Mens Rea* Canon

A statute creating a criminal offense whose elements are similar to those of a common-law crime will be presumed to require a culpable state of mind (*mens rea*) in its commission. All statutory offenses imposing substantial punishment will be presumed to require at least awareness of committing the act.

> "We have 'on a number of occasions read a state-of-mind component into an offense even when the statutory definition did not in terms so provide.'"
>
> *Dean v. United States*,
> 556 U.S. 568, 574–75 (2009) (per Roberts, C.J.).[1]

The ancient rule of the common law was contained in the maxim *actus non facit reum nisi mens sit rea*: An act does not constitute a crime unless there is criminal intent. As Blackstone put it: "[A]s a vicious will without a vicious act is no civil crime, so, on the other hand, an unwarrantable act without a vicious will is no crime at all."[2] He describes as one instance excusing "defect of will" the fact of "*ignorance* or *mistake* . . . ; when a man, intending to do a lawful act, does that which is unlawful. . . . But this must be an ignorance or mistake of fact, and not an error in point of law."[3]

The *mens rea* canon still applies to criminal statutes that do not explicitly contain a *mens rea* requirement. As recently as 1994, the Supreme Court spoke approvingly of, and applied, "the background presumption of evil intent."[4] The problem is that the assumption of a *mens rea* requirement is not *always* applied—nor would anyone think it should be. Take, for example, a reckless-

---

1 Quoting *United States v. U.S. Gypsum Co.*, 438 U.S. 422, 437 (1978) (per Burger, C.J.).

2 4 William Blackstone, *Commentaries on the Laws of England* 21 (4th ed. 1770).

3 *Id.* at 27. *See* J.W. Cecil Turner, *Kenny's Outlines of Criminal Law* 60 (19th ed. 1966) ("[T]he mistake, however reasonable, must not relate to matters of law but to matters of fact. For it is a basic legal principle . . . that a mistake of law, even though inevitable, is not allowed to form any excuse for crime.").

4 *United States v. X-Citement Video, Inc.*, 513 U.S. 64, 70 (1994) (per Rehnquist, C.J.).

driving statute defining the offense as exceeding the posted speed limit by more than 15 miles per hour. "I did not realize I was driving so fast" is surely no defense.

The ancient principle and the modern difficulty of applying it are both described in Justice Robert H. Jackson's classic opinion for the Court in *Morissette v. United States*.[5] The discussion began:

> Crime, as a compound concept, generally constituted only from concurrence of an evil-meaning mind with an evil-doing hand, was congenial to an intense individualism and took deep and early root in American soil. As the states codified the common law of crimes, even if their enactments were silent on the subject, their courts assumed that the omission did not signify disapproval of the principle but merely recognized that intent was so inherent in the idea of the offense that it required no statutory affirmation.[6]

But the opinion goes on to describe the demise of the concept as an absolute rule—"a century-old but accelerating tendency, discernible both here and in England, to call into existence new duties and crimes which disregard any ingredient of intent."[7] Justice Jackson's description of the difficulty of discerning from the extant cases when evil intent will be required, and when not, is as true today as it was 60 years ago:

> Neither this Court nor, so far as we are aware, any other has undertaken to delineate a precise line or set forth comprehensive criteria for distinguishing between crimes that require a mental element and crimes that do not. We attempt no closed definition, for the law on the subject is neither settled nor static.[8]

The *Morissette* case itself involved a deer-hunter on a government-owned tract of land in Michigan used by the Air Force as a practice bombing range but regularly used by nearby residents for deer-hunting. After a fruitless day's hunt, Morissette decided

---

5   342 U.S. 246 (1952) (per Jackson, J.).

6   *Id.* at 251–52.

7   *Id.* at 253.

8   *Id.* at 260.

to cut his losses by salvaging some of the spent practice-bomb casings that were lying about rusting and that (according to his account) he believed to have been abandoned. He was convicted under a statute that subjected to fine and imprisonment "[w]hoever embezzles, steals, purloins, or knowingly converts to his use . . . or without authority sells, conveys, or disposes of any . . . thing of value of the United States . . . ."[9] The charge to the jury did not permit acquittal for good-faith belief that the property was abandoned.

The Supreme Court reversed the conviction, finding several factors requiring *mens rea*. The principal one was that "[s]tealing, larceny, and its variants and equivalents, were among the earliest offenses known to the law that existed before legislation" and for them "[s]tate courts of last resort . . . have consistently retained the requirement of intent."[10] The principle is akin to the presumption against change in common law (§ 52):

> Congressional silence as to mental elements in an Act merely adopting into federal statutory law a concept of crime already so well defined in common law and statutory interpretation by the states may warrant quite contrary inferences than the same silence in creating an offense new to general law, for whose definition the courts have no guidance except the Act.[11]
>
> .   .   .
>
> [W]here Congress borrows terms of art in which are accumulated the legal tradition and meaning of centuries of practice, it presumably knows and adopts the cluster of ideas that were attached to each borrowed word in the body of learning from which it was taken and the meaning its use will convey to the judicial mind unless otherwise instructed.[12]

Another factor was that none of the crimes that had been collected in the Code revision that produced the statute "fits the congres-

---

9   18 U.S.C. § 641.

10   342 U.S. at 260–61.

11   *Id.* at 262.

12   *Id.* at 263.

sional classification of a petty offense; each is, at its least, a mis-demeanor, and if the amount involved is one hundred or more dollars each is a felony."[13]

The first of those two factors—statutory embodiment of a common-law crime—is perhaps the most commonly used ground, and the only certain ground, for finding a *mens rea* element in a statute that does not expressly contain it. That is correct when the actual name of the common-law crime (burglary, fraud, theft) appears in the statute. It is merely one instance of the canon of imputed common-law meaning (see § 53). Beyond this, however, even when the statute does not use the common-law term but sets forth the elements of a crime that existed at common law—making the traditional elements of fraud, for example, a federal crime if perpetrated across state lines, or subjecting those traditional elements to especially harsh penalties if perpetrated in a certain context such as securities sales—the presumption of evil intent should apply to those elements as well.

This rule will as a practical matter require *mens rea* for the overwhelming majority of serious crimes: The common law developed prohibitions of serious crime over hundreds of years, and there is not much new serious crime under the sun. Except for an expansive application of this common-law-analogue rule, however, we can find no justification in consistent judicial practice for finding an intent requirement not expressed or textually implied. Some cases have suggested that doing so is proper when the offense is *malum in se* (inherently wrong) rather than *malum prohibitum* (wrong only because prohibited).[14] But there are many modern examples of crimes without an intent requirement that contradict this rule. For example, an evil-intent requirement would surely not be imposed on a statute that makes it a crime to drive so as to endanger human life—though such an action is wrong in itself.[15]

---

13 *Id.* at 268–69.

14 *See, e.g., United States v. Balint,* 258 U.S. 250, 252 (1922) (per Taft, C.J.).

15 Many statutes expressly negate a state-of-mind requirement. *See, e.g.,* Colo. Rev. Stat. § 18-3-205(1)(b)(I) (2003) (vehicular-assault statute) ("If a person operates or drives a motor vehicle while under the influence of alcohol . . . and this conduct is the proximate cause of a serious bodily injury to another, such person commits

Another factor often mentioned is the second one alluded to by Justice Jackson in *Morissette*: the severity of the punishment. As one authority describes it: "Other things being equal, the greater the possible punishment, the more likely some fault is required; and, conversely, the lighter the possible punishment, the more likely the legislature meant to impose liability without fault."[16] This is doubtless true as an empirical observation of what courts do, but it seems to us more a demonstration that hard cases make bad law than a principled basis for reading into a text what it does not contain. The proposition that harsh penalties imply a *mens rea* requirement is simply contradicted by too many laws.[17]

Some authorities point to other nontextual factors that might suggest eliminating a *mens rea* requirement (and, in their absence, the need for one), such as the seriousness of harm to the public, the defendant's ease of ascertaining the facts, the prosecution's difficulty of proving intent, and even the anticipated frequency of prosecution.[18] The sheer number of these factors (all of them "have a bearing . . . , but no single factor can be said to be controlling"[19]) suggests that they cannot be adopted as criteria for unenacted *mens rea*. When we are talking about reading into a text what it does not contain, we must have a clear and firm rule that the legislature can count on. Other than the common-law-analogue rule described

---

vehicular assault. This is a strict liability crime."); Ga. Code Ann. § 40-6-394 (1999) (injury-by-vehicle statute) ("Whoever, without malice, shall cause bodily harm to another . . . shall be guilty of the crime of serious injury by vehicle."); Tex. Penal Code Ann. § 49.07(a)(1) (2007) (intoxication-assault statute) ("A person commits an offense if the person, by accident or mistake . . . while operating a motor vehicle in a public place while intoxicated . . . causes serious bodily injury to another.").

16 1 Wayne LaFave, *Substantive Criminal Law* § 5.5(a), at 274–75 (2003).

17 *Id.* at 277. *See, e.g.*, 42 U.S.C. § 6928 (imprisonment for up to two years, and fine of $50,000 for each day of violation for anyone who without a permit "knowingly treats, stores, or disposes of any hazardous waste identified or listed under this subchapter"—*knowingly* seemingly applicable only to fact of treatment, storage, or disposal, not to unlawfulness); 33 U.S.C. § 1319(c)(1)(A) (imposing fines up to $25,000 per day and imprisonment up to one year for negligent violations of the Clean Water Act); 15 U.S.C. § 78ff(b) (penalty of $100 per day for failure to file under Securities Exchange Act).

18 *See* 1 LaFave, *Substantive Criminal Law* § 5.5(a), at 274–78.

19 *Id.* at 276.

above, the only rule that reflects consistent judicial practice (and that legislators thus have reason to assume) is that all crimes carrying significant penalties will be presumed to require what might be called the starting-point for *mens rea* (though it does not alone demonstrate fault or evil intent): the defendant's awareness that he was performing the act in question. When that awareness does not exist through no fault of the defendant's (as with sleepwalking but not drunkenness),[20] or when the act the defendant thought he was performing (if any) is lawful,[21] criminal liability will not attach. The sleepwalker will not be guilty of the jailable offense of dumping garbage into a river, nor the hallucinating madman who thinks he is filling the pit of hell. When legislators know that, apart from a statutory enactment of common-law crimes, the failure to specify an intent requirement means liability without fault, they will be more likely to specify (as they should) that element of the offense.

In cases where *mens rea* is not read into the statute, the harshness of the outcome is mitigated by the application of other exceptions to criminal liability regularly applied by common-law courts—exceptions prompted by the same consideration of fairness as the *mens rea* requirement but separate from it and more specific. For example, the rule excusing violations produced by government entrapment is one of the "generally applicable, background principles of assumed legislative intent"[22] against which all

---

20   *See, e.g., State v. Boyd*, 692 P.2d 769, 771 (Utah 1984) (reversing conviction for evading police because evidence showed defendant may have been suffering a fugue reaction); *State v. Overton*, 815 A.2d 517, 521 (N.J. Super. App. Div. 2003) (holding that defendant's sleepwalking while naked did not show he knowingly endangered the morals of a child). *Cf. State v. Welsh*, 508 P.2d 1041, 1044 (Wash. Ct. App. 1973) (conviction reversed and remanded to allow evidence that defendant suffered psychomotor seizure, possibly negating his intent to commit assault).

21   *See, e.g.,* 4 William Blackstone, *Commentaries on the Laws of England* 27 (4th ed. 1770) ("As if a man, intending to kill a thief or housebreaker in his own house, by mistake kills one of his own family. This is no criminal action."). *See also* J.W. Cecil Turner, *Kenny's Outlines of Criminal Law* 57 (19th ed. 1966) ("the man can claim that the facts were as he had mistakenly believed them to be, and not as they really were").

22   *Brogan v. United States*, 522 U.S. 398, 406 (1998) (per Scalia, J.).

laws are enacted. So is the defense of duress or coercion,[23] and the understanding that (unless otherwise indicated) criminal statutes do not apply to government agents in the lawful execution of their duties.[24] The government-agent exception would have applied in the classic case of *United States v. Kirby*,[25] in which a local sheriff who executed an arrest warrant (for murder) against a postman in the course of his rounds was prosecuted under a federal criminal statute prohibiting willful interference with the delivery of mail.[26] The driver who violates a criminal law against high-speed driving while taking a seriously injured person to the emergency room could be excused by the common-law defense of necessity, which "traditionally cover[s] the situation where physical forces beyond the actor's control rendered illegal conduct the lesser of two evils."[27]

Regrettably, saying that *mens rea* is required for crimes analogous to common-law offenses does not solve all problems relating to analyzing those crimes, since it is not always clear what qualifies as *mens rea*. At common law, for example, even negligence would suffice for manslaughter,[28] though apparently not for other crimes. A similar problem arises when a criminal statute imposes an express intent element, by employing the word *knowingly* or *willfully*. Does this mean only intentional doing of the act (e.g., taking the property), or also knowing the fact that makes the act unlawful

---

23 *See Dixon v. United States*, 548 U.S. 1, 6–7 (2006) (per Stevens, J.) ("The duress defense . . . allows the defendant to 'avoid liability . . . even though the necessary *mens rea* was present.'"); *Nall v. Commonwealth*, 271 S.W. 1059, 1059–60 (Ky. 1925) (defendant who was forced to act at gunpoint and then convicted of breaking and entering with intent to steal presented sufficient evidence for jury instruction on defense of coercion). *See also* Glanville L. Williams, *Textbook of Criminal Law* 577 (1978) ("A man may be 'compelled' by a threat to do something to which he is strongly averse. . . . Subject to certain rules, a threat that is sufficiently grave to be accounted 'duress' can operate as a defence.") (internal footnote omitted).

24 *Brogan*, 522 U.S. at 406.

25 74 U.S. (7 Wall.) 482 (1868) (per Field, J.).

26 The Supreme Court in *Kirby* reached the same result, but on the basis of the unbounded doctrine that "[t]he reason of the law in such cases should prevail over its letter." 74 U.S. (7 Wall.) at 487.

27 *United States v. Bailey*, 444 U.S. 394, 410 (1980) (per Rehnquist, J.).

28 *See* 2 Joel Prentiss Bishop, *Commentaries on the Criminal Law* § 696, at 382 (5th ed. 1872).

(e.g., that the property taken is owned by someone else). That was the context in which Justice Jackson adverted to severity of punishment—in connection with whether the *knowingly converts* portion of the *Morissette* statute required knowledge that the shell casings had not been abandoned. In such a case we are dealing not with the insertion of a requirement that the text does not contain but with the meaning of a requirement that it does. On that issue, severity of the punishment is relevant (though not necessarily determinative)—harsh punishment not ordinarily being imposed for innocent acts. Also relevant to the meaning of express scienter requirements are the other factors mentioned above and rejected as insufficient to establish an unenacted requirement of *mens rea*. For example, the extreme difficulty of proving knowledge of a certain element would suggest that the "knowingly" requirement should not be extended that far.

But even when the issue is the extent of a textual-intent requirement, a clear text prevails over factors appropriate for resolving ambiguity. We disapprove, for example, the Court's resolution in *United States v. X-Citement Video*,[29] which dealt with a provision that subjected to criminal penalty

(a) Any person who—

    (1) *knowingly* transports or ships . . . [in] interstate or foreign commerce . . . by any means including by computer or mails, any visual depiction, if—

        (A) the producing of such visual depiction involves the use of a minor engaging in sexually explicit conduct; and

        (B) such visual depiction is of such conduct.[30]

To preserve the constitutionality of this provision against First Amendment attack, the Court applied the *knowingly* requirement to sections of text clearly and unambiguously separated from subsection (a)(1)—namely, to (a)(1)(A) and (a)(1)(B).[31] Worse, they are entirely different clauses. There is no grammatical connection at all

---

29 513 U.S. 64 (1994) (per Rehnquist, C.J.).

30 18 U.S.C. § 2252(a)(1) (1988 & Supp. V 1988) (emphasis added).

31 *See* 513 U.S. at 80 (Scalia, J., dissenting).

between the adverb *knowingly* in the relative *who*-clause and the two conditional *if*-clauses. Applying the *knowingly* to those makes it a completely different law from what Congress passed. As one of us wrote in dissent in that case, "The equivalent, in expressing a simpler thought, would be the following: 'Anyone who knowingly double-parks will be subject to a $200 fine if that conduct occurs during the 4:30-to-6:30 rush hour.' It could not be clearer that the scienter requirement applies only to the double-parking, and not to the time of day."[32]

The scienter-invoking words *knowingly* and *willfully* present a recurrent problem. If people are prohibited from "knowingly violating this statute" or "willfully violating this subchapter," must they know about (1) the unlawfulness stemming from the statute or subchapter at issue? (2) the very statute or subchapter itself? or (3) merely the fact of committing the act that happens to be prohibited by the statute or subchapter? A relatively recent United States Supreme Court case dealing with the meaning of an express intent requirement is *Ratzlaf v. United States*.[33] The statute at issue there required each bank deposit of $10,000 or more to be reported to the government, and made it illegal to structure a transaction so as to circumvent the reporting requirement. It imposed criminal penalties for "willfully violating this subchapter."[34] After some highly successful gambling, Waldemar Ratzlaf purposely deposited just under $10,000 in each of several banks to avoid the reporting requirements (and presumably to avoid paying taxes). He was charged with and convicted of willfully structuring the transactions to evade reporting, and the Ninth Circuit affirmed his conviction. The Supreme Court reversed. There was no doubt that Ratzlaf intentionally structured the transactions to avoid reporting; but the Supreme Court held, applying the rule of lenity, that he was not properly convicted of "willfully violating" the subchapter because the jury was not charged with finding that he knew the evasive restructuring to be unlawful.[35]

---

32 *Id.* at 81–82.

33 510 U.S. 135 (1994) (per Ginsburg, J.).

34 31 U.S.C. §§ 5322(a), 5324.

35 510 U.S. at 148–49.

It exceeds the ambition of this treatise, and is perhaps beyond human endeavor, to identify all situations in which a requirement of *mens rea* ought to be read into a statutory text; to
state precisely what the *mens rea* requirement thus inserted ought
to consist of; and to describe what textual scienter requirements
such as *knowingly* and *willfully* import. An admirable effort to do
so, though exceedingly complicated, is to be found in the Model
Penal Code[36]—which does not, we hasten to warn, purport to be
a description of what the cases say, since they say just about everything.[37] Any criminal-law treatise will demonstrate (intentionally
or not) the unmanageable complexity of the enterprise.[38]

---

36 10A *Uniform Laws Annotated* §§ 2.01–2.05.

37 The Code was promulgated by the American Law Institute in 1962; as of 2001,
    two states had adopted its "major provisions . . . to a substantial degree." 10A
    Uniform Laws Annotated at 1. We have not investigated whether those states, or
    any others, have adopted the particular provisions under discussion here.

38 *See* J.W. Cecil Turner, *Kenny's Outlines of Criminal Law* 55 (19th ed. 1966) ("[I]t is
    not possible to formulate any general principle by which to decide to what extent
    mens rea is a constituent in statutory offences."). *See also* Rollin M. Perkins &
    Ronald N. Boyce, *Criminal Law* 826–934 (3d ed. 1982); Glanville L. Williams,
    Textbook of Criminal Law 68–106 (1978).

51. Presumption Against Implied Right of Action

A statute's mere prohibition of a certain act does not imply creation of a private right of action for its violation. The creation of such a right must be either express or clearly implied from the text of the statute.

The common law applied an equitable rule, *ubi jus, ibi remedium*: where there is a right, there is a remedy. It provided courts with a means to remedy injuries in equity and, later, violations of statutory prohibitions that injured private parties.[1] Some 19th-century American courts held that when a statute created a right but did not provide a remedy for a violation of that right, courts could use the common law to create a remedy.[2] The rule was not often invoked.

Many 20th-century courts, including federal courts (which, apart from select fields such as admiralty law, have no significant common-law powers), asserted a similar power to create private claims to accompany statutory prohibitions. In a 1964 case, for example, the Supreme Court of the United States said "it is the duty of the courts to be alert to provide such remedies as are necessary to make effective the congressional purpose."[3] The Court took a step away from that broad assertion of power in the landmark case

---

1   *See, e.g., Ashby v. White*, (1703) 87 E.R. 810, 815 (K.B.) (per Holt, C.J.) (holding that a violation of a statute granting a right to vote supported a claim for injury); *The Case of the Marshalsea*, (1612) 10 Co. Rep. 64, 70 (per Coke, C.J.) (allowing action for false imprisonment even though governing statute did not provide a remedy). *See also* "Privilege of Priests,"(1612) 12 Co. Rep. 100 (summarizing the outcome of a 16th-century case as "when any thing is prohibited by an Act, although that the Act doth not give an action, yet action lieth upon it.").

2   *See, e.g., Kneass v. Schuylkill Bank*, 14 F. Cas. 749, 750 (C.C.E.D. Pa. 1821) (No. 7,876) (noting that if Congress had not provided for damages in patent-infringement case, the common law could have provided a remedy); *Willis v. St. Paul Sanitation Co.*, 50 N.W. 1110, 1112–13 (Minn. 1892) (finding that a constitutional provision creating a right need not expressly provide for a remedy to enforce it); *Rose v. King*, 30 N.E. 267, 269 (Ohio 1892) (allowing suit against landlord for failure to comply with statute requiring a fire escape); *Stearns v. Atlantic & St. Lawrence R.R.*, 46 Me. 95, 111 (1858) (stating that when a statute creates a right, the common law provides a remedy).

3   *J.I. Case Co. v. Borak*, 377 U.S. 426, 433 (1964) (per Clark, J.).

of *Cort v. Ash*.[4] That case did not go so far as to hold, however, that the existence of private rights of action depended entirely on statutory creation. In finding a private claim for violations of § 10(b) of the Securities Exchange Act (even though the terms of the Act did not create it and did create private claims for violations of other provisions), the Court said that "indication of legislative intent, explicit or implicit, . . . to create such a remedy" is merely one factor to consider, along with whether the plaintiff is "one of the class for whose especial benefit the statute was enacted," whether it is "consistent with the underlying purposes of the legislative scheme to imply such a remedy," and whether "the cause of action [is] one traditionally relegated to state law."[5]

Another prominent case taking the same approach was *Cannon v. University of Chicago*,[6] in which a female applicant to two private medical schools sued under Title IX of the Educational Amendments of 1972,[7] alleging that her rejections had been unlawfully based on sex discrimination. The trial court dismissed the complaint, holding that the statute neither expressly nor impliedly created a private remedy to redress unlawful sex discrimination. The intermediate appellate court affirmed, declaring that the exclusive remedy was the termination of federal financial support after an agency hearing.[8] Relying on "the four factors that *Cort* [*v. Ash*] identifies,"[9] the Supreme Court reversed. It analyzed whether (1) the plaintiff belonged to the class for whose special benefit the statute was enacted, (2) whether the legislative history evidenced an intent to create a private right of action, (3) whether a private remedy would disturb any underlying legislative purpose, and (4) whether state law has been the traditional source for regulating the allegedly unlawful purpose.[10] Finding that all these factors supported creating a private claim, the Court held that a private right

4   422 U.S. 66 (1975) (per Brennan, J.).
5   *Id.* at 78.
6   441 U.S. 677 (1979) (per Stevens, J.).
7   20 U.S.C. § 1681.
8   *See* 20 U.S.C. § 1682.
9   441 U.S. at 688 (citing 422 U.S. 66 (1975)).
10   *Id.* at 689–709.

of action was created by implication—though admonishing Congress that when it intends to entrust parties with a private claim to support statutory rights, the preferred course is to make an explicit legislative grant rather than relying on judicial inference.[11]

Later in the same year, the Court's analysis essentially repudiated the approach of *Cannon* and *Cort v. Ash*. The case of *Touche Ross & Co. v. Redington*[12] involved § 17(a) of the Securities Exchange Act of 1934, which required brokerage firms that transact business through a national securities exchange to maintain records and reports that the SEC declared to be in the public interest or for the protection of investors. By regulation, the SEC obliged brokerage firms covered by § 17(a) to file annual reports certified by an independent public accountant. After Weis Securities, a member of the New York Stock Exchange, became insolvent and was liquidated, a private investor sued the accounting firm of Touche Ross, which had prepared the 1972 financial report that Weis had filed, claiming that the report was improperly audited and helped to conceal substantial operating losses. The Supreme Court held that a private claim did not exist:

> It is true that in *Cort v. Ash*, the Court set forth four factors that it considered "relevant" in determining whether a private remedy is implicit in a statute not expressly providing one. But the Court did not decide that each of these factors is entitled to equal weight. The central inquiry remains whether Congress intended to create, either expressly or by implication, a private cause of action. Indeed, the first three factors discussed in *Cort*—the language and focus of the statute, its legislative history, and its purpose—are ones traditionally relied upon in determining legislative intent.[13]

The architects of § 17(a), it found, sought to forestall bankruptcies, not to compensate victims through private damage claims: "[I]t is not for us to fill any *hiatus* Congress has left in this area."[14]

---

11 *Id.* at 717.

12 442 U.S. 560 (1979) (per Rehnquist, J.).

13 *Id.* at 575–76.

14 *Id.* at 579 (quoting *Wheeldin v. Wheeler*, 373 U.S. 647, 652 (1963) (per Douglas, J.)).

Later cases have adhered to this approach, rejecting the proposition that "our inquiry . . . cannot stop with the intent of Congress."[15] It is revealing to compare the Court's pre-*Touche Ross* opinion in *Cannon*, which held that there was a private right of action for intentional discrimination under Title IX of the Educational Amendments of 1972[16] with its opinion in *Alexander v. Sandoval*,[17] which held that no private right of action exists to enforce the disparate-impact regulations promulgated under Title VI. Without some discernible basis in the statute, the Court said, a right of action "does not exist and courts may not create a new one, no matter how desirable that might be as a policy matter, or how compatible with the statute."[18]

This is the proper approach where common-law power to create legal claims is not being exercised. Courts should not look at large for "congressional intent" (see § 67); they should look for the fair import of the statute. Does this mean that a private remedy can never be implied by the text of the statute? Not never. Imagine, for example, a statute that does not explicitly create one but that says: "In any private suit for violation of this statute, the victorious plaintiff will be entitled to attorney's fees." But that textual acknowledgment of the existence of a private action is a far cry from the mere facts that the statutory prohibition protects a particular class and that a private claim is "consistent with the underlying purposes of the legislative scheme." Such flimsy indications are inadequate to establish what is inherently implausible: that the statute has left creation of a private claim to implication. Subjection to private suit would be a major addition to the statute; its punitive effect would often exceed the governmental fine or sanction. Moreover, it would take responsibility for suit out of the hands of public officials, who will presumably exercise their discretion in the public interest, and place it in the hands of those who would use it for private gain. And the existence of the thousands

---

15   *Transamerica Mortg. Advisors, Inc. v. Lewis*, 444 U.S. 11, 23 (1979) (per Stewart, J.).

16   441 U.S. at 689–709.

17   532 U.S. 275 (2001) (per Scalia, J.).

18   *Id*. at 286–87.

of statutory prohibitions that *do* explicitly provide for private rights of action should lead us to be skeptical of implied rights.

So a private right of action cannot be found to be "implied" unless the implication both is clear and is based on the text of the statute—not exclusively on its purpose.

Stabilizing Canons

52. Presumption Against Change in Common Law

A statute will be construed to alter the common law only when that disposition is clear.

It has often been said that statutes in derogation of the common law are to be strictly construed.[1] That is a relic of the courts' historical hostility to the emergence of statutory law.[2] The better view is that statutes will not be interpreted as changing the common law unless they effect the change with clarity. There is no more reason to reject a fair reading that changes the common law than there is to reject a fair reading that repeals a prior statute (see § 55). For both, the alteration of prior law must be clear—but it need not be express, nor should its clear implication be distorted.

A fair construction ordinarily disfavors implied change. Consider, for example, the common-law rule that a pet is personal property for the negligent or willful injury of which the owner may recover damages.[3] In *Scharfeld v. Richardson*,[4] a 1929 District of Columbia statute provided that "[a]ny dog wearing [a] tax

---

1   *See, e.g., Robert C. Herd & Co. v. Krawill Mach. Corp.*, 359 U.S. 297, 304 (1959) (per Whittaker, J.); *Brown v. Barry*, 3 U.S. (3 Dall.) 365, 367 (1797) (per Ellsworth, C.J.); *Nowak v. City of Country Club Hills*, 958 N.E.2d 1021, 1026 (Ill. 2011); *Evans v. Evans*, 695 S.E.2d 173, 176 (Va. 2010); *Robbins v. People*, 107 P.3d 384, 388 (Colo. 2005).

2   *See* Harlan Fiske Stone, *The Common Law in the United States*, 50 Harv. L. Rev. 4, 18 (1936) (calling this relic an "ancient shibboleth"). *Compare* Roscoe Pound, *Common Law and Legislation*, 21 Harv. L. Rev. 383, 402 (1908) (stating that the "derogation canon" was not of English origin but in fact was "an American product of the nineteenth century") *with* Carleton Kemp Allen, *Law in the Making* 456–57 n.6 (7th ed. 1964) (conclusively showing that the derogation canon "was at least as old as the time of Edward III [1327–1377] and that the canon is "older than Professor Pound allows"), *and with* Samuel E. Thorne, *The Equity of a Statute and* Heydon's Case, 31 Ill. L. Rev. 202, 212 (1936) (Allen & Thorne citing English cases stating the derogation canon from as early as the 16th century).

3   *See Sentell v. New Orleans & C. R. Co.*, 166 U.S. 698, 700 (1897) (per Brown, J.) ("By the common law, as well as by the law of most, if not all, the states, dogs are so far recognized as property that an action will lie for their conversion or injury.").

4   133 F.2d 340 (D.C. Cir. 1942).

tag . . . shall be regarded as personal property in all the courts of said District, and any person injuring or destroying the same shall be liable to a civil action for damages."[5] Mr. Scharfeld's dog, Popo, attacked and killed Mrs. Erck's dog, Little Bits. At the time of the canine ruckus, Little Bits was not wearing a tax tag. The question was whether the statute eliminated the protection of untagged dogs, as Popo's owner claimed, thereby depriving Little Bits's owner of the $200 jury award. In an opinion by then-Judge Fred Vinson of the District of Columbia Circuit, the court decided that any legislative change of the common law requires "exactness of expression" and that a statute should not "be extended beyond the necessary and unavoidable meaning of its terms."[6] This holding is admittedly in tension with the negative-implication canon (§ 10) and even the presumption against ineffectiveness (§ 4). The outcome would have been different, naturally, if the statutory phrasing had been "only a dog wearing a tax tag," as opposed to "any dog wearing a tax tag."

The direct alteration of the common law by statute is to be distinguished from judicial alteration of a common-law rule when, because of statutory change, the reason for the rule no longer holds (*cessante ratione legis cessat lex ipsa*—see § 34, at 220). So, for example, when the so-called married-women's acts made married women capable of holding property and contracting, some courts understandably held that these statutes affected common-law doctrines about a husband's liability for his wife's torts, estates by the entireties, and similar matters.[7]

---

5   D.C. Code 1929, Tit. 20, § 918 (as quoted in *id.*).

6   133 F.2d at 341.

7   *See Rains v. Rains*, 46 P.2d 740, 742 (Colo. 1935) ("[W]here [the common-law fiction that husband and wife were one] is abolished, nonliability [of husband to wife] does not survive."); *Lee v. Blewett*, 77 So. 147, 148 (Miss. 1918) ("Since our statutes removing the disabilities of coverture . . . have conferred full testamentary capacity upon married women, the reason for the rule [that an unmarried woman's will is revoked when she gets married] has ceased, and consequently so has the rule itself."); *Johnson v. Johnson*, 77 So. 335, 337 (Ala. 1917) (state statutes abrogating the common-law fiction of legal unity of husband and wife enable a wife to sue her husband for assault and battery).

53. Canon of Imputed Common-Law Meaning

A statute that uses a common-law term, without defining it, adopts its common-law meaning.

The age-old principle is that words undefined in a statute are to be interpreted and applied according to their common-law meanings. This principle has been applied to such terms as *assault*,[1] *child*,[2] *defraud*,[3] *estate*,[4] *forge*,[5] *fraud*,[6] *next-of-kin*,[7] and *record of conviction*.[8] Even though federal law has no common-law criminal

---

1   *United States v. Guilbert*, 692 F.2d 1340, 1343 (11th Cir. 1982) ("the term 'assault' is not defined by the statute, but where 'a federal criminal statute uses a common law term without defining it, the term is given its common law meaning.'") (citing *United States v. Bell*, 505 F.2d 539, 540 (7th Cir. 1974), *cert. denied*, 420 U.S. 964 (1975)).

2   *Jung v. St. Paul Fire Dep't Relief Ass'n*, 27 N.W.2d 151, 154 (Minn. 1947) ("[the statute's] use of the term 'child' or 'children,' obviously does not by and of itself involve or effect any change in the common law so as to include illegitimates.").

3   *Neder v. United States*, 527 U.S. 1, 23 (1999) (per Rehnquist, C.J.) (applying the principle to *defraud*: "under the rule that Congress intends to incorporate the well-settled meaning of the common-law terms it uses, we cannot infer from the absence of an express reference to materiality that Congress intended to drop that element from the fraud statutes.").

4   *Citizens Action League v. Kizer*, 887 F.2d 1003, 1006 (9th Cir. 1989) ("Because Congress did not define 'estate' in the Act, we look to its common law meaning in construing this statutory section.").

5   *Gilbert v. United States*, 370 U.S. 650, 655 (1962) (per Harlan, J.) ("[I]t is therefore important to inquire . . . into the common-law meaning of forgery at the time the 1823 statute was enacted. For in the absence of anything to the contrary it is fair to assume that Congress used that word in the statute in its common-law sense.").

6   *Soza v. Hill* (*In re Soza*), 542 F.3d 1060, 1071 (5th Cir. 2008) (Weiner, J., concurring) ("I can only justify providing content to the Insurance Code's fraud provision by giving 'fraud' its *common law* meaning, not by torturing other incompatible statutes.").

7   *McCool v. Smith*, 66 U.S. (1 Black) 459, 469 (1861) (per Swayne, J.) (applying the principle to *next-of-kin*: "It is a sound rule, that whenever our Legislature use[s] a term without defining it, which is well known in the English law, and there has been a definite appropriate meaning affixed to it, they must be supposed to use it in the sense in which it is understood in the English law.").

8   *Commonwealth v. Minnich*, 95 A. 565, 567 (Pa. 1915) (applying the principle to *record of conviction*: "A word which has a settled common-law meaning, when used in an act upon the subject matter as to which it has acquired such meaning, is to be so understood.").

offenses—all federal offenses having been created by statute—the federal courts still look to common-law meaning.[9]

If the context makes clear that a statute uses a common-law term with a different meaning, the common-law meaning is of course inapplicable. For example, in the common law of New York, *chattels real* and *chattel interests* were interchangeable terms, as were *fee simple* and *fee simple absolute*, but in 1827 the legislative revisers in that state created subtle distinctions between both pairs.[10] The New York revisers also gave *real estate* a broader sense than it had had at common law—by embracing within it terms for years.[11] Interpreters must be vigilant about such legislative alterations.

---

9   *See Neder*, 527 U.S. at 23; *Gilbert*, 370 U.S. at 655; *Guilbert*, 692 F.2d at 1343.

10   *See* Robert Ludlow Fowler, *History of the Law of Real Property in New York* 103 (1895).

11   *Id.* at 98.

54. Prior-Construction Canon

If a statute uses words or phrases that have already received authoritative construction by the jurisdiction's court of last resort, or even uniform construction by inferior courts or a responsible administrative agency, they are to be understood according to that construction.

> "In adopting the language used in the earlier act, Congress 'must be considered to have adopted also the construction given by this Court to such language, and made it a part of the enactment.'"
>
> *Shapiro v. United States*,
> 335 U.S. 1, 16 (1948) (per Vinson, C.J.).[1]

The clearest application of the prior-construction canon occurs with reenactments: If a word or phrase has been authoritatively interpreted by the highest court in a jurisdiction, or has been given a uniform interpretation by inferior courts or the responsible agency, a later version of that act perpetuating the wording is presumed to carry forward that interpretation. But the canon goes beyond this and applies as well (though with less force) to interpretations of the same wording in related statutes.[2]

In England, the prior-construction canon (actually a broader version of it) is called "the rule in *Ex parte Campbell*,"[3] after an 1870 case in which Lord Justice James declared:

> Where once certain words in an Act of Parliament have received a judicial construction in one of the Superior Courts, and the Legislature has repeated them without any alteration in a subsequent statute, I conceive that the Legislature must be taken to have used them according to the meaning which a Court of competent jurisdiction has given to them.[4]

---

1   Quoting *Hecht v. Malley*, 265 U.S. 144, 153 (1924) (per Sanford, J.).

2   *See, e.g.*, *Bragdon v. Abbott*, 524 U.S. 624, 645 (1998) (per Kennedy, J.) ("When administrative and judicial interpretations have settled the meaning of an existing statutory provision, repetition of the same language in a new statute indicates, as a general matter, the intent to incorporate its administrative and judicial interpretations as well.").

3   [1870] L.R. 5 Ch. App. 703.

4   *Id.* at 706.

More than 60 years later, Lord Buckmaster called this principle "a salutary rule and one necessary to confer upon Acts of Parliament that certainty which, though it is often lacking, is always to be desired."[5] But in England, as here, the canon has its detractors. Lord Denning complained that according to this canon, whenever a legislature reenacts a statute, it "thereby gives statutory authority to every erroneous interpretation which has been put upon it."[6]

As we have been at pains to point out throughout this treatise, context is as important as sentence-level text. The entire document must be considered. If that is so, there is no such thing as a prior judicial opinion interpreting precisely the same word or phrase, unless it is interpreting the very same document. Hence to the textualist, this canon is a peculiar one.

On the other hand, when a statute uses the very same terminology as an earlier statute—especially in the very same field, such as securities law or civil-rights law—it is reasonable to believe that the terminology bears a consistent meaning. One might even say that the body of law of which a statute forms a part—especially if that body has been codified—is part of the statute's context. So even without the benefit of prior judicial interpretation, it is fair to argue that giving an ambiguous term one meaning rather than another would cause it to make no sense as used in an earlier-enacted statute—or, for that matter, in one enacted later—so that such an interpretation should be rejected. This is the macro-contextual reasoning that underlies the related-statutes canon (§ 39).

It might be possible to say that the prior-construction canon was based on this macro-contextual reasoning if it applied only to interpretive holdings of a court of last resort, which would give definitive meaning to the words or phrases used elsewhere. But in fact the canon does not apply only to holdings of the court of last

5   *Barrass v. Aberdeen Steam Trawling & Fishing Co.*, [1933] A.C. 402, 412.

6   *Royal Crown Derby Porcelain Co. Ltd v. Russell*, [1949] 2 K.B. 417, 429 (per Denning, L.J.). *See* Carlton Kemp Allen, *Law in the Making* 508 (7th ed. 1964) (stating that "if a word has once been given a particular meaning in any case of authority, however obscure, in connection with any statute, however recondite, the draftsman who uses that word in a later enactment is, so to speak, 'affected with notice' of the judicial interpretation, however remote it may be from the matter in hand").

resort. It applies as well to uniform holdings of lower courts[7] and even to well-established agency interpretations.[8] It applies whenever the judicial or administrative interpretation antedates the enactment, whereas macro-contextual reasoning would give the same effect to a later authoritative judicial interpretation as well.

Perhaps the best explanation for the prior-construction canon is this: The word or phrase at issue is a statutory term used in a particular field of law (to which the statute at issue belongs). When that term has been authoritatively interpreted by a high court, or has been given uniform interpretation by the lower courts or the responsible agency, the members of the bar practicing in that field reasonably enough assume that, in statutes pertaining to that field, the term bears this same meaning. The term has acquired, in other words, a technical legal sense (see § 6 [ordinary-meaning canon]) that should be given effect in the construction of later-enacted statutes. This footing is sounder than the fanciful presumption of legislative knowledge.

Defending the reasonable expectations of the bar in this regard comes at a price: A high court's prior construction, having now been enshrined in the statute, can no longer be overruled—even by the same high court. Worse still, the uniform lower-court or agency interpretation enshrined in a later-enacted statute will never have been, and thereafter never will be, subject to high-court review. These consequences can be avoided when the application of other sound rules of interpretation overcomes this canon. But when it does not, the stability achieved by the canon is probably worth the cost. High courts very rarely overrule their prior holdings pertaining to statutory construction anyway. And where

---

7   See, e.g., Manhattan Props., Inc. v. Irving Trust Co., 291 U.S. 320, 336 (1934) (per Roberts, J.) (interpreting the Bankruptcy Act to accord with "the rulings of the great majority of the lower federal courts" that were outstanding when the Act was several times amended).

8   See, e.g., FDIC v. Philadelphia Gear Corp., 476 U.S. 426, 437 (1986) (per O'Connor, J.) (interpreting the word *deposit* to accord with "the longstanding [agency] interpretation" of the word in a predecessor statute); *NLRB v. Bell Aerospace*, 416 U.S. 267, 275 (1974) (per Powell, J.) (adopting the Labor Board's interpretation that *employee* in the Taft-Hartley Act did not include managerial employees—an interpretation that had been consistent before the Act's amendment repeating the language.)

lower-court holdings are uniform and sufficiently numerous, or where a prominent agency interpretation has been in effect for a substantial period without judicial challenge, the possibility that the high court would disagree is remote.

There remains one significant issue relating to when the prior-construction canon applies. The bar is unquestionably justified in relying on a decision (even a single decision) of the jurisdiction's highest court regarding the meaning of a certain word or phrase that is repeated in a later statute. But how numerous must the lower-court opinions be, or how prominent and long-standing the administrative interpretation, to justify the level of lawyerly reliance that justifies the canon? What about two intermediate-court decisions? (We doubt it—though some cases have relied on just a single intermediate-court decision.[9]) Or seven courts of first instance? (Perhaps.) Will it suffice to cite the uniform views of state high courts in 15 jurisdictions other than the jurisdiction whose law governs? (That might be persuasive—but it has nothing to do with the present canon.) We cannot give conclusive numbers. The criterion ought to be whether the uniform weight of authority is significant enough that the bar can justifiably regard the point as settled law.

Roscoe Pound asserted, dubiously in our view, that there is a further extension of this rule:

> Where a state legislature enacts a statute in which it copies the language of a statute already obtaining in another state and already given a settled judicial interpretation in that state, it is presumed that the legislature acted with knowledge of that interpretation and intended the act to be so construed. The same presumption obtains where a provision, clause, or phrase is taken from the legislation of another state.[10]

---

9   *See, e.g., Commonwealth v. Flanagan*, 923 N.E.2d 101, 106 (Mass. App. Ct. 2010) (relying on a single intermediate appellate-court opinion construing prior vehicular-negligence law); *Grimes County Bail Bond Bd. v. Ellen*, 267 S.W.3d 310, 315 (Tex. App.—Houston [14th Dist.] 2008) (relying on a single intermediate appellate-court opinion construing prior Bail Bond Act).

10 3 Roscoe Pound, *Jurisprudence* 494 (1959).

Pound here extends the canon beyond reasonable justification. How is the competent lawyer (or the court, for that matter) to know that a statute has been "copied" from that of another state? Not by looking to legislative history (see § 66).

Finally, we emphasize that this canon applies only to presumed legislative approval of prior judicial or administrative interpretations in statutes adopted after those interpretations. The mere failure of a legislature to correct extant lower-court, intermediate-court, or agency interpretations is not, in our view, a sound basis for believing that the legislature has "adopted" them.[11] The bar may well have relied on those interpretations, but until they have been approved by the jurisdiction's highest court or implicitly adopted in a subsequent statute, they are not the law.[12]

---

11   *See, e.g., Sun Home Health Visiting Nurses v. Workers' Comp. Appeal Bd.*, 815 A.2d 1156, 1161 (Pa. Commw. Ct. 2003) (saying that the legislature's failure to amend the Workers' Compensation Act gave rise to the presumption that it agreed with the court's earlier interpretation of one of the Act's provisions).

12   The issues discussed in this section are considered in great detail in Caleb Nelson, *Statutory Interpretation* 418–594 (2011).

55. Presumption Against Implied Repeal

Repeals by implication are disfavored—"very much disfavored."[1] But a provision that flatly contradicts an earlier-enacted provision repeals it.

> "The rarity with which [the Court has] discovered implied repeals is due to the relatively stringent standard for such findings, namely, that there be an irreconcilable conflict between the two federal statutes at issue."
> *J.E.M. Ag Supply, Inc. v. Pioneer Hi-Bred Int'l, Inc.,*
> 534 U.S. 124, 142 (2001) (per Thomas, J.).

The essence of the presumption against implied repeals is that if statutes are to be repealed, they should be repealed with some specificity. The canon is hardly absolute: It speaks not to the possibility of an implied repeal but to the evidence necessary to support one. When a statute specifically permits what an earlier statute prohibited, or prohibits what it permitted, the earlier statute is (no doubt about it) implicitly repealed. This principle is well established enough to have been recited in *The Federalist* by Alexander Hamilton, who contrasted contradiction of an earlier statute with contradiction of the Constitution:

> The rule which has obtained in the courts for determining [conflicting statutes'] relative validity is that the last in order of time shall be preferred to the first. But this is a mere rule of construction, not derived from any positive law, but from the nature and reason of the thing. It is a rule not enjoined upon the courts by legislative provision but adopted by themselves, as consonant to truth and propriety, for the direction of their conduct as interpreters of the law. They thought it reasonable that between the interfering acts of an *equal* authority, that which was the last indication of its will should have the preference.[2]

The presumption disfavoring implied repeals is similarly a judicially created rule of construction. Its purpose has been explained by the Idaho Supreme Court:

---

1 James Kent, *Commentaries on American Law* *467 n.(y1) (Charles M. Barnes ed., 13th ed. 1884). *See United States v. Noce*, 268 U.S. 613, 619 (1925) (per Taft, C.J.) ("Implied repeals are not favored.").

2 *The Federalist*, No. 78, at 468 (Clinton Rossiter ed., 1961).

> Since laws are presumed to be passed with deliberation, and with full knowledge of existing ones on the same subject, it is but reasonable to conclude that the legislature, in passing a statute, did not intend to interfere with or abrogate any former law relating to the same matter, unless the repugnancy between the two is irreconcilable.[3]

We doubt that. The legislative omniscience assumed by this explanation is fanciful. What is not fanciful is the need for a code of laws whose application—or at least whose very existence—is clear. A doctrine of readily implied repealer would repeatedly place earlier enactments in doubt.

The Supreme Court of the United States long ago announced that an implied repeal may occur in either of two circumstances: "(1) Where provisions in the two acts are in irreconcilable conflict, the later act to the extent of the conflict constitutes an implied repeal of the earlier one; and (2) if the later act covers the whole subject of the earlier one and is clearly intended as a substitute, it will operate similarly as a repeal of the earlier act."[4] Though rare, implied repeals of each type are hardly unknown.

A Nevada case, *Washington v. State*,[5] provides an illustration of the Type 1 implied repeal. A 1977 Nevada statute made it a felony to sell or offer to sell certain controlled substances or imitations of those substances.[6] A 1983 statute made the same acts a misdemeanor.[7] As the court wrote on appeal, "the only true difference between [the two legislative provisions] is the penalty"[8]—and the penalties were utterly inconsistent. Hence the court held that "the

---

3   *Meade v. Freeman*, 462 P.2d 54, 62 (Idaho 1969). *Cf. M. DeMatteo Constr. Co. v. City of New London*, 674 A.2d 845, 849 (Conn. 1996) ("[T]he General Assembly is always presumed to know all the existing statutes and the effect that its action or non-action will have upon any one of them.") (quoting *In re Ralph M.*, 559 A.2d 179 (Conn. 1989)).

4   *Posadas v. National City Bank of N.Y.*, 296 U.S. 497, 503 (1936) (per Sutherland, J.).

5   30 P.3d 1134 (Nev. 2001).

6   Nev. Rev. Stat. § 453.323.

7   *Id.* § 453.332.

8   30 P.3d at 1138.

earlier statute . . . [was] repealed by implication since its entire substance is covered by [the later statute]."[9]

Another example of a Type 1 implied repeal occurred in *Moyle v. Director, Office of Workers' Compensation Programs*,[10] decided by the Ninth Circuit. The issue was whether disability benefits could be garnished to pay delinquent spousal support. The Longshore and Harbor Workers' Compensation Act, enacted in 1927, *prohibited* the garnishment in express terms: "compensation and benefits [payable under the Act] shall be exempt from all claims of creditors and from levy, execution, and attachment or other remedy for recovery or collection of a debt, which exemption may not be waived."[11] But the Social Security Act garnishment provision, enacted 48 years later in 1975, *permitted* the garnishment in express terms: "moneys . . . due from or payable by, the United States [or its agencies or instrumentalities] to any individual . . . shall be subject [to any legal action brought] . . . to enforce the legal obligation of the individual to provide child support or alimony."[12] The Ninth Circuit held that because these two statutes were irreconcilable, the later-enacted provision allowing garnishment impliedly repealed the earlier provision that prohibited the garnishment. The court made no mention of the general/specific canon (§ 28), and rightly so, since neither statute had general application.

In constitutional law, we see a Type 1 implied repeal in the Seventeenth Amendment, which provides: "The Senate of the United States shall be composed of two Senators from each State, elected by the people thereof . . . ." No express mention is made of Article I, § 3: "The Senate of the United States shall be composed of two Senators from each State, chosen by the Legislature thereof . . . ." But the repeal by contradictory provision is inescapable.

As for Type 2, a good example occurred in the aftermath of the Civil War.[13] In 1867, Congress passed an amendment to the

---

9 *Id.*

10 147 F.3d 1116 (9th Cir. 1998).

11 33 U.S.C. § 916.

12 42 U.S.C. § 659(a).

13 *Murdock v. City of Memphis*, 87 U.S. (20 Wall.) 590 (1875) (per Miller, J.).

Judiciary Act of 1789. One section replicated the jurisdictional provisions of the original act, but it differed in subtle changes and omissions. In particular, federal courts were now authorized, when hearing disputes removed from state courts, to decide state-law matters as well as federal questions. At issue was the effect of "the omission . . . of two important provisions"[14] in the new act, coupled with the fact that "there is no repeal by positive new enactments inconsistent in terms with the old law."[15] Did the omitted provisions remain good law? No. As the Court explained about the Act taken as a whole:

> A careful comparison of these two sections . . . can leave no doubt that it was the intention of Congress, by the latter statute, to revise the entire matter to which they both had reference . . . and to substitute their will in that regard entirely for the old law upon the subject.
>
> . . .
>
> The result of this reasoning is that . . . the act of 1789 is technically repealed, and . . . the act of 1867 has taken its place. What of the statute of 1789 is embraced in that of 1867 is of course the law now and has been ever since it was first made so. What is changed or modified is the law as thus changed or modified. That which is omitted ceased to have any effect from the day that the substituted statute was approved.[16]

While the implication of a later enactment will rarely be strong enough to repeal a prior provision, it will often change the meaning that would otherwise be given to an earlier provision that is ambiguous. That is so because a law is to be construed as a whole (including later-added and later-revised provisions),[17] and because laws *in pari materia* (including later-enacted laws) are to be interpreted together.[18] And just as later-enacted laws can change the meaning of earlier ones, earlier laws can change the interpretation

---

14 *Id.* at 616.

15 *Id.* at 616–17.

16 *Id.* at 617.

17 *See* § 24 (whole-text canon).

18 *See* § 39 (related-statutes canon).

that would otherwise be given to later-enacted laws. As the Supreme Court of the United States has explained:

> Where a statutory term presented to us for the first time is ambiguous, we construe it to contain that permissible meaning which fits most logically and comfortably into the body of both previously and subsequently enacted law. We do so not because that precise accommodative meaning is what the lawmakers must have had in mind (how could an earlier Congress know what a later Congress would enact?), but because it is our role to make sense rather than nonsense out of the *corpus juris*.[19]

What if the earlier ambiguous provision has already been construed by the jurisdiction's high court to have a meaning that does not fit as well with a later statute as another meaning? Stare decisis is not an insuperable obstacle to giving effect to the implication of the later statute; it is, after all, a new total law (or a new *corpus juris*) to which the tools of construction are being applied. At this point, however, the need for stability intervenes. A clear, authoritative judicial holding on the meaning of a particular provision should not be cast in doubt and subjected to challenge whenever a related though not utterly inconsistent provision is adopted in the same statute or even in an affiliated statute. Legislative revision of law clearly established by judicial opinion ought to be by express language or by unavoidably implied contradiction. We know of no case to the contrary, and we think that is as it should be.

Doubts about the law will arise whenever a statute that directly contradicts an earlier enactment is not held to repeal it. The rule of law is harmed by decisions such as the United States Supreme Court's opinion in *Watt v. Alaska*.[20] There the addition of the word *minerals* to § 401(a) of the Wildlife Refuge Revenue Sharing Act[21] caused that Act to provide that 25% of the revenues from mineral leases on wildlife refuges would be paid to the counties wherein

---

19 *West Virginia Univ. Hosps. v. Casey*, 499 U.S. 83, 100–01 (1991) (per Scalia, J.) (internal citation omitted).

20 451 U.S. 259 (1981) (per Powell, J.).

21 49 Stat. 383, as amended, 16 U.S.C. § 751s(c). The amendment was enacted by Pub. L. 88-523, 78 Stat. 701.

the refuge lies, and the remainder would be used by the Department of the Interior for public purposes. This contradicted § 35 of the Mineral Leasing Act of 1920,[22] which provided that (for Alaska) 90% of the revenues would go to the State and the remainder to the United States Treasury. The contradiction between the two texts could not have been clearer. The Court held, however, that the new provision (though not, apparently, the rest of § 401(a)) applied only to newly acquired refuge lands—a limitation nowhere contained in the text. "Sole reliance on the 'plain language' of § 401(a)," the Court said, "would assume the answer to the question at issue."[23] For its abridgment of the text, the Court relied on the fact that the legislative history contained "no explanation" for the insertion of the word *minerals* in § 401(a),[24] and the Justices' perception that "it is almost inconceivable that Congress knowingly would have changed substantially a longstanding formula for distribution of substantial funds without a word of comment."[25] The circumstances of the statute's enactment, the Court said, "may persuade a court that Congress did not intend words of common meaning to have their literal effect."[26] It is no surprise that the Court cited for that proposition the infamous *Holy Trinity Church v. United States*,[27] a case reflecting the same philosophy that it is the function of the courts to improve faulty legislation. An interesting cross-section of the Court—Justice Stewart, joined by Chief Justice Burger and Justice Marshall—dissented.

What, precisely, is an express repeal? The phrase *is hereby repealed* is not necessary. Any language expressly stating that the prior provision is no longer operative will suffice—for example, a statement that a certain provision is "amended to read as follows,"[28]

---

22 30 U.S.C. § 191.

23 451 U.S. at 266.

24 *Id.* at 270.

25 *Id.* at 271 n.13.

26 *Id.* at 266.

27 143 U.S. 457 (1892) (per Brewer, J.). *See supra*, pp. 11–13.

28 *Goodno v. City of Oshkosh*, 31 Wis. 127, 129 (1872) (citing *State v. Ingersoll*, 17 Wis. 631 (1864), and explaining that "amended so as to read as follows" in a venue statute repealed all of the former statute's provisions that were not repeated in the amended statute); *State v. Andrews*, 20 Tex. 230, 231 (1857) (holding that

or a statement that a certain disposition is "adopted in lieu of" a prior statutory disposition.[29]

---

the phrasing *shall hereafter read as follows* in an amending act effected a complete repeal of unrepeated provisions of former act).

29 *Gossler v. Goodrich*, 10 F. Cas. 836 (C.C.D. Mass. 1867) (No. 5,631).

56. Repeal-of-Repealer Canon

The repeal or expiration of a repealing statute does not reinstate the original statute.

When a statute is repealed, it falls irretrievably into oblivion. It is not half-buried in expectation of resurrection. Hence a repeal of a repealer does not revivify the statutory corpse. The common law, which is timeless, revives. Interestingly, this view has not always held sway. In the 19th century, James Kent (following Blackstone) wrote that "[i]f a statute be repealed, and afterwards the repealing act be repealed, this revives the original act . . . ."[1] But modern authorities favor the opposite conclusion. The relevant federal statute provides: "Whenever an Act is repealed, which repealed a former Act, such former Act shall not thereby be revived, unless it shall be expressly so provided."[2]

Jeremy Bentham mocked the old revitalizing view, confessing himself "guilty of a legal heresy" with these words: "With regard to men, if *Secundus* kills *Primus*, it certainly is not *Tertius*, killing *Secundus*, that will bring *Primus* back to life again. I see not why it should be otherwise with respect to statutes."[3] Bentham sensibly believed that "the indirect method of revival can have no advantage over the direct one: it is as easy to say, that such a Statute shall be revived, as that another shall be repealed."[4]

Perhaps because of historical doubts about the result courts might reach absent specification, legislatures at times have been admirably explicit. In California, for example, when the entire

---

1   1 James Kent, *Commentaries on American Law* *465–66 (Charles M. Barnes ed., 13th ed. 1884). *Cf.* 1 William Blackstone, *Commentaries on the Laws of England* 90 (4th ed. 1770) ("If a statute, that repeals another, is itself repealed afterwards, the first statute is hereby revived.").

2   1 U.S.C. § 108. Cf. Unif. Statute & Rule Construction Act § 15 (1995) ("The repeal of a repealing statute or rule does not revive the statute or rule originally repealed or impair the effect of a savings clause in the original repealing statute or rule.").

3   Jeremy Bentham, *A Comment on the Commentaries: A Criticism of William Blackstone's Commentaries on the Laws of England* 148–49 (1776; Charles Warren Everett ed., 1928).

4   *Id.*

Civil Code was enacted in 1872, § 20 provided that "all statutes, laws, and rules heretofore in force in this State, whether consistent or not with the provisions of this Code, . . . are repealed or abrogated."[5] But with abundant caution, the text continued: "This repeal or abrogation does not revive any former law heretofore repealed."[6]

The question of an *expiring* repealer has also been raised, and an expiration is generally held not to revive the "suspended" act.[7]

---

5   Cal. Civ. Code § 20.

6   *Id.*

7   *See The Chancellor's Case*, 1 Bland. 595, 665 n.(w) (Md. Ch. 1826) (quoting *Hanson's Laws of Maryland*, ch. 33 (1765) ("[T]he repealing clause of [an] act, notwithstanding its expiration, is still in force.")).

57. Desuetude Canon

A statute is not repealed by nonuse or desuetude.

> "It is only within the past ten or fifteen years that there have
> been suggestions in some judicial opinions to the effect
> that courts, faced with an obsolete statute and a history of
> legislative inaction, may take matters into their own hands and
> do whatever justice and good sense may seem to require."
>
> Grant Gilmore,
> *The Ages of American Law* 97 (1977).

The bright-line rule is that a statute has effect until it is repealed. If 10, 20, 100, or even 200[1] years pass without any known
cases applying the statute, no matter: The statute is on the books
and continues to be enforceable until its repeal.[2] This is the essence of the desuetude (pronounced /des-wi-tyood/) canon. Its
operation is starkly exemplified in the 1983 case of *Commonwealth
v. Stowell*,[3] in which a woman was criminally prosecuted for adul-
tery—and, on conviction, was fined $50. The Supreme Judicial
Court of Massachusetts upheld the conviction, saying:

> We are not unaware that . . . the crime of adultery is rare-
> ly made the subject of criminal prosecution. . . . It seems
> beyond dispute that the statute defining or punishing the
> crime of . . . adultery has fallen into a very comprehensive
> desuetude. . . . To recognize that fact is not to say that this
> statute has become invalid or judicially unenforceable. . . . If
> any lack of prosecution of the crime of adultery indicates a
> general public disfavor with the statute, appropriate means

---

1   *See Attorney-General v. H.R.H. Prince Ernest Augustus of Hanover,* [1957] A.C.
    436, [1957] 1 All E.R. 49 (holding that a 1705 statute was still valid in 1914,
    despite its startling implications.). *See also* R.W.M. Dias, *Jurisprudence* 228–29
    (4th ed. 1976).

2   *See* A.K.R. Kiralfy, *The English Legal System* 110 (3d ed. 1960) ("Statutes never
    become obsolete with the passage of time."); James Kent, *Commentaries on Ameri-
    can Law* *466 n.(g) (Charles M. Barnes ed., 13th ed. 1884) ("A statute cannot be
    repealed by non-user . . ."). *Cf. Northern Ind. Pub. Serv. Co. v. Carbon County Coal
    Co.,* 799 F.2d 265, 274 (7th Cir. 1986) (per Posner, J.) ("We do not believe that
    we have the power to declare a constitutional statute invalid merely because we,
    or for that matter everybody, think [sic] the statute has become obsolete.").

3   449 N.E.2d 357 (Mass. 1983).

exist to address such disfavor to the Legislature, which has the power to change or repeal the statute.[4]

One noted commentator has proposed that courts ought to be able to declare statutes invalid by reason of desuetude.[5] The practical problem with this proposal is that it introduces considerable doubt into the rather fundamental question of what laws exist. How much time must pass before repeal by nonuse takes effect? And the more significant problem, in our view, is the theoretical one. Neither the judiciary nor the executive branch has the power to invalidate lawful enactments: "In reason, and by most authorities, the power alone which can make a law is competent to annul one."[6]

Only West Virginia cases hold that desuetude invalidates.[7] We think they are wrong. One of those cases discussing the issue most extensively is *Committee on Legal Ethics of the West Virginia State Bar v. Printz*.[8] There a West Virginia attorney faced discipline for giving an accused embezzler a choice of either restoring the embezzled funds or facing criminal charges. This offer not to prosecute in exchange for restitution was a misdemeanor.[9] The West Virginia Supreme Court assumed for itself the power to "judge each statute individually to determine if it is void due to desuetude,"[10] using for that purpose a three-part test: (1) Does the statute prohibit only acts that are *malum prohibitum*, as opposed

---

4   *Id.* at 360–61 (internal quotations and bracket omitted).

5   Guido Calabresi, *A Common Law for the Age of Statutes* 101–02 (1982).

6   Joel Prentiss Bishop, *Commentaries on the Written Laws and Their Interpretation* § 149, at 135 (1882).

7   *See, e.g., State v. Donley*, 607 S.E.2d 474, 479–80 (W. Va. 2004); *State ex rel. Canterbury v. Blake*, 584 S.E.2d 512, 517 (W. Va. 2003). *See also Desuetude*, 119 Harv. L. Rev. 2209, 2209 (2006) ("Desuetude, the obscure doctrine by which a legislative enactment is judicially abrogated following a long period of nonenforcement, currently enjoys recognition in the courts of West Virginia and nowhere else."). *Cf.* William N. Eskridge Jr., *Dynamic Statutory Interpretation*, 135 U. Pa. L. Rev. 1479, 1496 (1987) (arguing that as a statute becomes more distant in time, the court should give more weight to "evolutive" factors and be less constrained by the text's words).

8   416 S.E.2d 720 (W. Va. 1992).

9   W. Va. Code § 61-5-19.

10 416 S.E.2d at 726.

to *malum in se*? (2) Have there been open, notorious, and pervasive violations of the statute for a long period? (3) Has there been a "conspicuous policy of nonenforcement"?[11] Apart from the serious indeterminateness of this test, the incompatibility of the entire enterprise with democratic government is demonstrated by the statement with which the court concludes that portion of its opinion: "[T]he Legislature may revitalize any statute simply by repassing it."[12]

The rationale for this supposed doctrine of "desuetudinous repealer" is that "a penal enactment which is linguistically clear, but has been notoriously ignored by both its administrators and the community for an unduly extended period, imparts no more notice of its proscriptions than a statute which is phrased in vague terms."[13] But that cannot be true: If it is "notoriously ignored," then it is well known. And what is an "unduly extended period"? Most people know that in most parts of the country, jaywalking laws are rarely enforced because police generally have more pressing matters in need of their attention. But the reasonable jaywalker, if there is such a person, knows that he crosses illegally at the risk of receiving a citation.

As Judge Richard A. Posner correctly observes: "[T]he concept of statutory 'obsolescence' is so vague that a liberal judge could easily believe, in good faith, that only illiberal statutes obsolesce."[14] He does not make the reverse observation that a conservative judge could easily believe, in good faith, that only liberal statutes obsolesce—perhaps because modernity tends to equate with liberality. But the fact is that a judge of any political bent could believe, in good faith, that only statutes antithetical to his beliefs obsolesce. And that is what used to be called chancellor's-foot justice—when

---

11 *Id.*

12 *Id.*

13 Arthur E. Bonfield, *The Abrogation of Penal Statutes by Nonenforcement*, 49 Iowa L. Rev. 389, 416 (1964).

14 Richard A. Posner, *Legal Formalism, Legal Realism, and the Interpretation of Statutes and the Constitution*, 37 Case Western L. Rev. 179, 197 (1986–1987).

justice in the courts of equity was waggishly said to be measured by the length of the chancellor's foot.[15]

The real point, however, is that only the legislature has the power both to enact and to disenact statutes.

---

15   *See Black's Law Dictionary* 263 (9th ed. 2009) (s.v. chancellor's foot).

Thirteen Falsities Exposed

58. The false notion that the spirit of a statute should prevail over its letter.

"There is nothing more dangerous than the common axiom: *the spirit of the laws is to be considered.* To adopt it is to give way to the torrent of opinions."

Cesare Beccaria,
An Essay on Crimes and Punishments 24 (1793).

Some of the canons we have discussed apply not only to statutes but to legal texts in general; others are peculiar to statutes. Among the statute-specific canons are rules that reflect the spirit of the common law—for example, the rule of lenity (§ 49); and rules that can be said to reinforce the structure of the Constitution—for example, the rule that a federal statute will be presumed not to preempt state law (§ 47). Some authorities believe that after all these rules have been considered and applied, the resulting determination of statutory meaning can be overridden by a judicially perceived, at-large "spirit" of the law that overcomes its letter.

This interpretive notion sprang up when statutory law was sparse and spotty in the Middle Ages. An early example occurred in 1550, when a statute providing a remedy specifically against the warden of Fleet Prison was interpreted to apply to all jailers.[1] In that era, the problem was more pervasive than this simple example might suggest: Some medieval lawyers took the stance that any unreasonable statute could be disregarded.[2] Fortunately, even in Tudor times, this view "bore little fruit in the practice of the courts."[3]

The mere statement of the spirit-over-letter concept gives reason to doubt its validity. No one has ever set forth any principles for perceiving an at-large spirit that overcomes the letter. The concept is, in practice, a bald assertion of an unspecified and hence unbounded judicial power to ignore what the law says, leading to "completely unforeseeable and unreasonable results."[4]

---

1 J.H. Baker, *An Introduction to English Legal History* 209 (4th ed. 2002).

2 *Id.*

3 *Id.*

4 Frederick J. de Sloovère, *Textual Interpretation of Statutes*, 11 N.Y.U. L.Q. Rev. 538, 542 (1934).

It is true that Chief Justice John Marshall often referred to the "spirit" of the United States Constitution.[5] But as even he owned, although "the spirit of an instrument, especially a constitution, is to be respected not less than its letter . . . the spirit is to be collected chiefly from its words."[6] In an 1821 case, Marshall rebuked counsel who pressed his "extravagantly absurd" point "with much ingenuity" by making an argument that was "founded, not on the words of the [C]onstitution, but on its spirit, a spirit extracted, not from the words of the instrument, but from his [counsel's] view of the nature of our Union."[7]

The common view in the 18th and 19th centuries closely equated the spirit with the letter. Here is how a noted British judge put it in 1852: "Perhaps the most efficacious mode of procuring good laws, certainly the only one allowable to a Court of Justice, is to act fully up to the spirit and language of bad ones, and to let their inconvenience be fully felt by giving them full effect."[8]

Today, however, the "spirit" of laws is the unhappy interpretive conception of a supposedly better policy than can be found in the words of an authoritative text. It is an unreliable nonstandard. As one important commentator remarked a century after Marshall's day: "The requirements of good faith and common sense . . . do not justify the interpreter . . . to seek the spirit or equitable meaning of the statute in disregard of its textual implications. These doctrines lead more often than the doctrine of literalness to spurious

---

5   *See, e.g.*, *Cohens v. Virginia*, 19 U.S. (6 Wheat.) 264, 383 (1821) (per Marshall, C.J.) (asking rhetorically whether "the spirit of the constitution" would justify Virginia's exempting itself from the federal constitution); *McCulloch v. Maryland*, 17 U.S. (4 Wheat.) 316, 421 (1819) (per Marshall, C.J.) ("Let the end be legitimate, let it be within the scope of the constitution, and all means which are appropriate, which are plainly adapted to that end, which are not prohibited, but consistent with the letter and *spirit* of the constitution, are constitutional" [emphasis added]).

6   *Sturges v. Crowninshield*, 17 U.S. (4 Wheat.) 122, 202 (1819) (per Marshall, C.J.).

7   *Cohens v. Virginia*, 19 U.S. (6 Wheat.) 264, 422 (1821) (per Marshall, C.J.).

8   *Pocock v. Pickering*, [1852] 18 Q.B. 789, 798 (per Coleridge, J.). *Cf.* Ulysses S. Grant, *Inaugural Address*, 4 Mar. 1869 ("I know of no method to secure the repeal of bad or obnoxious laws so effective as their stringent execution.") (as quoted in Frontispiece, 2 Green Bag 2d (Winter 1999)).

interpretation and to completely unforeseeable and unreasonable results."[9]

Baron de Montesquieu, the political philosopher celebrated for his 1748 book *The Spirit of Laws*, might be thought to have promoted a spirit-over-letter approach. But he did not. He well understood that it is the legislator who enacts the public will, *not* the judge: "The nearer a government approaches towards a republic, the more the manner of judging becomes settled and fixed."[10] He rightly contrasted the arbitrariness of despotism with the predictability of a juster system of adjudication: "In despotic governments . . . the judge himself is his own rule . . . . In republics, *the very nature of the constitution requires the judges to follow the letter of the law*; otherwise the law might be explained to the prejudice of every citizen, in cases where their honor, property, or life is concerned."[11] The idea underlying legislation is that plain words must evoke predictable meanings: "It is an essential article that the words of the laws should excite in everybody the same ideas."[12] Most important: "The very nature of the constitution requires the judges to follow the letter of the law."[13]

In *Roe v. Wade*,[14] the Supreme Court declared unconstitutional state statutes that in no way contradicted any specific provision of the Constitution. This nebulous type of unconstitutionality ignored what had long been the unimpeachable doctrine:

> [N]o court is at liberty to pronounce a statute unconstitutional unless the fact that it is repugnant to some particular designated clause or portion of the constitution is distinctly alleged and clearly shown, or unless it is made indubitably to appear that the statute is contrary to some

---

9   Frederick J. de Sloovère, *Textual Interpretation of Statutes*, 11 N.Y.U. L.Q. Rev. 538, 542 (1934).

10 Montesquieu, *The Spirit of Laws* (pt. 1) 75 (Thomas Nugent trans., 1949).

11 *Id.* (emphasis added).

12 *Id.* (pt. 2) at 165.

13 *Id.* (pt. 1) at 75.

14 410 U.S. 113 (1973) (per Blackmun, J.).

one or more of the implied restrictions upon the power of the legislature."[15]

It is telling that on this same issue—abortion—the normally purposivist Lord Denning invoked democracy and literalism as the more prudent course: "Abortion is a subject on which many people feel strongly. . . . Emotions run so high on both sides that I feel that we as judges must go by the very words of the statute—without stretching it one way or the other—and writing nothing in which is not there."[16] It should not require high-running emotions among the public to encourage judges to follow the letter of the law.

---

15 Henry Campbell Black, *In Defense of the Judiciary*, 1 Const. Rev. 23, 32 (1917). *See* Thomas M. Cooley, *A Treatise on the Constitutional Limitations Which Rest upon the Legislative Power of the States of the American Union* 72–73 (1868) ("[A] statute cannot be declared void because opposed to a supposed general intent or spirit which it is thought pervades or lies concealed in the Constitution, but wholly unexpressed, or because, in the opinion of the court, it violates fundamental rights or principles.").

16 *Royal Coll. of Nursing of the U.K. v. Department of Health & Soc. Sec.*, [1981] A.C. 800, 805.

59. The false notion that the quest in statutory interpretation is to do justice.

"Our unwillingness to soften the import of Congress' chosen words even if we believe the words lead to a harsh outcome is longstanding."
Lamie v. United States Trustee,
540 U.S. 526, 538 (2004) (per Kennedy, J.).

In 1933, Justice Benjamin Cardozo wrote: "We do not pause to consider whether a statute differently conceived and framed would yield results more consonant with fairness and reason. We take the statute as we find it."[1] Chief Justice Earl Warren echoed the sentiment: "[W]e are bound to operate within the framework of the words chosen by Congress and not to question the wisdom of the latter in the process of construction."[2] This used to be not just the judicial aspiration; it was, by and large, the judicial reality. In 1935, Max Radin wrote of his salutary realization that "in the ordinary processes of legal adjustment, whatever lip-service is rendered to the idea of justice, no real account is taken of justice, but a great deal of account is taken of particular words in statutes, particular words in documents . . . ."[3]

In more recent years, this orthodoxy has often been replaced by what Learned Hand called the school of thought whereby the judge "must conform his decision to what honest men would think right, and it is better for him to look into his own heart to find out what that is."[4] This was not a parody. Since the mid-20th century, legal theorists have been prodding judges to make policy from the

---

1   *Anderson v. Wilson*, 289 U.S. 20, 27 (1933) (per Cardozo, J.).

2   *Richards v. United States*, 369 U.S. 1, 10 (1962) (per Warren, C.J.). *See People ex rel. Davies v. Cowles*, 13 N.Y. 350, 360 (1856) ("Courts are not responsible that only wise laws shall be made; they have no power given to them to judge of the wisdom of the legislature, nor to revise and alter that which has been enacted to be the law."). *Cf.* W. Nembhard Hibbert, *Jurisprudence* 95 (1932) ("The prime rule of interpretation of a statute is to give to the words thereof their ordinary meaning if the language is clear, irrespective of what the Judges may think the legislature meant, and irrespective of what pernicious results may flow therefrom.").

3   Max Radin, "A Juster Justice, a More Lawful Law," in *Legal Essays in Tribute to Orrin Kip McMurray* 537, 537 (Max Radin & A.M. Kidd eds., 1935).

4   Learned Hand, "How Far Is a Judge Free in Rendering a Decision?" in *The Spirit of Liberty* 79, 83 (1952).

bench. Here is an example from 1955: "Judges should make law when necessary to the ends of justice. . . . Our legal system could not operate without a great amount of judicial lawmaking in all fields of law."[5]

The problem is that although properly informed human minds may agree on what a text means, human hearts often disagree on what is right. That is why we vote (directly or through our representatives) on what the law ought to be, but leave it to experts of interpretation called judges to decide what an enacted law means. It is doubtless true, as a descriptive matter, that judges will often strain to avoid what they consider an unjust result. But we decline to elevate that human tendency to an approved principle of interpretation.

The soundest, most defensible position is one that requires discipline and self-abnegation. If judges think no further ahead than achieving justice in the dispute now at hand, the law becomes subject to personal preferences and hence shrouded in doubt. It is age-old wisdom among mature, experienced legal thinkers that procedure matters most: how things should be done, as opposed to what should be done. And for judges the "how" is fidelity to law. But it is a hard lesson to learn, and harder to follow.

5   Quintin Johnstone, *An Evaluation of the Rules of Statutory Interpretation*, 3 U. Kan. L. Rev. 1, 9 (1955).

60. The false notion that when a situation is not quite covered by a statute, the court should reconstruct what the legislature would have done had it confronted the issue.

"The question ... is not what Congress 'would have wanted' but what Congress enacted."

Argentina v. Weltover, Inc.,
504 U.S. 607, 618 (1992) (per Scalia, J.).

The classical expression for circumstances not contemplated by the drafters of a legal instrument is *casus incogitati*. There was once a historical tradition that besought judges to deal with *casus incogitati* by asking how the lawgiver would have wanted them to be resolved. This approach would never have become even a tributary of a historical tradition were it not for 16th-century remarks by Edmund Plowden, who seems to have been contemplating the monarch as a one-man legislator.[1] Recall a time in which statutes were relatively scarce, the monarch was the de jure and de facto head of state, and statutes were regarded as derogating from the common law. Here is Plowden's statement from 1574:

> [I]n order to form a right judgment when the letter of a statute is restrained, and when enlarged, by equity, it is a good way, when you peruse a statute, to suppose that the lawmaker is present, and that you have asked him the question you want to know touching the equity; then you must give yourself such an answer as you imagine he would have done, if he had been present .... And if the lawmaker would have followed the equity, notwithstanding the words of the law ..., you may safely do the like.[2]

But today, in the words of a leading commentator, the question "How would you intend your words to apply to the facts of this case?" is meaningless when applied to a full legislature.[3] So although we acknowledge that this what-would-the-legislature-

---

1   *See* Rupert Cross, *Precedent in English Law* 172 (1961).

2   2 Edmund Plowden, *Commentaries, or Reports of Cases Decided in the Superior Courts During the Reigns of Edward VI, Mary and Elizabeth I* 459, 467 (note to *Eyston v. Studd*, (1574) 2 Plow. 459a, 467).

3   *See* Rupert Cross, *Precedent in English Law* 172 (1961).

have-wanted strain existed in Anglo-American law, today it is anomalous and philosophically indefensible as violating the separation of powers, and it produces considerable judicial mischief.

The view of the judge as a telepathic time-traveler and collaborative lawmaker ignores the reality that it is, in Judge Easterbrook's words, "impossible for a court—even one that knows each legislator's complete table of preferences—to say what the whole body would have done with a proposal it did not consider in fact."[4] Further: "[J]udicial predictions of how the legislature would have decided issues it did not in fact decide are bound to be little more than wild guesses."[5]

In truth, many *casus incogitati* are fully covered by a statute: Although the legislators did not consider a particular circumstance, the text plainly applies or does not apply by its very words.[6] If it does not apply, the circumstance is probably a *casus omissus*— in which case the principle explained in § 8 squarely applies. No metaphysics necessary. A British judge, Lord Millett, thought through the question with great acuity: "Effect cannot be given to an unenacted intention. So, judges are not supposed to give effect to an intention which Parliament would have had if it had thought about it, which it did not."[7]

Modern theorists have devised (or perhaps resurrected) an approach allied to imaginative reconsideration. They call it "preference elicitation," whereby a court should decide cases based not

---

4   Frank H. Easterbrook, *Statutes' Domains*, 50 U. Chi. L. Rev. 533, 547–48 (1983).

5   *Id.* at 548.

6   *Smith v. Chicago Sch. Reform Bd. of Trs.*, 165 F.3d 1142, 1150 (7th Cir. 1999) (per Easterbrook, J.) (observing that "statutory words often have effects in addition to those contemplated by their authors.").

7   Lord Millett, *Construing Statutes*, 20 Statute L. Rev. 107, 110 (1999). *Cf.* Lord Oliver of Aylmerton, *A Judicial View of Modern Legislation*, 14 Statute L. Rev. 1, 5 (1993) ("Too often, I think, the referee is tempted to shift the goal-posts in reliance upon his own speculation about what it would have been sensible for Parliament to do if Parliament had thought of doing it."); *British Assessment Catering Trades Ass'n v. Westminster City Council*, [1987] 1 W.L.R. 977, 982 (H.L.) (per Balcombe, L.J.) ("[W]here . . . the language of the statute is clear, the fact that it may have effects which were not in contemplation when the Act was passed is a matter for the legislature, not the courts.").

on what the enacting legislature would have wanted to do but on what the current legislature would want to do.[8] Something like this theory was practiced in Justinian's day[9] and in 14th-century England[10] (and soon after rejected), but it has not been adopted by any postmedieval English-speaking court that we know of—and, we trust, never will be. This is not the role of judicial decision-makers in the modern Anglo-American tradition. The jurisprudent Lon Fuller wrote that this procedure "has always failed, and no thoughtful adviser would recommend it to any government today."[11]

---

8   *See* Frank B. Cross, *The Theory and Practice of Statutory Interpretation* 16 (2009). *Cf.* Charles P. Curtis, *A Better Theory of Legal Interpretation*, 3 Vand. L. Rev. 407, 415 (1950) ("courts would do better to try to anticipate the wishes of their present and future masters than divine their past intentions.").

9   1 Dig. 17, 2, 21.

10 Theodore F.T. Plucknett, *A Concise History of the Common Law* 293 (2d ed. 1936).

11 Lon L. Fuller, *Anatomy of the Law* 30 (1968).

61. The half-truth that consequences of a decision provide the key to sound interpretation.

Some outcome-pertinent consequences—what might be called textual consequences—are relevant to a sound textual decision—specifically, those that:

(1) cause a private instrument or governmental prescription to:
 - be ineffective (§ 4 [presumption against ineffectiveness]);
 - be invalid (§ 5 [presumption of validity]);
 - contain a provision that only duplicates another provision (§ 26 [surplusage canon]);
 - contain a provision that contradicts another provision (§ 27 [harmonious-reading canon]); or
 - produce an absurd result (§ 37 [absurdity doctrine]); or
(2) cause a provision of a governmental prescription to:
 - be of questionable constitutionality (§ 38 [constitutional-doubt canon]);
 - have retroactive effect (§ 41 [presumption against retroactivity]);
 - eliminate sovereign immunity (§ 46 [presumption against waiver of sovereign immunity]);
 - preempt state law (§ 47 [presumption against federal preemption]);
 - expand liability for punishment or increase the degree of punishment (§ 49 [rule of lenity]);
 - create a criminal offense similar to a common-law offense (§ 50 [*mens rea* canon]); or
 - create a private right of action (§ 51 [presumption against implied right of action]).

But so-called *consequentialism* invokes a quite different type of consequence, suggested by such questions as "Who wins?" "Will this decision help future plaintiffs?" "Will it help future defendants?" "Is this decision good for the 'little guy'?" "Is it good for business?" "Will it advance the rights of women? Of minorities?" Questions like these are appropriately asked by those who write the laws, but not by those who apply them. The provision of the federal judicial oath that promises to "administer justice without respect to persons, and do equal right to the poor and to the rich" rules them out of bounds. In sum, "[w]hen once the meaning is plain, it is not the province of a court to scan its wisdom or its policy."[1]

When one asks, as the consequentialists do, "Will this decision produce a good or a bad result?"[2] it is not even clear from what perspective that question should be asked and answered. Consider the Michigan case involving a statute authorizing prosecutors to offer immunity in exchange for testimony. It provided: "No person required to answer [potentially incriminating] questions shall thereafter be prosecuted for any offense concerning which such answers may have tended to incriminate him."[3] Charles McIntire, who the prosecution thought had been an accomplice in a homicide committed by Thomas Fleck, was given immunity for his grand-jury testimony. Ten years later, Fleck confessed that he and McIntire had committed the murder. The state sought to prosecute McIntire, arguing that providing truthful answers was an implicit condition of the immunity agreement. The Michigan Supreme Court said no: "The text of the statute is clear and un-ambiguous. It simply does not condition transactional immunity on *truthful* testimony."[4] A regrettable outcome, arguably, but an honest textualist result.

How would consequentialists decide that case? Some of them would want to ensure that McIntire would not go scot-free because he added perjury to murder. But others would consider the long-term effect of giving McIntire his just deserts. If lying invalidates the immunity agreement, the immunized witness will be guaranteed nothing except that the government must prove

---

1   G. Granville Sharp & Brian Galpin, *Maxwell on the Interpretation of Statutes* 5 (10th ed. 1953).

2   *See generally* Adrian Vermeule, *Judging Under Uncertainty: An Institutional Theory of Legal Interpretation* (2006); Cass R. Sunstein, *Must Formalism Be Defended Empirically?* 66 U. Chi. L. Rev. 636 (1999).

3   Mich. Comp. Laws § 767.6.

4   *People v. McIntire*, 599 N.W.2d 102, 106 (Mich. 1999) (emphasis in original).

he was lying before a later prosecution could be successful—not a very attractive deal. So the ability to offer testimonial immunity would become much less helpful to prosecutors. Should one be a consequentialist on a wholesale or on a retail level? To this question the consequentialists have no satisfactory answer.

62. The false notion that words should be strictly construed.

"Literalness may strangle meaning."
Utah Junk Co. v. Porter,
328 U.S. 39, 44 (1946) (per Frankfurter, J.).

One of the earliest references to "strictness" of interpretation appeared in 1343, in a pronouncement by Thorpe, J.: "Statutes are to be interpreted strictly."[1] This statement and many others of the time were perhaps a reaction to an earlier period in which courts stretched statutes considerably or else ignored them altogether.[2] If by *strict* one simply meant that the interpreter holds tight to the fair meaning of the law, then the doctrine would be sound.

But in the 19th century, a "strict" construction came to mean a narrow, crabbed reading of a text. In the words of Justice Joseph Story, what is needed is reasonableness, not strictness, of interpretation:

> If . . . we are to give a reasonable construction to this in-strument, as a constitution of government established for the common good, we must throw aside all notions of sub-jecting it to a strict interpretation, as if it were subversive of the great interests of society, or derogated from the inher-ent sovereignty of the people.[3]

Story expounded this view not just as a legal commentator, but also as a Justice: "The words [of the Constitution] are to be taken

---

1   Y.B. 17 & 18 Edw. III (Rolls Series, vol. 10, No. 9) (Hilary term, 1343–1344), 440, 446 (per Thorpe, J.) ("[A]ccording to the intent of the Statute, which is *stricti juris* . . ."); Y.B. 18 Edw. III (Rolls Series, vol. 11, No. 31) (Easter term, 1344), 131, 131 ("[*S*]*tatutes are stricti juris.*").

2   Theodore F.T. Plucknett, *A Concise History of the Common Law* 296–97 (2d ed. 1936). *See* Frank Hall Childs, *Where and How to Find the Law* 76 (1926) ("Some-times hostile construction amends or even abrogates the legislative [meaning]. A good illustration of this was the construction placed upon the old English 'statute of uses,' which was held by the courts not to apply in so many situations that it had little practical effect.").

3   1 Joseph Story, *Commentaries on the Constitution of the United States* § 423, at 300 (2d ed. 1858). *Cf.* Lackland H. Bloom Jr., *Methods of Interpretation: How the Supreme Court Reads the Constitution* 6 (2009) (showing that Chief Justice John Marshall likewise "rejected strict construction as a rule of interpretation designed to promote judicial restraint").

in their natural and obvious sense, and not in a sense unreasonably restricted or enlarged."[4] This enlightened view prevailed in the mid-19th century, when the Pennsylvania Supreme Court explained that "strictness, which has run into an aphorism, means no more than that [a law] is to be interpreted according to its language . . . . [W]e have only to say what the very words mean."[5] Strict constructionism understood as a judicial straitjacket is a long-outmoded approach deriving from a mistrust of all enacted law.

Adhering to the *fair meaning* of the text (the textualist's touchstone) does not limit one to the hyperliteral meaning of each word in the text. In the words of Learned Hand: "a sterile literalism . . . loses sight of the forest for the trees."[6] The full body of a text contains implications that can alter the literal meaning of individual words. To give but three examples: (1) the rule of *ejusdem generis*, which narrows the literal meaning of a tagalong general term (see § 32 [*ejusdem generis* canon]); (2) the rule that a provision whose literal meaning is evidently absurd can be taken to be an error if the rest of the text shows that only another meaning makes sense (see § 37 [absurdity doctrine]); and (3) the principle that an act not literally authorized is authorized as a necessary predicate of an authorized act (see § 30 [predicate-act canon]).

Textualists should object to being called strict constructionists. Whether they know it or not, that is an irretrievably pejorative term,[7] as it ought to be. Strict constructionism, as opposed to fair-reading textualism, is not a doctrine to be taken seriously. Consider some cases.

Case #1: This case was posed by Pufendorf and repeated by Blackstone. A law forbids a layman "to *lay hands* on a priest." Does this mean only that the layman's hands must not touch the

---

4   *Martin v. Hunter's Lessee*, 14 U.S. (1 Wheat.) 304, 326 (1816) (per Story, J.).

5   *Commonwealth v. Cooke*, 50 Pa. 201, 207 (1865).

6   *New York Trust Co. v. Commissioner*, 68 F.2d 19, 20 (2d Cir. 1933) (per L. Hand, J.).

7   *See, e.g.*, James Willard Hurst, *The Growth of American Law* 186 (1950) (stating that after the 1870s, "strict construction of statutes . . . put a primarily obstructive, if not destructive connotation on the process of statutory interpretation").

priest, or does it include kicking, head-butting, even the use of a weapon (such as a cudgel) on the priest? If the statute is "strictly" construed, the kicking, head-butting, and cudgeling could be done with impunity. But as Blackstone rightly observed, a fair reading prohibits these acts—according to the words' "usual and most known signification."[8] Indeed, Pufendorf states that the literal reading amounts to "[q]uibbles . . . too gross and frivolous."[9] "Don't you lay a hand on me!" is a warning not to harm physically in any way. Although *lay hands on* would be an odd phrasing for a modern statute (employing as it does the figure of speech synecdoche), its meaning is plain. To read the phrase hyperliterally is to destroy its sense.

Case #2: A law punishes severely whoever "draws blood in the streets." Does this prohibition extend to a surgeon who opens the vein of a person who has fallen down in the street with a fit? Both Pufendorf and Blackstone would say no by applying the absurdity doctrine (see § 37).[10] We agree with that result, but think it should rest on the same ground as Case #1: the conventional meaning of the language. As a learned commentator notes, *drawing blood* has (and, 300 years ago, had) two quite different idiomatic meanings.[11] One, applicable to violent encounters with man or beast, refers to a breaking of the skin, no matter how much blood is thereby drawn; the other, applicable to medical procedures, refers precisely to the extraction of blood. The former was obviously meant by the penal law.

Case #3: A statute prescribes that to convict a person, the charging instrument must allege that what he did was "against the peace of the state." A prisoner's indictment omitted the second definite article and instead alleged that his felonious act was

---

8   1 William Blackstone, *Commentaries on the Laws of England* § 2, at 60 (4th ed. 1770).

9   Samuel Pufendorf, *Of the Law of Nature and Nations* 5.12.3, at 536 (Basil Kennett trans., 4th ed. 1729).

10   *Id.* at 540 (calling the bloodletter a "barber"); 1 William Blackstone, *Commentaries on the Laws of England* § 2, at 60 (4th ed. 1770) (calling the bloodletter a "surgeon").

11   *See* John F. Manning, *The Absurdity Doctrine*, 116 Harv. L. Rev. 2387, 2461 (2003).

"against the peace of state."[12] Does he go free? No. The sense is the same, and the omission of the definite article does not vitiate the indictment.

Case #4: The Official Secrets Act makes it a crime to obstruct a member of the armed forces "in the vicinity of" a prohibited place, such as a military base. Antinuclear protesters disrupt military operations on a restricted military airfield and are prosecuted under the Act. Their defense is that they were not "in the vicinity of" the prohibited place—they were actually *in* that place.[13] Do they get off? No: the phrase *in the vicinity of* includes *in*, and any other outcome would be ludicrous.

12　Ex. adapted from Learned Hand, "How Far Is a Judge Free in Rendering a Decision?" (1935), in *The Spirit of Liberty* 103, 107 (Irving Dilliard ed., 1952).

13　*Adler v. George*, [1964] 2 Q.B. 7.

63. The false notion that tax exemptions— or any other exemptions for that matter— should be strictly construed.

United States Supreme Court cases often set forth a requirement of a higher-than-normal level of clarity to support an exemption from taxation. This is variously expressed as a rule that "exemptions from taxation are to be construed narrowly,"[1] that they must be "unambiguously proved,"[2] that they "are not to be implied,"[3] and that doubts regarding them "must be resolved against the taxpayer."[4] Yet many Supreme Court cases denying an exemption make no mention of this rule,[5] and even some cases granting an exemption ignore it.[6]

Indeed, until the early 20th century, the rule applicable to exemptions from federal taxes was the reverse. As the Supreme Court stated in 1873: "If there is a doubt as to the liability of an instrument to taxation, the construction is in favor of the exemption, because, in the language of Pollock, C.B., . . . 'a tax cannot be

---

1   *E.g., Mayo Found. for Med. Educ. & Research v. United States*, 131 S.Ct. 704, 715 (2011) (per Roberts, C.J.) (quoting *Bingler v. Johnson*, 394 U.S. 741, 752 (1969) (per Stewart, J.)).

2   *E.g., Chickasaw Nation v. United States*, 534 U.S. 84, 95 (2001) (per Breyer, J.).

3   *E.g., United States v. Wells Fargo Bank*, 485 U.S. 351, 354 (1988) (per Brennan, J.). *See also United States Trust Co. of N.Y. v. Helvering*, 307 U.S. 57, 60 (1939) (per Black, J.) ("Exemptions from taxation do not rest upon implication.").

4   *Helvering v. New York Trust Co.*, 292 U.S. 455, 470 (1934) (Roberts, J., dissenting).

5   *See Portland Golf Club v. Commissioner*, 497 U.S. 154 (1990) (per Blackmun, J.) (denying exemption without mention of elevated standard); *O'Connor v. United States*, 479 U.S. 27 (1986) (per Scalia, J.) (same); *United States v. American Coll. of Physicians*, 475 U.S. 834 (1986) (per Marshall, J.) (same); *Bob Jones Univ. v. United States*, 461 U.S. 574 (1983) (per Burger, C.J.) (same); *HCSC-Laundry v. United States*, 450 U.S. 1 (1981) (per curiam) (same); *Helvering v. Le Gierse*, 312 U.S. 531 (1941) (per Murphy, J.) (same); *Merchants Nat'l Bank of Baltimore v. United States*, 214 U.S. 33 (1909) (per White, J.) (same). *See also Heiner v. Colonial Trust Co.*, 275 U.S. 232, 235 (1927) (per Stone, J.) (denying exemption, saying only that "[t]ax exemptions are never lightly to be inferred").

6   *See Lederer v. Stockton*, 260 U.S. 3, 8 (1922) (per Taft, C.J.) (exemption for charitable corporations granted to a trust whose beneficiary was a charitable corporation; to hold otherwise "would be to defeat the beneficent purpose of Congress"); *Helvering v. New York Trust Co.*, 292 U.S. 455 (1934) (per Butler, J.) (upholding exemption from normal tax rates for capital gains).

imposed without clear and express words for that purpose."[7] This notion accords with the rule applicable to governmental acquisition of private property by other means, such as the imposition of penalties (see § 49 [rule of lenity]). Even the rule that public grants were to be construed "strictly against the grantees" did not exclude "what is given, either expressly *or by necessary or fair implication.*"[8]

Why the reversal of this rule? During the 19th century, the vast majority of federal cases dealing with exemption from taxation involved *state* taxes that were assertedly precluded by a state commitment enforceable under the Contracts Clause[9] or by the operation of some federal statute.[10] Whereas a mere exemption from a tax can be eliminated by the taxing sovereign, these cases claimed that the state had, by its contractual commitment or by federal law, been deprived of its power to withdraw the exemption—that is, deprived of its power to tax. Small wonder that extraordinary clarity would be required to produce this result. The long line of Contracts Clause cases denying the claim of a federally guaranteed exemption from state taxation begins with Chief Justice Marshall's 1839 opinion in *Providence Bank v. Billings,*[11] rejecting the bald assertion that the mere grant of a corporate charter implied an exemption. The abandonment of the power to tax, Marshall said, "ought not to be presumed, in a case in which the deliberate purpose of the state to abandon it does not appear."[12] Later cases, in which grounds were asserted for the exemption beyond the mere fact of a corporate charter, provoked expression of a stricter rule:

---

7   *United States v. Isham*, 84 U.S. (17 Wall.) 496, 504 (1873) (per Hunt, J.) (quoting *Gurr v. Scudds*, [1855] 11 Exch. 190, 192).

8   *United States v. Denver & R.G. Ry. Co.*, 150 U.S. 1, 14 (1893) (per Jackson, J.) (emphasis added).

9   *E.g., Bailey v. Magwire*, 89 U.S. (22 Wall.) 215 (1874) (per Davis, J.) (tax exemption asserted to have been conferred by corporate charter); *The Delaware R.R. Tax*, 85 U.S. (18 Wall.) 206 (1873) (per Field, J.) (same).

10 *E.g., Territory of N.M. v. United States Trust Co. of N.Y.*, 174 U.S. 545 (1899) (per McKenna, J.) (exemption from territorial taxes on railroad right-of-way assertedly conferred by federal statute).

11 29 U.S. (4 Pet.) 514 (1830) (per Marshall, C.J.).

12 *Id.* at 561.

The taxing power is vital to the functions of government. It helps to sustain the social compact and to give it efficacy. It is intended to promote the general welfare. It reaches the interests of every member of the community. It may be restrained by contract in special cases for the public good, where such contracts are not forbidden. But the contract must be shown to exist. There is no presumption in its favor. Every reasonable doubt should be resolved against it. Where it exists it is to be rigidly scrutinized, and never permitted to extend, either in scope or duration, beyond what the terms of the concession clearly require. It is in derogation of public right, and narrows a trust created for the good of all.[13]

The strong presumption against a state's waiver, or the federal government's elimination, of a state's power to tax is analogous to the entirely proper strong presumption against a state's waiver, or the federal government's elimination, of state sovereign immunity (see § 46).

Unsurprisingly, the 19th-century state-tax exemption cases become the principal authorities cited for the "strict construction" rule applied to federal-tax exemptions. For example, in the 1940 case of *United States v. Stewart*,[14] Justice William O. Douglas's opinion for the Court cites five cases for the proposition that "[e]xemptions from taxation cannot rest upon mere implications" and are to be "construed narrowly."[15] Three of the five are state-tax cases; one of the two federal-tax cases in fact does not express such a rule but engages in ordinary textual interpretation;[16] and the other case cites in support of its statement that "[e]xemptions from

---

13 *Tucker v. Ferguson*, 89 U.S. (22 Wall.) 527, 575 (1874) (per Swayne, J.). *See also Central R.R. & Banking Co. v. Georgia*, 92 U.S. (2 Otto) 665, 674–75 (1875) (per Strong, J.) ("[I]t is a well-settled principle that a claim for exemption from taxation cannot be supported, unless the statute alleged to confer it is so plain as to leave no room for controversy. No presumption can be made in support of the exemption; and, if there be a reasonable doubt, it must be resolved in favor of the State.").

14 311 U.S. 60 (1940) (per Douglas, J.).

15 *Id.* at 71.

16 *Murdock v. Ward*, 178 U.S. 139 (1900) (per Shiras, J.).

taxation do not rest upon implication" nothing but four state-tax cases.[17]

But whatever the worthy or unworthy origins of the rule that exemptions from taxation are to be strictly construed, we agree with the Supreme Court opinions ignoring it.[18] Like any other governmental intrusion on property or personal freedom, a tax statute should be given its fair meaning, and this includes a fair interpretation of any exceptions it contains. So when one statutory provision imposes a categorical tax, any exception assertedly imported by another provision must be clear. But it can be clearly implied no less than clearly expressed, and the terms of the exception ought to be reasonably, rather than strictly, construed.

But never mind tax exemptions. The cases are many stating that exemptions from all sorts of statutes are to be narrowly construed.[19] Sometimes (though rarely) there is at least some textual basis for that prescription—as in the provision of the federal Freedom of Information Act stating that it does not "authorize withholding of information or limit the availability of records to the public, except as specifically stated."[20] But almost always, the only announced justification for the rule is to the effect that it is necessary to achieve the beneficial purposes of the law.[21] Yet

---

17 *United States Trust Co. of N.Y. v. Helvering*, 307 U.S. 57, 60 (1939) (per Black, J.).

18 *See supra* nn.5 & 6.

19 *See, e.g., Piedmont & N. Ry. Co. v. ICC*, 286 U.S. 299, 311–12 (1932) (per Roberts, J.) (declaring that exemptions to Transportation Act should be narrowed and limited to effect the remedy intended); *Abshire v. County of Kern*, 908 F.2d 483, 485 (9th Cir. 1990) (stating that exemption to the Fair Labor Standards Act must be narrowly construed); *Osborne v. Dumoulin*, 55 So.3d 577, 586 (Fla. 2011) (narrowly construing homestead exemptions in bankruptcy); *Simpson Strong-Tie Co. v. Gore*, 230 P.3d 1117, 1123 (Cal. 2010) (exemptions to anti-SLAPP statute must be construed narrowly).

20 5 U.S.C. § 552(d).

21 *See, e.g., Hampton Police Ass'n v. Town of Hampton*, 20 A.3d 994, 998 (N.H. 2011) (exemptions to Right-to-Know Law are narrowly construed "with a view to providing the utmost information to best effectuate the statutory and constitutional objective of facilitating access to all public documents"); *Abshire*, 908 F.2d at 485 (purpose of narrow construction of FLSA is "to further Congress' goal of providing broad federal employment protection"); *Skinner v. Steele*, 730 S.W.2d 335, 337 (Tenn. Ct. App. 1987) (finding that narrowly construing exemption to consumer-protection act serves statute's purpose).

as we have discussed earlier (see pp. 18–21), the limitations on a statute's scope are as much a part of the statute's "purpose" as the scope itself. Without some textual indication, there is no reason to give statutory exceptions anything other than a fair (rather than a "narrow") interpretation. The expressions to the contrary find their source either in a judicial proclivity to make difficult interpretive questions easy, or else in an inappropriate judicial antagonism to limitations on favored legislation.

64. The false notion that remedial statutes should be liberally construed.

Here we contradict an oft-repeated and age-old formulation[1] that needlessly invites judicial lawmaking. True, the rule was invoked by the first Chief Justice, John Jay, in *Chisholm v. Georgia*, in 1793.[2] "But this liberality of exposition," as Justice Joseph Story explained in the mid-19th century, "is clearly inadmissible, if it extends beyond the just and ordinary sense of the terms."[3] Hence a fair reading is all that is required. One can well understand Jeremy Bentham's objection to the idea that certain statutes were to be "liberally and beneficially expounded." Bentham retorted: "As if other statutes were to be expounded illiberally and unbeneficially."[4]

The first problem with the remedial-statute rule is the difficulty of determining what constitutes a remedial statute. Is any statute *not* remedial? Does any statute *not* seek to remedy an unjust or inconvenient situation? Blackstone defined the troublesome term as follows:

---

1   *See* 3 Norman J. Singer & J.D. Shambie Singer, *Statutes and Statutory Construction* § 60:2, at 268 (7th ed. 2007) ("[I]f a statute is considered remedial, it should be given a liberal interpretation and should be construed to give the terms used the most extensive meaning to which they are reasonably susceptible."). *See also, e.g., Peyton v. Rowe*, 391 U.S. 54, 65 (1968) (per Warren, C.J.) ("remedial statutes should be liberally construed"); *Beley v. Naphtaly*, 169 U.S. 353, 360 (1898) (per Peckham, J.) ("[The act] is a remedial statute, and one entitled to a liberal construction."); *City of Mason v. West Tex. Utils. Co.*, 237 S.W.2d 273, 280 (Tex. 1951) ("If a statute is curative or remedial . . . it [should] be given the most comprehensive and liberal construction possible."); *Miami County v. City of Dayton*, 110 N.E. 726, 728 (Ohio 1915) ("[A] remedial statute . . . should receive a broad and liberal construction.").

2   2 U.S. (2 Dall.) 419, 476 (1793) (opinion of Jay, C.J.) ("The question now before us [is the clause of the Constitution that] . . . extends the judicial power 'to controversies between a state and citizens of another state.' . . . This extension of power is remedial, because it is to settle controversies. It is therefore, to be construed liberally.").

3   1 Joseph Story, *Commentaries on the Constitution of the United States* § 429, at 304 (2d ed. 1858).

4   Jeremy Bentham, *A Comment on the Commentaries: A Criticism of William Blackstone's Commentaries on the Laws of England* 143 (1776; Charles Warren Everett ed., 1928).

> Remedial statutes are those which are made to supply such defects, and abridge such superfluities, in the common law, as arise [from] either the general imperfection of all human laws, from change of time and circumstances, from the mistakes and unadvised determinations of unlearned (or even learned) judges, or from any other cause whatsoever.[5]

This passage causes one to suspect that the remedial-statute rule was just an antidote to the unreasonable rule that statutes in derogation of the common law were to be strictly construed. If the object was to change the common law, they were to be "liberally" construed—which probably meant only "not strictly" (see § 62). As Blackstone's capacious description ("any other cause whatsoever") would suggest, all sorts of statutes have been held to be "remedial" within the meaning of the rule.[6] The law reports teem with cases holding that statutes must be liberally construed because they are remedial.[7]

The other problem with the remedial-statute rule is that identifying what a "liberal construction" consists of is impossible—which means that it is an open invitation to engage in "purposive" rather than textual interpretation, and generally to engage in

---

5   1 William Blackstone, *Commentaries on the Laws of England* 86 (4th ed. 1770).

6   *See, e.g., Pineda v. Williams-Sonoma Stores, Inc.*, 246 P.3d 612, 617–18 (Cal. 2011) (Credit Card Act); *Barr v. NCB Mgmt. Servs., Inc.*, 711 S.E.2d 577, 583 (W. Va. 2011) (West Virginia Consumer Credit and Protection Act); *S.M. Hentges & Sons, Inc. v. Mensing*, 777 N.W.2d 228, 232 (Minn. 2010) (prelien notice requirement); *Austin v. Alabama Check Cashers Ass'n*, 936 So.2d 1014, 1026 (Ala. 2005) (Alabama Small Loan Act); *International Ass'n of Fire Fighters v. City of Everett*, 42 P.3d 1265, 1267 (Wash. 2002) (statute awarding attorney's fees); *Jarrett v. Woodward Bros., Inc.*, 751 A.2d 972, 981 (D.C. 2000) (liquor-control law); *Gordon Sel-Way, Inc. v. Spence Bros., Inc.*, 475 N.W.2d 704, 716 (Mich. 1991) (statute governing award of interest on civil judgments); *Muzzy v. Chevrolet Div., Gen. Motors Corp.*, 571 A.2d 609, 614 (Vt. 1989) (lemon law); *Flores v. United Air Lines Inc.*, 757 P.2d 641, 647 (Haw. 1988) (employment-discrimination statute); *Southland Ref. Co. v. State Indus. Comm'n*, 27 P.2d 827, 828 (Okla. 1933) (workers'-compensation law); *Nelson v. HSBC Bank USA*, 929 N.Y.S.2d 259, 262–63 (App. Div. 2011) (local civil-rights statute).

7   *See, e.g., Cruz v. Sullivan*, 912 F.2d 8, 11 (2d Cir. 1990) ("The [Social Security] Act must be liberally applied, for it is a remedial statute intended to include not exclude."); *Barker v. State*, 402 N.E.2d 550, 555 (Ohio 1980) ("these remedial [expungement] provisions are to be liberally construed to promote their purposes"); *Martin Marietta Corp. v. Faulk*, 407 P.2d 348, 349 (Colo. 1965) ("The Workmen's Compensation Act should be given a liberal construction because its purpose is highly remedial and beneficent.").

judicial improvisation. Of course, "liberal construction" does have an identifiable meaning if it means (as we suspect it originally did mean) nothing more than rejection of "strict construction" and insistence on fair meaning. The canon is therefore today either incomprehensible or superfluous.

65. The false notion that a statute cannot oust courts of jurisdiction unless it does so expressly.

Subject to constitutional limitations such as the provision restricting suspension of the writ of habeas corpus,[1] federal courts have only that jurisdiction conferred by Congress.[2] The same is true of state courts except where their jurisdiction has been constitutionally prescribed.[3] But where jurisdiction has previously been conferred by statute, it can be eliminated by implication of a later statute. How might this occur? In a jurisdiction in which state and county courts by statute have concurrent jurisdiction over certain cases, let us say that a new statute provides that for some of those cases "the state courts shall have exclusive jurisdiction." For those cases, the county courts have thereby been ousted of jurisdiction.

The text should be given its fair meaning, in accordance with rules that we have described. Ouster of jurisdiction is already adequately protected by (1) the presumption against implied repeal (§ 55)[4] and (2) the rule disfavoring an interpretation that raises

1 U.S. Const. art. I, § 9, cl. 2.

2 *Buel v. Van Ness*, 21 U.S. (8 Wheat.) 312, 324 (1823) (per Johnson, J.) ("If the United States have jurisdiction over all causes arising under their own laws, Congress must possess the power of determining to what extent that jurisdiction shall be vested in this Court."); *Cary v. Curtis*, 44 U.S. (3 How.) 236, 245 (1845) (per Daniel, J.) ("Congress . . . possess[es] the sole power of creating the tribunals (inferior to the Supreme Court) for the exercise of the judicial power, and of investing them with jurisdiction either limited, concurrent, or exclusive, and of withholding jurisdiction from them.").

3 *See, e.g., Chenault v. Phillips*, 914 S.W.2d 140, 141 (Tex. 1996) ("This Court's jurisdiction, like that of all Texas courts, is conferred solely by the Texas Constitution and state statutes. We do not have jurisdiction to decide any case absent an express constitutional or statutory grant."); *Lucas v. Biller*, 130 S.E.2d 582, 585 (Va. 1963) ("The subjects over which the various courts of this State shall have jurisdiction, if not fixed by the Constitution, shall be determined only by the legislature . . ."); *Humphrys v. Putnam*, 178 N.E.2d 506, 509 (Ohio 1961) ("It is fundamental, however, that courts have only such jurisdiction as is conferred upon them by the Constitution or by the Legislature acting within its constitutional authority."). *See also* James V. Calvi & Susan E. Coleman, *American Law and Legal Systems* 48 (5th ed. 2004).

4 *See, e.g., Examining Bd. of Eng'rs, Architects & Surveyors v. Flores de Otero*, 426 U.S. 572, 594–95 (1976) (per Blackmun, J.) (holding that Congress did not intend to repeal by implication the jurisdiction of the federal district court of Puerto Rico to hear federal civil-rights cases); *Colorado River Water Conservation Dist. v. United States*, 424 U.S. 800, 808 (1976) (per Brennan, J.) (holding that the

constitutional doubts (§ 38). Any additional thumb on the scales amounts to self-serving judicial arrogance. Although there is a presumption of judicial review of unlawful executive action,[5] the question whether the presumption has been overcome, and whether court jurisdiction over any other matters has been excluded, ought *not* to be governed by any special rules.

Perhaps the jurisdictional-ouster presumption might be justified as reflecting ordinary meaning—on the theory that ouster of jurisdiction is so extraordinary that it will not lightly be assumed. But we doubt it. The presumption seems to us founded quite simply on judicial self-interest—or, to put a better face on it, judicial policy that court jurisdiction will not be yielded lightly. Consider that even in some cases in which the ouster is quite clear, it has been disregarded.[6]

McCarran Amendment did not repeal the jurisdiction of district courts to entertain federal water suits); *Rosecrans v. United States*, 165 U.S. 257, 262 (1897) (per Brewer, J.) ("When there are statutes clearly defining the jurisdiction of the courts, the force and effect of such provisions should not be disturbed by a mere implication flowing from subsequent legislation.").

5   *See Kucana v. Holder*, 130 S.Ct. 827, 839 (2010) (per Ginsburg, J.) (recognizing "a familiar principle of statutory construction: the presumption favoring judicial review of administrative action"); *Gutierrez de Martinez v. Lamagno*, 515 U.S. 417, 434 (1995) (per Ginsburg, J.) ("Because the statute is reasonably susceptible to divergent interpretation, we adopt the reading that accords with traditional understandings and basic principles: that executive determinations generally are subject to judicial review . . ."); *Bowen v. Michigan Acad. of Family Physicians*, 476 U.S. 667, 681 (1986) (per Stevens, J.) ("We ordinarily presume that Congress intends the executive to obey its statutory commands and, accordingly, that it expects the courts to grant relief when an executive agency violates such a command."); *Abbott Labs. v. Gardner*, 387 U.S. 136, 140 (1967) (per Harlan, J.) ("[A] survey of our cases shows that judicial review of a final agency action by an aggrieved person will not be cut off unless there is persuasive reason to believe that such was the purpose of Congress.").

6   *See, e.g.*, *Hamdan v. Rumsfeld*, 548 U.S. 557 (2006) (Stevens, J., plurality opinion).

66. The false notion that committee reports and floor speeches are worthwhile aids in statutory construction.

"[H]ow often words introduced for the purpose of explanation are themselves the means of creating doubt or ambiguity!"

License Cases,
46 U.S. (5 How.) 504, 612 (1847) (opinion of Daniel, J.).

From the beginnings of the republic, American law followed what is known as the "no-recourse doctrine"—that in the interpretation of a text, no recourse may be had to legislative history. You will find scant mention of legislative history in the pre-20th-century law. Blackstone had this to say about statutory construction:

> The fairest and most rational method to interpret the will of the legislator, is by exploring his intentions at the time when the law was made, by *signs* the most natural and probable. And these signs are either the words, the context, the subject matter, the effects and consequence, or the spirit and reason of the law.[1]

Chancellor James Kent's 19th-century *Commentaries on American Law* expressed a reluctance even to use the title of an act or the preamble as an aid in its construction.[2] The use of debates leading up to enactment is not even considered.

That has been our history. In English practice, a complete disregard of legislative history remained the firm rule from 1769, when it was first announced,[3] until 1992, when the House of Lords changed the practice[4]—probably under the spell of unfortunate American influences.

---

1   1 William Blackstone, *Commentaries on the Laws of England* 59 (4th ed. 1770) (emphasis added).

2   1 James Kent, *Commentaries on American Law* *560 (Charles M. Barnes ed., 13th ed. 1884).

3   *Millar v. Taylor,* [1769] 4 Burr. 2303, 2332 (K.B.).

4   *Pepper v. Hart,* [1992] 3 W.L.R. 1032; [1993] 1 All E.R. 42 (H.L.) (ruling by a 6-to-1 margin—with Lord Mackay dissenting—that reference to Hansard could be made under limited circumstances). *See* James A. Holland & Julian S. Webb, *Learning Legal Rules* 275-84 (7th ed. 2010) (suggesting already the "fall" of this ruling in Britain, or at least its significant retrenchment). *Cf. Crilly v. T. & J. Farrington Ltd.,* [2001] 3 I.R. 251, [2000] 1 I.L.R.M. 548 (in which the Supreme

Let us consider our history in more detail. In 1796, for example, Representative Robert Harper, speaking against a motion before Congress, referred to the "universal practice of Courts of Law, who, when called on to explain acts of the Legislature, never resorted to the debates which preceded it—to the opinions of members about its signification—but inspected the act itself, and decided by its own evidence."[5] One of Harper's opponents that day, Representative Albert Gallatin, a proponent of the motion, was pointed out as having said on an earlier occasion: "[A] law must be construed from the face of it, and . . . nothing extraneous to it could be admitted."[6] To this view Gallatin assented, insisting that "whatever might have been the views of the members who framed it, that could not derogate from the nature of the law."[7] There was, in short, agreement on the importance of disregarding legislative history.

From the 18th century on, legal thinkers held firmly to the conviction that meaning derives from text, not from outside sources such as legislative history:

- **Alexander Hamilton (1791):** "[W]hatever may have been the intention of the framers of the constitution, or of a law, that intention is to be sought for in the instrument itself."[8]

- **Marshall, C.J. (1819):** "The words of an instrument, unless there be some sinister design that shuns the light,

---

Court of Ireland outright rejected all uses of legislative history in statutory construction); Lord Millett, *Construing Statutes*, 20 Statute L. Rev. 107, 110 (1999) (calling *Pepper v. Hart* a "regrettable decision").

5   5 Annals of Cong. 462 (1796). For this early example, we are indebted to Hans W. Baade, *"Original Intent" in Historical Perspective: Some Critical Glosses*, 69 Tex. L. Rev. 1001 (1991).

6   5 Annals of Cong. at 453.

7   *Id.* at 466.

8   Alexander Hamilton, "Final Version of an Opinion on the Constitutionality of an Act to Establish a Bank," in 8 *The Papers of Alexander Hamilton* 97, 111 (Harold C. Syrett ed., 1965).

will always represent the intention of those who frame it."[9]

- **James Madison (1821):** "As a guide in expounding and applying the provisions of the Constitution, the debates and incidental decisions of the Convention can have no authoritative character."[10]

- **Marshall, C.J., again (1827):** "To say that the intention of the instrument must prevail; that this intention must be collected from its words; that its words are to be understood in that sense in which they are generally used by those for whom the instrument was intended; that its provisions are neither to be restricted into insignificance, nor extended to objects not comprehended in them, nor contemplated by its framers;—is to repeat what has been already said more at large, and is all that can be necessary."[11]

- **Story, J. (1843):** "What passes in [C]ongress upon the discussion of a bill can hardly become a matter of strict judicial inquiry; and if it were, it could scarcely be affirmed, that the opinions of a few members, expressed either way, are to be considered as the judgment of the whole house, or even of a majority. But, in truth, little reliance can or ought to be place[d] upon such sources of interpretation of a statute. . . . [I]n truth, courts of justice are not at liberty to look at considerations of this sort. We are bound to interpret the act as we find it, and to make such an interpretation as its language and its apparent objects require. We must take it to be true, that the legislature intend precisely what they say, and to the

---

9 "Marshall's 'A Friend to the Union' Essays, Philadelphia Union, April 24–28, 1819," in *John Marshall's Defense of* McCulloch v. Maryland 78, 85 (Gerald Gunther ed., 1969).

10 Letter from James Madison to Thomas Richie (15 Sept. 1821), reprinted in 9 *The Writings of James Madison* 71 n.1 (Gaillard Hunt ed., 1910).

11 *Ogden v. Saunders*, 25 U.S. (12 Wheat.) 213, 332 (1827) (opinion of Marshall, C.J.).

extent which the provisions of the act require, for the purpose of securing their just operation and effect."[12]

- **Taney, C.J. (1845):** "The law as it passed is the will of the majority of both houses, and the only mode in which that will is spoken is in the act itself."[13]

The Supreme Court first made use of legislative history in 1859—not to determine the meaning of the law, but rather to reflect (by concession of both parties) the facts in existence when the law was enacted.[14] As late as 1897, the Supreme Court pronounced that there was "a general acquiescence in the doctrine that debates in [C]ongress are not appropriate sources of information from which to discover the meaning of the language of a statute passed by that body."[15]

The Supreme Court's retreat from that principle is fascinating. In 1911, in its first opinion interpreting the Sherman Act, the Court used the legislative debates as follows: "Although," it said, "debates may not be used as a means for interpreting a statute . . . that rule, in the nature of things, is not violated by resorting to debates as a means of ascertaining the environment at the time of the enactment of a particular law; that is, the history of the period when it was adopted."[16] Twenty years later, when it came to interpret the "unfair methods of competition" provision of the Federal Trade Commission Act, it said:

---

12 *Mitchell v. Great Works Milling & Mfg. Co.*, 17 F. Cas. 496, 498–99 (C.C.D. Me. 1843) (No. 9,662) (per Story, J.).

13 *Aldridge v. Williams*, 44 U.S. (3 How.) 9, 15 (1845) (per Taney, C.J.).

14 *Dubuque & Pac. R.R. v. Litchfield*, 64 U.S. (23 How.) 66, 87–88 (1859) (per Catron, J.) (interpreting a congressional land grant, a private bill, in a dispute in which the parties agreed that the facts stated in a House committee report were accurate).

15 *United States v. Trans-Missouri Freight Ass'n*, 166 U.S. 290, 318 (1897) (per Peckham, J.).

16 *Standard Oil Co. v. United States*, 221 U.S. 1, 50 (1911) (per White, C.J.). *Cf. Omaechevarria v. Idaho*, 246 U.S. 343, 351 (1918) (per Brandeis, J.) (referring to "the reports of the Secretary of the Interior upon whose recommendation the Act was introduced, the reports of the committees of Congress, and the debates thereupon" as indicating legislative purpose).

> It is true, at least generally, that statements made in debate cannot be used as aids to the construction of a statute. But the fact that throughout the consideration of this legislation there was common agreement in the debate as to the great purpose of the act[,] may properly be considered in determining what that purpose was and what were the evils sought to be remedied.[17]

In the course of this opinion, the Court proceeded, without feeling the need for justification, to note the fact that the Senate language (*unfair competition*) had been altered in conference to the adopted language (*unfair methods of competition*). Then it surmised that "[d]ebate apparently convinced the sponsors of the legislation that [the original] words, which had a well settled meaning at common law, were too narrow"—and concluded that "[u]ndoubtedly the substituted phrase has a broader meaning."[18]

By 1940, a treatise on statutory construction described the landscape in this country as follows:

> Although there seems to be considerable conflict in the cases, the weight of authority apparently refuses to regard the opinions, the motives, and the reasons expressed by the individual members of the legislature, even in debate, as a proper source from which to ascertain the meaning of an enactment. . . . A number of cases, however, make a distinction between legislative debates and the reports of legislative committees, and it must be admitted that the latter undoubtedly possess a more reliable or satisfactory source of assistance.[19]

The author optimistically concluded: "The time will undoubtedly come when the courts will generally resort to the debates for whatever assistance—be it ever so minute—that may be found there."[20]

He proved prophetic. According to a study that appeared in the *Jurimetrics Journal*, in 1938 the Supreme Court cited legislative

---

17 *FTC v. Raladam Co.*, 283 U.S. 643, 650 (1931) (per Sutherland, J.).

18 *Id.* at 648.

19 Earl T. Crawford, *The Construction of Statutes* § 213, at 375–76, 382 (1940).

20 *Id.* § 215, at 382.

history 19 times—in 1979, 405 times.[21] The high point of 445 was reached in 1974.[22] The frequency of citing legislative history in statutory cases was 100% in 1981–1982,[23] nearly 75% in 1988–1989,[24] but only 18% by 1992–1993.[25] Statistics vary from term to term and may vary from statistician to statistician. One analyst puts the 1996–1997 figure at "about half";[26] another puts the 2004 number at 17%.[27]

Not everyone welcomed the invasion of legislative history into judicial interpretation. For example, Justice Robert H. Jackson wrote: "I, like other opinion writers, have resorted not infrequently to legislative history as a guide to the meaning of statutes. I am coming to think it is a badly overdone practice, of dubious help to true interpretation and one which poses serious practical problems for a large part of the legal profession."[28] About the same time, Max Radin expressed incredulity at the warm embrace: "That we had taken 'legislative history' to our bosom as a method of interpretation is an instance of following after strange gods when we have a better one at home."[29] He reasoned that the enterprise is inconsistent with our very form of government:

---

21 Jorge L. Carro & Andrew R. Brann, *The U.S. Supreme Court and the Use of Legislative Histories*, 22 Jurimetrics J. 294, 303 (1982).

22 *Id.*

23 *See* Patricia M. Wald, *Some Observations on the Use of Legislative History in the 1981 Supreme Court Term*, 68 Iowa L. Rev. 195, 197–99 (1983).

24 *See* Patricia M. Wald, *The Sizzling Sleeper: The Use of Legislative History in Construing Statutes in the 1988–89 Term of the United States Supreme Court*, 39 Am. U. L. Rev. 277, 288 (1990).

25 *See* Thomas W. Merrill, *Textualism and the Future of the* Chevron *Doctrine*, 72 Wash. U. L.Q. 351, 355 (1994).

26 *See* Jane S. Schacter, *The Confounding Common Law Originalism in Recent Supreme Court Statutory Interpretation: Implications for the Legislative History Debate and Beyond*, 51 Stan. L. Rev. 1, 14–15 (1998).

27 *See* James J. Brudney & Corey Ditslear, *The Decline and Fall of Legislative History? Patterns of Supreme Court Reliance in the Burger and Rehnquist Eras*, 89 Judicature 220, 222 (2006). *See also* Frank B. Cross, *The Theory and Practice of Statutory Interpretation* 136–38 (2009).

28 Robert H. Jackson, *The Meaning of Statutes: What Congress Says or What the Court Says*, 34 A.B.A. J. 535, 537–38 (1948).

29 Max Radin, *A Case Study in Statutory Interpretation:* Western Union Co. v. Lenroot, 33 Cal. L. Rev. 219, 224 (1945).

> [T]he constitutional power granted to Congress to legis-
> late is granted only if it is exercised in the form of vot-
> ing on specific statutes. If all the legislators in the halls of
> Congress or outside, in exactly similar words orally uttered
> what was in their minds, that would not be a statute and
> therefore no law. They are empowered to make law only in
> one fashion and that is by voting on proposed statutes.[30]

Apart from this political problem and a torrent of practical
problems, to which we will shortly turn, the use of legislative history poses a major theoretical problem: It assumes that what we are
looking for is the intent of the legislature rather than the meaning
of the statutory text. That puts things backwards. To be "a government of laws, not of men" is to be governed by what the laws *say*,
and not by what the people who drafted the laws intended. Jurists
from Chancellor Kent to Justice Frankfurter have recognized this.
Kent wrote in his *Commentaries on American Law* that "the great
object of the maxims of interpretation is, to discover the true intention of *the law*,"[31] and lest his meaning be mistaken he added
in a footnote:

> The English judges have frequently observed, in answer to
> the remark that the legislature meant so and so, that they
> in that case have not so expressed themselves, and therefore
> the maxim applied, *quod voluit non dixit* [What it wanted
> it did not say].[32]

Similarly, Justice Oliver Wendell Holmes wrote: "We do not inquire what the legislature meant; we ask only what the statute
means."[33]

---

30 *Id.* at 223.

31 1 James Kent, *Commentaries on American Law* 467 (1826) (emphasis added).

32 *Id.*

33 Oliver Wendell Holmes, "The Theory of Legal Interpretation," in *Collected Legal
Papers* 203, 207 (1920) (quoted with approval in *Schwegmann Bros. v. Calvert
Distillers Corp.*, 341 U.S. 384, 397 (1951) (Jackson, J., concurring)). *Cf. Magor
& St. Mellons Rural Dist. Council v. Newport Corp.*, [1952] A.C. 189, 191 (H.L.)
(per Lord Simonds) ("The duty of the court is to interpret the words that the legislature has used; those words may be ambiguous, but, even if they are, the power
and duty of the court to travel outside them on a voyage of discovery are strictly
limited.").

A reliance on legislative history also assumes that the legislature even *had* a view on the matter at issue. This is pure fantasy. In the ordinary case, most legislators could not possibly have focused on the narrow point before the court. The few who did undoubtedly had varying views. There is no reason to believe, in other words, that a "legislative intent" ever existed (see § 67).

Even if legislative intent did exist, there would be little reason to think it might be found in the sources that the courts consult. Floor statements may well have been (and in modern times very probably were) delivered to an almost-empty chamber—or even inserted into the *Congressional Record* as a virtually invisible "extension of remarks" after adjournment. Even if the chamber was full, there is no assurance that everyone present listened, much less agreed. As for committee reports, they are drafted by committee staff and are not voted on (and rarely even read) by the committee members, much less by the full house. And there is little reason to believe that the members of the committee reporting the bill hold views representative of the full chamber. Quite to the contrary, the conventional wisdom is that the Committee on Agriculture, for example, will be dominated by representatives from farming states. (While some political scientists have challenged that view, it is at least clear that the representativeness of committees is unproved.) Statements in committee hearings are so far removed from what the full house could possibly have had in mind that their asserted relevance is comical. And all these doings in one of the houses of a bicameral legislature could not possibly have entered into the thinking of the other house—or of the President who signed the bill. The stark reality is that the only thing that one can say for sure was agreed to by both houses and the President (on signing the bill) is the text of the statute. The rest is legal fiction.

Further, the use of legislative history to find "purpose" in a statute is a legal fiction that provides great potential for manipulation and distortion. The more the courts have relied on legislative history, the less reliable that legislative history has become. In earlier days, when the sole purpose of floor statements and committee reports really was to inform the other members who were to vote on the committee's bill, it was not as absurd (though still absurd enough) to pretend that most or all of those members had heard the floor statement or read the committee report and agreed with it. But nowadays, when legislators expect judges to take those statements and reports as authoritative expressions of "legislative intent," the primary purpose of the exercise has become influencing the courts rather than informing congressional colleagues.

So whereas courts used to refer to legislative history because it existed, today it exists—in all its ever-increasing, profuse detail—*because* the courts refer to it.[34] Legislators engage in floor colloquies (again, typically before an empty house) precisely to induce courts to accept their views about how the statute works. (They have been known to preface a colloquy with, "Let's make some legislative history."[35]) Anyone familiar with the congressional scene knows that one of the regular jobs of Washington law firms is to *draft* legislative history—to be read on the floor or inserted into committee reports.

Legislative history creates mischief both coming and going—not only when it is made but also when it is used. With major legislation, the legislative history has something for everyone. Judge Harold Leventhal of the District of Columbia Circuit once likened its use to entering a crowded cocktail party and looking over the heads of the guests for one's friends.[36] Moreover, because there are no rules about which categories of statements are entitled to how much weight, the history can be either hewed to as determinative or disregarded as inconsequential—as the court

---

34 R.W.M. Dias, *Jurisprudence* 237 (4th ed. 1976) ("In America the suspected insertion by astute politicians of colouring matter into Congress debates and the proceedings of committees with a view to persuading the courts to take a certain view of a statute when it has been passed is proving to be an embarrassment . . .").

35 *See, e.g.*, 11 *Legislative History: Civil Rights Act of 1964* 5821 (1965) ("MR. HUMPHREY: Why does not the Senator finish the article and then we will *make some legislative history.* MR. SMATHERS: Yes, let us *make some legislative history.* I am for it. I read further from the article: . . ."); United States Senate Committee on the Judiciary, *Hearings* 148 (1972) ("MR. KENNEDY: We are trying to make some legislative history.").

36 Patricia M. Wald, *Some Observations on the Use of Legislative History in the 1981 Supreme Court Term*, 68 Iowa L. Rev. 195, 214 (1983) (quoting a personal conversation).

desires. Legislative history greatly increases the scope of manipulated interpretation, making possible some interpretations that the traditional rules of construction could never plausibly support.

But its use in that fashion is admittedly exceptional. The vast majority of citations of legislative history are makeweights, supporting a disposition that the court would have reached anyway. Using it this way may be relatively harmless to the judicial process (though it can greatly expand the length of opinions), but it still distorts the legislative process and imposes substantial work on the lawyers who must consult the entrails of legislative history on pain of malpractice, and substantial costs on the clients who must foot the bill.

Lest it be thought that our insistence on reestablishing the no-recourse doctrine is eccentric, we set forth below a few of the many criticisms of legislative history over the years:

- **1933:** "[A] little thought will reveal its [the no-recourse doctrine's] wisdom. For, even assuming that the records of the debates are complete, it is impossible for the Court to know which speeches (if any) influenced either House in its actual votes, or in what direction; while a prolonged discussion of Parliamentary speeches in Court would not only increase the length and consequent expense of trials of cases, but might lead to the importation of a political atmosphere into the precincts of justice."[37]

- **1936:** "Even the majority who vote for complex legislation do not have any common intention as to its detailed provisions. Their vote indicates party dragooning rather than approval and appreciation of the measure. . . . The intention of the legislature is a myth, and the only possible value of parliamentary reports and debates is to give clues to the social purpose which was the driving force behind the bill."[38]

---

37 Edward Jenks, *The New Jurisprudence* 91 (1933).

38 J.A. Corry, *Administrative Law and the Interpretation of Statutes*, 1 U. Toronto L.J. 286, 290 (1936).

- **1947:** "[I]t is becoming increasingly common to manufacture 'legislative history' during the course of legislation. The accusations of outside participation made in Congress, and the elaborate interpretations in some passages in the committee reports, suggest the danger that this occurred during consideration of the Taft–Hartley amendments."[39]

- **1951:** "[P]olitical controversies which are quite proper in the enactment of a bill . . . should have no place in its interpretation."[40]

- **1957:** "Is the task of the Court to decide what the *legislature* meant or what the *statute* means? If it is the latter, resort to extrinsic aids becomes largely irrelevant, since an imperfectly disclosed meaning should not bind the parties or the Court."[41]

- **1960:** "Even specific statements of meaning may have been planted in the legislative history with the knowledge that their inclusion in the final bill would prevent its passage and with the specific intent that they would be subsequently 'written into' the statute by the Supreme Court."[42]

- **1963:** "The *Congressional Record* is full of inclusions placed there by members of Congress in deference to their constituents, material which may be noticed by Congressmen's legislative assistants or clerks but not called to their superiors' attention. . . . [T]he fact that it is in writing

39 Archibald Cox, *Some Aspects of the Labor Management Relations Act, 1947*, 61 Harv. L. Rev. 1, 44 (1947).

40 *Schwegmann Bros. v. Calvert Distillers Corp.*, 341 U.S. 384, 396 (1951) (Jackson, J., concurring).

41 Charles B. Nutting, *The Supreme Court and Extrinsic Aids to Statutory Interpretation*, 43 A.B.A. J. 266, 266 (1957).

42 Samuel J. Henry & Thomas O. Moore, *A Decade of Legislative History in the Supreme Court: 1950–1959*, 46 Va. L. Rev. 1408, 1437 (1960).

does not mean that all who must vote on an issue have seen the material."[43]

- **1972:** "It is now possible to pick and choose one's 'evidence' from that mountain; in effect, to pick and choose any reasonable legislative intent. Charles Curtis stated the accusation more strongly, accusing the courts of 'fumbling about in the ashcans of the legislative process for the shoddiest unenacted expressions of intention.'"[44]

- **1987:** "Legislative history . . . minimizes or ignores the role of the Executive. In carrying out his constitutionally ordained functions, the President passes upon legislation, and as a practical matter does so without the benefit of legislative history. In this regard, the President's view of the statute may be different from that of the Congress, and from the subsequent interpretation rendered by the courts. Judicial interpolation of the statute based upon legislative materials thus has the potential to create a statute that the President would not have signed."[45]

- **1988:** "[C]ommittee reports are written by staff and rarely read . . . . [T]hey may be the work of people who couldn't get a majority for their statutory language, . . . [and] words uttered on the floor are more apt to reflect Quixotic views of maverick legislators than the sense of the whole body. . . . No one can vote against a report, and the President cannot veto the language of a report."[46]

- **1989:** "[J]udicial reliance on legislative intent, whether or not derived on the basis of legislative history, suffers

---

43 Stephen L. Wasby, *Legislative Materials as an Aid to Statutory Interpretation: A Caveat*, 12 J. Pub. L. 262, 263–64 (1963).

44 Richard I. Nunez, *The Nature of Legislative Intent and the Use of Legislative Documents as Extrinsic Aids to Statutory Interpretation: A Reexamination*, 9 Cal. W. L. Rev. 128, 132 (1972).

45 Kenneth W. Starr, *Observations About the Use of Legislative History*, 1987 Duke L.J. 371, 376.

46 Frank H. Easterbrook, *The Role of Original Intent in Statutory Construction*, 11 Harv. J.L. & Pub. Pol'y 59, 59 (1988).

from . . . basic difficulties. The first is that Congress enacts statutes rather than its own views about what those statutes mean; those views, while relevant, are not controlling unless they are in the statute. . . . The second set of problems is that legislative intent, like legislative purpose, is largely a fiction in hard cases—a problem aggravated by the extraordinary difficulties of aggregating the 'intentions' of a multimember body."[47]

- **1997:** "If something appears in the legislative history—clarification of how a term applies, a stated preference for a given interpretive approach, etc.—then someone in the enactment process necessarily anticipated the point. This makes it at least theoretically possible for Congress to address the question in the legislation itself. The sole impediment is the burden of enacting the already-identified legal principle into law through bicameralism and presentment—a burden that the Constitution expressly contemplates and requires."[48]

- **2000:** "[O]ur legislatures speak only through their statutes; statutes are their only voice; statutes are law, extrinsic materials are not. If a legislature speaks only through its statutes, then anyone subject to its rule should have to listen only to those statutes."[49]

A few of the pro-legislative-history statements in the literature, together with our responses to them, are as follows:

- **1965:** "Legislative history can have important functions. It may suggest lines of analysis for the judges; it may

---

47 Cass R. Sunstein, *Interpreting Statutes in the Regulatory State*, 103 Harv. L. Rev. 405, 431, 433 (1989).

48 John F. Manning, *Textualism as a Nondelegation Doctrine*, 97 Colum. L. Rev. 673, 728 (1997).

49 Michael B.W. Sinclair, *Guide to Statutory Interpretation* 103 (2000). *Cf.* P.S. Atiyah, "Judicial–Legislative Relations in England," in *Judges and Legislators: Toward Institutional Comity* 129, 146 (Robert A. Katzmann ed., 1988) ("Parliament speaks to judges in a very formal way: through statutes. Officially, it does not speak to the judges in any other way.").

serve as a check on the analysis reached, giving the judicial analyst reason to retrace his steps."[50] [These functions do not justify treating legislative history as authoritative. It is not.]

- **1988:** "[T]he legislative reports and debates may provide examples of the meaning that the statutory words might bear. Often, a generalist interpreter hasn't the foggiest idea of what a technical statute is all about; the legislative history provides a window on the specialist world."[51] [We do not object to using legislative history for the same purpose as one might use a dictionary or a treatise. That has nothing to do with treating it as authoritative for the meaning of the text.]

- **1989:** "Ignoring the legislature's understanding of statutes burdens the process of enactment with additional uncertainties. . . . An interpretative rule that ignores legislative intent will impose undue burdens on the legislative process, hindering the ability of the democratic branches to function effectively."[52] [This wrongly assumes that there was an "understanding" on the point at issue; and the "ability of the democratic branches to function effectively" is not enhanced by allowing individual legislators or a single committee to write law that the full house does not know of.]

- **1992:** "A statute's language might seem fairly clear. The language might produce a result that does not seem absurd. Yet legislative history nonetheless might clearly show that the result is wrong because of a drafting error that courts should correct."[53] [A drafting error that is

---

50 William Robert Bishin, *The Law Finders: An Essay in Statutory Interpretation*, 38 S. Cal. L. Rev. 1, 16 (1965).

51 T. Alexander Aleinikoff, *Updating Statutory Interpretation*, 87 Mich. L. Rev. 20, 55 (1988).

52 Daniel A. Farber, *Statutory Interpretation and Legislative Supremacy*, 78 Geo. L.J. 281, 291 (1989).

53 Stephen Breyer, *On the Uses of Legislative History in Interpreting Statutes*, 65 S.

not evident on the face of the statute is an error of the drafter, not of the house that voted for the draft; and citizens seeking to obey the law should not have to comb legislative history for covert drafting errors.]

- **1998:** "[W]hen legislative history is excluded, the remaining interpretive tools available to a judge effectively permit unfettered discretion."[54] [Nothing is more unfetteredly discretionary than the selective use of legislative history. Since the proponents of legislative history do not assert that it replaces rather than supplements the traditional principles of interpretation, it is unfettered discretion added to unfettered discretion.]

- **2010:** "At the very least, [legislative history] can help us to determine whether the difficulty in applying the statute results from an unfortunate choice of statutory language chosen to effectuate a legislative goal that becomes clearer once one investigates the matter."[55] [At most this can identify the "unfortunate choice" of the drafting legislator or committee: The "legislative goal" of the entire Congress is presumably expressed by the language (however "unfortunate") that the Members of Congress voted for—which is also the language (however "unfortunate") that citizens must obey.]

The only goals inarguably sought by a legislative majority are those embodied in the enacted text. Even were it otherwise, we are governed not by unexpressed or inadequately expressed "legislative goals" but by *the law.*

The unprincipled heyday of legislative history came in the 1970s and 1980s, reaching its lowest point in *Citizens to Preserve*

Cal. L.J. 845, 849 (1992).

54 Stephen F. Ross & Daniel Tranen, *The Modern Parol Evidence Rule and Its Implications for New Textualist Statutory Interpretation*, 87 Geo. L.J. 195, 196 (1998) (internal quotation marks omitted).

55 Lawrence M. Solan, *The Language of Statutes: Laws and Their Interpretation* 87 (2010).

Overton Park, Inc. v. Volpe,[56] where Justice Thurgood Marshall wrote for the Court:

> The legislative history . . . is ambiguous. . . . Because of this ambiguity it is clear that we must look primarily to the statutes themselves to find the legislative intent.[57]

Thus Justice Felix Frankfurter's *reductio ad absurdum* from a quarter-century before—his quip that "when the legislative history is doubtful, go to the statute"[58]—became straight-faced reality in volume 401 of the *United States Reports.*

The only plausible justification for giving effect to legislative history is that the legislature is far too busy to consider the minute details of the bills that it considers—that it expects, it wishes, them to be resolved by the members and committees that draft the legislation and bring it to the floor. We have no idea whether this assessment of legislative expectations and desires is correct; there are forceful assertions of congressional sentiment to the contrary. Consider, for example, the following illuminating (and amusing) exchange between the senator from Colorado and the chairman of the Senate Finance Committee on a tax bill:

> MR. ARMSTRONG: My question, which may take [the chairman of the Committee on Finance] by surprise, is this: Is it the intention of the chairman that the Internal Revenue Service and the Tax Court and other courts take guidance as to the intention of Congress from the committee report which accompanies this bill?
>
> MR. DOLE: I would certainly hope so . . . .
>
> MR. ARMSTRONG: Mr. President, will the Senator tell me whether or not he wrote the committee report?
>
> MR. DOLE: Did I write the committee report?

---

56 401 U.S. 402 (1971) (per Marshall, J.).

57 *Id.* at 412 n.29. *See* Philip P. Frickey, *From the Big Sleep to the Big Heat: The Revival of Theory in Statutory Interpretation,* 77 Minn. L. Rev. 241, 243 (1992) (calling Justice Marshall's inversion an "outright blooper").

58 *Greenwood v. United States,* 350 U.S. 366, 374 (1956) (per Frankfurter, J.). *See* Felix Frankfurter, *Some Reflections on the Reading of Statutes,* 47 Colum. L. Rev. 527, 543 (1947) (warning that "[s]purious use of legislative history must not swallow the legislation so as to give point to the quip that only when the legislative history is doubtful do you go to the statute").

MR. ARMSTRONG: Yes.

MR. DOLE: No; the Senator from Kansas did not write the committee report.

MR. ARMSTRONG: Did any Senator write the committee report?

MR. DOLE: I have to check.

MR. ARMSTRONG: Does the Senator know of any Senator who wrote the committee report?

MR. DOLE: I might be able to identify one, but I would have to search. I was here all during the time it was written, I might say, and worked carefully with the staff as they worked . . . .

MR. ARMSTRONG: Mr. President, has the Senator from Kansas, the chairman of the Finance Committee, read the committee report in its entirety?

MR. DOLE: I am working on it. It is not a bestseller, but I am working on it.

MR. ARMSTRONG: Mr. President, did members of the Finance Committee vote on the committee report?

MR. DOLE: No.

MR. ARMSTRONG: Mr. President, the reason I raise the issue is not perhaps apparent on the surface, and let me just state it: . . . The report itself is not considered by the Committee on Finance. It was not subject to amendment by the Committee on Finance. It is not subject to amendment now by the Senate. . . . If there were matter within this report which was disagreed to by the Senator from Colorado or even by a majority of all Senators, there would be no way for us to change the report. I could not offer an amendment tonight to amend the committee report. . . . [F]or any jurist, administrator, bureaucrat, tax practitioner, or others who might chance upon the written record of this proceeding, let me just make the point that this is not the law, it was not voted on, it is not subject to amendment, and we should discipline ourselves to the task of expressing congressional intent in the statute.[59]

---

59 128 Cong. Rec. 16,918–19 (1982).

Even if it made sense to believe that legislators gave committees power to determine statutory details, and even if it made sense to regard un-voted-on (and probably unread) committee reports as representing the views of the committees, it would not make good constitutional law. The Framers envisioned an executive bureaucracy (though perhaps not the behemoth it has come to be) in which many agents of the President, acting with his authority and in his name, would administer the laws. The Framers did not envision a legislative bureaucracy any more than they envisioned a judicial bureaucracy. It is rudimentary that legislative power, like judicial power, is *nondelegable*. Judges may have all the law clerks, and legislators all the committees, administrative assistants, committee counsel, and chiefs of staff that the budget will allow. But they are there to *assist* the judges and legislators in their decision-making—not to make the decisions for them. Even if the members of each house wish to do so, they cannot assign responsibility for making law—or the details of law—to one of their number, or to one of their committees. The law is what the legislature says; and what the legislature says is to be found nowhere but in the laws that each full house has enacted.

As the great theorist John Locke put it in 1689, the legislative power consists in the power "to make laws, . . . not to make legislators."[60] The use of legislative history also spawns a separation-of-powers problem: It entrusts the legislature (or more precisely some legislators) with the interpretation of provisions that it has enacted—a function that is the preeminent and exclusive responsibility of the courts.

There is one use of legislative history that does not attribute the words of one or several legislators to the entire Congress, and does not depend on a theory of delegation of legislative power. It has been described thus in a United States Supreme Court case rejecting the apparent meaning of a statutory amendment:

> We find it difficult to believe that Congress in this manner adopted an amendment which would work such an alteration to the basic thrust of the draft bill amending

---

60 John Locke, *Second Treatise of Government* 87 (1689; Richard Cox ed., 1982).

§ 6103. . . . [Such an alteration] would have, it seems to us, at a minimum engendered some debate in the Senate and resulted in a rollcall vote. More importantly, Senator Haskell's remarks clearly indicate that he did not mean to revise § 6103(b)(2) in this fashion. He . . . gives no intimation that his amendment would [effect such a change]. All in all, we think this is a case where common sense suggests, by analogy to Sir Arthur Conan Doyle's 'dog that didn't bark,'[61] that an amendment having the effect petitioner ascribes to it would have been differently described by its sponsor, and not nearly as readily accepted by the floor manager of the bill.[62]

In other words, the failure of the sponsor *and of the entire Congress* to say in legislative history that the statute did what the statute does means that the statute does not do it. One of your authors discussed this principle of interpretation in a later Supreme Court case relying on it:

I have often criticized the Court's use of legislative history because it lends itself to a kind of ventriloquism. The Congressional Record or committee reports are used to make words appear to come from Congress's mouth which were spoken or written by others (individual Members of Congress, congressional aides, or even enterprising lobbyists). The Canon of Canine Silence the Court invokes today introduces a reverse—and at least equally dangerous—phenomenon, under which courts may refuse to believe Congress's *own* words unless they can see the lips of others moving in unison.[63]

Happily, the Supreme Court of the United States has not always applied the Canon of Canine Silence, and indeed has sometimes explicitly rejected it.[64]

---

61 The allusion is to an Arthur Conan Doyle short story entitled *Silver Blaze* (1892), in which one of the clues enabling Sherlock Holmes to solve the crime was the "curious incident" that a dog did not bark.

62 *Church of Scientology of Cal. v. IRS*, 484 U.S. 9, 17–18 (1987) (per Rehnquist, C.J.).

63 *Koons Buick Pontiac GMC, Inc. v. Nigh*, 543 U.S. 50, 73–74 (2004) (Scalia, J., dissenting).

64 *See, e.g., Morales v. Trans World Airlines, Inc.*, 504 U.S. 374, 385 n.2 (1992) (per Scalia, J.) ("[L]egislative history need not confirm the details of changes in the

Using legislative history to establish what the legislature "intended" is quite different from using it for other purposes. For example, for the purpose of establishing linguistic usage—showing that a particular word or phrase is capable of bearing a particular meaning—it is no more forbidden (though no more persuasive) to quote a statement from the floor debate on the statute in question than it is to quote the *Wall Street Journal* or the *Oxford English Dictionary*. Similarly, legislative history can be consulted to refute attempted application of the absurdity doctrine—to establish that it is indeed thinkable that a particular word or phrase should mean precisely what it says. For to establish thinkability (so to speak), just as to establish linguistic usage, one does not have to make the implausible leap of attributing the quoted statement to the entire legislature. It suffices that a single presumably rational legislator, or a single presumably rational committee, viewed the allegedly absurd result with equanimity. This use of legislative history will be very rare (your judicial author recalls encountering it only once in 29 years on the appellate bench[65]), and it is a worthwhile check on the tendency to call absurd what is merely ill-advised.

It could be argued that because resort to legislative history has been standard judicial practice since the mid-20th century, by disapproving its use (without any power to forbid its use) we undermine the values of certainty and predictability that we elsewhere uphold. The principled answer to that is that use of legislative history is not just wrong; it violates constitutional requirements of nondelegability, bicameralism, presidential participation, and the supremacy of judicial interpretation in deciding the case presented. The pragmatic answer is that anyone who thinks that by excluding legislative history we will be excluding predictable results has not read the cases. It would be more accurate to say that we will be excluding predictable uncertainty. Rather than resolving uncertainty, legislative history normally induces it. Predicting when it will be entirely ignored, on the one hand, or considered

---

law effected by statutory language before we will interpret that language according to its natural meaning.").

65 *See Green v. Bock Laundry Mach. Co.*, 490 U.S. 504, 527 (1989) (Scalia, J., concurring in the judgment).

dispositive, on the other, is—not to put too fine a point on it—a crapshoot.

࠲ࠫ   ࠲ࠫ   ࠲ࠫ

Consider an example of roundabout lawmaking through legislative history. In 1952, the McCarran–Walter Act set forth grounds for excluding from entry into the United States certain aliens, including those "afflicted with psychopathic personality . . . or mental defect."[66] In *Boutilier v. INS*,[67] the question arose whether this provision justified exclusion based on homosexuality. Both *psychopathic personality* and *mental defect* were well-known technical terms in the 1950s.[68] But instead of inquiring into these historical meanings to the best of its ability, the Supreme Court of the United States relied exclusively on legislative history, part of which consisted of this supposedly determinative assertion in a Senate report: "The Public Health Service has advised that the provision for the exclusion of aliens afflicted with psychopathic personality or a mental defect . . . is sufficiently broad to provide for the exclusion of homosexuals and sex perverts."[69] Never did the Court even begin its proper investigation: the meaning of the relevant terms, as technical labels, in 1952.[70] As an illustration of just how tendentiously legislative history can be employed, the Court cited the withdrawal from the bill of an explicit reference

---

66 Immigration and Nationality (McCarran–Walter) Act, ch. 477, 66 Stat. 163, 182 (1952) (codified at 8 U.S.C. § 1182(a)(4)).

67 387 U.S. 118 (1967) (per Clark, J.).

68 *See* David Kennedy Henderson & Robert Dick Gillespie, *A Text-book of Psychiatry for Students and Practitioners* 571 (1950) (defining *mental defect* as an intellectual deficiency present at birth or developed early in life); Raymond Bernard Cattell, *Personality: A Systematic Theoretical and Factual Study* 13 (1950) (defining *mental defect* as including poor reasoning skills and low intelligence); Edmund Bergler, *The Basic Neurosis* 240 (1949) ("Homosexuality per se has nothing to do with psychopathy."); 2 Paul William Preu, "The Concept of Psychopathic Personality," in *Personality and the Behavior Disorders: A Handbook Based on Experimental and Clinical Research* 922 (J. McVicker Hunt ed., 1944) (citing and discussing four different definitions of *psychopathic personality*).

69 S. Rep. No. 1137, 82d Cong., 2d Sess. 9 (1952).

70 *Cf.* 387 U.S. at 125–27, 130–31 (Douglas, J., dissenting) (attempting to define the terms as developed by medical studies from the 1940s and 1950s).

to homosexuals, as though this change somehow buttressed rather than contradicted its conclusion.[71] None of this legislative history should have mattered one whit.

❧   ❧   ❧

Ponder how curious it is that the most virulent critics of originalism are typically the very same people who rummage through legislative history to figure out what the enactors intended. This brings us to the next section.

---

71   387 U.S. at 120–21.

67. The false notion that the purpose of interpretation is to discover intent.

> "We are to be governed not by Parliament's
> intentions but by Parliament's enactments."
>
> Lord Scarman,
> 418 H.L. Official Rep. Col. 65 (9 Mar. 1981).

Literary critics often invoke "authorial intent" in discussions of literature. It can be useful to consider whether, for example, Shakespeare meant a word such as Macbeth's *intrenchant* to mean "cuttable" or "not cuttable," or perhaps both, in a play that is otherwise rife with purposeful ambiguities.[1] While such inquiries may sometimes be difficult, they at least look for something that almost certainly existed: Unless he was being uncharacteristically sloppy, Shakespeare meant "cuttable" or "not cuttable," or perhaps both.

That is not the case when one probes the "intent" behind a document crafted by multiple authors—especially multiple authors who may not have had the same objects in mind. Take what happens with a contract. Two parties, each represented by counsel, want to reach an important deal. One party's lawyer prepares the first draft of the contract, which favors that lawyer's client in all sorts of ways. On receiving the draft, the other lawyer revises the document to eliminate the lopsided provisions, to insert others, and to change the wording of many others. After much negotiation, they agree on final language—but only after compromises that leave some provisions purposely vague. For example, one side wanted a right to terminate within 45 days after the occurrence of a specified event; the other wanted that right to exist only within 5 days after the occurrence. Finally they fell back on the language "within a reasonable time after the occurrence." The lawyer on one side privately told the client that a court would probably say that 30 days would be commercially reasonable; the other lawyer privately told the client that a court would probably say that 48 hours would be commercially reasonable (a week at the outside).

---

1   Bryan A. Garner, *A Note on the Ambiguity of Macbeth's "Intrenchant,"* Am. Notes & Queries, vol. 20, nos. 3 & 4, pp. 39–43 (Nov./Dec. 1981).

So the parties signed, each believing that if a dispute arose, his view would carry the day.

In many important ways, the parties who are affected by a legal document are potential adversaries collaborating only because they need to consummate a transaction. There simply is no meeting of the minds—or *consensus ad idem*, as the older authorities called it. Nor, contrary to popular myth, is a meeting of the minds necessary to the creation of an enforceable contract.[2] There may be as many internal disagreements over predictions about how a court would apply the contractual terms—perhaps dozens in a ten-page contract.

Now transfer this vignette to the context of legislation, in which collective intent is pure fiction because dozens if not hundreds of legislators have their own subjective views on the minutiae of bills they are voting on—or perhaps no views at all because they are wholly unaware of the minutiae.[3] The Whigs disagree with the Tories on how a court will someday apply a given provision—or they *would* disagree if they took the time to consider it. A couple of Whigs speak out on the issue, or perhaps a couple of Tories, but only a smattering of those in the full legislative assembly. Each member voting for the bill has a slightly different reason for doing so. There is no single set of intentions shared by all. The state of the assembly's collective psychology is a hopeless stew of intentions:

> Legislators do not have common objectives, so the basis for imputing agreement to them is weaker than the foundation for this technique in private law. . . . Statutes are drafted by multiple persons, often with conflicting objectives. There will not be a single objective, and discretionary

2   *See, e.g.,* 1 Samuel Williston, *A Treatise on the Law of Contracts* § 4:1, at 330-35 (Richard A. Lord ed., 4th ed. 2007); Grant Gilmore, *The Death of Contract* 43 (1974).

3   *See* Robert E. Keeton, *Keeton on Judging in the American Legal System* 210–11 (1999) ("'[L]egislative intent' . . . is a legal fiction. Only a natural person can have a state of mind such as intent. No legal entity such as a legislature can have an 'intent' in a strictly factual sense."); John Chipman Gray, *The Nature and Sources of the Law* 170 (2d ed. 1921) (stating that "the psychic transference of the thought of an artificial body must stagger the most advanced of the ghost hunters").

interpretation favors some members of the winning coalition over others.[4]

Yet a majority has undeniably agreed on the final language that passes into law. That is all they have agreed on—and that is the sole means by which the assembly has authority to make law.

It is unfashionable in many circles to speak of "objectivity" and "subjectivity." But the law uses these concepts all the time, and they are indispensable. The "reasonable person" in the tort law of negligence is an objectivizing construct—the "anthropomorphic conception of justice,"[5] as a British judge termed the idea. In our view, the fair meaning of a statutory text is determined by a similar objectivizing construct—the "reasonable reader," a reader who is aware of all the elements (such as the canons) bearing on the meaning of the text, and whose judgment regarding their effects is invariably sound. Never mind that no such person exists. Without positing his existence—as tort law posits the existence of the "reasonable person"—we could never subject the meaning of a statute to an objective test.

An influential legal philosopher, Tony Honoré, suggests that the notion of legislative intent is also a useful fiction:

> [T]here is good reason, I think, to say that the interpreter should try to discover the intention of the legislature or the parties to a contract or treaty. A statute, contract, or treaty is a compromise between different views. Perhaps no member of the legislature, and no party to the contract or treaty, would themselves have chosen the text that was finally agreed, if it depended on them alone. The point of speaking of the intention of the legislature or the contracting parties is not that any particular person's views should govern the interpretation of the text. It is rather that the interpreter should treat the text as if it represented the view

---

4 Frank H. Easterbrook, *What Does Legislative History Tell Us?* 66 Chi.-Kent L. Rev. 441, 446–47 (1990). *Cf.* Frank H. Easterbrook, *Text, History, and Structure in Statutory Interpretation*, 17 Harv. J.L. & Pub. Pol'y 61, 68 (1994) ("Peer inside the heads of legislators and you will find a hodgepodge.").

5 *Davis Contractors Ltd. v. Fareham U.D.C.*, [1956] A.C. 696, 728–29 (per Lord Radcliffe).

of a single individual, and make it as coherent as the words permit.[6]

Although this makes "legislative intent" a cogent fiction, those who search for it do not use the phrase this way. As their affection for legislative history demonstrates, they are looking for the genuine intent of the legislators. The use of the term *legislative intent* encourages this search for the nonexistent. What Professor Honoré ought to suggest is not an idiosyncratic definition of *legislative intent* but replacement of the term with *statutory intent*. Although even this term invites a search for some subjective intent, it accords more precisely with what Professor Honoré believes.

True, the courts have often repeated the incantation that their goal is "to ascertain the legislative intent, and, if possible, to effectuate the purposes of the lawmakers."[7] The aspirational declarations have never been holdings of the courts—always dicta. And we believe them to be erroneous. The correct, clear-headed view is as stated by Lord Reid: "We often say that we are looking for the intention of Parliament, but that is not quite accurate. We are seeking the meaning of the words which Parliament used. We are seeking not what Parliament meant but the true meaning of what they said."[8] And by Judge Robert E. Keeton: "[T]he search is for the objectively manifested meaning, not for somebody's unexpressed state of mind."[9]

We believe that references to *intent* have led to more poor interpretations than any other phenomenon in judicial decision-making. Consider this retrograde bit of judicial lawmaking in Texas:

---

6   Tony Honoré, *About Law* 94 (1995).

7   *ICC v. Baird*, 194 U.S. 25, 38 (1904) (per Day, J.). *See also Philbrook v. Glodgett*, 421 U.S. 707, 713 (1975) (per Rehnquist, J.) ("Our objective . . . is to ascertain the congressional intent and give effect to the legislative will."); *United States v. American Trucking Ass'ns*, 310 U.S. 534, 542 (1940) (per Reed, J.) ("[T]he function of the courts . . . is to construe the language so as to give effect to the intent of Congress.").

8   *Black Clawson Int'l Ltd. v. Papierwerke Waldhof-Aschaffenburg AG*, [1975] A.C. 591, 613. *See* Charles Fried, *Sonnet LXV and the "Black Ink" of the Framers' Intention*, 100 Harv. L. Rev. 751, 759 (1987) ("[W]ords and text are chosen to embody intentions and thus replace inquiries into subjective mental states. In short, the text *is* the intention of the authors or the framers.").

9   Robert E. Keeton, *Keeton on Judging in the American Legal System* 207 (1999).

"Only when it is necessary to give effect to the clear legislative intent can we insert additional words into a statutory provision."[10] Or this, from Missouri: "[C]ourts have not hesitated to hold that legislative intent will prevail over common meaning."[11]

The truth is that "[a]scertaining the 'intention of the legislature' . . . boils down to finding the meaning of the words used."[12] If courts do otherwise, they engage in policy-based lawmaking, as John Chipman Gray noted more than a century ago: "[I]n almost all [cases of statutory interpretation], it is probable, and . . . in most of them it is perfectly evident, that the makers of the statutes had no real intention, one way or another, on the point in question; that if they had, they would have made their meaning clear; and that when the judges are professing to declare what the Legislature meant, they are, in truth, themselves legislating to fill up *casus omissi*."[13]

It is perhaps easy to understand how common-law courts got into the habit of referring to (and purporting to discern) "legislative intent." References to the concept date back to the Middle Ages, when statutes "had very little in common with modern legislation."[14] The judges and the lawmakers were synonymous: "Do not gloss the statute," Chief Justice Hengham admonished counsel in 1305, "for we know better than you: we made it."[15] At that time, the judges were never troubled by questions of intent because they were the chief drafters.[16] By the mid-1300s, however, the judges had become separated from the legislature "to such an extent that they treat[ed] legislation as the product of an alien body, of which they knew nothing save from the words of the

---

10 *Hunter v. Fort Worth Capital Corp.*, 620 S.W.2d 547, 552 (Tex. 1981).

11 *Christian Disposal, Inc. v. Village of Eolia*, 895 S.W.2d 632, 634 (Mo. Ct. App. 1995).

12 R.W.M. Dias, *Jurisprudence* 219 (4th ed. 1976).

13 John Chipman Gray, *The Nature and Sources of the Law* § 370, at 165 (1909).

14 Theodore F.T. Plucknett, *A Concise History of the Common Law* 295 (2d ed. 1936).

15 *Aumeye v. Anonymous*, Y.B. 33–35 Edw. I (Rolls Series), 78, 82 (1305) (referring to the Second Statute of Westminster (1285)).

16 Plucknett, *A Concise History of the Common Law* at 295.

statute itself, and from that wording alone [could] they infer its intention—and with the rise of this idea we reach the modern point of view."[17] Yet the old terminology has lingered more than 600 years. As many respected authorities agree,[18] it is high time that further uses of *intent* in questions of legal interpretation be abandoned.

---

17 *Id.*

18 *See, e.g.*, Lord Millett, *Construing Statutes*, 20 Statute L. Rev. 107, 109 (1999) ("My own experiences . . . led me to abandon the use of the expression 'the intention of Parliament.' It was a fiction too far."); Eva H. Hanks, Michael E. Herz & Steven S. Nemerson, *Elements of Law* 249 (1994) ("[W]hat if the search for intent is so difficult because the thing being searched for is not there? Legislative intent may be like the Loch Ness Monster: for years many have believed (generally against their better judgment) that it exists, and some claim even to have glimpsed it, but in reality there just is no such thing. If there is no 'legislative intent,' then the whole theory of intentionalism must be wrong."); John W. MacDonald, *The Position of Statutory Construction in Present Day Law Practice*, 3 Vand. L. Rev. 369, 371 (1950) ("[A]nyone who has ever dealt with the legislative process knows how conspicuously absent is a collective legislative intention."); Max Radin, *The Law and Mr. Smith* 183 (1938) ("Lawyers and courts . . . never have satisfactorily explained . . . what they mean by the [so-called] 'intent' and just how they propose to discover it.").

68. The false notion that the plain language of a statute is the "best evidence" of legislative intent.

"[A] law is the best expositor of itself."
Pennington v. Coxe,
6 U.S. (2 Cranch) 33, 52 (1804) (per Marshall, C.J.).

Intentionalist theorists and courts promote the idea that enacted texts merely evoke or suggest—as opposed to state—what the true law is. This fallacy follows from the previous one. Consider how a textbook-writer phrases this notion: "What a legislature says in the text of a statute is considered the best evidence of the legislative intent or will."[1] Even the Supreme Court of the United States gave voice to this view when it said that a statute's language is "the most reliable evidence of [congressional] intent."[2] The statute is not the law, but only *evidence* of it? Some unenacted intent (which collectively never actually existed) is what we mean by law? If this were true, then it would hardly be possible ever to reach a consensus about the law.

The traditional view is that an enacted text is itself the law. As the Supreme Court of the United States wrote in 1850: "The sovereign will is made known to us by legislative enactment."[3] And it is made known in no other way. Or as an early-20th-century theorist put the point: "[W]henever a law is adopted, all that is really agreed upon is the words."[4]

---

1 2A Norman J. Singer & J.D. Shambie Singer, *Statutes and Statutory Construction* § 46:3, at 165 (7th ed. 2007). *See* Jane S. Schacter, *The Pursuit of "Popular Intent": Interpretive Dilemmas in Direct Democracy,* 105 Yale L.J. 107, 118 (1996) ("[M]any courts . . . explicitly characterize statutory language as the *best evidence of intent.*") (emphasis added).

2 *United States v. Turkette,* 452 U.S. 576, 593 (1981) (per White, J.). *Cf. United States v. American Trucking Ass'ns,* 310 U.S. 534, 543 (1940) (per Reed, J.) ("There is, of course, no more persuasive evidence of the purpose of a statute than the words by which the legislature undertook to give expression to its wishes.").

3 *Wheeler v. Smith,* 50 U.S. (9 How.) 55, 78 (1850) (per McLean, J.).

4 Josef Kohler, "Judicial Interpretation of Enacted Law," in *Science of Legal Method: Select Essays by Various Authors* 187, 196 (1917). *See Davies, Jenkins & Co. v. Davies,* [1968] A.C. 1097, 1121 (per Lord Morris) ("It is well accepted that the beliefs and assumptions of those who frame Acts of Parliament cannot make the law.").

Naturally, if one views the text as defining and therefore confining, there is hardly a better way to unshackle oneself than to minimize it by calling it mere "evidence." Mainstream legal thinkers express astonishment at this view. Laurence H. Tribe writes: "I never cease to be amazed by the arguments of judges, lawyers, or others who proceed as though legal texts were little more than interesting documentary evidence of what some lawgiver had in mind."[5] He adds: "[I]t is the *text's* meaning, and not the content of anyone's expectations or intentions, that binds us as law."[6] And Charles Fried aptly notes that "we would not consider an account of Shakespeare's mental state at the time he wrote a sonnet to be a more complete or better account of the sonnet than the sonnet itself."[7]

The rationale for rejecting the law-as-evidence-of-law view is that it "demean[s] the constitutionally prescribed method of legislating to suppose that its elaborate apparatus for deliberation on, amending, and approving a text is just a way to create some *evidence* about the law, while the *real* source of legal rules is the mental processes of legislators."[8] There is no satisfactory answer to this point.

---

5 Laurence H. Tribe, "Comment," in Antonin Scalia, *A Matter of Interpretation: Federal Courts and the Law* 65, 65 (1997).

6 *Id.* at 66 (emphasis in original). *Cf.* Lord Millett, *Construing Statutes*, 20 Statute L. Rev. 107, 110 (1999) ("Effect cannot be given to an unenacted intention.").

7 Charles Fried, *Sonnet LXV and the "Black Ink" of the Framers' Intention*, 100 Harv. L. Rev. 751, 758 (1987).

8 *In re Sinclair*, 870 F.2d 1340, 1344 (7th Cir. 1989) (per Easterbrook, J.).

69. The false notion that lawyers and judges, not being historians, are unqualified to do the historical research that originalism requires.

> "Lawyers are ... necessarily historians .... If they do not take this task seriously, they will not cease to be historians. They merely will be bad historians."
>
> Max Radin, *The Law and You* 188–89 (1948).

Originalism admittedly requires lawyers and judges to engage in historical semantics.[1] It is often charged that they are ill-equipped for the task: "It is quite true that lawyers are for the most part extremely bad historians. They often make up an imaginary history and use curiously unhistorical methods."[2] The leveler of that charge, Max Radin, cited a British example of a 1939 judicial misinterpretation of sources dating back to 1215—in a different language altogether (medieval Latin and Law French). The example serves as a useful admonition. But note that Radin was an originalist:

> We have thus imposed a new burden on the lawyer on the bench. Besides all the other things asked of him, he is also to be a historian. But there is no help for it. There is simply no way by which the law can be made either simple or easy.[3]

---

1   3 Roscoe Pound, *Jurisprudence* 491 (1959) ("In the case of constitutional provisions historical interpretation is often necessary."); R.W.M. Dias, *Jurisprudence* 221 (4th ed. 1976) ("[I]n the case of antique enactments, whose framers have long since disappeared, . . . [i]t is the judges on whom the task devolves to ascertain the meaning as best they can."); Van Vechten Veeder, *The Judicial Characteristics of the Late Lord Bowen*, 10 Harv. L. Rev. 351, 365 (1897) (quoting Lord Bowen as averring that "[t]he only reasonable and the only satisfactory way of dealing with English law is to bring to bear upon it the historical method"). *Cf.* Walter F. Murphy, "The Art of Constitutional Interpretation: A Preliminary Showing," in *Essays on the Constitution of the United States* 130, 150 (M. Judd Harmon ed., 1978) ("[T]o allow the plain words of the Constitution to settle a controversy, judges must either become linguistic historians or adopt some version of the doctrine that the Constitution's meaning changes over time.").

2   Max Radin, *Law as Logic and Experience* 138 (1940).

3   *Id.* at 140. *Cf.* Dahlia Lithwick, "Justice Grover vs. Justice Oscar," *Slate* (6 Dec. 2006) http://www.slate.com/id/2154993/ ("Breyer says that if the only thing that matters is historical truths from the time of the Constitution, 'we should

Nor is it a valid refutation of originalism that "no one can reconstruct original understanding precisely."[4] Our charge is to try.

Fortunately for American interpreters, we are generally dealing with a continuous linguistic tradition: We speak what linguists call "Modern English" (Shakespeare's 16th-century writings were in Early Modern English). What was written and spoken in the 18th century was likewise Modern English (which evolved from Middle English in the late 15th century). Further, legal drafting ordinarily employs an especially stable form of English: a variation on standard written English known as "legal English." It changes glacially, on the whole. For terms that undergo shifts in meaning, we have superb linguistic resources in the form of historical dictionaries.[5]

But the originalist's inquiry goes well beyond determining the historical usage of words. For example, in the *Heller* case,[6] which upheld the individual right to possess firearms, one of the significant aspects of the Second Amendment was that it did not purport to *confer* a right to keep and bear arms. It did not say that "the people shall have the right to keep and bear arms," or even that "the government shall not prevent the people from keeping and bearing arms," but rather that "the right of the people to keep and bear arms" (implying a *preexisting* right) "shall not be infringed." This triggered historical inquiry showing that the right to have arms for personal use (including self-defense) was regarded at the time of the framing as one of the fundamental rights of Englishmen. Once the history was understood, it was difficult to regard the guarantee of the Second Amendment as no more than a guarantee of the right to join a militia. Moreover, the prefatory clause of the Second Amendment ("A well regulated militia being necessary for the defense of a free state") could not be logically reconciled with a personal right to keep and bear arms without the

---

have nine historians on the Court.' Scalia says . . . that a court of nine historians sounds better than a court of nine ethicists.").

4   Kent Greenawalt, *Legal Interpretation: Perspectives from Other Disciplines and Private Texts* 168 (2010).

5   *See, e.g.*, *The Oxford English Dictionary* (2d ed. 1989).

6   *District of Columbia v. Heller*, 554 U.S. 570 (2008) (per Scalia, J.).

historical knowledge (possessed by the framing generation) that the Stuart kings had destroyed the people's militia by disarming those whom they disfavored. Here the opinion was dealing with history in a broad sense.

It is reasonable to ask whether lawyers and judges can adequately perform historical inquiry of this sort. Those who oppose originalism exaggerate the task. In some cases, to be sure, it *is* difficult, and originalists will differ among themselves on the correct answer.[7] But that is the exception, not the rule. In most cases—and especially the most controversial ones—the originalist answer is entirely clear. There is no historical support whatever for the proposition that any provision in the Constitution guaranteed a right to abortion, or to sodomy, or to assisted suicide. Those acts were criminal in all the states for two centuries. Nor is there any historical support for the proposition that the Eighth Amendment (which prohibits cruel and unusual punishments) prohibited the death penalty, which was the *only* penalty for a felony (indeed, the definition of a felony) at the time of the framing.

Today's lawyers and judges, when analyzing historical questions, have more tools than ever before. They can look to an ever-growing body of scholarship produced by the legions of academic legal historians populating law and history faculties at our leading universities.[8] No history faculty of any note would consider itself complete without legal experts; and no law faculty would consider itself complete without its share of expert historians.

Judges also benefit from increasingly sophisticated and thorough—sometimes too thorough—amicus briefs that are filed on nearly every appellate case of note. In 1988, when the Supreme Court considered whether the Eighth Amendment barred the execution of someone who was under the age of 16 at the time of

---

7   *See, e.g., McIntyre v. Ohio Elections Comm'n*, 514 U.S. 334 (1995) (in which Scalia, J., and Thomas, J., reached different conclusions regarding the question whether "the freedom of speech" guaranteed by the First Amendment included the right to speak anonymously).

8   *See, e.g.,* Neil M. Richards, *Clio and the Court: A Reassessment of the Supreme Court's Uses of History*, 13 J.L. & Pol. 809, 819–20 (1997); Lawrence M. Friedman, *American Legal History: Past and Present*, 34 J. Legal Educ. 563 (1984) (discussing "booming" field of American legal history).

the offense,[9] any Justice interested in the original meaning of the phrase *cruel and unusual punishments* would look in vain for help from the parties or their amici. Briefs about child psychology—yes. Briefs about international law—plenty. But not a single brief reflecting on the history of the Eighth Amendment or the practices it was understood to condemn at the time of the founding. Twenty years later, in the *Heller* case, the amicus briefing presented an array of historical material whose thoroughness would have been unthinkable earlier. One amicus brief included an appendix consisting of a nearly 200-page collection of historical materials relating to the "right to bear arms" as it was understood at the time of the founding. Several amicus briefs were submitted on behalf of professors of history and professors of law specializing in Anglo-American legal history, the history of the founding era, and American constitutional history. The Court had the help of many experts who gathered and presented the relevant evidence needed to interpret the Second Amendment's meaning.

Originalism does not always provide an easy answer, or even a clear one. Originalism is not perfect. But it is more certain than any other criterion. And this is not even a close question. In ease of lawyerly application (never mind legitimacy and predictability), originalism surpasses competing approaches. Lawyers are trained to read statutes. They are not trained to be moral philosophers, which is what it takes to evaluate whether there should be (and hence is) a right to abortion, sodomy, assisted suicide, and many another proposed innovation. History is a rock-hard science compared to moral philosophy. Even those questions that are the easiest for the originalist—abortion, assisted suicide, sodomy, the death penalty—pose enormous difficulties for nonoriginalists, who must agonize over what the modern Constitution *ought to* mean with regard to each of them. And since times change, they must agonize over the very same questions every five or ten years.

---

9   *Thompson v. Oklahoma*, 487 U.S. 815 (1988) (Stevens, J., plurality opinion).

70. The false notion that the Living Constitution is an exception to the rule that legal texts must be given the meaning they bore when adopted.

"The meaning of the constitution is fixed when it is
adopted, and it is not different at any subsequent time
when a court has occasion to pass upon it."
Thomas M. Cooley,
A Treatise on the Constitutional Limitations
Which Rest upon the Legislative Power of the
States of the American Union 55 (1868).

Although judges generally decline theorists' calls to update unamended statutes, the updating of constitutional provisions is very much in vogue. Many now embrace the notion that the Constitution is a "living document" whose meaning evolves as the times require. These constitutional evolutionists pay little heed to what the Framers were doing. Consider this representative passage from a modern author:

> Legal indeterminacy is more than a necessity: It is also a
> *positive* factor in a constitutional system. Dynamic rather
> than static interpretations of concepts such as "due process"
> and "equal protection" allow future generations to respond
> to new ideas of justice arguably superior to those possessed
> by the framers . . . . A jurisprudence that goes beyond past
> ideas to include newer ones incorporates the values not
> only of the framers but also of the intervening generations
> and of the present. Any or all of these ideas may be wrong,
> unjust, or incomplete. But surely that risk is preferable to
> a limited approach that ensures that the errors of the past
> will be frozen into law beyond correction.[1]

What possible justification is there for treating the Constitution differently from all other legal texts? Some commentators point out that "[t]he language of the Constitution does not say whether the original understanding controls its meaning."[2] But

---

1   Judith A. Baer, "The Fruitless Search for Original Intent," in *Judging the Constitution: Critical Essays on Judicial Lawmaking* 49, 65 (Michael W. McCann & Gerald L. Houseman eds., 1989).

2   Cass R. Sunstein, *The Partial Constitution* 102 (1993). *Cf.* Jack N. Rakove, *Original Meanings: Politics and Ideas in the Making of the Constitution* 368 (1996) ("If nothing in the text of the Constitution literally constrains or even instructs us

neither does the language of statutes, and we do not allow courts to "update" them. Moreover, there was no need for the Framers to specify that their product was to be treated as an "originalist" text. There were no other sorts of legal texts. There were no 18th-century textual evolutionists. Blackstone made it very clear that original meaning governed,[3] and the supporters of evolving meanings in legal texts can point to no contemporaneous commentators who differed with him.[4]

One might suppose that the Framers of the Constitution never envisioned that their text would endure for 250 or more years, and that they would not have wanted to confine future interpreters to their own historical visions. This is pure speculation, and implausible speculation at that. The Framers knew very well that Magna Carta, drafted in 1215, was still the law of England in the late 1700s—more than 570 years later.[5] The lawyers among the Framers knew very well, as all informed lawyers of the day would have, that cases arose from time to time on the basis of its wording.[6] Steeped in classical learning, the Framers thought about and

---

to read it as its framers and ratifiers might have done, we may still have soundly Madisonian reasons for attempting to recover its original meanings.").

3   1 William Blackstone, *Commentaries on the Laws of England* 60 (4th ed. 1770).

4   *See* John O. McGinnis & Michael B. Rappaport, *Original Methods Originalism: A New Theory of Interpretation and the Case Against Construction*, 103 Nw. U. L. Rev. 751, 802 (2009) ("Nothing in the historical record . . . suggests that the original methods included living constitutionalism or other principles permitting interpreters to update the Constitution to reflect changing values."). *See also* Thomas M. Cooley, *A Treatise on the Constitutional Limitations Which Rest upon the Legislative Power of the States of the American Union* 54 (1868) ("A principal share of the benefit expected from a written constitution would be lost if the rules they established were so flexible as to bend to circumstances or be modified by public opinion.").

5   *See, e.g.*, Daines Barrington, *Observations on the More Ancient Statutes: From Magna Charta to the Twenty-First of James I. Cap. XXVII* 1 (5th ed. 1796) (noting, in its very first sentence, that "particular chapters of Magna Charta . . . may at present be enforced").

6   *See, e.g.*, *R. v. Inhabitants of the W. Riding of Yorkshire*, [1770] 5 Burrow 2594, 2597 (observing that the plain language of Magna Carta did not obligate a town to build or maintain a bridge); *Tonson v. Collins*, [1761] 1 Blackstone W. 321, 340 (in which the court was called on to apply the language of Magna Carta to a copyright matter); *Digges's Lessee v. Beale*, 1 H. & McH. 67 (Prov. Ct. Md. 1726) (in which the argument was that a minor had the right to present a defense under Magna Carta).

used precedents hundreds and even thousands of years old. As we have shown, the idea that legal texts might be subject to semantic drift was alien to their modes of thought. The evolutionists sometimes appeal to Chief Justice Marshall's famous line in *McCulloch v. Maryland* that "we must never forget, that it is a *constitution* we are expounding."[7] But far from suggesting that the Constitution evolves, its whole point was just the opposite. Marshall said it to justify his holding that the word *necessary* in the Necessary and Proper Clause[8] should not be construed to "exclude . . . the choice of means, and leave . . . to Congress, in each case, that only which is most direct and simple."[9] Why? Precisely because "[t]his provision is made in a constitution, intended to endure for ages to come, and, consequently, to be adapted to the various *crises* of human affairs."[10] There would be no need to give the provision an expansive reading if today's narrow reading could be changed ("evolved") tomorrow as the need arises. In a later case, Marshall affirmed that the Constitution was "an instrument, which was intended to be perpetual."[11]

Yet the constitutional evolutionists will say that we have been living under the Living Constitution for so long that it is too late to go back. In fact, however, the notion of a Living Constitution, or at least general acceptance of that notion, is pretty new, dating from the time of the Warren Court (1953–1969). Yes, there were willful judicial distortions of the Constitution before that time (willful judges have always been with us). For example, the Court added to the tripartite federal government a headless

---

7   17 U.S. (4 Wheat.) 316, 407 (1819) (per Marshall, C.J.). This has been such a rallying cry for the constitutional evolutionists that it is the title of a publication on the website of the American Constitution Society for Law and Public Policy, a group that favors the Living Constitution. *See We Must Never Forget, That It Is a Constitution We Are Expounding: Collected Writings on Interpreting Our Founding Document* at http://www.acslaw.org/pdf/ACS_Expounding_FNL.pdf.

8   U.S. Const., art. I, § 8, cl. 18.

9   *McCulloch*, 17 U.S. at 413.

10   *Id.* at 415.

11   *Ogden v. Saunders*, 25 U.S. (12 Wheat.) 213, 355 (1827) (opinion of Marshall, C.J.).

Fourth Branch in *Humphrey's Executor v. United States*[12] (in which the Court held that Congress could make certain agency heads immune from presidential removal and control) and expanded the Commerce Clause beyond all reason in *Wickard v. Filburn*[13] (in which the Court held that a farmer's cultivation of wheat for his own consumption affected interstate commerce and thus could be regulated under the Commerce Clause). But earlier judges went about revising the Constitution the good old-fashioned way: They distorted its meaning. You will find no indication in *Humphrey's Executor* or *Wickard* that it was anything other than the *original* principle of presidential power or the *original* scope of the Commerce Clause being applied. But plausible distortion has its limits: No one would believe, for example, that the Eighth Amendment prohibited the death penalty, since that was the only penalty for a felony (it was the definition of a felony) when the Eighth Amendment was adopted. But a Living Constitution can get us there easily.

One defender of the Living Constitution asserts that most of the important constitutional language "was almost certainly selected for its open-endedness and its capacity for *redefinition* over time."[14] Open-endedness, yes; redefinition, no. There is simply no evidence to support this notion. And there is a mountain of evidence to the contrary, including many expressions of belief in an unchanging Constitution (see § 7 [fixed-meaning canon]). Amendable, yes;[15] changing, no.

---

12 295 U.S. 602 (1935) (per Sutherland, J.).

13 317 U.S. 111 (1942) (per Jackson, J.).

14 Alan M. Dershowitz, "The Sovereignty of Process: The Limits of Original Intention," in *Politics and the Constitution: The Nature and Intent of Interpretation* 11, 12 (1990) (emphasis added). *Cf.* Cass R. Sunstein, *The Partial Constitution* 99 (1993) ("The breadth of the words of the Constitution invites the view that its meaning is capable of change over time."); Laurence H. Tribe, "Comment," in Antonin Scalia, *A Matter of Interpretation: Federal Courts and the Law* 87 (1997) (stating that "constitutional provisions . . . are launched upon [a] historic journey" and that they "speak across generations, projecting a set of messages undergoing episodic revisions").

15 *But see* William Van Alstyne, "Clashing Visions of a 'Living' Constitution: Of Opportunists and Obligationists," in *Cato Supreme Court Review 2010–2011* 13, 20 (2011) (arguing that nonoriginalism weakens amendability: "[T]here is a greater collective suspicion of 'new' amendments because, I believe, it is feared

Then there is the commonsense point: If an open-ended provision whose application to extant phenomena can be "redefined"—a First Amendment, for example, that can be redefined not to protect offensive speech—it is an open-ended guarantee that guarantees nothing at all. A Cruel and Unusual Punishments Clause ensuring merely that future generations do nothing *they* consider cruel—a clause that means, in effect, "to thine own self be true"—is of little use. The open-ended provisions of our Constitution permit or forbid forever those extant phenomena that they were understood to permit or forbid when adopted. And their application to future new phenomena must accord with their application to then-extant phenomena. So the Eighth Amendment's prohibition of cruel and unusual punishments prohibits neither the death penalty nor any manner of imposing that penalty that is less cruel than hanging, which was an accepted manner in 1791. It is not left to future judges to determine in the abstract, with no governing standards, whether electrocution or lethal injection is "cruel." Otherwise, they might be equally free to find that burning at the stake is not cruel.

Further, why would anyone think that the judges are appropriate spokesmen for "the people"? Do they have some special capacity to discern what people think? Quite to the contrary: Judges have no expertise whatever in assessing public opinion. Extremely few federal judges have ever even run for office. And in all their other judicial work (apart, that is, from revising the meaning of the Constitution) they are forbidden to consult public opinion. Whenever they invalidate a federal statute that violates the Bill of Rights, they tell public opinion to get lost. And in all their cases they have no capacity to conduct surveys, since they are limited to what litigants tell them and what may be found in the public record. The most accurate spokesmen for the people of each generation are the legislators that those people elect to represent them.

Which means that if the Living Constitution advocates are correct, if the American Constitution should mean whatever each

today that enactment of additional text may just give judges and others still greater license to use that language as one more springboard for reshaping our constitutional regime.").

successive generation of Americans thinks it ought to mean, then
Marbury v. Madison[16] was wrongly decided. The members of Congress take the same oath to support the Constitution that the Justices do.[17] *Marbury v. Madison's* holding that the Supreme Court
can disregard Congress's determination of what the Constitution
requires is firmly rooted in the reasoning that the Constitution is
a law, whose meaning, like that of other laws, can be discerned
by law-trained judges. If it is not that, but is instead an open invitation for each generation to give its capacious terms whatever
meaning that generation favors, then our Constitution, like that
of England's, should be whatever the legislature believes it to be.[18]
Or to put the point differently: Only in the theater of the absurd
does an aristocratic, life-tenured, unelected council of elders set
aside laws enacted by the people's chosen representatives on the
ground that the people do not want those laws.

Yet in announcing its Living Constitution opinions, the Supreme Court has not relied on the will of the people. In its earliest expansion of the Eighth Amendment, in 1977, it purported
to do so, observing that only one state continued to impose the
death penalty for the rape of an adult.[19] (This as though the fact
that other states had abolished it showed that they had concluded
that it was not only unnecessary or excessive but positively beyond
the pale.) But in later cases, the supposed "national consensus" of
unconstitutionality to which the Court pointed became less and
less plausible, reaching the zenith of implausibility in an opinion
asserting that society's belief that it is unconstitutional to impose
the death penalty for a murder committed by someone under the
age of 18 was demonstrated by the fact that 18 of the 38 states

---

16   5 U.S. (1 Cranch) 137 (1803) (per Marshall, C.J.).

17   *See* Art. VII, cl. 3.

18   Some academics follow Living Constitutionalism to this logical conclusion. *See
     generally* Larry D. Kramer, *The People Themselves: Popular Constitutionalism and
     Judicial Review* (2004); Robert C. Post & Reva B. Siegel, *Legislative Constitu-
     tionalism and Section Five Power: Policentric Interpretation of the Family Medical
     Leave Act*, 112 Yale L.J. 1943 (2003).

19   *Coker v. Georgia*, 433 U.S. 584, 595–96 (1977) (per White, J.).

retaining the death penalty imposed that limitation.[20] Ultimately, the Court abandoned the pretense and said straight-out that what the people think does not matter: "[I]n the end our own judgment will be brought to bear on the question of the acceptability of the death penalty under the Eighth Amendment."[21]

Let us consider this hypothesis: that courts are authorized to give a different meaning to the Constitution not as perceivers of what the people want but as the wise dispensers of judgments about social changes required in the fullness of time. Is there any basis whatever for believing that that is what the Framers, and those who ratified the Constitution, understood? No. The Amendment Clause, article V,[22] prescribes a rigorous and cumbersome method for amending the document; it is implausible that the design was for this to be short-circuited by simply persuading the Supreme Court that interpretive reform is a good idea. "What a court is to do," wrote the celebrated 19th-century jurist Thomas M. Cooley, "is to *declare the law as written*, leaving it to the people themselves to make such changes as new circumstances may require."[23]

The fact that the Constitution uses general terms is no indication that courts can change their meaning—any more than that would hold true for the many statutes that speak in generalities. The acid test is whether the Constitution would have been ratified if it had stated expressly what evolutionists assert that it implies: "The general terms of this Constitution have no fixed application, but permit and forbid what the Supreme Court may from time to time hold that they ought to permit and forbid." Not likely.

The very name *Living Constitution* is misleading. It conveys the impression of a system designed to be flexible and adaptable.

---

20 *Roper v. Simmons*, 543 U.S. 551, 564–68 (2005). The Court transformed these statistics into a proof that "the majority of states" believed that under-18 murderers deserve a special "juvenile" exemption from the death penalty by counting within that majority the states that did not have the death penalty at all. *Id.* at 567. *See also id.* at 609–11 (Scalia, J., dissenting).

21 *Id.* at 563 (quoting *Coker*, 433 U.S. at 597).

22 U.S. Const. art. V.

23 Thomas M. Cooley, *A Treatise on the Constitutional Limitations Which Rest upon the Legislative Power of the States of the American Union* 55 (1868) (emphasis in original).

This quality is touted by the advocates of the system, who speak metaphorically of the Constitution as a "living organism" that must grow with society or else "become brittle and snap." It is not a living organism—any more than any other legal prescription is. And the notion that the advocates of the Living Constitution want to bring us flexibility and openness to change is a fraud and a delusion. All one needs for flexibility and change is a ballot box and a legislature. The advocates of the Living Constitution want to bring us what constitutions are designed to impart: rigidity and difficulty of change. The originalists' Constitution produces a flexible and adaptable political system. Do the people want the death penalty? The Constitution neither requires nor forbids it, so they can impose or abolish it, as they wish. And they can change their mind—abolishing it and then reinstituting it when the incidence of murder increases. When, however, Living Constitutionalists read a prohibition of the death penalty into the Constitution— and no fewer than four Supreme Court Justices who served during the tenure of your judicial coauthor would have done so—all flexibility is at an end. It would thereafter be of no use debating the merits of the death penalty, just as it is of no use debating the merits of prohibiting abortion. The subject has simply been eliminated from the arena of democratic choice.[24] And that is not, we reemphasize, an accidental consequence of the Living Constitution: It is the whole purpose that this fictitious construct is designed to serve. Persuading five Justices is so much easier than persuading Congress or 50 state legislatures—and what the Justices enshrine in the Constitution lasts forever. In practice, the Living Constitution would better be called the Dead Democracy.

---

24 *See* Gerald N. Rosenberg, *The Hollow Hope: Can Courts Bring About Social Change?* 12 (2d ed. 2008) (warning of "the danger that litigation by the few will replace political action by the many and reduce the democratic nature of the American polity"). *Cf.* James Bradley Thayer, *John Marshall* 107 (1901) (observing that the "tendency of a common and easy resort" to litigation to achieve the invalidation of statutes passed by democratically accountable branches of government would "dwarf the political capacity of the people").

Afterword

We have set forth what we consider to be the best available approach to textual interpretation—an approach both linguistic and historical. Some will argue that a widespread adoption of these techniques would be to "turn back the clock"—that it would be an unacceptable retrenchment on the privacy protections and much of the Bill of Rights law that developed in the latter half of the 20th century. One Living Constitutionalist writes: "[I]t should be clear that an extraordinarily radical purge of established constitutional doctrine would be required if we candidly and consistently applied the pure interpretive model. Surely that makes out at least a prima facie case against the model."[1]

Proponents of the Living Constitution worry about a "radical purge" of society's settled practices and beliefs? That is what the Living Constitution has been all about, from *Baker v. Carr*[2] to *Lawrence v. Texas*.[3] While it once pretended to reflect at least the current society's revised beliefs (always as perceived by judges, to be sure), in recent years that pretense has been abandoned, and it has been explicitly acknowledged that the Living Constitution means what reform-minded judges think it should mean. So abortion and homosexual sodomy, which society so much disapproved that they were criminal under the laws of most states and had been for centuries, are now constitutionally protected—and off-limits to the democratic process.

In any case, originalism would not produce the "extraordinarily radical purge of established constitutional doctrine" that its critics say they fear. The chief barrier against such a wrenching purge—by originalism or any other theory of interpretation—is the doctrine of stare decisis. The critics assume that originalism alone, originalism uniquely, is unconstrained by that barrier. It is

---

1   Thomas C. Grey, "Do We Have an Unwritten Constitution?" in *Stanford Legal Essays* 179, 189 (1975). *Cf.* Cass R. Sunstein, *The Partial Constitution* 98 (1993) ("A return to a narrowly described 'original understanding' would result in the elimination, in one bold stroke, of many constitutional safeguards.").

2   369 U.S. 186 (1962) (per Brennan, J.).

3   539 U.S. 558 (2003) (per Kennedy, J.).

not. We do not propose that all the decisions made, and doctrines adopted, in the past half-century or so of unrestrained constitutional improvisation be set aside—only those that fail to meet the criteria for stare decisis. These include consideration of (1) whether harm will be caused to those who justifiably relied on the decision,[4] (2) how clear it is that the decision was textually and historically wrong,[5] (3) whether the decision has been generally accepted by society,[6] and (4) whether the decision permanently places courts in the position of making policy calls appropriate for elected officials.[7] Different proponents of originalism will weigh these vari-

---

4   *See Walton v. Arizona*, 497 U.S. 639, 673 (1990) (Scalia, J., concurring in part & concurring in the judgment) (explaining that stare decisis has little applicability when the earlier caselaw has spawned uncertainty because the doctrine's purpose is that of "introducing certainty and stability into the law and protecting the expectations of individuals and institutions that have acted in reliance on existing rules"); *South Carolina v. Gathers*, 490 U.S. 805, 824 (1989) (Scalia, J., dissenting) ("The freshness of error not only deprives [the earlier case] of the respect to which long-established practice is entitled, but also counsels that the opportunity of correction be seized at once, before state and federal laws and practices have been adjusted to embody it."). *See also* Thomas M. Cooley, *A Treatise on the Constitutional Limitations Which Rest upon the Legislative Power of the States of the American Union* 52 (1868) ("Before [disregarding stare decisis], . . . it will be well to consider whether the point involved is such as to have become a rule of property, so that titles have been acquired in reliance upon it, and vested rights will be disturbed by any change.").

5   *See Payne v. Tennessee*, 501 U.S. 808, 834 (1991) (Scalia, J., concurring) (supporting the overruling of *Booth v. Maryland*, 482 U.S. 496 (1987): "If there was ever a case that defied reason, it was *Booth* . . . , imposing a constitutional rule that had absolutely no basis in constitutional text, in historical practice, or in logic."); *United States v. International Boxing Club of N.Y., Inc.*, 348 U.S. 236, 249 (1955) (Frankfurter, J., dissenting) ("That doctrine [of stare decisis] is not, to be sure, an imprisonment of reason.").

6   *See* John O. McGinnis & Michael B. Rappaport, *A Pragmatic Defense of Originalism*, 31 Harv. J. L. & Pub. Pol'y 917, 922 (2008) (noting that the Constitution, containing entrenched norms with substantial consensus, "creates legitimacy, allegiance, and even affection as citizens come to regard the entrenched norms as part of their common bond").

7   *See Tennessee v. Lane*, 541 U.S. 509, 556 (2004) (Scalia, J., dissenting) (declining to give stare decisis effect to "congruence and proportionality" tests for § 5 of the Fourteenth Amendment). *See also, e.g., Ewing v. California*, 538 U.S. 11, 31–32 (2003) (Scalia, J., concurring) (declining to give stare decisis effect to a "proportionality" test for violation of the Eighth Amendment); *Stenberg v. Carhart*, 530 U.S. 914, 954–56 (2000) (Scalia, J., dissenting) (declining to give stare decisis effect to the "undue burden" standard of *Planned Parenthood of S.E. Pa. v. Casey*, 505 U.S. 833 (1992) (plurality opinion)).

ous factors in different ways.[8] Your authors, for example, believe that the Supreme Court should not give stare decisis effect to *Roe v. Wade*,[9] which even its defenders acknowledge was an analytically unsound opinion that has not received general acceptance, and which (as revised by *Casey*[10]) places judges in the position of making the policy call whether particular restrictions on abortion impose an "undue burden."[11] We would, on the other hand, accept as settled law the incorporation doctrine[12]—whereby the Bill of Rights is made applicable to the states by interpreting the Fourteenth Amendment's Due Process Clause as encompassing it—even though it is based on an interpretation of the Due Process Clause (so-called substantive due process) that the words will not bear. And we would accept most, though not all, other prior applications of substantive due process, though we would not apply that atextual doctrine anew in the future.

Stare decisis—a doctrine whose function "is to make us say that what is false under proper analysis must nonetheless be held to be true, all in the interest of stability"[13]—is not a part of

---

8   *See, e.g.*, Charles A. Beard, "Judicial Review and 'the Intent of the Framers'" (1912), in *Essays in Constitutional Law* 20, 23–24 (Robert G. McCloskey ed., 1957) ("When the judge or the scholar is faced by a seeming conflict between historical intent and orthodox interpretation, no naive rule-of-thumb is available to make his task easy. He is forced to a delicate choice which might involve, for a beginning, such factors as the conclusiveness of the historical evidence, the weight of the precedents that have been built up to support a counter-view, and the disturbance to settled institutions threatened by the proposed change.").

9   410 U.S. 113 (1973) (per Blackmun, J.). *See Helvering v. Hallock*, 309 U.S. 106, 121 (1940) (per Frankfurter, J.) ("This Court, unlike the House of Lords, has from the beginning rejected a doctrine of disability at self-correction.").

10 *Planned Parenthood of S.E. Pa. v. Casey*, 505 U.S. 833 (1992) (plurality opinion).

11 *See, e.g.*, *Gonzales v. Carhart*, 550 U.S. 124, 146 (2007).

12 *See, e.g.*, *Wallace v. Jaffree*, 472 U.S. 38, 48–49 (1985) (per Stevens, J.) (explaining applicability of First Amendment's Establishment Clause to the states through the Fourteenth Amendment); *Malloy v. Hogan*, 378 U.S. 1, 6 (1964) (per Brennan, J.) (holding that Fifth Amendment's prohibition of compulsory self-incrimination is protected by the Fourteenth Amendment against abridgment by the States).

13 Antonin Scalia, *A Matter of Interpretation: Federal Courts and the Law* 138–40 (1997). *See Patterson v. McLean Credit Union*, 491 U.S. 164, 172 (1989) (per Kennedy, J.) (unanimously reaffirming, in the interests of stability, *Runyon v. McCrary*, 427 U.S. 160 (1976) (per Stewart, J.), though some Justices considered the precedent incorrect).

textualism. It is an exception to textualism (as it is to any theory of interpretation) born not of logic but of necessity. Courts cannot consider anew every previously decided question that comes before them. Stare decisis has been a part of our law from time immemorial, and we must bow to it. All we categorically propose here is that, when a governing precedent deserving of stare decisis effect does not dictate a contrary disposition, judges ought to use proper methods of textual interpretation. If they will do that, then over time the law will be more certain, and the rule of law will be more secure.

Appendix A

A Note on the Use of Dictionaries

> "When [lawyers and judges] look up a word in a dictionary—and
> they often do—they are as likely as not to select a poor dictionary."
> —Max Radin, "A Juster Justice, a More Lawful Law,"
> in *Legal Essays in Tribute to Orrin Kip McMurray*
> 537, 538 (Max Radin & A.M. Kidd eds., 1935).

Lord Macmillan was hardly overstating the case in 1938 when he said that "one of the chief functions of our courts is to act as an animated and authoritative dictionary."[1] The reason is that with legal interpretation, inevitably "[t]he words used by one set of persons have to be interpreted by another set of persons."[2] So it is understandable that so-called judicial dictionaries have been assembled over the years—sometimes vast compilations of judicial pronouncements about what a given word or phrase means. In that genre, the leading American text is the 132-volume set of *Words and Phrases* (permanent edition updated yearly); the leading British text is the 3-volume *Stroud's Judicial Dictionary* (6th ed. 2000).

Unsurprisingly, in their work as part-time lexicographers, judges frequently have occasion to consult the work of professional lexicographers. In § 6, we criticized an appellate judge for relying on a "nonscholarly" dictionary—the 1980 edition of the *Oxford American Dictionary* (see p. 75). In lexicographic circles, that book is known to have been hastily put together by two editors on short notice, and very much on the cheap. The main part of the dictionary runs to only 816 pages. The look and feel of the book do not impress the user as being scholarly. By *scholarly* we mean weighty. Not superficial. Chock-full of erudition. Later editions of that dictionary, by contrast, are better works of scholarship.

Consider an illuminating example of how an uncritical approach to dictionaries can mislead judges—an example akin to

---

1   Lord Macmillan, *Law and Other Things* 163 (1938).

2   *Id.*

one we have already considered. Let us say that you are a judge called on to decide whether fighting cocks qualify as *poultry* under a recent statute that gives a tax deduction for any person who "rears poultry." And assume, for the purposes of this hypothetical decision, that cockfighting is not illegal in your jurisdiction. You consult a dictionary for whatever light it might shine on this definitional issue. But which one? If you are linguistically naive, you might suppose that dictionaries are all basically the same. You have in your office five dictionaries of not-too-distant vintage whose definitions are as follows:

- **1951:** "domestic fowls collectively, as chickens, turkeys, guinea fowls, ducks, and geese."[3]

- **1956:** "domestic fowls, generally or collectively, as hens, ducks, etc."[4]

- **1975:** "domestic fowls, as chickens, ducks, turkeys, and geese."[5]

- **1999:** "chickens, turkeys, ducks, and geese; domestic fowl."[6]

- **2003:** "domestic fowls collectively."[7]

You might be tempted to reason from these definitions that (1) fighting cocks are raised in pens and are not found in the wild—and to that extent are "domesticated"; (2) the definitions stress generality and collectiveness, so this type of fowl would seem to qualify; and (3) fighting cocks as a matter of fact are chickens, and chickens are explicitly mentioned in three of the five definitions.

And if you so reasoned, you would arrive at an incorrect result mainly because of the unreliable, rather threadbare definitions you have consulted.

---

3   *The American College Dictionary* 949 (1951).

4   *Funk & Wagnalls New College Standard Dictionary* 919 (1956).

5   *The Doubleday Dictionary for Home, School, and Office* 568 (1975).

6   *The Concise Oxford Dictionary* 1121 (10th ed. 1999).

7   *The Times English Dictionary and Thesaurus* 920 (2d ed. 2003).

The all-important element found in unabridged dictionaries— and even in the better desktop dictionaries—is that poultry is used for food. These definitions are much superior because they are fuller and more explanatory:

- **1934:** "any domesticated birds which serve as a source of food, either eggs or meat."[8]

- **1971:** "domesticated birds kept for eggs or meat."[9]

- **1987:** "domesticated fowl collectively, esp. those valued for their meat and eggs, as chickens, turkeys, ducks, geese, and guinea fowl."[10]

- **1993:** "Domestic fowl; birds commonly reared for meat, eggs, or feathers in a yard, barn or other enclosure, as chickens, ducks, geese, turkeys, or guinea-fowl (usu. excluding game-birds, as pigeons, pheasants, etc.). Also, such birds as a source of food."[11]

- **2007:** "domestic fowls raised for meat or eggs; chickens, turkeys, ducks, geese, etc. collectively."[12]

- **2011:** "domesticated fowl, such as chickens, turkeys, ducks, or geese, raised for meat or eggs."[13]

Because these definitions give a much different view of the word's scope, they would almost certainly prevent a judge from coming to the false conclusion that fighting cocks qualify as poultry.

Hence a comparative weighing of dictionaries is often necessary.[14] In one case, the Supreme Court of the United States had to decide whether *modify* in a telecommunications statute meant

---

8   *Webster's Second New International Dictionary* 1934 (1934).

9   *Webster's Seventh New Collegiate Dictionary* 665 (1971) (same definition in 11th ed. 2003).

10   *Random House Dictionary of the English Language* 1515 (2d ed. 1987).

11   2 *The New Shorter Oxford English Dictionary* 2312 (4th ed. 1993).

12   *Webster's New World College Dictionary* 1127 (4th ed. 2007).

13   *American Heritage Dictionary of the English Language* 1380 (5th ed. 2011).

14   *See* Michael B.W. Sinclair, *Guide to Statutory Interpretation* 137 (2000) ("[I]f you use a dictionary, use more than one and check editions from the date of enactment as well as current.").

"to change moderately" or "to change fundamentally."[15] The petitioners cited only a single dictionary supporting the fundamental-change sense—the notoriously permissive *Webster's Third New International Dictionary* (1961)—when all the other cited dictionaries supported the moderate-change sense.[16] The Court properly rejected the idea that the out-of-step definition created a genuine ambiguity.[17]

But courts must take care in such analyses. Occasionally most dictionaries will define a word inadequately—without accounting for its semantic nuances as they may shift from context to context—and a given dictionary will improve on the others. When that is so, the more advanced semantic analysis will be preferable.

The primary principles to remember in using dictionaries are these:

- A dictionary definition states the core meanings of a term. It cannot delineate the periphery.

- Because common words typically have more than one meaning, you must use the context in which a given word appears to determine its aptest, most likely sense.

- You must consult the prefatory material to understand the principles on which the dictionary has been assembled. The ordering of senses provides a classic example. Although many people assume that the first sense listed in a dictionary is the "main" sense, that is often quite untrue.[18] Some dictionaries list senses from oldest in the language (putting obsolete or archaic senses first) to newest. Others list them according to current frequency. Using a dictionary know-

---

15   *MCI Telecomms. Corp. v. AT&T Co.*, 512 U.S. 218 (1994) (per Scalia, J.) (interpreting 47 U.S.C. § 203(b)(2)).

16   *Id.* at 225–26.

17   *Id.* at 226–28.

18   *See Muscarello v. United States*, 524 U.S. 125, 128 (1998) (per Breyer, J.) (erroneously suggesting that the first meaning listed in the *Oxford English Dictionary* is the "primary meaning," as opposed to the oldest). *Cf. Mississippi Poultry Ass'n, Inc. v. Madigan*, 992 F.2d 1359, 1369 (5th Cir. 1993) (Reavley, J., dissenting) ("I cannot imagine that the majority favors interpreting statutes by choosing the first definition that appears in a dictionary."), *aff'd on reh'g*, 31 F.3d 293 (5th Cir. 1994) (en banc).

ledgeably requires a close reading of the principles discussed at the outset.

- Dictionaries tend to lag behind linguistic realities—so a term now known to have first occurred in print in 1900 might not have made its way into a dictionary until 1950 or even 2000. If you are seeking to ascertain the meaning of a term in an 1819 statute, it is generally quite permissible to consult an 1828 dictionary.
- Historical dictionaries, such as *The Oxford English Dictionary* (20 vols.; 2d ed. 1989; updated online) or the out-of-print *Century Dictionary* (12 vols.; last revised 1914), are the most reliable sources for historical terms. But they are often least useful for very recent shifts in meaning.

Among contemporaneous-usage dictionaries—those that reflect meanings current at a given time—the following are the most useful and authoritative for the English language generally and for law. Note, however, that *The Oxford English Dictionary* is also useful for each period because it shows the historical development of word-senses.

1750–1800

English Language

1755: Samuel Johnson, *A Dictionary of the English Language*, 2 vols. (appearing also in a second edition of 1756, a third of 1765, and a fourth of 1773; the final edition in Johnson's lifetime was the fifth edition of 1784)

1757: Nathan Bailey, *A Universal Etymological English Dictionary* (14th ed.—issued in many editions of roughly comparable quality)

1760: Thomas Dyche & William Pardon, *A New General English Dictionary* (12th ed.—issued in many editions of roughly comparable quality)

1775: John Ash, *The New and Complete Dictionary of the English Language*, 2 vols.

Law

1771: Timothy Cunningham, *A New and Complete Law Dictionary*, 2 vols. (2d ed. 1771; 3d ed. 1783)

1772: Giles Jacob, *A New Law Dictionary* (9th ed. 1772; 10th ed. 1782)

1792: Richard Burn, *A New Law Dictionary*, 2 vols.

1797–1798: William Marriot, *A New Law Dictionary*, 4 vols. (an updating of Cunningham[19])

1801–1850

English Language

1806: Noah Webster, *A Comprehensive Dictionary of the English Language* (an abridged dictionary containing brief definitions of only the most common terms)

1818: Samuel Johnson, *A Dictionary of the English Language*, 5 vols. (H.J. Todd ed.)

1828: Noah Webster, *An American Dictionary of the English Language*, 2 vols. (an unabridged dictionary)

1850: John Boag, *A Popular and Complete English Dictionary*, 2 vols.

Law

1803: Thomas Potts, *A Compendious Law Dictionary*

1816: Thomas Walter Williams, *A Compendious and Comprehensive Law Dictionary*

1829: James Whishaw, *A New Law Dictionary*

1835: Thomas Edlyne Tomlins, *The Law-Dictionary*, 2 vols. (also in 1809 and 1820 editions)

1839: John Bouvier, *A Law Dictionary*, 2 vols. (1st ed.)

1847: Henry James Holthouse, *A New Law Dictionary* (Henry Penington ed., Am. ed.)

---

19 *See* Bryan A. Garner, Introduction to William Marriot, *A New Law Dictionary* (1797; repr. 2011) (demonstrating that Marriot's work was not a new dictionary, but only a new edition of Cunningham).

1850: Alexander M. Burrill, *A New Law Dictionary and Glossary*

1851–1900

English Language

1860: Joseph Worcester, *A Dictionary of the English Language* (or other editions during the period)

1882: Robert Gordon Latham, *A Dictionary of the English Language*, 2 vols. (an updating of Johnson)

1882: James Stormonth, *A Dictionary of the English Language*

1882: Noah Webster, *A Dictionary of the English Language* (or other editions during the period)

1895: *The Century Dictionary and Cyclopedia*, 10 vols.

1897: Robert Hunter & Charles Morris, *The Universal Dictionary of the English Language*, 4 vols.

Law

1859: Alexander M. Burrill, *A Law Dictionary and Glossary* (2d ed.)

1860: J.J.S. Wharton, *Law Lexicon, or Dictionary of Jurisprudence* (2d Am. ed.)

1879: Benjamin Vaughn Abbott, *Dictionary of Terms and Phrases Used in American or English Jurisprudence*, 2 vols.

1883: John Bouvier, *A Law Dictionary*, 2 vols. (15th ed.)

1883: Stewart Rapalje & Robert L. Lawrence, *A Dictionary of American and English Law*, 2 vols.

1890: William C. Anderson, *A Dictionary of Law*

1891: Henry Campbell Black, *A Dictionary of Law*

1893: J. Kendrick Kinney, *A Law Dictionary and Glossary*

1901–1950

English Language

1903: *The Century Dictionary and Cyclopedia,* 10 vols. (or other editions during the period)

1933: *The Oxford English Dictionary* (the first complete edition was called *The New English Dictionary*[20])

1934: *Webster's Second New International Dictionary*

1943: *Funk & Wagnalls New Standard Dictionary of the English Language,* 2 vols. (rev. ed.)

Law

1901: Walter A. Shumaker & George Foster Longsdorf, *The Cyclopedic Dictionary of Law*

1910: Henry Campbell Black, *A Law Dictionary,* (2d ed. 1910; 3d ed. [retitled *Black's Law Dictionary*] 1933)

1911: J.J.S. Wharton, *Wharton's Law Lexicon* (W.H. Aggs ed., 11th ed.)

1919: Benjamin W. Pope, *Legal Definitions,* 2 vols.

1940: *Bouvier's Law Dictionary* (William Edward Baldwin ed.) (or other editions during the period)

1951–2000

English Language

1961: *Webster's Third New International Dictionary* (a dictionary to be used cautiously because of its frequent inclusion of doubtful, slipshod meanings without adequate usage notes[21])

---

20 *See* Edward Jenks, *The New Jurisprudence* 90 (1933) ("As a matter of fact, a copy of the *New Oxford Dictionary* has become an almost essential feature of the libraries of most of the English higher tribunals, for the purpose of assisting them in the interpretation of statutes.").

21 *See generally Dictionaries and That Dictionary* (James Sledd & Wilma R. Ebbitt, eds., 1962). *See also MCI Telecomms. Corp. v. AT&T Co.,* 512 U.S. 218, 228 n.3 (1994) (per Scalia, J.) (noting that "[u]pon its long-awaited appearance in 1961, *Webster's Third* was widely criticized for its portrayal of common error as proper

1969: *American Heritage Dictionary of the English Language* (2d ed. 1980; 3d ed. 1996; 4th ed. 2001)

1987: *The Random House Dictionary of the English Language* (2d unabridged ed.)

1989: *The Oxford English Dictionary* (2d ed.)

1993: *Merriam-Webster's Collegiate Dictionary* (10th ed.; 11th ed. 2003)

1996: *Webster's New World College Dictionary* (3d ed.; 4th ed. 2007)

Law

1969: James A. Ballentine, *Ballentine's Law Dictionary* (William S. Anderson ed., 3d ed.)

1970: Max Radin, *Law Dictionary* (Lawrence G. Greene ed., 2d ed.)

1990: *Black's Law Dictionary* (4th ed. 1951; 5th ed. 1981; 6th ed. 1990; 7th ed. 1999)

1995: Bryan A. Garner, *A Dictionary of Modern Legal Usage* (2d ed.)

1996: *Merriam-Webster's Dictionary of Law*

2001–present

English Language (up-to-date editions)

The Oxford English Dictionary (online edition)

American Heritage Dictionary of the English Language

Merriam-Webster's Collegiate Dictionary

The New Oxford American Dictionary

The New Shorter Oxford English Dictionary

Webster's New World College Dictionary

The Cambridge Guide to English Usage

Garner's Modern American Usage

---

usage," and citing as an instance "its approval (without qualification) of the use of 'infer' to mean 'imply'").

Law

2009: *Black's Law Dictionary* (9th ed.)

2011: *Merriam-Webster's Dictionary of Law* (2d ed.)

2011: *Garner's Dictionary of Legal Usage* (3d ed.)

When using modern desktop dictionaries, be sure you have the current edition; they are periodically updated and improved.

Appendix B

A Glossary of Legal Interpretation

absurdity doctrine: The doctrine that a provision may be either disregarded or judicially corrected as an error (when the correction is textually simple) if failing to do so would result in a disposition that no reasonable person could approve (§ 37).

ambiguity: 1. An uncertainty of meaning based not on the scope of a word or phrase but on a semantic dichotomy that gives rise to any of two or more quite different but almost equally plausible interpretations. **2.** Loosely, VAGUENESS. ● We adhere to sense 1 in this text.

antiformalism: An interpretive method that encourages a judge to consider nontextual sources such as purpose, legislative intent, and public policy, thereby giving the courts more discretion to make or create law.—**antiformalist,** n. Cf. FORMALISM.

application: The process by which a decision-maker ascertains the legal category under which the facts at issue should be placed and hence the rule of law that is to govern them.

artificial-person canon: The doctrine that the word *person* includes corporations and other entities, but not the sovereign (§ 44).

associated-words canon: The doctrine that associated words bear on one another's meaning (§ 31). See *noscitur a sociis*.

bicameralism: A system of government with two legislative or parliamentary chambers, both of which must pass a bill before it can become law.

borrowed-statute doctrine: The proposition that if a legislature enacts a statute copied (borrowed) from another jurisdiction, it also borrows the existing settled construction of the statute in the lending state. ● We believe the proposition to be false (see § 54 [prior-construction canon]).

canon of construction: A principle that guides the interpreter of a text on some phase of the interpretive process.

canon of imputed common-law meaning: The doctrine that a statute that uses a common-law term, without defining it, adopts its common-law meaning (§ 53).

casus incogitatus (/**kah**-zəs in-koj-i-**tah**-təs/): A situation unthought of by the author of a legal instrument. Pl. *casus incogitati* (/**kah**-zəs in-koj-i-**tah**-tee/).

casus male inclusus (/**kah**-zəs **mahl**-ee in-**kloo**-səs/): A situation literally provided for by a legal text, but wrongly so in the judge-interpreter's eyes, because the provision's literal application has unintended, undesirable, or even absurd consequences.

casus ōmissus (/**kah**-zəs oh-**mis**-əs/): A situation not provided for by a legal text. Pl. *casus omissi* (/**kah**-zəs oh-**mis**-ee/).

clear-statement rule: A doctrine holding that a legal instrument, esp. a statute, will not have some specified effect unless that result is unquestionably produced by the text. • Examples are the constitutional-doubt canon (§ 38), the presumption against retroactivity (§ 41), and the presumption against waiver of sovereign immunity (§ 46).

conjunctive/disjunctive canon: The doctrine that *and* joins a conjunctive list, *or* a disjunctive list—but with negatives, plurals, and various specific wordings there are nuances (§ 12).

consequentialism: An interpretive theory that assesses the rightness or wrongness of a judge-interpreter's reading according to its extratextual consequences. (See § 61.)

constitutional-avoidance rule: The doctrine that a case should not be resolved by deciding a constitutional question if it can be resolved in some other fashion. • This rule of judicial procedure is not a canon of construction.

constitutional-doubt canon: The doctrine that a statute should be interpreted in a way that avoids placing its constitutionality in doubt (§ 38).

construction: 1. The act or process of interpreting or explaining the meaning of a legal text; the ascertainment of a document's sense in accordance with established judicial standards. **2.** According to some theorists, the judicial imputation of meaning where the text is silent. ● In this treatise and in accordance with prevailing usage, we use *construction* in sense 1—essentially as a synonym of *interpretation*. See INTERPRETATION.

> *purposive construction*: An interpretation that looks to the "evil" that the statute is trying to correct (i.e., the statute's purpose, usually conceived broadly and apart from the limitations of the text).

> *strict construction*: **1.** A narrow, crabbed interpretation. **2.** An interpretation according to the literal meaning of the words, as contrasted with what the words denote in context according to a fair reading.

contra proferentem **rule** (/kon-trə proh-fə-ren-təm/) [fr. Latin *verba chartarum fortius accipiuntur contra proferentem* "the words of a writing are taken more strongly against the person offering them"]: The doctrine that, in the interpretation of private documents, doubts and ambiguities are to be construed unfavorably to the drafter.

derogation canon: The old doctrine that statutes in derogation of the common law are to be strictly construed. ● The fair-reading method rejects this doctrine. (See § 52.)

desuetude (des-wi-tyood): **1.** The longtime discontinuance of a practice or custom. **2.** The civil-law doctrine that if a statute or treaty is left unenforced long enough, it ceases to have legal effect even though it has not been repealed. ● This doctrine has no applicability in common-law systems. (See § 57.)

desuetude canon: The doctrine that a statute is not repealed by nonuse or desuetude (§ 57).

distributive-phrasing canon: The doctrine that distributive phrasing applies each expression to its appropriate referent (§ 33). ● The Latin name for this canon is *reddendo singula singulis* (/rə-den-doh sing-gyə-lə sing-gyə-lees/), meaning (freely translated) "by interpreting distributive terms as distributive." It is often shortened to *reddendo singula.*

eisegesis (/ɪ-sə-**jee**-səs/): The act of reading into a text one's own desired meaning.

ejusdem generis **canon** (/ee-**yoos**-dem **jen**-ə-ris/): The doctrine that where general words follow an enumeration of two or more things, they apply only to persons or things of the same general kind or class specifically mentioned (§ 32). ● The Latin phrase means "of the same kind or class."

equity of the statute: The supposed fair application intended for an enactment, as the interpreter's paramount concern—allowing departures from the statute's literal words. ● This statute-specific ally of purposivism arose in the Middle Ages, mostly fell into disuse by the Renaissance, was thoroughly rejected for most of the 19th century, and has made spasmodic comebacks in American law since then. See PURPOSIVISM.

exegesis (/eks-ə-**jee**-səs/): The explanation of the meaning of a text through close reading.

expressio unius est exclusio alterius (/ek-**spres**-ee-oh **oo**-nee-əs est eks-**kloo**-zee-oh ahl-**tair**-ee-əs/): The expression of one thing is the exclusion of another. (See § 10 [negative-implication canon].)

extraterritoriality canon: The doctrine that a statute presumptively has no extraterritorial application (*statuta suo clauduntur territorio, nec ultra territorium disponunt*) (§ 43).

fair reading: The interpretation that would be given to a text by a reasonable reader, fully competent in the language, who seeks to understand what the text meant at its adoption, and who considers the purpose of the text but derives purpose from the words actually used.

fixed-meaning canon: The doctrine that words must be given the meaning they had when the text was adopted; ORIGINALISM (§ 7). ● "The 'will of Congress' we look to is not a will evolving from Session to Session, but a will expressed and fixed in a particular enactment."[1]

formalism: Decision-making on the basis of form rather than substance; specif., an interpretive method whereby the judge adheres to the words rather than pursuing the text's unexpressed purposes (purposivism) or evaluating its consequences (consequentialism). ● The term is often pejorative. The conclusive argument against a dismissive attitude toward formalism is that the rule of law *is* form—from the requirements for enacting law (majority of both houses, unless the President refuses to sign, in which case two-thirds) to the requirements for applying law (a properly constituted court that has jurisdiction and that follows the dictates of the statute).—**formalist,** n. Cf. ANTIFORMALISM.

gender/number canon: The doctrine that in the absence of a contrary indication, the masculine includes the feminine (and vice versa) and the singular includes the plural (and vice versa) (§ 14).

generalia specialibus non derogant (/jən-ə-**rah**-lee-ə spesh-ee-**ah**-lee-boos non **der**-oh-gahnt/): Things general do not restrict (or detract from) things special. (See § 28 [general/specific canon].)

generalia verba sunt generaliter intelligenda (/jən-ə-**rah**-lee-ə vər-bə suunt jen-ə-**rah**-li-tər in-tel-ə-**jen**-də/): General words are to be understood in a general sense. (See § 9 [general-terms canon].)

general/specific canon: The doctrine that if there is a conflict between a general provision and a specific provision, the specific provision prevails (*generalia specialibus non derogant*) (§ 28).

general-terms canon: The doctrine that general terms are to be given their general meaning (*generalia verba sunt generaliter intelligenda*) (§ 9).

---

1   *West Virginia Univ. Hosp., Inc. v. Casey,* 499 U.S. 83, 101 n.7 (1991) (per Scalia, J.).

grammar canon: The doctrine that words are to be given the meaning that proper grammar and usage would assign them (§ 17).

harmonious-reading canon: The doctrine that the provisions of a text should be interpreted in a way that renders them compatible, not contradictory (§ 27).

Heydon's Case, **rule in:** see MISCHIEF RULE.

imaginative reconstruction: An interpretive approach whereby the judge seeks to resolve a *casus omissus* (an omitted case) by putting himself in the place of the enacting legislature and trying to divine what the collective body would have wanted done. (See § 60.)

inclusio unius est exclusio alterius: see EXPRESSIO UNIUS EST EXCLUSIO ALTERIUS.

in pari materia (/in **pahr**-ee mə-**teer**-ee-ə/) [Latin "in the same matter"]: On the same subject; relating to the same matter. • It is a canon of construction that statutes *in pari materia* should be construed together, so that ambiguities in one statute may be resolved by looking at another statute on the same subject (see § 39 [related-statutes canon]).

interpretation: 1. Properly, the ascertainment of a text's meaning; specif., the determination of how a text most fittingly applies to particular facts. Cf. APPLICATION. **2.** Loosely, the imputation or creation of meaning that is absent from a text. • "Current legislative terminology, by implying a single concept of 'statutory interpretation,' tends to obscure the important difference between the finding of meaning, on the one hand, and the imputation of meaning or the judicial creation of law, on the other."[2] In this treatise, we use *interpretation* in sense 1. See CONSTRUCTION.

liberal interpretation: Broad interpretation of a text's language beyond its permissible meanings, usually with the object of

---

2   Reed Dickerson, Introduction to *Symposium on Judicial Law Making in Relation to Statutes*, 36 Ind. L.J. 411, 413 (1961).

producing the result that the interpreter thinks desirable. (See § 64.)

literal interpretation: An interpretation based strictly on the exact grammatical sense of unambiguous words.

purposive interpretation: **1.** An interpretation that looks to the "evil" that the statute is trying to correct (i.e., the statute's purpose). **2.** See *teleological interpretation*.

spurious interpretation: An interpretation that makes, un-makes, or remakes meaning rather than discovering it. ● According to Roscoe Pound, spurious interpretation "puts a meaning into the text as a juggler puts coins, or what not, into a dummy's hair, to be pulled forth presently with an air of discovery."[3]

strict interpretation: An interpretation according to the most narrow, literal meaning of the words without regard for context and other permissible meanings. (See § 62.)

teleological interpretation: An interpretation arrived at through imaginative reconstruction (q.v.), whereby the judge attempts to read the text as he believes the drafter would have wished to phrase it in order to achieve the drafter's desired end.

textual interpretation: An interpretation based purely on the words of a governing text, in their context, as the sole legitimate guides to meaning.

viperine interpretation: An interpretation that essentially destroys the text. ● Here is what Thomas Hobbes said in 1651 about the phenomenon (without actually using the phrase): "[B]y the craft of an Interpreter, the Law may be made to beare a sense, contrary to that of the Soveraign; by which means the Interpreter becomes the Legislator."[4]

interpretation principle: The doctrine that every application of a text to particular circumstances entails interpretation (§ 1).

---

3   3 Roscoe Pound, *Jurisprudence* 479–80 (1959).

4   Thomas Hobbes, *Leviathan* 190 (Richard Tuck ed., rev. student ed. 1996) (spelling and capitalization thus in original).

interpretive-direction canon: The doctrine that definition sections and interpretation clauses are to be carefully followed (§ 36).

irreconcilability canon: The doctrine that if a text contains truly irreconcilable provisions at the same level of generality, and they have been simultaneously adopted, neither provision should be given effect (§ 29).

last-antecedent canon: The doctrine that a pronoun, relative pronoun, or demonstrative adjective generally refers to the nearest reasonable antecedent (§ 18). • Strictly speaking, "last antecedent" denotes a noun or noun phrase referred to by a pronoun or relative pronoun—since grammatically speaking, only pronouns are said to have antecedents. But in modern practice, and despite the misnomer, it is common to refer to the *last-antecedent canon* when what is actually meant is the *nearest-reasonable-referent canon* (§ 20).

legislative free-riding: A legislature's passive reliance on the judiciary to ameliorate poor legal drafting by "interpreting" statutory provisions by means other than the fair-reading method, as by creating equitable exceptions to plainly worded mandates or by filling *casus omissi* with judicially fabricated gap-fillers.

legislative history: The proceedings leading to the enactment of a statute, including legislative hearings, committee reports, and floor debates. Cf. STATUTORY HISTORY.

legislative intent: The design or plan that the enacting legislature had for the application of a statute to specific situations that might arise. • When this design or plan is not apparent from the text, it is a fictional intent that cannot be reliably ascertained.

Living Constitutionalism: The doctrine that a constitutional provision should be interpreted in light of the knowledge, needs, and mores existing at the time when the interpretive decision is rendered.—**Living Constitutionalist,** n.

living-tree doctrine: A Canadian doctrine of constitutional interpretation characterizing the constitution as a "living tree" capable of growth and expansion and mandating that it be given a "large and liberal interpretation." • This doctrine, which is equivalent to Living Constitutionalism, was first announced in a 1930 decision of the Judicial Committee of the Privy Council.[5] It has no applicability to legislation and none whatsoever to American law.

mandatory/permissive canon: The doctrine that mandatory words impose a duty; permissive words grant discretion (§ 11).

mens rea (/menz **ray-ə**/): Evil intent, as traditionally required for statutes defining crimes or imposing penalties. ● This traditional concept is often expressed but inconsistently applied and frequently ignored. As a reliable canon, we think it can apply only to offenses that are analogous to common-law crimes.

mens rea **canon:** The doctrine that a statute creating a criminal offense whose elements are similar to those of a common-law crime will be presumed to require a culpable state of mind (*mens rea*) in its commission (§ 50).

mischief rule: The interpretive doctrine that a statute should be interpreted by first identifying the problem (or "mischief") that the statute was designed to remedy and then adopting a construction that will suppress the problem and advance the remedy. ● This is a primarily British name for purposivism. The classic and most ancient statement of the rule occurred in *Heydon's Case*:

> For the sure and true interpretation of all statutes in general (be they penal or beneficial, restrictive or enlarging of the common law) four things are to be discerned and considered: first, what was the common law before the making of the act. Second, what was the mischief and defect for which the common law did not provide. Third, what remedy the Parliament hath resolved and appointed to cure the disease of the Commonwealth. And fourth, the true reason of the remedy; and then the office of all the judges is always to make such construction as shall suppress the mischief, and advance the remedy, and to suppress subtle inventions and evasions for continuance of the mischief, and pro privato commodo, and to add force and life to the

---

5   *Edwards v. A.G. for Canada*, [1930] A.C. 124.

cure and remedy, according to the true intent of the makers
of the act, pro bono publico.[6]

The prevailing scholarly view today is that the mischief rule represents "the last remnant of the equity of a statute."[7] See PURPO-
SIVISM.

nearest-reasonable-referent canon: The doctrine that when the
syntax involves something other than a parallel series of nouns
or verbs, a prepositive or postpositive modifier normally applies
only to the nearest reasonable referent (§ 20).

negative-implication canon: The doctrine that the expression of
one thing implies the exclusion of others (*expressio unius est exclusion alterius*) (§ 10).

nonentrenchment doctrine: see REPEALABILITY CANON.

nonoriginalism: The view that a text need not be interpreted in
accordance with its original meaning (that is, the understanding
of informed readers at the time of its adoption), but rather may
be given new meanings to accord with the times.

no-recourse doctrine: The traditional common-law rule barring
recourse to legislative history as an aid in statutory interpretation. • The rule was first announced in the famous copyright
case of *Millar v. Taylor*: "The sense and meaning of an Act of
Parliament must be collected from what it says when passed into
a law; and not from the history of changes it underwent in the
house where it took its rise. That history is not known to the
other house, or to the Sovereign."[8] The no-recourse rule was well
accepted in 18th-century America.[9] (See § 66.)

noscitur a sociis (/**noh**-shee-tər [*or* **nos**-ə-tər] ah **soh**-shee-is/):
[Latin "it is known by its associates"] A canon of construction
holding that the meaning of an unclear word or phrase, espe-

---

6   *Heydon's Case*, (1584) 3 Rep. 7a.

7   J.H. Baker, *An Introduction to English Legal History* 212 (4th ed. 2002).

8   [1769] 4 Burr. 2303, 2332, 98 Eng. Rep. 201, 217 (K.B.) (per Willes, J.).

9   *See* Hans W. Baade, *"Original Intent" in Historical Perspective: Some Critical Glosses*, 69 Tex. L. Rev. 1001, 1010–11 (1991).

cially one in a list, should be determined by the words immediately surrounding it (§ 31 [associated-words canon]).

omitted-case canon: The doctrine that nothing is to be added to what the text states or reasonably implies (*casus omissus pro omisso habendus est*). That is, a matter not covered is to be treated as not covered (§ 8). See CASUS OMISSUS.

ordinary-meaning canon: The doctrine that words are to be understood in their ordinary, everyday meanings—unless the context indicates that they bear a technical sense (§ 6).

original intent: The subjective intention of the framers or ratifiers of a legal instrument, esp. a governmental text. ● When it goes beyond what is apparent from the words of the text, original intent as applied to the product of a collective body almost always denotes a legal fiction, and when not that, an unascertainable reality.

originalism: 1. The doctrine that words are to be given the meaning they had when they were adopted; specif., the canon that a legal text should be interpreted through the historical ascertainment of the meaning that it would have conveyed to a fully informed observer at the time when the text first took effect. (See § 7 [fixed-meaning canon].) **2.** The doctrine that a legal text should be interpreted to effect the intent of those who prepared it or gave it legal effect. ● Sense 1 is our preferred use of the term: It is an objective test. Sense 2 embodies a subjective test.

original meaning: The understanding of a text, esp. an important text such as the Constitution, reflecting what an informed, reasonable member of the community would have understood at the time of adoption according to then-prevailing linguistic meanings and interpretive principles. (See § 7 [fixed-meaning canon].)

penalty/illegality canon: The doctrine that a statute penalizing an act makes it unlawful (§ 48).

pending-action canon: The doctrine that when statutory law is altered during the pendency of a lawsuit, the courts at every level must apply the new law unless doing so would violate the presumption against retroactivity (§ 42).

plain-meaning rule: 1. The doctrine that if the text of a statute is unambiguous, it should be applied by its terms without recourse to policy arguments, legislative history, or any other matter extraneous to the text—unless this application leads to an absurdity. ● Here is a classic 1929 statement of the rule by the Supreme Court of the United States: "[W]here the language of an enactment is clear, and construction according to its terms does not lead to absurd or impracticable consequences, the words employed are to be taken as the final expression of the meaning intended."[10] The doctrine is essentially sound but largely unhelpful, since determining what is unambiguous is eminently debatable. **2.** Loosely, the ordinary-meaning canon. See ORDINARY-MEANING CANON (§ 6).

pragmatism: An approach to statutory construction applying a "best policy" standard. ● This approach is a relatively unstructured problem-solving process involving common sense, a respect for stare decisis, and a sense of social needs.[11] Some commentators' efforts to structure pragmatism by injecting a list of other considerations fail to provide certainty and objectivity as long as "best policy" remains a defining factor.

preamble: An introductory statement in a constitution, statute, or other document explaining the document's basis and objective; esp., a statutory recital of the inconveniences for which the statute is designed to provide a remedy. (See § 34 [prefatory-materials canon].)

predicate-act canon: The doctrine that authorization of an act also authorizes a necessary predicate act (§ 30).

prefatory-materials canon: The doctrine that a preamble, purpose clause, or recital is a permissible indicator of meaning (§ 34).

---

10   *United States v. Missouri Pac. R.R.*, 278 U.S. 269, 278 (1929) (per Butler, J.).

11   *See* Frank B. Cross, *The Theory and Practice of Statutory Interpretation* 13 (2009).

presumption against federal preemption: The doctrine that a federal statute is presumed to supplement rather than displace state law (§ 47).

presumption against change in common law: The doctrine that a statute will be construed to alter the common law only when that disposition is clear (§ 52).

presumption against implied repeal: The doctrine that repeals by implication are disfavored—very much disfavored—but a provision that flatly contradicts an earlier enacted provision repeals it (§ 55).

presumption against implied right of action: The doctrine that a statute's mere prohibition of a certain act does not imply creation of a private right of action for its violation (§ 51).

presumption against ineffectiveness: The doctrine that a textually permissible interpretation that furthers rather than obstructs the document's purpose should be favored (§ 4).

presumption against retroactivity: The doctrine that a statute presumptively has no retroactive application (§ 41).

presumption against waiver of sovereign immunity: The doctrine that a statute does not waive sovereign immunity—and a federal statute does not eliminate state sovereign immunity—unless that disposition is unequivocally clear (§ 46).

presumption of consistent usage: The doctrine that a word or phrase is presumed to bear the same meaning throughout a text; a material variation in terms suggests a variation in meaning (§ 25).

presumption of nonexclusive "include": The doctrine that the verb *to include* introduces examples, not an exhaustive list (§ 15).

presumption of validity: The doctrine that an interpretation that validates outweighs one that invalidates (§ 5). See UT RES MAGIS VALEAT QUAM PEREAT.

principle of interrelating canons: The doctrine that no canon of interpretation is absolute. Each may be overcome by the strength of differing principles that point in other directions (§ 3).

prior-construction canon: The doctrine that if a statute uses words or phrases that have already received authoritative construction by the jurisdiction's court of last resort, or even uniform construction by inferior courts or a responsible administrative agency, they are to be understood according to that construction (§ 54).

proviso canon (/prə-vɪ-zoh/): The doctrine that a proviso conditions only the principal matter that it qualifies—almost always the matter immediately preceding (§ 21).

punctuation canon: The doctrine that punctuation is a permissible indicator of meaning (§ 23).

purpose clause: A usu. prefatory or introductory clause that explains the reasons for the existence of a legal instrument. (See § 34.)

purposivism: The doctrine that a drafter's "purposes," as perceived by the interpreter, are more important than the words that the drafter has used; specif., the idea that a judge-interpreter should seek an answer not in the words of the text but in its social, economic, and political objectives. ● Broadly speaking, *purposivism* is synonymous with *mischief rule.* Cf. EQUITY-OF-THE-STATUTE.

recital: In a contract or deed, a preliminary statement showing that specified facts exist, or explaining the background of the transaction or the reasons for entering into it. (See § 34.)

reddendo singula singulis: see DISTRIBUTIVE-PHRASING CANON.

reenactment canon: The doctrine that if the legislature amends or reenacts a provision other than by way of a consolidating statute or restyling project, a significant change in language is presumed to entail a change in meaning (§ 40).

related-statutes canon: The doctrine that statutes *in pari materia* are to be interpreted together, as though they were one law (§ 39).

remedial statute: Any statute other than a private bill. ● This is a term redolent of doubt and uncertainty. Blackstone defined it as follows: "Remedial statutes are those which are made to supply such defects, and abridge such superfluities, in the common law, as arise either from the general imperfection of all human laws, from change of time and circumstances, from the mistakes and unadvised determinations of unlearned judges, or from any other cause whatsoever."[12] Even on Blackstone's test, every statute is remedial—and every statute certainly remedies a problem. The term is unhelpful except as a means of invoking the incantation that "remedial statutes are to be liberally construed" and of thereby evading the fair reading of the text. (See § 64.)

repealability canon: The doctrine that the legislature cannot derogate from its own authority or the authority of its successors (§ 45).

repealer: A legislative act that abrogates an earlier law.

repeal-of-repealer canon: The doctrine that the repeal or expiration of a repealing statute does not reinstate the original statute (§ 56).

rule in *Heydon's Case*: see MISCHIEF RULE.

rule of lenity: The doctrine that ambiguity in a statute defining a crime or imposing a penalty should be resolved in the defendant's favor (§ 49).

rule of the last antecedent: see LAST-ANTECEDENT CANON.

scope-of-subparts canon: The doctrine that material within an indented subpart relates only to that subpart; material contained in unindented text relates to all the following or preceding indented subparts (§ 22).

scrivener's error: A drafter's or typist's technical error—such as transposing characters or omitting an obviously needed word—that can be rectified without serious doubt about the correct reading. (See § 37.)

separation of powers: The division of governmental authority into three branches—legislative, executive, and judicial—each

12 1 William Blackstone, *Commentaries on the Laws of England* 86 (4th ed. 1770).

with specified duties on which neither of the other branches can rightfully encroach. • The first tentative formulation of the proposition that this is the most desirable form of government appeared in John Locke's *Two Treatises of Government* (1689) and was later elaborated more fully in Montesquieu's *Spirit of Laws* (1748).

series-qualifier canon: The doctrine that when there is a straightforward, parallel construction that involves all nouns or verbs in a series, a prepositive or postpositive modifier normally applies to each item in the series (§ 19).

statuta suo clauduntur territorio, nec ultra territorium disponunt: see EXTRATERRITORIALITY CANON.

statutory history: The enacted lineage of a statute, including prior laws, amendments, codifications, and repeals. Cf. LEGISLATIVE HISTORY.

strict construction: see CONSTRUCTION.

strict interpretation: see INTERPRETATION.

subordinating/superordinating canon: The doctrine that subordinating language (signaled by *subject to*) or superordinating language (signaled by *notwithstanding* or *despite*) merely shows which provision prevails in the event of a clash—but does not necessarily denote a clash of provisions (§ 13).

supremacy-of-text principle: The doctrine that the words of a governing text are of paramount concern, and what they convey, in their context, is what the text means (§ 2).

surplusage canon: The doctrine that, if possible, every word and every provision is to be given effect (*verba cum effectu sunt accipienda*) (§ 26). • According to this canon, "if a [textual] provision lends itself to two possible interpretations, and if one of those interpretations would make another provision in the [text] superfluous, then interpreters ordinarily should prefer the other interpretation."[13]

---

13   Caleb Nelson, *What Is Textualism?* 91 Va. L. Rev. 347, 355 (2005).

technical-meaning exception: The doctrine that the ordinary-meaning canon does not apply when a word or phrase that has acquired a specialized or peculiar meaning in a given context appears in that context. (See § 6 [ordinary-meaning canon].)

teleological interpretation: see INTERPRETATION.

textualism: The doctrine that the words of a governing text are of paramount concern, and what they convey in their context is what the text means.—**textualist,** adj. & n.

title-and-headings canon: The doctrine that the title and headings are permissible indicators of meaning (§ 35).

unintelligibility canon: The doctrine that an incomprehensible text is inoperative (§ 16).

ut res magis valeat quam pereat (/ət [*or* oot] rays **mah**-jis **vah**-lee-aht kwam **peer**-ee-aht/): (Interpret the law, contract, etc.) So that the matter may have force rather than perish. (See § 5 [presumption of validity].) See PRESUMPTION OF VALIDITY.

vagueness: 1. Uncertain breadth of meaning. **2.** Loosely, ambiguity.

verba cum effectu sunt accipienda (/vər-bə kəm ə-**fek**-too suunt ak-si-pee-**en**-də/) [Latin]: Words must be taken so as to have effect (§ 26 [surplusage canon]).

viperine interpretation: see INTERPRETATION.

whole-text canon: The doctrine that the text must be construed as a whole (§ 24).

Table of Cases

Bibliography

The literature on legal interpretation is stupendously voluminous. The works here listed are among those that we consulted and that influenced us in some way while we researched this book. Although we could lengthen the list, we seek here to draw attention to only the most pertinent sources.

Books

Abbott, L.W. *Law Reporting in England 1485–1585*. London: Athlone Press, 1973.

Abel-Smith, Brian; and Robert Stevens. *In Search of Justice*. London: Penguin, 1968.

Abel-Smith, Brian; and Robert Stevens. *Lawyers and the Courts: A Sociological Study of the English Legal System 1750–1965*. London: Heinemann, 1967.

Ackerman, Bruce A. *Reconstructing American Law*. Cambridge, Mass.: Harvard Univ. Press, 1984.

Ackerman, Bruce A. *We the People: Foundations*. Vol. 1. Cambridge, Mass.: Belknap Press, 1981.

Ackerman, Bruce A. *We the People: Transformations*. Vol. 2. Cambridge, Mass.: Belknap Press, 1998.

Adler, Matthew D.; and Kenneth Einar Himma (eds.). *The Rule of Recognition and the U.S. Constitution*. N.Y.: Oxford Univ. Press, 2009.

Allen, Carleton Kemp. *Law and Orders: An Inquiry into the Nature and Scope of Delegated Legislation and Executive Powers in England*. London: Stevens & Sons, 1945.

Allen, Carleton Kemp. *Law in the Making*. 7th ed. Oxford: Oxford Univ. Press, 1964.

Amar, Akhil Reed. *America's Constitution: A Biography*. N.Y.: Random House, 2005.

Amar, Akhil Reed. *The Bill of Rights: Creation and Reconstruction*. New Haven: Yale Univ. Press, 1998.

American Jurisprudence 2d. Vol. 17A (*Contracts*) §§ 1–732 (2004 & Supp. 2011).

American Jurisprudence 2d. Vol. 17A (*Statutes*) §§ 1–319 (2004 & Supp. 2011).

Anastaplo, George. *Reflections on Constitutional Law*. Lexington, Ky.: Univ. Press of Kentucky, 2006.

Antieau, Chester James; and (in vols. 2 & 3) William J. Rich. *Modern Constitutional Law*. 3 vols. St. Paul: West Group, 1997.

Arkes, Hadley. *The Return of George Sutherland*. Princeton, N.J.: Princeton Univ. Press, 1994.

Association of American Law Schools (ed.) *Select Essays in Anglo-American Legal History*. 3 vols. Boston: Little, Brown & Co., 1907.

Atiyah, P.S. *An Introduction to the Law of Contract*. 4th ed. N.Y.: Oxford Univ. Press, 1989.

Atiyah, P.S. *Law and Modern Society*. Oxford: Oxford Univ. Press, 1983.

Atiyah, P.S.; and Robert S. Summers. *Form and Substance in Anglo-American Law*. Oxford: Clarendon Press, 1987.

Austin, John. *Lectures on Jurisprudence, or the Philosophy of Positive Law*. 2 vols. Robert Campbell, ed. Jersey City, N.J.: Frederick D. Linn & Co., 1910.

Austin, John. *The Province of Jurisprudence Determined* [1832]. H.L.A. Hart, ed. N.Y.: Noonday Press, 1954.

Babington, Anthony. *The Rule of Law in Britain from the Roman Occupation to the Present Day: The Only Liberty*. Chichester: Barry Rose, 1995.

Baer, Judith A. *Equality Under Law: Reclaiming the Fourteenth Amendment*. Ithaca: Cornell Univ. Press, 1983.

Baer, Judith A. *Our Lives Before the Law: Constructing a Feminist Jurisprudence*. Princeton, N.J.: Princeton Univ. Press, 1999.

Bagwell, J. Timothy. *American Formalism and the Problem of Interpretation*. Houston, Tex.: Rice Univ. Press, 1986.

Baker, J.H. *Baker and Milsom Sources of English Legal History: Private Law to 1750*. 2d ed. Oxford: Oxford Univ. Press, 2010.

Baker, J.H. *An Introduction to English Legal History*. 4th ed. London: Butterworths Lexis/Nexis, 2002.

Balkin, Jack M. *Living Originalism*. Cambridge, Mass.: Harvard Univ. Press, 2011.

Barak, Aharon. *Purposive Interpretation in Law*. Sari Bashi, trans. Princeton, N.J.: Princeton Univ. Press, 2005.

Barber, Sotirios A.; and James E. Fleming. *Constitutional Interpretation: The Basic Questions*. Oxford: Oxford Univ. Press, 2007.

Barnett, Randy E. *Restoring the Lost Constitution: The Presumption of Liberty*. Princeton, N.J.: Princeton Univ. Press, 2004.

Barnett, Randy E. (ed.). *The Rights Retained by the People: The History and Meaning of the Ninth Amendment*. Fairfax, Va.: George Mason Univ. Press, 1989.

Barrington, Daines. *Observations on the More Ancient Statutes: From Magna Charta to the Twenty-First of James I. Cap. XXVII*. 5th ed. London: J. Nichols, 1796.

Beal, Edward. *Cardinal Rules of Legal Interpretation*. Rev. A.E. Randall. 3d ed. London: Stevens & Sons, 1924.

Beale, Joseph H. *A Treatise on the Conflict of Laws*. 3 vols. N.Y.: Baker, Voorhis & Co., 1935.

Beccaria, Cesare. *An Essay on Crimes and Punishments*. Trans. anon. New ed. Phil.: William Young, 1793.

Beckman, Robert C.; Brady S. Coleman; and Joel Lee. *Case Analysis and Statutory Interpretation*. 2d ed. Singapore: Humanities Press, 2001.

Bell, John. *Policy Arguments in Judicial Decisions*. Oxford: Clarendon Press, 1983.

Bell, John; Sophie Boyron; and Simon Whittaker. *Principles of French Law*. Oxford: Oxford Univ. Press, 1998.

Belz, Herman A. *A Living Constitution or Fundamental Law? American Constitutionalism in Historical Perspective*. Lanham, Md.: Rowman & Littlefield, 1998.

Bennett, Robert W.; and Lawrence B. Solum. *Constitutional Originalism: A Debate*. Ithaca: Cornell Univ. Press, 2011.

Bennion, Francis. *Statutory Interpretation*. 4th ed. London: Butterworths, 2002.

Bennion, Francis. *Understanding Common Law Legislation: Drafting and Interpretation*. Oxford: Oxford Univ. Press, 2001.

Benson, Robert. *The Interpretation Game: How Judges and Lawyers Make the Law*. Durham, N.C.: Carolina Academic Press, 2008.

Bentham, Jeremy. *A Comment on the Commentaries: A Criticism of William Blackstone's Commentaries on the Laws of England* [1776]. Charles Warren Everett, ed. Oxford: Clarendon Press, 1928.

Bentham, Jeremy. *An Introduction to the Principles of Morals and Legislation* [1789]. Laurence J. Lafleur, ed. N.Y.: Hafner Pub. Co., 1948.

Bentham, Jeremy. *Of Laws in General*. H.L.A. Hart, ed. London: Athlone Press, 1970.

Bentham, Jeremy. *Theory of Legislation*. 2 vols. R. Hildreth, ed. Boston: Weeks, Jordan & Co., 1840.

Bentham, Jeremy. *The Works of Jeremy Bentham*. 11 vols. John Bowring, ed. Edinburgh: William Tait, 1843.

Berger, Raoul. *Congress v. The Supreme Court*. Cambridge, Mass.: Harvard Univ. Press, 1969.

Berger, Raoul. *Government by Judiciary*. Cambridge, Mass.: Harvard Univ. Press, 1977.

Berger, Raoul. *Selected Writings on the Constitution*. Cumberland, Va.: James River Press, 1987.

Berlins, Marcel; and Clare Dyer. *The Law Machine*. 2d ed. Harmondsworth: Penguin, 1986.

Bickel, Alexander M. *The Least Dangerous Branch: The Supreme Court at the Bar of Politics*. Indianapolis: Bobbs-Merrill, 1962.

Bickel, Alexander M. *The Supreme Court and the Idea of Progress*. N.Y.: Harper & Row Pubs., 1970.

Bienenfeld, F.R. *Rediscovery of Justice*. London: George Allen & Unwin Ltd., 1947.

Bingham, Tom. *The Rule of Law*. London: Allen Lane, 2010.

Bird, Otto A. *The Idea of Justice*. N.Y.: Frederick A. Praeger, 1967.

Birks, Peter (ed.). *English Private Law*. 2 vols. Oxford: Oxford Univ. Press, 2000.

Bishin, William Robert; and Christopher D. Stone. *Law, Language, and Ethics: An Introduction to Law and Legal Method*. Mineola, N.Y.: Foundation Press, Inc., 1972.

Bishop, Joel Prentiss. *Commentaries on the Criminal Law*. 5th ed. Boston: Little, Brown & Co., 1872.

Bishop, Joel Prentiss. *Commentaries on the Law of Contracts*. Chicago: Flood & Co., 1887.

Bishop, Joel Prentiss. *Commentaries on the Law of Statutory Crimes*. Boston: Little, Brown & Co., 1873.

Bishop, Joel Prentiss. *Commentaries on the Written Laws and Their Interpretation*. Boston: Little, Brown & Co., 1882.

Bix, Brian. *Jurisprudence: Theory and Context*. 2d ed. London: Sweet & Maxwell, 1999.

Blachly, Frederick F.; and Miriam E. Oatman. *Administrative Legislation and Adjudication*. Washington, D.C.: Brookings Institution, 1934.

Black, Henry Campbell. *Handbook on the Construction and Interpretation of the Laws*. 2d ed. St. Paul: West 1911.

Black, Henry Campbell. *The Relation of the Executive Power to Legislation*. Princeton, N.J.: Princeton Univ. Press, 1919.

Black, Hugo. *One Man's Stand for Freedom: Mr. Justice Black and The Bill of Rights*. Irving Dilliard, ed. N.Y.: Knopf, 1971.

Black's Law Dictionary. Bryan A. Garner, ed. 9th ed. St. Paul: Thomson/West, 2009.

Blackstone, William. *Commentaries on the Laws of England*. 4 vols. 4th ed. Oxford: Clarendon Press, 1770.

Bloom, Lackland H., Jr. *Methods of Interpretation: How the Supreme Court Reads the Constitution*. N.Y.: Oxford Univ. Press, 2009.

Bobbitt, Philip Chase. *Constitutional Fate: Theory of the Constitution*. N.Y.: Oxford Univ. Press, 1982.

Bodenheimer, Edgar. *Jurisprudence: The Philosophy and Method of the Law*. Rev. ed. Cambridge, Mass.: Harvard Univ. Press, 1974.

Borda, Aldo Zammit (ed.). *Legislative Drafting*. London: Routledge, 2011.

Bork, Robert H. *Coercing Virtue: The Worldwide Role of Judges*. Washington, D.C.: AEI Press, 2003.

Bork, Robert H. *Slouching Towards Gomorrah: Modern Liberalism and American Decline*. N.Y.: HarperCollins, 1996.

Bork, Robert H. *The Tempting of America: The Political Seduction of the Law*. N.Y.: Free Press, 1990.

Bork, Robert H. *A Time to Speak*. Wilmington, Del.: ISI Books, 2008.

Botha, Christo. *Statutory Interpretation: An Introduction for Students*. 3d ed. Kenwyn, S.A.: Juta & Co., 1998.

Bowers, Frederick. *Linguistic Aspects of Legislative Expression*. Vancouver: Univ. of British Columbia Press, 1989.

Bradford, M.E. *Original Intentions: On the Making and Ratification of the United States Constitution*. Athens & London: Univ. of Georgia Press, 1993.

Branch, Thomas. *Principia Legis et Aequitatis: Being an Alphabetical Collection of Maxims, Principles or Rules, Definitions, and Memorable Sayings, in Law and Equity*. London: J. & W.T. Clarke, 1824.

Breyer, Stephen. *Active Liberty: Interpreting a Democratic Constitution*. N.Y.: Oxford Univ. Press, 2008.

Breyer, Stephen. *Making Our Democracy Work: A Judge's View*. N.Y.: Vintage Books, 2011.

Brigham, John. *Constitutional Language: An Interpretation of Judicial Decision*. Westport, Conn.: Greenwood Press, 1978.

Broom, Herbert. *A Selection of Legal Maxims*. Joseph Gerald Pease & Herbert Chitty, eds. 8th ed. London: Sweet & Maxwell, 1911.

Browen, W. Jethro. *The Underlying Principles of Modern Legislation*. 6th ed. London: John Murray, 1920.

Brumbaugh, Jesse Franklin. *Legal Reasoning and Briefing*. Indianapolis: Bobbs-Merrill, 1917.

Burdick, Charles Kellogg. *The Law of the American Constitution*. N.Y.: G.P. Putnam's Sons, 1922.

Burgess, John W. *Political Science and Comparative Constitutional Law*. 2 vols. Boston: Ginn & Co., 1890.

Burrows, Roland. *Interpretation of Documents*. London: Butterworths, 1943.

Burton, Steven J. *Elements of Contract Interpretation*. N.Y.: Oxford Univ. Press, 2009.

Bybee, Keith J. *All Judges Are Political, Except When They Are Not*. Stanford, Cal.: Stanford Univ. Press, 2010.

Cabot, Richard C. *The Meaning of Right and Wrong*. N.Y.: The Macmillan Co., 1933.

Cahill, Fred V., Jr. *Judicial Legislation: A Study in American Legal Theory*. N.Y.: Ronald Press Co., 1952.

Cairns, Huntington. *Legal Philosophy from Plato to Hegel*. Baltimore: Johns Hopkins Univ. Press, 1949.

Cairns, Huntington. *The Theory of Legal Science*. Chapel Hill: Univ. of North Carolina Press, 1941.

Calabresi, Guido. *A Common Law for the Age of Statutes*. Cambridge, Mass.: Harvard Univ. Press, 1982.

Calabresi, Steven G. (ed.). *Originalism: A Quarter-Century of Debate*. Washington, D.C.: Regnery Pub., 2007.

Calvi, James V.; and Susan E. Coleman. *American Law and Legal Systems*. 5th ed. Upper Saddle River, N.J.: Pearson Prentice Hall, 2004.

Campos, Paul F.; Pierre Schlag; and Steven D. Smith. *Against the Law*. Durham, N.C.: Duke Univ. Press, 1996.

Cardozo, Benjamin N. *The Growth of the Law*. Hartford: Yale Univ. Press, 1924.

Cardozo, Benjamin N. *The Paradoxes of Legal Science*. N.Y.: Columbia Univ. Press, 1928.

Carp, Robert A.; Ronald Stidham; and Kenneth L. Manning. *Judicial Process in America*. 7th ed. Washington, D.C.: CQ Press, 2007.

Carpenter, William Seal. *Foundations of Modern Jurisprudence*. N.Y.: Appleton-Century-Crofts, Inc., 1958.

Carter, Lief H. *Reason in Law*. 8th ed. N.Y.: Longman, 2010.

Chamberlayne, Charles Frederic. *A Treatise on the Modern Law of Evidence*. 5 vols. Albany: Matthew Bender & Co., 1916.

Chemerinsky, Erwin. *Constitutional Law: Principles and Policies*. Frederick, Md.: Wolters Kluwer Law & Business, 2011.

Chemerinsky, Erwin. *Interpreting the Constitu-tion.* N.Y.: Praeger Pubs., 1987.

Childs, Frank Hall. *Where and How to Find the Law.* Chicago: La Salle Extension Univ., 1926.

Chitty, Joseph. *A Practical Treatise on the Law of Contracts Not Under Seal.* Boston: Wells & Lilly, 1827.

Choper, Jesse H. *Judicial Review and the Na-tional Political Process: A Functional Reconsid-eration of the Role of the Supreme Court.* Chi-cago: Univ. of Chicago Press, 1980.

Clark, E.C. *Practical Jurisprudence: A Comment on Austin.* Cambridge: Cambridge Univ. Press, 1883.

Clark, S.H. *Interpretation of the Printed Page.* Chicago: Row, Peterson & Co., 1915.

Cockram, Gail-Maryse. *Interpretation of Stat-utes.* 2d ed. Cape Town: Juta & Co., 1983.

Cohen, Felix S. *The Legal Conscience: Selected Papers of Felix S. Cohen.* Lucy Kramer Cohen, ed. New Haven: Yale Univ. Press, 1960.

Cohen, Julius. *Materials and Problems on Leg-islation.* 2d ed. Indianapolis: Bobbs-Merrill, 1967.

Cohen, Morris R. *Law and the Social Order: Essays in Legal Philosophy.* N.Y.: Harcourt, Brace & Co., 1933.

Cohen, Morris R. *Reason and Law.* N.Y.: Free Press, 1950.

Cohen, Morris R.; and Felix S. Cohen (eds.). *Readings in Jurisprudence and Legal Philoso-phy.* Boston: Little, Brown & Co., 1951. 2d ed. Philip Schuchman, ed. Boston: Little, Brown & Co., 1979.

Coigne, Armand B. *Statute Making: A Treatise on the Means and Methods for the Enactment of Statute Law in the United States.* 2d ed. N.Y.: Commerce Clearing House, 1965.

Coke, Edward. *The First Part of the Institutes of the Laws of England, or a Commentary upon Littleton* [1628]. 14th ed. Dublin: Moore, 1791.

Coke, Edward. *The Fourth Part of the Institutes of the Laws of England* [1644]. 15th ed. Lon-don: E. & R. Brooke, 1797.

Collier, Charles W. *Meaning in Law: A Theory of Speech.* N.Y.: Oxford Univ. Press, 2009.

Condorcet, M. *A Commentary and Review of Montesquieu's Spirit of Laws.* Philadelphia: William Duane, 1811.

Coode, George. *On Legislative Expression, or, The Language of Written Law.* 2d ed. London: Thomas Turpin, 1852.

Cooley, Thomas M. *A Treatise on the Constitu-tional Limitations Which Rest upon the Legisla-tive Power of the States of the American Union.* Boston: Little, Brown & Co., 1868.

Coquillette, Daniel R. *The Anglo-American Le-gal Heritage.* Durham, N.C.: Carolina Aca-demic Press, 1999.

Corpus Juris Secundum. Vols. 17, 17A, 17B (*Contracts*) §§ 1–1069 (2011 & Supp. 2011).

Corpus Juris Secundum. Vol. 82 (*Statutes*) §§ 1–616 (2011 & Supp. 2011).

Coté, Pierre André. *The Interpretation of Leg-islation in Canada.* 2d ed. Cowansville, Que-bec: Les Editions Yvon Blais, Inc., 1992.

Countryman, Vern; et al. *Law in Contemporary Society: The Orgain Lectures.* Austin: Univ. of Texas Press, 1973.

Cox, Archibald. *The Role of the Supreme Court in American Government.* N.Y.: Oxford Univ. Press, 1976.

Cox, Archibald. *The Warren Court: Consti-tutional Adjudication as an Instrument of Reform.* Cambridge, Mass.: Harvard Univ. Press, 1968.

Craies, William Feilden. *A Treatise on Statute Law.* 2d ed. London: Stevens & Haynes, 1911.

Crawford, Earl T. *The Construction of Statutes.* St. Louis: Thomas Law Book Co., 1940.

Cross, Frank B. *Decision Making in the U.S. Courts of Appeals.* Stanford, Cal.: Stanford Univ. Press, 2007.

Cross, Frank B. *The Theory and Practice of Stat-utory Interpretation.* Stanford, Cal.: Stanford Univ. Press, 2009.

Cross, Rupert. *Precedent in English Law.* Ox-ford: Clarendon Press, 1961. 4th ed. (with J.W. Harris). Oxford: Clarendon Press, 1991.

Cross, Rupert. *Statutory Interpretation.* John Bell & George Engle, eds. 3d ed. London: LexisNexis, 1995.

Currie, David P. *The Constitution in the Supreme Court: The First Hundred Years, 1789-1888.* Chicago: Univ. of Chicago Press, 1985.

Curtis, Charles P. *It's Your Law.* Cambridge, Mass.: Harvard Univ. Press, 1954.

Cushing, Luther Stearns. *Elements of the Law and Practice of Legislative Assemblies in the United States of America.* 2d ed. Boston: Little, Brown & Co., 1866.

Dale, William. *Legislative Drafting: A New Approach.* London: Butterworths, 1977.

Davies, Jack. *Legislative Law and Process in a Nutshell.* 3d ed. St. Paul: West, 2007.

Davitt, Thomas E., Jr. *The Elements of Law.* Boston: Little, Brown & Co., 1959.

Denning, Lord. *The Discipline of Law.* London: Butterworths, 1979.

Denning, Lord. *The Due Process of Law.* Lon-don: Butterworths, 1980.

Denning, Lord. *Landmarks in the Law*. London: Butterworths, 1984.

Denning, Lord. *What Next in the Law?* London: Butterworths, 1982.

De Sloovère, Frederick J. *Cases on the Interpretation of Statutes*. St. Paul: West Pub. Co., 1931.

De Tourtoulon, Pierre. *Philosophy in the Development of Law*. Martha McC. Read, trans. N.Y.: Macmillan, 1922.

Devenish, G.E. *Interpretation of Statutes*. Cape Town: Juta & Co., 1992.

Devlin, Patrick. *The Judge*. N.Y.: Oxford Univ. Press, 1979.

Devlin, Patrick. *Samples of Lawmaking*. London: Oxford Univ. Press, 1962.

Dias, R.W.M. *Jurisprudence*. 4th ed. London: Butterworths, 1976.

Dickerson, Reed. *The Fundamentals of Legal Drafting*. 2d ed. Boston: Little, Brown & Co., 1986.

Dickerson, Reed. *The Interpretation and Application of Statutes*. Boston: Little, Brown & Co., 1975.

Dickerson, Reed. *Legislative Drafting*. Boston: Little, Brown & Co., 1954.

Dickerson, Reed (ed.). *Professionalizing Legislative Drafting—The Federal Experience*. Chicago: American Bar Association, 1973.

Dillon, John F. *The Laws and Jurisprudence of England and America*. Boston: Little, Brown & Co., 1894.

Dodd, David. *Statutory Interpretation in Ireland*. Haywards Heath: Tottel Pub., 2008.

Douglas, William O. *A Living Bill of Rights*. Garden City, N.Y.: Doubleday & Co., 1961.

Dowling, Noel T.; Edwin Wilhite Patterson; and Richard R.B. Powell. *Materials for Legal Method*. Brooklyn: Foundation Press, 1952.

Driedger, E.A. *The Composition of Legislation*. Ottawa: Edmond Cloutier, 1957. 2d ed. Ottawa: Dep't of Justice, 1976.

Driedger, E.A. *The Construction of Statutes*. Toronto: Butterworths, 1974.

Ducat, Craig R. *Constitutional Interpretation*. 6th ed. St. Paul: West Pub. Co., 1996.

Duxbury, Neil. *Patterns of American Jurisprudence*. Oxford: Clarendon Press, 1995.

Dwarris, Fortunatus. *A General Treatise on Statutes: Their Rules of Construction, and the Proper Boundaries of Legislation and of Judicial Interpretation*. 2d ed. London: William Benning & Co., 1848. Platt Potter, ed. 1st Am. ed. Albany: William Gould & Sons, 1871.

Dworkin, Ronald. *Justice for Hedgehogs*. Cambridge, Mass.: Belknap Press, 2011.

Dworkin, Ronald. *Law's Empire*. Cambridge, Mass.: Belknap Press, 1986.

Dworkin, Ronald. *A Matter of Principle*. Cambridge, Mass.: Harvard Univ. Press, 1985.

Dworkin, Ronald (ed.). *The Philosophy of Law*. Oxford: Oxford Univ. Press, 1991.

Dworkin, Ronald. *Taking Rights Seriously*. Cambridge, Mass.: Harvard Univ. Press, 1977.

Eisenberg, Melvin Aron. *The Nature of the Common Law*. Cambridge, Mass.: Harvard Univ. Press, 1988.

Elhauge, Einer. *Statutory Default Rules: How to Interpret Unclear Legislation*. Cambridge, Mass.: Harvard Univ. Press, 2008.

Ely, John Hart. *Democracy and Distrust: A Theory of Judicial Review*. Cambridge, Mass.: Harvard Univ. Press, 1980.

Endlich, G.A. *A Commentary on the Interpretation of Statutes*. Jersey City, N.J.: F.D. Linn & Co., 1888.

Epstein, Richard A. *Design for Liberty: Private Property, Public Administration, and the Rule of Law*. Cambridge, Mass.: Harvard Univ. Press, 2011.

Erskine, John. *An Institute of the Law of Scotland*. 2 vols. James Baldenach Nicolson, ed. Edinburgh: Bell & Bradfute, 1871.

Eskridge, William N., Jr. *Cases and Materials on Legislation*. 4th ed. St. Paul: West, 2007.

Eskridge, William N., Jr. *Dynamic Statutory Interpretation*. Cambridge, Mass.: Harvard Univ. Press, 1994.

Eskridge, William N., Jr.; and John A. Ferejohn. *A Republic of Statutes: The New American Constitution*. New Haven: Yale Univ. Press, 2010.

Eskridge, William N., Jr.; Philip P. Frickey; and Elizabeth Garrett. *Legislation and Statutory Interpretation*. 2d ed. N.Y.: Foundation Press, 2006.

Eskridge, William N., Jr.; Philip P. Frickey; and Elizabeth Garrett (eds.). *Statutory Interpretation Stories*. N.Y.: Foundation Press, 2010.

Evans, Jim. *Statutory Interpretation: Problems of Communication*. Auckland: Oxford Univ. Press, 1988.

Farber, Daniel A.; and Philip P. Frickey. *Law and Public Choice: A Critical Introduction*. Chicago: Univ. of Chicago Press, 1991.

Farber, Daniel A.; and Suzanna Sherry. *Beyond All Reason: The Radical Assault on Truth in American Law*. N.Y.: Oxford Univ. Press, 1997.

Farnsworth, E. Allan. *Farnsworth on Contracts*. 2d ed. N.Y.: Aspen Law and Business, 1998.

Farnsworth, Ward. *The Legal Analyst: A Toolkit for Thinking About the Law*. Chicago: Univ. of Chicago Press, 2007.

Faulkner, Robert K. *The Jurisprudence of John Marshall*. Princeton, N.J.: Princeton Univ. Press, 1968.

Fay, E. Stewart. *Discoveries in the Statute-Book*. London: Sweet & Maxwell, 1939.

Feldman, David (ed.). *English Public Law*. Oxford: Oxford Univ. Press, 2004.

Fifoot, C.H.S. *English Law and Its Background*. London: G. Bell & Sons Ltd., 1932.

Finch, Henry. *Law, or a Discourse Thereof*. London: Henry Lintot, 1759.

Finnis, J.M. *1973 Annual Survey of Commonwealth Law*. London: Butterworths, 1974.

Fortescue, John. *De Laudibus Legum Angliæ: A Treatise in Commendation of the Laws of England*. [ca. 1470] Francis Gregor, trans. Andrew Amos, ed. Cincinnati: Robert Clarke & Co., 1874.

Fox, Charles M. *Working with Contracts: What Law School Doesn't Teach You*. 2d ed. N.Y.: Practising Law Institute, 2008.

Frame, Alex. *Salmond: Southern Jurist*. Wellington, N.Z.: Victoria Univ. Press, 1995.

Frank, Jerome. *Courts on Trial*. Princeton, N.J.: Princeton Univ. Press, 1950.

Frank, Jerome. *Law and the Modern Mind*. N.Y.: Brentano's, 1930.

Frank, W.F. *The General Principles of English Law*. 4th ed. London: George G. Harrap & Co., 1969.

Frankfurter, Felix; and James M. Landis. *The Business of the Supreme Court: A Study in the Federal Judicial System*. N.Y.: Macmillan, 1928.

Frankfurter, Felix. *Felix Frankfurter on the Supreme Court: Extrajudicial Essays on the Court and the Constitution*. Philip B. Kurland, ed. Cambridge, Mass.: Harvard Univ. Press, 1970.

Frankfurter, Felix. *Mr. Justice Holmes and the Supreme Court*. 2d ed. Cambridge, Mass.: Belknap Press, 1961.

Freund, Ernst. *Standards of American Legislation*. 2d ed. Chicago: Univ. of Chicago Press, 1965.

Freund, Paul A. *On Law and Justice*. Cambridge, Mass.: Harvard Univ. Press, 1968.

Freund, Paul A. *On Understanding the Supreme Court*. Boston: Little, Brown & Co., 1949.

Fried, Charles. *Contract as Promise: A Theory of Contractual Obligation*. Cambridge, Mass.: Harvard Univ. Press, 1981.

Fried, Charles. *Saying What the Law Is: The Constitution in the Supreme Court*. Cambridge, Mass.: Harvard Univ. Press, 2004.

Friedman, Barry. *The Will of the People: How Public Opinion Has Influenced the Supreme Court and Shaped the Meaning of the Constitution*. N.Y.: Farrar, Straus & Giroux, 2009.

Friedman, Lawrence M. *Total Justice: What Americans Want from the Legal System*. Boston: Beacon Press, 1985.

Friedman, Lawrence M.; and Harry N. Scheiber (eds.). *American Law and the Constitutional Order: Historical Perspectives*. Cambridge, Mass.: Harvard Univ. Press, 1978.

Friedmann, W. *Legal Theory*. London: Stevens & Sons, 1947.

Friendly, Henry J. *Benchmarks*. Chicago: Univ. of Chicago Press, 1967.

Fuller, Lon L. *Anatomy of the Law*. N.Y.: New Am. Lib., 1968.

Fuller, Lon L. *Legal Fictions*. Stanford, Cal.: Stanford Univ. Press, 1967.

Gadamer, Hans-Georg. *Philosophical Hermeneutics*. David E. Linge, trans. Berkeley: Univ. of California Press, 1976.

Gadamer, Hans-Georg. *Truth and Method*. Joel Weinsheimer & Donald G. Marshall, trans. 2d ed. N.Y.: Crossroad, 1989.

Gall, Gerald L. *The Canadian Legal System*. Toronto: Carswell, 1977.

Garner, Bryan A. *Garner's Dictionary of Legal Usage*. 3d ed. N.Y.: Oxford Univ. Press, 2011.

Garner, Bryan A. *Garner's Modern American Usage*. 3d ed. N.Y.: Oxford Univ. Press, 2009.

Garner, Bryan A. *Guidelines for Drafting and Editing Court Rules*. Wash., D.C.: Administrative Office of the U.S. Courts, 1996.

Garner, Bryan A. *Legal Writing in Plain English*. Chicago: Univ. of Chicago Press, 2001.

Garvey, Gerald. *Constitutional Bricolage*. Princeton, N.J.: Princeton Univ. Press, 1971.

Geldart, William. *Introduction to English Law*. D.C.M. Yardley, ed. 9th ed. Oxford: Oxford Univ. Press, 1984.

George, Robert P. (ed.). *The Anatomy of Law: Essays on Legal Positivism*. Oxford: Oxford Univ. Press, 1996.

Gerken, Joseph L. *What Good Is Legislative History?* Buffalo: William S. Hein & Co., 2007.

Gilmore, Grant. *The Ages of American Law*. New Haven: Yale Univ. Press, 1977.

Gilmore, Grant. *The Death of Contract*. Columbus, Ohio: Ohio St. Univ. Press, 1974.

Goldberg, Arthur J. *Equal Justice: The Warren Era of the Supreme Court*. N.Y.: Noonday Press, 1972.

Goldford, Dennis J. *The American Constitution and the Debate over Originalism.* N.Y.: Cambridge Univ. Press, 2005.

Golding, Martin P. *Philosophy of Law.* Englewood Cliffs, N.J.: Prentice Hall, 1975.

Goldstein, Joseph. *The Intelligible Constitution: The Supreme Court's Obligation to Maintain the Constitution as Something We the People Can Understand.* N.Y.: Oxford Univ. Press, 1992.

Goldstein, Laurence. *Precedent in Law.* Oxford: Clarendon Press, 1987.

Goldstein, Leslie Friedman. *In Defense of the Text: Democracy and Constitutional Theory.* Savage, Md.: Rowman & Littlefield Pubs., Inc., 1991.

Goldstone, Lawrence. *The Activist: John Marshall, Marbury v. Madison, and the Myth of Judicial Review.* N.Y.: Walker & Co., 2008.

Goodenow, John Milton. *Historical Sketches of the Principles and Maxims of American Jurisprudence.* Steubenville, Ohio: James Wilson, 1819.

Gray, John Chipman. *The Nature and Sources of the Law.* 2d ed. N.Y.: Macmillan, 1921.

Greenawalt, Kent. *Legal Interpretation: Perspectives from Other Disciplines and Private Texts.* N.Y.: Oxford Univ. Press, 2010.

Greenawalt, Kent. *Statutory Interpretation: 20 Questions.* N.Y.: Foundation Press, 1999.

Groat, George Gorham. *Attitudes of American Courts in Labor Cases: A Study in Social Legislation.* N.Y.: Columbia Univ. Press, 1911.

Grotius, Hugo. *The Rights of War and Peace* [1625]. A.C. Campbell, trans. N.Y.: M. Walter Dunne, 1901.

Guest, A.G. (ed.). *Oxford Essays in Jurisprudence.* Oxford: Oxford Univ. Press, 1961.

Hägerström, Axel. *Inquiries into the Nature of Law and Morals.* Karl Olivecrona, ed. C.D. Broad, trans. Stockholm: Almqvist & Wiksell, 1953.

Hahlo, H.R.; and Ellison Kahn. *The South African Legal System and Its Background.* Cape Town: Juta & Co., 1968.

Haines, Charles Grove. *The American Doctrine of Judicial Supremacy.* N.Y.: Russell & Russell, 1959.

Hall, James Parker; and James DeWitt Andrews (eds.). *American Law and Procedure.* Vol. 14 ["Statutory Construction"]. Rev. ed. Chicago: La Salle Extension Univ., 1948.

Hall, Jerome (ed.). *Readings in Jurisprudence.* Indianapolis: Bobbs-Merrill, 1938.

Hall, Kermit L.; and Kevin T. McGuire (eds.). *The Judicial Branch.* N.Y.: Oxford Univ. Press, 2005.

Hamburger, Philip. *Law and Judicial Duty.* Cambridge, Mass.: Harvard Univ. Press, 2008.

Hamilton, Burritt. *Practical Law.* Rev. ed. Battle Creek, Mich.: Ellis Pub. Co., 1912.

Hanbury, H.G. *English Courts of Law.* 2d ed. Oxford: Oxford Univ. Press, 1953.

Hanks, Eva H.; Michael E. Herz; and Steven S. Nemerson. *Elements of Law.* Cincinnati: Anderson Pub. Co., 1994.

Harlan, John M. *The Evolution of a Judicial Philosophy: Selected Opinions and Papers of Justice John M. Harlan.* David L. Shapiro, ed. Cambridge, Mass.: Harvard Univ. Press, 1969.

Harmon, M. Judd (ed.). *Essays on the Constitution of the United States.* Port Washington, N.Y.: Nat'l Univ. Pubs., 1978.

Harris, J.W. *Legal Philosophies.* 2d ed. London: LexisNexis UK, 1997.

Hart, Henry M.; and Albert M. Sacks. *The Legal Process: Basic Problems in the Making and Application of Law.* William N. Eskridge Jr. & Philip P. Frickey, eds. 1958. Repr. Westbury, N.Y.: Foundation Press, 1994.

Hart, H.L.A.; and Tony Honoré. *Causation in the Law.* 2d ed. Oxford: Oxford Univ. Press, 1985.

Hatton, Christopher. *A Treatise Concerning Statutes.* London: Richard Tonson, 1677.

Hayek, F.A. *The Road to Serfdom: The Definitive Edition.* Bruce Caldwell ed. Chicago: Univ. of Chicago Press, 2007.

Hazard, Geoffrey C.; and W. William Hodes. *The Law of Lawyering: A Handbook on the Model Rules of Professional Conduct.* 2d ed. Englewood Cliffs, N.J.: Prentice Hall Law & Business, 1990.

Helmholz, R.H. (ed.). *The Oxford History of the Laws of England: The Canon Law and Ecclesiastical Jurisdiction from 597 to the 1640s.* Vol. 1. Oxford: Oxford Univ. Press, 2004.

Hennessey, Edward F. *Judges Making Law.* Boston: Franklin N. Flaschner Judicial Institute, 1994.

Herget, James E. *American Jurisprudence, 1870–1970: A History.* Houston: Rice Univ. Press, 1990.

Heron, Denis Caulfield. *The Principles of Jurisprudence.* London: Longmans, Green & Co., 1873.

Hetzel, Otto J.; Michael E. Libonati; and Robert F. Williams. *Legislative Law and Statutory Interpretation: Cases and Materials.* 3d ed. N.Y.: Lexis Pub., 2001.

Hibbert, W. Nembhard. *Jurisprudence.* London: Sweet & Maxwell, 1932.

Hirsch, E.D. *Validity in Interpretation.* New Haven: Yale Univ. Press, 1967.

Hirschl, Ron. *Towards Juristocracy: The Origins and Consequences of the New Constitutionalism*. Cambridge, Mass.: Harvard Univ. Press, 2004.

Hoadly, Benjamin. *Sixteen Sermons*. London: John & Paul Knapton, 1754.

Hobbes, Thomas. *Leviathan* [1651]. Richard Tuck, ed. Rev. student ed. Cambridge: Cambridge Univ. Press, 1996.

Hoffer, Peter Charles. *A Nation of Laws: America's Imperfect Pursuit of Justice*. Lawrence, Kan.: Univ. of Kansas Press, 2010.

Holdsworth, William. *A History of English Law*. 16 vols. 2d ed. London: Methuen & Co., 1937.

Holdsworth, William. *Some Makers of English Law*. Cambridge: Cambridge Univ. Press, 1966.

Holdsworth, William. *Sources and Literature of English Law*. Oxford: Clarendon Press, 1925.

Holland, James A.; and Julian S. Webb. *Learning Legal Rules*. 7th ed. Oxford: Oxford Univ. Press, 2010.

Holmes, Oliver Wendell. *Collected Legal Papers*. N.Y.: Harcourt, Brace & Howe, Inc., 1920.

Holmes, Oliver Wendell. *The Common Law*. Boston: Little, Brown & Co., 1881.

Holmes, Oliver Wendell. *Justice Oliver Wendell Holmes: His Book Notices and Uncollected Letters and Papers*. Harry C. Shriver, ed. N.Y.: Central Book Co., 1936.

Holmes, Oliver Wendell. *Speeches*. 2d ed. Boston: Little, Brown & Co., 1934.

Honoré, Tony. *About Law*. Oxford: Clarendon Press, 1995.

Honoré, Tony. *Making Law Bind*. Oxford: Clarendon Press, 1987.

Hook, Sidney (ed.). *Law and Philosophy: A Symposium*. N.Y.: N.Y. Univ. Press, 1964.

Horack, Frank E., Jr. *Cases and Materials on Legislation*. 2d ed. Chicago: Callaghan, 1954.

Hughes, Charles Evans. *The Supreme Court of the United States*. N.Y.: Columbia Univ. Press, 1928.

Huhn, Wilson. *The Five Types of Legal Argument*. Durham, N.C.: Carolina Academic Press, 2002.

Hurst, James Willard. *Dealing with Statutes*. N.Y.: Columbia Univ. Press, 1982.

Hurst, James Willard. *The Growth of American Law*. Boston: Little, Brown & Co., 1950.

Huscroft, Grant; and Bradley W. Miller (eds.). *The Challenge of Originalism: Theories of Constitutional Interpretation*. N.Y.: Cambridge Univ. Press, 2011.

Ilbert, Courtenay. *Legislative Methods and Forms*. London: Henry Frowde and Steven & Sons, 1901.

Ilbert, Courtenay. *The Mechanics of Law Making*. N.Y.: Columbia Univ. Press, 1914.

Ilbert, Courtenay. *Parliament: Its History, Constitution, and Practice*. London: Williams & Norgate, 1911.

Irons, J. Campbell. *The Scottish Justices' Manual*. Edinburgh: William Green & Sons, 1900.

Irons, Peter H. *Brennan vs. Rehnquist: The Battle for the Constitution*. N.Y.: Knopf, 1994.

Jackson, R.M. *The Machinery of Justice in England*. 5th ed. Cambridge: Cambridge Univ. Press, 1967.

Jackson, Robert H. *Full Faith and Credit: The Lawyer's Clause of the Constitution*. N.Y.: Columbia Univ. Press, 1945.

Jackson, Robert H. *The Struggle for Judicial Supremacy*. N.Y.: Knopf, 1941.

Jacob, Giles. *The Statute-Law Common-plac'd*. London: Bernard Lintot, 1731.

Jaffa, Harry V. *Original Intent and the Framers of the Constitution: A Disputed Question*. Washington, D.C.: Regnery Gateway, 1994.

Jaffe, Louis L. *English and American Judges as Lawmakers*. Oxford: Clarendon Press, 1969.

Jellum, Linda D. *Mastering Statutory Interpretation*. Durham, N.C.: Carolina Academic Press, 2008.

Jellum, Linda D.; and David Charles Hricik. *Modern Statutory Interpretation: Problems, Theories, and Lawyering Strategies*. Durham, N.C.: Carolina Academic Press, 2006. 2d ed. 2009.

Jenks, Edward. *The Book of English Law*. P.B. Fairest, ed. 6th ed. Athens, Ohio: Ohio Univ. Press, 1967.

Jenks, Edward. *The New Jurisprudence*. London: John Murray, 1933.

Jenks, Edward. *A Short History of English Law from the Earliest Times to the End of the Year 1911*. Boston: Little, Brown & Co., 1913.

Jennings, W. Iver. *Parliament*. N.Y.: Macmillan, 1940.

Jones, Chester Lloyd. *Statute Law Making in the United States*. Boston: Boston Book Co., 1912.

Jordan, Elijah. *Theory of Legislation: An Essay on the Dynamics of Public Mind* [1930]. Chicago: Univ. of Chicago Press, 1952.

Judson, Frederick N. *The Judiciary and the People*. New Haven: Yale Univ. Press, 1913.

Kames, Lord. *Historical Law-Tracts*. 2d ed. Edinburgh: A. Kincaid, 1761.

Karlen, Delmar. *Appellate Courts in the United States and England*. N.Y.: N.Y. Univ. Press, 1963.

Katzmann, Robert A. (ed.). *Judges and Legislators: Toward Institutional Comity*. Washington, D.C.: Brookings Institution, 1988.

Keefe, William S.; and Morris S. Ogul. *The American Legislative Process*. 10th ed. Upper Saddle River, N.J.: Prentice Hall, 2001.

Keeton, George W. *English Law: The Judicial Contribution*. Newton Abbot, Devon.: David & Charles, 1974.

Keeton, Robert E. *Keeton on Judging in the American Legal System*. Charlottesville: Lexis Law. Pub., 1999.

Keeton, Robert E. *Venturing to Do Justice: Reforming Private Law*. Cambridge, Mass.: Harvard Univ. Press, 1969.

Kelly, David St. Leger (ed.). *Essays on Legislative Drafting*. Adelaide: Adelaide Law Rev. Ass'n, 1988.

Kelsen, Hans. *General Theory of Law and State*. Anders Wedberg, ed. Cambridge, Mass.: Harvard Univ. Press, 1945.

Kelsen, Hans. *The Pure Theory of Law*. Max Knight, trans. Berkeley: Univ. of Cal. Press, 1967.

Kent, Edward Allen (ed.). *Law and Philosophy: Readings in Legal Philosophy*. N.Y.: Appleton-Century-Crofts, 1970.

Kent, Harold S. *In on the Act: Memoirs of a Lawmaker*. London: Macmillan, 1979.

Kent, James. *Commentaries on American Law*. [1826] 4 vols. Charles M. Barnes, ed. 13th ed. Boston: Little, Brown & Co., 1884.

Kerruish, Valerie. *Jurisprudence as Ideology*. London: Routledge, 1991.

Kim, Yule. *Statutory Interpretation: General Principles and Recent Trends*. N.Y.: Nova Science Pubs. Inc., 2009.

Kiralfy, A.K.R. *The English Legal System*. London: Sweet & Maxwell, 1954. 3d ed. 1960.

Kocourek, Albert; and John Henry Wigmore (eds.). *Formative Influences of Legal Development*. Boston: Little, Brown & Co. 1918.

Korkunov, N.M. *General Theory of Law*. W.G. Hastings, trans. 2d ed. N.Y.: Augustus M. Kelley, 1922.

Kornstein, Daniel. *The Music of the Laws*. N.Y.: Everest House Pubs., 1982.

Kramer, Larry D. *The People Themselves: Popular Constitutionalism and Judicial Review*. Oxford: Oxford Univ. Press, 2004.

Kramer, Matthew H. *Objectivity and the Rule of Law*. Cambridge: Cambridge Univ. Press, 2007.

LaFave, Wayne. *Substantive Criminal Law*. 2d ed. Eagan, Minn.: Thomson/West, 2003.

Laski, Harold J. *Studies in Law and Politics*. New Haven: Yale Univ. Press, 1932.

Law Commission. *A New Interpretation Act: To Avoid "Prolixity and Tautology."* Wellington, N.Z.: Law Commission, 1990.

Leach, W.A. *Legal Interpretation for Surveyors*. London: Estates Gazette Ltd., 1966.

Lee, Rex E. *A Lawyer Looks at the Constitution*. Provo, Utah: Brigham Young Univ. Press, 1981.

Leflar, Robert A. *One Life in the Law: A 60-Year Review*. Fayetteville, Ark.: Univ. of Arkansas Press, 1985.

Leiter, Brian (ed.). *Objectivity in Law and Morals*. N.Y.: Cambridge Univ. Press, 2001.

Lenhoff, Arthur. *Comments, Cases, and Other Materials on Legislation*. Buffalo: Dennis, 1949.

Levi, Edward H. *An Introduction to Legal Reasoning*. Chicago: Univ. of Chicago Press, 1949.

Levin, Joel. *How Judges Reason: The Logic of Adjudication*. N.Y.: Peter Lang Pub., 1992.

Levinson, Sanford. *Constitutional Faith*. 2d ed. (with new afterword). Princeton: Princeton Univ. Press, 2011.

Levinson, Sanford; and Steven Mailloux (eds.). *Interpreting Law and Literature: A Hermeneutic Reader*. Evanston, Ill.: Northwestern Univ. Press, 1988.

Levy, Beryl Harold. *Cardozo and the Frontiers of Legal Thinking*. N.Y.: Oxford Univ. Press, 1938.

Levy, Leonard W. *Seasoned Judgments: The American Constitution, Rights, and History*. New Brunswick: Transaction Pubs., 1995.

Leyh, Gregory (ed). *Legal Hermeneutics: History, Theory, and Practice*. Berkeley: University of California Press, 1992.

Lieber, Francis. *Legal and Political Hermeneutics, or Principles of Interpretation and Construction in Law and Politics*. Boston: Little & Brown, 1839. Rev. William G. Hammond. 3d ed. St. Louis: F.H. Thomas & Co., 1880.

Lieber, Francis. *Manual of Political Ethics, Designed Chiefly for the Use of Colleges and Students at Law*. 2 vols. Boston: Little & Brown, 1838.

Lieber, Francis. *On Civil Liberty and Self-Government*. Theodore D. Woolsey, ed. 3d ed. Philadelphia: J.B. Lippincott & Co., 1883.

Lile, William M.; Henry S. Redfield; Eugene Wambaugh; Alfred F. Mason; and James E. Wheeler. *Brief Making and the Use of Law Books*. 3d ed. St. Paul, Minn.: West Pub. Co., 1914.

Linde, Hans A.; and George Bunn. *Legislative and Administrative Processes*. Mineola, N.Y.: Foundation Press, 1976.

Liu, Goodwin; Pamela S. Karlan; and Christopher H. Schroeder. *Keeping Faith with the Constitution*. N.Y.: Oxford Univ. Press, 2010.

Llewellyn, Karl. *The Bramble Bush*. [1930.] Dobbs Ferry, N.Y.: Oceana, 1960.

Llewellyn, Karl. *The Common Law Tradition: Deciding Appeals*. Boston: Little, Brown, 1960.

Llewellyn, Karl. *Jurisprudence: Realism in Theory and Practice*. Chicago: Univ. of Chicago Press, 1962.

Llewellyn, Karl. *The Karl Llewellyn Papers*. William Twining, ed. Chicago: Univ. of Chicago Law School, 1968.

Llewellyn, Karl. *The Theory of Rules*. Frederick Schauer, ed. Chicago: Univ. of Chicago Press, 2011.

Lloyd, Dennis. *The Idea of Law*. Baltimore: Penguin, 1964.

Lloyd, Dennis. *Introduction to Jurisprudence*. Rev. ed. N.Y.: Frederick A. Praeger, 1965.

Locke, John. *An Essay Concerning Human Understanding* [1689]. Edinburgh: Mundell & Son, 1801. Kenneth P. Winkler, ed. Indianapolis, Ind.: Hackett Pub. Co., 1996.

Locke, John. *Second Treatise of Government*. [1689]. Richard Cox, ed. Arlington Heights, Ill.: H. Davidson, 1982.

Lord, Richard A. *Williston on Contracts*. 4th ed. Eagan, Minn.: Thomson/West, 2007.

Luce, Robert. *Legislative Problems: Development, Status, and Trend of the Treatment and Exercise of Lawmaking Powers*. Boston: Houghton Mifflin, 1935.

Lunt, Dudley Cammett. *The Road to the Law*. N.Y.: McGraw-Hill, 1932.

Lynch, Joseph M. *Negotiating the Constitution: The Earliest Debates over Original Intent*. Ithaca: Cornell Univ. Press, 1999.

Lyons, David. *Moral Aspects of Legal Theory*. N.Y.: Cambridge Univ. Press, 1993.

MacCormick, D. Neil. *Legal Reasoning and Legal Theory*. Oxford: Clarendon Press, 1978.

MacCormick, D. Neil; and Robert S. Summers (eds.). *Interpreting Statutes: A Comparative Study*. London: Dartmouth Pub. Co., 1991.

MacCormick, D. Neil; and Peter Birks (eds.). *The Legal Mind: Essays for Tony Honoré*. Oxford: Clarendon Press, 1986.

Macmillan, Lord. *Law and Other Things*. Cambridge: Cambridge Univ. Press, 1938.

Madison, James. *The Writings of James Madison*. 9 vols. Gaillard Hunt, ed. N.Y.: G.P. Putnam's Sons, 1910.

Maine, Henry Sumner. *Ancient Law*. Frederick Pollock, ed. 4th Am. ed. fr. 10th London ed. N.Y.: Henry Holt & Co., 1906.

Maitland, Frederic William *The Constitutional History of England*. Cambridge: Cambridge Univ. Press, 1909.

Maitland, Frederic William; and Francis C. Montague. *A Sketch of English Legal History*. N.Y. & London: G.P. Putnam's Sons, 1915.

Mammen, Christian E. *Using Legislative History in American Statutory Interpretation*. The Hague: Kluwer Law International, 2002.

Manchester, Colin; David Salter; Peter Moodie; and Bernadette Lynch. *Exploring the Law: The Dynamics of Precedent and Statutory Interpretation*. Sydney: Law Book Co., 1996.

Manning, John F.; and Matthew C. Stephenson. *Legislation and Regulation*. N.Y.: Thomson Reuters, 2010.

Mansfield, Harvey C., Jr. *America's Constitutional Soul*. Baltimore: Johns Hopkins Univ. Press, 1991.

Marcus, Maeva. *Truman and the Steel Seizure Case: The Limits of Presidential Power*. N.Y.: Columbia Univ. Press, 1971.

Mason, Alpheus Thomas. *The Supreme Court from Taft to Warren*. N.Y.: W.W. Norton & Co., 1958.

Mayers, Lewis. *The American Legal System*. Rev. ed. N.Y.: Harper & Row, 1964.

McBain, Howard Lee. *The Living Constitution: A Consideration of the Realities and Legends of Our Fundamental Law*. N.Y.: Macmillan, 1927.

McCaffrey, Francis J. *Statutory Construction*. N.Y.: Central Book Co., 1953.

McCarthy, Charles. *The Wisconsin Idea*. N.Y.: Macmillan, 1912.

McCloskey, Robert G. *The American Supreme Court*. Sanford Levinson, ed. 2d ed. Chicago: Univ. of Chicago Press, 1994.

McDowell, Gary L. *The Language of Law and the Foundations of American Constitutionalism*. Cambridge: Cambridge Univ. Press, 2010.

McGowan, Miranda. *Do as I Do, Not as I Say: An Empirical Investigation of Justice Scalia's Ordinary Meaning Method of Statutory Interpretation*. 78 Miss. L.J. 129 (2008).

McKinney's Consolidated Laws of New York Annotated. Vol. 1 ["Statutes"]. St. Paul: West Pub. Co., 1971.

McWhinney, Edward. *Judicial Review in the English-Speaking World*. Toronto: Univ. of Toronto Press, 1956.

Meador, Daniel J.; Thomas E. Baker; and Joan E. Steinman. *Appellate Courts: Structures, Functions, Processes, and Personnel*. 2d ed. Newark: LexisNexis, 2006.

Megarry, R.E. *A New Miscellany-at-Law*. Bryan A. Garner, ed. Oxford: Hart Pub., 2005.

Megarry, R.E. *A Second Miscellany-at-Law*. London: Sweet & Maxwell, 1973.

Mellinkoff, David. *The Language of the Law*. Boston: Little, Brown & Co., 1963.

Merman, Samuel. *Law and the Legal System: An Introduction*. Boston: Little, Brown & Co., 1973.

Merryman, John Henry. *The Civil Law Tradition*. Stanford, Cal.: Stanford Univ. Press, 1969.

Merryman, John Henry (ed.). *Stanford Legal Essays*. Stanford, Cal.: Stanford Univ. Press, 1975.

Micklem, Nathaniel. *Law and the Laws: Being the Marginal Comments of a Theologian*. London: Sweet & Maxwell, 1952.

Mikva, Abner J.; and Eric Lane. *An Introduction to Statutory Interpretation and the Legislative Process*. N.Y.: Aspen Law & Bus., 1997.

Miller, Charles A. *The Supreme Court and the Uses of History*. Cambridge, Mass.: Belknap Press, 1969.

Minor, John B. *Institutes of Common and Statute Law*. 4 vols. Richmond, Va.: J.W. Randolph Co., 1891.

Mishkin, Paul J. *On Law in Courts: An Introduction to Judicial Development of Case and Statute Law*. Brooklyn: Foundation Press, 1965.

Moncrieff, F.C. *The Wit and Wisdom of the Bench and Bar*. London: Cassell, Petter, Galpin & Co., 1882.

Montesquieu, Charles Louis, II [Baron de Montesquieu]. *The Spirit of Laws* [1748]. Thomas Nugent, trans. N.Y.: Hafner Pub. Co., 1949.

Morris, Clarence (ed.). *The Great Legal Philosophers: Selected Readings in Jurisprudence*. Philadelphia: Univ. of Pennsylvania Press, 1963.

Morris, Clarence. *The Justification of the Law*. Philadelphia: Univ. of Pennsylvania Press, 1971.

Morton, William Kinniburgh. *Manual of the Law of Scotland*. Edinburgh: William Green & Sons, 1896.

Muller, James W. (ed.). *The Revival of Constitutionalism*. Lincoln: Univ. of Nebraska Press, 1988.

Murphy, Walter F.; James E. Fleming; A. Barber; and Stephen Macedo. *American Constitutional Interpretation*. 4th ed. N.Y.: Foundation Press, 2008.

Murray, John Edward. *Murray on Contracts*. 2d rev. ed. Indianapolis: Bobbs-Merrill, 1974.

Nelson, Caleb. *Statutory Interpretation*. N.Y.: Foundation Press, 2011.

Nelson, William E. *Americanization of the Common Law*. Cambridge, Mass.: Harvard Univ. Press, 1975.

Newman, Frank C.; and Stanley S. Surrey. *Legislation*. Englewood Cliffs, N.J.: Prentice Hall, 1955.

Newman, Ralph A. (ed.). *Essays in Jurisprudence in Honor of Roscoe Pound*. Indianapolis: Bobbs-Merrill, 1962. [Cf. Sayre.]

Nutting, Charles B.; Shelden D. Elliott; and Reed Dickerson. *Cases and Materials on Legislation*. 4th ed. St. Paul: West, 1969.

O'Brien, David M. (ed.). *Judges on Judging: Views from the Bench*. 1st ed. Chatham, N.J.: Chatham House Pubs., Inc., 1997. 2d ed. Washington, D.C.: CQ Press, 2004.

Office of Legal Policy of the Department of Justice. *The Constitution in the Year 2000: Choices Ahead in Constitutional Interpretation*. Washington, D.C.: GPO, 1988.

O'Neill, Johnathan. *Originalism in American Law and Politics: A Constitutional History*. Baltimore: Johns Hopkins Univ. Press, 2005.

Parkinson, Thomas I. *Cases and Materials on Legislation*. N.Y.: Columbia Univ. Press, 1933.

Partington, Martin. *Introduction to the English Legal System, 2010–2011*. Oxford: Oxford Univ. Press, 2010.

Paton, G.W. *A Textbook of Jurisprudence*. G.W. Paton & David P. Derham, eds. 4th ed. Oxford: Clarendon Press, 1972.

Patterson, Edwin Wilhite. *Jurisprudence: Men and Ideas of the Law*. Brooklyn: Foundation Press, 1953.

Peabody, Bruce (ed.). *The Politics of Judicial Independence: Courts, Politics, and the Public*. Baltimore: Johns Hopkins Univ. Press, 2011.

Pearce, D.C. *Statutory Interpretation in Australia*. Sydney: Butterworths, 1981.

Pennock, J. Roland; and John W. Chapman (eds.). *The Limits of the Law*. N.Y.: Lieber-Atherton, 1974.

Perillo, Joseph M. *Calamari and Perillo on Contracts*. 6th ed. St. Paul: Thomson/West, 2009.

Perkins, Rollin M.; and Ronald N. Boyce. *Criminal Law*. 3d ed. Mineola, N.Y.: Foundation Press, 1982.

Perry, Michael J. *The Constitution, the Courts, and Human Rights: An Inquiry into the Legitimacy of Constitutional Policymaking by the Judiciary*. New Haven: Yale Univ. Press, 1982.

Philbrick, Frederick A. *Language and the Law: The Semantics of Forensic English*. N.Y.: Macmillan, 1949.

Phillips, O. Hood; and A.H. Hudson. *A First Book of English Law*. 7th ed. London: Sweet & Maxwell, 1977.

Pierson, Charles W. *Our Changing Constitution*. N.Y.: Doubleday, Page & Co., 1922.

Piesse, E.L. *The Elements of Drafting*. J.K. Aitken & Peter Butt, eds. 10th ed. Sydney: Lawbook Co., 2004.

Pigeon, Louis-Philippe. *Drafting and Interpreting Legislation*. Toronto: Carswell, 1988.

Plowden, Edmund. *Commentaries, or Reports of Cases Decided in the Superior Courts During the Reigns of Edward VI, Mary, and Elizabeth I* [1571]. London: S. Brooke, 1816.

Plucknett, Theodore F.T. *A Concise History of the Common Law*. 2d ed. London: Butterworth & Co., 1936. 5th ed. London: Butterworth & Co., 1956.

Plucknett, Theodore F.T. *Statutes and Their Interpretation in the First Half of the Fourteenth Century*. Cambridge: Cambridge Univ. Press, 1922.

Politics and the Constitution: The Nature and Extent of Interpretation. Washington, D.C.: Nat'l Legal Ctr. & Am. Studs. Ctr., 1990.

Pollack, Ervin H. *Jurisprudence: Principles and Applications*. Columbus: Ohio St. Univ. Press, 1979.

Pollock, Frederick. *Essays in Jurisprudence and Ethics*. London: Macmillan, 1882.

Pollock, Frederick. *Essays in the Law*. London: Macmillan, 1922.

Pollock, Frederick. *A First Book of Jurisprudence for Students of the Common Law*. London: Macmillan, 1896.

Pollock, Frederick. *The Genius of the Common Law*. N.Y.: Columbia Univ. Press, 1912.

Pollock, Frederick. *An Introduction to the History of the Science of Politics*. London: Macmillan, 1906.

Pollock, Frederick. *Oxford Lectures and Other Discourses*. London: Macmillan, 1890.

Pollock, Frederick; and Frederic William Maitland. *The History of English Law Before the Time of Edward I*. 2 vols. 2d ed. Cambridge: Cambridge Univ. Press, 1898.

Popkin, William D. *A Dictionary of Statutory Interpretation*. Durham, N.C.: Carolina Academic Press, 2007.

Popkin, William D. *Materials on Legislation*. 5th ed. N.Y.: Foundation Press, 2009.

Popkin, William D. *Statutes in Court: The History and Theory of Statutory Interpretation*. Durham, N.C: Duke Univ. Press, 1999.

Posner, Richard A. *The Federal Courts: Crisis and Reform*. Cambridge, Mass.: Harvard Univ. Press, 1985.

Posner, Richard A. *How Judges Think*. Cambridge, Mass.: Harvard Univ. Press, 2008.

Posner, Richard A. *Law and Legal Theory in England and America*. Oxford: Clarendon Press, 1996.

Posner, Richard A. *Law and Literature: A Misunderstood Relation*. 3d ed. Cambridge, Mass.: Harvard Univ. Press, 2009.

Posner, Richard A. *Overcoming Law*. Cambridge, Mass.: Harvard Univ. Press, 1995.

Posner, Richard A. *The Problems of Jurisprudence*. Cambridge, Mass.: Harvard Univ. Press, 1990.

Post, C. Gordon. *An Introduction to the Law*. Englewood Cliffs, N.J.: Prentice Hall, 1963.

Potter, Harold. *An Historical Introduction to English Law and Its Institutions*. London: Sweet & Maxwell, 1848.

Pound, Roscoe. *Contemporary Juristic Theory*. Claremont, Cal.: The Claremont Colleges, 1940.

Pound, Roscoe. *The Future of the Common Law*. Cambridge, Mass.: Harvard Univ. Press, 1937.

Pound, Roscoe. *Interpretations of Legal History*. Cambridge, Mass.: Harvard Univ. Press, 1946.

Pound, Roscoe. *An Introduction to the Philosophy of Law*. New Haven: Yale Univ. Press, 1922.

Pound, Roscoe. *Jurisprudence*. 4 vols. St. Paul: West Pub. Co., 1959.

Pound, Roscoe. *Justice According to Law*. New Haven: Yale Univ. Press, 1951.

Pound, Roscoe. *The Spirit of the Common Law*. Francestown, N.H.: Marshall Jones Co., 1921.

Pound, Roscoe. *The Task of Law*. Lancaster, Pa.: Franklin & Marshall College, 1944.

Powell, Thomas Reed. *Vagaries and Varieties in Constitutional Interpretation*. N.Y.: Columbia Univ. Press, 1956.

Probert, Walter. *Law, Language and Communication*. Springfield, Ill.: Charles C. Thom Pub., 1972.

Pufendorf, Samuel. *Of the Law of Nature and Nations*. Basil Kennett, trans. 4th ed. London: J. Walthoe et al., 1729.

Pufendorf, Samuel. *Two Books of the Elements of Universal Jurisprudence*. [late 17th c.]. William Oldfather, trans. 1931; Thomas Behme, ed. Indianapolis: Liberty Fund, 2009.

Radin, Max. *Handbook of Anglo-American Legal History*. St. Paul: West. Pub. Co., 1936.

Radin, Max. *The Law and You.* N.Y.: New Am. Lib., 1948.

Radin, Max. *Law as Logic and Experience.* New Haven, Conn.: Yale Univ. Press, 1940.

Rakove, Jack N. *Original Meanings: Politics and Ideas in the Making of the Constitution.* N.Y.: Knopf, 1996.

Rakove, Jack N. (ed.). *Interpreting the Constitution: The Debate over Original Intent.* Boston: Northeastern Univ. Press, 1990.

Rapalje, Stewart; and Robert L. Lawrence. *A Dictionary of American and English Law.* Jersey City, N.J.: Frederick D. Linn & Co., 1888.

Raz, Joseph. *The Authority of Law.* N.Y.: Oxford Univ. Press, 1979.

Read, Horace E.; John W. McDonald; and Jefferson B. Fordham. *Cases and Other Materials on Legislation.* 2d ed. Brooklyn: Foundation Press, 1959.

Rehnquist, William H., *The Supreme Court: How It Was, How It Is.* N.Y.: William Morrow & Co., 1987.

Reid, John Philip. *Chief Justice: The Judicial World of Charles Doe.* Cambridge, Mass.: Harvard Univ. Press, 1967.

Reinsch, Paul Samuel. *American Legislatures and Legislative Methods.* N.Y.: Century Co., 1907.

Renton, Lord (ed.). *The Preparation of Legislation.* London: Her Majesty's Stationery Office Pubs., 1975.

Research and Documentation Corp. (ed.). *Drafting Contracts and Commercial Instruments.* Greenvale, N.Y.: Research and Document Corp., 1971.

Restatement (Second) of Contracts §§ 200–230. St. Paul: American Law Institute Pubs., 1981.

Richards, I.A. *Interpretation in Teaching.* N.Y.: Harcourt, Brace & Co., 1938.

Riddall, J.G. *Jurisprudence.* 2d ed. London: Butterworths, 1999.

Robinson, Edward Stevens. *Law and the Lawyers.* N.Y.: Macmillan, 1935.

Robinson, Stanley. *Drafting.* London: Butterworths, 1973.

Robson, William A. *Civilisation and the Growth of Law.* N.Y.: Macmillan, 1935.

Roche, John P. *Courts and Rights: The American Judiciary in Action.* N.Y.: Random House, 1961.

Rosenberg, Gerald N. *The Hollow Hope: Can Courts Bring About Social Change?* 2d ed. Chicago: Univ. of Chicago Press, 2008.

Rosenberg, J. Mitchell. *Jerome Frank: Jurist and Philosopher.* N.Y.: Philosophical Lib., 1970.

Ross, Alf. *On Law and Justice.* Berkeley.: Univ. of Cal. Press, 1959.

Rossum, Ralph A. *Antonin Scalia's Jurisprudence: Text and Tradition.* Lawrence, Kan.: Univ. Press of Kansas, 2006.

Rottschaefer, Henry. *Handbook of Constitutional Law.* St. Paul: West, 1939.

Rotunda, Ronald D.; and John E. Nowak. *Treatise on Constitutional Law: Substance and Procedure.* 4 vols. 3d ed. St. Paul: West Group, 1999.

Rubenfeld, Jed. *Revolution by Judiciary: The Structure of American Constitutional Law.* Cambridge, Mass.: Harvard Univ. Press, 2005.

Russell, F.A.A. *Essays and Excursions in Law.* London: Sweet & Maxwell, 1929.

Salmond, John. *Essays in Jurisprudence and Legal History.* London: Stevens & Sons, 1891.

Salmond, John. *Jurisprudence.* Glanville L. Williams, ed. 10th ed. London: Sweet & Maxwell, 1947.

Savigny, Frederick Charles von. *Of the Vocation of Our Age for Legislation and Jurisprudence.* Abraham Hayward, trans. London: Littlewood & Co., 1831.

Sawer, Geoffrey. *Law in Society.* Oxford: Clarendon Press, 1965.

Sayre, Paul (ed.). *Interpretations of Modern Legal Philosophies: Essays in Honor of Roscoe Pound.* N.Y.: Oxford Univ. Press, 1947. [Cf. Newman, Ralph A.]

Scalia, Antonin; and Bryan A. Garner. *Making Your Case: The Art of Persuading Judges.* St. Paul: Thomson/West, 2008.

Scalia, Antonin. *A Matter of Interpretation: Federal Courts and the Law.* Princeton, N.J.: Princeton Univ. Press, 1997.

Schauer, Frederick. *Playing by the Rules: A Philosophical Examination of Rule-Based Decision-Making in Law and in Life.* N.Y.: Oxford Univ. Press, 1991.

Schlag, Pierre. *The Enchantment of Reason.* Durham, N.C.: Duke Univ. Press, 1998.

Schleiermacher, F.D. *Hermeneutics: The Handwritten Manuscripts.* Heinz Kimmerle, ed. James Duke & Jack Forstman, trans. Missoula, Mont.: Scholars Press, 1977.

Schubert, Glendon (ed.). *Judicial Decision-Making.* N.Y.: Free Press of Glencoe, 1963.

Schur, Edwin M. *Law and Society: A Sociological View.* N.Y.: Random House, 1968.

Science of Legal Method: Select Essays by Various Authors. Ernest Bruncken & Layton B. Register, trans. Boston: Boston Book Co., 1917.

Seagle, William. *The Quest for Law.* N.Y.: Knopf, 1941.

Sedgwick, Theodore; and John Norton Pomeroy. *A Treatise on the Rules Which Govern the Interpretation and Construction of Statutory and Constitutional Law*. N.Y.: John S. Voorhies, 1857. 2d ed. N.Y.: Baker, Voorhis & Co., 1874.

Seidman, Louis Michael. *Our Unsettled Constitution: A New Defense of Constitutionalism and Judicial Review*. New Haven: Yale Univ. Press, 2001.

Shaman, Jeffrey M. *Constitutional Interpretation*. Westport, Conn.: Greenwood Press, 2001.

Shambaugh, Benjamin F. (ed.). *Statute-Making in Iowa*. Applied History vol. 3. Iowa City: State Historical Soc'y of Iowa, 1916.

Shanks, Hershel. *The Art and Craft of Judging: The Decisions of Judge Learned Hand*. N.Y.: Macmillan, 1968.

Shapiro, Martin M. *Courts: A Comparative and Political Analysis*. Chicago: Univ. of Chicago Press, 1981.

Shapiro, Martin M. *Who Guards the Guardians?: Judicial Control of Administration*. Athens, Ga.: Univ. of Georgia Press, 1988.

Shapiro, Scott J. *Legality*. Cambridge, Mass.: Harvard Univ. Press, 2011.

Sharp, G. Granville; and Brian Galpin. *Maxwell on the Interpretation of Statutes*. 10th ed. London: Sweet & Maxwell, 1953.

Shartel, Burke. *Our Legal System and How It Operates*. Ann Arbor: Univ. of Mich. Law School, 1951.

Shklar, Judith N. *Legalism*. Cambridge, Mass.: Harvard Univ. Press, 1964.

Simpson, A.W.B. *Invitation to Law*. Oxford: Blackwell Pub., 1988.

Sinclair, Michael B.W. *Guide to Statutory Interpretation*. Albany: Lexis, 2000.

Singer, Norman J.; and J.D. Shambie Singer. *Statutes and Statutory Construction*. 14 vols. 7th ed. St. Paul: West, 2007. [This is a successor to *Sutherland on Statutes and Statutory Construction*, by Jabez Gridley Sutherland.]

Smith, E. Fitch. *Commentaries on Statute and Constitutional Law and Statutory and Constitutional Construction*. 2d ed. N.Y.: Albany, Banks & Bros., 1876.

Snowiss, Sylvia. *Judicial Review and the Law of the Constitution*. New Haven: Yale Univ. Press, 1990.

Solan, Lawrence M. *The Language of Statutes: Laws and Their Interpretation*. Chicago: Univ. of Chicago Press, 2010.

Staab, James B. *The Political Thought of Justice Antonin Scalia: A Hamiltonian on the Supreme Court*. Lanham, Md.: Rowman & Littlefield Pubs., 2006.

Stevens, Robert. *The Independence of the Judiciary: The View from the Lord Chancellor's Office*. Oxford: Oxford Univ. Press, 1993.

Stimson, Frederic Jesup. *Popular Law-Making: A Study of the Origin, History, and Present Tendencies of Law-Making by Statute*. N.Y.: Charles Scribner's Sons, 1910.

Stone, Julius. *Legal System and Lawyers' Reasoning*. Stanford, Cal.: Stanford Univ. Press, 1968.

Story, Joseph. *Commentaries on the Constitution of the United States*. 2 vols. 2d ed. Boston: Little, Brown & Co., 1858.

Story, Joseph. *Commentaries on the Law of Promissory Notes, and Guaranties of Notes*. 3d ed. Boston: Little & Brown, 1851.

Story, Joseph. *A Familiar Exposition of the Constitution of the United States*. N.Y.: Am. Book Co., 1840.

Story, William W. *A Treatise on the Law of Contracts Not Under Seal*. 2 vols. Melville M. Bigelow, ed. 5th ed. Boston: Little, Brown & Co., 1874.

Strauss, David A. *The Living Constitution*. N.Y.: Oxford Univ. Press, 2010.

Strauss, Peter L. *Legislation: Understanding and Using Statutes*. N.Y.: Foundation Press, 2006.

Summers, Robert S.; D. Neil MacCormick; and John Bell. *Legal Reasoning and Statutory Interpretation: Rotterdam Lectures in Jurisprudence*. Jan van Dunné, ed. Arnhem, Neth.: Gouda Quint, 1989.

Sunstein, Cass R. *A Constitution of Many Minds*. Princeton, N.J.: Princeton Univ. Press, 2009.

Sunstein, Cass R. *One Case at a Time: Judicial Minimalism on the Supreme Count*. Cambridge, Mass.: Harvard Univ. Press, 1999.

Sunstein, Cass R. *The Partial Constitution*. Cambridge, Mass.: Harvard Univ. Press, 1993.

Sutherland, Arthur E. (ed.). *Government Under Law*. Cambridge, Mass.: Harvard Univ. Press, 1956.

Sutherland, George. *Constitutional Power and World Affairs*. N.Y.: Columbia Univ. Press, 1919.

Sutherland, Jabez Gridley. *See* Singer, Norman J.

Swindler, William F. *Court and Constitution in the 20th Century: The Modern Interpretation*. Indianapolis: Bobbs-Merrill, 1974.

Symonds, Arthur. *The Mechanics of Law-Making*. London: E. Churton, 1835.

Tamanaha, Brian Z. *Beyond the Formalist–Realist Divide: The Role of Politics in Judging*. Princeton: Princeton Univ. Press, 2010.

Tamanaha, Brian Z. *Law as a Means to an End: Threat to the Rule of Law.* Cambridge: Cambridge Univ. Press, 2006.

Tamanaha, Brian Z. *On the Rule of Law: History, Politics, Theory.* Cambridge: Cambridge Univ. Press, 2004.

Tamen, Miguel. *Manners of Interpretation: The Ends of Argument in Literary Studies.* Albany: State Univ. of New York Press, 1993.

Thayer, James Bradley. *John Marshall.* Boston: Houghton Mifflin, 1901.

Thibaut, Anton Friedrich Justus. *An Introduction to the Study of Jurisprudence.* Nathaniel Lindley, trans. Philadelphia: T. & J.W. Johnson, 1855.

Thorne, Samuel E. (ed.). *A Discourse upon the Exposicion and Understandinge of Statutes with Sir Thomas Egerton's Additions.* [ca. 1565]. San Marino, CA: Huntington Lib. Press, 1942.

Thornton, G.C. *Legislative Drafting.* 4th ed. London: Butterworths, 1996.

Thring, Henry. *Practical Legislation.* London: H.M. Stationery Office, 1878.

Thring, Henry. *Simplification of the Law.* London: R.J. Bush, 1875.

Tiedeman, Christopher G. *The Unwritten Constitution of the United States: A Philosophical Inquiry into the Fundamentals of American Constitutional Law.* N.Y.: G.P. Putnam's Sons, 1890.

Tribe, Laurence H. *American Constitutional Law.* 3d ed. N.Y.: Foundation Press, 2000.

Tribe, Laurence H. *God Save This Honorable Court.* N.Y.: Random House, 1985.

Tribe, Laurence H. *The Invisible Constitution.* N.Y.: Oxford Univ. Press, 2008.

Tribe, Laurence H.; and Michael C. Dorf. *On Reading the Constitution.* Cambridge, Mass.: Harvard Univ. Press, 1991.

Turner, J.W. Cecil. *Kenny's Outlines of Criminal Law.* 19th ed. Cambridge: Cambridge Univ. Press, 1966.

Tushnet, Mark. *Red, White, and Blue: A Critical Analysis of Constitutional Law.* Cambridge, Mass.: Harvard Univ. Press, 1988.

Tushnet, Mark. *Taking the Constitution Away from the Courts.* Princeton, N.J.: Princeton Univ. Press, 1999.

Tushnet, Mark. *Why the Constitution Matters.* New Haven: Yale Univ. Press, 2010.

Twining, William; and David Miers. *How to Do Things with Rules: A Primer of Interpretation.* 5th ed. Cambridge: Cambridge Univ. Press, 2010.

United States Department of Justice. *Using and Misusing Legislative History: A Reevaluation of the Status of Legislative History in Statutory Interpretation.* Washington, D.C.: Office of Legal Policy, 1989.

Vanderbilt, Arthur T. *Men and Measures of the Law.* N.Y.: Knopf, 1949.

Vandevelde, Kenneth J. *Thinking Like a Lawyer: An Introduction to Legal Reasoning.* Boulder, Colo.: Water View Press, 1996.

Vermeule, Adrian. *Judging Under Uncertainty: An Institutional Theory of Legal Interpretation.* Cambridge, Mass.: Harvard Univ. Press, 2006.

Vermeule, Adrian. *Law and the Limits of Reason.* N.Y.: Oxford Univ. Press, 2009.

Vinogradoff, Paul. *The Collected Papers of Paul Vinogradoff.* 2 vols. Oxford: Clarendon Press, 1928.

Vinogradoff, Paul. *Common-Sense in Law.* London: Williams & Norgate, 1925.

Vinogradoff, Paul. *Essays in Legal History.* London: Oxford Univ. Press, 1913.

Vinogradoff, Paul. *Outlines of Historical Jurisprudence.* Oxford Univ. Press, 1920.

Von Savigny. *See* Savigny.

Wagner, Anne; Wouter Werner; and Deborah Cao (eds.). *Interpretation, Law, and the Construction of Meaning: Collected Papers on Legal Interpretation in Theory, Adjudication and Political Practice.* Dordrecht, Neth.: Springer, 2010.

Walker, Timothy. *Introduction to American Law.* Philadelphia: P.H. Nicklin & T. Johnson, 1837. Clement Bates, ed. 10th ed. Boston: Little, Brown, 1895.

Walkland, S.A. *The Legislative Process in Great Britain.* London: George Allen & Unwin, 1968.

Ward, Kenneth D.; and Cecilia R. Castillo (eds.). *The Judiciary and American Democracy.* Albany: State Univ. of New York Press, 2005.

Warmington, L. Crispin (ed.). *Stephen's Commentaries on the Laws of England.* 4 vols. 21st ed. London: Butterworth & Co., 1950.

Warren, Charles. *The Supreme Court in United States History.* 2 vols. Boston: Little, Brown & Co., 1926.

Wasserstrom, Richard A. *The Judicial Decision: Toward a Theory of Legal Justification.* Stanford, Cal.: Stanford Univ. Press, 1961.

Watson, Alan. *Failures of the Legal Imagination.* Phil.: Univ. of Pennsylvania Press, 1988.

Watson, Alan. *Legal Origins and Legal Change.* London: Hambledon Press, 1991.

Webster, Daniel. *The Works of Daniel Webster.* 6 vols. Boston: C.C. Little & J. Brown, 1851.

Wellington, Harry H. *Interpreting the Constitution: The Supreme Court and the Process of Adjudication.* New Haven: Yale Univ. Press, 1990.

Wheare, K.C. *Modern Constitutions.* 2d ed. London: Oxford Univ. Press, 1966.

White, G. Edward. *The American Judicial Tradition.* 3d ed. N.Y.: Oxford Univ. Press, 2007.

White, G. Edward. *The Constitution and the New Deal.* Cambridge, Mass.: Harvard Univ. Press, 2000.

Whittington, Keith E. *Constitutional Construction: Divided Powers and Constitutional Meaning.* Cambridge, Mass.: Harvard Univ. Press, 1999.

Whittington, Keith E. *Constitutional Interpretation: Textual Meaning, Original Intent, and Judicial Review.* Lawrence, Kan.: Univ. Press of Kansas, 1999.

Wigmore, John Henry. *Problems of Law: Its Past, Present, and Future.* N.Y.: Charles Scribner's Sons, 1920.

Wilberforce, Edward. *Statute Law: The Principles Which Governs the Construction and Operation of Statutes.* London: Stevens & Co., 1881.

Wilkinson, J. Harvie, III. *Cosmic Constitutional Theory.* N.Y.: Oxford Univ. Press, 2012.

Willard, Ashton R. *A Legislative Handbook.* Boston: Houghton Mifflin, 1890.

Williams, Glanville L. *Learning the Law.* 9th ed. Stevens & Sons, 1973. A.T.H. Smith, ed. 12th ed. London: Sweet & Maxwell, 2002.

Williams, Glanville L. *Textbook of Criminal Law.* London: Stevens & Sons, 1978.

Williston, Samuel. *A Treatise on the Law of Contracts.* Richard A. Lord, ed. 4th ed. Eagan, Minn.: Thomson/West, 2007.

Winfield, Percy H. *The Chief Sources of English Legal History.* Cambridge, Mass.: Harvard Univ. Press, 1925.

Wolfe, Christopher. *The Rise of Modern Judicial Review: From Constitutional Interpretation to Judge-Made Law.* Rev. ed. Lanham, Md.: Rowman & Littlefield, 1994.

Wortley, B.A. *Jurisprudence.* Manchester: Univ. of Manchester Press, 1967.

Wright, Charles Alan. *The Law of Federal Courts.* 5th ed. St. Paul: West, 1994.

Wright, Charles Alan; et al. *Federal Practice and Procedure.* 31 vols. St. Paul: West Pub. Co., 2011.

Wright, Lord, of Durley. *Legal Essays and Addresses.* Cambridge: Cambridge Univ. Press, 1939.

Wyzanski, Charles E., Jr. *Whereas—A Judge's Premises: Essays in Judgment, Ethics, and the Law.* Boston: Little, Brown & Co., 1965.

Yale Law Faculty. *Two Centuries' Growth of American Law: 1701–1901.* N.Y.: Charles Scribner's Sons, 1901.

Zander, Michael. *The Law-Making Process.* 4th ed. London: Butterworths, 1994.

Zander, Michael. *A Matter of Justice: The Legal System in Ferment.* London: I.B. Tauris & Co., 1988.

Articles

Abraham, Kenneth S. *Statutory Interpretation and Literary Theory: Some Common Concerns of an Unlikely Pair.* 32 Rutgers L. Rev. 676 (1979).

Abrahamson, Shirley S.; and Robert L. Hughes. *Shall We Dance? Steps for Legislators and Judges in Statutory Interpretation.* 75 Minn. L. Rev. 1045 (1991).

Ackerman, Bruce A. *The Living Constitution.* 120 Harv. L. Rev. 1737 (2007).

Adler, Donna D. *A Conversational Approach to Statutory Analysis: Say What You Mean & Mean What You Say.* 66 Miss. L.J. 37 (1996).

Aigler, Ralph W. *Legislation in Vague or General Terms.* 21 Mich. L. Rev. 831 (1923).

Aleinikoff, T. Alexander. *Updating Statutory Interpretation.* 87 Mich. L. Rev. 20 (1988).

Aleinikoff, T. Alexander; and Theodore M. Shaw. *The Costs of Incoherence: A Comment on Plain Meaning,* West Virginia University Hospitals, Inc. v. Casey, *and Due Process of Statutory Interpretation.* 45 Vand. L. Rev. 687 (1992).

Alexander, Larry A. *On Statutory Interpretation: Fancy Theories of Interpretation Aren't.* 73 Wash. U. L.Q. 1081 (1995).

Alexander, Larry A. *Painting Without the Numbers: Noninterpretive Judicial Review.* 8 U. Dayton L. Rev. 447 (1983).

Alexander, Larry A.; and Saikrishna Prakash. *Mother May I? Imposing Mandatory Prospective Rules of Statutory Interpretation.* 20 Const. Comment. 97 (2003).

Amar, Akhil Reed. *Intratextualism.* 112 Harv. L. Rev. 747 (1999).

Amar, Akhil Reed. *On Lawson on Precedent.* 17 Harv. J.L. & Pub. Pol'y 39 (1994).

Amar, Akhil Reed. *On Text and Precedent.* 31 Harv. J.L. & Pub. Pol'y 961 (2008).

Amar, Akhil Reed. *Rethinking Originalism: Original Intent for Liberals (and for Conservatives and Moderates, Too).* Slate, 21 Sept. 2005. http://www.slate.com/id/2126680.

Amar, Akhil Reed. *The Supreme Court, 1999 Term—Foreword: The Document and the Doctrine.* 114 Harv. L. Rev. 26 (2000).

Amos, Maurice Sheldon. *The Interpretation of Statutes.* 5 Cambridge L.J. 163 (1934).

Andrews, James DeWitt. "Statutory Construction," in 14 *American Law and Procedure.* James Parker Hall & James DeWitt Andrews, eds. Rev. ed. Chicago: La Salle Extension Univ., 1948.

Aprill, Ellen P.; and Nancy Staudt. *Theories of Statutory Interpretation (and Their Limits).* 38 Loy. L.A. L. Rev. 1899 (2005).

Araujo, Robert John. *Method in Interpretation: Practical Wisdom and the Search for Meaning in Public Legal Texts.* 68 Miss. L.J. 225 (1998).

Araujo, Robert John. *Suggestions for a Foundation Course in Legislation.* 15 Seton Hall Legis. J. 17 (1991).

Ard, B.J. *Interpreting by the Book: Legislative Drafting Manuals and Statutory Interpretation.* 120 Yale L.J. 185 (2010).

Arnold, Morris S. *The Enterprise of Judging: Panel I—The Diversity of the Federalist Society.* 17 Harv. J.L. & Pub. Pol'y 5 (1994).

Atiyah, P.S. "Judicial–Legislative Relations in England," in *Judges and Legislators: Toward Institutional Comity.* Robert A. Katzmann, ed. Washington, D.C.: Brookings Institution, 1988.

Attanasio, John B. *Everyman's Constitutional Law: A Theory of the Power of Judicial Review.* 72 Geo. L.J. 1665 (1984).

Auchie, Derek. *The Undignified Death of the Casus Omissus Rule.* 25 Statute L. Rev. 40 (2004).

Ayers, Marc James. *Unpacking Alabama's Plain-Meaning Rule of Statutory Construction.* 67 Ala. Law. 31 (2006).

Baade, Hans W. *"Original Intent" in Historical Perspective: Some Critical Glosses.* 69 Tex. L. Rev. 1001 (1991).

Baade, Hans W. *"Original Intention": Raoul Berger's Fake Antique.* 70 N.C. L. Rev. 1523 (1992).

Baade, Hans W. *Time and Meaning: Notes on the Intertemporal Law of Statutory Construction and Constitutional Interpretation.* 43 Am. J. Comp. L. 319 (1995).

Baer, Judith A. "The Fruitless Search for Original Intent," in *Judging the Constitution: Critical Essays on Judicial Lawmaking.* Michael W. McCann & Gerald L. Houseman, eds. Glenview, Ill.: Scott, Foresman, 1989.

Baker, Scott; and Kimberly D. Krawiec. *The Penalty Default Canon.* 72 Geo. Wash. L. Rev. 663 (2004).

Balkin, Jack M. *Abortion and Original Meaning.* 24 Const. Comment. 291 (2007).

Balkin, Jack M. "Fidelity to Text and Principle," in *The Constitution in 2020.* Jack M. Balkin & Reva B. Siegel, eds. N.Y.: Oxford Univ. Press, 2009.

Balkin, Jack M. *Original Meaning and Constitutional Redemption.* 24 Const. Comment. 427 (2007).

Balkin, Jack M. *Tradition, Betrayal, and the Politics of Deconstruction.* 11 Cardozo L. Rev. 1613 (1990).

Barak, Aharon. Foreword, *A Judge on Judging: The Role of a Supreme Court in a Democracy.* 116 Harv. L. Rev. 16 (2002).

Barker, William B. *Statutory Interpretation, Comparative Law, and Economic Theory: Discovering the Grund of Income Taxation.* 40 San Diego L. Rev. 821 (2003).

Barnett, Randy E. *The Choice Between Madison and FDR.* 31 Harv. J.L. & Pub. Pol'y 1005 (2008).

Barnett, Randy E. *An Originalism for Nonoriginalists.* 45 Loy. L. Rev. 611 (1999).

Barnett, Randy E. *The Original Meaning of the Commerce Clause.* 68 U. Chi. L. Rev. 101 (2001).

Barnett, Randy E. *Scalia's Infidelity: A Critique of Faint-Hearted Originalism.* 75 U. Cin. L. Rev. 7 (2006).

Barnett, Randy E. *Trumping Precedent with Original Meaning: Not as Radical as It Sounds.* 22 Const. Comment. 527 (2005).

Barrett, Amy Coney. *Statutory Stare Decisis in the Courts of Appeals.* 73 Geo. Wash. L. Rev. 317 (2005).

Bassett, Debra Lyn. *Statutory Interpretation in the Context of Federal Jurisdiction.* 76 Geo. Wash. L. Rev. 52 (2007).

Bates, T. St. J. N. *Parliamentary Material and Statutory Construction: Aspects of the Practical Application of* Pepper v. Hart. 14 Statute L. Rev. 46 (1993).

Batey, Robert. *Vagueness and the Construction of Criminal Statutes—Balancing Acts.* 5 Va. J. Soc. Pol'y & L. 1 (1997).

Beaney, William M. *Civil Liberties and Statutory Construction.* 8 J. Pub. L. 66 (1959).

Beard, Charles A. *The Living Constitution.* 185 Annals Am. Acad. Pol. & Soc. Sci. 29 (1936).

Beard, Charles A. "Judicial Review and 'the Intent of the Framers'" (1912), in *Essays in Constitutional Law.* Robert G. McCloskey, ed. N.Y.: Knopf, 1957.

Beaulac, Stéphane. *Parliamentary Debates in Statutory Interpretation: A Question of Admissibility or of Weight?* 43 McGill L.J. 287 (1998).

Bell, Bernard W. *Interpreting and Enacting Statutes in the Constitution's Shadows: An Introduction.* 32 U. Dayton L. Rev. 307 (2007).

Bell, Bernard W. *Legislative History Without Legislative Intent: The Public Justification Approach to Statutory Interpretation.* 60 Ohio St. L.J. 1 (1999).

Bell, Bernard W. *"No Motor Vehicles in the Park": Reviving the Hart–Fuller Debate to Introduce Statutory Construction.* 48 J. Legal Educ. 88 (1998).

Bell, Bernard W. *R-E-S-P-E-C-T: Respecting Legislative Judgments in Interpretive Theory.* 78 N.C. L. Rev. 1253 (2000).

Bell, Bernard W. *Using Statutory Interpretation to Improve the Legislative Process: Can It Be Done in the Post-Chevron Era?* 13 J.L. & Pol. 105 (1997).

Bell, John. "Policy Arguments in Statutory Interpretation," in *Legal Reasoning and Statutory Interpretation.* Jan van Dunné, ed. Arnhem, Neth.: Gouda Quint, 1989.

Bennett, Robert W. *Objectivity in Constitutional Law.* 132 U. Pa. L. Rev. 445 (1984).

Bennett, Robert W. *Originalism: Lessons from Things That Go Without Saying.* 45 San Diego L. Rev. 645 (2008).

Bennett, Robert W. *Originalist Theories of Constitutional Interpretation.* 73 Cornell L. Rev. 355 (1988).

Bennett, Robert W. *The Supreme Court and Textualism.* 49 Tax Notes 109 (1990).

Bentil, J. Kodwo. *Statutory Surplusage.* 12 Statute L. Rev. 64 (1991).

Berger, Raoul. *Constitutional Interpretation and Activist Fantasies.* 82 Ky. L.J. 1 (1993).

Berger, Raoul. *Doctor Bonham's Case: Statutory Construction or Constitutional Theory?* 117 U. Pa. L. Rev. 521 (1969).

Berger, Raoul. *Mark Tushnet's Critique of Interpretivism.* 51 Geo. Wash. L. Rev. 532 (1983).

Berger, Raoul. *New Theories of "Interpretation": The Activist Flight from the Constitution.* 47 Ohio St. L.J. 1 (1986).

Berger, Raoul. *Original Intent: The Rage of Hans Baade.* 71 N.C. L. Rev. 1151 (1993).

Berger, Raoul. *Original Intent: A Response to Hans Baade.* 70 Tex. L. Rev. 1535 (1992).

Berger, Raoul. *Original Intention in Historical Perspective.* 54 Geo. Wash. L. Rev. 296 (1986).

Berger, Raoul. *Originalist Theories of Constitutional Interpretation.* 73 Cornell L. Rev. 350 (1988).

Berger, Raoul. *Some Reflections on Interpretivism.* 55 Geo. Wash. L. Rev. 1 (1986).

Berman, Mitchell N. *Originalism and Its Discontents (Plus a Thought or Two About Abortion).* 24 Const. Comment. 383 (2007).

Berman, Mitchell N. *Originalism Is Bunk.* 84 N.Y.U. L. Rev. 1 (2009).

Betti, Emilio. *On a General Theory of Interpretation: The Raison d' Etre of Hermeneutics.* 32 Am. J. Juris. 245 (1987).

BeVier, Lillian R. *The Integrity and Impersonality of Originalism.* 19 Harv. J.L. & Pub. Pol'y 283 (1996).

BeVier, Lillian R. *Judicial Restraint: An Argument from Institutional Design.* 17 Harv. J.L. & Pub. Pol'y 7 (1994).

Binder, Guyora. *Institutions and Linguistic Conventions: The Pragmatism of Lieber's Legal Hermeneutics.* 16 Cardozo L. Rev. 2169 (1995).

Birch, Christopher. *The Connotation/Denotation Distinction in Constitutional Interpretation.* 5 J. App. Prac. & Process 445 (2003).

Bishin, William Robert. *The Law Finders: An Essay in Statutory Interpretation.* 38 S. Cal. L. Rev. 1 (1965).

Bishop, Thomas A. *The Death and Reincarnation of Plain Meaning in Connecticut: A Case Study.* 41 Conn. L. Rev. 825 (2009).

Black, Henry Campbell. *In Defense of the Judiciary.* 1 Const. Rev. 23 (1917).

Blatt, William S. *The History of Statutory Interpretation: A Study in Form and Substance.* 6 Cardozo L. Rev. 799 (1985).

Blatt, William S. *Interpretive Communities: The Missing Element in Statutory Interpretation.* 95 Nw. U. L. Rev. 629 (2001).

Blatt, William S. *Missing the Mark: An Overlooked Statute Redefines the Debate over Statutory Interpretation.* 64 U. Miami L. Rev. 641 (2010).

Bonfield, Arthur E. *The Abrogation of Penal Statutes by Nonenforcement.* 49 Iowa L. Rev. 389 (1964).

Bork, Robert H. *The Impossibility of Finding Welfare Rights in the Constitution.* 1979 Wash. U. L.Q. 695.

Bork, Robert H. *Neutral Principles and Some First Amendment Problems.* 47 Ind. L.J. 1 (1971).

Boudreau, Cheryl; Mathew D. McCubbins; and Daniel B. Rodriguez. *Statutory Interpretation and the Intentional(ist) Stance.* 38 Loy. L.A. L. Rev. 2131 (2005).

Bowen, Serena Perretti. *Extrinsic Aids to Statutory Interpretation—The New Jersey View.* 8 Rutgers L. Rev. 486 (1954).

Boyle, James. *The Politics of Reason: Critical Legal Theory and Local Social Thought.* 133 U. Pa. L. Rev. 685 (1985).

Brazil, P. *Legislative History and the Sure and True Interpretation of Statutes in General and the Constitution in General.* 4 U. Queens L. Rev. 1 (1961).

Breen, John M. *Statutory Interpretation and the Lessons of Llewellyn.* 33 Loy. L.A. L. Rev. 263 (2000).

Breitel, Charles D. "The Courts and Law-Making," in *Legal Institutions Today and Tomorrow.* Monrad G. Paulsen, ed. N.Y.: Columbia Univ. Press, 1959.

Brennan, William J., Jr. *The Constitution of the United States: Contemporary Ratification.* 27 S. Tex. L. Rev. 433 (1986).

Bressman, Lisa Schultz. *Deference and Democracy.* 75 Geo. Wash. L. Rev. 761 (2007).

Brest, Paul. *The Misconceived Quest for the Original Understanding.* 60 B.U. L. Rev. 204 (1980).

Breyer, Stephen. *On the Uses of Legislative History in Interpreting Statutes.* 65 S. Cal. L. Rev. 845 (1992).

Bronaugh, Richard; Peter Barton; and Aileen Kavanagh. *The Idea of a Living Constitution.* 16 Can. J.L. & Jurisprudence 55 (2003).

Brossard, Eugene Edward. *Punctuation of Statutes.* 24 Or. L. Rev. 157 (1945).

Brown, Rebecca L. *History for the Non-Originalist.* 26 Harv. J.L. & Pub. Pol'y 69 (2003).

Brudner, Alan. *The Ideality of Difference: Toward Objectivity in Legal Interpretation.* 11 Cardozo L. Rev. 1133 (1990).

Brudney, James J.; and Corey Ditslear. *Canons of Construction and the Elusive Quest for Neutral Reasoning.* 58 Vand. L. Rev. 1 (2005).

Brudney, James J.; and Corey Ditslear. *The Decline and Fall of Legislative History? Patterns of Supreme Court Reliance in the Burger and Rehnquist Eras.* 89 Judicature 220 (2006).

Brudney, James J.; and Corey Ditslear. *The Warp and Woof of Statutory Interpretation: Comparing Supreme Court Approaches in Tax Law and Workplace Law.* 58 Duke L.J. 1231 (2009).

Brugger, Winfried. *Concretization of Law and Statutory Interpretation.* 11 Tul. Eur. & Civ. L.F. 207 (1996).

Bruncken, Ernest. *Interpretation of the Written Law.* 25 Yale L.J. 129 (1915).

Bucholtz, Barbara K. *The Interpretive Project and the Problem of Legitimacy.* 11 Tex. Wesleyan L. Rev. 377 (2005).

Buchwald, Delf. *Statutory Interpretation in the Focus of Legal Justification: An Essay in Coherentist Hermeneutics.* 25 U. Tol. L. Rev. 735 (1994).

Burrows, J.F. *The Cardinal Rule of Statutory Construction in New Zealand.* 3 N.Z. Univ. L. Rev. 253 (1969).

Burrows, J.F. *Inconsistent Statutes.* 3 Otago L. Rev. 601 (1976).

Burrows, J.F. *Statutory Interpretation in New Zealand.* 11 N.Z. Univ. L. Rev. 1 (1984).

Butler, Judith. *Deconstruction and the Possibility of Justice: Comments on Bernasconi, Cornell, Miller, Weber.* 11 Cardozo L. Rev. 1715 (1990).

Buzbee, William W. *The One-Congress Fiction in Statutory Interpretation.* 149 U. Pa. L. Rev. 171 (2000).

Calabresi, Steven G. *A Critical Introduction to the Originalism Debate.* 31 Harv. J.L. & Pub. Pol'y 875 (2008).

Calabresi, Steven G. *The Originalist and Normative Case Against Judicial Activism: A Reply to Professor Barnett.* 103 Mich. L. Rev. 1081 (2005).

Calabresi, Steven G. *Text vs. Precedent in Constitutional Law.* 31 Harv. J.L. & Pub. Pol'y 947 (2008).

Calabresi, Steven G.; and Julia T. Rickert. *Originalism and Sex Discrimination.* 90 Tex. L. Rev. 1 (2011).

Campos, Paul F. *That Obscure Object of Desire: Hermeneutics and the Autonomous Legal Text.* 77 Minn. L. Rev. 1065 (1993).

Campos, Paul F. *Three Mistakes About Interpretation.* 92 Mich. L. Rev. 388 (1993).

Carro, Jorge L.; and Andrew R. Brann. *The U.S. Supreme Court and the Use of Legislative Histories.* 22 Jurimetrics J. 294 (1982).

Carrol, Peter H., III. *Literalism: The United States Supreme Court's Methodology for Statutory Construction in Bankruptcy Cases.* 25 St. Mary's L.J. 143 (1993).

Carroll, Kristy L. *Whose Statute Is It Anyway? Why and How Courts Should Use Presidential Signing Statements When Interpreting Federal Statutes.* 46 Cath. U. L. Rev. 475 (1997).

Carter, Ross. *Statutory Interpretation in New Zealand's Court of Appeal: When "May" Means "Must," Section Headings Affect Interpretation, and Latent Acts Have Effect.* 22 Statute L. Rev. 20 (2001).

Carter, Ross. *Statutory Interpretation Using Legislated Examples: Bennion on Multiple Consumer Credit Agreements.* 32 Statute L. Rev. 86 (2011).

Cavanaugh, Earl J. *The Effect of the Statutory Construction Act in Pennsylvania.* 12 U. Pitt. L. Rev. 283 (1951).

Cavanaugh, Maureen B. *Order in Multiplicity: Aristotle on Text, Context, and the Rule of Law.* 79 N.C. L. Rev. 577 (2001).

Chafee, Zechariah, Jr. *The Disorderly Conduct of Words*. 41 Colum. L. Rev. 381 (1941).

Chamberlain, J.P. *The Courts and Committee Reports*. 1 Chi. L. Rev. 81 (1933).

Chandler, Jim. *Statutory Construction: Effect of Congressional Acknowledgement of Judicial Construction*. 16 Okla. L. Rev. 221 (1963).

Channick, Susan A. Estate of MacDonald: *A Case for Logical over Literal Statutory Construction*. 28 Idaho L. Rev. 919 (1992).

Chemerinsky, Erwin. *Foreword: The Vanishing Constitution*. 103 Harv. L. Rev. 43 (1989).

Chibundu, Maxwell O. *Structure and Structuralism in the Interpretation of Statutes*. 62 U. Cin. L. Rev. 1439 (1994).

Choate, Guy D. *Introduction*. 38 Tex. Tech L. Rev. 237 (2006).

Clark, Charles E. *Special Problems in Drafting and Interpreting Procedural Codes and Rules*. 3 Vand. L. Rev. 493 (1950).

Clark, Robert C. *Judicial Decisionmaking and the Growth of the Law*. 17 Harv. J.L. & Pub. Pol'y 1 (1994).

Clark, Walter M. *The Doctrine of Ejusdem Generis in Missouri*. 1952 Wash. U. L.Q. 250.

Cleveland, Steven J. *Judicial Discretion and Statutory Interpretation*. 57 Okla. L. Rev. 31 (2004).

Coffman, Claude T. *Essay on Statutory Interpretation*. 9 Mem. St. U. L. Rev. 57 (1978).

Cogan, Efrat Massry. *Executive Nonacquiescence: Problems of Statutory Interpretation and Separation of Powers*. 60 S. Cal. L. Rev. 1143 (1987).

Cohen, Julius. *Judicial "Legisputation" and the Dimensions of Legislative Meaning*. 36 Ind. L.J. 414 (1961).

Colby, Thomas B.; and Peter J. Smith. *Living Originalism*. 59 Duke L.J. 239 (2009).

Coldiron, William. *The Use of Extrinsic Aids in Statutory Interpretation in Kentucky*. 36 Ky. L.J. 190 (1948).

Colinvaux, Roger. *What Is Law? A Search for Legal Meaning and Good Judging Under a Textualist Lens*. 72 Ind. L.J. 1133 (1997).

Conference Committee Materials in Interpreting Statutes. 4 Stan. L. Rev. 257 (1952).

Coombe, Rosemary J. *"Same As It Ever Was": Rethinking the Politics of Legal Interpretation*. 34 McGill L.J. 603 (1989).

Corns, Christopher. *Purposive Construction of Legislation and Judicial Autonomy*. 58 Law Inst. J. 391 (1984).

Cornwell, Joel R. *Smoking Canons: A Guide to Some Favorite Rules of Construction*. CBA Record, May 1996, at 43.

Corrigan, Maura D.; and J. Michael Thomas. *"Dice Loading" Rules of Statutory Interpretation*. 59 N.Y.U. Ann. Surv. Am. L. 231 (2003).

Corry, J.A. *Administrative Law and the Interpretation of Statutes*. 1 U. Toronto L.J. 286 (1936).

Corry, J.A. *The Use of Legislative History in the Interpretation of Statutes*. 32 Can. B. Rev. 624 (1954).

Costello, George A. *Average Voting Members and Other "Benign Fictions": The Relative Reliability of Committee Reports, Floor Debates, and Other Sources of Legislative History*. 1990 Duke L.J. 39.

Cox, Archibald. *Judge Learned Hand and the Interpretation of Statutes*. 60 Harv. L. Rev. 370 (1947).

Cox, Archibald. *Some Aspects of the Labor Management Relations Act, 1947*. 61 Harv. L. Rev. 1 (1947).

Cox, Paul N. *Ruminations On Statutory Interpretation in the Burger Court*. 19 Val. U. L. Rev. 287 (1985).

Coxon, Benedict. *Open to Interpretation: The Implication of Words into Statutes*. 30 Statute L. Rev. 1 (2009).

Crabbe, V.C.R.A.C. *Punctuation in Legislation*. 1988 Statute L. Rev. 87.

Craig, Robin Kundis. *The Stevens/Scalia Principle and Why It Matters: Statutory Conversation and a Cultural Critical Critique of the Strict Plain Meaning Approach*. 79 Tul. L. Rev. 955 (2005).

Cramton, Roger C. *Nonstatutory Review of Federal Administrative Action: The Need for Statutory Reform of Sovereign Immunity, Subject Matter Jurisdiction, and Parties Defendant*. 68 Mich. L. Rev. 387 (1970).

Crespi, Gregory Scott. *The Influence of a Decade of Statutory Interpretation Scholarship on Judicial Rulings: An Empirical Analysis*. 53 SMU L. Rev. 9 (2000).

Cross, Frank B. *The Significance of Statutory Interpretive Methodologies*. 82 Notre Dame L. Rev. 1971 (2007).

Cuevas, Carlos J. *The Rehnquist Court, Strict Statutory Construction, and the Bankruptcy Code*. 42 Clev. St. L. Rev. 435 (1994).

Culotta, Michael L. *The Use of Committee Reports in Statutory Interpretation: A Suggested Framework for the Federal Judiciary*. 60 Ark. L. Rev. 687 (2007).

Cunningham, Clark D.; Judith N. Levi; Georgia M. Green; and Jeffrey P. Kaplan. *Plain Meaning and Hard Cases*. 103 Yale L.J. 1561 (1994) (reviewing Lawrence M. Solan, *The Language of Judges* (1993)).

Curd, Thomas H.S. *Substance and Procedure in Rule Making.* 51 W. Va. L.Q. 34 (1948).

Currie, David P. *His Accidency.* 5 Green Bag 2d 151 (2002).

Curtis, Charles P. *A Better Theory of Legal Interpretation.* 3 Vand. L. Rev. 407 (1950).

Dale, William. *Principles, Purposes, and Rules.* 1988 Statute L. Rev. 15.

D'Amato, Anthony. *Can Legislatures Constrain Judicial Interpretation of Statutes?* 75 Va. L. Rev. 561 (1989).

D'Amato, Anthony. *The Injustice of Dynamic Statutory Interpretation.* 64 U. Cin. L. Rev. 911 (1996).

Danner, Richard A. *Justice Jackson's Lament: Historical and Comparative Perspectives on the Availability of Legislative History.* 13 Duke J. Comp. & Int'l L. 151 (2003).

Davies, D.J. Llewelyn. *The Interpretation of Statutes in the Light of Their Policy by the English Courts.* 35 Colum. L. Rev. 519 (1935).

Davies, Ross E. *A Public Trust Exception to the Rule of Lenity.* 63 U. Chi. L. Rev. 1175 (1996).

Davis, Elliott M. *The Newer Textualism: Justice Alito's Statutory Interpretation.* 30 Harv. J.L. & Pub. Pol'y 983 (2007).

Davis, Kenneth Culp. *Legislative History and the Wheat Board Case.* 31 Can. B. Rev. 1 (1935).

Dawson, John P. "The Functions of the Judge," in *Talks on American Law.* Harold J. Berman, ed. Rev. ed. 2d ed. N.Y.: Vintage Books, 1971.

Dershowitz, Alan M. "The Sovereignty of Process: The Limits of Original Intention," in *Politics and the Constitution: The Nature and Intent of Interpretation.* Washington, D.C.: Nat'l Legal Ctr. for the Public Interest & Am. Studs. Ctr., 1990.

De Sloovère, Frederick J. *Contextual Interpretation of Statutes.* 5 Fordham L. Rev. 219 (1936).

De Sloovère, Frederick J. *The Equity and Reason of a Statute.* 21 Cornell L. Rev. 591 (1936).

De Sloovère, Frederick J. *Extrinsic Aids in the Interpretation of Statutes.* 88 U. Pa. L. Rev. 527 (1940).

De Sloovère, Frederick J. *The Functions of Judge and Jury in the Interpretation of Statutes.* 46 Harv. L. Rev. 1086 (1933).

De Sloovère, Frederick J. *The Local Law Theory and Its Implications in the Conflict of Laws.* 41 Harv. L. Rev. 421 (1928).

De Sloovère, Frederick J. *Preliminary Questions in Statutory Interpretation.* 9 N.Y.U. L.Q. Rev. 1 (1932).

De Sloovère, Frederick J. *Steps in the Process of Interpreting Statutes.* 10 N.Y.U. L.Q. Rev. 1 (1932).

De Sloovère, Frederick J. *Textual Interpretation of Statutes.* 11 N.Y.U. L.Q. Rev. 538 (1934).

Devabhakthuni, Sanjeev. *How to Win the Read Vote: A Profile of the Statutory Interpretation Method of Associate Judge Susan P. Read from a Practical Viewpoint.* 73 Alb. L. Rev. 993 (2010).

Dickerson, Reed. *The Difficult Choice Between "And" and "Or."* 46 A.B.A. J. 310 (1960).

Dickerson, Reed. *The Diseases of Legislative Language.* 1 Harv. J. on Legis. 5 (1964).

Dickerson, Reed. *How to Write a Law.* 31 Notre Dame L. Rev. 14 (1955).

Dickerson, Reed. *Legal Drafting: Writing as Thinking, or, Talk-Back from Your Draft and How to Exploit It.* 29 J. Legal Educ. 373 (1978).

Dickerson, Reed. *Legislative Drafting: A Challenge to the Legal Profession.* 40 A.B.A. J. 635 (1954).

Dickerson, Reed. *Legislative Drafting: American and British Practices Compared.* 44 A.B.A. J. 865 (1958).

Dickerson, Reed. *Legislative Drafting and the Law Schools.* 7 J. Legal Educ. 472 (1955).

Dickerson, Reed. *Legislative Drafting in London and in Washington.* 1959 Cambridge L.J. 49.

Dickerson, Reed. *Obscene Telephone Calls: An Introduction to the Reading of Statutes.* 22 Harv. J. on Legis. 173 (1985).

Dickerson, Reed. *Plain English Statutes and Readability.* 64 Mich. B.J. 567 (1985).

Dickerson, Reed. *Professionalizing Legislative Drafting: A Realistic Goal.* 60 A.B.A. J. 562 (1974).

Dickerson, Reed. *Statutes and Constitutions in an Age of Common Law.* 48 U. Pitt. L. Rev. 773 (1987).

Dickerson, Reed. *Statutory Interpretation: Core Meaning and Marginal Uncertainty.* 29 Mo. L. Rev. 1 (1964).

Dickerson, Reed. *Statutory Interpretation: A Peek Into the Mind and Will of a Legislature.* 50 Ind. L.J. 206 (1975).

Dickerson, Reed. *Statutory Interpretation: The Uses and Anatomy of Context.* 23 Case W. Res. L. Rev. 353 (1972).

Dickerson, Reed. *Statutory Interpretation in America: Dipping into Legislative History—I.* 1984 Statute L. Rev. 76.

Dickerson, Reed. *Statutory Interpretation in America: Dipping into Legislative History—II.* 1984 Statute L. Rev. 141.

Dickerson, Reed. Introduction to *Symposium on Judicial Law Making in Relation to Statutes*. 36 Ind. L.J. 411 (1961).

Dickerson, Reed. *United States v. McGoff: Can Lawyers Be Taught How to Read Statutes?* 15 Seton Hall Legis. J. 1 (1991).

Dietz, George A. *Statutory Construction: Ejusdem Generis Versus Legislative Intent.* 3 U. Fla. L. Rev. 258 (1950).

Dittoe, Michael J. *Statutory Revision by Common Law Courts and the Nature of Legislative Decision Making—A Response to Professor Calabresi.* 28 St. Louis U. L.J. 235 (1984).

Diver, Colin S. *Statutory Interpretation in the Administrative State.* 133 U. Pa. L. Rev. 549 (1985).

Dixon, John A., Jr. *Judicial Method in Interpretation of Law in Louisiana.* 42 La. L. Rev. 1661 (1982).

Dolan, Joseph. *Law School Teaching of Legislation.* 22 J. Legal Educ. 63 (1969).

Donato, James. *Dworkin and Subjectivity in Legal Interpretation.* 40 Stan. L. Rev. 1517 (1988).

Dorf, Michael C. *Integrating Normative and Descriptive Constitutional Theory: The Case of Original Meaning.* 85 Geo. L.J. 1765 (1997).

Dortzbach, Kenneth R. *Legislative History: The Philosophies of Justice Scalia and Breyer and the Use of Legislative History by the Wisconsin State Courts.* 80 Marq. L. Rev. 161 (1996).

Dougherty, Veronica M. *Absurdity and the Limits of Literalism: Defining the Hand Result in Statutory Interpretation.* 44 Am. U. L. Rev. 127 (1994).

Drake, Joseph H. *Sociological Interpretation of Law.* 16 Mich. L. Rev. 599 (1917).

Driedger, E.A. *New Approach to Statutory Interpretation.* 29 Can. B. Rev. 839 (1951).

Duperson, Robert A. *Interpretation Acts—Impediments to Legal Certainty and Access to the Law.* 26 Statute L. Rev. 64 (2005).

Durden, Stephen M. *Textualist Canons: Cabining Rules or Predilective Tools.* 33 Campbell L. Rev. 115 (2010).

Dwan, Ralph H.; and Ernest R. Fiedler. *The Federal Statutes—Their History and Use.* 22 Minn. L. Rev. 1008 (1938).

Dworkin, Ronald. *The Arduous Virtue of Fidelity: Originalism, Scalia, Tribe, and Nerve.* 65 Fordham L. Rev. 1249 (1997).

Dworkin, Ronald. *The Forum of Principle.* 56 N.Y.U. L. Rev. 469 (1981).

Dworkin, Ronald. *Law as Interpretation.* 60 Tex. L. Rev. 527 (1982).

Easterbrook, Frank H. *Abstraction and Authority.* 59 U. Chi. L. Rev. 349 (1992).

Easterbrook, Frank H. *Alternatives to Originalism?* 19 Harv. J.L. & Pub. Pol'y 479 (1996).

Easterbrook, Frank H. "Approaches to Judicial Review," in *Politics and the Constitution: The Nature and Extent of Interpretation.* Wash., D.C.: Nat'l Legal Ctr. for the Public Interest & Am. Studs. Ctr., 1990.

Easterbrook, Frank H. *The Demand for Judicial Review.* 88 Nw. U. L. Rev. 372 (1993).

Easterbrook, Frank H. *Do Liberals and Conservatives Differ in Judicial Activism?* 73 U. Colo. L. Rev. 1401 (2002).

Easterbrook, Frank H. *Formalism, Functionalism, Ignorance, Judges.* 22 Harv. J. Law & Pub. Pol'y 13 (1998).

Easterbrook, Frank H. *Judges as Honest Agents.* 33 Harv. J.L. & Pub. Pol'y 915 (2010).

Easterbrook, Frank H. *Judicial Discretion in Statutory Interpretation.* 57 Okla. L. Rev. 1 (2004).

Easterbrook, Frank H. *Legal Interpretation and the Power of the Judiciary.* 7 Harv. J.L. & Pub. Pol'y 87 (1984).

Easterbrook, Frank H. *Method, Result, and Authority: A Reply.* 98 Harv. L. Rev. 622 (1985).

Easterbrook, Frank H. *Originalism.* 31 Harv. J.L. & Pub. Pol'y 901 (2008).

Easterbrook, Frank H. *Pragmatism's Role in Interpretation.* 31 Harv. J. Law & Pub. Pol'y 901 (2008).

Easterbrook, Frank H. *Presidential Review.* 40 Case W. Res. L. Rev. 905 (1989–1990).

Easterbrook, Frank H. *The Role of Original Intent in Statutory Construction.* 11 Harv. J.L. & Pub. Pol'y 59 (1988).

Easterbrook, Frank H. *Stability and Reliability in Judicial Decisions.* 73 Cornell L. Rev. 422 (1988).

Easterbrook, Frank H. *Statutes' Domains.* 50 U. Chi. L. Rev. 533 (1983).

Easterbrook, Frank H. *Text, History, and Structure in Statutory Interpretation.* 17 Harv. J.L. & Pub. Pol'y 61 (1994).

Easterbrook, Frank H. *Textualism and the Dead Hand.* 66 Geo. Wash. L. Rev. 1119 (1998).

Easterbrook, Frank H. *Unitary Executive Interpretation: A Comment.* 15 Cardozo L. Rev. 313 (1993).

Easterbrook, Frank H. *What Does Legislative History Tell Us?* 66 Chi.-Kent L. Rev. 441 (1990).

Easterbrook, Frank H. *What's So Special About Judges?* 61 Univ. Colo. L. Rev. 773 (1990).

Edelman, Paul H.; David E. Klein; and Stefanie A. Lindquist. *Consensus, Disorder, and Ideology on the Supreme Court.* 9 J. Empirical Legal Studs. 129 (2012).

Edwards, Harry T. *The Growing Disjunction Between Legal Education and the Legal Profession*. 91 Mich. L. Rev. 34 (1992).

Edwards, Harry T. *The Judicial Function and the Elusive Goal of Principled Decision Making*. 1991 Wis. L. Rev. 837.

Eisenberg, Melvin Aron. *Strict Textualism*. 29 Loy. L.A. L. Rev. 13 (1995).

Elphinstone, Howard W. *On the Limits of Rules of Construction*. 1 L.Q. Rev. 466 (1885).

Engel, Anthony L. *Questionable Uses of Canons of Statutory Interpretation: Why the Supreme Court Erred When It Decided "Any" Only Means "Some."* 96 J. Crim. L. & Criminology 877 (2006).

Engholm, Rudy. *Logic and Laws: Relief from Statutory Obfuscation*. 9 U. Mich. J.L. Reform 322 (1976).

Englert, Gregory R. *The Other Side of Ejusdem Generis*. 11 Scribes J. Legal Writing 51 (2007).

Epstein, Richard A. *The Pitfalls of Interpretation*. 7 Harv. J.L. & Pub. Pol'y 101 (1984).

Eskridge, William N., Jr. *All About Words: Early Understandings of the "Judicial Power," in Statutory Interpretation, 1776–1806*. 101 Colum. L. Rev. 990 (2001).

Eskridge, William N., Jr. *America's Statutory Construction*. 41 U.C. Davis L. Rev. 1 (2007).

Eskridge, William N., Jr. *The Case of the Speluncean Explorers: Twentieth-Century Statutory Interpretation in a Nutshell*. 61 Geo. Wash. L. Rev. 1731 (1993).

Eskridge, William N., Jr. *Dynamic Interpretation of Economic Regulatory Legislation (Countervailing Duty Law)*. 21 Law & Pol'y Int'l Bus. 663 (1990).

Eskridge, William N., Jr. *Dynamic Statutory Interpretation*. 135 U. Pa. L. Rev. 1479 (1987).

Eskridge, William N., Jr. *Gadamer/Statutory Interpretation*. 90 Colum. L. Rev. 609 (1990).

Eskridge, William N., Jr. *Interpreting Legislative Inaction*. 87 Mich. L. Rev. 67 (1988).

Eskridge, William N., Jr. *Legislative History Values*. 66 Chi.-Kent L. Rev. 365 (1990).

Eskridge, William N., Jr. *The New Textualism*. 37 UCLA L. Rev. 621 (1990).

Eskridge, William N., Jr. *No Frills Textualism*. 119 Harv. L. Rev. 2041 (2006).

Eskridge, William N., Jr. *Norms, Empiricism, and Canons in Statutory Interpretation*. 66 U. Chi. L. Rev. 671 (1999).

Eskridge, William N., Jr. *Overriding Supreme Court Statutory Interpretation Decisions*. 101 Yale L.J. 331 (1991).

Eskridge, William N., Jr. *Overruling Statutory Precedents*. 76 Geo. L.J. 1361 (1988).

Eskridge, William N., Jr. *Politics Without Romance: Implications of Public Choice Theory for Statutory Interpretation*. 74 Va. L. Rev. 275 (1988).

Eskridge, William N., Jr. *Public Values in Statutory Interpretation*. 137 U. Pa. L. Rev. 1007 (1989).

Eskridge, William N., Jr. *Should the Supreme Court Read the Federalist but Not Statutory Legislative History?* 66 Geo. Wash. L. Rev. 1301 (1998).

Eskridge, William N., Jr. *Textualism: The Unknown Ideal?* 96 Mich. L. Rev. 1509 (1998).

Eskridge, William N., Jr.; and Gary Peller. *The New Public Law Movement: Moderation as a Postmodern Cultural Form*. 89 Mich. L. Rev. 707 (1991).

Eskridge, William N., Jr.; and John A. Ferejohn. *Super-Statutes*. 50 Duke L.J. 1215 (2001).

Eskridge, William N., Jr.; and Judith N. Levi. *Regulatory Variable and Statutory Interpretation*. 73 Wash. U. L.Q. 1103 (1995).

Eskridge, William N., Jr.; and Lauren E. Baer. *The Continuum of Deference: Supreme Court Treatment of Agency Statutory Interpretations from Chevron to Hamdan*. 96 Geo. L.J. 1083 (2008).

Eskridge, William N., Jr.; and Philip P. Frickey. *Foreword: Law as Equilibrium*. 108 Harv. L. Rev. 26 (1994).

Eskridge, William N., Jr.; and Philip P. Frickey. *Legislation Scholarship and Pedagogy in the Post-Legal Process Era*. 48 U. Pitt. L. Rev. 691 (1987).

Eskridge, William N., Jr.; and Philip P. Frickey. *The Making of the Legal Process*. 107 Harv. L. Rev. 2031 (1994).

Eskridge, William N., Jr.; and Philip P. Frickey. *Quasi-Constitutional Law: Clear Statement Rules as Constitutional Lawmaking*. 45 Vand. L. Rev. 593 (1992).

Eskridge, William N., Jr.; and Philip P. Frickey. *Statutory Interpretation as Practical Reasoning*. 42 Stan. L. Rev. 321 (1990).

Evans, Larry; Jarrell Wright; and Neal Devins. *Congressional Procedure and Statutory Interpretation*. 45 Admin. L. Rev. 239 (1993).

Fallon, Richard H., Jr. *A Constructivist Coherence Theory of Constitutional Interpretation*. 100 Harv. L. Rev. 1189 (1987).

Fallon, Richard H., Jr. *How to Choose a Constitutional Theory*. 87 Cal. L. Rev. 535 (1999).

Fallon, Richard H., Jr. *Non-Legal Theory in Judicial Decisionmaking*. 17 Harv. J.L. & Pub. Pol'y 87 (1994).

Farber, Daniel A. *Do Theories of Statutory Interpretation Matter? A Case Study.* 94 Nw. U. L. Rev. 1409 (2000).

Farber, Daniel A. *Earthquakes and Tremors in Statutory Interpretation: An Empirical Study of the Dynamics of Interpretation.* 89 Minn. L. Rev. 848 (2005).

Farber, Daniel A. *The Hermeneutic Tourist: Statutory Interpretation in Comparative Perspective.* 81 Cornell L. Rev. 513 (1996).

Farber, Daniel A. *The Inevitability of Practical Reason: Statutes, Formalism, and the Rule of Law.* 45 Vand. L. Rev. 533 (1992).

Farber, Daniel A. *Legislative Deals and Statutory Bequests.* 75 Minn. L. Rev. 667 (1991).

Farber, Daniel A. *The Originalism Debate: A Guide for the Perplexed.* 49 Ohio St. L.J. 1085 (1989).

Farber, Daniel A. *Playing the Baseline: Civil Rights, Environmental Law, and Statutory Interpretation.* 91 Colum. L. Rev. 676 (1991) (reviewing Cass R. Sunstein, *After the Rights Revolution: Reconceiving the Regulatory State* (1990)).

Farber, Daniel A. *Statutory Interpretation and Legislative Supremacy.* 78 Geo. L.J. 281 (1989).

Farber, Daniel A. *Statutory Interpretation and the Idea of Progress.* 94 Mich. L. Rev. 1546 (1996).

Farber, Daniel A. *Statutory Interpretation, Legislative Inaction, and Civil Rights.* 87 Mich. L. Rev. 2 (1988).

Farber, Daniel A.; and Brett H. McDonnell. *"Is There a Text in This Class?" The Conflict Between Textualism and Antitrust.* 14 J. Contemp. Legal Issues 619 (2005).

Farber, Daniel A.; and Philip P. Frickey. *The Jurisprudence of Public Choice.* 65 Tex. L. Rev. 873 (1987).

Farber, Daniel A.; and Philip P. Frickey. *Legislative Intent and Public Choice.* 74 Va. L. Rev. 423 (1988).

Farina, Cynthia R. *Statutory Interpretation and the Balance of Power in the Administrative State.* 89 Colum. L. Rev. 452 (1989).

Farnsworth, E. Allan. *"Meaning" in the Law of Contracts.* 76 Yale L.J. 939 (1967).

Farnsworth, E. Allan. "Some Considerations in the Drafting of Agreements," in *Drafting Contracts and Commercial Instruments.* Greenvale, N.Y.: Research and Documentation Corp., 1971.

Farnsworth, Ward; Dustin Guzior; and Anup Malani. *Ambiguity About Ambiguity: An Empirical Inquiry into Legal Interpretation.* 2 J. Legal Analysis 257 (2010).

Fein, Bruce E. *Original Intent and the Constitution.* 47 Md. L. Rev. 196 (1987).

Ferejohn, John A.; and Barry R. Weingast. *Limitation of Statutes: Strategic Statutory Interpretation.* 80 Geo. L.J. 565 (1992).

Ferejohn, John A.; and Barry R. Weingast. *A Positive Theory of Statutory Interpretation.* 12 Int'l Rev. L. & Econ. 263 (1992).

Finley, Elizabeth. *Crystal Gazing: The Problem of Legislative History.* 45 A.B.A. J. 1281 (1959).

Fiorina, Morris. *Legislator Uncertainty, Legislative Control, and the Delegation of Legislative Power.* 2 J.L. Econ. & Org. 33 (1986).

Fish, Stanley. *Intentional Neglect.* N.Y. Times, 19 July 2005.

Fish, Stanley. *Interpretation and the Pluralist Vision.* 60 Tex. L. Rev. 495 (1982).

Fish, Stanley. *There Is No Textualist Position.* 42 San Diego L. Rev. 629 (2005).

Fisher, Glendon M., Jr.; and William J. Harbison. *Trends in the Use of Extrinsic Aids in Statutory Interpretation.* 3 Vand. L. Rev. 586 (1950).

Fisher, Louis. *Statutory Construction: Keeping a Respectful Eye on Congress.* 53 SMU L. Rev. 49 (2000).

Fiss, Owen M. *Objectivity and Interpretation.* 34 Stan. L. Rev. 739 (1982).

Fitz-Gerald, Roger M. *The Judicial Process in Statutory Construction.* 1960 U. Ill. L. Rev. 443.

Fleming, James E. *The Balkanization of Originalism.* 67 Md. L. Rev. 10 (2007).

Fletcher, C. Edward, III. *Principlist Models in the Analysis of Constitutional and Statutory Texts.* 72 Iowa L. Rev. 891 (1987).

Fordham, Jefferson B.; and Russell J. Leach. *Interpretation of Statutes in Derogation of the Common Law.* 3 Vand. L. Rev. 438 (1950).

Foster, Sydney. *Should Courts Give Stare Decisis Effect to Statutory Interpretation Methodology?* 96 Geo. L.J. 1863 (2008).

Foy, H. Miles, III. *On Judicial Discretion in Statutory Interpretation.* 62 Admin. L. Rev. 291 (2010).

Foy, H. Miles, III. *Some Reflections on Legislation, Adjudication, and Implied Private Actions in the State and Federal Courts.* 71 Cornell L. Rev. 501 (1986).

Frank, Jerome. *Words and Music: Some Remarks on Statutory Interpretation.* 47 Colum. L. Rev. 1259 (1947).

Frankfurter, Felix. *Some Reflections on the Reading of Statutes.* 47 Colum. L. Rev. 527 (1947).

Frankfurter, Felix. *A Symposium on Statutory Construction: Foreword.* 3 Vand. L. Rev. 365 (1950).

Frankham, Markley. *Some Comments Concerning the Use of Legislative Debates and Committee Reports in Statutory Interpretation.* 2 Brook. L. Rev. 173 (1933).

Franklin, Mitchell. *A Study of Interpretation in the Civil Law.* 3 Vand. L. Rev. 557 (1950).

Freund, Ernst. *Interpretation of Statutes.* 65 U. Pa. L. Rev. 207 (1917).

Freund, Ernst. *The Use of Indefinite Terms in Statutes.* 30 Yale L.J. 437 (1921).

Freund, Paul A. "An Analysis of Judicial Reasoning," in *Law and Philosophy: A Symposium.* Sidney Hook, ed. N.Y.: N.Y. Univ. Press, 1964.

Freund, Paul A. "The Supreme Court," in *Talks on American Law.* Harold J. Berman, ed. 2d ed. N.Y.: Vintage Books, 1971.

Frickey, Philip P. *Faithful Interpretation.* 73 Wash. U. L.Q. 1085 (1995).

Frickey, Philip P. *From the Big Sleep to the Big Heat: The Revival of Theory in Statutory Interpretation.* 77 Minn. L. Rev. 241 (1992).

Frickey, Philip P. *Getting from Joe to Gene (McCarthy): The Avoidance Canon, Legal Process Theory, and Narrowing Statutory Interpretation in the Early Warren Court.* 93 Cal. L. Rev. 397 (2005).

Frickey, Philip P. *Interpretation on the Borderline: Constitution, Canons, Direct Democracy.* 1 N.Y.U. J. Legis. & Pub. Pol'y 105 (1997).

Frickey, Philip P. *Interpretive-Regime Change.* 38 Loy. L.A. L. Rev. 1971 (2005).

Frickey, Philip P. *Revisiting the Revival of Theory in Statutory Interpretation: A Lecture in Honor of Irving Younger.* 84 Minn. L. Rev. 199 (1999).

Fried, Charles. *Reply to Lawson.* 17 Harv. J.L. & Pub. Pol'y 35 (1994).

Fried, Charles. *Sonnet LXV and the "Black Ink" of the Framers' Intention.* 100 Harv. L. Rev. 751 (1987).

Fried, Michael S. *A Theory of Scrivener's Error.* 52 Rutgers L. Rev. 589 (2000).

Friedman, Lawrence M. *American Legal History: Past and Present.* 34 J. Legal Educ. 563 (1984).

Friedmann, W. *The Interpretation of Statutes in Modern British Law.* 3 Vand. L. Rev. 544 (1950).

Friedmann, W. *Statute Law and Its Interpretation in the Modern State.* 26 Can. B. Rev. 1277 (1948).

Friendly, Henry J. "Mr. Justice Frankfurter and the Reading of Statutes," in *Felix Frankfurter: The Judge.* Wallace Mendelson, ed. N.Y.: Reynal & Co., 1964.

Fuller, Lon L. *American Legal Realism.* 82 U. Pa. L. Rev. 429 (1934).

Fuller, Lon L. *The Case of the Speluncean Explorers.* 62 Harv. L. Rev. 616 (1949).

Fuller, Lon L. *Positivism and Fidelity to Law—A Reply to Professor Hart.* 71 Harv. L. Rev. 630 (1958).

Fung, Spring Yuen-Ching. *The Rise and Fall of the Proviso.* 18 Statute L. Rev. 104 (1997).

Garrett, Elizabeth. *The Purposes of Framework Legislation.* 14 J. Contemp. Legal Issues 717 (2005).

Gebbia-Pinetti, Karen M. *Statutory Interpretation, Democratic Legitimacy and Legal-System Values.* 21 Seton Hall Legis. J. 233 (1997).

Gillman, Howard. *The Collapse of Constitutional Originalism and the Rise of the Notion of the "Living Constitution" in the Course of American State-Building.* 11 Studs. Am. Pol. Dev. 191 (1997).

Givati, Yehonatan. *Strategic Statutory Interpretation by Administrative Agencies.* 12 Am. L. & Econ. Rev. 95 (2010).

Givati, Yehonatan; and Matthew C. Stephenson. *Judicial Deference to Inconsistent Agency Statutory Interpretations.* 40 J. Legal Studs. 85 (2011).

Glendon, Mary Ann. "Comment," in Antonin Scalia, *A Matter of Interpretation: Federal Courts and the Law.* Princeton, N.J.: Princeton Univ. Press, 1997.

Gluck, Abbe R. *The States as Laboratories of Statutory Interpretation: Methodological Consensus and the New Modified Textualism.* 119 Yale L.J. 1750 (2010).

Gluck, Abbe R. *Statutory Interpretation Methodology as "Law": Oregon's Path-Breaking Interpretive Framework and Its Lessons for the Nation.* 47 Willamette L. Rev. 539 (2011).

Golanski, Alani. *Linguistics in Law.* 66 Alb. L. Rev. 61 (2002).

Gold, Andrew S. *Absurd Results, Scrivener's Errors, and Statutory Interpretation.* 75 U. Cin. L. Rev. 25 (2006).

Goldstein, Jared A. *Equitable Balancing in the Age of Statutes.* 96 Va. L. Rev. 485 (2010).

González, Carlos E. *Reinterpreting Statutory Interpretation.* 74 N.C. L. Rev. 585 (1996).

González, Carlos E. *Statutory Interpretation: Looking Back. Looking Forward.* 58 Rutgers L. Rev. 703 (2006).

González, Carlos E. *Trumps, Inversions, Balancing, Presumptions, Institution Prompting, and Interpretive Canons: New Ways for Adjudicating Conflicts Between Legal Norms.* 45 Santa Clara L. Rev. 233 (2005).

Goodman, Maxine D. *Reconstructing the Plain Language Rule of Statutory Construction: How and Why.* 65 Mont. L. Rev. 229 (2004).

Grabow, John C. *Congressional Silence and the Search for Legislative Intent: A Venture into Speculative Realities.* 64 B.U. L. Rev. 737 (1984).

Graff, Gerald. *"Keep Off the Grass," "Drop Dead," and Other Indeterminacies: A Response to Sanford Levinson.* 60 Tex. L. Rev. 405 (1982).

Graglia, Lino A. *Do Judges Have a Policy-Making Role in the American System of Government?* 17 Harv. J.L. & Pub. Pol'y 119 (1994).

Graglia, Lino A. *"Interpreting" the Constitution: Posner on Bork.* 44 Stan. L. Rev. 1019 (1992).

Graham, Barbara Luck. *Supreme Court Policymaking in Civil Rights Cases: A Study of Judicial Discretion in Statutory Interpretation.* 7 St. Louis U. Pub. L. Rev. 401 (1988).

Graham, Randal N.M. *A Unified Theory of Statutory Interpretation.* 23 Statute L. Rev. 91 (2002).

Graham, Randal N.M. *In Defence of Maxims.* 22 Statute L. Rev. 45 (2001).

Graham, Randal N.M. *What Judges Want: Judicial Self-Interest and Statutory Interpretation.* 30 Statute L. Rev. 38 (2009).

Grant, Ulysses S. *Inaugural Address,* 4 Mar. 1869, reprinted in Frontispiece, 2 Green Bag 2d (Winter 1999).

Green, Christopher R. *Originalism and the Sense-Reference Distinction.* 50 St. Louis U. L.J. 555 (2006).

Greenawalt, Kent. *Are Mental States Relevant for Statutory and Constitutional Interpretation?* 85 Cornell L. Rev. 1609 (2000).

Greenawalt, Kent. *How Law Can Be Determinate.* 38 UCLA L. Rev. 1 (1990).

Greenawalt, Kent. *Variations on Some Themes of a "Disporting Gazelle" and His Friend: Statutory Interpretation as Seen by Jerome Frank and Felix Frankfurter.* 100 Colum. L. Rev. 176 (2000).

Greenberg, Mark D.; and Harry Litman. *The Meaning of Original Meaning.* 86 Geo. L.J. 569 (1998).

Greenberger, Steven R. *Civil Rights and the Politics of Statutory Interpretation.* 62 U. Colo. L. Rev. 37 (1991).

Greene, Abner S. *The Missing Step of Textualism.* 74 Fordham L. Rev. 1913 (2006).

Greene, Jamal. *On the Origins of Originalism.* 88 Tex. L. Rev. 1 (2009).

Greene, Jamal. *Selling Originalism.* 97 Geo. L.J. 657 (2009).

Gregory, Robert J. *Overcoming Text in an Age of Textualism: A Practitioner's Guide to Arguing Cases of Statutory Interpretation.* 35 Akron L. Rev. 451 (2002).

Gregory, Robert J. *When a Delegation Is Not a Delegation: Using Legislative Meaning to Define Statutory Gaps.* 39 Cath. U. L. Rev. 725 (1990).

Grey, Thomas C. *"Do We Have an Unwritten Constitution?"* in *Stanford Legal Essays.* John Henry Merryman, ed. Stanford, Cal.: Stanford Univ. Press, 1975.

Griffin, Stephen M. *Rebooting Originalism.* 2008 U. Ill. L. Rev. 1185.

Grossman, Seth. *Tricameral Legislating: Statutory Interpretation in an Era of Conference Committee Ascendancy.* 9 N.Y.U. J. Legis. & Pub. Pol'y 251 (2005).

Gudridge, Patrick O. *Legislation in Legal Imagination: Introductory Exercises.* 37 U. Miami L. Rev. 493 (1983).

Gutteridge, H.C. *A Comparative View of the Interpretation of Statute Law.* 8 Tul. L. Rev. 1 (1933).

Hadfield, Gillian K. *Incomplete Contracts and Statutes: Comment on Shepsle, "Congress Is a 'They' Not an 'It.'"* 12 Int'l Rev. L. & Econ. 257 (1992).

Hamilton, Alexander. *"Final Version of an Opinion on the Constitutionality of an Act to Establish a Bank"* (1791), in *The Papers of Alexander Hamilton.* Vol. 8. Harold C. Syrett, ed. N.Y.: Columbia Univ. Press, 1965.

Hand, Learned. *"How Far Is a Judge Free in Rendering a Decision?"* (1935), in *The Spirit of Liberty.* Irving Dilliard, ed. N.Y.: Knopf, 1952.

Handelman, Gwen T. *Zen & The Art of Statutory Construction: A Tax Lawyer's Account of Enlightenment.* 40 DePaul L. Rev. 611 (1991).

Harrison, John. *Forms of Originalism and the Study of History.* 26 Harv. J.L. & Pub. Pol'y 83 (2003).

Harrison, John. *Reconstructing the Privileges or Immunities Clause.* 101 Yale L.J. 1385 (1992).

Hart, H.L.A. *Positivism and the Separation of Law and Morals.* 71 Harv. L. Rev. 593 (1958).

Healy, Michael P. *The Attraction and Limits of Textualism: The Supreme Court Decision PUD No. 1 of Jefferson County v. Washington Department of Ecology.* 5 N.Y.U. Envtl. L.J. 382 (1996).

Healy, Michael P. *Communis Opinio and the Methods of Statutory Interpretation: Interpreting Law or Changing Law.* 43 Wm. & Mary L. Rev. 539 (2001).

Healy, Michael P. *Legislative Intent and Statutory Interpretation in England and the United States: An Assessment of the Impact of Pepper v. Hart.* 35 Stan. J. Int'l L. 231 (1999).

Hellwege, Jean. *Connecticut Abandons "Plain-Meaning" Rule for Statutory Interpretation.* 39 Trial 86 (June 2003).

Henderson, H. McN.; and Bates, T. St. J. N. *Teaching Legislation in Edinburgh: An Outline.* 1980 Statute L. Rev. 151.

Henry, Samuel J.; and Thomas O. Moore. *A Decade of Legislative History in the Supreme Court: 1950–1959.* 46 Va. L. Rev. 1408 (1960).

Henry Thring—A Hundred Years On. 28 Statute L. Rev. iii (2007).

Hermann, Donald H.J. *Phenomenology, Structuralism, Hermeneutics, and Legal Study: Applications of Contemporary Continental Thought to Legal Phenomena.* 36 U. Miami L. Rev. 379 (1982).

Herrero, Mariano Magide. *Judicial Interpretation: Hart and European Legal Reasoning.* 20 Statute L. Rev. 164 (1999).

Hertko, Matthew J. *Statutory Interpretation in Illinois: Abandoning the Plain Meaning Rule for an Extratextual Approach.* 2005 U. Ill. L. Rev. 377.

Herz, Michael E. *Imposing Unified Executive Branch Statutory Interpretation.* 15 Cardozo L. Rev. 219 (1993).

Herz, Michael E. *Purposivism and Institutional Competence in Statutory Interpretation.* 2009 Mich. St. L. Rev. 89.

Herz, Michael E. *Textualism and Taboo: Interpretation and Deference for Justice Scalia.* 12 Cardozo L. Rev. 1663 (1991).

Hetzel, Otto J. *Instilling Legislative Interpretation Skills in the Classroom and the Courtroom.* 48 U. Pitt. L. Rev. 663 (1987).

Hewart, Lord, of Bury. *"Law, Ethics, and Legislation,"* in *Essays and Observations.* London: Cassell & Co., 1930.

Hirsch, E.D. *Past Intentions and Present Meanings.* 23 Essays in Criticism 79 (1983).

Hirsch, Werner Z. *Reducing Law's Uncertainty and Complexity.* 21 UCLA L. Rev. 1233 (1974).

Holder, Russell. *Say What You Mean and Mean What You Say: The Resurrection of Plain Meaning in California Courts.* 30 U.C. Davis L. Rev. 569 (1997).

Holdheim, Wolfgang. *A Hermeneutic Thinker.* 16 Cardozo L. Rev. 2153 (1995).

Holmes, Oliver Wendell. *The Theory of Legal Interpretation.* 12 Harv. L. Rev. 417 (1899).

Hopkins, E. Russell. *The Literal Canon and the Golden Rule.* 15 Can. B. Rev. 689 (1937).

Horack, Frank E., Jr. *Congressional Silence: A Tool of Judicial Supremacy.* 25 Tex. L. Rev. 247 (1947).

Horack, Frank E., Jr. *Constitutional Liberties and Statutory Construction.* 29 Iowa L. Rev. 448 (1944).

Horack, Frank E., Jr. *Cooperative Action for Improved Statutory Interpretation.* 3 Vand. L. Rev. 382 (1950).

Horack, Frank E., Jr. *The Disintegration of Statutory Construction.* 24 Ind. L.J. 335 (1949).

Horack, Frank E., Jr. *In the Name of Legislative Intention.* 38 W. Va. L.Q. 119 (1932).

Horack, Frank E., Jr. *Statutory Interpretation—Light from Plowden's Reports.* 19 Ky. L.J. 211 (1931).

Horenstein, Mike Robert. *The Virtues of Interpretation in a Jural Society.* 16 Cardozo L. Rev. 2273 (1995).

Houy, Joshua. *State v. Janklow: "Shall" Means Shall.* 50 S.D. L. Rev. 529 (2005).

Howe, Lord. *Managing the Statute Book.* 13 Statute L. Rev. 165 (1992).

Hudson, A.H. *Legislation and Reality: A Clash.* 1988 Statute L. Rev. 66.

Hunt, Alan Reeve. *Validity of Canon That Statutes in Derogation of the Common Law Should Be Strictly Construed.* 52 Mich. L. Rev. 756 (1954).

Hupp, Linda L. *Statutory Construction—The Role of the Court.* 71 W. Va. L. Rev. 382 (1969).

Hyde, Charles Cheney. *Concerning the Interpretation of Treaties.* 3 Am. J. Int'l L. 46 (1909).

Ilbert, Courtenay. *The Improvement of the Statute Law.* 189 Q. Rev. 172 (1899).

Imwinkelried, Edward J. *An Extended Footnote to "Statutory Construction: Not for the Timid."* 30 Champion 36 (May 2006).

Imwinkelried, Edward J. *A More Modest Proposal than a Common Law for the Age of Statutes: Greater Reliance in Statutory Interpretation on the Concept of Interpretive Intention.* 68 Alb. L. Rev. 949 (2005).

Imwinkelried, Edward J. *Moving Beyond "Top Down" Grand Theories of Statutory Construction: A "Bottom Up" Interpretive Approach to the Federal Rules of Evidence.* 75 Or. L. Rev. 389 (1996).

Imwinkelried, Edward J. *Using a Contextual Construction to Resolve the Dispute over the Meaning of the Term "Plan" in Federal Rule of Evidence 404(b).* 43 U. Kan. L. Rev. 1005 (1995).

Israelit, Ronald H. *The Plain Meaning Rule in the Reflection of Current Trends and Proclivities.* 26 Temp. L.Q. 174 (1952).

Jackson, Bernard S. *Who Enacts Statutes?* 18 Statute L. Rev. 177 (1997).

Jackson, Robert H. *The Meaning of Statutes: What Congress Says or What the Court Says.* 34 A.B.A. J. 535 (1948).

Jackson, Robert H. *Problems of Statutory Interpretation.* 8 F.R.D. 121 (1948).

Jacobs, Francis G. "Approaches to Interpretation in a Plurilingual Legal System," in *A True European: Essays for Judge David Edward.* Mark Hoskins & William Robinson, eds. Oxford: Hart Pub., 2003.

Jaffe, Louis L. *The Right to Judicial Review I.* 71 Harv. L. Rev. 401 (1958).

Jaffe, Louis L. *The Right to Judicial Review II.* 71 Harv. L. Rev. 769 (1958).

Jamieson, N.J. *The Pathology of Legislation.* 1984 Statute L. Rev. 87.

Jamieson, N.J. *Towards a Systematic Statute Law.* 3 Otago L. Rev. 543 (1976).

Jeffries, John Calvin, Jr. *Legality, Vagueness, and the Construction of Penal Statutes.* 71 Va. L. Rev. 189 (1985).

Jellum, Linda D. *The Art of Statutory Interpretation: Identifying the Interpretive Theory of the Judges of the United States Court of Appeals for Veterans' Claims and the United States Court of Appeals for the Federal Circuit.* 49 U. Louisville L. Rev. 59 (2010).

Jellum, Linda D. *"Which Is to Be Master," the Judiciary or the Legislature? When Statutory Directives Violate Separation of Powers.* 56 UCLA L. Rev. 837 (2009).

Johansen, Steven J. *What Does Ambiguous Mean? Making Sense of Statutory Analysis in Oregon.* 34 Willamette L. Rev. 219 (1998).

Johnstone, Quintin. *The Use of Extrinsic Aids to Statutory Construction in Oregon.* 29 Or. L. Rev. 1 (1949).

Jonakait, Randolph N. *The Supreme Court, Plain Meaning, and the Changed Rules of Evidence.* 68 Tex. L. Rev. 745 (1990).

Jones, Harry Willmer. *Extrinsic Aids in the Federal Courts.* 25 Iowa L. Rev. 737 (1940).

Jones, Harry Willmer. *The Plain Meaning Rule and Extrinsic Aids in the Interpretation of Federal Statutes.* 25 Wash. U. L.Q. 2 (1939).

Jones, Harry Willmer. *Statutory Doubts and Legislative Intention.* 40 Colum. L. Rev. 957 (1940).

Jones, J. Woodfin. *The Absurd-Results Principle of Statutory Construction in Texas.* 15 Rev. Litig. 81 (1996).

Jones, Lisa G. *Statutory Construction.* 35 U. Louisville J. Fam. L. 208 (1996–1997).

Jones, Theodore E., II. *Approaching Statutory Interpretation in New Mexico.* 8 Natural Resources J. 689 (1968).

Jones, Theodore W. *Textualism and Legal Process Theory: Alternative Approaches to Statutory Interpretation.* 26 J. Legis. 45 (2000).

Jordan, William S., III. *Judicial Review of Informal Statutory Interpretations: The Answer Is Chevron Step Two, Not Christensen or Mead.* 54 Admin. L. Rev. 719 (2002).

Kannar, George. *Strenuous Virtues, Virtuous Lives: The Social Vision of Antonin Scalia.* 12 Cardozo L. Rev. 1845 (1991).

Kaplow, Louis. *Rules Versus Standards: An Economic Approach.* 42 Duke L.J. 557 (1992).

Kavanagh, Aileen. *Original Intention, Enacted Text, and Constitutional Interpretation.* 47 Am. J. Juris. 255 (2002).

Kay, Richard S. *Adherence to the Original Intentions in Constitutional Adjudication: Three Objections and Responses.* 82 Nw. U. L. Rev. 226 (1988).

Kaye, Judith S. *State Courts at the Dawn of a New Century: Common Law Courts Reading Statutes and Constitutions.* 70 N.Y.U. L. Rev. 1 (1995).

Kaye, Judith S. *Things Judges Do: State Statutory Interpretation.* 13 Touro L. Rev. 595 (1997).

Kean, Gordon. *The Title-Body Clause and the Proposed Statutory Revision.* 8 La. L. Rev. 113 (1947).

Keenan, Thomas. *Deconstruction and the Impossibility of Justice.* 11 Cardozo L. Rev. 1675 (1990).

Kelley, William K. *Avoiding Constitutional Questions as a Three-Branch Problem.* 86 Cornell L. Rev. 831 (2001).

Kelso, J. Clark; and Charles D. Kelso. *Statutory Interpretation: Four Theories in Disarray.* 53 SMU L. Rev. 81 (2000).

Kelso, R. Randall. *Statutory Interpretation Doctrine on the Modern Supreme Court and Four Doctrinal Approaches to Judicial Decision-Making.* 25 Pepp. L. Rev. 37 (1997).

Kende, Mark S. *A Misguided Statutory Interpretation Theory: The Élian Gonzalez Cuban Asylum Case.* 18 B.U. Int'l L.J. 201 (2000).

Kennedy, John David. *Statutory Construction in Maine.* 7 Me. B.J. 148 (1992).

Kernochan, John M. *Continuous Statutory Revision and Compilation.* 36 A.B.A. J. 939 (1950).

Kernochan, John M. *Statutory Interpretation: An Outline of Method.* 3 Dalhousie L.J. 333 (1976).

Kesavan, Vasan; and Michael Stokes Paulsen. *The Interpretive Force of the Constitution's Secret Drafting History.* 91 Geo. L.J. 1113 (2003).

Kesavan, Vasan; and Michael Stokes Paulsen. *Is West Virginia Unconstitutional?* 90 Cal. L. Rev. 291 (2002).

Kestenband, Jeffrey C. Conway v. Town of Wilton: *Statutory Construction, Stare Decisis, and Public Policy in Connecticut's Recreational Use Statute.* 30 Conn. L. Rev. 1091 (1998).

Keyes, John Mark. *Expressio Unius: The Expression That Proves the Rule.* 1989 Statute L. Rev. 1.

Keyes, John Mark. *Incorporation by Reference in Legislation.* 25 Statute L. Rev. 180 (2004).

Kilgour, D.G. *The Rule Against the Use of Legislative History: "Canon of Construction or Counsel of Caution?"* 30 Can. B. Rev. 769 (1952).

Kiracofe, Adam W. *The Codified Canons of Statutory Construction: A Response and Proposal to Nicholas Rosenkranz's Federal Rules of Statutory Interpretation.* 84 B.U. L. Rev. 571 (2004).

Kirby, Michael. "Statutory Interpretation and the Rule of Law—Whose Rule, What Law?" in *Essays on Legislative Drafting.* David St. Leger Kelly, ed. Adelaide: Adelaide Law Rev. Ass'n, 1988.

Kirby, Michael. *Towards a Grand Theory of Interpretation: The Case of Statutes and Contracts.* 24 Statute L. Rev. 95 (2003).

Kirk, Maurice. *Legal Drafting: Curing Unexpressive Language.* 3 Tex. Tech. L. Rev. 23 (1971).

Kirk, Maurice. *Legal Drafting: The Ambiguity of "And" and "Or."* 2 Tex. Tech. L. Rev. 235 (1971).

Klein, Mark A. *Analysis of Statutory Construction Problems Resulting from Slight Changes in Wording from Former Statutes.* 21 Hastings L.J. 1303 (1970).

Kleinberg, Alexander. *Demystifying Ambiguous Statutes with the Maxims of Statutory Interpretation: A Closer Look at* J.D. Tan, LLC v. Summers. 26 Seattle U. L. Rev. 149 (2002).

Kloepfer, Stephen. *Ambiguity and Vagueness in the Criminal Law: An Analysis of Types.* 27 Crim. L.Q. 94 (1984).

Klotz, Gary W. *Emerging Standards for Implied Actions Under Federal Statutes.* 9 U. Mich. J.L. Reform 294 (1976).

Knapp, Steven; and Walter Benn Michaels. *Against Theory.* 8 Critical Inquiry 723 (1982).

Kniffin, Margaret N. "Interpretation of Contracts," in 5 *Corbin on Contracts.* St. Paul: West Pub., 1998.

Kochan, Donald J. *The Other Side of the Coin: Implications for Policy Formation in the Law of Judicial Interpretation.* 6 Cornell J.L. & Pub. Pol'y 463 (1997) (reviewing Antonin Scalia, *A Matter of Interpretation: Federal Courts and the Law* (1997)).

Kohler, Josef. "Judicial Interpretation of Enacted Law," in *Science of Legal Method: Select Essays by Various Authors.* Ernest Bruncken & Layton B. Register, trans. Boston: Boston Book Co., 1917.

Kozinski, Alex. *Should Reading Legislative History Be an Impeachable Offense?* 31 Suffolk U. L. Rev. 807 (1998).

Kramer, Larry D. *Two (More) Problems with Originalism.* 31 Harv. J.L. & Pub. Pol'y 907 (2008).

Kress, Ken. *Legal Indeterminacy.* 77 Cal. L. Rev. 283 (1989).

Krishnakumar, Anita S. *The Hidden Legacy of Holy Trinity Church: The Unique National Institution Canon.* 51 Wm. & Mary L. Rev. 1053 (2009).

Krishnakumar, Anita S. *Passive-Voice References in Statutory Interpretation.* 76 Brook. L. Rev. 941 (2011).

Krishnakumar, Anita S. *Statutory Interpretation in the Roberts Court's First Era: An Empirical and Doctrinal Analysis.* 62 Hastings L.J. 221 (2010).

Krislov, Samuel. "Legislatures and the Judiciary," in 3 *Encyclopedia of the American Legislative System.* Joel J. Silbey, ed. N.Y.: C. Scribner's Sons, 1994.

Kristol, William. *The Judiciary: Conservatism's Lost Branch.* 17 Harv. J.L. & Pub. Pol'y 131 (1994).

Kysar, Rebecca M. *Listening to Congress: Earmark Rules and Statutory Interpretation.* 94 Cornell L. Rev. 519 (2009).

Landau, Jack L. *The Intended Meaning of "Legislative Intent" and Its Implications for Statutory Construction in Oregon.* 76 Or. L. Rev. 47 (1997).

Landau, Jack L. *Interpreting Statutes Enacted by Initiative: An Assessment of Proposals to Apply Specialized Interpretive Rules.* 34 Willamette L. Rev. 487 (1998).

Landau, Jack L. *Oregon as a Laboratory of Statutory Interpretation.* 47 Willamette L. Rev. 563 (2011).

Landau, Jack L. *Some Observations About Statutory Construction in Oregon.* 32 Willamette L. Rev. 1 (1996).

Landau, Jack L. *Some Thoughts About Constitutional Interpretation.* 115 Penn St. L. Rev. 837 (2011).

Landis, James M. *A Note on "Statutory Interpretation."* 43 Harv. L. Rev. 886 (1930).

Landis, James M. "Statutes and the Sources of Law," in *Harvard Legal Essays Written in Honor of and Presented to Joseph Henry Beale and Samuel Williston.* Cambridge, Mass.: Harvard Univ. Press, 1934.

Lane, Eric. *Legislative Process and Its Judicial Renderings: A Study in Contrast.* 48 U. Pitt. L. Rev. 639 (1987).

LaRue, L.H. *Statutory Interpretation: Lord Coke Revisited.* 48 U. Pitt. L. Rev. 733 (1987).

Lash, Kurt T. *Originalism, Popular Sovereignty, and Reverse Stare Decisis.* 93 Va. L. Rev. 1437 (2007).

Latham, E.G. *Legislative Purpose and Administrative Policy Under the National Labor Relations Act.* 5 Geo. Wash. L. Rev. 433 (1937).

Lattin, Ward E. *Legal Maxims and Their Use in Statutory Interpretations.* 26 Geo. L.J. 1 (1937).

Lavery, Urban A. *Punctuation in the Law.* 9 A.B.A. J. 225 (1923).

Lawson, Gary. *The Constitutional Case Against Precedent.* 17 Harv. J. L. & Pub. Pol'y 23 (1994).

Lawson, Gary. *On Reading Recipes . . . and Constitutions.* 85 Geo. L.J. 1823 (1997).

Lawson, Gary. *Proving the Law.* 86 Nw. U.L. Rev. 859 (1992).

Lawson, Gary. *Stare Decisis and Constitutional Meaning.* 17 Harv. J.L. & Pub. Pol'y 23 (1994).

Lawson, Gary; and Guy Seidman. *Originalism as a Legal Enterprise.* 23 Const. Comment. 47 (2006).

Lee, Frederic P. *Legislative and Interpretive Regulations.* 29 Geo. L.J. 1 (1940).

Lee, Natalie. *A Purposive Approach to the Interpretation of Tax Statutes?* 20 Statute L. Rev. 124 (1999).

Leedes, Gary C. *A Critique of Illegitimate Noninterpretivism.* 8 U. Dayton L. Rev. 533 (1983).

Leib, Ethan J. *The Perpetual Anxiety of Living Constitutionalism.* 24 Const. Comment. 353 (2007).

Leib, Ethan J.; and Michael Serota. *The Costs of Consensus in Statutory Construction.* 120 Yale L.J. Online 47 (2010).

Leitch, William A. *Interpretation and the Interpretation Act 1978.* 1980 Statute L. Rev. 5.

Lenhoff, Arthur. *Extra-Legislational Progress of Law—The Place of the Judiciary in the Shaping of New Law.* 28 Neb. L. Rev. 542 (1949).

Lenhoff, Arthur. *On Interpretive Theories: A Comparative Study in Legislation.* 27 Tex. L. Rev. 312 (1949).

Lerner, Max. *Constitution and Court as Symbols.* 46 Yale L.J. 1290 (1937).

Lessig, Lawrence. *Fidelity in Translation.* 71 Tex. L. Rev. 1165 (1993).

Lester, Lord. *Pepper v. Hart Revisited.* 15 Statute L. Rev. 10 (1994).

Levi, Edward H. "The Nature of Judicial Reasoning," in *Law and Philosophy: A Symposium.* Sidney Hook, ed. N.Y.: N.Y. Univ. Press, 1964.

Levin, Hillel Y. *The Food Stays in the Kitchen: Everything I Needed to Know About Statutory Interpretation I Learned by the Time I Was Nine.* 12 Green Bag 2d 337 (2009).

Levinson, Sanford. *The Democratic Faith of Felix Frankfurter.* 25 Stan. L. Rev. 430 (1972).

Levinson, Sanford. *Law as Literature.* 60 Tex. L. Rev. 373 (1982).

Levinson, Sanford. *On Dworkin, Kennedy, and Ely: Decoding the Legal Past.* 51 Partisan Rev. 248 (1984).

Levinson, Sanford. *Some Reflections on the Rehabilitation of the Privileges or Immunities Clause of the Fourteenth Amendment.* 12 Harv. J. Law & Pub. Pol'y 71 (1989).

Levinson, Sanford. *The Turn Toward Functionalism in Constitutional Theory.* 8 U. Dayton L. Rev. 567 (1983).

Levinson, Sanford. *What Do Lawyers Know (and What Do They Do with Their Knowledge)? Comments on Schauer and Moore.* 58 S. Cal. L. Rev. 41 (1985).

Lieber, Francis. *Legal and Political Hermeneutics, or Principles of Interpretation and Construction in Law and Politics, with Remarks on Precedents and Authorities.* 16 Cardozo L. Rev. 1883 (1995).

LiMandri, Gina. *Realism and Reasonableness in Statutory Interpretation:* People v. Anderson. 40 Hastings L.J. 805 (1989).

Linde, Hans A. *Due Process of Lawmaking.* 55 Neb. L. Rev. 197 (1976).

Lipkin, Robert Justin. *Indeterminacy, Justification, and Truth in Constitutional Theory.* 60 Fordham L. Rev. 595 (1992).

Little, Rory K. *The Federal Death Penalty: History and Some Thoughts About the Department of Justice's Role.* 26 Fordham Urb. L.J. 347 (1999).

Livingston, Michael A. *Congress, the Courts & the Code: Legislative History & the Interpretation of Tax Statutes.* 69 Tex. L. Rev. 819 (1991).

Llewellyn, Karl. *Remarks on the Theory of Appellate Decision and the Rules or Canons About How Statutes Are to Be Construed.* 3 Vand. L. Rev. 395 (1950).

Llewellyn, Karl. "Rule of Thumb and Principle," in *The Karl Llewellyn Papers.* William Twining, ed. Chicago: Univ. of Chicago Law School, 1968.

Ludwig, Alfred J. *Authority with the Force of Law: Statutory Interpretation as Policymaking in* Gonzales v. Oregon. 71 Mo. L. Rev. 1141 (2006).

Luneburg, William V. *Justice Rehnquist, Statutory Interpretation, the Policies of Clear Statement, and Federal Jurisdiction.* 58 Ind. L.J. 211 (1982).

Lyell, Nicholas. Pepper v. Hart: *The Government Perspective.* 15 Statute L. Rev. 1 (1994).

Lyman, Sherwin. *The Absurdity and Repugnancy of the Plain Meaning Rule of Interpretation.* 3 Man. L.J. 53 (1969).

MacCallum, Gerald C., Jr. *Legislative Intent.* 75 Yale L.J. 754 (1966).

MacCormick, D. Neil; and Zenon Bankowski. "Some Principles of Statutory Interpretation," in *Legal Reasoning and Statutory Interpretation.* Jan van Dunné, ed. Arnhem, Neth.: Gouda Quint, 1989.

MacDonald, John W. *The Position of Statutory Construction in Present Day Law Practice.* 3 Vand. L. Rev. 369 (1950).

Macey, Jonathan R. *Originalism as an "Ism".* 19 Harv. J.L. & Pub. Pol'y 301 (1996).

Macey, Jonathan R. *Promoting Public-Regarding Legislation Through Statutory Interpretation: An Interest Group Model.* 86 Colum. L. Rev. 223 (1986).

Macey, Jonathan R.; and Geoffrey P. Miller. *The Canons of Statutory Construction and Judicial Preferences.* 45 Vand. L. Rev. 647 (1992).

Mackay, Lord. *Finishers, Refiners, and Polishers: The Judicial Role in the Interpretation of Statutes.* 10 Statute L. Rev. 151 (1989).

Maggs, Gregory E. *Reducing the Costs of Statutory Ambiguity: Alternative Approaches and the Federal Courts Study Committee.* 29 Harv. J. on Legis. 123 (1992).

Maher, G.; and B. Litt. *Statutory Interpretation and Overruling in the House of Lords.* 1981 Statute L. Rev. 77.

Maichel, Warren R. *Role of the Common Law in the Interpretation of Statutes in Missouri.* 1952 Wash. U. L.Q. 101.

Maltz, Earl M. *The Legacy of* Griggs v. Duke Power Co.: *A Case Study in the Impact of a Modernist Statutory Precedent.* 1994 Utah L. Rev. 1353.

Maltz, Earl M. *Rhetoric and Reality in the Theory of Statutory Interpretation: Underenforcement, Overenforcement, and the Problem of Legislative Supremacy.* 71 B.U. L. Rev. 767 (1991).

Maltz, Earl M. *Statutory Interpretation and Legislative Power: The Case for a Modified Intentionalist Approach.* 63 Tul. L. Rev. 1 (1988).

Mann, F.A. *The Interpretation of Uniform Statutes.* 62 L.Q. Rev. 278 (1946).

Manning, John F. *The Absurdity Doctrine.* 116 Harv. L. Rev. 2387 (2003).

Manning, John F. *Clear Statement Rules and the Constitution.* 110 Colum. L. Rev. 399 (2010).

Manning, John F. *Competing Presumptions About Statutory Coherence.* 74 Fordham L. Rev. 2009 (2006).

Manning, John F. *Deriving Rules of Statutory Interpretation from the Constitution.* 101 Colum. L. Rev. 1648 (2001).

Manning, John F. *Legal Realism and the Canons' Revival.* 5 Green Bag 2d 283 (2002).

Manning, John F. *Putting Legislative History to a Vote: A Response to Professor Siegel.* 53 Vand. L. Rev. 1529 (2000).

Manning, John F. *Second-Generation Textualism.* 98 Cal. L. Rev. 1287 (2010).

Manning, John F. *Separation of Powers as Ordinary Interpretation.* 124 Harv. L. Rev. 1939 (2011).

Manning, John F. *Textualism and the Equity of the Statute.* 101 Colum. L. Rev. 1 (2001).

Manning, John F. *Textualism as a Nondelegation Doctrine.* 97 Colum. L. Rev. 673 (1997).

Manning, John F. *What Divides Textualists from Purposivists?* 106 Colum. L. Rev. 70 (2006).

Manson, Carl H. *The Drafting of Statute Titles.* 10 Ind. L.J. 155 (1934).

Marcin, Raymond B. *Epieikeia: Equitable Lawmaking in the Construction of Statutes.* 10 Conn. L. Rev. 377 (1978).

Marcin, Raymond B. *Punctuation and the Interpretation of Statutes.* 9 Conn. L. Rev. 227 (1977).

Markman, Stephen J. *Resisting the Ratchet.* 31 Harv. J.L. & Pub. Pol'y 983 (2008).

Marshall, Enid A. *Interpretation by a Superior Court.* 90 L.Q. Rev. 170 (1974).

Marshall, H.H. *The Drafting of Statutes: The Commonwealth Experience.* 1980 Statute L. Rev. 135.

Marshall, John. "Marshall's 'A Friend to the Union' Essays, Philadelphia Union, April 24–28, 1819," in *John Marshall's Defense of* McCulloch v. Maryland. Gerald Gunther, ed. Stanford, Cal.: Stanford Univ. Press, 1969.

Marshall, Lawrence C. *The Canons of Statutory Construction and Judicial Constraints: A Response to Macey and Miller.* 45 Vand. L. Rev. 673 (1992).

Marshall, Lawrence C. *Let Congress Do It: The Case for an Absolute Rule of Statutory Stare Decisis.* 88 Mich. L. Rev. 177 (1989).

Martineau, Robert J. *Craft and Technique, Not Canons and Grand Theories: A Neo-Realist View of Statutory Construction.* 62 Geo. Wash. L. Rev. 1 (1993).

Marx, Jonathan. *How to Construe a Hybrid Statute*. 93 Va. L. Rev. 235 (2007).

Mashaw, Jerry L. *Textualism, Constitutionalism, and the Interpretation of Federal Statutes*. 32 Wm. & Mary L. Rev. 827 (1991).

May, John. *Statutory Construction: Not For the Timid*. 30 The Champion 28 (Jan./Feb. 2006).

Mayfield, Frank M., Jr. *Common Law Methods of Construing a Civil Law Statute*. 1951 Wash U. L.Q. 249.

Mayton, William T. *Law Among the Pleonasms: The Futility and Aconstitutionality of Legislative History in Statutory Construction*. 41 Emory L.J. 113 (1992).

McClain, Emlin. "Construction and Interpretation," in 1 *Cyclopedia of American Government*. 2d ed. Andrew C. McGlaughlin & Albert Bushness Hart, eds. N.Y.: P. Smith, 1942.

McConnell, Michael W. *On Reading the Constitution*. 73 Cornell L. Rev. 359 (1987).

McConnell, Michael W. *Originalism and the Desegregation Decisions*. 81 Va. L. Rev. 947 (1995).

McCubbins, Mathew D.; and Daniel B. Rodriguez. *What Is New in the New Statutory Interpretation?* 14 J. Contemp. Legal Issues 535 (2005).

McDowell, Gary L. Introduction to *Politics and the Constitution: The Nature and Extent of Interpretation*. Washington, D.C.: Nat'l Legal Ctr. for the Public Interest & Am. Studs. Ctr., 1990.

McGinnis, John O.; and Michael B. Rappaport. *Original Methods Originalism: A New Theory of Interpretation and the Case Against Construction*. 103 Nw. U. L. Rev. 751 (2009).

McGinnis, John O.; and Michael B. Rappaport. *A Pragmatic Defense of Originalism*. 31 Harv. J.L. & Pub. Pol'y 917 (2008).

McGowan, Miranda Oshige. *Against Interpretation*. 42 San Diego L. Rev. 711 (2005).

McGreal, Paul E. *Slighting Context: On the Illogic of Ordinary Speech in Statutory Interpretation*. 52 U. Kan. L. Rev. 325 (2004).

McGreal, Paul E. *There Is No Such Thing as Textualism: A Case Study in Constitutional Method*. 69 Fordham L. Rev. 2393 (2001).

McIntosh, Simeon C.R. *Legal Hermeneutics: A Philosophical Critique*. 35 Okla. L. Rev. 1 (1982).

McKenna, James. *The Law Court's Philosophy of Statutory Interpretation: The Legislature as Architect, The Court as Builder*. 19 Me. B.J. 164 (2004).

McKenna, M. Scott. *Discerning Legislative Intent*. 17 Nev. Law. 20 (Feb. 2009).

McManes, Kenmore M. *Effect of Legislative History on Judicial Decision*. 5 Geo. Wash. L. Rev. 235 (1937).

McNellie, Elizabeth A. *The Use of Extrinsic Aids in the Interpretation of Popularly Enacted Legislation*. 89 Colum. L. Rev. 157 (1989).

McNollgast. *Legislative Intent: The Use of Positive Political Theory in Statutory Interpretation*. 57 J. Law & Contemp. Probs. 3 (1994). ["McNollgast" is a pseudonym for three authors: Mathew D. McCubbins, Roger G. Noll, and Barry R. Weingast.]

McNollgast. *Positive Canons: The Role of Legislative Bargains in Statutory Interpretation*. 80 Geo. L.J. 705 (1992).

Meek, Bert Bookham, Jr. *Statutes: The Use of Code Headings as Constructional Aids*. 33 Cal. L. Rev. 155 (1945).

Meese, Edwin, III. *The Battle for the Constitution*. Pol'y Rev., Winter 1986, at 32.

Meese, Edwin, III. *Toward a Jurisprudence of Original Intent*. 11 Harv. J.L. & Pub. Pol'y 5 (1988).

Melnick, R. Shep. Book Review. *Statutory Reconstruction: The Politics of Eskridge's Interpretation*. 84 Geo. L.J. 91 (1995).

Mendelson, Wallace. *Mr. Justice Frankfurter on the Construction of Statutes*. 43 Cal. L. Rev. 652 (1955).

Merrill, Maurice H. *Uniformly Correct Construction of Uniform Laws*. 49 A.B.A. J. 545 (1963).

Merrill, Thomas W. *The Conservative Case for Precedent*. 31 Harv. J.L. & Pub. Pol'y 977 (2008).

Merrill, Thomas W. *A Modest Proposal for a Political Court*. 17 Harv. J.L. & Pub. Pol'y 137 (1994).

Merrill, Thomas W. *Originalism, Stare Decisis, and the Promotion of Judicial Restraint*. 22 Const. Comment. 271 (2005).

Merrill, Thomas W. *Textualism and the Future of the Chevron Doctrine*. 72 Wash. U. L.Q. 351 (1994).

Merz, Michael R. *The Meaninglessness of the Plain Meaning Rule*. 4 U. Dayton L. Rev. 31 (1979).

Meyer, Bernard S. *Legislative History and Maryland Statutory Construction*. 6 Md. L. Rev. 311 (1942).

Meyer, Bernard S. *Some Thoughts on Statutory Interpretation with Special Emphasis on Jurisdiction*. 15 Hofstra L. Rev. 167 (1987).

Meyler, Bernadette. *Towards a Common Law Originalism*. 59 Stan. L. Rev. 551 (2006).

Miano, Timothy J. *Formalist Statutory Construction and the Doctrine of Fair Warning: An Examination of* United States v. Councilman. 14 Geo. Mason L. Rev. 513 (2007).

Michaels, Walter Benn. *Constitutional Interpretation: Response to Perry and Simon*. 58 S. Cal. L. Rev. 673 (1985).

Michel, Paul R. *Text and History in Statutory Construction: Introduction*. 17 Harv. J.L. & Pub. Pol'y 57 (1994).

Michell, Paul. *Just Do It! Eskridge's Critical Pragmatic Theory of Statutory Interpretation*. 41 McGill L.J. 713 (1996).

Michelman, Frank I. *Law's Republic*. 97 Yale L.J. 1493 (1988).

Mickells, Adrienne L. *The Uniform Statute and Rule Construction Act: Help, Hindrance, or Irrelevancy?* 44 U. Kan. L. Rev. 423 (1996).

Miers, David. *Legislation, Linguistic Adequacy and Public Policy*. 1986 Statute L. Rev. 90.

Miers, David; and Alan Page. *Teaching Legislation in Law Schools*. 1980 Statute L. Rev. 23.

Mikva, Abner J. *Reading and Writing Statutes*. 48 U. Pitt. L. Rev. 627 (1987).

Mikva, Abner J. *A Reply to Judge Starr's Observations*. 1987 Duke L.J. 380.

Mikva, Abner J. *Statutory Interpretation: Getting the Law to Be Less Common*. 50 Ohio St. L.J. 979 (1989).

Miller, Arthur S. *Statutory Language and the Purposive Use of Ambiguity*. 42 Va. L. Rev. 23 (1956).

Miller, Clarence A. *The Value of Legislative History of Federal Statutes*. 73 U. Pa. L. Rev. 158 (1925).

Miller, Geoffrey P. *Pragmatics and the Maxim of Interpretation*. 1990 Wis. L. Rev. 1179.

Miller, Geoffrey P. *The Unitary Executive in a Unified Theory of Constitutional Law: The Problem of Interpretation*. 15 Cardozo L. Rev. 201 (1993).

Miller, Jeffrey G. *Evolutionary Statutory Interpretation: Mr. Justice Scalia Meets Darwin*. 20 Pace L. Rev. 409 (2000).

Miller, Jeremy M. *The Language of Justice: Vagueness, Discretion and Sophistry in Criminal Law*. 13 W. St. U. L. Rev. 129 (1985).

Miller, John A. *Indeterminacy, Complexity, and Fairness: Justifying Rule Simplification in the Law of Taxation*. 68 Wash. L. Rev. 1 (1993).

Millett, Lord. *Construing Statutes*. 20 Statute L. Rev. 107 (1999).

Milsom, S.F.C. "The Past and the Future of Judge-Made Law," in *Studies in the History of the Common Law*. London: Hambledon Press, 1985.

Minow, Martha. *The Supreme Court, 1986 Term—Foreword: Justice Engendered*. 101 Harv. L. Rev. 10 (1987).

Minow, Martha; and Elizabeth V. Spelman. *In Context*. 63 S. Cal. L. Rev. 1597 (1990).

Moglen, Eben; and Richard J. Pierce Jr. *Sunstein's New Canons: Choosing the Fictions of Statutory Interpretation*. 57 U. Chi. L. Rev. 1203 (1990).

Moldafsky, Milton I. *Criminal Law—Statutory Construction*. 2 Mo. L. Rev. 367 (1937).

Molot, Jonathan T. *The Rise and Fall of Textualism*. 106 Colum. L. Rev. 1 (2006).

Monaghan, Henry Paul. *Stare Decisis and Constitutional Adjudication*. 88 Colum. L. Rev. 723 (1988).

Montrose, J.L. *Ambiguous Words in a Statute*. 76 L.Q. Rev. 359 (1960).

Moore, John Norton. *Treaty Interpretation, The Constitution, and the Rule of Law*. 42 Va. J. Int'l L. 163 (2001).

Moore, Michael S. *The Interpretive Turn in Modern Theory: A Turn for the Worse?* 41 Stan. L. Rev. 871 (1989).

Moore, Michael S. *A Natural Law Theory of Interpretation*. 58 S. Cal. L. Rev. 277 (1985).

Moore, Michael S. *The Semantics of Judging*. 54 S. Cal. L. Rev. 151 (1981).

Morrison, Trevor W. *Constitutional Avoidance in the Executive Branch*. 106 Colum. L. Rev. 1189 (2006).

Movsesian, Mark L. *Are Statutes Really "Legislative Bargains"? The Failure of the Contract Analogy in Statutory Interpretation*. 76 N.C. L. Rev. 1145 (1998).

Mullane, Michael. *Statutory Interpretation in Arkansas: How Arkansas Courts Interpret Statutes*. 2005 Ark. L. Notes 73.

Mullane, Michael. *Statutory Interpretation in Arkansas: How Should a Statue Be Read? When Is It Subject to Interpretation? What Our Courts Say and What They Do*. 2004 Ark. L. Notes 85.

Mullins, Morell E., Sr. *Coming to Terms with Strict and Liberal Construction*. 64 Alb. L. Rev. 9 (2000).

Mullins, Morell E., Sr. *Tools, Not Rules: The Heuristic Nature of Statutory Interpretation*. 30 J. Legis. 1 (2003).

Munson, F. Granville. *The Drafting of Federal Statute Law*. 43 Am. L. Rev. 121 (1909).

Munzer, Stephen R. *Realistic Limits on Realist Interpretation*. 58 S. Cal. L. Rev. 459 (1985).

Murphy, Arthur W. *Old Maxims Never Die: The "Plain-Meaning Rule" and Statutory Interpretation in the "Modern" Federal Courts*. 75 Colum. L. Rev. 1299 (1975).

Murphy, Walter F. "The Art of Constitutional Interpretation: A Preliminary Showing," in *Essays on the Constitution of the United States*. M. Judd Harmon, ed. Port Washington, N.Y.: Nat'l Univ. Pubs., 1978.

Nagle, John Copeland. Delaware & Hudson *Revisited*. 72 Notre Dame L. Rev. 1495 (1997).

Nagle, John Copeland. *Newt Gingrich, Dynamic Statutory Interpreter*. 143 U. Pa. L. Rev. 2209 (1995).

Nagle, John Copeland. *The Worst Statutory Interpretation Case in History*. 94 Nw. U. L. Rev. 1445 (2000).

Nard, Craig Allen. *Deference, Defiance, and the Useful Arts*. 56 Ohio St. L.J. 1415 (1995).

Nehf, James P. *Textualism in the Lower Courts: Lessons from Judges Interpreting Consumer Legislation*. 26 Rutgers L.J. 1 (1994).

Nelson, Caleb. *Judicial Review of Legislative Purpose*. 83 N.Y.U. L. Rev. 1784 (2008).

Nelson, Caleb. *Originalism and Interpretive Conventions*. 70 U. Chi. L. Rev. 519 (2003).

Nelson, Caleb. *The Persistence of General Law*. 106 Colum. L. Rev. 503 (2006).

Nelson, Caleb. *Preemption*. 86 Va. L. Rev. 225 (2000).

Nelson, Caleb. *A Response to Professor Manning*. 91 Va. L. Rev. 451 (2005).

Nelson, Caleb. *Stare Decisis and Demonstrably Erroneous Precedents*. 87 Va. L. Rev. 1 (2001).

Nelson, Caleb. *Statutory Interpretation and Decision Theory*. 74 U. Chi. L. Rev. 329 (2007).

Nelson, Caleb. *What Is Textualism?* 91 Va. L. Rev. 347 (2005).

Nelson, William E. *History and Neutrality in Constitutional Adjudication*. 72 Va. L. Rev. 1237 (1986).

Neuborne, Burt. *Background Norms for Federal Statutory Interpretation*. 22 Conn. L. Rev. 721 (1990).

Newland, Sarah. *The Mercy of Scalia: Statutory Construction and the Rule of Lenity*. 29 Harv. C.R.-C.L. L. Rev. 197 (1994).

Newman, Frank C. *How Courts Interpret Regulations*. 35 Cal. L. Rev. 509 (1947).

Niranjan, V. *Was the Death of the Casus Omissus Rule "Undignified"?* 30 Statute L. Rev. 73 (2009).

Nourse, Victoria. *Misunderstanding Congress: Statutory Interpretation, the Supermajoritarian Difficulty, and the Separation of Powers*. 99 Geo. L.J. 1119 (2011).

Nunez, Richard I. *The Nature of Legislative Intent and the Use of Legislative Documents as Extrinsic Aids to Statutory Interpretation: A Reexamination*. 9 Cal. W. L. Rev. 128 (1972).

Nutting, Charles B. *The Ambiguity of Unambiguous Statutes*. 24 Minn. L. Rev. 509 (1940).

Nutting, Charles B. *The Relevance of Legislative Intention Established by Extrinsic Evidence*. 20 B.U. L. Rev. 601 (1940).

Nutting, Charles B. *Subjective Standards and Objective Language: Can Taste Be Codified*. 2 Harv. J. Legis. 175 (1965).

Nutting, Charles B. *The Supreme Court and Extrinsic Aids to Statutory Interpretation*. 43 A.B.A. J. 266 (1957).

O'Connor, Gary E. *Restatement (First) of Statutory Interpretation*. 7 N.Y.U. J. Legis. & Pub. Pol'y 333 (2004).

Ogune, Theo I. *Judges and Statutory Construction: Judicial Zombism or Contextual Activism?* 30 U. Balt. L.F. 4 (2000).

Oliver, Lord, of Aylmerton. *A Judicial View of Modern Legislation*. 14 Statute L. Rev. 1 (1993).

Oman, Nathan. *Statutory Interpretation in Econotopia*. 25 Pace L. Rev. 49 (2004).

Osborn, John G. *Legal Philosophy and Judicial Review of Agency Statutory Interpretation*. 36 Harv. J. on Legis. 115 (1999).

Osgood, Russell K. *The Enterprise of Judging*. 17 Harv. J.L. & Pub. Pol'y 13 (1994).

Outzs, Lori L. *A Principled Use of Congressional Floor Speeches in Statutory Interpretation*. 28 Colum. J.L. & Soc. Probs. 297 (1995).

Page, Barbara. *Statutes in Derogation of Common Law: The Canon as an Analytical Tool*. 1956 Wis. L. Rev. 78.

Paradise, Christina. *Statutory Interpretation*. 12 Roger Williams U. L. Rev. 661 (2007).

Patterson, Dennis M. *The Poverty of Interpretive Universalism: Toward the Reconstruction of Legal Theory*. 72 Tex. L. Rev. 1 (1993).

Patterson, Dennis M. *Interpretation in Law— Toward a Reconstruction of the Current Debate*. 29 Vill. L. Rev. 671 (1984).

Paulsen, Michael Stokes. *A Government of Adequate Powers*. 31 Harv. J.L. & Pub. Pol'y 991 (2008).

Paulsen, Michael Stokes. *The Intrinsically Corrupting Influence of Precedent*. 22 Const. Comment. 289 (2005).

Paulsen, Michael Stokes. *The Irrepressible Myth of Marbury*. 101 Mich. L. Rev. 2706 (2003).

Paulson, Stanley L. *Kelsen on Legal Interpretation*. 10 Legal Studs. 136 (1990).

Peñalver, Eduardo M. *Restoring the Right Constitution?* 116 Yale L.J. 732 (2007).

Perry, Michael J. *The Authority of Text, Tradition, and Reason: A Theory of Constitutional Interpretation.* 58 S. Cal. L. Rev. 551 (1985).

Person, Debora A. *Legislative Histories and the Practice of Statutory Interpretation in Wyoming.* 10 Wyo. L. Rev. 559 (2010).

Peterson, Sandra. *Gender-Neutral Drafting: Historical Perspective.* 19 Statute L. Rev. 93 (1998).

Peterson, Sandra. *Gender-Neutral Drafting: Recent Commonwealth Developments.* 20 Statute L. Rev. 35 (1999).

Phelps, Arthur W. *Factors Influencing Judges in Interpreting Statutes.* 3 Vand. L. Rev. 456 (1950).

Phelps, Teresa Godwin; and Jenny Ann Pitts. *Questioning the Text: The Significance of Phenomenological Hermeneutics for Legal Interpretation.* 29 St. Louis U. L.J. 353 (1985).

Pierce, Richard J., Jr. *The Supreme Court's New Hypertextualism: An Invitation to Cacophony and Incoherence in the Administrative State.* 95 Colum. L. Rev. 749 (1995).

Plass, Stephen A. *The Illusion and Allure of Textualism.* 40 Vill. L. Rev. 93 (1995).

Podger, Ellen S. *Vagueness and Statutory Construction.* 22 Champion 61 (May 1998).

Pogue, Richard W. *Legislation—Invalidity of Statutes Framed in Vague Terms.* 51 Mich. L. Rev. 941 (1953).

Poirier, Marc R. *On Whose Authority? Linguists' Claim of Expertise to Interpret Statutes.* 73 Wash. U. L.Q. 1025 (1995).

Pool, Joseph H. *Bulk Revision of Texas Statutes.* 39 Tex. L. Rev. 469 (1961).

Popkin, William D. *The Collaborative Model of Statutory Interpretation.* 61 S. Cal. L. Rev. 541 (1988).

Popkin, William D. *Foreword: Nonjudicial Statutory Interpretation.* 66 Chi.-Kent L. Rev. 301 (1990).

Popkin, William D. *An "Internal" Critique of Justice Scalia's Theory of Statutory Interpretation.* 76 Minn. L. Rev. 1133 (1992).

Popkin, William D. *Judicial Use of Presidential Legislative History: A Critique,* 66 Ind. L.J. 699 (1991).

Popkin, William D. *Law-Making Responsibility and Statutory Interpretation,* 68 Ind. L.J. 865 (1993).

Popkin, William D. *William N. Eskridge, Jr.: Dynamic Statutory Interpretation.* 45 J. Legal Educ. 297 (1995).

Posner, Eric; and Adrian Vermeule. *Legislative Entrenchment: A Reappraisal.* 111 Yale L.J. 1665 (2002).

Posner, Richard A. *Economics, Politics, and the Reading of Statutes and the Constitution.* 49 U. Chi. L. Rev. 263 (1982).

Posner, Richard A. *Legal Formalism, Legal Realism, and the Interpretation of Statutes and the Constitution.* 37 Case W. Res. L. Rev. 179 (1986).

Posner, Richard A. "Pragmatic Adjudication," in *The Revival of Pragmatism: New Essays on Social Thought, Law, and Culture.* Morris Dickstein, ed. Durham, N.C.: Duke Univ. Press, 1998.

Posner, Richard A. *Reply: The Institutional Dimension of Statutory and Constitutional Interpretation.* 101 Mich. L. Rev. 952 (2003).

Posner, Richard A. "The Separation of Powers," in *Politics and the Constitution: The Nature and Extent of Interpretation.* Washington, D.C.: Nat'l Legal Ctr. for the Public Interest & Am. Studs. Ctr., 1990.

Posner, Richard A. *Statutory Interpretation—in the Classroom and in the Courtroom.* 50 U. Chi. L. Rev. 800 (1983).

Post, Robert C.; and Reva B. Siegel. *Legislative Constitutionalism and Section Five Power: Policentric Interpretation of the Family Medical Leave Act.* 112 Yale L.J. 1943 (2003).

Post, Robert C.; and Reva B. Siegel. *Originalism as a Political Practice: The Right's Living Constitution.* 75 Fordham L. Rev. 545 (2006).

Pound, Roscoe. *Common Law and Legislation.* 21 Harv. L. Rev. 383 (1908).

Pound, Roscoe. *The Political and Social Factor in Legal Interpretation.* 45 Mich. L. Rev. 599 (1947).

Pound, Roscoe. *Spurious Interpretation.* 7 Colum. L. Rev. 379 (1907).

Pound, Roscoe. *The Theory of Judicial Decision.* 36 Harv. L. Rev. 641 (1923).

Pound, Roscoe. *What of Stare Decisis?* 10 Fordham L. Rev. 1 (1941).

Powell, H. Jefferson. *The Executive and the Avoidance Canon.* 81 Ind. L.J. 1313 (2006).

Powell, H. Jefferson. *The Original Understanding of Original Intent.* 98 Harv. L. Rev. 885 (1985).

Powell, Richard R.B. *Construction of Written Instruments—Part I.* 14 Ind. L.J. 199 (1939).

Powell, Richard R.B. *Construction of Written Instruments—Part II.* 14 Ind. L.J. 309 (1939).

Powell, Richard R.B. *Construction of Written Instruments—Part III.* 14 Ind. L.J. 397 (1939).

Pryor, William H., Jr. *The Demand for Clarity: Federalism, Statutory Construction, and the 2000 Term.* 32 Cumb. L. Rev. 361 (2002).

Pueser, Janice M. *Rules of Statutory Construction for Legislative Drafting.* 17 F.R.D. 143 (1955).

Pulvers, Roy; and Wendy Willis. *Revolution and Evolution: What Is Going On with Statutory Interpretation in the Oregon Courts?* Or. St. B. Bull. 13 (Jan. 1996).

Quarles, James C. *Some Statutory Construction Problems and Approaches in Criminal Law.* 3 Vand. L. Rev. 531 (1950).

Radin, Max. *A Case Study in Statutory Interpretation:* Western Union Co. v. Lenroot. 33 Cal. L. Rev. 219 (1945).

Radin, Max. *The Doctrine of the Separation of Powers in Seventeenth Century Controversies.* 86 U. Pa. L. Rev. 842 (1938).

Radin, Max. *Early Statutory Interpretation in England.* 38 Ill. L. Rev. 16 (1943).

Radin, Max. "A Juster Justice, a More Lawful Law," in *Legal Essays in Tribute to Orrin Kip McMurray.* Max Radin & A.M. Kidd, eds. Berkeley: Univ. of California Press, 1935.

Radin, Max. *Legal Realism.* 31 Colum. L. Rev. 824 (1931).

Radin, Max. *Realism in Statutory Construction and Elsewhere.* 23 Cal. L. Rev. 156 (1935).

Radin, Max. *A Short Way with Statutes.* 56 Harv. L. Rev. 388 (1942).

Radin, Max. *Solving Problems by Statute.* 14 Or. L. Rev. 90 (1934).

Radin, Max. *Statutory Interpretation.* 43 Harv. L. Rev. 863 (1930).

Rakoff, Todd D. *Statutory Interpretation as a Multifarious Enterprise.* 104 Nw. U. L. Rev. 1559 (2010).

Randolph, A. Raymond. *Dictionaries, Plain Meaning, and Context in Statutory Interpretation.* 17 Harv. J.L. & Pub. Pol'y 71 (1994).

Randolph, A. Raymond. *Originalism and History: The Case of* Boumediene v. Bush. 34 Harv. J. L. & Pub. Pol'y 89 (2011).

Ratner, Gershon M. *The Federal Circuit's Approach to Statutory and Regulatory Construction, with Emphasis on Veterans Law.* 6 Fed. Cir. B.J. 243 (1996).

Raz, Joseph. "Intention in Interpretation," in *The Autonomy of Law: Essays on Legal Positivism.* Robert P. George, ed. Oxford: Clarendon Press; N.Y.: Oxford Univ. Press, 1996.

Redish, Martin H. *Federal Common Law, Political Legitimacy, and the Interpretive Process: An "Institutionalist" Perspective.* 83 Nw. U. L. Rev. 761 (1989).

Redish, Martin H.; and Dennis Murashko. *The Rules Enabling Act and the Procedural–Substantive Tension: A Lesson in Statutory Interpretation.* 93 Minn. L. Rev. 26 (2008).

Redish, Martin H.; and Theodore T. Chung. *Democratic Theory and the Legislative Process: Mourning the Death of Originalism in Statutory Interpretation.* 68 Tul. L. Rev. 803 (1994).

Rehnquist, William H. *The Notion of a Living Constitution.* 54 Tex. L. Rev. 693 (1976).

Renton, Lord. *Interpretation of Legislation.* 1982 Statute L. Rev. 7.

Re-reading Justice Scalia. 32 Statute L. Rev. iii (2011).

Rhodes, Robert M.; John Wesley White; and Robert S. Goldman. *The Search for Intent: Aids to Statutory Construction in Florida.* 6 Fla. St. U. L. Rev. 383 (1978).

Rhyne, Charles S. *Statutory Construction in Resolving Conflicts Between State and Local Legislation.* 3 Vand. L. Rev. 509 (1950).

Richards, David A. J. *Interpretation and Historiography.* 58 S. Cal. L. Rev. 489 (1985).

Richards, Neil M. *Clio and the Court: A Reassessment of the Supreme Court's Uses of History.* 13 J.L. & Pol. 809 (1997).

Richardson, James R. *Judicial Law Making: Intent of Legislature v. Literal Interpretation.* 39 Ky. L.J. 79 (1950).

Rickershauser, Charles E., Jr. *Statutory Construction: Conflicting Acts Passed at the Same Session: Higher Chapter Number Prevails.* 3 UCLA L. Rev. 417 (1956).

Riesenfeld, Stefan A. *Law Making and Legislative Precedent in American Legal History.* 33 Minn. L. Rev. 103 (1949).

Ritchie, Marguerite E. *Alice Through the Statutes.* 21 McGill L.J. 685 (1975).

Roberts, Hugh. *Mr. Justice Bryson on Statutory Interpretation: A Comment.* 13 Statute L. Rev. 165 (1992).

Rodriguez, Daniel B. *The Presumption of Reviewability: A Study in Canonical Construction and Its Consequences.* 45 Vand. L. Rev. 743 (1992).

Rodriguez, Daniel B. *Statutory Interpretation and Political Advantage.* 12 Int'l Rev. L. & Econ. 217 (1992).

Rodriguez, Daniel B. *The Substance of the New Legal Process.* 77 Cal. L. Rev. 919 (1989) (reviewing William N. Eskridge Jr. & Philip P. Frickey, *Cases and Materials on Legislation: Statutes and the Creation of Public Policy* (1988)).

Rodriguez, Daniel B.; and Barry R. Weingast. *The Paradox of Expansionist Statutory Interpretations.* 101 Nw. U. L. Rev. 1207 (2007).

Rogers, C. Paul, III. *Judicial Reinterpretation of Statutes: The Example of Baseball and the Antitrust Laws.* 14 Hous. L. Rev. 611 (1977).

Romero, Alan R. *Interpretive Directions in Statutes.* 31 Harv. J. on Legis. 211 (1994).

Root, Elihu. *The Importance of an Independent Judiciary*. 72 Independent 704 (1912).

Rosenfeld, Michael. *Deconstruction and Legal Interpretation: Conflict, Indeterminacy and the Temptations of the New Legal Formalism*. 11 Cardozo L. Rev. 1211 (1990).

Rosenkranz, Nicholas Quinn. *Federal Rules of Statutory Interpretation*. 115 Harv. L. Rev. 2085 (2002).

Roskill, Lord. *Some Thoughts on Statutes, New and Stale*. 1981 Statute L. Rev. 77.

Ross, Jeremy L. *A Rule of Last Resort: A History of the Doctrine of the Last Antecedent in the United States Supreme Court*. 39 Sw. L. Rev. 325 (2009).

Ross, Stephen F. *Statutory Interpretation as a Parasitic Endeavor*. 44 San Diego L. Rev. 1027 (2007).

Ross, Stephen F. *Where Have You Gone, Karl Llewellyn? Should Congress Turn Its Lonely Eyes to You?* 45 Vand. L. Rev. 561 (1992).

Ross, Stephen F.; and Daniel Tranen. *The Modern Parol Evidence Rule and Its Implications for New Textualist Statutory Interpretation*. 87 Geo. L.J. 195 (1998).

Rubin, Edward L. *Beyond Public Choice: Comprehensive Rationality in the Writing and Reading of Statutes*. 66 N.Y.U. L. Rev. 1 (1991).

Rubin, Edward L. *Modern Statutes, Loose Canons, and the Limits of Practical Reason: A Response to Farber and Ross*. 45 Vand. L. Rev. 579 (1992).

Rules of Drafting Adopted by the Conference of Commissioners on Uniformity of Legislation in Canada. 26 Can. B. Rev. 1231 (1948).

Russell, F.A.A. "The Interpretation of Statutes," in *Essays and Excursions in Law*. London: Sweet & Maxwell, 1929.

Safranek, Stephen J. *Scalia's Lament*. 8 Tex. Rev. L. & Pol. 315 (2004).

Sager, Lawrence G. *Constitutional Triage*. 81 Colum. L. Rev. 707 (1981).

Samaha, Adam M. *Originalism's Expiration Date*. 30 Cardozo L. Rev. 1295 (2008).

Samuels, Alec. *De Minimis Non Curat Lex*. 1985 Statute L. Rev. 167.

Samuels, Alec. *The Eiusdem Generis Rule in Statutory Interpretation*. 1984 Statute L. Rev. 180.

Samuels, Alec. *Errors in Bills and Acts*. 1982 Statute L. Rev. 94.

Samuels, Alec. *Henry Thring: the First Modern Drafter*. 24 Statute L. Rev. 91 (2003).

Samuels, Alec. *The Interpretation of Statutes*. 1980 Statute L. Rev. 86.

Samuels, Alec. *The Misuse of Rules of Statutory Interpretation*. 1980 Statute L. Rev. 166.

Samuels, Alec. *Retrospective Retitling*. 19 Statute L. Rev. 129 (1998).

Sanders, Paul H.; and John W. Wade. *Legal Writings on Statutory Construction*. 3 Vand. L. Rev. 569 (1950).

Sands, C. Dallas. *Statutory Construction and National Development*. 18 Int'l & Comp. L.Q. 206 (1969).

Scalia, Antonin. *Assorted Canards of Contemporary Legal Analysis*. 40 Case W. Res. L. Rev. 581 (1990).

Scalia, Antonin. *Originalism: The Lesser Evil*. 57 U. Cin. L. Rev. 849 (1989).

Scalia, Antonin. *The Rule of Law as a Law of Rules*. 56 U. Chi. L. Rev. 1175 (1989).

Schacter, Jane S. *The Confounding Common Law Originalism in Recent Supreme Court Statutory Interpretation: Implications for the Legislative History Debate and Beyond*. 51 Stan. L. Rev. 1 (1998).

Schacter, Jane S. *Metademocracy: The Changing Structure of Legitimacy in Statutory Interpretation*. 108 Harv. L. Rev. 593 (1995).

Schacter, Jane S. *The Pursuit of "Popular Intent": Interpretive Dilemmas in Direct Democracy*. 105 Yale L.J. 107 (1996).

Schanck, Peter C. *An Essay on the Role of Legislative Histories in Statutory Interpretation*. 80 Law Libr. J. 391 (1988).

Schanck, Peter C. *Understanding Postmodern Thought and Its Implications for Statutory Interpretation*. 65 S. Cal. L. Rev. 2505 (1992).

Schauer, Frederick. Ashwander *Revisited*. 1995 Sup. Ct. Rev. 71 (1995).

Schauer, Frederick. *An Essay on Constitutional Language*. 29 UCLA L. Rev. 797 (1982).

Schauer, Frederick. *Formalism*. 97 Yale L.J. 509 (1988).

Schauer, Frederick. *The Practice and Problems of Plain Meaning: A Response to Aleinikoff and Shaw*. 45 Vand. L. Rev. 715 (1992).

Schauer, Frederick. *Precedent and the Necessary Externality of Constitutional Norms*. 17 Harv. J.L. & Pub. Pol'y 45 (1994).

Schauer, Frederick. *Statutory Construction and the Coordinating Function of Plain Meaning*. 1990 Sup. Ct. Rev. 231.

Schnapper, Eric. *Statutory Misinterpretations: A Legal Autopsy*. 68 Notre Dame L. Rev. 1095 (1993).

Schneider, Daniel M. *Empirical Research on Judicial Reasoning: Statutory Interpretation in Federal Tax Cases*. 31 N.M. L. Rev. 325 (2001).

Schreiber, Sidney M. *Statutory Interpretation: Some Comments on Two Judicial Viewpoints*. 10 Seton Hall L. Rev. 94 (1979).

Schultz, Matthew. *Equitable Repudiation: Toward a Doctrine of Fallible Perfection in Statutory Interpretation.* 29 Fla. St. U. L. Rev. 303 (2001).

Schutter, David C. *The Invalidation of Statutes for Hypothetical Unconstitutionality: A Tale of Two Absurdities.* 7 Ariz. L. Rev. 252 (1966).

Schwartz, Bernard. *Brennan v. Rehnquist— Mirror Images in Constitutional Construction.* 19 Okla. City U. L. Rev. 213 (1994).

Schwartz, David S. *Correcting Federalism Mistakes in Statutory Interpretation: The Supreme Court and the Federal Arbitration Act.* 67 Law & Contemp. Probs. 5 (2004).

Schwartz, Jack; and Amanda Stakem Conn. *The Court of Appeals at the Cocktail Party: The Use and Misuse of Legislative History.* 54 Md. L. Rev. 432 (1995).

Scott, Robert E. *The Case for Formalism in Relational Contract.* 94 Nw. U. L. Rev. 847 (2000).

Scott, Warwick Potter. *The Judicial Power to Apply Statutes to Subjects to Which They Were Not Intended to Be Applied.* 14 Temp. L.Q. 318 (1940).

Sentell, R. Perry, Jr. *The Canons of Construction in Georgia: "Anachronisms" in Action.* 25 Ga. L. Rev. 365 (1991).

Sentell, R. Perry, Jr. *Statutes in Derogation of the Common Law: In the Georgia Supreme Court.* 53 Mercer L. Rev. 41 (2001).

Sentell, R. Perry, Jr. *Statutes of Nonstatutory Origin.* 14 Ga. L. Rev. 239 (1980).

Shaman, Jeffrey. *The Constitution, the Supreme Court, and Creativity.* 9 Hastings Const. L.Q. 257 (1982).

Shanfield, Louis. *The Scope of Judicial Independence of the Legislature in Matters of Procedure and Control of the Bar.* 19 St. Louis L. Rev. 163 (1934).

Shapiro, David L. *Continuity and Change in Statutory Interpretation.* 67 N.Y.U. L. Rev. 921 (1992).

Shapiro, Martin M. *Judicial Decisionmaking: The Role of Text, Precedent, and the Rule of Law.* 17 Harv. J.L. & Pub. Pol'y 155 (1994).

Sheets, Wallace J. *The Use of Contemporaneous Circumstances and Legislative History in the Interpretation of Statutes in Missouri.* 1952 Wash. U. L.Q. 265.

Shepherd, Pete. *Oregon State Statutory Interpretation: Blind to History, but Useful in Application.* 47 Willamette L. Rev. 587 (2011).

Siegel, Jonathan R. *The Polymorphic Principle and the Judicial Role in Statutory Interpretation.* 84 Tex. L. Rev. 339 (2005).

Siegel, Jonathan R. *Textualism and Contextualism in Administrative Law.* 78 B.U. L. Rev. 1023 (1998).

Siegel, Jonathan R. *The Use of Legislative History in a System of Separated Powers.* 53 Vand. L. Rev. 1457 (2000).

Siegel, Jonathan R. *What Statutory Drafting Errors Teach Us About Statutory Interpretation.* 69 Geo. Wash. L. Rev. 309 (2001).

Silving, Helen. *A Plea for a Law of Interpretation.* 98 U. Pa. L. Rev. 499 (1950).

Simamba, Bilika H. *The Placing and Other Handling of Definitions.* 27 Statute L. Rev. 73 (2006).

Simmons, Courtney. *Unmasking the Rhetoric of Purpose: The Supreme Court and Legislative Compromise.* 44 Emory L.J. 117 (1995).

Simon, Larry G. *The Authority of the Framers of the Constitution: Can Originalist Interpretation Be Justified?* 73 Cal. L. Rev. 1482 (1985).

Sinclair, Michael B.W. *Law and Language: The Role of Pragmatics in Statutory Interpretation.* 46 U. Pitt. L. Rev. 373 (1985).

Sinclair, Michael B.W. *Legislative Intent: Fact or Fabrication?* 41 N.Y.L. Sch. L. Rev. 1329 (1997).

Sinclair, Michael B.W. *Statutory Reasoning.* 46 Drake L. Rev. 299 (1997).

Sither, Charles A. *Statutory Interpretation and the Plain Meaning Rule.* 37 Ky. L.J. 66 (1948).

Skinner, Louis V. *Statutes in Derogation of the Common Law.* 14 Or. L. Rev. 290 (1935).

Slade, Michael B. *Democracy in the Details: A Plea for Substance over Form in Statutory Interpretation.* 37 Harv. J. on Legis. 187 (2000).

Slawson, W. David. *Legislative History and the Need to Bring Statutory Interpretation Under the Rule of Law.* 44 Stan. L. Rev. 383 (1992).

Slocum, Brian G. *Overlooked Temporal Issues in Statutory Interpretation.* 81 Temp. L. Rev. 635 (2008).

Slocum, Brian G. *The Problematic Nature of Contractionist Statutory Interpretations.* 102 Nw. U. L. Rev. Colloquy 307 (2008).

Smith, Herbert A. *Interpretation in English and Continental Law.* 9 J. Comp. Legis. & Int'l L. 3d ser. 153 (1927).

Smith, Michael R. *Linguistic Hooks: Overcoming Adverse Cognitive Stock Structures in Statutory Interpretation.* 8 Legal Comm. & Rhetoric: J. Ass'n Legal Writing Directors 25 (2011).

Smith, Steven D. *Law Without Mind.* 88 Mich. L. Rev. 104 (1989).

Smith, Steven D. *Why Should Courts Obey the Law?* 77 Geo. L.J. 113 (1988).

Smith, Steven E. *Legislative Intent: In Search of the Holy Grail.* 53 Cal. St. B.J. 294 (1978).

Sneath, G.R. *Statutory Presumptions—Hidden Effects and Uncertain in Operation.* 1982 Statute L. Rev. 23.

Sneed, Joseph T. *The Art of Statutory Interpretation.* 62 Tex. L. Rev. 665 (1983).

Snyder, Fritz. *Legislative History and Statutory Interpretation: The Supreme Court and the Tenth Circuit.* 49 Okla. L. Rev. 573 (1996).

Socarras, Michael. *Judicial Modification of Statutes: A Separation of Powers Defense of Legislative Efficiency.* 4 Yale L. & Pol'y Rev. 228 (1985).

Solan, Lawrence M. *Language and Lenity.* 40 Wm. & Mary L. Rev. 57 (1998).

Solan, Lawrence M. *Learning Our Limits: The Decline of Textualism in Statutory Cases.* 1997 Wis. L. Rev. 235.

Solan, Lawrence M. *Private Language, Public Laws: The Central Role of Legislative Intent in Statutory Interpretation.* 93 Geo. L.J. 427 (2005).

Solan, Lawrence M. *Statutory Interpretation, Morality, and the Text.* 76 Brook. L. Rev. 1033 (2011).

Solum, Lawrence B. District of Columbia v. Heller *and Originalism.* 103 Nw. U. L. Rev. 923 (2009).

Solum, Lawrence B. *Incorporation and Originalist Theory.* 18 J. Contemp. Legal Issues 409 (2009).

Solum, Lawrence B. *On the Indeterminacy Crisis: Critiquing Critical Dogma.* 54 U. Chi. L. Rev. 462 (1987).

Solum, Lawrence B. *The Supreme Court in Bondage: Constitutional Stare Decisis, Legal Formalism, and the Future of Unenumerated Rights.* 9 U. Pa. J. Const. L. 155 (2006).

Southerland, Harold P. *Theory and Reality in Statutory Interpretation.* 15 St. Thomas L. Rev. 1 (2002).

Sparkman, John. *Legislative History and the Interpretation of Laws.* 2 Ala. L. Rev. 189 (1950).

Spence, Muriel Morisey. *The Sleeping Giant: Textualism as Power Struggle.* 67 S. Cal. L. Rev. 585 (1994).

Stack, Kevin M. *The Divergence of Constitutional and Statutory Interpretation.* 75 U. Colo. L. Rev. 1 (2004).

Stammier, Rudolf. *Legislation and Judicial Decision.* 23 Mich. L. Rev. 362 (1925).

Stapleton, Sara. *Ensuring a Fair Trial in the International Criminal Court: Statutory Interpretation and the Impermissibility of Derogation.* 31 N.Y.U. J. Int'l L. & Pol. 535 (1999).

Starr, Kenneth W. *Observations About the Use of Legislative History.* 1987 Duke L.J. 371.

Staszewski, Glen. Introduction to *Symposium on Administrative Statutory Interpretation.* 2009 Mich. St. L. Rev. 1.

Staudt, Nancy; Lee Epstein; Peter Wiedenbeck; René Lindstädt; and Ryan J. Vander Wielen. *Judging Statutes: Interpretive Regimes.* 38 Loy. L.A. L. Rev. 1909 (2005).

Stempel, Jeffrey W. *The Rehnquist Court, Statutory Interpretation, Inertial Burdens, and a Misleading Version of Democracy.* 22 U. Tol. L. Rev. 583 (1991).

Stephenson, Matthew C. *The Price of Public Action: Constitutional Doctrine and the Judicial Manipulation of Legislative Enactment Costs.* 118 Yale L.J. 2 (2008).

Stevens, John Paul. *The Shakespeare Canon of Statutory Construction.* 140 U. Pa. L. Rev. 1373 (1992).

Stevens, John Paul. *The Life-Span of a Judge-Made Rule.* 58 N.Y.U. L. Rev. 1 (1983).

Stone, Harlan Fiske. *The Common Law in the United States.* 50 Harv. L. Rev. 4 (1936).

Stone, Julius. *Uncommitted Relativism in Modern Theories of Justice.* 16 Sw. L.J. 171 (1962).

Stone, Julius; and G. Tarello. *Justice, Language and Communication.* 14 Vand. L. Rev. 331 (1960).

Strang, Lee J. *Originalism and the "Challenge of Change": Abduced-Principle Originalism and Other Mechanisms by Which Originalism Sufficiently Accommodates Changed Social Conditions.* 60 Hastings L.J. 927 (2009).

Strauss, David A. *Common Law Constitutional Interpretation.* 63 U. Chi. L. Rev. 877 (1996).

Strauss, David A. *Originalism, Precedent, and Candor.* 22 Const. Comment. 299 (2005).

Strauss, David A. *Why Conservatives Shouldn't Be Originalists.* 31 Harv. J.L. & Pub. Pol'y 969 (2008).

Sullivan, Craig A. *Statutory Construction in Missouri.* 59 J. Mo. B. 120 (2003).

Sullivan, Grant T.; and John R. Webb. *Consistency in Statutory Interpretation.* 38 Colo. Law. 67 (June 2009).

Summers, Robert S. "Statutory Interpretation in the United States," in *Interpreting Statutes: A Comparative Study.* D. Neil MacCormick & Robert S. Summers, eds. Brookfield, Vt.: Dartmouth Pub. Co., 1991.

Summers, Robert S.; and Geoffrey Marshall. *The Argument from Ordinary Meaning in Statutory Interpretation.* 43 N. Ireland L.Q. 213 (1992).

Sunstein, Cass R. *Five Theses on Originalism.* 19 Harv. J.L. & Pub. Pol'y 311 (1996).

Sunstein, Cass R. *Interpreting Statutes in the Regulatory State*. 103 Harv. L. Rev. 405 (1989).

Sunstein, Cass R. *Law and Administration After Chevron*. 90 Colum. L. Rev. 2071 (1990).

Sunstein, Cass R. *Must Formalism Be Defended Empirically?* 66 U. Chi. L. Rev. 636 (1999).

Sunstein, Cass R. *Nondelegation Canons*. 67 U. Chi. L. Rev. 315 (2000).

Sunstein, Cass R. *Principles, Not Fictions*. 57 U. Chi. L. Rev. 1247 (1990).

Sunstein, Cass R.; and Adrian Vermeule. *Interpretation and Institutions*. 101 Mich. L. Rev. 885 (2003).

Sunstein, Cass R.; and Adrian Vermeule. *Interpretive Theory in Its Infancy: A Reply to Posner*. 101 Mich. L. Rev. 972 (2003).

Sutton, Dale E. *Use of "Shall" in Statutes*. 4 John Marshall L.Q. 204 (1938–1939).

Sutton, Jeffrey S. *A Review of Richard A. Posner, How Judges Think*. 108 Mich. L. Rev. 859 (2010).

Sutton, Jeffrey S. *The Role of History in Judging Disputes About the Meaning of the Constitution*. 41 Tex. Tech. L. Rev. 1173 (2009).

Tabb, Charles Jordan; and Robert M. Lawless. *Of Commas, Gerunds, and Conjunctions: The Bankruptcy Jurisprudence of the Rehnquist Court*. 42 Syracuse L. Rev. 823 (1991).

Talmadge, Philip A. *A New Approach to Statutory Interpretation in Washington*. 25 Seattle U. L. Rev. 179 (2001).

Tate, Albert. J. *Techniques of Judicial Interpretation in Louisiana*. 22 La. L. Rev. 727 (1962).

Taylor, George H. *Structural Textualism*. 75 B.U. L. Rev. 321 (1995).

TenBroek, Jacobus. *Admissibility of Congressional Debates in Statutory Construction by the United States Supreme Court*. 25 Cal. L. Rev. 326 (1937).

Thayer, James Bradley. *The Origin and Scope of the American Doctrine of Constitutional Law*. 7 Harv. L. Rev. 129 (1893).

Thomas, James C. *Statutory Construction When Legislation Is Viewed as a Legal Institution*. 3 Harv. J. on Legis. 191 (1966).

Thorne, Samuel E. *The Equity of a Statute and Heydon's Case*. 31 Ill. L. Rev. 202 (1936).

Thornton, H.M. *Contrary Intention*. 15 Statute L. Rev. 182 (1994).

Thornton, John Edward. *Intent of the Draftsman as a Device to Construe Written Instruments*. 5 Ala. L. Rev. 36 (1952).

Tiefer, Charles. *The Reconceptualization of Legislative History in the Supreme Court*. 2000 Wis. L. Rev. 206.

Tiersma, Peter M. *The Ambiguity of Interpretation: Distinguishing Interpretation from Construction*. 73 Wash. U. L.Q. 1095 (1995).

Tiersma, Peter M. *A Message in a Bottle: Text, Autonomy, and Statutory Interpretation*. 76 Tul. L. Rev. 431 (2001).

Tiersma, Peter M. *The Textualization of Precedent*. 82 Notre Dame L. Rev. 1187 (2007).

Tiffany, H.T. "Interpretation and Construction," in *American and English Encyclopaedia of Law*. Vol. 17. David S. Garland & Lucius P. McGehee, eds. 2d ed. N.Y.: Edward Thompson Co., 1900.

Tillman, Nora Rotter; and Seth Barrett Tillman, *A Fragment on Shall and May*. 50 J. Am. Legal Hist. 453 (2010).

Tokeley, Kate. *Trends in Statutory Interpretation and the Judicial Process*. [2002] Victoria U. Wellington L. Rev. 41.

Torbert, Preston M. *Globalizing Legal Drafting: What the Chinese Can Teach Us About Ejusdem Generis and All That*. 11 Scribes J. Legal Writing (2007).

Traynor, Roger J. *Is This Conflict Really Necessary?* 37 Tex. L. Rev. 657 (1959).

Traynor, Roger J. *The Limits of Judicial Creativity*. 63 Iowa L. Rev. 1 (1977).

Tribe, Laurence H. "Comment," in Antonin Scalia, *A Matter of Interpretation: Federal Courts and the Law*. Princeton, N.J.: Princeton Univ. Press, 1997.

Tribe, Laurence H. *Judicial Interpretation of Statutes: Three Axioms*. 11 Harv. J.L. & Pub. Pol'y 51 (1988).

Tribe, Laurence H. *The Puzzling Persistence of Process-Based Constitutional Theories*. 89 Yale L. J. 1063 (1980).

Tunks, Lehan K. *Assigning Legislative Meaning: A New Bottle*. 37 Iowa L. Rev. 372 (1952).

Turley, Jonathan. *Through a Looking Glass Darkly: National Security and Statutory Interpretation*. 53 SMU L. Rev. 205 (2000).

Tushnet, Mark V. *A Comment on the Critical Method in Legal History*. 6 Cardozo L. Rev. 997 (1985).

Tushnet, Mark V. *Following the Rules Laid Down: A Critique of Interpretivism and Neutral Principles*. 96 Harv. L. Rev. 781 (1983).

Tushnet, Mark V. *Heller and the New Originalism*. 69 Ohio St. L.J. 609 (2008).

Tushnet, Mark V. *Judges and Constitutional Theory: A View from History*. 63 U. Colo. L. Rev. 425 (1992).

Tushnet, Mark V. *Legal Realism, Structural Review, and Prophecy*. 8 U. Dayton L. Rev. 809 (1983).

Tushnet, Mark V. *A Note on the Revival of Textualism in Constitutional Theory*. 58 S. Cal. L. Rev. 683 (1985).

Tushnet, Mark V. *Theory and Practice in Statutory Interpretation*. 43 Tex. Tech L. Rev. 1185 (2011).

Tyler, Amanda L. *Continuity, Coherence, and the Canons*. 99 Nw. U. L. Rev. 1389 (2005).

Tyler, Gus. *Court Versus Legislature*. 27 Law & Contemp. Probs. 390 (1962).

Uys, J.F. *Interpretation of Statutes*. 1963 Ann. Surv. S. African L. 553.

Van Alstyne, William. "Clashing Visions of a 'Living' Constitution: Of Opportunists and Obligationists," in *Cato Supreme Court Review 2010–2011*. Wash., D.C.: Center for Constitutional Studies, Cato Institute, 2011.

Van Alstyne, William. *Interpreting This Constitution: The Unhelpful Contributions of Special Theories of Judicial Review*. 35 U. Fla. L. Rev. 209 (1983).

Veeder, Van Vechten. *The Judicial Characteristics of the Late Lord Bowen*. 10 Harv. L. Rev. 351 (1897).

Vermeule, Adrian. *The Cycles of Statutory Interpretation*. 68 U. Chi. L. Rev. 149 (2001).

Vermeule, Adrian. *Interpretation, Empiricism, and the Closure Problem*. 66 U. Chi. L. Rev. 698 (1999).

Vermeule, Adrian. *Interpretive Choice*. 75 N.Y.U. L. Rev. 74 (2000).

Vermeule, Adrian. *The Judiciary Is a They, Not an It: Interpretive Theory and the Fallacy of Division*. 14 J. Contemp. Legal Issues 549 (2005).

Vermeule, Adrian. *Legislative History and the Limits of Judicial Competence: The Untold Story of Holy Trinity Church*. 50 Stan. L. Rev. 1833 (1998).

Vermeule, Adrian. *Saving Constructions*. 85 Geo. L.J. 1945 (1997).

Vermeule, Adrian. *Three Strategies of Interpretation*. 42 San Diego L. Rev. 607 (2005).

Vermeule, Adrian; and Ernest A. Young. *Hercules, Herbert, and Amar: The Trouble with Intratextualism*. 113 Harv. L. Rev. 730 (2000).

Vogenauer, Stefan. *What Is the Proper Role of Legislative Intention in Judicial Interpretation?* 18 Statute L. Rev. 235 (1997).

Von Mehren, Arthur. "The Judicial Conception of Legislation in Tudor England," in *Interpretations of Modern Legal Philosophies: Essays in Honor of Roscoe Pound*. Paul Sayre, ed. N.Y.: Oxford Univ. Press, 1947.

Vranken, Martin. *Statutory Interpretation and Judicial Policy Making: Some Comparative Reflections*. 12 Statute L. Rev. 31 (1991).

Wald, Patricia M. *The Sizzling Sleeper: The Use of Legislative History in Construing Statutes in the 1988–89 Term of the United States Supreme Court*. 39 Am. U. L. Rev. 277 (1990).

Wald, Patricia M. *Some Observations on the Use of Legislative History in the 1981 Supreme Court Term*. 68 Iowa L. Rev. 195 (1983).

Wald, Stephanie. *The Use of Legislative History in Statutory Interpretation Cases in the 1992 U.S. Supreme Court Term; Scalia Rails but Legislative History Remains on Track*. 23 Sw. U. L. Rev. 47 (1993).

Walker, John M., Jr. *Judicial Tendencies in Statutory Construction: Differing Views on the Role of the Judge*. 58 N.Y.U. Ann. Surv. Am. L. 203 (2001).

Wasby, Stephen L. *Legislative Materials as an Aid to Statutory Interpretation: A Caveat*. 12 J. Pub. L. 262 (1963).

Weaver, Russell L. *Challenging Regulatory Interpretation*. 23 Ariz. St. L.J. 109 (1991).

Webster, Peter D.; Sylvia H. Walbolt; and Christine R. Davis. *Statutory Construction in Florida: In Search of a Principled Approach*. 9 Fla. Coastal L. Rev. 435 (2008).

Wechsler, Herbert. "The Nature of Judicial Reasoning," in *Law and Philosophy: A Symposium*. Sidney Hook, ed. N.Y.: N.Y. Univ. Press, 1964.

Wechsler, Herbert. *Toward Neutral Principles of Constitutional Law*. 73 Harv. L. Rev. 1 (1959).

Weisberg, Robert. *The Calabresian Judicial Artist: Statutes and the New Legal Process*. 35 Stan. L. Rev. 213 (1983).

Wheeler, Franklin J.; and Thomas B. Wheeler. *Statute Revision: Its Nature, Purpose and Method*. 16 Tul. L. Rev. 165 (1942).

Whitebread, Charles H. *Habeas, Civil and Criminal Statutory Interpretation*. 2004 Orange County Law. 34.

Whittington, Keith E. *The New Originalism*. 2 Geo. J.L. & Pub. Pol'y 599 (2004).

Widiss, Deborah A. *Shadow Precedents and the Separation of Powers: Statutory Interpretation of Congressional Overrides*. 84 Notre Dame L. Rev. 511 (2009).

Williams, Clifton. *Expressio Unius Est Exclusio Alterius*. 15 Marq. L. Rev. 185 (1931).

Williams, David. *Legitimation and Statutory Interpretation: Conquest, Consent, and Community in Federal Indian Law*. 80 Va. L. Rev. 403 (1994).

Williams, Glanville L. *Language and the Law—I*. 61 L.Q. Rev. 71 (1945).

Williams, Glanville L. *Language and the Law—II*. 61 L.Q. Rev. 179 (1945).

Williams, Glanville L. *Language and the Law—III.* 61 L.Q. Rev. 293 (1945).

Williams, Glanville L. *Language and the Law—IV.* 61 L.Q. Rev. 384 (1945).

Williams, Glanville L. *Language and the Law—V.* 62 L.Q. Rev. 387 (1946).

Williams, Glanville L. *The Meaning of Literal Interpretation—I.* 131 New L.J. 1128 (1981).

Williams, Glanville L. *The Meaning of Literal Interpretation—II.* 131 New L.J. 1149 (1981).

Williams, Robert F. *Statutes as Sources of Law Beyond Their Terms in Common-Law Cases.* 50 Geo. Wash. L. Rev. 554 (1982).

Williams, Stephen F. *Non-Legal Theory in Judicial Decisionmaking: "Legal" Versus "Non-Legal" Theory.* 17 Harv. J.L. & Pub. Pol'y 79 (1994).

Willis, John. *Statute Interpretation in a Nutshell.* 16 Can. B. Rev. 1 (1938).

Wilson, W.A. *The Complexity of Statutes.* 37 Modern L. Rev. 497 (1974).

Wilson, W.A. *Questions of Interpretation.* 1987 Statute L. Rev. 142.

Wilson, W.A. *Trials and Try-ons: Modes of Interpretation.* 13 Statute L. Rev. 1 (1992).

Winckel, Anne. *The Contextual Role of a Preamble in Statutory Interpretation.* 23 Melb. U. L. Rev. 184 (1999).

Winder, W.H.D. *The Interpretation of Statutes Subject to Case-Law.* 58 Juridical L. Rev. 93 (1946).

Winter, Steven L. *Indeterminacy and Incommensurability in Constitutional Law.* 78 Cal. L. Rev. 1441 (1990).

Witherspoon, Joseph P. *Administrative Discretion to Determine Statutory Meaning: "The High Road."* 35 Tex. L. Rev. 63 (1956).

Witherspoon, Joseph P. *Administrative Discretion to Determine Statutory Meaning: "The Low Road."* 38 Tex. L. Rev. 392 (1960).

Witherspoon, Joseph P. *Administrative Discretion to Determine Statutory Meaning: "The Middle Road": I.* 40 Tex. L. Rev. 751 (1962).

Witherspoon, Joseph P. *The Essential Focus of Statutory Interpretation.* 36 Ind. L.J. 411 (1961).

Wofford, John G. *The Blinding Light: The Use of History in Constitutional Interpretation.* 31 U. Chi. L. Rev. 502 (1964).

Wood, J.C.E. *Statutory Interpretation: Tupper and the Queen.* 6 Osgoode Hall L.J. 92 (1968).

Wormser, Maurice I. *The Development of the Law.* 23 Colum. L. Rev. 701 (1923).

Worthy, Albert W., Jr. *Statutes—Refusal to Apply Statutory Definitions to Terms Used in the Act.* 28 Tex. L. Rev. 733 (1950).

Wright, Abby. *For All Intents and Purposes: What Collective Intention Tells Us About Congress and Statutory Interpretation.* 154 U. Pa. L. Rev. 983 (2006).

Wydick, Richard C. *Should Lawyers Punctuate?* 1 Scribes J. Legal Writing 7 (1990).

Yoo, John Choon. *Marshall's Plan: The Early Supreme Court and Statutory Interpretation.* 101 Yale L.J. 1607 (1992).

Young, Ernest A. *Constitutional Avoidance, Resistance Norms, and Preservation of Judicial Review.* 78 Tex. L. Rev. 1549 (2000).

Young, Ernest A. *The Constitution Outside the Constitution.* 117 Yale L.J. 408 (2007).

Young, Ernest A. *The Continuity of Statutory and Constitutional Interpretation: An Essay for Phil Frickey.* 98 Cal. L. Rev. 1371 (2010).

Young, Robert P., Jr. *A Judicial Traditionalist Confronts Justice Brennan's School of Judicial Philosophy.* 33 Okla. City U. L. Rev. 263 (2008).

Zelenak, Lawrence. *The Court and the Code: A Response to the Warp and Woof of Statutory Interpretation.* 58 Duke L.J. 1783 (2009).

Zeppos, Nicholas S. *Chief Justice Rehnquist, the Two Faces of Ultra-Pluralism, and the Originalist Fallacy.* 25 Rutgers L.J. 679 (1994).

Zeppos, Nicholas S. *Judicial Candor and Statutory Interpretation.* 78 Geo. L.J. 353 (1989).

Zeppos, Nicholas S. *Justice Scalia's Textualism and the "New" New Legal Process.* 12 Cardozo L. Rev. 1597 (1991).

Zeppos, Nicholas S. *Legislative History and the Interpretation of Statutes: Toward a Fact-Finding Model of Statutory Interpretation.* 76 Va. L. Rev. 1295 (1990).

Zeppos, Nicholas S. *The Use of Authority in Statutory Interpretation: An Empirical Analysis.* 70 Tex. L. Rev. 1073 (1992).

Zweigert, Konrad; and Hans-Jürgen Puttfarken. *Statutory Interpretation—Civilian Style.* 44 Tul. L. Rev. 704 (1970).

Index

Colophon

The pages of this book were designed and laid out by Jeff Newman in the offices of LawProse, Inc., in Dallas, Texas. The authors collaborated in and approved the design, which drew on influences of classical law treatises. The body type is Caslon. Designed by the English typefounder William Caslon (1692–1766), the face was prevalent in England and America into the early-20th century. It was the face chosen for the first printed versions of the United States Declaration of Independence. The typeface used here is a modern cut, Adobe Caslon, designed by Carol Twombly based on Caslon's specimen pages from the mid-18th century. Twombly also helped design Myriad, the complementary face used here for epigraphs throughout.